D0123522

Contents

Plan of the Series

. . . Almost the most prodigious asset of a country, and perhaps its most precious possession, is its native literary product—when that product is fine and noble and enduring.

Mark Twain*

The advisory board, the editors, and the publisher of the *Dictionary of Literary Biography* are joined in endorsing Mark Twain's declaration. The literature of a nation provides an inexhaustible resource of permanent worth. We intend to make literature and its creators better understood and more accessible to students and the reading public, while satisfying the standards of teachers and scholars.

To meet these requirements, *literary biography* has been construed in terms of the author's achievement. The most important thing about a writer is his writing. Accordingly, the entries in *DLB* are career biographies, tracing the development of the author's canon and the evolution of his reputation.

The purpose of *DLB* is not only to provide reliable information in a convenient format but also to place the figures in the larger perspective of literary history and to offer appraisals of their accomplishments by qualified scholars.

The publication plan for *DLB* resulted from two years of preparation. The project was proposed to Bruccoli Clark by Frederick C. Ruffner, president of the Gale Research Company, in November 1975. After specimen entries were prepared and typeset, an advisory board was formed to refine the entry format and develop the series rationale. In meetings held during 1976, the publisher, series editors, and advisory board approved the scheme for a comprehensive biographical dictionary of persons who contributed to North American literature. Editorial work on the first volume began in January 1977, and it was published in 1978. In order to make *DLB* more than a reference tool and to compile volumes that individually have claim to status as literary history, it was decided to organize volumes by topic, period, or genre. Each of these freestanding volumes provides a biographical-bibliographical guide and overview for a particular area of literature. We are convinced that this organization—as opposed to a single alphabet method—constitutes a valuable innovation in the presentation of reference material. The volume plan necessarily requires many decisions for the placement and treatment of authors who might properly be included in two or three volumes. In some instances a major figure will be included in separate volumes, but with different entries emphasizing the aspect of his career appropriate to each volume. Ernest Hemingway, for example, is represented in *American Writers in Paris, 1920-1939* by an entry focusing on his expatriate apprenticeship; he is also in *American Novelists, 1910-1945* with an entry surveying his entire career. Each volume includes a cumulative index of the subject authors and articles. Comprehensive indexes to the entire series are planned.

With volume ten in 1982 it was decided to enlarge the scope of *DLB*. By the end of 1986 twenty-one volumes treating British literature had been published, and volumes for Commonwealth and Modern European literature were in progress. The series has been further augmented by the *DLB Yearbooks* (since 1981) which update published entries and add new entries to keep the *DLB* current with contemporary activity. There have also been *DLB Documentary Series* volumes which provide biographical and critical source materials for figures whose work is judged to have particular interest for students. One of these companion volumes is entirely devoted to Tennessee Williams.

We define literature as the *intellectual commerce of a nation:* not merely as belles lettres but as that ample and complex process by which ideas are generated, shaped, and transmitted. *DLB* entries are not limited to "creative writers" but extend to other figures who in their time and in their way influenced the mind of a people. Thus the series encompasses historians, journalists, publishers, and screenwriters. By this means

*From an unpublished section of Mark Twain's autobiography, copyright © by the Mark Twain Company

readers of *DLB* may be aided to perceive literature not as cult scripture in the keeping of intellectual high priests but firmly positioned at the center of a nation's life.

DLB includes the major writers appropriate to each volume and those standing in the ranks immediately behind them. Scholarly and critical counsel has been sought in deciding which minor figures to include and how full their entries should be. Wherever possible, useful references are made to figures who do not warrant separate entries.

Each *DLB* volume has a volume editor responsible for planning the volume, selecting the figures for inclusion, and assigning the entries. Volume editors are also responsible for preparing, where appropriate, appendices surveying the major periodicals and literary and intellectual movements for their volumes, as well as lists of further readings. Work on the series as a whole is coordinated at the Bruccoli Clark Layman editorial center in Columbia, South Carolina, where the editorial staff is responsible for accuracy of the published volumes.

One feature that distinguishes *DLB* is the illustration policy—its concern with the iconography of literature. Just as an author is influenced by his surroundings, so is the reader's understanding of the author enhanced by a knowledge of his environment. Therefore *DLB* volumes include not only drawings, paintings, and photographs of authors, often depicting them at various stages in their careers, but also illustrations of their families and places where they lived. Title pages are regularly reproduced in facsimile along with dust jackets for modern authors. The dust jackets are a special feature of *DLB* because they often document better than anything else the way in which an author's work was perceived in its own time. Specimens of the writers' manuscripts are included when feasible.

Samuel Johnson rightly decreed that "The chief glory of every people arises from its authors." The purpose of the *Dictionary of Literary Biography* is to compile literary history in the surest way available to us—by accurate and comprehensive treatment of the lives and work of those who contributed to it.

The *DLB* Advisory Board

Introduction

This volume of the *Dictionary of Literary Biography* comprises literary biographies of the first generation of seventeenth-century nondramatic poets. All but one of them were born before the English defeat of the Spanish Armada (and the birth of Thomas Hobbes) in 1588; most of them were dead years before King Charles I went to the scaffold outside Whitehall Palace in 1649. The majority began to compose poems during the last decade and a half of the reign of the last Tudor monarch, Queen Elizabeth I (1558-1603); and (with the possible exception of John Donne, if we believe Ben Jonson's claim that Donne composed "all his best pieces" before 1598) all wrote the majority of their poems during the reign of the first Stuart monarch, James I (1603-1625). They lived and wrote during one of the most volatile and decisive periods of religious, social, and political change in English history, the period of the Pilgrims' exodus to Amsterdam and Plymouth, of the English Civil Wars, and of the start of the Thirty Years War; but above all they lived and wrote in the period which might rightly be viewed as the severing of the Christocentric medieval world from the secularized modern world—a split epitomized literally and symbolically in the *legal* execution of a monarch who had been said to rule by "divine" right. All periods, of course, are periods of change and continuity, but this one was especially characterized by change; thus the importance of recalling the paradoxes which seem to define the literary biographies of these authors—none of whom would probably have even imagined much less condoned the events in the street outside the Stuart Banqueting House on that January morning in 1649 when Charles I was executed. Their literary careers offer apt examples of the current of change and the symptoms of radical disruption in the fabric of the nation that were to be realized at the midpoint of their century and that became also the turning point of the world as we know it.

Inheritors of the Renaissance tradition of Christian humanist learning, with its Ciceronian emphasis on "eloquent" service to church and state, and advocates of the medieval political theology fundamental to the Tudor monarchy, these poets were all firm believers in the Christocentric universe of Providential order and benevolence. They are most profitably viewed, by preference and occasion, as "the last Elizabethans." Despite the range and variety of their individual religious confessions (from the Erasmian Roman Catholicism which Donne and Sir John Beaumont had inherited from their families—to which Ben Jonson the High Church Anglican was once converted—to Edward, Lord Herbert of Cherbury's deism, Josuah Sylvester's Calvinism, and the "Scottish" Protestantism of Sir Robert Aytoun, Sir William Alexander, and William Drummond—differences with which the Tudor queen had largely avoided outright conflict through a broad, although not always consistently or evenly applied "Settlement"), all these poets would have agreed on certain basic principles. Man was the central creature in God's Creation, like the sun at the center of the elemental macrocosm which humoral man mirrored in shape and form; he maintained vestiges of the *imago dei* in the tripartite (memory-reason-will) structure of his rational soul or "erect wit," despite the adamant proclivities of his "fallen will"; and he could be saved by God's Grace from the damnation which he naturally deserved. To be "the last Elizabethans," in other words, was largely to accept and maintain, with little modification, the divine cosmos and Christian economy of the Middle Ages. Regardless of their chosen positions viz-à-viz the Reformation, all would have generally agreed with the interpretation of man's condition as dramatized in the first half of the late-medieval Catholic morality play *Everyman*. Their major disagreements stemmed from the interpretation and authority of the "Holicherche" and "Good Deeds" central to the Catholic theology of sanctifying Grace in the second half of the play. Certainly, they chose different (in some cases *many* different) confessional stances and undoubtedly would have been worried about the eternal condition of the souls of those who disagreed with their choices. In some cases they might have been willing (and anxious) to coerce others to accept what they believed to be the Truth: "unmoved thou / Of force must one, and forc'd but one allow; / And the right," Donne wrote in his 1595 meditation on the state of religious and political "Power" in the last years of the Tudor reign. Not even the curious "School of Night" with which some of the more skeptical or adventuresome poets of the age were associated would have denied in general Donne's reminder in that third *Satyre* that the surest "cure" for the "worne maladies" of the fallen world was to "Seeke true religion":

> on a huge hill
> Cragged and steep, Truth stands, and hee that will
> Reach her, about must, and about must goe;
> And what the'hills suddenes resists, winne so;
> Yet strive so, that before age, deaths twilight,
> Thy Soule rest, for none can worke in that night.
> . . . .
> So perish Soules, which more chuse mens unjust
> Power from God claym'd, then God himselfe to
>   trust.

In this sense, then, it is more likely that his later warning in *The First Anniversary* (1611), with its reliance on the medieval typology of Christ as the Phoenix and its alarm at the privileging of the subjective self, is less a frightened recoil from the innovations of Copernicus's heliocentric universe (which Donne consistently mocks in his love lyrics and in early prose tracts such as *Ignatius his conclave*, 1611) than it is the traditional *contemptus mundi* response to man's inevitable failures in moral and intellectual insight:

> new Philosophy calls all in doubt,
> . . . .
> 'Tis all in pieces, all cohærence gone;
> All just supply, and all Relation:
> Prince, Subject, Father, Sonne, are things forgot,
> For every man alone thinkes he hath got
> To be a Phœnix, and that there can bee
> None of that kinde, of which he is, but hee.

Donne's "intellectual curiosity in scientific speculation provided him with convenient illustrations in *The First Anniversary* of the decay and disorder of the world and in the *Second Anniversary* [1612] of the soul's ignorance," F. P. Wilson suggests; but the novelty or "wit" of these poems which is representative of the philosophical meditations of his contemporaries does not lie in their quite conventional and medieval meditations on habitual failures of mankind to maintain the *imago dei* within. Thus, even in its reliance on the planes of corre-

spondence between the microcosm and macrocosm to indict an age in which "art is lost, and correspondence too," Donne's tense anatomy of man's plight *sub lege* is generally continuous with the final warnings of the Doctor in *Everyman*, the sermons on Order and obedience in the official *Book of Homilies*, or Ulysses' speech on "degree" in Shakespeare's *Troilus and Cressida* (1609):

> The heavens themselves, the planets, and this
>   centre
> Observe degree, priority, and place,
> Insisture, course, proportion, season, form,
> Office, and custom in all line of order;
> And therefore is the glorious planet Sol
> In noble eminence enthron'd and spher'd
> Amidst the other; whose med'cinable eye
> Corrects the ill aspects of planets evil,
> And posts like the commandment of a king,
> Sans check, to good and bad. . . . .
> . . . . .O, when degree in shak'd,
> Which is the ladder of all high designs,
> The enterprise is sick. . . . .
> Take but degree away, untune that string,
> And hark what discord follows. Each thing meets
> In mere oppugnancy: the bounded waters
> Should lift their bosoms higher than the shores,
> And make a sop of all this solid globe;
> Strength should be lord of imbecility,
> And the rude son should strike his father dead;
> Force should be right, or rather, right and wrong
> (Between whose endless jar justice resides)
> Should lose their names, and so should justice
>   too!
> Then every thing include itself in power,
> Power into will, will into appetite,
> And appetite, an universal wolf
> (So double seconded with will and power),
> Must make perforce an universal prey,
> And last eat up himself.

Indeed, that Andrew Marvell in 1650 could make the subject of a commendatory *Horatian Ode* a "forward youth" who "could not cease / In the inglorious arts of peace, / But through advent'rous war / Urged his active star" in order to overthrow a king and, as "the Wars' and Fortune's son," was urged to remember *above all* that "The same arts that did gain / A *power* must it maintain" (however equivocal or ambiguous the poet's own opinion of Oliver Cromwell) is a revealing indication of how far from the world of Shakespeare's *Troilus and Cressida* and how deeply into the world of Hobbes's *Leviathan* (1651) that England went during the life of this first generation of seventeenth-century British poets.

The major dilemma facing the majority of these poets, however, was not on which side they would fight during the Civil Wars. Rather, as indicated in the contours of their poems individually and as a group, it was that of maintaining the medieval worldview (and its endemic aesthetic) during the late Elizabethan and Jacobean period. The difficulty with their position was that it lacked adequate support in the centers of social and cultural power in Jacobean England. The brilliance (but also the precariousness or, to use the favorite term of the Tudor fin de siècle poets, the "mutability" of the Elizabethan Settlement) was dependent largely upon the force of character and personal charisma of that remarkable queen. (She might have rightly deserved that term "royal actor" which Marvel so tentatively strove later to apply to Charles I.) But the integrity of the Settlement was already beginning to decline in her waning years, and it could not be sustained by the Stuarts. They seemed not to understand that it could not be formalized by rigorous defenses of a theory of "the divine rights of kings" or maintained by the insistent performance of a sort of daily royal "masque" which obtained only the illusion of medieval political theology. Neither James nor his son was able to inspire the personal confidence and devotion that had helped Elizabeth shape England—through the genius of her chosen counselors and advisers, of course—into a confident, international state proud of its traditions and image. The offensive absolutism of James's divine-right theory, which lacked any basis in English custom and any appeal to the increasingly restless gentry and commercial classes—much less to the Puritans whom James, in the Hampton Court Conference of 1604, threatened to "harry out of the country," or to the radical sectarians (the Catholics?) who had engineered the Gunpowder Plot in November 1605, not long after the king's accession—was muted by the muddling moderation of his policies, the endless befuddlements of the "Spanish Match," and, perhaps, although certainly beyond his control, was dealt a sort of deadly blow in 1612 by "the untimely death of the incomparable Prince, Henry." The nearly ubiquitous response to the death of this Prince of Wales—comparable in number only with the elegiac response to Sir Philip Sidney's death in 1586, at the height of Elizabeth's regime—was the sole instance of any sort of general poetic engagement with the court, even in light of the several poets such as Jonson and Aurelian Townshend who contributed some

of the best masques to the royal entertainment. After the failures and melancholic results of James's rule, the efforts of Charles to make the divine-right theory into a reality on the Gallic model was simply a recipe for disaster.

Despite the status and renown of its kings as among the world's greatest collectors and connoisseurs of art—perhaps the most significant and ironically symbolic example being the Continental baroque paintings which Charles commissioned Peter Paul Rubens to paint on the ceiling of the Banqueting House under which the king moved on his way to the scaffold outside that building, constructed by Inigo Jones for the king's self-celebrations and art collection—the Stuart court yet provided no traditional cultural substance for these poets to celebrate and defend. Except for the opportunities to participate in the masques' (questionable) defenses of their divine power, the Stuarts provided no articulate norms to furnish a context for the classical poetical structures in which these Renaissance humanist poets had been educated. (A life-pension of one hundred marks to Jonson, after his fulsome description of James as "best of poets," does not qualify.) Thus, the penchant of the emerging poets of the 1590s—Donne, Jonson, Joseph Hall, Samuel Rowlands, George Chapman—for classical genres of a conventionally conservative tendency (epigram and formal verse satire) was of considerable consequence (or at least should have been) in alerting reader and ruler to a general disillusionment with the waning of the Elizabethan Settlement; but it was at the same time of no consequence eventually because of the Stuart court's inability to offer a celebratory alternative. It is not surprising, then, that these poets—and those who continued to tap the resources of the genres popular to the Elizabethan age—became ineluctably drawn into a *private*, effectually subversive mode in the absence of a credible public ideal.

Of course, from a broader perspective, it is possible that the sort of crisis of aesthetic identity which these poets confronted (or which confronted them)—as an effusion of both Elizabethan disillusionment and Jacobean melancholy—was merely the culmination of a general and specific assault on nonsecular society which can be traced back (at least) to King Henry VIII's placing of his own dynastic and amatory/sexual desires before the demands of the spiritual courts, perhaps even back to the culmination on English soil of a general secularizing movement whose origin some would find in Martin Luther's posting of his personal demands on the outside of the cathedral in Wittenberg (1517). And some have found the foundation of the age's sense of urgent questioning and skepticism (as fulfilled in the compelling figure of Montaigne) in the discovery of the "new" heliocentric universe by Copernicus (and its confirmation in the work of Galileo and Johannes Kepler) or in the philosophical "innovations" of Francis Bacon and Réne Descartes and their "new" brand of metaphysical rationalism.

An equally compelling explanation for the momentum of this general antiauthoritarian movement in English would see Jacobean melancholy as merely the extension of the late Elizabethan disillusionment. Just when England had achieved its miraculous victory over its major international enemy in the Channel, instead of engaging in a wave of patriotic celebration the nation turned to all those social, religious, and political problems which had lain dormant, resulting in a series of widespread and divisive quarrels. Cynthia's sailor came home as John Marston's Malcontent; Edmund Spenser's epic praise of Astraea was displaced by Thomas Lodge's verse satires; and, shortly, Shakespeare's "mirror of all Christian kings" would be confronted on the boards by Jonson's humorists. While the nation had been striving for its place, identity, and security, Elizabeth's subjects seemed largely willing to accept the general outlines of her able counselors' Settlement; but as those men of vision and acumen—such as Sir Francis Walsingham and William Cecil, Baron Burghley—were replaced by men of less ability and vision, and the entire system of patronage and "honour" on which the queen had founded her "cult" became increasingly corrupt, at that precise time the nation turned its attention to internal problems. This view of Jacobean melancholy and social unrest as merely the ebb tide of Elizabethan disillusionment and activism is compelling. However, it remains true that the Stuart project failed in large part because of its own failure to establish continuity with the *successes* of Elizabeth's appeal and authority. The self-involved reluctances of James to respond to widespread complaint and the increasingly severe and repressive responses to urgent social and spiritual unrest by his son only served to exacerbate, increase, and accelerate the disillusionment of the troubled final years of Elizabeth's "Golden Age."

The first generation of poets of the seventeenth century cannot be understood apart from this general movement toward the scaffolding outside Whitehall Palace. From the perspective of their desire to establish and maintain a continuity with their medieval/Tudor cultural past, even the new genres to which they turned in the last years of Elizabeth's rule (which were really not "new" but vehicles with which their education had made them thoroughly familiar)—and the new directions in which they took those forms they inherited—actually confirm the poets' desire to maintain the worldview they saw being called into question. But since James's corrupt and venal court could hardly pass for a defender of this tradition, these conservative poets actually were engaging in a subversion of the regime that was eroding the culture of feudal England. The nostalgia central to Michael Drayton's epic allegory, for instance, or the transformation of the amatory sonnet into a vehicle of religious meditation and contemplation by John Beaumont and Donne—and nearly every other poet of the period—and the preference for formal verse satire by Rowlands, Hall, and Donne constitute less a break with the norms and forms of their predecessors than a fervent attempt to arrest the decay of those traditions. Even when practiced by the rising generation of new intellectuals at the Inns of Court, satire remains a largely conservative vehicle. Hall's defense of his *Virgidemiae* (1597, 1598) explains,

> Now is Parnassus turned to the stews,
> And on Bay-stocks the wanton Myrthle grows.
> Cytheon hill's become a Brothel-bed,
> And Pyrene sweet, turned to a poisoned head
> Of coal-black puddle: whose infectious stain
> Corrupteth all the lowly fruitful plain.

Hall is indebted as much to Spenser as to Horace; several poems in *Virgidemiae* seem framed to pursue specifically the Blatant Beast which had shed the chains of Calidore's Courtesy to attack the court at the (more than minimally disillusioned) conclusion of the Elizabethan allegorist's unfinished epic. Even the saucy vernacularisms of Rowland's "Blood-Letting" participate in the accommodation of classical and native English materials to the Tudor-Stuart scene, fully in the spirit of the medieval-Renaissance traditions of Christian humanist *imitatio*. Even Donne's fashionable adaptations of Horace's urbane ridicule to the scourging of Juvenalian criminals—as in his attack on the poet-lawyer Coscus as one whose "lyes. . . . like a Kings favorite, yea like a King," seem to "rore" [like the] winds in our ruin'd

Abbeys"—merely applies its witty, new "coarse attire" to the plea for a return to the best of a past age; "Where," he cries at the conclusion of *Satyre II*, his imitation of Horace's *Satire* 2.1,

> are those spred woods which cloth'd
>   hertofore
> Those bought lands? not built, nor burnt within
>   dore.
> Where's th'old landlords troops, and almes? . . .

In this same sense, the seemingly radical changes that the amatory sonnet underwent when refashioned by the brilliant mental dexterity of Donne's hyperbolic defense of romantic and sexual love merely continue the testing of the mode and morality of international Petrarchism that was central to Sir Philip Sidney's sequence. Some of the genres preferred by Elizabeth's courtly makers fell out of general use—the madrigal, eclogue, verse narrative, and heroical epistle (although later revived by the new Spenserians). Yet even those which emerged as the dominant or most popular genres—such as the epigram, as exemplified in the centos of Latin epigrams by John Owen, the perfection of the English potentiality of the Latinate contours of the form in those of Jonson, or, once again, the application of the strategies of Martial's witty condensed vessels of surprise to the argumentative possibilities of the love lyric by Donne—served to establish links with the entire program of *studia humanitatis* central to the Renaissance of Tudor England. Likewise, the development of the verse epistle into a widespread and sophisticated vehicle of personal conversation and moral-spiritual debate—as seen in the companion poems of Sir Henry Wotton most clearly—serves to remind that these "last Elizabethans" could trace their poems back to the originary moments of the Renaissance, to Petrarch's discovery and subsequent publication of Cicero's private *sermones* with Brutus.

Of course, once this attempt to reestablish the lineaments of a Christian humanist poetic confronted the Stuart court it came in conflict with a form of absolutism, as articulated by James, which was not compatible with the humanism of the Renaissance. This "official" denial of the "old" Elizabethan aesthetic was followed by a foreign policy which destroyed in large part patriotic appeal and by the courtly collusion with the new money economy—which were then accentuated by the public display of James's succumbing to the appeal and authority of George Villiers (later duke of Buckingham) and by the general corruption of the old system of "honour" by the endless bestowing of titles. It is not surprising, then, that the poetry of the Jacobeans began to reflect (and to engage) a failure of confidence or a reluctance to participate in the sort of national poetic endeavor which had both celebrated and been incremental to the height of the English humanist Renaissance in the previous regime. Perhaps Donne's response to the request for his contribution of an epithalmion to the courtly celebration of the (scandalous) marriage of Robert Carr, Earl of Somerset, to the divorced Frances Howard, Lady Essex (1613), is representative:

> If my Muse were onely out of fashion, and but wounded and maimed like Free Will in the *Roman Church*, I should adventure to put her to an Epithalamion. But since she is dead, like Free-will in our Church, I have not so much Muse left as to lament her losse.
>
> (letter to Sir Robert Ker, 1613)

These lines are a considerable distance from Spenser's optimistic description of the poet's aim to "fashion a worthy gentlemen or noble person in virtuous and gentle discipline" (letter to Walter Ralegh, 23 January 1590).

Of course, before his death in 1599, Spenser himself had become somewhat disillusioned about the potential of the poet's mission, and the witty denial of the vatic functions of the poet in Donne's refusal does not itself measure the gap between the medieval and modern world which the age was to experience. But this gap does indicate that the symptoms of that major cultural change were evident in the poems of this first generation of Jacobean poets. Donne's statement does indicate one way in which the disillusionment with the Elizabethan Settlement became more severe under the Stuarts. The decadence of the "new" age is manifested, in fact, in the *diffuseness* of the poetry, in the general absence of the sort of Sidneyan poetic which had dominated the court-centered poetry of Elizabeth's reign. It is most obvious, however, in the general movement of the poets from a courtly to an essentially private poetry, as is exemplified in the three major poets of the Jacobean period, Donne, Drayton, and Jonson: a Recusant wit, an archconservative allegorist, and a High Church neoclassicist.

Perhaps the outstanding feature of the poetry of Donne—especially given his own personal ambitions and, after his marriage in 1601, his need for public acceptance and employment—is the near absence of public poetry in his canon or the limitations of the few specimens he did compose. His canon does offer outstanding examples of his skill in the most popular of the "new" old genres of the age, the satirical epigram, poems which proved to be among the most frequent in the commonplace books of the century:

> I am unable, yonder begger cries,
> To stand, or move; if he say true, hee *lies*.

> If in his Studie Hamon hath such care
> To'hang all old strange things, let his wife beware.

And he could employ this skill to the celebration of public figures, as in his lapidarian epigram on Sir John Wingfield, the sole gentle casualty of Robert Devereaux, second Earl of Essex's successful English siege of Cadiz (1596), in which Donne participated:

> Beyond th'old Pillers many'have travailed
> Towards the Suns cradle, and his throne, and bed.
> A fitter Piller our Earle did bestow
> In that late Iland; for he well did know
> Farther then Wingefield no man dares to go.

The pillaging of the *impressa* (in which the sun rises between the pillars of Hercules) and motto (*plus oultra*, or "farther than") of the Spanish king by the poet, and his application of them to Wingfield, confirm both Donne's wit and his ability to pen the "patriotic" encomium. "Who shall doubt, Donne, where I a Poet bee," wrote Jonson, "When I dare send my *Epigrammes* to thee."

Unlike Jonson, Donne published none of his epigrams, and with the exception of his *Anniversaries*, very few of his poems—even though he was at the vanguard of the "new" literature of the age. As Alastair Fowler points out, the major direction of the age—the movement "away from the flowing amplitude of the Elizabethans [and] their copiousness or poignant incident" to a "wit" which showed itself in compression—is first evident in the epigrams of Donne (and Jonson); even Donne's lyrics, as Joseph Spence pointed out, are essentially "a tissue of epigrams." But Donne shared his poems with only the small coterie of readers of his own choosing. The few poems he did make public, such as those two magnificently troubled elegies on the death of Elizabeth Drury, he regretted having published (for they are, after all, finally less poems of public patronage than private meditations on the progress of decay in this "cinder" of a world). Even when he did attempt public poetry, as in his joining the nearly ubiquitous response to the death of Prince Henry or the few epithalamia he did finally agree to compose, the performances were so obscure or so strained that they have remained largely unread. In fact, sometime around 1614 he tried to call in even the manuscript poems in circulation; only in 1633, two years after his death, did his *Poems* reach the public.

This turn from public panegyric, vatic allegory, and courtly *institutio* to meditation and satire, from publication to manuscript circulation, in Donne is less the affectation of a would-be gentleman who deigns not to publish his poems than it is an outright rejection of the courtly aesthetic of the Sidney-Spenser circle of poets. His explicit attacks on the court in his satires and verse epistles ("Here's no more news than virtue"), his denial of the pattern of behavior formalized by Baldassare Castiglione's *Book of the Courtier* (1528) in both his poems ("Rules to make Courtiers, . . . being understood / May make good Courtiers, but who Courtiers good?"—*Satyre V*) and his prose ("I am no Courtier for without having lived there desirously I cannot have sinned enough to have deserved that reprobate name"— letter to Sir Henry Wotton, 1600?) are best seen and defended in the sheer brilliance of his witty adaptations of the Ovidian elegy to the defense of both an anti-court ethos and a private vision of unorthodox integrity. In "Loves Warre," for instance, Donne illustrates his clear understanding of the generic properties of the love elegy as the alternative to the allegorical epic that was central to the Elizabethan scene. Eroticizing the worn-out metaphor of love as a sea voyage in order to illustrate the harsh realities of war and the politics of "honour" (reminiscent of his treatment of the grand American project as little more than a meritricious form of suicide in *Satyre III*)—"Long voyages are long consumptions / And ships are carts for execution"—he concludes by scoffing at the general course of the religious wars by urging that his best "service" (that term central to Castiglione's visionary textbook and Sidney's own guide to English poetics) to the state is to stay home and make love, not war:

> Thousands we see which travaile not
> To warrs; but stay swords, armes, and shott
> To make at home; And shall not I do then
> More glorious service staying to make men?

When Elizabeth forced him into rustication in 1579 because of his overly aggressive opposition to her diplomatic maneuverings, Sidney had written his *Defence of Poetry* as an illustration of how the poetry of his enforced separation from the court still fulfilled his public duty and spiritual commitment. Donne's Ovidian elegies (the generic choice itself a challenge to the norms of the august court) appropriate the rudiments of that poetic in order to defend the integrity of the private mode (of life and poetry). This is certainly a long way from Sidney's defense of the poet as "the prince of learning [who] with the force of a divine breath [can] bestow a Cyrus upon the world to make many Cyruses," thus doing "honor to the heavenly Maker of that maker"—not only in Donne's saucy eroticizing of Sidney's "maker" motif but in its aggressive denial of the *public* project it teases.

Another example of how Donne's comic undercuttings of the Sidney-Spenser poetic bespeak more than their delightfully witty turns of epigrammatic surprise and spirited high jinks is *Elegy XIX* ("Going to Bed"), which lay unpublished until 1669. It follows Donne's later directive in a sermon that "in all Metricall compositions . . . the force of the whole piece, is for the most part left to the shutting up; the whole frame of the Poem is a beating out of a piece of gold, but the last clause is as the impression of the stamp, and that it is that makes it currant. . . ." We can see in its "last clause" how this delightfully naughty strip-tease poem uncovers—or at least outrageously hints at—some bases of the poet's rejection of the court aesthetic. Following more than forty lines of indiscreet comparisons between sexual, imperial, colonial, and religious "extasies," in which the *dis*-covering of the woman's body is not only a private experience of the national project in the New World—

> O my America! my new-found-land,
> My kingdome, safeliest when with one man man'd,
> My Myne of precious stones, my Emperie,
> How blest am I in this discovering thee!

—but also a personalized erotic version of divine revelation in which seeing the woman's vagina is equated with spiritual ecstasy, the concluding epigram reads:

> To teach thee I am naked first; why then
> What needs thou have more covering than a man?

Donne later admitted that he attached some "fear" and "shame" to his satires and elegies; perhaps this couplet suggests why, in the manner in which it plays with the "currant" Protestant doctrine of "imputed grace" by which Christ's human lovers are covered by the redemptive clothing of His blood—continuing the wide range of metonymies used throughout the poem to "teach" the paradisical "innocence" which "License[s]" the "whole joyes" of sexual "labour." From the perspective of the "currant" theological position of Donne as a recusant Catholic (the great-grandnephew of the martyred Sir Thomas More; the brother of Henry, who died in prison for his belief; the nephew of the Jesuit leader Jasper Heywood), *Elegy XIX* is much more than a "shameful" display of Ovidian sensuality. If Donne's *chosen* reader, to whom his manuscript poem would have been sent—"I will have no such Readers as I can teach," he urged in *Metempsychosis*—and who was already on the outside of the Establishment with the poet, would have recalled another image which the concluding lines of this Lady Day poem might evoke even amid its Ovidian excesses—the image of the recently martyred Margaret Clitherow in her "white lynnen," guilty of "no pennance" for her recusancy, being mercifully crushed by the body of her executioner—then this poem may take on some elements of the "fear" with which Donne later associated it. Whether Margaret Clitherow is actually in the poem or not, however, it is certainly clear that Sidney's poetic is not; in fact, as suggested by the annotations of one contemporary reader of the elegy, it is likely that the poem is intended in part as a send-up of the *Epithalamion* of the foremost proponent of the Sidneyan aesthetic, Spenser (just as Donne's elegy known as "Love's Progress" is directed primarily at the sort of Neoplatonic idealizings characteristic of Elizabeth's "sage and serious" Spenser). It is possible, then, that Donne's private poetry and his insistence that it be kept private are grounded in his spiritual/religious alienation from the Protestant project which underlay both Sidney's *Defence* and Spenser's attempts to fulfill its goals in his *Faerie Queene* (1590, 1596).

Indeed, even in his love lyrics Donne consistently defines himself and his poetry in opposition to the "currant" court aesthetic. Certainly the individuality and intimacy of his "dialogue[s] of one" rest in part on his skill with the charged compressions of an epigrammatic style and the colloquial cadences of spoken language, his crisp, pointed wit powerfully condensed into conceits which convey above all the power of his mental life. But, at the same time, this creation of an intimate, private voice is accentuated by a convincing spontaneity that finds its point of departure in the flaunting of its distance from the claims of the public world:

> Let sea-discoverers to new worlds have gone,
> Let Maps to others, worlds on worlds have showne,
> Let us possesse one world, each hath one, and is
>   one.
>
> ("The Good-morrow")

It is not just the subject that is private here, in other words, but the style of the definition itself in its mental acuity and purposeful obscurity, its outright refusal to conform to the metrical, syntactical, or patriarchial rules of the world:

> For Godsake hold your tongue, and let me love,
>   Or chide my palsy, or my gout,
> My five gray haires, or ruin'd fortune flout,
>   With wealth your state, your minde with Arts improve,
>   Take you a course, get you a place,
>   Observe his honour, or his grace,
>   Or the Kings reall, or his stamped face
>   Contemplate, what you will, approve,
>   So you will let me love.
>
> ("The Canonization")

No one or no thing can qualify the private response; Copernicus's "new" sun is demoted to his Ptolemaic status as old Sol circling the earth in search of value, a "Busie old foole" who is told to

> Goe tell Court-huntsman, that the King will ride,
> Call countrey ants to harvest offices
> . . . .
> Aske for those Kings whom thou saw'st yesterday,
> And thou shalt heare, All here in one bed lay.
> . . . .
> This bed thy center is, these walls, thy sphaere.
>
> ("The Sunne Rising")

Anyone who dares, in fact, to violate or intrude the integrity of this private world is threatened:

> Who ever guesses, thinks, or dreames he knowes
> Who is my mistris, wither by this curse;
> . . . .
> May he dreame Treason, and beleeve, that hee
> Meant to performe it, and confesse, and die,
>   And no record tell why:
>   His sonnes, which none of his may bee,

Inherite nothing but his infamie[.]

> ("The Curse")

Such violation amounts, in other words, to a sort of sacrilegious invasion of the holy by the secular.

In fact, it is likely, once again, that the conceit (the figure of *thought*) by which the amatory and the religious are identified is more that the "evaporations" of "wit." Once again the "last clause" of many of these lyrics calls on the language of "currant" theological debate in order to reiterate that the speaker's amatory and spiritual confessions stand united in opposition to the Protestant poetry of the Sidneyan Petrarchists. In the *Satyres* the speaker says he is "like Papists," and when confronted by the court agent "felte [him] self then / Becomming Traytor" for defending his "Mistresse, faire Religion." In many of his lyrics Donne works a variation on this equation; borrowing the lexicon of Counter-Reformation theological debate about the "absent presence" of Christ's body in the Feast of Love, he frames a speaker who uses the terms and argument of the current Recusant position concerning the hermeneutics of the sacraments and a protesting, scornful auditor who is given those of the current Protestant position, which are then amplified in such a way that at times these two modes of the private life are indistinguishable. (This stance is even more pointed, in fact, if Arthur Marotti is correct in his claim that "Love is not love" in the Elizabethan and early Jacobean Protestant poets' lyrics but actually only a metaphor by which they explore political and religious arenas of thought and brokerage.) Structured in accordance with the frame of the Ignatian meditation in which Catholics were educated (a heritage Donne repeatedly recalls in his prose works), the lyrics often focus attention in their "last clause" on the ways in which the speaker's romantic love and the Catholics' confession of faith share a denial of the "currant" dispensation. In "The Extasie," for instance, after invoking the Protestant emphasis on the "booke" (the Bible) to defend the presence of the body in human love, the lyricist concludes that the Platonic reader (like those the Protestant poets accrue) would see such "love reveal'd" as merely "Small change." This is, in fact, the precise term Cardinal Bellarmine used to describe the divine presence of Catholic transubstantiation. In "The Canonization," after borrowing the ecclesiastical *processus* which the Catholic church

used to determine "sainthood," the alienated
speaker asserts that the protesting, intrusive
"layetie" who tried to silence him and restrict his
devotion to his mistress at the start of the poem
would not be able to understand their love even
if he "approved" it. At best such a "Protestant"
reader would see it as a "pattern" "from above,"
the precise terms which John Calvin used to describe how the metonymical Holy Supper of the
Protestant church is merely the engagement with
a "pattern" of divinity that is located only in
Christ's presence in heaven "above."

Even Donne's most outrageously bawdy lyr-
ics, such as "The Flea," play serious but witty variations on the image of lovers as saints who must
"die" for their devotion, who must realize the
full "martyrdom" of their life in the sacrifice of
their bodies to Love. Even if these conceits are
read only as the blasphemous efforts of the poet
to separate himself from the Establishment, they
remain testaments to Donne's consistent and conscious choice of a style and an aesthetic that separate him from the Protestant world. And just as
the world of the lyrics is defined in terms of its similarity to the world of Donne's own outlawed religion, so the construction of his private devotion
in the Holy Sonnets rests on its similarity to his private love life:

> as in my idolatrie
> I said to all my profane mistresses,
> Beauty, of pitty, foulness onely is
> A signe of rigour; so I say to thee,

he confesses to Christ,

> To wicked spirits are horrid shapes assign'd,
> This beauteous forme assures a pitious minde.

The religious devotion stirred by his vision of the
"picture of Christ crucified" in his heart (another
Catholic baroque image recalled probably from
his Catholic heritage and education) is finally defined in terms of its inversion of the code of
Petrarchan frustration. Even in the religious sonnets of Donne, that is, the private is like only the
private.

In some essential ways, then, Donne is unrep-
resentative of the Jacobean melancholy of his generation, in the sense that he was alienated from
the court aesthetic through his Catholicism even
before the Stuart accession. His poetry is nevertheless a compelling symptom of the aversion or disappointment which these poets felt towards the
"new age." The major influence that his poems

had on other Jacobean poets—even when available only in manuscript—and the growth of his
popularity as a model for the next generation of
poets after the 1633 edition of his *Poems*—
suggest that—even as the responses of an "out-
law" recusant Catholic poet already opposed to
the residing aesthetic of the court—his poems, in
their contribution to the diffuseness of the poetic
response to the court and their choice of the private mode that Donne's contemporaries also
chose, record the temper of the times quite
clearly.

If Donne's alienation from the court aesthetic even before 1603 qualifies his status as representative of the major current of the age, however, then an even more drastic example of the
turn of the Jacobean poets away from the court
aesthetic to the private mode—although not as
compelling poetically as Donne's—is provided by
the Jacobean Spenserians, those poets who remained fervently dedicated to the religious and artistic norms, forms, and themes of the Elizabethan court. Just as John of Gaunt's moving
reminiscences about medieval England as "this
seat of Mars, / This other Eden, demi-paradise, /
This fortress built by Nature for herself, . . . /
This blessed plot, this earth, this realm" (*Richard
II*, 1597), in Shakespeare's depiction of the fall of
the last Angevin king, offered a critique of both
the failures of the tragic king and the "new man"
who opposed him, so the Spenserians' remembrance of things past illustrates another mode of
meditative privacy that is parallel to Donne's opposition to the court but which is at the same time disapproving of that particular form of retreat (and
its doctrinal bases). While Drayton and his poetic
allies saw themselves as professional poets in the
mold of the Protestant Sidneyan poetic and its militant anti-Catholicism, and thus distinct from the
amateur musings of a meditative satirist, yet they
too, in their earnest and gentle attempts to return to the splendor and heroism of British landscape and history, also eventually found themselves, as a result of their antiquarian vision,
equally alienated from the Stuart court.

In his first extant published work, *The
Shadow of Night* (1594), Chapman's allegorical
"Hymnus in Cynthiam" expressed in some of his
most obscure but anxious lines the growing fear
that the disappearance of Cynthia (that is,
Elizabeth) from the world would bring universal
darkness and chaos to England:

> Peacefull, and warlike, and the powre of fate,
> In perfect circle of whose sacred state,
> The circles of our hopes are compassed:
> All wisedome, beautie, maiestie and dread,
> Wrought in the speaking pourtrait of thy face:
> Great Cynthia. . . . .
> . . . if the enuious forehead of the earth
> Lowre on thy age, and claime thee as her birth:
> Tapers, nor torches, nor the forrests burning,
> Soule-winging musicke, nor teare-stilling mourning,
> (Vsd of old Romanes and rude Macedons
> In thy most sad, and blacke discessions)
> We know can nothing further thy recall,
> When Nights darke robes (whose obiects blind vs all)
> Shall celebrate thy changes funerall.

Like the *Mutabilitie Cantos* which both disrupt and conclude Spenser's Elizabethan epic, and which also confront the mutability of the queen, Chapman shadows forth a "speaking picture" of the fear that the Jacobean Spenserians found a fearful and vexing reality. Except for Prince Henry—to whom (until his death in 1612) they dedicated a majority of their works and who had in fact become the focus of rivalry with his father—the neo-Spenserians of the seventeenth century saw the Stuart court, with its general and specific failures, as proof that Chapman's greatest fears had become reality.

Drayton's awesome allegorical survey of England, *Poly-Olbion* (1612), is representative. Part of that first major revival of Spenserian poetry in the age, following closely upon the assassination of Henri IV of France (1610), as a plea for James to take a more active role in the struggles against the Hapsburg Catholic forces, and perhaps even as a panegyric for the type of pious Protestant leadership which the Sidney/Spenser school admired in Henry, the young Prince of Wales, Drayton's "heroic" poem opens with an engraving of "Albion" which resembles remarkably that of Queen Elizabeth in the frontispiece of Christopher Saxton's atlas of England and Wales and in the Ditchley portrait of her. The letter "To the Generall *Reader*" of *Poly-Olbion* begins with complaints about "this lunatique Age" and "his Majesties . . . distressed fortunes." Henry (depicted in his armor) is called the nation's "best hope, and the world's delight"; and this opinion is dangerously recorded in the text itself when the catalogue of English monarchs abruptly stops with Elizabeth—a loud silence that might best reiterate the veiled satires of James scattered through Drayton's earlier work, the *Pastorals* of

1610. Representative of an informal "circle" which included William Browne of Tavistock, William Drummond of Hawthornden, John Davies of Hereford, George Sandys, Josuah Sylvester, and especially the caustic (and oft-arrested) George Wither, Drayton continued to practice those genres favored by the Elizabethans—eclogue, madrigal, sonnet, heroical epistle, and allegorical verse narrative; in fact, much of the subsequent development and eventual prominence of the pentameter couplet in English poetry is due to his practice. But what is equally remarkable about his verse is its expression of the alienation and opposition to the Stuart ethos. As Richard Helgerson points out, the extent of this detachment—which finally turns into a petulant nostalgia for the lost "Eden" of Spenser's Elizabethan moral landscape and the "heroic" aggression of Sidney's militant Protestantism—is evinced in the dedicatory poems which head the continuation of *Poly-Olbion* (1622). Poised there to confirm and defend the eminent panegyric of Ralegh (whose execution in 1618 was believed the result of James's submission to Spanish pressure), to underline the praise of those English kings who had defeated *Scottish* armies, and to support the criticism of James's policies that is evident in nearly every line of his fulsome tribute to Elizabeth, the commendatory poems of his younger Spenserians identify Drayton as the sole survivor of the heroic past, "England's brave genius" whose recollection of the national landscape reiterates their own disgust with the vacuum at the (former) center of their culture. As Browne of Tavistock wrote,

> All met not Death,
> When wee intoomb'd our deare *Elizabeth*.
> Immortall *Sydney*, honoured *Colin Clout*,
> Presaging what wee feele, went timely out.
> Then why lives *Drayton*, when the *Times* refuse,
> Both *Meanes* to live, and *Matter* for a *Muse?*

"An intensely patriotic attachment to the land and its depiction and an equally intense nostalgia for the age of Elizabeth went hand in hand with a disdain for the Stuart monarch and his court," Helgerson says. To be a Spenserian poet in the Stuart age meant to serve the country *instead of* the crown; and when the court responded with increased censorship ("I fear, as I do stabbing," wrote Drayton, "this word *state*"), these poets found additional support for their withdrawal into the literal and allegorical "woods" which had sung so sweetly in Spenser's melodious hymns to English culture and court.

Like those meditative poets to whom they so vociferously compared their patriotic defenses of retreat from the court—those whose "Verses are wholly deduc't to Chambers," said Drayton in the "To the generall *Reader*," of the first *Poly-Olbion*—the new Spenserians in their relentless reiteration of the topos of withdrawal to the country contributed to the failure of the age to attain a unifying poetic. Even when the monarch is praised by these poets—as in Phineas Fletcher's allegory of the Gunpowder Plot, in which James is figured as the ideal enemy of the Catholics—the work is often dedicated to Prince Henry or his memory, and the veil of the allegory frequently slips in order to warn James that he should emulate the militancy of his offspring. Insistently, that is, these poets borrow the basic plot of book 1 of Spenser's *Faerie Queene*, emphasizing and expanding its pastoral elements, in order to figure the land and the landscape as a pristine Una who needs the regal protection of another Arthurian warrior knight. Browne's Aletheia wanders through book 1 of *Britannia's Pastorals* (1613) because Adulation dominates the court which refuses her admission. And the simmering discontent that underlies much of his first book becomes explicit outrage and satirical rejection of the court in the second book (1616), paralleling and reenforcing the numerous and bitter satires of Wither. Thus, even when Drayton concludes his roll call of great English poets for the "Dearely-loved Friend Henery Reynolds" with an attack on those

> whose poems, be they nere so rare,
> In private chambers, that incloistered are,
> And by transcription daintyly must goe;
> As though the world unworthy were to know,
> Their rich composures, let those men that keepe
> Those wonderous reliques in their judgement deepe,
> And cry them up so, let such Peeces bee
> Spoke of those that shall come after me,
> I passe not for them,

his frustrated annoyance at the end of the Elizabethan poetic of Sidney and Spenser, which had led to the retreat of his circle of fellow poets from the realm of court poetry, ironically records the same dismay with the absence of an invigorating Stuart poetic which had led those private manuscript poets to their "chambers." Although they would not have condoned the recourse to nostalgia to which Drayton's "Rightly borne Poets" turned—as prominently displayed in Corbett's wry "*New* Ballad" lamenting the disappearance of "The Faeryes" from Stuart England—whether these sprites recall the "old religion" or the old aesthetic as seen also in Drayton's *Nymphidia* (1627)—yet those "incloistered" poets agreed in principle with the modern "ancients." Wotton's "Upon the sudden Restraint of the Earle of Somerset" (a poem by a prominent public figure, ambassador to Venice, whose major poems are private verse epistles to Donne the manuscript poet) plainly articulates why they all found it necessary to move from the public to the private mode:

> Then, since fortunes favours fade,
> You, that in her armes do sleepe,
> Learne to swim, and not to wade;
> For, the Hearts of Kings are deepe.
>
> But, if Greatness be so blind,
> As to trust in towers of Aire,
> Let it be with Goodness lin'd,
> That at'least, the Fall be faire.
>
> Then though darkened, you shall say,
> When Friends faile, and Princes frowne,
> *Vertue* is the roughest way,
> But proves at night a *Bed* of *Downe*.

Thus, even though Donne (master of verses which "must only passe by Transcription," exemplar of the amateur poet whom Drayton disparaged) and the disciples of Spenser were as far apart politically and poetically as Donne and Eliza's Spenser had been, they responded as poets committed to the national need for "Vertue" in a similar fashion—choosing either the traditional structures of the Ignatian meditation or the antique forms of the pastoral allegory to offset the "deepe" vacuities they found at the heart of Stuart "policy." The very diversity of the strains of patriotic British allegory in the period tells the same story. Whether approximating the cerebral wit of Donne, as in the Fletchers' striking epithets and startling paradoxes amid their Spenserian methodology, or imitating the pastoral regionalism of Spenser's *Shepheardes Calender* (1579), as in the charming sentiments of William Basse, the poets move away from the court to find their voices. Sandys turned to moralizing Ovid to maintain his Christian humanist roots; Basse turned to a sort of literalized image of the landscape in Spenser's early poetry; and the Fletchers—in the strangely grotesque metamorphoses of book 2 of Spenser's *Faerie Queene* into *The Purple Island* (1633) and in the sensuous yet dazzlingly witty conjunctions of *Christs Victorie and Triumph* (1610)—showed the lengths to which the conservative Spenserians would go to maintain connections with the "Muses of Elizium."

In the same general vein, Aemelia Lanyer's Renaissance refashioning of the Chaucerian "legende of good women" in *Salve Deus Rex Judæorum* (1611), in spite of its full praises of Queen Anne and Princess Elizabeth (or in addition to them), dedicates the majority of its encomia to present the paradigmatic Protestant virtue of Margaret Russell, Countess of Cumberland, and her daughter, Anne Clifford, Countess of Dorset—both of whom played little part in the politics of the court and returned from the court to the country. In the last part of Lanyer's "Description of Cookeham" (which challenges Jonson's "To Penshurst" as the first English country-house poem) the praise for the "divinity" of withdrawal from the court to the country is mitigated by another elegiac lament for the passing away of that way of life in "this blessed isle," recalling again the complaints against cultural decay that had sounded in the verse satire at the start of the Jacobean regime.

Even those located at the nucleus of the Stuart court, such as Sidney's niece Lady Mary Wroth (who had had a coveted role in Jonson and Inigo Jones's *Masque of Blackness* in 1605), evince the same tendency toward an unrelenting melancholy displayed in Wroth's *Pamphilia to Amphilanthus*, the first sonnet sequence written by an Englishwoman. Even Wroth's masterpiece, *The Countesse of Mountgomeries Urania* (1621), focuses attention on a consciousness in conflict with societal values as much because of the corruption of the courtly world as because of her gender. Even those persons whom one might have thought rightly to have assumed a central position in the court—such as Lord Herbert of Cherbury—strove to find ways to transcend the cultural malaise through a sort of obscure philosophical poeticizing, not perhaps in itself so unusual but significant in terms of the general attitude toward a court that had once been the center of British culture.

The Jacobean poet who would seem to be the most notable exception to this general movement to the private mode would be Jonson. Heir to the "social mode" of Henry Howard, Lord Surrey's originary English neoclassicism, collaborator

with Inigo Jones in the principal royal masques of the day, the author of numerous panegyrics on court figures, raised to the status of poet laureate by James's life pension to him in 1616, England's first professional poet seems, in fact, to have admired (or at least to have wanted to admire) the first Stuart king. Infrequently, in fact, does Jonson turn from the world; even when enumerating the *Contemptus mundi* catalogue, as in "To the World" (*Forest* 4), for example, he turns to face it with the same poised, urbane courage and stoic control he showed in his well-known elegy on the death of his son:

> But I will bear these, with that scorne,
>   As shall not need thy false reliefe.
> Nor for my peace will I goe farre.
>   As wandrers doe, that still doe rome
> But make my strengths, such as they are,
>   Here in my bosome, and at home.

However, the final note, the emphatic "at home" of the final foot, evokes a turn to the stability of the private mode that is consistently voiced by Jonson, even in his most "public" verse.

Jonson did write a panegyric to the king—

> How, best of Kings, do'st thou a scepter beare!
>   How best of *Poets*, do'st thou laurell weare!

—but this flattery is balanced immediately by equivocal qualifications:

> For such a *Poet*, while thy dayes were greene,
>   Thou wert, as chiefe of them are said to'haue beene.

We should not forget, that is, as he told William Herbert, Earl of Pembroke, in the dedication to his *Epigrams*, that satire was "the ripest of [Jonson's] studies," or that, as a professional poet, Jonson depended on his writing to survive. From this point of view his praise of court figures is qualified and perhaps even pointed; one often feels that the tension of the poems is less his disinclination to flatter than the intensity of his begging those figures to try to live up to his expectations and his descriptions of them. In fact, one must wonder whether Jonson's many published epigrams and the effects of their juxtaposition to his panegyrics would have pleased or embarrassed James and his court. In a sense, Jonson, despite his many collaborations in court festivities, after all, adamantly remained the perennial outsider, because of his status as the son of a bricklayer or because of the volatility of his temper or because of the steadfast courage of his moral perspecuity. In the 1616 folio arrangement of his poems, for instance, his panegyrics to Robert Cecil, Earl of Salisbury (numbers 43, 63, and 64), are followed immediately (number 65) by a poem in which he attacks himself for writing poems to "a worthless lord." It was Jonson, after all, who dared to call Cecilia Bulstrode (kin to the powerful Lucy Harington, Countess of Bedford) "the Court Pucelle" (*Underwood* 49) and who dared to chide the court for failing to recognize William Parker, Lord Monteagle's pivotal role in discovering the Gunpowder Plot (Epigram 60). Indeed, Jonson went to lengths to announce his role as a public poet in the tradition of the Sidneyan poetic, associating himself repeatedly with the Sidney dynasty. In addition to the dedication of *Epigrams* to the son of Sir Philip's sister, the second poem of *The Forest* is addressed to Philip's younger brother, Sir Robert Sidney, Lord Lisle (later the earl of Leceister), and others are addressed to Sir Philip's daughter, Elizabeth Sidney, Countess of Rutland, and to Sir Robert Wroth, husband to Sidney's niece. But rather than mere panegyrics to their nobility or (what the court wanted and needed) essays of how the concord of James's rule was evinced in the harmonious life of the gentry, these poems often sound a chord of disillusionment that borders on anticourt satire. "To Sir Robert Wroth," for instance, is a defense of withdrawal from the court ("How blesst art thou, canst loue the countrey, Wroth") which ironically recalls Donne's own outrageous defenses of his "service" to his country in other ways than attendance on the court: "happy: Such be thou" Jonson says, "To doe thy countrey seruice, thy selfe right" in moving to the country.

Even in the most memorable of his poems to the Sidney heirs, "To Penshurst," there is less praise for any "peace" which England's self-proclaimed "*parens patriae*" has brought to the countryside than there is outright defense (however hyperbolic and idealized its contours) of Sir Robert's abandonment of the court for the true site of "noble parts, / . . . manners, armes, and arts." Indeed, the appearance of "King Iames . . . / With his braue sonne" in the world of the estate is figured in the poem as their accidental discovery of this center where "thy lord dwells": their idle, royal peregrinations (they are "hunting late") only providentially bring them to where "they saw thy fires / Shine bright on euery

harth," and they then become "guests" invited to see firsthand the embodiment of the chivalric past of England. Sir Robert's restoration and expansion of the estate in 1612 (proudly accomplished *without* the aid of Spanish pensions, as was Cecil's) aimed, in what Dan Wayne calls the "self-conscious medievalism" of its Tudor culture, to be an expression "in forms and images that represented history as an unbroken tradition"—to be, that is, a monument to that same tradition of British moral culture whose loss Donne bemoaned at the end of *Satyre II* and whose norms and forms the neo-Spenserians had striven to regain in their own nostalgic regionalisms. This poem might well be seen, in fact, as an essay of the central crisis of the Jacobean age, the relation of gentry to royalty; only here Jonson focuses attention less on the decay of those hierarchic values he believed central to civilization than on the "noble" alternative which Sir Robert's desertion of the court embodied. One has only to recall the difference between Sir Robert's attitude toward his residence at Penshurst and the near-despair with which Sir Philip had approached his "rustication" when expelled from the courtly world of Queen Elizabeth in order to see how Jonson's poem associates him with that general movement from the public to the private mode in seventeenth-century poetry. Here Jonson "figures forth" (Sir Philip's term for "right poetry") the residence of true "honour" and "religion" (ostensibly different from a world in which George Villiers, the second son of an indigent knight, moved from earl to marquis to duke of Buckingham in less than a decade, less on the devoutness of his "service" than the amatory devotion of the king). Here are the "better marks" of contact with England's historic and sacramental past, rather than an inflation of "honour" at the court, "a fortune of this age, but rarely known." Here is the "gentleman" who "courtiers good"—but in Kent, not Whitehall, London. And if one doubts that Jonson's turn to private mode is incremental even to his most public poems, one has only to turn to "Inviting a Friend to Supper," where once again the entertainments of the court are rejected for "The entertaynment perfect" of the private life of civilized conduct. Just as the visit of James to Penshurst was figured as an "entertainment" but less appealing in its "zeal" to the sort of sacramental meal in which the poet participated, so in Epigram 101 "my poore home" is repeatedly praised as a contrast to the world of courtly intrigue and decadent excess:

Of this we will sup free, but moderately,
  And we will haue no *Pooly'*, or *Parrot* by;
Nor shall our cups make any guiltie men:
  But, at our parting, we will be, as when
We innocently met. No simple word,
  That shall be vtter'd at our mirthfull boord,
Shall make vs sad next morning; or affright
  The libertie, that wee'll enioy to night.

Here is the poetry of civilization in the "plain style" of one of its most exquisite spokesmen— but, as in the idealized encomium to the ancient nobility that lived at Penshurst, it finds its center in the world of the private celebration of the lord's table.

Jonson, then, despite his continual associations with the court of James, remained the perennial outsider who strove at pivotal moments in his poetic career to privilege the private voice for the same reason as the majority of the other poets of his generation. Committed, like Donne and Drayton, to reach that "huge hill [where] Truth stands," he could not finally commit his life and his art to any culture which had "left [its] roots." As Donne said, those who

  having left their roots, and themselves given
To the streames tyrannous rage, alas, are driven
Through mills, and rockes, and woods, and, at last, almost
Consum'd in going, in the sea are lost:
So perish Soules, which more chuse mens unjust
Power from God claym'd, then God himselfe to trust.

The rival claims about the sources of that "Power," of course, were to dominate the wars of Truth and the civil wars of the next generation. The diffuseness of the poetic landscape of this first generation of seventeenth-century poets and the variety and contradictions in their search for a poetic center in meditative, in antique, or in vatic mode provide a revealing and compelling portrait of the tensions and paradoxes endemic to a generation on the cusp between the medieval and the modern worlds.

—*M. Thomas Hester*

Acknowledgments

This book was produced by Bruccoli Clark Layman, Inc. Karen L. Rood, senior editor for the *Dictionary of Literary Biography* series, and Henry Cuningham were the in-house editors.

Production coordinator is James W. Hipp. Projects manager is Charles D. Brower. Photography editors are Edward Scott and Timothy C. Lundy. Layout and graphics supervisor is Penney L. Haughton. Copyediting supervisor is Bill Adams. Typesetting supervisor is Kathleen M. Flanagan. Systems manager is George F. Dodge. The production staff includes Rowena Betts, Steve Borsanyi, Teresa Chaney, Patricia Coate, Rebecca Crawford, Margaret McGinty Cureton, Bonita Dingle, Mary Scott Dye, Denise Edwards, Sarah A. Estes, Robert Fowler, Mary Lee Goodwin, Avril E. Gregory, Ellen McCracken, Kathy Lawler Merlette, John Myrick, Pamela D. Norton, Thomas J. Pickett, Maxine K. Smalls, and Jennifer C. J. Turley.

Walter W. Ross and Dennis Lynch did library research. They were assisted by the following librarians at the Thomas Cooper Library of the University of South Carolina: Jens Holley and the interlibrary-loan staff; reference librarians Gwen Baxter, Daniel Boice, Faye Chadwell, Jo Cottingham, Cathy Eckman, Rhonda Felder, Gary Geer, Jackie Kinder, Laurie Preston, Jean Rhyne, Carol Tobin, Virginia Weathers, and Connie Widney; circulation-department head Thomas Marcil; and acquisitions-searching supervisor David Haggard.

Seventeenth-Century British Nondramatic Poets
First Series

Dictionary of Literary Biography

Sir William Alexander, Earl of Stirling

(1577? - 1640)

Robert D. Beckett
Southwest Missouri State University

BOOKS: *A Short Discourse of the Good Ends of the higher providence in the late attemptat against his Maiesties Person* (Edinburgh: Printed by Robert Waldegrave, 1600);

The Tragedie of Darius (Edinburgh: Printed by Robert Waldegrave, 1603);

Aurora (London: Printed by R. Field for Edward Blount, 1604);

A Paraenesis To The Prince (London: Printed by R. Field for Edward Blount, 1604);

The Monarchick Tragedies [*Darius, Croesus, A Paraenesis to the Prince, Aurora, Some Verses Written to his Majestie by the Authour at the time of his Maiesties first entrie into England, Some Verses Written shortly thereafter by reason of an inundation of Douen, a water neere vnto the Authors house, wherevpon his Maiestie was sometimes wont to Hawke*] (London: Printed by V. S. for Edward Blount, 1604); enlarged as *The Monarchicke Tragedies; Crœsus, Darius, the Alexandræan, Julius Caesar* (London: Printed by V. Simmes for Edward Blount, 1607; revised, British English version, London: Printed by William Stansby, 1616);

An Elegie on the Death of Prince Henrie (Edinburgh: Printed by Andro Hart, 1612);

Doomes-Day, or, The Great Day of the Lords Ivdgement [four books, or "Hours"] (Edinburgh: Printed by Andro Hart, 1614);

An Encouragement to Colonies (London: Printed by W. Stansby, 1624); republished as *The Mapp and Description of New-England* (London: Printed by W. Stansby for N. Butler, 1630);

Recreations With The Muses (London: Printed by Thomas Harper, 1637)—revised texts of the tragedies and *A Paraenesis*, a much-enlarged version of *Doomes-Day*, and *Jonathan*, a fragment of a heroic poem.

Editions: "Poems of Stirling," in *The Works of the English Poets*, 21 volumes, edited by Alexander Chalmers (London: Printed for J. Johnson and 48 others, 1810), V: 288-439;

A Short Discourse of the Good Ends of the higher providence, in *Adversaria, Notices Illustrative of some of the Earlier Works printed for the Bannatyne Club*, edited by David Laing (Edinburgh: Printed by T. Constable, 1867);

Anacrisis, in *Critical Essays of the Seventeenth Century*, 3 volumes, edited by J. E. Spingarn (Oxford: Clarendon Press, 1908), I: 180-189;

The Poetical Works of Sir William Alexander Earl of Stirling, 2 volumes, edited by L. E. Kastner and H. B. Charlton, Manchester University Publications, English series, no. 10 (Manchester: Manchester University Press / London & New York: Longmans, Green, 1921, 1929).

OTHER: "Supplement To a Defect In The Third Book of 'Arcadia,' " in *The Countesse of Pembrokes Arcadia. Now the Fourth Time Published, With Some New Additions* (London: Printed by H. Lownes for S. Waterson, 1613);

The Psalmes of King David, Translated by King James, mainly translated by Alexander (Oxford: Printed by W. Turner, 1631);

Sir William Alexander, Earl of Stirling (portrait by an unknown artist; Scottish National Portrait Gallery)

Anacrisis, in *The Works of William Drummond, of Hawthornden* (Edinburgh: Printed by James Watson, 1711).

Sir William Alexander, first Earl of Stirling, was one of the Scots nobles who went to England with James VI of Scotland when, as James I, he succeeded Elizabeth to the throne of England in 1603. Representative of the courtly writing encouraged, patronized, and influenced by that monarch, Alexander's works include a youthful sonnet sequence; occasional poems for his royal patron Prince Henry; an elegy on the occasion of that prince's death in 1612; *Doomes-Day* (1614, 1637), which influenced John Milton's *Paradise Lost* (1667); many (perhaps most) of the metrical psalms attributed to James I; a fragment of a poem on the biblical Jonathan; and, most significant among his poetical works, four Senecan closet dramas—*The Tragedie of Darius* (1603), *Croesus* (1604), *The Alexandræan* (1607), and *Julius Caesar* (1607)—written in the fashion of French trage-

dian Robert Garnier. Alexander also wrote literary prose. Of greatest historical interest is his continuation (1613) of Sir Philip Sidney's incomplete romance, *The Countess of Pembrokes Arcadia* (1590). His undistinguished effort at literary criticism, *Anacrisis*, probably written in 1634, was not published until the eighteenth century. He also wrote a prose tract published under two titles, *An Encouragement to Colonies* (1624) and *The Mapp and Description of New-England* (1630).

The only son of Alexander Alexander and Marion Graham Alexander, William Alexander was born in Menstrie, Scotland, most probably in 1577. The Alexanders were an ancient, large, and honored family. William appears to have been educated at the University of Glasgow (which he later patronized and to which his sons were sent) and the University of Leyden in Holland. There is no record of his taking a degree at either university. In the company of the young Archibald Campbell, seventh Earl of Argyll, he toured the Continent in 1597, visiting France,

Alexander's birthplace, the manor house in Menstrie, Scotland, built on land granted to his family before 1505

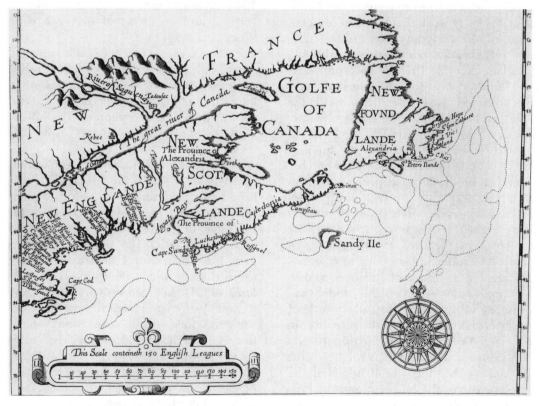

Map published in An Encouragement to Colonies *(1624), part of Alexander's unsuccessful campaign to encourage Scottish settlement of Nova Scotia, territory granted to him by James I*

Spain, and Italy. In 1601 Alexander married Janet, the only daughter of Sir William Erskine, of the family of the earls of Mar. Eleven children were born of this marriage. It is not clear when he met King James VI of Scotland, but it is quite likely that his friend and kinsman the earl of Argyll was the agent of that meeting, probably after their return from the Grand Tour. An unsigned prose work, *A Short Discourse of the Good Ends of the higher providence in the late attemptat against his Majesties Person* (1600), most likely referring to the 4 October 1594 defeat of King James's forces at the Battle of Glenlivet, shows that Alexander early began to seek recognition and favor by means of his writing. When James VI of Scotland became James I of Great Britain and removed his court to London, Alexander moved south and became attached to the court. Soon after James came to the throne in 1603, Alexander had his first signed publication, *The Tragedie of Darius* (1603), followed the next year by three books: *Aurora*, *A Paraenesis To The Prince*, and *The Monarchick Tragedies*. The second and third of these works reveal his continued interest in attracting royal favor.

Despite his close association with the court of James, Alexander worked hard to revise Scotticisms out of his early work. Each of the consecutive editions of the Senecan plays (1604, 1607, 1616, 1637) reflects Alexander's concern with Anglicizing his language. By 1616 he had completed most of the literary works for which he is remembered. His collected works, *Recreations With The Muses* (1637), published near the end of his life, adds no work written after 1616.

Knighted by 1609, Alexander was appointed master of requests for Scotland in 1614 and became a member of the Scottish privy council in 1615. In 1621, a year after the Jamestown settlement, James I conferred on Alexander title to the territory known as Nova Scotia; indeed, the name was given to the area by Alexander. In 1624, to help Alexander in his efforts at colonization, James created an order of baronets, and in 1626—the same year in which Alexander was named secretary of state for Scotland—Charles I authorized armorial bearings for the province, in effect providing Alexander with the opportunity to sell titles in order to raise funds for his effort at colonization. Neither the sale of titles nor the colonization was successful, however, and the British occupation forces, under ·the command of Alexander's son, Sir William Alexander the younger, were forced to abandon Port Royal to the French. Alexander's prose tract *An Encouragement to Colonies* (1624), written to stir interest in settling this land, traces the history of colonizing from the time of the sons of Noah, emphasizes the importance of carrying Christianity to foreign shores, and urges the plantation development of New Scotland. It was Alexander's ambition that colonists would carry into unexplored tracts the civilizing influences of British culture and the elevating influence of Christianity. Alexander, however, had little success in urging Scots to emigrate, and his financial problems, as well as the competing claims of the French to the region, led to the surrender of the grant to the French in 1632. Financially strapped, Alexander, who was appointed an extraordinary judge of the Court of Sessions in 1631, was provided another opportunity to mend his fortunes by issuing debased coins, but this effort earned him only the hatred and contempt of his fellow Scots. Coupled with this unpopular effort to debase the coinage, his attempt to force an English Bible on the church in Scotland caused him to be scorned and reviled by his countrymen. Thus, despite his honors—he was created Viscount Stirling in 1630 and earl of Stirling in 1633—Alexander died in 1640 in much reduced circumstances, bereft of fortune and an object of derision to his fellow Scots.

An Encouragement to Colonies belongs to "literature" only if the term is construed in the broadest sense. Alexander's other writings, however, belong to the history of literature in the special sense. Indeed, they epitomize the kinds of writing attempted by courtly poets of the early seventeenth century.

Although not his earliest publication, *Aurora* (1604) was probably the first-written of his published works, dating from before his connection with the court of James Stuart, even before his marriage in 1601. This Petrarchan-metaphysical sequence includes 104 sonnets, 10 songs, 3 elegies, 2 sestinas, and 4 madrigals. *Aurora* reflects the influence of Sir Philip Sidney's *Astrophel and Stella* (1591). Like Sidney's sequence, Alexander's is notable for its metrical experiments. One of the songs, for example, is an "echo" song quite similar in its structure to one of the "eclogues" in Sidney's *Arcadia*. Although his sonnets show a strong preference for the octave rhyming *abba cddc* and the sestet rhyming *effe gg*, he employs many other rhyming patterns in the sestets. The content is quite conventionally Petrarchan, and *Aurora* is never vividly presented.

THE TRAGEDIE
OF DARIVS.

By VVilliam Alexander
of Menstrie

Omne tulit punctum qui miscuit vtile dulci.

EDINBVRGH
Printed by Robert VValde-graue
Printer to the Kings Maiestie. 1603
Cum Privilegio Regio.

Title page and address to the reader for the first of the poetic closet dramas in which Alexander depicts the dangers of monarchic ambition

To the Reader.

LO heere, gentle Reader, I present to thy favourable viewe and censure the first essay of my rude & vn-skilfull Muse in a Tragicall Poeme. Wherein I thought my time and paines better emploied, as in a subject both pleasant and profitable, then in those idle & vaine toyes, which by their sweet allurementes infect the mindes both of the writer, and reader with the contagion of vice and brutishe sensualitie. The language of this Poeme is (as thou feest) mixt of the English and Scottish Dialects; which perhaps may be vn-pleasant and irksome to some readers of both nations. But I hope the gentle and judicious Englishe reader will beare with me, if I retaine some badge of mine owne countrie, by vsing sometimes words that are peculiar therevnto, especiallie when I finde them propre, and significant. And as for my owne countrie-men, they may not justly finde fault with me, if for the more parte I vse the English phrase, as worthie to be preferred before our owne for the elegancie and perfection thereof. Yea I am perswaded that both countrie-men will take in good part the mixture of their Dialects, the rather for that the bountiful providence of God doth invite them both to a straiter vnion and conjunction aswell in language, as in other respectes.

As for the other defectes and deformities of this

3   Poeme,

To the Reader.

Poeme, I hope, gentle Reader, thou wilt the more sparinglie and courteouslie censure them, for that they are the first faultes of one who is but a young prentice in the arte of Poesie, and for that the imperfection of the worke is supplied with the worthinesse of the matter, and with an earnest desire of procuring thereby the profite and delite. If thou accept gratiouslie these first frutes of my Muse, it will (God-willing) both encourage and enable her to bring foorth heereafter frute of the same kinde, more pleasant and aggreeable to thy delicate taste.

In the meane time, and alwaies, I
bid thee hartelie fare-well.

Sir Robert Aytoun

(25 February 1570 - 25 February 1638)

Sandra Bell
Queen's University at Kingston

BOOKS: *Basia: sive strena Cal. Jan. ad Jacobum Hayum equitem* (Printed by M. Bradwood, 1605);

In obitum Thomæ Rhædi, epicedium (Printed by E. Allde, 1624);

The tragedie of Phillis, complaining of the disloyall love of Amyntas (Printed by M. Flesher for H. Gosson, circa 1625);

Lessus in funere Raphaelis Thorii (Printed by E. Allde for T. Walkley, 1626);

The Poems of Sir Robert Aytoun, edited by Charles Roger[s] (Edinburgh: Adam & Charles Black, 1844);

The Poems of Sir Robert Aytoun, edited by Rogers (London: Privately printed, 1871);

The English and Latin Poems of Sir Robert Aytoun, edited by Charles B. Gullans (Edinburgh: Printed for the Scottish Text Society by W. Blackwood, 1963).

OTHER: *Delitiae Poetarum Scotorum*, includes 24 poems by Aytoun, 2 volumes (Amsterdam, 1637), I: 40-75;

"Poems by Sir Robert Ayton," edited by David Laing, in *Bannatyne Miscellany*, 1 (Edinburgh: Printed by Ballantyne, 1827), pp. 299-324;

"New Poems by Sir Robert Ayton," edited by Charles B. Gullans, *Modern Language Review*, 55 (April 1960): 161-168.

Robert Aytoun's career marks the progress of a poet of Scotland and England at the union of the crowns in 1603, when King James VI of Scotland became King James I of England. Aytoun's verses record his own political advancement, contemporary politics and scandal, as well as the changing styles of court poetry and song. His early works are in literary Scots and influenced by the Castalian movement and by King James, while the later works, especially his amorous verse, are adapted to the English courtly fashion. These poems show the influence of English courtly music, which they themselves influenced.

Frequently quoted in commonplace books, many of his poems and songs enjoyed a popularity in both Scotland and England and reveal Aytoun to be part of the literary traditions of both North and South. Though obscure today, Aytoun was a noteworthy courtier, poet, and patron during the English Renaissance.

Aytoun's vernacular verse was collected by his nephew Sir John Aytoun. Though a preface to this manuscript, which is now in the British Library, reveals that this collection was prepared for publication, it did not reach the press. Most of Aytoun's Latin verse was collected in *Delitiae Poetarum Scotorum* (1637). David Laing published the first collection of Aytoun's English poems in 1827, including a brief biographical sketch. Charles Rogers published an edition of the Latin and English works in 1844, which was revised in 1871 because of the discovery of more material. A more accurate and complete text is Charles B. Gullans's 1963 edition, published for the Scottish Text Society, which includes the Latin and vernacular poems as well as a biography and a collection of letters.

There is some difficulty in dating Aytoun's verse. His epitaphs and poems relating to specific political events or court scandal can be more closely dated than the generic verse. Aytoun's Scottish "diers," poems in which the speaker is near death for love, are dated by Gullans from 1590 to 1603, and the sonnets from 1600 to 1605 or perhaps earlier, as the vogue for sonnets in England was in the 1590s. According to Helena Mennie Shire, the movement from earlier to later poems is marked by stylistic changes, especially those reflecting changes in court music, and corresponds to Aytoun's change from Castalian poet to Cavalier.

Aytoun was born on 25 February 1570 to a large landowning family of Fifeshire, the second of four sons and two daughters born to Andrew Aytoun and his wife, Mariona (née Lundie). He matriculated in March 1584 at St. Leonard's College, St. Andrews, receiving his B.A. in Novem-

Monument to Sir Robert Aytoun in Westminster Abbey (frontispiece to Charles Rogers, ed., The Poems of Sir Robert Aytoun, *1871)*

ber 1588 and an M.A. in March 1589. He received an inheritance on his father's death in 1590. This information is all that is recorded of Aytoun's life in Scotland.

Aytoun's verses reveal the influence of Scotland on his poetry. It is unknown whether he ever approached King James's court in Scotland or knew any of the members of the Castalian band of court makars (poets). King James's *Essayes of a Prentise, in the divine art of Poesie* with its treatise for Scottish poetry appeared in 1584, the same year that Aytoun entered college, and its probable influence is reflected in several of Aytoun's poems which follow the fashion of King James's poetry. Alexander Montgomerie, "chief poet" of James's Scottish court and one whose verses are frequently quoted in the treatise, also influenced Aytoun's style and content.

Although Aytoun was not a member of the Castalian band, he continues a Scottish tradition, and Shire calls him the "Last Castalian." His early verse follows the fashion of poets in Scotland in the 1590s. A group of seven poems referred to as the "Diaphantus" poems were written by Aytoun in conjunction with Sir William Alexander (later earl of Stirling) and Alexander Craig, a fellow undergraduate at St. Leonard's. The poems are a collection of extended love laments in literary Scots. The first is a plaint of absence; the other six are diers. Highly rhetorical and in "poulter's measure," they may be influenced by a love lament written by King James at the request of Queen Anne, which was quite popular in Scotland in the 1590s. The second and sixth of the Diaphantus poems, "Quhen Diaphantus Knew" and "Will thow, remorsles fair," are by Aytoun; Alexander wrote the fourth and fifth poems, and the third, "Craiges passionado," is most likely by Craig. These poems, the only extant Scottish poems by Aytoun and Alexander, reveal a group of Scottish poets working together much as the members of the earlier Castalian band.

The style of the dier or *passionado* was not fashionable in early-seventeenth-century England, so that, although Aytoun later modified the "uncouth" Scots of the Diaphantus collection for publication in England, it caused little stir in that country. (No copy of this published version is known to exist.) The fashions of Scotland, which lagged behind those of England, may have hindered the acceptance of Aytoun's verse in England, but they provided a welcome ground for some of his later songs, which remained popular in Scotland throughout the seventeenth century.

Very little is known of Aytoun's movements in the period from 1590 to 1603. He was in Paris for all or part of this time, perhaps continuing studies of civil law. Thomas Dempster, in *Historia Ecclesiastica Gentis Scotorum* (1627), recorded that in France Aytoun "for long cultivated the arts and left there a name for virtue and distinguished proof of his achievement" and that he wrote French and Greek (nonextant) as well as Latin and Scots poems. An influence of the French vocabulary and *air de cour* is apparent in some of Aytoun's verse.

Aytoun reappears in recorded history in 1603, when his more than four-hundred-line Latin panegyric to King James was published in Paris. He won favor with King James and enjoyed a fairly rapid rise at court. In 1608 he became groom of the privy chamber, and in 1609 he conveyed James's defense of the right of kings to demand an oath of allegiance to Protestant princes in Germany. He was knighted on 30 August 1612 and in that same year succeeded Sir William Fowler as secretary to Queen Anne. Aytoun also served as secretary to Queen Henrietta Maria, after Charles I became king in 1625, and remained at that post until death in 1638.

Aytoun's positions at court afforded him communication with important political and noble persons, as well as court playwrights, poets, and musicians. According to William Drummond of Hawthornden, Ben Jonson claimed "That Sir Robert Aiton loved him dearly." Another contemporary, John Aubrey, stated that "Sir Robert was one of the best poets of his time—Mr John Dreyden says he has seen verses of his, some of

the best of that age." Aubrey continued, "He was acquainted with all the witts of his time in England. He was a great acquaintance of Mr. Thomas Hobbes of Malmesbury, whom Mr. Hobbes told me he had made use of (together with Ben Johnson [*sic*]) for an Aristarchus, when he made his Epistle Dedicatory to his translation of Thucydides." In his notes on Hobbes, Aubrey wrote, "*Aiton*, Scoto-Britannus, a good poet and critique and good scholar."

Aytoun's vernacular occasional verses provide some measure of his acquaintances. He continued his friendship with Craig and Alexander, and founded new ones with both vernacular and Latin poets. His position required him to respond to such events as the deaths of Prince Henry in 1612 and Queen Anne in 1619. The death of the prematurely born Prince Charles on 13 May 1629 occasioned one of Aytoun's finest poems, "on the Princes death, to the King." His poems to George Villiers, first Duke of Buckingham, do not so much claim an intimate relationship, as they further confirm the power wielded by the king's favorite. Two poems to King James, "Where Thebes staitely Towres did threat the skye" and "The old Records of annalized fame," use the image of Phoebus and praise the king as a provider and preserver of life.

Not all of Aytoun's occasional verse is praise, however. In an overtly skeptical statement on the court, "Vpon Mr Thomas Murrays fall," sparked by an unknown incident, he parallels the illumination offered by a small boy on a dark night to the illumination needed by the court:

> they that take
> The way from whence I came, have neede to make
> A light there guide, for I dare boldly say
> Its ten to one, but they shall lose there way.

Another poem which questions the movements of the court is a sonnet on the River Tweed. Aytoun notes that the Tweed, which formerly divided the kingdoms of England and Scotland, now "conjoynes two Diadems in one." This poem is foreboding, as the river is asked to be the "Trinchman," or interpreter, of the news of this union to "that Religious place" where lies Robert the Bruce, champion of Scottish independence. An emendation in Sir John Aytoun's manuscript substitutes "Captivers" for "Captaines" in the line "our Captaines last farewell," which further emphasizes that the union of the two kingdoms, while in the interest of King James (the

Transcription of a poem by Aytoun as it appears in the first Dalhousie manuscript, a collection of poems by John Donne and others copied by an unknown hand between 1613 and 1624 from manuscripts in the collection of Robert Devereux, second Earl of Essex (Texas Tech University Library, Dalhousie I, f. 15v)

"Captiver" who leads his Scottish subjects into captivity), may not be in the best interest of Scotland.

Aytoun was also highly regarded as a Scottish Latinist by his contemporaries, and his impressive and intricate classical Latin verses played a large role in his life at court. Most of these verses are occasional and refer to the nobility or those in court service: panegyrics to the king; congratulations to Buckingham on his dual office of master of the horse and master of the fleet; letters accompanying New Year's gifts to James Hay, a Scottish favorite at court, and Raphael Thorius, a French physician who wrote Latin poetry; epitaphs on several courtiers, as well as on Buckingham and Prince Henry. Some of his verses refer to contemporary political concerns: the Gunpowder Plot of Guy Fawkes (1605); the rumored assassination of King James; the foreboding comet which appeared just before Queen Anne's death; the conflicting duties of King James as father and as king at the onset of the Thirty Years' War in Europe. (The last two lines of this poem are quoted in a pamphlet urging militant action, *Tom Tell Troath, or a Free Discourse Touching the Manners of the Tyme*, possibly written by Joseph Swetnam and printed circa 1626.)

Aytoun also recorded court scandal in his Latin poems. "Legitimas quicunque audes traducere taedas," circulated in manuscript in 1613, is headed "Vpon the Countess of Essex Divorce" in Sir John Aytoun's manuscript. Commenting on the annulment of the marriage between Robert Devereux, third Earl of Essex, and Lady Frances Howard, this satiric epigram questions the laws that forbid an unsatisfied wife to bestow her "kingdom" on a more able man than her husband. A second poem followed in 1616, shortly after the discovery of the joint crime of Lady Frances and her new husband, Robert Carr, Earl of Somerset, both convicted of arranging the murder of Sir Thomas Overbury, who had acted as their go-between before Lady Frances's divorce. "Haec Caro Carina suo mandata salutem" is headed "Carina Caro" and models itself on the erotic epistles of Ovid's *Heroides*. Both Carina and Caros are imprisoned for poisoning one of the nobility, and Carina's execution is imminent by the end of the poem.

A small number of Aytoun's Latin verses reveal that his own progress at court was not without its disappointments. In the blossoming of his career, he related his own condition to that of the spring, and gave thanks to King James for rec-

ognition and admittance into the privy chamber. In "Aulae valedicit," however, he bids good-bye to the royal court—his hopes for advancement and favor dashed; this poem was probably written after his (unsuccessful) attempt to become provost of Eton in 1623-1624. "Expostulatio cum Iacobo Rege" is a lamentation in which Aytoun asks why he has been forgotten by his king. In a short epigram he thanks the king for his praise but says he would rather receive a more substantial reward. While these poems reveal Aytoun's occasional frustrations, it is pleasing to know that this last poem, "Carmina quae scripsi, laudasti maxime Princeps," was written before the more substantial reward of the position of groom of the privy chamber in 1608. Aytoun's poems both reflected and affected his position at court.

There are extant contemporary translations of a few of Aytoun's Latin poems. "De Rebus Bohemicis" becomes "Whiles thy sonnes rash vnluckye armes attempt," and there are several translations of his congratulatory poem on Buckingham's receipt of a dual office; one translation may have been made by King James. Aytoun also wrote English poems on some of the same topics covered in his Latin verse. "Vpon the :5: th of November" recalls the Gunpowder Plot, and two poems, one to Prince Charles, the other to King James, lament the death of Prince Henry in 1612. The majority of Aytoun's vernacular verse, however, deals not with topical or political subjects, but focuses on love.

Aytoun's courtly position also influenced his amorous poems. The clear, graceful verses capture the rhythm of courtly speech and develop a more intricate argument than his early pieces. His lighthearted, sometimes flippant approach to matters of love is part of the courtly fashion of Platonic and Petrarchan verse, especially stylish under Queen Henrietta Maria, and has earned him the title "father of the Cavaliers." His use of paradox in poems such as "There is none, no, none but I" shapes the recurrent theme of the failed attempt of the ever-constant lover to conquer the "cruel fair" mistress, as well as the theme of the pleasant pain of unrequited love.

Lovely eyes and Loveless heart,
Why doe you soe disagree?
How can sweetness cause such smart
Or smarting soe delightful be?

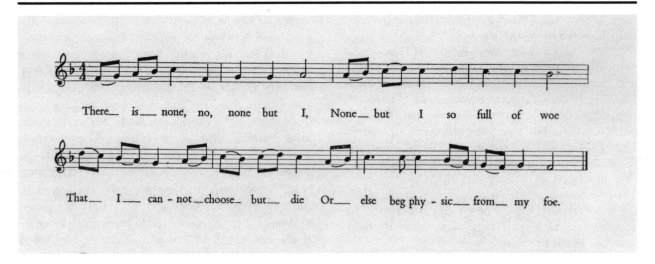

Opening lines of "There is none, no, none but I," lyrics by Aytoun set to music by Thomas Campion

These two themes, variously presented as the virtue and the vice of the mistress, run throughout Aytoun's love poetry.

This Platonic love theme is often made ambiguous by the common Renaissance pun on "die." Yet a poem such as "Lov's like a game at Irish where the dye," in which "When you are on, you must throw home and hye," is not ambiguous at all. Sexual punning is one method Aytoun uses to play with the court taste for Platonic love. He more explicitly mocks this fashion in "Vpon Platonick Love: To Mistress Cicely Crofts, Maide of Honor":

> Thus doe your raptures reach to that degree
>   In loves Phylosiphy
> That you can figure to your selfe a fyre,
> Void of all heat, a love without desire.

In this poem, a real love is not inspirational or divine, but one of bodily satisfaction: "My senses tell me if I please not them / My love is butt a dottage or a dreame." Aytoun switches with ease from the role of the Petrarchan or Platonic lover to the sensual Cavalier and reveals the changes occurring in court poetry.

Shire examines how the changing fashion of court music influenced Aytoun's poetry and how his songs reflect the practice of songwriting over two reigns. Some of his songs were set to (and written for) traditional Scottish ayres. "Thou Wilt Not Goe" was popular in Scotland from 1610 to 1665, but the Englished lyric, while popular, has no recorded music. Another lyric, "I do confess thou'rt smooth and fair," was Scotticized and set to a Scottish ayre as "I do confess thou art sae fair / I had been ower the lugs in love." Other verses underwent translations in the North or South and were then set to music that reflected the tastes of the particular country. In some cases the words were written for popular tunes—and thus shaped by the music; in others Aytoun's verses were popular enough to have music written specifically for them—thus influencing the shape of court song.

Aytoun's early songwriting period at court is what Shire calls the "Ayton-Campion conjunction." Aytoun was probably acquainted with Thomas Campion and some of Aytoun's lyrics were set to Campion's music. At this time "tuneful airs" were popular and required short lyrics with light and moving rhythms. The music was usually written for one stanza and repeated for subsequent stanzas, creating the need for them to match the form of the first closely. The arguments were witty, but not too involved, and demanded a natural phrasing and direct expression. In the nature of the Cavalier lyric, these songs often discussed witty reasonings of love. One very popular example, Aytoun's "There is no wordly pleasure here below," underwent a metamorphosis over time, and eventually incorporated a rejoinder to Aytoun's call for moderation in love.

Under the influence of Henry Lawes, court musician from 1625 to 1662 (omitting the Civil War years), the fashion moved from the tuneful air to a "declamatory" court style, which captured the rhythms and emphasis of speech in music. Because this declamatory style of music was freer in structure, succeeding stanzas of a lyric did not have to follow the rhyme scheme and metrical form of the first. This change led to multiple variations in versions of the songs.

The lyrics were also influenced by "dramatic song" settings of Dr. John Wilson, singer and musician in the courts of James I and Charles I. In Wilson's resetting of "There is none, no, none but I" (an answer to "There is none, O, none but you," already set to a "tuneful air" by Campion), he no longer places the emphasis on the witty argument and paradoxical conclusion, but on the emotions of this Cavalier lyric. There is also a significant change in some wording to accommodate the new musical setting. The adaptability of Aytoun's lyrics ensured their survival, albeit in revised form.

Some of Aytoun's verses have at least three musical settings, each with slightly different wording. The resettings of "Upon a ringe Queen Anne sent to Sir Robert Aytoune" reveal the popularity and flexibility of Aytoun's verse, as the meaning and emphasis of the song change from the older *air de cour* style, to the mid-century version found in John Gamble's songbook, and finally to the declamatory style of musician John Playford. Aytoun could take advantage of musical styles to popularize his own verse, but the use of his lyrics by Jacobean and Carolinian musicians suggests that he directly influenced the shape of court music in these two reigns.

Aytoun died on 25 February 1638 and was buried in the south aisle of the choir in Westminster Abbey, near the steps leading into Henry VII's chapel. A copper bust of Aytoun was erected at his burial place.

Aytoun's move to England and involvement in the English court and English fashions did not sever his connection to Scotland. William Lithgow records Aytoun's importance in the continuity of a Scottish literary tradition in the preface to *The Pilgrimes Farewell to his Native Country of Scotland* (1618): "Brave Murray ah is dead, Aiton supplies his place." The line of Scottish makars flows from Alexander Montgomerie to his apprentice, John Murray, and so to Aytoun. The assertion that this line is then continued by Robert Burns is debatable, but the original words of "Old long syne," very much in Aytoun's style, are found in an Aytoun manuscript, and were first attributed to Aytoun by Rogers in 1871. Burns also rewrote "I doe confess th'art smooth, and faire," included as one of the four "Doubtful poems" in Gullans's edition. Whether Burns in the eighteenth century did continue Aytoun's line or not, in the seventeenth century Aytoun's verse found a popularity in both the North and South rarely experienced by a poet born in Scotland.

References:

Helena Mennie Shire, Commentary in *A Choice of Poems and Songs by Robert Aytoun*, edited by Shire (Cambridge: University Press, 1961);

Shire, *Song, Dance and Poetry of the Court of Scotland Under King James VI* (Cambridge: University Press, 1969).

Papers:

Aytoun's English poems were copied by his nephew Sir John Aytoun and are preserved at the British Library (Add.MSS. 10308).

William Basse

(circa 1583 - 1653)

Brian M. Blackley
University of Kentucky

BOOKS: *Sword and Buckler: or, a Serving-mans Defence* (London: Printed by F. Kingston for M. Lownes, 1602);

Three Pastoral Elegies of Anander, Anetor, and Muridella (London: Printed by V. Simmes for J. Barnes, 1602);

Great Brittaines Sunnes-set bewailed with a shower of teares (Oxford: Printed by Joseph Barnes, 1613).

Edition: *Poetical Works of William Basse (1602-1653)*, edited by R. Warwick Bond (London: Ellis & Elvey, 1893).

OTHER: William Browne, *Britannia's Pastorals. The second Booke*, includes a commendatory verse by Basse (London: Printed by T. Snodham for G. Norton, 1616);

E. Allde, ed., *Ballads*, includes "Maister Basse his careere, or the new hunting of the hare" ["The Hunter's Song"] by Basse (London: Printed by E. Allde, circa 1620);

John Donne, *Poems. With elegies on the authors death*, includes "Elegy on Shakespeare" by Basse (London: Printed by M. Flesher for G. Marriot, 1633);

M. Walbancke, ed., *Annalia Dubrensia*, includes "To the Noble and Fayre Assemblies" by Basse (London: Printed by R. Raworth for M. Walbancke, 1636);

Izaak Walton, *The Compleat Angler*, includes "The Angler's Song" by Basse (London: Printed by T. Maxey for Rich. Marriot, 1653).

Known primarily for his occasional poetry, William Basse has a small but secure place as a Spenserian poet of considerable note among his contemporaries. His "Elegy on Shakespeare," which was not properly credited to Basse until Edmond Malone's edition of Shakespeare in 1790, and "The Angler's Song," appearing in Izaak Walton's *The Compleat Angler* (1653), are the primary works which have established his reputation. His verse is characterized by unpretentious

diction, a pleasant and flowing prosody, and frequent allusion to the celebrated persons he knew.

Basse appears to be from Moreton, near Thame, in Oxfordshire: in *Athenæ Oxonienses* (1691-1692) Anthony Wood called him "sometime a retainer to Lord Wenman of Thame Park." Lord Wenman was the former Sir Richard Wenman, created an Irish peer by the title of Viscount Wenman of Tuam in July 1628. Other contemporary mention of Basse is included in the entries of the *Thame Parish Register*, which records the baptism of an Elizabeth Basse (20 November 1625); the burial of "Jane ye daughter of Wm. Basse" (10 September 1634); the marriage of Richard Furt and Dorothy Basse "by banns" (24 July 1637); and the burial of "Helinor ye wife of William Basse" (23 September 1637). There also seems to have been a Thomas Basse in the neighborhood, but of the citations regarding William Basse there can be no doubt.

The information pertaining to the life of Basse is perhaps unusually scarce, much of it derived from the contents, dedications, or titles of his poems. The year 1602 marks Basse's first publication, *Sword and Buckler: or, a Serving-mans Defence*. The work has two prefatory verses; the second, "To the Reader," begins

> Reade if you will: And if you will not chuse,
> My booke (Sir) shall be read though you refuse:
> But if you doe, I pray commend my wit,
> For, by my faith, 'tis first that ere I writ.

There is no reason to disbelieve the author's claim that the poem is his first effort. The poem is an argument on behalf of the serving class, insisting on the fine qualities and loyalty of most servants despite frequent abuses at the hands of their "hard commanders." His purpose and the meaning of his title become fully apparent in stanza 23:

> Who let's us now to finde our owne defence
> Against all such encounters offer'd thus?
> Who is so void of loue, or bare of sence,

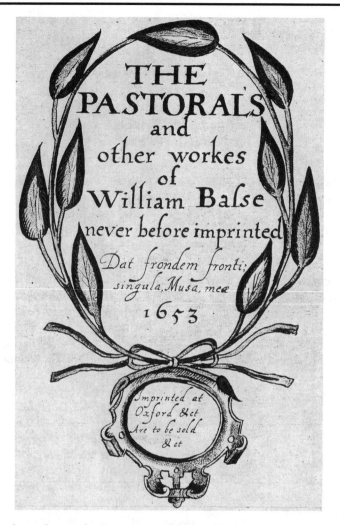

Title page for the manuscript volume of poems that Basse prepared for possible publication in 1653 (from Poetical Works of William Basse [1602-1653], *edited by R. Warwick Bond, 1893)*

To thinke it any misdemeasne in us,
    If we, to right our selves, doe fall againe
    Into our ancient Sword and Buckler vaine?

Yet Basse insists that he is not suggesting insurrection; his is but a "speaking fight." He addresses accusations that "ev'ry Serving-man doth love a whore" and that such men "love Dronkenesse" and stand accused of "idlenes." In stanza 73 he asserts that he has "served but a little while" and lives himself "in the place and manner of a Page." This information is important in determining how he came to Thame Park.

The first Lady Wenman, Agnes, was a daughter of Sir George Fermor of Easton Neston in Northamptonshire, a lady of much learning and some literary achievement. (The Cambridge University Library holds manuscript volumes containing her English translation of John Zonaras's twelfth-century *Historyes and Chronicles of the World*.) It is probable that the attention of this "lerned lady" at some time was drawn to William Basse, a promising young scholar at the Northampton Free Grammar School, and that upon the occasion of her marriage to Sir Robert Wenman, an event which most likely took place shortly after he received his knighthood in 1596, the boy William accompanied her to Thame Park in the capacity of page. Further support for placing Basse originally in Northampton appears in the fourth eclogue in the manuscript volume of his *Pastorals and other workes*. A reference in the margin identifies "yon Towne" as Northampton, which is contrasted in the poem with Oxford. Thus Basse seems likely a native of Northampton who came to work and live virtually his entire life in Oxfordshire at Thame Park in service to Lord Wenman.

Three Pastoral Elegies of Anander, Anetor, and Muridella, also published in 1602, shows Edmund

Spenser to be the strongest single influence on Basse's works. R. Warwick Bond, editor of the only collected edition of Basse's poetry, suggested that Basse knew Spenser, but there is no solid evidence of such a personal connection between them. The direct and emphatic nature of Basse's verses in the third of his *Three Pastoral Elegies*, which refer to Colin Clout, Spenser's persona in his *Shepheardes Calender* (1579), does, however, raise the possibility of a personal relationship:

> when I was Collins loued boy,
> (Ah, Collin, for thee, Collin, weep I now,)
> For thou art dead, ah, that to me didst joy,
> As Coridon did to Alexis vow.
> But (as I sed,) when I was Collins boy,
> His deare young boy, and yet of yeares inow,
> To leade his willing heard along the plaine,
> I on his pipe did learne this singing vaine.
>
> And oh, (well mote he now take rest therfore,)
> How oft in pray'rs and songs he pray'd and sung,
> That I (as had himselfe full long before,)
> Mought liue a happy shepheard and a young;
> And many vowes, and many wishes more,
> When he his Pipe into my bosome flung:
> And said, though Collin ne're shall be surpast,
> Be while thou liu'st, as like him as thou maist.

These lines also could record only a thorough literary debt to the Court poet, however; and, indeed, such a debt might be seen in the predictability of *Three Pastoral Elegies* as far as the conventions of love poetry during the end of the Elizabethan period, with the loyal and melancholy lover crying over his unrequited love of the cold and beautiful mistress: "the strictnes of a Ladies will" and "the hardship of a Louer's ill." Anander is the lovesick shepherd who loves Muridella; Anetor is the intermediary to whom Anander's woes are told. In the second elegy the blazon enumerating Muridella's beauty employs the usual hyperbole and similes, but is perhaps taken to even greater detail than some others working within the tradition:

> How comely, Lord, (me thinks) hir backe was made,
> How right hir shoulders to the same were knit;
> How excellently both hir sides were laide;
> How straight, how long hir armes were, and how
>   fit.

This partial stanza also presents a common characteristic of Basse's writing, the use of the same word to begin several successive lines. The ele-

gies are otherwise undistinguished, except for their rather striking detail in describing country life, enhancing the reality of the events described. Basse freely acknowledges his debt to Spenser, and he successfully captures some of Spenser's flowing style and moral tone, yet with fewer archaisms and less power or intensity.

Still, judging by the quality of these 1602 publications, their metrical skill and control over language, the author is unlikely to have been much younger than eighteen. It is probably accurate, then, to fix his date of birth about 1583. If, however, Basse is merely writing in character, there is the possibility that he was born earlier and lived to be more than seventy years old.

Also uncertain is the date of Basse's marriage to his wife, Helinor. It is most likely that on the occasion of Basse's marriage, and no doubt through the goodwill and generosity of Sir Richard, Basse acquired a home of his own at Moreton, within a mile or thereabouts of Thame Park. By all indications, he lived there until his death.

The first poem after 1602 for which there is any sure indication of composition date is the long narrative poem *Urania: The Woman in the Moone*, which, since it is dedicated to Prince Henry, must have been written before his death in 1612. Basse's most original work and possibly his best achievement, *Urania* is a light and playful satire against women, quite reminiscent of Ovid's *Metamorphoses*. In *Urania*, which consists of four cantos (quarters of the moon), Jupiter is dissatisfied with the state of the earth and dispatches two Olympians to investigate and report. They both fall in love with their Ethiopian hostess on earth and, in order to entice her to surrender to their passions, reveal their deity to her. She agrees to fulfill their desires, provided they reveal to her first how to ascend to the heavens. They do, and she at once sprouts wings and flies to Olympus, distancing their pursuit. Her arrival confounds and disrupts the Immortals, and Jove holds a council, which decides to place her in the moon, rather than imperil heaven's peace by allowing her to stay or risk betrayal of their secrets by sending her back to earth. Her final revenge is to subject all women to her influence. The wit and good-natured fun of the work are best exemplified in the exasperation the Olympians feel when the "audacious Dame" arrives:

> Some of the Court are angry, some are glad,
> The elder frowne, the younger flock about her,

> But (of all other) Iuno was horne-mad,
> She of great Ioue did so extreamly doubt her:
> And Venus waxed leane, with strong suspect
> That Mars would favour this, & her neglect.

The poem is smooth and pleasing, written in six-line stanzas of iambic pentameter, rhyming *ababcc* (the same rhyme scheme as *Sword and Buckler*). An additional section, "The Story Morallized," seems unnecessary and may have been added much later—unless, of course, it is intended to recall the rather obtuse glosses provided by "E. K." at the end of each month of *The Shepheardes Calender*, and the careful explanation that Spenser makes of his "darke conceit" in the introduction to *The Faerie Queene* (1590), and thus to acknowledge again Basse's imitation of the Elizabethan mythic poet.

Prince Henry's death in 1612 is lamented by Basse in his elegy *Great Brittaines Sunnes-set*, which was published in Oxford in 1613. Far from his best work, the elegy is written in a difficult eight-line stanza ending in two Alexandrines with rhymed hemistichs. The form may have outmatched his inspiration:

> Like to a changeling (in his sleepes) become
> Rob'd of his sexe, by some prodigious cause;
> I am turn'd woman: wat'rish feares benumbe
> My Heate: my Masculine existence thawes
> To teares, wherein I could againe entombe
> His tombe, or penetrate hir marble jawes:
> But, O, why should I twice entombe him! O what folly
> Were it to pierce (with sighes) a monument so holy!

The conceited thought which he expresses here is not typical of his verse, and the strain in his comparisons is a rare problem. The frequent use of parentheses is a common mark in Basse's verse, as well as the use of slant rhyme, such as "twice" and "sighes."

Basse seems to have justified his position in the Wenman household by the occasional offering of a poem in honor of some member of the family or some special guest. A sort of family poet laureate, he was probably exempted from personal service in order that he might visit the library and enhance his literary skills. *Polyhymnia*, a volume prepared for publication but never printed, offers several instances of such verse. Among those individuals whom he honored with

his poetry were Lady Penelope Dynham, eldest daughter of his patron; Elizabeth, Viscountess Falkland, wife of Sir Henry Cary, Viscount Falkland, the Irish lord deputy; Sir William, Lord Knollys, of Caversham House (later earl of Banbury); and Mary Herbert, Countess of Pembroke, sister of Sir Philip Sidney. She appears several times under the name "Poemenarcha" and is the subject of eclogue 2 in Basse's *Pastorals*, where she is praised for her generosity to shepherds (encouragement to poets): the "shepheards Queene," who "lends us light." Her departure for Belgium in 1616 is lamented by Orpin in eclogue 5, and her death in 1621 is lamented by Tomkin in eclogue 8, together with her brother "Philisiden":

> To tell thee plaine, I mean Philisiden
> And his deare sister, that renowned Dame
> We Poemenarcha call'd; he that of men
> The wonder was, she of her sex the same.

There is only one person for whom all these allusions would have been applicable: the countess of Pembroke. Few of Basse's poetic pseudonyms are so obvious as "Philisiden," a name for Philip Sidney borrowed from Spenser's "Ruines of Time."

Basse's connection with the Wenman family also implies connection with their relatives, the Norreys, also from the Oxfordshire area. They lived in Rycote, a little north of the high road between Thame and Oxford and within a few miles of Thame Park. The *Polyhymnia* volume was dedicated to Bridget, Countess of Lindsey, owner of Rycote. The opening poem is addressed to Francis, Lord Norreys, Earl of Berkshire and grandfather of the countess.

There were originally two manuscript versions of *Polyhymnia*. One, which Bond calls the Cole Manuscript, was described by William Cole (1714-1782) in his manuscript "Collections for an Anthenæ Cantabrigienses." Joseph Hunter (1783-1861), in his manuscript "Chorus Vatum Anglicorum," referred to the Cole manuscript, but it has since disappeared. The other was acknowledged by Thomas Corser as part of his manuscript collection in *Notes and Queries* (9 March 1850) and was also mentioned in John Payne Collier's *Bibliographical and Critical Account of the Rarest Books in the English Language* (1865). Corser's manuscript was sold in 1868 to a bookseller, a Mr. Honnor, who was a purchasing agent for private collectors. Honnor died in 1883, leaving no record of the disposition of the manuscript. As a result of the loss of both manuscripts, only the notices by Cole and Hunter, and the articles by Corser and Collier, remain as testimony to the existence of the work. Each manuscript included works absent in the other; Bond collates the fragments quoted in these sources in his edition.

Corser reported that his manuscript had fifty-two leaves, was "beautifully written without any corrections" and "in the original binding" with the autograph of Francis, Lord Norreys, on the flyleaf. Corser asserts it was a presentation copy from Basse. Since Norreys was created Viscount Thame and earl of Berkshire in 1621 and died in 1623, the compilation and presentation of the volume must fall within that two-year period. "The Youth in the Boat" was the longest work in the collection. Divided into two parts, it had 59 four-line stanzas in the first and 163 in the second, not including a finishing 11-stanza "Morall." Only a 16-stanza beginning fragment remains.

The general content of Basse's verse, the occasional Latinisms and abundant allusions to Ovid's *Metamorphoses* and classical mythology in general, encourages the assumption that Basse was a university man. However, his name is not on the registers of those who graduated from Oxford or Cambridge between 1567 and 1610. The William Basse of Suffolk who was admitted a sizar of Emanuel College, Cambridge, in 1629 (A.B. 1632, and A.M. in 1636) was not related. There was a William Basse of Benhall, Suffolk, who died at age eighty-five in 1607, survived by a son, Thomas, and a grandson, William, most likely the Cambridge student. The poet Basse's relations with the two Oxfordshire houses make any connection to Suffolk unlikely. Basse evinces clear interest in Oxford in his work whether its source was from actual study at the university or simply from residence in its neighborhood. In 1613 he wrote some verses on the consecration of the chapel of Wadham College, Oxford, and included them in *Polyhymnia*. Individuals mentioned in his poetry include many Oxford men, such as Ralph Bathurst, who wrote a commendatory verse to Basse's manuscript *Pastorals and other workes*; Clement Barksdale, identified as "Jasper" in *The Metamorphosis of the Walnut Tree of Borestall*; and William Browne, who wrote *Britannia's Pastorals* (1613, 1616), for the second book of which Basse wrote a prefatory verse of commendation. From the placement of Basse's verse along with the verses by George Wither and Ben Jonson in

the 1616 folio edition of Browne's book, printed apart from those of other contributors, we may infer some association among the four poets.

Basse's best-known poem, the "Elegy on Shakespeare," may have been written as early as 1616 and certainly no later than 1623, when Jonson alluded to it. Printed initially in the first edition of John Donne's poetry in 1633 and thus mistakenly attributed to him, it was removed in the 1635 edition not to reappear; this confusion over authorship was probably due to Donne's having possessed a manuscript copy of Basse's poem. Malone wrote an extensive note on its authorship in his edition of Shakespeare in 1790. There are ten manuscripts for the poem; Bond grants greatest authority to the Lansdowne manuscript version in William Browne's hand (British Library, Lansdowne 777, fo.67b). However, he includes in his collection the Fennell manuscript version (location now unknown) for comparison. Malone said of the manuscript he used that it "appears to have been written soon after the year 1621." Two of the manuscripts omit lines 13 and 14, presumably thinking the poem to be a sonnet and shortening it to fourteen lines. In none of the manuscripts does the location of the graves of Geoffrey Chaucer, Sir Francis Beaumont, and Spenser agree with the actual position of their resting places in Westminster Abbey. Probably Basse had the chronological order of the poets' deaths in mind when he composed the lines, arriving at the Chaucer-Spenser-Beaumont sequence that the spatial logic of the lines suggests, as he calls on them to make room for Shakespeare. This way, the idea in line 9 on "precedency in death" accords with the meaning of the opening sentence.

The poem was quite well received and widely circulated among Basse's contemporaries. Jonson's allusion to Basse's "Elegy" in his own poem, "To the Memory of my beloved, the Author, Mr. William Shakespeare," prefixed to the 1623 folio, proves that Jonson not only was aware of Basse's poem in manuscript (Basse's elegy was not published until 1633 when it was attributed to Donne), but that he admired it and respected its popular reception. Basse's "Elegy" begins:

Renowned Spenser, lye a thought more nye
To learned Chaucer, and rare Beaumond, lye
A little neerer Spenser, to make roome
For Shakespeare in your threefold, fowerfold
    Tombe.

Jonson opens his own work with these responding lines alluding to the fact that Shakespeare is not buried in Westminster Abbey (a monument to him was placed there in 1740):

> My Shakespeare, rise; I will not lodge thee by
> Chaucer or Spenser, or bid Beaumont lie
> A little further to make thee a room.
> Thou art a Moniment, without a tombe.

It is also worth noting that the version of Basse's elegy in William Browne's hand suggests perhaps an even closer relationship between these two poets than Basse's commendatory verse on Browne's *Britannia's Pastorals* alone would indicate.

Further connections between Basse and the foremost poets of his age may be inferred from the appearance of one of his poems in the collection *Annalia Dubrensia* (1636). The collection praises Robert Dover and his revival of the Cotswold Games. Held on the Cotswold Hills in Gloucestershire by leave of King James I, the games were attended by nobility and gentry, some of whom traveled sixty miles to see them. The games were held annually for some forty years and included events of playing at cudgels, wrestling, broad jump, pitching the bar, hammer throw, dancing, hunting, and marksmanship, all depicted on the woodcut prefacing the volume. Each year a poet was chosen to herald and praise the event in verse; thirty-four of these contributions were collected in the 1636 volume. Basse's poem is sixteenth—and his name is sixteenth in the sequence of the authors' names on the title page, which corresponds precisely to the order of their poems—suggesting that Basse's poem was composed for the games in 1618. In ten eight-line stanzas of iambic tetrameter, Basse salutes the sportsmanship and honor of the competition:

> But where men meet, not for delight
> So much, as for delight to meet;
> And where, to use their Pastime right,
> They make it not so great, as sweete;
> Where Love doth, more then gaine, invite,
> Hands part at last as first they greete;
>   And loosers none, where all that's plaid
>   With friendship won may not be weigh'd.

Along with Basse's verses in the volume were contributions from Michael Drayton, Thomas Randolph, Ben Jonson, Owen Felltham, Thomas Heywood, and others.

Among some of Basse's best light verses are "The Hunter's Song" and "The Angler's Song," both representative of Basse's metrical precision and easy rhyme. Their musicality has led to suggestions that Basse possessed some technical knowledge of music, but there has been no evidence discovered in support for his musicianship. "The Hunter's Song" is set to music in a collection titled *Wit and Drollery* (1682) and also in *Old Ballads* (1725). The tune apparently became famous under the title "Maister Basse his careere," and was published under that title in a collection titled *Ballads* (circa 1620). "Tom of Bedlam," another short work, was set to music and is printed in *Choice Ayres, Songs and Dialogues* (1675) and in Thomas Percy's *Reliques of Ancient English Poetry* (1765). Neither of these works has generated the renown of "The Angler's Song," which was written at the request of a literary friend, Izaak Walton, for *The Compleat Angler* (1653).

In Walton's book, Coridon offers to sing a song "if any body wil sing another." Piscator replies:

> I'l promise you I'l sing a song that was lately made at my request by Mr. William Basse, one that has made the choice Songs of the "Hunter in his carrere" and of "Tom of Bedlam," and many others of note; and this that I wil sing is in praise of Angling.

At the end of Piscator's song, Coridon has high praise for the song, stating that Piscator "paid his debt in good coyn," and calls for the hostess to bring another round so that they may drink to him. The first two stanzas of the poem serve well as an example of Basse's work:

> As inward love breeds outward talk,
> The Hound some praise, and some the Hawk;
> Some, better pleas'd with private sport,
> Use tenis; some a Mistris court:
>   But these delights I neither wish,
>   Nor envy, while I freely fish.
>
> Who hunts, doth oft in danger ride;
> Who hauks, lures oft both far & wide;
> Who uses games, may often prove
> A loser; but who fals in love,
>   Is fettered in fond Cupids snare:
>   My Angle breeds me no such care.

The smoothness and humorous subtleties of this simple verse make it noteworthy. The play on "private sport" and the tennis "court" in contrast with a mistress to "court" (perhaps at court), all

Illustration for the first eclogue in Basse's manuscript for The Pastorals and other workes *(from* Poetical Works of William Basse [1602-1653], *edited by R. Warwick Bond, 1893)*

combine to develop the options in "angling," that is, to use artful or wily means to catch a person or thing, or to follow the practices and customs of those who have descended from the tribe of Angles. Also, the possible pun in what the contrasted activities "breed" increases the variety of meanings; the "care" bred from "Cupids snare" may be more than emotional. The control of language in its sound and meaning, the fluency and facility in this poem and in some other works by Basse must be the means by which he was so well received by his contemporaries.

The other major work of Basse's life is *The Pastorals and other workes*. The only extant manuscript volume of Basse's poems in his hand, this collection was in the possession of publishers Ellis and Elvey when Bond compiled his edition of Basse's poems in 1893. *The Pastorals and other*

workes is a folio prepared for publication in 1653, but some incident, most likely the author's death, precluded its printing. The collection includes Basse's most mature work, the nine eclogues of the *Pastorals* and *The Metamorphosis of the Walnut Tree of Boarstall*, as well as the earlier *Urania*. The dating of *Metamorphosis* is possible, but only to the seven-year period between the siege of the Boarstall House under Philip Skippon and Thomas Fairfax in 1646 (alluded to in canto III, stanzas 6 and 7), and the intended publication date. The dating of the *Pastorals* is impossible except by allusions in individual eclogues. For example, eclogue 8 must have been composed after 1640 due to its reference to the death of Lord Wenman, "that good Lord of th'ancient house of Thame." Eclogue 3 celebrates the generosity of "Lord Viscount Wenman" in acrostic form, plac-

ing it before his death, yet after his 1628 elevation to the peerage.

The story of *The Metamorphosis* is framed as
a tale told by one shepherd, Jefferye, to another,
Jasper. A Raven discovers that his old friend, the
Walnut tree at Boarstall, is dead. He decides to
honor him by bringing other trees to Boarstall
for a memorial. Only nut-bearing trees are
invited—the Hazel, Walnut, Filbert, and Chest-
nut. Through the power of the muse, they up-
root themselves and travel to Boarstall, where
they debate over whether they should allow the
oak tree to attend and then invite him as well.
Two sawyers (carpenters) are brought to perform
an autopsy and determine cause of death. They
find the tree is sound, so it is sawed into planks
to form a wainscoting for a gallery in the
Boarstall Church. The trees then return to their
respective homes. Jefferye explains that the
Raven laments the death of the good (making
the bird a poet figure) and the nut trees are "fruitful" and noble people. Those who bear no fruit
cannot expect in return the sort of charity the Walnut received: "Best honors are with hardest la-
bours won."

The selection of these particular works for
The Pastorals and other workes was almost certainly
made by Basse. The handwriting in the dedication to Lord Wenman (amended "As it was in his
dayes intended"), the apology to Clio, the note to
the reader, and all nine eclogues appear in a
clear and legible hand which is identical to the author's signature. We can be certain Basse intended this text for publication because Dr.
Ralph Bathurst contributed a poem, "To Mr. W.
Basse upon the intended publication of his
poems," on 13 January 1651.

The eclogues are obviously patterned after
Spenser's *The Shepheardes Calender*, but instead of
months of the year Basse improvises with the eclogues representing the days of the week and celebrating several virtues. He interrupts the pattern
with other poems, however, and there is no eclogue for Sunday. The intent of the eclogues is
strictly didactic, and they adapt Spenser's technique of cloaking all in the garb of the pastoral
(but rarely so much as to disguise completely).
Monday expresses a lover's complaint just as
Spenser's *Calender* does in January. Basse uses
the name Colliden to represent himself, just as
Spenser used Colin Clout.

Spenser and Basse are nonetheless widely different. There is ample evidence that Basse conducted close study of the master, but their work

stands apart in theme: Basse's creations are troubled by none of the public affairs or crises that
trouble Spenser's swains. No allegory of political
events of the day is perceptible. Instead, with
Basse we have a far more visual landscape covered with silver beeches and crystal streams. Further, the swains speak of their husbandry as if
they truly are swains, with details on farming, medicinal herbs, and the various flora and fauna of
their world. It may be Basse's infusion of actual experience from so many years of country living
that grants the work its finest distinction. In
works such as *Urania* and *The Metamorphosis* there
is substantially less, if anything, to link Basse to
Spenser. In fact, the stories and tone of the two
works are more reminiscent of Chaucer, especially since *The Metamorphosis* uses Chaucer's rime
royal.

Basse's power as a fluent storyteller, his ability to expand a simple tale into a flowing work
without tedium, is considerable. While Basse may
rarely offer a truly memorable line, he never
provides an arhythmic one, even at the cost of an
occasional questionable inversion. His poetry is
marked more by restraint and artistic sensibility
than by innovation, yet his excellent ear for the
sound of verse makes his better works consistently enjoyable. He remains, thus, an example of
the variety of Spenserian imitation current to the
seventeenth-century scene and of how that type
of humanist poetics could engender delightful innovations.

Several works have been doubtfully attributed to Basse. *That which Seemes Best is Worst*, a
translation of Juvenal's tenth satire printed in
1617 under the initials "W.B.," seems most likely
to be the work of William Barksted, who did
other similar translations. *A Helpe to Discourse,
or a miscelany of Merriment. Together with the
countrymans counsellour* (1619) is a book in two
parts by "W. B. & E. P." The second part, "The
countrymans Covnsellor," is attributed to "E. P.
Philomathem," on its own title page, possibly indicating that W. B. is responsible for the first part
of the book. Norman Ault argues persuasively
that a poem in the first part, "A memento for
mortalitie. Taken from the view of Sepulchres of
so many Kings and Nobles, as lye interred in the
Abbey of Westminster," is Basse's. He is almost
certainly correct, but the possibility of Basse's
merely having contributed one of his poems to a
work by an acquaintance such as Barksted or
Browne still remains. None of the other works in
the first part has generated any similar claims;

they are largely epigrams, riddles, and other humorous verse. Another work often attributed to Basse is a similar text, *A Helpe to Memory and Discourse* (1620), which includes two poems by Donne, but no one supposes that Donne was involved in the authorship of the volume. *A Helpe to Discourse* was so popular that it went through fourteen editions by 1640. If Basse were the author of so successful a work, it seems highly unlikely that he would hesitate to publish his more substantial and serious works. Too many questions remain to attribute any of these works to Basse with confidence.

References:

Norman Ault, "A Memento for Mortalitie," *Times*

Literary Supplement, 12 January 1933, p. 24;

J. Payne Collier, "William Basse and his Poems," *Notes and Queries*, 1 (26 January 1850): 200-201;

Thomas Corser, "William Basse and his Poems," *Notes and Queries*, 1 (9 March 1850): 295-297;

Edward F. Rimbault, "William Basse and his Poems," *Notes and Queries*, 1 (23 February 1850): 265-266.

Papers:

Manuscript copies of Basse's poems are scattered among holdings at the Bodleian Library, Oxford; Winchester College Library; the British Library; and the Chetham Library, Manchester.

Sir John Beaumont

(1583? - April 1627)

Charles A. Huttar
Hope College

BOOK: *The Metamorphosis of Tabacco* (London: Printed by F. Kingston for J. Flasket, 1602; facsimile, Amsterdam: Theatrum Orbis Terrarum / New York: Da Capo Press, 1971).

Editions: *Bosworth-field: with a taste of the variety of other poems, left by sir J. Beaumont, baronet, deceased*, edited by John Beaumont, Jr. (London: Printed by F. Kyngston for H. Seile, 1629);

"The Poems of Sir John Beaumont," in volume 6 of *The Works of the English Poets*, edited by Alexander Chalmers (London: Printed for J. Johnson and forty-seven others, 1810), pp. 1-48; facsimile, Anglistica & Americana (Hildesheim & New York: Georg Olms, 1970);

The Poems of Sir John Beaumont, Bart., edited by Alexander B. Grosart, Fuller Worthies' Library (Blackburn: C. Tiplady, 1869);

The Theatre of Apollo, edited by W. W. Greg (London: F. Etchells & H. Macdonald, 1926);

The Shorter Poems of Sir John Beaumont: A Critical Edition with an Introduction and Commentary, edited by Roger D. Sell, Acta Academiae

Aboensis, series A, 49 (Abo: Abo Akademi, 1974).

John Beaumont (he acquired the "Sir" only about ten weeks before his death) wrote poetry across a quarter-century, nearly all of it serious work and much of it religious in theme. His earliest published work appeared in 1602 when he was eighteen or nineteen, and he was writing occasional verse—an elegy and a devotional poem—in late March 1627 during the last few weeks of his life. From the beginning his work displayed a wide-ranging intellect, critical acumen, and a firm grasp of the poetic craft, especially that of the heroic couplet.

Beaumont was born circa 1583 into a family long and firmly connected to the legal profession and to the Catholic faith. His was the third generation in which the sons were educated at the Inns of Court. His father, Judge Francis Beaumont, conformed to the Church of England and indeed was known for his severity in dealing with recusants; he sat on the panel of judges which in 1595 condemned the Jesuit Sir Henry Walpole;

nevertheless he seems to have retained Catholic sympathies in private life. John's mother, Anne Pierrepoint Beaumont, furthered the recusant cause in various ways. Her brother, Gervase Pierrepoint, was imprisoned in 1581 for aiding another missionary priest, Edmund Campion. Later, two cousins on the Beaumont side were implicated in the Gunpowder Plot of November 1605. John himself was indicted several times for refusing to attend the established church, and on one occasion, when suspected of hiding a fugitive priest, he paid a threatening informant one hundred pounds in protection money.

The Beaumonts were an old Anglo-Norman family. Their ancestors had briefly enjoyed a peerage which was brought to an end by the Wars of the Roses (1455-1485). Following the Dissolution under Henry VIII the family acquired a substantial estate in 1538, Grace Dieu Priory, in Charnwood Forest, Leicestershire. Here John was brought up along with an elder brother, Henry; Francis, a year younger, who became a playwright; and a younger sister, Elizabeth. From here the three brothers went together to Oxford in February 1597 and enrolled in Broadgates Hall, the predecessor of Pembroke College. In November John and Henry left Oxford and, following family tradition, enrolled in London's Inner Temple. In April 1598 their father died, leaving his property to the eldest son, Henry, who, on the accession of King James I, was knighted in April 1603. Henry later married but died in July 1605 without male issue, leaving the second son, John, as heir.

Up until he inherited the estate, John must have lived in London, where he developed some acquaintances in literary circles, notably Ben Jonson—also in that period a Catholic—and Michael Drayton. A lasting friendship developed with Drayton, twenty years his senior, to whom he dedicated his first published work and with whom he exchanged commendatory verses. In his "Eighth Eglog" Drayton spoke warmly of visiting John and Francis ("those hopefull Boyes") and their sister at the family estate in Charnwood. Later, in "To Henry Reynolds," Drayton described the two poets as "bosome friends."

John Beaumont also associated with the recusant community in London. Church attendance laws were then being enforced with new rigor. Proceedings were brought against him in October 1605; the bureaucracy moved slowly, but on 22 September 1607, following an apparently uncontested conviction, two-thirds of his possessions were confiscated and given to Sir James Sempill, a royal favorite, for so long as Beaumont's recusancy continued, and Beaumont was ordered to leave London and stay within five miles of Grace Dieu. He was married by this time, to Elizabeth Fortescue, daughter of a Catholic merchant dwelling in the city. The first of their eleven children was born in 1607. Despite the loss of property he remained independently wealthy and settled into the life of a cultured country gentleman, including occasional verse composition—one of his elegies can be dated as early as 1610—and perhaps one or more of his larger poetic projects. Some of his translations may belong to this period. His livelihood was threatened in 1611 by a lawsuit over the inheritance, brought on behalf of Sir Henry's posthumous daughter, Barbara, but Beaumont won the case by a precedent-setting decision which the legal authority Sir Edward Coke duly recorded. He continued to avoid the established church, but the restriction on travel seems to have been relaxed, for his writings show him conversant to a degree with the London scene.

John and his wife both could trace royal ancestry—in *The Crowne of Thornes* he refers to an ancestor who ruled the Latin kingdom of Jerusalem—and he was a child of his time in his regard for rank. A prospect of improved fortunes came around 1620 with the rise to royal favor of George Villiers as Marquess, later Duke, of Buckingham; his mother, Maria Beaumont Villiers, was John's distant cousin. Through verse Beaumont unabashedly cultivated Buckingham's patronage on numerous occasions: in an epithalamium for Buckingham's 20 May 1620 wedding to Lady Katherine Manners, a pair of sonnets for a royal visit to Buckingham's home on 3 August 1621 (one poem was probably spoken as a prologue in Jonson's masque *The Gypsies Metamorphos'd*, commissioned for the occasion), congratulatory poems on the births of Buckingham's children, a congratulation to his brother, John Villiers, on recovered health, and so on. There were also poems to King James and Prince Charles: in January 1622 when James escaped drowning in a riding accident, in February 1623 when Charles went to Spain to woo the infanta, in October when he returned without her, and on the first anniversary of his return. Early in 1625 he had completed a masque, *The Theatre of Apollo* (1626), for representation at court with James in the unspeaking title role, when the performance was forestalled by the King's death on 27 March. Beaumont wrote an elegy, then an epithalamium for Charles's marriage to Henrietta Maria, a panegyric for Charles's much-delayed coronation in February 1626, and a pair of sonnets celebrating his first year on the throne.

Beaumont also maintained associations with prominent recusants during these years at court—years when persons of influence were at least sympathetic to the Catholic cause. He backed Edmund Bolton's scheme for a Royal Academy of Honour, designed to advance noble virtue and to hold up heroic examples for public praise.

The somewhat perfunctory tone of the later poems to Charles may suggest that Beaumont's life at court was more troubled than it had been in the previous reign, but on 31 January 1627 his courtship of the powerful brought its reward: he was made a baronet. On 19 April he was buried, at age forty-four, in Westminster Abbey. Drayton's later comment, "Thy care for that which was not worth thy breath, / Brought on too soone thy much lamented death," sheds little light on the immediate cause, but it may chide Beaumont's courtly ambitions.

Two of his sons wrote poetry: John, who succeeded to the baronetcy, brought out his father's literary remains under the title *Bosworth-field* in 1629, and died in action in 1644 as a Royalist colonel; and Francis, a Jesuit.

From the Restoration on down to William Wordsworth, Beaumont's work was considered a model for the heroic couplet, combining technical mastery of the form with intellectual substance. Alexander Pope ranked him above Richard Crashaw and George Herbert but below John Donne. Alexander B. Grosart and other nineteenth-century critics thought the religious poetry his best claim to fame; it was misunderstood, however, for received opinion called Beaumont "Puritan." His contemporaries valued him not only for those achievements but as an exemplar of solid Christian humanism, a teacher of virtue whose teaching could also delight, and, in the words of William Burton, "a Gentleman of great learning, grauity and worthinesse."

All three aspects of his work are reflected in two poems of literary criticism, "Concerning the true forme of English Poetry" and "Of the excellent use of Poems," addressed to King James and Prince Charles respectively. The poem on form presents and at the same time exemplifies neoclassical precepts. A poet who is himself "serious" and "modest," avoiding ostentation, must strike a mean between "light dancing tunes" and "heavy prose"; his "sweet Musick" should "like a

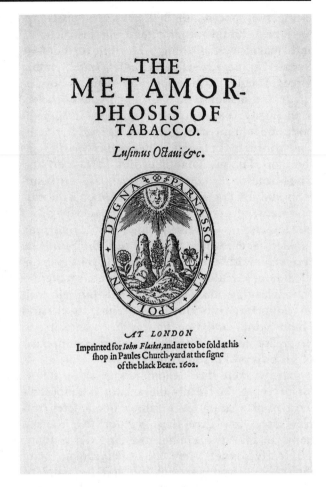

Title page for the poem in which Beaumont traces the use of tobacco back to the ancients

milky torrent flow"—phraseology that echoes Jonson and anticipates Sir John Denham. Eschewing the lame metrics of "most" poets and their artful display—the "strange conceits" and "darksome words"—the ideal poet should imitate a classical purity of diction, "affect" learning neither in vocabulary nor in comparisons, and use rhyme judiciously, preferably in couplets, not stanzas padded with "needlesse repetition." If the subject is "noble," excellent poetry that makes "actions by the liuely sound appeare" will be "easie." Beaumont begins by praising the king's own youthful work as a critic (reprinted in 1616 in the folio edition of King James's *Works*)—though Beaumont's own criticism shows no sign of its influence—and he closes with the patriotic wish that, despite the disadvantages of a northern climate, English poets may arouse "wonder" rather than "scorne" in southern literati.

In the poem to Charles, on the use of poems, Beaumont follows Robert Southwell in insisting that poetry, though by some "onely apt for loue," should rather offer "sage instructions" and "make celestiall things / More fit for humane eares": "graue *Urania*" and "soft *Thalia*" joining forces. Poetic "harmony" is both a metaphor for virtue and a spur to it. The poet's role in society is to purify "barb'rous deedes" and "Language" both. Beaumont cites the example of Tyrtaeus, who through verse could move the Spartans as the more famous Timotheus did Alexander, and who wrote of his country's heroic past—as Beaumont did for England. Beaumont laments the current decay of poetry and the ascendancy of prose but hopes, "now in this realme," for a returning "golden age" when "this sacred fire" will be renewed—with the "great *Prince*" as its patron. Beaumont's mature theory thus combines the devotional single-mindedness of a Southwell with an antimannerism that owes much to classical Philip Sidney and Ben Jonson and something to pragmatic Francis Bacon, and adds an emphasis of his own on king and country.

How well did Beaumont's practice follow his precepts? Metrically the answer is simple: almost all his writing was in iambic pentameter couplets. The few exceptions include five translations, an ode, two epithalamia, and ten sonnets. The early sonnets were Shakespearean in form, the later Petrarchan, but all end in couplets. There are also seven poems of sonnet length entirely in couplets. Beaumont's earliest production, a largely narrative poem imitating, at times translating, Ovid, already displays a remarkable command of the Jonsonian principle of the couplet as the unit of both thought and meter. His (undated) translations from the Greek Anthology move away from the enjambment of the originals to closed-couplet form. Beaumont gives less consistent attention to other elements that would come to characterize neoclassical heroic couplet style— matters of internal structure such as caesura and rhetorical balance, or the close argumentation of larger paragraph units. There are exceptions: for example, the witty patterning of "Defi'd the heauen, and defild the Earth" in *The Metamorphosis of Tabacco* (1602), or "Upon the Two Great Feasts of the Annunciation and Resurrection Falling on the Same Day, March 25, 1627," where he adopts an antithetical style matching the paradoxical possibilities implicit in the theme. In "Bosworth Field," the inner debate of Norfolke over issues of loyalty and policy is a good example of heroic couplet argument; it ends with the sententious line, notable alike for its rhetoric and its

divine-right sentiment, "*I hate his vices, but adore the King.*" Sometimes in translating first-century Latin poets, Beaumont inherits a style more nearly Augustan. It remained for Edmund Waller and his contemporaries to refine the heroic couplet, but Beaumont laid down the critical principles, and his verse, with hints from Jonson, was developing in this direction. Already at the start Beaumont's verse had the metrical smoothness and polish which kept his name alive for two centuries. It could also hint at Augustan diction, as in line 333 of "Bosworth Field": "The feather'd wood they from their bowes let flie."

The following account of Beaumont's works considers first those in the humanist tradition (including classical translations), then religious poems, court poems, and assorted other occasional verse. Contemporary testimony assigns to John Beaumont the anonymous *Metamorphosis of Tabacco*; inferences from dedicatory verses support the ascription, and there is no compelling reason to doubt it. Informed by patriotism, academic learning, and high-spirited wit, the poem is described in the dedication as "my first-borne rimes," and two of the commendatory verses emphasize the author's youth. He frequently glosses his own learned allusions and conceits. The poem could well be the work of a student who found his poetic talent blossoming in the cultural life of the capital.

Two literary fashions, during the four years Beaumont had been in London, helped shape his *Metamorphosis of Tabacco*: Ovidian epyllia and tobacco pamphlets. English writings on tobacco had begun to appear in the 1570s, straightforward accounts and exaggerated reports of its medicinal powers. During the last decade of Elizabeth's reign, references to tobacco appeared with increasing frequency in satires and other poetry, in prose writings, and onstage. In 1602 controversy erupted with the publication of *Work for Chimnysweepers: or a Warning for Tabacconists. Describing the pernicious use of Tabacco*. Within four months, three rejoinders were registered and, presumably, printed; Beaumont's *Metamorphosis of Tabacco*, entered 30 March, was the second of these. Defending the weed was, clearly, politically correct: not for another two years would the new monarch, James, weigh in with *A Counter-blaste to Tobacco* (1604). Defending the Virginian variety in particular, as Beaumont did, as opposed to that of West Indian origin, was a display of patriotism even if not of connoisseurship.

Of the four pamphlets, Beaumont's was the only one in verse: an epyllion of 528 heroic couplets in the current Ovidian fashion. The earlier handling of Ovid in terms of erotic interest or moralization was increasingly giving way to a less respectful approach, with room for the comic and ironic. Beaumont signals his playful intent from the outset: his epigraph from Virgil's *Gnat* announced classical precedent for his lighthearted irreverence. Part of the game may have been for the two brothers John and Francis to write companion (or rival) epyllia; but whereas Francis's *Salmacis and Hermaphroditus* (1602) starts with a tale from Ovid's book 4, John plunges at once into mythopoeic invention, one of the conventions of the genre. His choosing to build his own transformation myth on a theme not inherently mythical may have been inspired by Sir John Harington's prose *Metamorphosis of Ajax* (1596).

Beaumont begins by rejecting, in lines that mock the lofty epic style, lesser love themes. Instead of lauding feminine beauty, as "loue-sick Poets" do, he will rise "a pitch aboue" them with "the sound of great *Tabaccoes* praise / . . . / *The Cornu-copia* of all earthly pleasure, / . . . / The blessed offspring of an vncouth land." Tobacco itself is to be his muse, able to "gently rul[e] the sturdiest *Caniball*" and inspire "the *Indian* Priests" to prophetic (though, in Beaumont's Eurocentric view, "barbrous") poetic utterance; in these lines he mocks the introductory poem in *Work for Chimny-sweepers* (also in iambic pentameter couplets) and praises tobacco for the same reasons that led the earlier poet to condemn it as a "Pagan Idol."

Beaumont proceeds to announce his epic theme with a question: Which of the gods was so "bounteous to the humane race" as to create tobacco? He then answers the question twice, devising two mythical narratives. In the first the four elements hold council in "the Americke Ile" (which Beaumont identifies with Plato's Atlantis), to condole with Prometheus concerning his punishment for creating humanity and stealing fire, and if possible to complete the work Prometheus left unfinished. In defiance of Jove and Fate, Earth brings forth an herb which makes the theft of fire worthwhile, for being kindled it will give "sweete life and breath" to the lifeless form "wise Prometheus" had "compos'd"; but Jove, still angry, "Did hide it long from the world's better part," that is, Europe. When the Graces happened upon "this celestiall fume" "in the palace of great *MuteZume*," they refused to return to "Our petie world," and "false" Europe was left with quarrels and flattering in place of friendship and delight until the search for the Graces led to the discovery of America. Thus Beaumont's first myth ends in satire.

The second myth tells of a "faire Nymph" dwelling "Along the valleys of *Wingandekoe*" (since renamed Virginia in honor of one still "more beauteous") who outshines the sun and has upset the cosmic order: "The Sphæres of Planets with a sudden chaunge / Make her the center of their circled raunge." To describe her beauty requires all the hyperbolic clichés of love poetry. Jove, disguised as a shepherd, courts her with stories of the gods' love affairs, but "the darke malicious night" spies on them and reports to Juno, who transforms the nymph into a plant. But Jove cannot forget her and, adorning the herb with earthly and heavenly powers, makes it "a *Microcosme* of good" and the soil where it springs— Virginia—"a cordiall . . . / . . . all euils to asswage." There ensues "the famous golden age," which Beaumont describes in detail, closely following Ovid—at twice the length. Proserpina then vengefully destroys "this sacred plant" and thus brings on the Iron Age, for which Beaumont returns to Ovid. From this point he is necessarily more inventive, for tobacco is not in Ovid. In Beaumont's somewhat Christianized cosmology, impious pride was not eradicated by the flood but

> continued in the humane race,
> Creeping vnseene, subiecting eu'ry part,
> Till it possest our chiefest towre, our hart;
> Which thus infected did a battell wage
> Gainst the remainders of the golden age.

Earth, water, air, and fire are all corrupted, deaths begin to occur prematurely, and only divine intervention preserves the world. Aesculapius reveals tobacco "to our new golden age" and invents a smoking pipe. Tobacco assuages sorrow and inspires physicians to deliver men from sickness and death.

Should this explanation not satisfy, Beaumont is ready with yet another. The gods cannot have "knowne this smokes delicious smack," or it would have replaced ambrosia and nectar, and "the vault of heau'n" would by now be blackened. In a tireless pursuit of *copia*, Beaumont offers more than a score of ways that legend, history, and poetry would read differently if ancient heroes and peoples had known tobacco. By this discovery the modern world far excels the ancient;

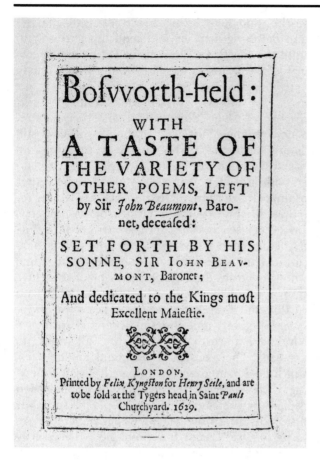

Title page for the collection in which the title poem is Beaumont's version of the battle in which Richard III was defeated by Henry VII

it is "the ioy of mortals," which sets man apart from beasts, it is a "dumbe Oratour" with great powers of persuasion, worthy of celebration in "a new *Tobacconalia*" replacing the Roman feast of Saturn; though admittedly its abuse can bring sickness or death, still it contains "all pleasures," is "as needfull" as *Tullies* friendship, or the Sunnie light," is the greatest of medicines (here Beaumont echoes Edmund Spenser and John Lyly) and the philosophers' stone. It is responsible for the refining of "all Arts, all tongues" in this "blest age" and the revival of learning from "dunsticall, and monkish barbarisme"; *a fortiori* in England, where "our moderne Muse" Elizabeth, "In whose respect the Muses barb'rous are," has

> spread the Colours of our *English* Rose
> In the farre countries, where *Tabacco* growes,
> And tam'd the sauage nations of the West,
> Which of this iewell were in vaine possest.

But the Spaniards, "farre more sauage than the *Sauages*," dominate the trade in both gold and

the yet nobler tobacco—a cordial better than music, a peacemaker, a beautifier that works better than a love potion, a substitute if need be for food and drink. The conceits go on, until Beaumont abruptly says, "Peace pratling Muse," and brings his poem to a close.

The Golden Age reappears, in a political context, at the beginning of Beaumont's "Bosworth Field," a historical poem of 818 lines in the Daniel-Drayton tradition with epic intentions:

> The Winter's storme of Ciuill warre I sing,
> Whose end is crown'd with our eternall Spring,
> Where Roses ioin'd, their colours mixe in one,
> And armies fight no more for *Englands* throne.

Though some of Beaumont's poems can be dated from their occasions, for "Bosworth Field" there is only internal evidence. A reference to Prince Charles as heir apparent indicates that it was written no earlier than 1612; from a possible veiled allusion to another Stuart, Roger D. Sell argues cogently for a date of circa 1624. The choice of subject—the 1485 battle in which Henry Tudor, Earl of Richmond, defeated Richard III and won the throne, becoming Henry VII—reflects not only a patriot's loyalty to the Tudor-Stuart establishment but also Beaumont's known interest in history, especially that of his native Leicestershire: he lived only a few miles from the battlefield. For his poem he may have collected surviving oral traditions; he used Raphael Holinshed's *Chronicles* (1577), improved the order of material (perhaps with a hint from William Shakespeare in putting Richard's speech before Richmond's), and invented additional details. His present-tense narrative boasts the machinery of epic, from invocation ("Thou gracious Lord, direct my feeble Pen") and abundant epic similes to presaging dreams, a brief catalogue of warriors, and hand-to-hand combat accompanied by noble speeches and chivalric behavior. The similes are mostly literary, though the occasional local reference ("Caister's bankes," "rocky Charnwood") suggests the possibility of direct observation. The poet's motive is more than literary, however. The attention he devotes to exemplary characters such as Norfolke and Stanley, as well as his readiness to take advantage of the heroic couplet's sententious proclivities—for example:

> *All dangers clouded with the mist of feare,*
> *Seeme great farre off, but lessen comming neare*

—suggests a dedication to the poet's role as moral teacher. "Bosworth Field" may, in fact, be Beaumont's contribution to the program of moral reform announced by Edmund Bolton in 1617 in his plan for a royal academy, in which Beaumont was to be a participant.

Beaumont's Richard III is conventionally villainous: guilt-ridden, he is awakened early by "hideous dreams" which flattering counselors persuade him to disregard; donning his helmet as a "maske" to "make his wrinkled visage faire," he feels it press on his temples with "vnusuall paines" which some take as evil omens; he coldbloodedly kills a sleeping sentry and jeers; though credited with courage and skill in battle, he exults ungenerously over the fallen foe. Henry, by contrast, sleeps peacefully, his "soule ... cleare," soothed by a dream in which he is saluted as the "iust scourge of murder, vertue's light" and foreshown emblematically the family tree of his descendants and the "golden age" of James's reign. This passage realizes the potential double focus, 1485 and 1603, of the reference to union in the opening lines.

The symmetry of Beaumont's structure continues as Richard summons "trusty *Norfolke*" to join his troops; the duke, though warned that the king's prospects are slim, and though aware of Richard's murder of the boys in the Tower, accepts the ethical distinction between the monarch's public and private faces—"*I hate his vices, but adore the King*"—and resolves to keep his oath. Richard then addresses his troops in a speech of twenty-six lines full of self-praise and of disdain for his enemy's French upbringing and Welsh lineage and, ironically, for Merlin's prophecy of a king of Celtic blood. A well-shaped couplet tells the response: "Some, with loud shouting, make the valleyes ring, / But most with murmur sigh, *God saue the king*." These scenes are nicely balanced by Henry's sending for Lord Stanley to join him, followed by Henry's twenty-six-line speech to his men. Like Norfolke, "Noble Stanley" faces an ethical dilemma, for Richard holds his son hostage and threatens to kill him. Stanley replies, "*If with my* Georges *bloud, he staine his throne, / I thanke my God, I haue more sonnes than one*," but he agrees to stay out of the combat entirely, joining neither side. Henry, respecting his integrity, shows neither "feare nor anger"—a departure from Holinshed. Beaumont's portrayal of Stanley also displays a depth of psychological insight greater than that found in Drayton's version of the same story in the complete *Poly-Olbion*

(1622). Henry's ensuing speech draws enthusiastic acclaim. He brands Richard a "*Tyrant*," "*Usurper*," and "*crooked Monster*" who instead of healing the nation's "*vnclosed wound*" has "*made his owne white Rose as red as ours*," and who will inevitably fall from his arrogant height.

Beaumont then provides a clear, workmanlike piece of descriptive narrative in which it is easy to follow the ebb and flow of battle as first one side, under Norfolke, then the other, under Oxford, briefly has the mastery. Stanley decides to modify his neutrality and send a few handpicked men to Henry's aid; Richard commands the execution of his son, Lord Strange, and only at the last moment is dissuaded. Three scenes then focus on individual heroism—Beaumont follows a pattern as old as the *Iliad*—exalting such virtues as loyalty, compassion, and friendship. The focus shifts to Richard himself, who with no lack of courage carries the attack directly to Richmond. A succession of similes liken the king to a raven, a "rolling fire" that consumes the harvest, a thunderbolt, and a tiger. The villain's strength and skill are acknowledged—he kills two soldiers before finally meeting Henry—but then he is forced to "confess ... with an angry frowne, / His riuall not vnworthy of the crowne." When the fleeing Catesby urges "*swift retreate* ... / ... *t'auoide the graue*," Richard courageously "scorn[s] his aduice, as foule and base." The outcome finally is decided by Providence—the same agent that in the outset of the poem was credited with the present "dayes of peace." Henry is protected "with a heau'nly shield"; Richard is borne down and trampled by sheer number of foes and dies, unrepentant, clinging to the last to "his rights pretence."

Beaumont chose for translation poems strongly ethical in theme and close to his personal concerns. He seems to have had no fixed theory of translation: he tends to follow his originals faithfully while avoiding graceless literalism, and where he expands it is more often for clarity or forcefulness than for the sake of rhyme or measure. The poems always have contemporary relevance, and occasionally he goes beyond that to adaptation: Horace's town and country mice live in a Jacobean society; Horace's and Juvenal's "rostra" become "pulpits"—but that translation is not unique to Beaumont. Twice he translated Christian writings, the "Funerall Hymne" of Prudentius and the so-called Sibylline prophetic verses with their acrostic on IESVS CHRIST SONNE OF GOD SAVIOVR; and Virgil's millen-

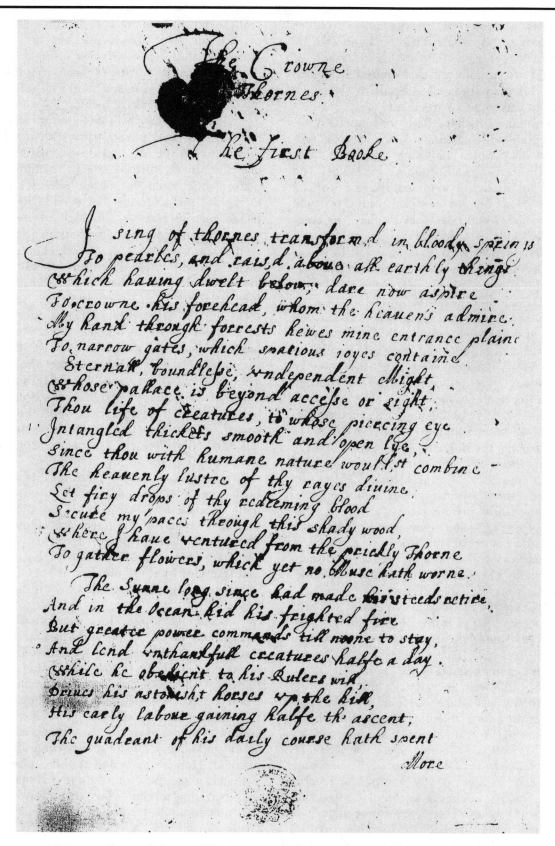

The Crowne
Thornes:

The first Booke.

I sing of thornes transform'd in bloody spires
To pearles, and rais'd aboue all earthly things
Which hauing dwelt below, dare now aspire
To crowne his forehead, whom the heauen's admire.
My hand through forrests hewes mine entrance plaine
To narrow gates, which spatious ioyes containe
Eternall, boundlesse, vndependent might,
Whose pallace is beyond accesse or sight,
Thou life of creatures, to whose piercing eye
Intangled thickets smooth and open lye,
Since thou with humane nature would'st combine
The heauenly lustre of thy rayes diuine,
Let firy drops of thy redeeming blood
Secure my paces through this shady wood,
Where I haue ventured from the prickly Thorne
To gather flowers, which yet no Muse hath worne.

The Sunne long since had made his steeds retire,
And in the Ocean hid his frighted fire,
But greater power commands till noone to stay,
And lend vnthankfull creatures halfe a day.
While he obedient to his Rulers will
Driues his astonisht horses vp the hill,
His early labour gaining halfe th'ascent,
The quadrant of his daily course hath spent

More

First page of the scribal copy of The Crowne of Thornes *(British Library, Add. Ms. 33, 392)* nial Eclogue 4 had long since been baptized. His other originals, even when Epicurean or Stoic, provided teachings harmonious with Christianity, not antithetical. Sometimes there is an explicit Christian overlay, as when "natura" in Ausonius becomes "corrupted nature." But satires by Juvenal and Persius on the vanity of human wishes, Claudian's epigram and Horace's epode on the "happy man" topos, other poems by Horace on the advantages of a retired life, and Ausonius on the discipline of self-examination all express sentiments congenial to a man whose own religious fidelity had required him to find contentment, if at all, in the simple country life. Through all these poems runs the Christian-Stoic theme of self-reliance expressed in "Horace, Ode 29, Book III":

> He master of himselfe, in mirth may liue,
> Who saith, I rest well pleas'd with former
>   dayes,
>   Let God from heau'n to morrow giue
>   Blacke clouds, or Sunny rayes.

Similar sentiments appear in some of Beaumont's original sacred poems such as "Against the desire of greatnesse," "Of the miserable state of Man," and "Of true Liberty." Others, like "Against inordinate loue of Creatures," "Of Teares," "Of Sinne," and "Of Sicknesse," approach their set topics in a similar tone of objective meditation, but from a more narrowly Christian standpoint. More dramatic than meditative is "A Dialogue between the World, a Pilgrim, and Vertue," which is built on the traditional "choice" between the easy descent ("th' infernall steepenesse") and the difficult upward path, beset with "prickly thornes" but offering an "immortall wreath" at the end. All these poems are marked by a love of paradox, of sudden turns in the argument, and of the visual and emblematic. "Against inordinate love of Creatures" gives an example of Beaumont's irony: "God is iust, / And hath ordain'd the obiects of our loue / To be our scourges, when we wanton proue" (a Christianized echo of *King Lear*); "Against the desire of greatnesse" declares that the ultimate punishment for sinful ambition is success. In "Of Teares," however, there is a more benign turn: though our tears are "full of bitter paines" because of the Fall, repentance changes them to pearls. Contrary to the traditional iconography of "the painters," Death, in the poem "Of Sicknesse," proves to be a "friend" and escort to Paradise. The reminiscence here of George Her-

bert ("Death") is still stronger in Beaumont's more subjective poems of devotion—"An act of Contrition," "An Act of Hope," and the companion pieces "In Desolation" and "In spirituall comfort." Other meditative poems use Ignatian methods to focus on observances in the liturgical calendar—the Annunciation and Resurrection coinciding, the Epiphany, the Ascension, the Transfiguration, and the Assumption of Mary. Here the abundant play with theological paradox and with words, especially the favorite *sun/Son* pun, invites comparison rather with the divine poems of Donne. Characteristic of Beaumont is the flower and color symbolism in "Upon the two great Feasts of the Annunciation and Resurrection falling on the same day, March 25. 1627." In "An Ode of the blessed Trinitie" the poet finds his "Muse" too "dull and weake" for the theme: beyond restating the creedal formulas, it must give way to "humble silence." Its forte is painting "humane shapes," employing the conventional Petrarchan conceits. Two other poems take up this last theme. "Against abused Loue" castigates "wanton Writers" who misuse the word "love" in celebrating lust; yet it ends, as does "A description of Loue," by granting that there can be, between persons, a noble love in which "may shine / Impressions of the Loue diuine."

Beaumont's magnum opus is *The Crowne of Thornes*, an unpublished poem of twelve books surviving in a unique scribal copy at the British Library. It was known and admired by the poet's contemporaries but then, for three centuries, supposed to have disappeared. Ruth Wallerstein described it in detail in 1954.

The work enjoyed the patronage or at least encouragement of his wife's relative Henry Wriothesley, third Earl of Southampton, possibly while Beaumont was still in forced retirement at Grace Dieu, but was completed only after Southampton's death in 1624 and, indeed, after Charles came to the throne. Encyclopedic in scope after the fashion of Josuah Sylvester's *Divine Weeks* (1598-1608), it is a meditation that radiates out from Christ's crown of thorns to virtually all imaginable implications of the crown figure—Christ's Passion, his followers' suffering, his and their victory, the crown of kingly authority, the ivy crown of Bacchic worship, the circle as symbol of perfection, the arc of the Milky Way, and so on—and, in similar fashion, all meanings and associations of thorns. Many of his symbols have the ingenuity of medieval exegesis or Metaphysical poetry. The work displays wide-

The passage in the manuscript for The Crowne of Thorns *that supports the argument for Beaumont's authorship of the poem*
(British Library, Add. Ms. 33, 392)

ranging knowledge, especially of antiquity and natural history, all presented with a thoroughness that suggests nearly unlimited leisure.

Its structure is a triad. The first four books meditate on the successive scenes of Christ's Passion, with careful attention to every detail. The crown of thorns is plaited, and Jesus is stripped naked—a detail which leads to comparisons with Noah and David, then to Christ's earlier stripping of himself to wash the disciples' feet, which in turn is allegorized as an ablution that guards against temptation ("the serpent's art") so that the apostles can "tread on angry snakes and find no harm"; then to Job's nakedness and that of Adam and Eve, and the symbolic meaning of the fig leaves and the animal skins they were given to wear. That covers some 300 lines—about one-fourth of book 1, which continues with other scenes of Christ's mocking. Book 2, Christ before Pilate, offers a meditation on the failure of paganism, with much reference to Egyptian and Roman myths and rites. Book 3, Christ mocked by the Jews, is full of anti-Jewish sentiment and rejoices that the rejection of Christ by his own people opened the way for Gentiles to enter God's kingdom. Book 4, the Crucifixion, moves quickly from *compositio loci* into the symbolism of the Cross figure, the number *four*, and the circle (crown, wreath) and square; then a vividly realized Descent into Hell, the Ascension, and the beginnings of the spread of Christianity; and then, after nearly 350 lines in which the reader is urged to accept Christ's crown of thorns as his/her own, the first section of the poem closes with allusions to the labyrinth of Daedalus and to the *Odyssey*, allegorized.

Books 5-8 expand the theme to a celebration of Christ as the almighty Creator who became incarnate, thus joining in himself macro-

cosm and microcosm. Beaumont ransacks mythology for parallels; as one example of his syncretizing of paganism and Christianity, Jesus is "our true God of wine," a "painefull treader" who "drownes the wine-presse with his precious blood." Beaumont uses the schema of the four elements again, having each relate the crown/thorns motif to its part of the created order. He takes up the problem of evil and heresy in book 7 and recounts in book 8 stories of Old Testament "types" prefiguring Christ.

The historical organization now begun is continued in the last four books, which complete the design by carrying the story down to the present. In the first Christian centuries the apostles make Christ's crown(s) their own, and much is made of duodecimal symbolism. Later, martyrs and, especially, kings take up Christ's work, from the Crusades on down to Britain's James; and, finally, Catholic queens. James's mother, Mary, Queen of Scots, and Charles's wife, Henrietta Maria, both become aftertypes of Mary the Queen of Heaven, and Beaumont's poem reaches its climax with the hope that the Catholic faith may be restored. It is no wonder the poem was not published.

Beaumont's court poems offer special problems for a reader approaching them from the cultural distance of the late twentieth century. Beaumont believed, for example, in the divine right of kings, and while by no means unaware of the failings of the great, he nevertheless held toward their rank an attitude which enabled him to utter what appears today as blatant sycophancy. In "Of true Greatnesse: to my Lord Marquesse of Buckingham," Beaumont begins, "Sir, you are truely great," but then proceeds to give his patron an evidently needed lecture on virtue: "No pow'r can make the slaue of passions great," therefore "he must aspire" beyond earthly desires and "fixe his sight" on God, who "buildes a Paradise within his brest." He could catalogue James's achievements in statecraft and culture with perspicuity and dignity—and in the same elegy make the king a bit too godlike. He could gracefully evoke a new Golden Age in the epithalamium for King Charles. But some inner tensions are nevertheless suggested in those poems where exaggerated compliment, witty conceits, technical smoothness, or convoluted argument proves insufficient to conceal thinness of conception and a flagging of intellectual rigor.

The Theatre of Apollo, discovered among the Royal MSS. in the British Library, is a masque-like entertainment but without dancing. It seats King James onstage as the new Apollo (in whose favor the sun has abdicated), surrounded by his progeny and with Buckingham prominent in the wings. Apollo holds a laurel wreath, to be awarded to the one who "best should sing his praise," and the winner is announced as he "whom greatest *Villiers* brought vnknowne, / Before *Apollo's* throne," to "sing / With heave'nly tunes, the greatnes of his *King*." A marginal note in the manuscript provides the identification of Beaumont. The rest of the entertainment is given to a characteristically Beaumontian exposition of the symbolism of precious stones which are prominent in the stage scenery. They represent four kinds of poets, and while the whole conception is couched in terms of classical mythology, the exposition here becomes explicitly Christian. The highest kind of poets "to *Heau'n* have rays'd their song" to celebrate the redemption, but of these we are now "forlorne." Next are the "pure, and spotlesse *Poetts*" who present "*morall action*"; far below them are the poets of "*Loues* fond desire. / . . . a poyson, worse then *Serpents* sting," and the poets of war. Finally, a fifth rock represents Death; but the poem ends with the hope "that this our bright *Apollo* long may live." James did not; the work was never performed.

Apart from poems written for friends' books, the rest of Beaumont's verse comprises a dozen or so elegies and epitaphs and a poem which was printed in 1629 but excised from all known copies of the book, "On the death of many good People slain by the fall of a floore at

a Catholike Sermon in Black Friers." Especially in the elegies on friends and on his young son, he is on firmer ground emotionally than in the court poems and writes with greater conviction. His various strategies of wit and irony for dealing with death and his praise of virtue ring true.

Biographies:
Mark Eccles, "A Biographical Dictionary of Elizabethan Authors," *Huntington Library Quarterly*, 5 (April 1942): 293-300;

Roger D. Sell, "The Life of Sir John Beaumont, ?1583-1627," in *The Shorter Poems of Sir John Beaumont*, edited by Sell, Acta Academiae Aboensis, series A, 49 (Abo: Abo Akademi, 1974), pp. 3-26;

Eccles, "Sir John Beaumont," *Studies in Philology*, 79 (Fall 1982): 13.

References:
A. B. Chambers, *Transfigured Rites in Seventeenth-Century English Poetry* (Columbia: University of Missouri Press, 1992);

Jeffrey Knapp, "Elizabethan Tobacco," *Representations*, no. 21 (Winter 1988): 27-66;

William Kupersmith, *Roman Satirists in Seventeenth-Century England* (Lincoln: University of Nebraska Press, 1985), pp. 24-36;

William Bowman Piper, *The Heroic Couplet* (Cleveland & London: Press of Case Western Reserve University, 1969), pp. 75-78, 231-239;

Randolph Lincoln Wadsworth, Jr., "The Bound, and Frontier of Our Poetrie: A Study of Sir John Beaumont (1583-1627)," Ph.D. dissertation, Stanford University, 1967;

Ruth Wallerstein, "Sir John Beaumont's *Crowne of Thornes*, a Report," *Journal of English and Germanic Philology*, 53 (1954): 410-434;

George Williamson, "The Rhetorical Pattern of Neo-classical Wit," *Modern Philology*, 33 (August 1935): 55-81.

Papers:
The manuscript for Beaumont's *Crowne of Thornes* is at the British Library (Ms. Add. 33, 392). A microfilm copy is in part 3, reel 39 of *British Literary Manuscripts from the British Library, London*, series one, The English Renaissance, c. 1500-1700 (Brighton, Sussex, England: Harvester Press Microform Publications, 1984).

William Browne of Tavistock
(circa 1590 - 1645)

James A. Riddell
California State University, Dominguez Hills

BOOKS: *Britannia's Pastorals* (London: Printed by T. Snodham for G. Norton, 1613);

The Shepheards Pipe (London: Printed by N. Okes for G. Norton, 1614);

Britannia's Pastorals. The Second Booke (London: Printed by T. Snodham for G. Norton, 1616);

The Works of William Browne, 3 volumes, edited by Thomas Davies (London: Printed for T. Davies, 1772);

Original Poems, Never before Published, edited by Sir Egerton Brydges (Ickham: Printed at the private press of Lee Priory by Johnson & Warwick, 1815);

Britannia's Pastorals: A Third Book, edited by T. Crofton Croker (London: Printed for the Percy Society by T. Richards, 1852);

The Whole Works of William Browne, 2 volumes, edited by W. Carew Hazlitt (London: Printed for the Roxburghe Library, 1868, 1869).

Editions: *Poems of William Browne of Tavistock*, 2 volumes, edited by Gordon Goodwin, with an introduction by A. H. Bullen, The Muses' Library (London: Routledge / New York: Dutton, 1894);

The Masque of the Inner Temple (Ulysses and Circe), edited by R. F. Hill, in *A Book of Masques in Honour of Allardyce Nicoll*, edited by T. J. B. Spencer and Stanley Wells (Cambridge: Cambridge University Press, 1967).

OTHER: "An Elegy on the Bewailed Death of the Truly Beloved and Most Virtuous Henry, Prince of Wales," in *Two Elegies, Consecrated to the Never-dying Memorie of the Most Worthily Admyred; Most Hartily Loved; and Generally Bewayled Prince; Henry Prince of Wales*, by Christopher Brooke (London: Printed by T. Snodham for R. More, 1613);

"Thirsis *praise of his Mistresse*," in *Englands Helicon*, second edition, enlarged (London: Printed by T. Snodham for R. More, 1614);

"To his worthy and ingenious Friend *the Author*," *The Ghost of Richard the Third*, by Brooke (London: Printed by G. Eld for L. Lisle, 1614);

"An Elegy consecrated to the memory of the truly worthy and learned Sir *Thomas Overbury Knight*," in *Sir Thomas Overburie, his Wife with new elegies* (London: Printed by E. Griffin for L. L'isle, 1616);

"To My Honor'd Friend, Mr. Drayton," in *The Second Part, or a Continuance of Poly-Olbion*, by Michael Drayton (London: Printed by A. Mathewes for J. Marriott, J. Grismand & T. Dewe, 1622);

"To the worthy Gentleman the Translator," in *The Rogue*, by Mateo Aleman, translated by James Mabbe (London: Printed at Eliot's Court Press for E. Blount, 1622);

"On the Dowager Countess of Pembroke," in *Remaines, Concerning Britaine*, third edition, edited by William Camden (London: Printed by N. Okes for S. Waterson, 1623).

William Browne of Tavistock has enjoyed a modest but persistent reputation from the time his earliest poetry was made public. His best-known work has always been *Britannia's Pastorals*; its first two books (1613, 1616), published when he was in his twenties, were the only parts he saw in print. In them he celebrates in a fanciful, exuberant, and somewhat desultory manner the West Country where he was raised. Another early work, also in the pastoral vein, is the substantial portion that Browne contributed to *The Shepheards Pipe* (1614). Book 3 of *Britannia's Pastorals*, written about ten years after books 1 and 2, was not published until the mid nineteenth century. Indeed, at his death almost as much of his verse was left in manuscript as in print, and much of the unpublished work, including book 3 of *Britannia's Pastorals*, was personal lyric rather than pastoral narrative.

It is because of Browne's early, published work that he is known as one of the "Spenserian Poets" of the first part of the seventeenth century, along with Michael Drayton, George Wither, Giles and Phineas Fletcher, and other lesser-known figures. These poets share values such as political patriotism, a love of the English countryside, and a regard for what might be called "traditionalism," especially as represented in the poetry of Edmund Spenser. All of them consciously imitated Spenser, not only in the subject matter of their verse, but also (in one respect) in its form—they all wrote long poems.

The Spenserians continued a mode of poetry which remained almost constantly before the public in the few years following Spenser's death in 1599. Collections of Spenser's poems were printed several times beginning in 1609. Furthermore, Josuah Sylvester's translation of *The Devine Weeks and Works* of the French poet Guillume de Saluste, Sieur Du Bartas—an encyclopedic poem which had influenced Spenser to some extent and the Spenserians to a larger extent—enjoyed extraordinary popularity in the first years of the seventeenth century, with editions appearing in 1605, 1608, 1611, and onward. Both Spenser and Du Bartas repeatedly emphasized the traditional view of the poet as a vatic creator, and both poets repeatedly expressed a contempt for transitory fame. These are, to be sure, generally shared concerns; the relationship of Du Bartas and the Spenserians is largely general, though in some instances quite specific. As Joan Grundy points out, "although the influence of *The Divine Weeks and Works* on the style, especially the diction and imagery, of seventeenth-century poetry has long been recognised, . . . the effect it had in modifying people's feelings about poetry, about its nature and objectives, in other words its *general* effect upon taste" is of central importance. In the case of Browne, a satisfactorily representative Spenserian, Du Bartas's (or Sylvester's) influence is clearly traceable, for Browne's "diction, which frequently includes compounds, [is] either borrowed directly from Sylvester, or formed in imitation of his." Perhaps even Browne's choice of the couplet form shows the influence of Sylvester.

William Browne was born in the medieval town of Tavistock, the son of Joan (née Lene)

and Thomas Brown (who seems to have spelled his surname usually without the *e*). According to John Prince, the poet's father was most likely a descendant of the "Knightly family of Browne, of Brownes-Ilarsh, in the Parish of Langtree, near Great Torrington, in Devon." William Browne went from Tavistock grammar school to Exeter College, Oxford, and left without a degree. He then entered Clifford's Inn, and went from there to the Inner Temple in November 1611. Like many poets of the age, shortly after arriving there, he was called to respond to the death of Prince Henry in 1612; among the numerous public expressions of grief was the *Two Elegies* put together (presumably) by Christopher Brooke and printed in 1613; the first elegy, by Brooke, is followed by one signed "W. B. Inter: Templ:," which would seem to be Browne's first published work. The year 1613 also saw the publication of the text on which he may have been working for some time, book 1 of *Britannia's Pastorals*. It attracted considerable public attention after it was published, but also had attracted significant notice even before, as it was prefaced by commendatory verses by such eminent figures as John Selden and his "chamber fellow" Edward Heyward, Michael Drayton, and Christopher Brooke.

Browne's work in the Spenserian mode continued in 1614 with the publication of *The Shepheards Pipe*, comprised of seven eclogues by Browne and four by others. Dedicated, like book 1 of *Britannia's Pastorals*, to Edward, Lord Zouche, it also includes two eclogues separately dedicated to intimates of Browne; he courted important men, and did it well. Various figures in the eclogues, such as Roget (George Wither), are identified by the poet, whose own persona throughout the eclogues (as in *Britania's Pastorals*) is Willie. This work in pursuit of patronage was followed in 1616 by book 2 of *Britannia's Pastorals*, which is dedicated to William Herbert, Earl of Pembroke. Although the first two books of *Britannia's Pastorals* were republished together in 1625, Browne's publishing career was, in effect, finished by 1616. Book 2 of *Britannia's Pastorals* was prefaced by an even more impressive collection of commendatory verses than had accompanied book 1: poems by Thomas Wenman of the Inner Temple, John Davies of Hereford, Wither, and Ben Jonson. Even more striking than the names of some of these poets, however, are the encomia to Browne of these poems. The emphasis throughout is on the friendship the contributors feel for Browne and on his agreeable character.

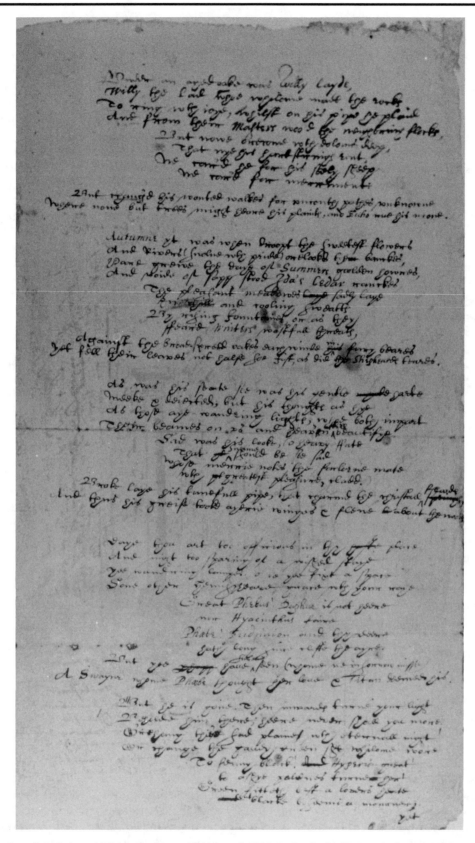

*Manuscript for three short lyrics, which remained unpublished until 1893, and a draft of Browne's elegy on Thomas Manwood, pub-
lished as the fourth eclogue in Browne's 1614 book,* The Shepheards Pipe *(Salisbury Cathedral Library, T. 2. 45)*

Browne is "so rare, / So innocent in all his ways / As in his lays," the "brightest swain / That woons, or haunts or hill or plain," and "him that merits best." His book is "a precious balsam for the sore. / 'Tis honey, nectar, balsam most devine: / Or one word for them all; my friend, 'tis thine." The tone of these poems is in contrast not only to that of the average collection of such verses, but also to that of the commendatory verses in the 1613 volume. One might expect commendatory verses to be friendly, but rarely are many, much less an entire collection, so pointedly concerned with the author's character. It would seem that the reception of *Britannia's Pastorals* was in no small part a result of the personal esteem that Browne himself enjoyed. In an age in which John Donne described "friendship" as his "second religion," Browne would seem to be an exemplary illustration of the significance of such social virtue.

The force of the poet's individual appeal does not, of course, explain the enduring appeal of his poem. *Britannia's Pastorals* has not attracted readers for nearly four hundred years because of the carefully woven plot; indeed, it has none. As K. M. Briggs points out, "Something of almost everything can be found in it—political satire, local legends and references, classical allusions, Jacobean conceits, fresh clear-cut pictures of the countryside, descriptions and similies drawn from crafts and country sports; everything but straightforward narrative." Everywhere in it one finds a cheerful patriotism and a fondness for local history and lore that seem always to have been attractive to English readers. These oft-quoted lines from song 3, book 2, are representative:

> Hail, thou my native soil! thou blessed plot
> Whose equall all the world affordeth not!
> Show me who can so many crystal rills,
> Such sweet-cloth'd valleys or aspiring hills;
> Such wood-ground, pastures, quaries, wealthy
>   mines;
> Such rocks in whom the diamond fairly shines;
> And if the earth can show the like again,
> Yet will she fail in her sea-ruling men.
> Time never can produce men to o'ertake
> The fames of Grenville, Davies, Gilbert, Drake,
> Or worthy Hawkins, or of the thousands more
> That by their power made the Devonian shore
> Mock the proud Tagus; for whose richest spoil
> The boasting Spaniard left the Indian soil
> Bankrupt of store, knowing it would quit the cost
> By winning this, though all the rest were lost.

Seldom since John of Gaunt's rueful paean to "this England" in Shakespeare's *Richard II* has the nationalism born and nurtured in the age of Elizabeth and James been so forcefully expressed. Even when he turns to political satire in his epic (again in the tradition of the epic as inherited from Ariosto and Englished by Spenser), Browne is relatively mild; for although he can be vigorous in his insights, the subjects of his satire are sufficiently abstract that particular persons could scarcely take offense; it is more the sins against his "blessed plot" that stirs his Horatian counsel than any Juvenalian fear of imminent doom. Furthermore, the satiric passages are sporadic, and Browne seems always willing, or even glad, to turn from them to more serene contemplations. In fact, there is but little satire in book 1, and, although there is more in book 2, it is not extensive, dealing mostly with general complaints, such as the enclosure of lands and the building of vast private houses, perhaps more in the spirit of Spenser's allegorical *Shepheardes Calender* (1579) than that of the personalized formal verse satire that was the favorite of the university wits of Browne's day. For example, only a few lines after one of the longer satirical passages in book 2 (about sixty lines), Browne deliberately turns to other matters:

> But stay, sweet Muse, forbear this harsher strain!
> Keep with the shepherds; leave the satyr's vein;
> Coop not with bears; let Icarus alone
> To scorch himself within the torid zone.

This self-address seems intended, again, to distance Browne deliberately from the fashionable modes of satire in favor of a conservative return to the stability of the Spenserian allegory and its support of the court.

Conspicuous imitation can have its drawbacks, of course, and as Browne strives, along with his muse, to "keep with the shepherds" in *Britannia's Pastorals*, his poetry is consciously derivative, consciously artificial. He owes most, of course, to Spenser but also a great deal to Italian and French court poets and to Michael Drayton, whose *Poly-Olbion* (1612) influenced Browne when he wrote *Britannia's Pastorals*, particularly book 2. *The Faerie Queene* (1590, 1596) and *Poly-Olbion* are "national" poems. Browne's is a regional poem, but he takes pains to expand its implications. The fame of the Devonshire worthies mentioned in the passage above, and others like them, "made the Devonian shore / Mock the

Title page for the 1616, combined edition of books 1 and 2 of the pastoral narratives that inspired John Davies of Hereford to proclaim: "Fame shall euer say, to thy renowne, / The Shepherds-Star, *or bright'st in* Skie, *is* Browne!"

proud Tagus," the Spanish river now properly put in its place. The topos of river as a national emblem is an ancient one. Browne's immediate antecedents are Spenser, especially in "The Ruines of Time," and Drayton. As those two poets celebrate the Thames, Browne celebrates his native Tavy. In the early lines of book 1, song 1, he makes clear the associations he intends to pursue as he sings of "Tavy's straggling spring":

What need I tune the swains of Thessaly?
Or, bootless, add to them of Arcadie?
. . . .
My Muse for lofty pitches shall not roam,
But homely pipen of her native home;
And to the swains, love rural minstrelsy;
Thus, dear Britannia, will I sing of thee.

Thus the regional poet, by way of synecdoche, celebrates his nation. Yet, even though Browne intends the Tavy to represent Britannia as the Thames does in Spenser and Drayton, Browne constantly returns to his own, strictly local, observations. Those observations have a great deal to do with the life that Browne experienced in Devon and little to do with the courtly tradition that he was keen to exploit. While he certainly belongs in that group of poets who have come to be known as Spenserians, he is also a West Country poet.

One or two early references to *Britannia's Pastorals* may be mentioned, each in its own way slightly mysterious. In his commendatory poem, which appears in book 2, Ben Jonson made a point of praising Browne for the conciseness of his work as well as its excellence: "I wou'd / More of our writers would like thee, not swell / With the *how much* they set forth, but th' *how well*." Yet one of the chief qualities of Browne's work is its rambling nature, and it can yield up such not-so-well-set-forth passages as these lines in book 2, song 1:

Thrice sacred Powers! (if sacred Powers there be
Whose mild aspect engyrland Poesy)
Ye happy sisters of the learned Spring,
Whose heavenly notes the woods are ravishing!
Brave Thespian maidens, at whose charming lays
Each moss-thrumb'd mountain bends, each current
    plays!
Piërian singers! O ye blessed Muses!
Who as a gem too dear the world refuses!

Perhaps Jonson was being ironic or didactic, or both. As this passage—and others such as: "whereon then fed / Of gallant Steeres, full many a thousand head"—appear early in book 2 (Browne's rich tribute to Jonson appears about one-third of the way into the second song in that book) such lines can hardly have escaped his notice. It is possible that an acute contemporary reader of Browne was hoping to nudge the young poet into writing the kind of verse for which he had already been praised.

Another early evaluation, of a sort, was advanced by William Winstanley in 1687 and perpetuated by John Prince a few years later. It has long been recognized that *Britannia's Pastorals* was in part influenced by Sir Philip Sidney's *Arcadia* (1590); one example of that influence may be Sidney's description of Mopsa: "Her hair pure crapal stone; her mouth O heavenly wide; / Her skin like burnished gold, her hands like silver ore untried." Although the "ugly girl" who appears in *Britannia's Pastorals* is merely a comic figure and Browne does not employ irony in the manner that Sidney does in his mock-blazon, this description in book 2, song 1, of *Britannia's Pastorals* is similar to Sidney's:

> The fishes yawn, the oysters gapen wide:
> So broad her mouth was. . . .
> . . . .
> Her nose (O crooked nose!) her mouth o'erhung,
> As it would be directed by her tongue:
> Her forehead such, as one might near avow
> Some ploughman had lately been at plough.

Presumably these are some of the lines that Winstanley had in mind when, in *The Lives of the Most Famous English Poets*, he gave Browne credit for the following, and about as many lines more:

> And is she not the Queen of Drabs,
> Whose Head is periwigg'd with scabs?
> Whose hair hangs down in curious flakes,
> All curl'd and crisp'd like crawling snakes;
> The breath of whose perfumed Locks
> Might choke the Devil with a Pox;
> Whose dainty twinings did entice
> The whole monoply of Lice;
> Her Forehead next is to be found,
> Resembling much the new-plough'd ground,
> Furrowed like stairs, whose windings led
> Unto the chimney of her head.

These lines were not written by Browne, but Prince, giving Winstanley due credit, cites the first eight lines as an example of Browne's work. Obviously, Winstanley did not check *Britannia's Pastorals* to make sure that his quotation was accurate, nor did Prince bother to verify Winstanley. It may be that Browne's description of the "ugly girl" had attracted enough attention that a whole subgenre of such descriptions was commonly, if vaguely, associated with Browne's poem—and that Winstanley's mistaken stab simply acknowledged as much. If so, *Britannia's Pastorals*, or at least some part of it, may be assumed to have passed into a body of poetry generally recognized by seventeenth-century readers.

Browne's *Masque of the Inner Temple (Ulysses and Circe)* was written in these early years and performed on 13 January 1615 (it was not published until 1772, however, when Thomas Davies, basing his text upon the manuscript copy in the library of Emmanuel College, Cambridge, included it in his collection of Browne's works). Browne seems to have based his version of the well-known and popular story of Ulysses and Circe in the *Odyssey* books 10 and 12, and in Ovid's *Metamorphoses*, book 14. It has been suggested that the story was refreshed in Browne's mind by his friend George Chapman's recently completed, soon to be published, translation of Homer. Browne moves away from the traditional reading of the episode as an example of the way that sensual appetite can turn men into beasts and treats it instead as a story of harmless dalliance—consistent once again with his reluctance to dwell on satirical elements in *Britannia's Pastorals*. To the extent that inferences can be drawn about Browne's temperament from his work, supported by further inferences that can be drawn from the commendatory verses that some of his friends wrote about book 2, it would seem that his early poetry was the work of a cheerful young man, anxious to explore the aspects of his patriotic vision in terms of those poets who had helped to forge the optimism and confidence of his nation, concerned to apply his vision to the virtues of his own region. He is always known as William Browne *of Tavistock*.

Little is known about Browne's personal and poetical activities in the several years following *Britannia's Pastorals*. In early 1624 he returned to Exeter College as tutor to Robert Dormer, who was to become the earl of Carnarvon. Later in the same year Oxford University created Browne master of arts. At about this time he traveled once or twice to France, perhaps in connection with his being tutor to Dormer. Also, at about this time he probably wrote most of the unfinished book 3 of *Britannia's Pastorals*. It was not published with the 1625 edition of the first two books, in reduced format, which could mean that he was still working on it after that date. Although Browne is sometimes assumed to have been married two, or even three, times, it is more likely that he was married only once, in 1628, to Timothy Eversfield, the daughter of Sir Thomas Eversfield of Horsham, Sussex, whom he seems to have wooed for some thirteen years. Two sons were born of this marriage; both were named Robert, and both died in infancy. That Browne has been supposed to have had more than one wife is the result of critics' too closely associating "characters" in his poetry with those in his own life. A. H. Bullen, for instance, assigns specific biographical implications to Browne's lovely epitaph "In Obitum M S, X° Maij, 1614":

> May! be thou never grac'd with birds that sing,
> Nor Flora's pride!

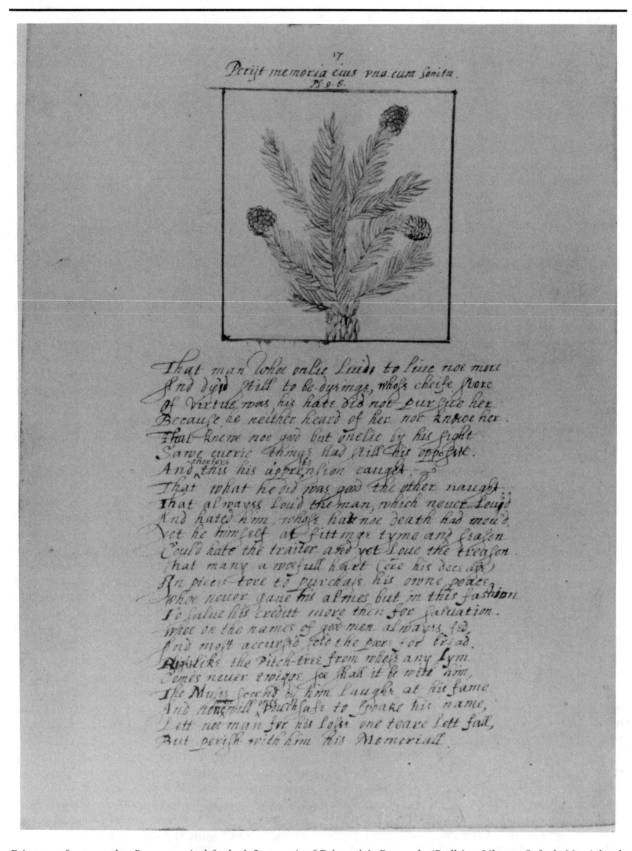

Fair copy of a poem that Browne revised for book 2, song 4, of Britannia's Pastorals *(Bodleian Library, Oxford; Ms. Ashmole 767, f. 12b). This version of the poem, under an emblem of a pitch tree, is in a manuscript book in which Browne drew emblems and wrote poems to accompany them.*

In thee all flowers and roses spring,
　Mine only died.

"The letters 'M S,' " says Bullen, "may well stand for "Maritæ Suæ [my wife]." Yet, as he notes, another epitaph in the same manuscript is titled "My own Epitaph" and is signed "Wm. Browne, 1614." Bullen is so eager to supply missing details for Browne's life that he overlooks the obvious undercutting of his own argument. Browne's epitaph for "M S" could have been just as much the product of pure imagination as the one for himself was.

The penchant to see Browne's work in autobiographical terms is encouraged, however, by the unfinished third book of *Britannia's Pastorals*, which consists of a completed first canto and an uncompleted second; it differs from the first two books in being much more concerned with the poet's personal experiences. The temptation to read biographical meanings into his earlier poetry may be the unfortunate fruit of critics' being familiar with book 3. Although the experiences are personal, they are not easy to sort out. One part of the difficulty lies in Browne's referring to more than one woman by the same name, Caelia, particularly since it seems that in one instance Browne is referring to a fictional character and in another instance is referring to the woman he married. Another part of the difficulty lies in the complication inherent in the poet's attempt to sing of (personal) love in the poem and to sing of the nation at the same time. This mingling of the personal and the public in book 3 is complicated further by the way in which book 3 is distanced from books 1 and 2 by the poet's celebrating Britannia not from the banks of the Tavy but from France (where he locates his narrator), even though it is to the Tavy that he unfailingly returns, as in the last lines of song 1:

　　　And Tavy in my rhymes
　Challenge a due; let it thy glory be,
　That famous Drake and I were born by thee!

Again like his English model, Browne's mixture of the various aspects of his pastoral epic—the fusion of the personal and the political into an attempted nationalistic or regional encomium—leaves the reader unsure of how clearly he intends one to separate the two. It is another feature he inherited from Spenser.

Sometime after his return from France, Browne took up residence with the Herbert fam-

ily at Wilton, in the county of Wiltshire (Philip Herbert, fourth Earl of Pembroke, was the father-in-law of Robert Dormer). A few years later, after his marriage, Browne seems to have settled near Dorking in Surrey, where he lived until his death in 1645. From these years there is preserved a letter (Ashmolean MS. 830) to Sir Benjamin Rudyerd, poet, man of letters, and politician, on a speech that Rudyerd delivered at the beginning of the Long Parliament.

> Sir,—I beseech you to pardon my interposing your most serious affairs with the remembrance of my service. The cause requires it, and every man who knows I have the honour to be known by you would think me stupid in not congratulating what every man thinks he hath a share in. I mean your late speech in Parliament, wherein they believe the spirit which inspired the Reformation and the genius which dictated the Magna Charta possessed you, In my poor cell and sequestration from all business I bless God and pray for more such members in the Commonwealth; and could you but hear (as it is pity but you should) what I do, it would add some years to your honored hairs. Believe it (Sir) you have given such a maintenance to the repute which your former deportment had begotten that it will need no other livelihood than a chronicle, which I hope our ensuing age will not see it want for. I have now done, ('Tis Sunday night) when I have prayed for my honored Lord the Lord Chamberlain, my good Lord and Master the Earl of Carnarvon, and for you and your good proceedings, I hope I shall wake the same thoughts again, and be ever
> 　　　Your most obliged servant
>
> 　　　　　Wm. Browne
>
> Dorking November 29
> 1640

This letter fills in several details for an otherwise particularly obscure period of Browne's life, as it establishes his residence, recalls his interest in political matters, and suggests his continuing connection with men of letters and his old patrons, Philip Herbert, Lord Pembroke (the lord chamberlain) and Dormer (the earl of Carnarvon). Virtually nothing is known about the rest of Browne's life. Anthony Wood talks of his having "a little body, so great a mind." Prince changes the phrasing to "He had a great mind in a little body," which form has been commonly retained, even when Wood is referred to as the source of the sentiment. It is the only reference to Browne's stature; no portrait of him has been recorded.

One of the more felicitous results of Browne's affiliation with the Herbert family is the best-known of his shorter poems, the epitaph for the mother of William and Philip Herbert, "On the Dowager Countess of Pembroke":

> Underneath this sable herse
> Lies the subject of all verse:
> Sidney's sister, Pembroke's mother:
> Death, ere thou hast slain another,
> Fair, and learn'd, and good as she,
> Time shall throw a dart at thee.
>
> Marble piles let no man raise
> To her name: for after days
> Some kind woman born as she,
> Reading this, like Niobe
> Shall turn marble, and become
> Both her mourner and her tomb.

The countess died in September 1621; the poem was first published, anonymously, in the third edition of William Camden's *Remaines, Concerning Britaine* in 1623. The first stanza, in particular, has been much admired. In it Browne points out the relationship of the family of his patrons, the Herberts, with the Sidney family; more important, he associates both families with the *idea* of a poetic tradition, going back ("Sidney's sister") to the penultimate decade of the previous century. It is the same idea that permeates most of Browne's writing, as it did that of the other Spenserians. Although he was, quite deliberately, a member of a group of poets who set out to write in a specific tradition, he found his own voice within it. The pastoral mode to which he was attracted provided for him a medium in which he could be both representative and original. Like the other Spenserians, Browne celebrated patriotic values and found suitable images for those values in the English countryside. Browne's countryside, however, was particularly his own. He wrote not so much of idealized, literary scenes, but of specific places in Devonshire. Illustrations of this practice can be found throughout his poetry but nowhere better than in *Britannia's Pastorals*, the poem for which he is chiefly known.

References:

K. M. Briggs, *The Anatomy of Puck* (London: Routledge & Kegan Paul, 1959), pp. 56-65;

Cedric C. Brown and Margherita Piva, "William Browne, Marino, France and the Third Book of *Britannia's Pastorals*," *Review of English Studies*, new series 29 (November 1978): 385-404;

Sukanta Chaudhuri, *Renaissance Pastoral and its English Developments* (Oxford: Clarendon Press, 1989);

Joan Grundy, *The Spenserian Poets* (London: Arnold, 1969);

Joshua McClennen, "William Browne as a Satirist," *Papers of the Michigan Academy of Science, Arts, and Letters*, 33 (1947): 355-361;

Frederic W. Moorman, *William Brown. His Britannia's Pastorals and the Pastoral Poetry of the Elizabethan Age* (Strasbourg: Trübner, 1978);

John Prince, *Danmonii Orientales Illustres: Or, The Worthies of Devon* (Exeter: Printed by Sam. Farley for Awnsham & John Churchill, London, and Charles Yeo & Philip Bishop, Exon., 1701);

William Winstanley, *The Lives of the Most Famous English Poets* (London: Printed by H. Clark for Samuel Manship, 1687).

Papers:
Manuscripts for Browne's love complaints are in the British Library (Lansdowne MS. 777). A manuscript for book 3 of *Britainia's Pastorals* is in Salisbury Cathederal Library. A manuscript for *The Inner Temple Masque* is at Emmanuel College, Cambridge.

George Chapman

(1559 or 1560 - 12 May 1634)

Gerald Snare
Tulane University

See also the Chapman entry in *DLB 62: Elizabethan Dramatists.*

BOOKS: Σκὶα νυκτὸς *The Shadow of Night: Containing Two Poeticall Hymnes* (London: Printed by R. F. for William Ponsonby, 1594);

Ouids Banquet of Sence (London: Printed by I. R. for Richard Smith, 1595);

Hero and Leander, parts 1 and 2 by Christopher Marlowe, parts 3-6 by Chapman (London: Printed by Felix Kingston for Paule Linley, 1598);

The Blinde Begger of Alexandria (London: Printed by J. Roberts for William Jones, 1598);

A Pleasant Comedy Entituled: An Humerous dayes Myrth (London: Printed by G. C. for Valentine Syms, 1599);

Al Fooles (London: Printed by G. Eld for Thomas Thorpe, 1605);

Eastward Hoe, by Chapman, Ben Jonson, and John Marston (London: Printed by G. Eld for William Aspley, 1605);

Sir Gyles Goosecappe Knight (London: Printed by John Windet for Edward Blunt, 1606);

The Gentleman Usher (London: Printed by Valentine Simmes for Thomas Thorppe, 1606);

Monsievr D'Olive (London: Printed by Thomas Creede for William Holmes, 1606);

Bussy D'Ambois (London: Printed by Eliot's Court Press for William Aspley, 1607);

The Conspiracie, and Tragedie of Charles Duke of Byron (London: Printed by George Eld for Thomas Thorppe, sold by L. Lisle, 1608);

Evthymiæ Raptvs; or the Teares of Peace (London: Printed by H. Lownes for Richard Bonian & H. Walley, 1609);

May-day (London: Printed by William Stansby for John Browne, 1611);

An Epicede or Funerall Song: On the most disastrous Death, of the Highborne Prince of Men, Henry Prince of Wales, & c. With The Funeralls, and Representation of the Herse (London: Printed by T. S. for John Budge, 1612);

The Widdowes Teares (London: Printed by William Stansby for John Browne, 1612);

The Revenge of Bussy D'Ambois (London: Printed by T. Snodham, sold by John Helme, 1613);

The Memorable Maske of the Honorable Houses or Inns of Court; the Middle Temple, and Lyncolns Inne (London: Printed by George Eld for George Norton, 1613);

Evgenia: Or Trve Nobilities Trance; For the Most Memorable Death, of the Thrice Noble and Religious; William Lord Rvssel (London, 1614);

Andromeda Liberata. Or The Nvptials of Persevs and Andromeda (London: Printed by Eliot's Court Press for Laurence L'Isle, 1614);

A Free and Offenceles Iustification, of a Lately Pvblisht and Most Maliciously Misinterpreted Poeme: Entitvled Andromeda Liberata (London: Printed by Eliot's Court Press for Laurence L'Isle, 1614);

Pro Vere, Avtvmni Lachrymae. Inscribed to the Immortal Memorie of the most Pious and Incomparable Souldier, Sir Horatio Vere, Knight (London: Printed by B. Alsop for Th. Walkley, 1622);

A Iustification of a Strange Action of Nero (London: Printed by Thomas Harper, 1629);

Caesar and Pompey (London: Printed by Thomas Harper, sold by G. Emondson & T. Alchorne, 1631);

The Tragedy of Chabot Admirall of France, by Chapman and James Shirley (London: Printed by Thomas Cotes for Andrew Crooke & William Cooke, 1639).

Editions: *The Comedies and Tragedies of George Chapman*, 3 volumes, edited by Richard Shepherd (London: John Pearson, 1873);

The Works of George Chapman, 3 volumes, edited by Shepherd and Algernon Charles Swinburne (London: Chatto & Windus, 1874-1875);

The Plays and Poems of George Chapman, 2 volumes, edited by Thomas Marc Parrott (London: Routledge / New York: Dutton, 1910, 1914);

The Poems of George Chapman, edited by Phyllis Brooks Bartlett (New York: Modern Lan-

George Chapman at age fifty-seven, portrait engraved by William Hole; from the verso of the title page of his Whole Works of Homer *(Henry E. Huntington Library and Art Gallery)*

guage Association of America / London: Oxford University Press, 1941);

Chapman's Homer: The Iliad, The Odyssey, and the Lesser Homerica, 2 volumes, edited by Allardyce Nicoll (New York: Pantheon, 1956);

The Divine Poem of Musæus, translated by Chapman, and *Hero and Leander*, completed by Chapman, in *Elizabethan Minor Epics*, edited by Elizabeth Story Donno (New York: Columbia University Press, 1963), pp. 70-126;

The Plays of George Chapman, volume 1, edited by Allan Holaday and Michael Kiernan (Urbana: University of Illinois Press, 1970); volume 2, edited by Holaday, G. Blakemore Evans, and Thomas Berger (Woodbridge, U.K. & Wolfeboro, N.H.: D. S. Brewer, 1987);

George Chapman's Minor Translations, edited by Richard Corballis (Salzburg: Institut für Anglistik und Amerikanistik, 1984).

PLAY PRODUCTIONS: See *DLB 62.*

OTHER: "De Guiana, Carmen Epicum," in *A Relation of the second Voyage to Guiana*, by Lawrence Keymis (London: Printed by T. Dawson, 1596);

Robert Allott, *Englands Parnassus*, includes eighty quotations from Chapman's poems (London: Printed by N. Ling, C. Burby & T. Hayes, 1600);

"Peristeros: or the Male Turtle," in *Loves Martyr: or, Rosalins Complaint*, by Robert Chester (London: Printed by R. Field for E. Blount, 1601);

"In Sejanum Ben. Jonsoni Et Musis, et sibi," in *Seianus His Fall*, by Ben Jonson (London: Printed by G. Elld for T. Thorpe, 1605);

"To his deare Friend, Benjamin Jonson his Volpone," in *Ben: Ionson his Volpone Or the Foxe* (London: Printed by G. Eld for Thomas Thorppe, 1607);

"To his loving friend M. Jo. Fletcher concerning his Pastorall, being both a Poem and a play," in *The Faithfvll Shepheardesse*, by John Fletcher (London: Printed by E. Allde for R. Bonian & H. Walley, 1609?);

"Mr. Geo: Chapman In worthye love of this new work, and the most Autenticall Aucthors," in *Parthenia or the Maydenhead of the first musicke that euer was printed for the Virginalls*, by William Byrd, John Bull, and Orlando Gibbons (London: Printed for M.^{ris} Dor: Evans, to be sould by G. Lowe, 1611?);

"To His Loved Sonne, Nat. Field, and His wethercocke woman," in *A Woman is a Weather-cocke*, by Nathan Field (London: Printed by W. Jaggard for J. Budge, 1612);

"To his Ingenuous, and much lov'd Friend, the Author," in *The Ghost of Richard the Third*, by Christopher Brooke (London: Printed by G. Eld for L. Lisle, 1614);

"To his long-lov'd and worthy friend, Mr. Edward Grimeston . . . ," in *A Table of Humane Passions*, by Nicolas Coeffeteau, translated by Edward Grimeston (London: Printed by N. Okes, 1621);

"To the Volume," in *The True History of the Tragicke Loves of Hipolito and Isabella, Neapolitans* (London: Printed by Tho: Harper & Nath. Feild, 1628).

TRANSLATIONS: *Seauen Bookes of the Iliades of Homere, Prince of Poets*, translated by Chapman from books 1, 2, 7-11 of Homer's *Iliad* (London: Printed by Iohn Windet, 1598);

Achilles Shield, translated by Chapman from book 18 of Homer's *Iliad* (London: Printed by Iohn Windet, 1598);

Homer Prince of Poets, translated by Chapman from books 1-12 of Homer's *Iliad* (London: Printed by H. Lownes for Samuel Macham, 1609);

The Iliads of Homer, translated by Chapman from all twenty-four books of Homer's *Iliad* (London: Printed by Richard Field for Nathaniell Butter, 1611);

Petrarchs Seuen Penitentiall Psalms, Paraphrastically Translated: With Other Philosophicall Poems

(London: Printed by R. Field for Matthew Selman, 1612);

The Whole Works of Homer Prince of Poetts, translated by Chapman (London: Printed by R. Field & W. Jaggard for Nathaniell Butter, 1616?);

The Divine Poem of Musaeus, translated by Chapman (London: Printed by R. Field & W. Jaggard, 1616);

The Georgicks of Hesiod, translated by Chapman (London: Printed by H. Lownes for Miles Partrich, 1618);

The Crowne of all Homers Workes Batrachomyomachia Or the Battaile of Frogs and Mise. His Hymn's— and—Epigrams, translated by Chapman (London: Printed by Eliot's Court Press for John Bill, 1624?).

George Chapman has retained to this day the considerable reputation he achieved in his own lifetime. Playwright, poet, translator, he is still considered an exceptionally important figure in the English Renaissance. His plays, particularly, were adapted for the stage throughout the Restoration, and, though his reputation dipped during most of the eighteenth century, the nineteenth saw a marked revival of interest in Chapman's works, perhaps best summed up in John Keats's well-known sonnet "On First Looking Into Chapman's Homer" (1816).

Chapman was born in Hitchin (as an allusion in *Euthymiæ Raptus; or the Teares of Peace* [1609] has it), a town in Hertfordshire some thirty miles from London. He was the second son of Thomas Chapman and Joan Nodes, the daughter of George and Margaret Grimeston Nodes and a cousin to Edward Grimeston the translator. Of his early life little is known except that he attended Oxford in 1574 and left before taking a degree. Upon Anthony Wood's testimony, Chapman was a person of "most reverend aspect, religious and temperate, qualities rarely meeting in a poet," one who excelled in Latin and Greek but not in logic and philosophy. We know that from at least 1583 through 1585 he was in the household of Sir Ralph Sadler, who was employed by both Queen Elizabeth and William Cecil, Lord Burghley. There is evidence to suggest that Chapman served in the military campaigns in the Low Countries in 1591 and 1592 and that he had returned to London before 1594.

If one can isolate a central passion in Chapman's life and works, it would be the cen-

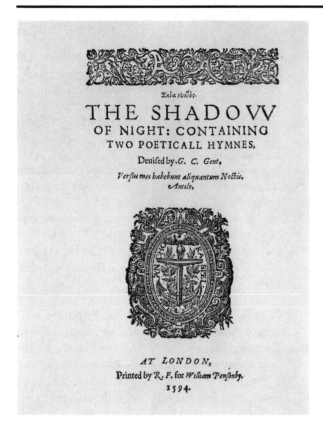

Σκιὰ ῥήκῖος·

THE SHADOW
OF NIGHT: CONTAINING
TWO POETICALL HYMNES,

Deuised by .G. C. Gent.

Versu mei habebunt aliquantum Noctis.
Antilo.

AT LONDON,
Printed by *R. F.* for *William Ponsonby.*
1594.

Title page for Chapman's first book, poems modeled on classi-cal Greek hymns but adapted to address the concerns of Chapman's contemporaries

tral project of Renaissance Christian humanism: an attempt to make literature (among the other disciplines) an instrument for both an upright private ethics and a benevolent and just public policy. In more parochial terms the project intended as well to establish a national literature powerful enough to rival the Latin and the Greek. In his poetic canon, including his Homeric translations, Chapman constantly aims at converting Greek and Latin poetry (classical as well as contemporary) to native English and claims as well an attempt to surpass his predecessors. If Chapman consistently borrows from other works (a practice hardly unknown in the period), he likewise consistently experiments with his borrowings, and that experimentation shows in his poems as well as in his plays. Since Algernon Charles Swinburne's essay in 1875, Chapman (until recently) has been taken as one of the most difficult and obscure poets in the Renaissance, a kind of moralist whose thought manifests itself in moral imperatives tortuously crammed into his dramatic or poetic works. Contemporary criticism, however, has sought to redeem Chapman from the reputation for pedantry and obscurity (largely a product of

late-nineteenth- and early-twentieth-century scholarship) and to take him as he was seen by his contemporaries, a learned translator, a novel poet, and a very successful dramatist.

Chapman's first published work was *The Shadow of Night* (1594), composed of two hymns, one to Night and one to Cynthia. They are modeled on Greek hymns of Proclus, Callimachus, and the Orphic hymns, even though they have a large number of borrowings and echoes from contemporary literature. Chapman may have found some of the Orphic hymns in Aldus's edition of *Hero and Leander* (1517), which he later used for his adaptation of that poem (1598). *The Shadow of Night* is, in essence, a heroic poem laced with lamentations by the supplicant poet for the loss of true knowledge, learning, and virtue in the world, a subject Chapman incessantly returned to throughout his career. A reader needs to observe that complaints about the vanity of the world and the prostitution of learning were commonplaces of the age. The pronounced defensive posture of many literati assumed an attack by a society convinced, for religious or political reasons, of the vanity of art. *The Shadow of Night* is only partly allegorical, as in the tale of Euthimya (whose name means "Cheerfulness") and the hunt (or chase of the passions) in "Cynthiam," and despite its reputation for obscurity, it displays throughout a quite remarkable and clear handling of syntax within some powerful pentameter couplets. We should take it as part of a whole program, in this instance, of Chapman's attempt to domesticate the Greek hymn, which can be noted clearly in the interpolated tale of the English victory over Alessandro Farnese, Duke of Parma, at Nymeghen (1590). The two poems are followed by glosses, a habit Chapman continued from his early work through his final edition of Homer late in his life. The poem thus clearly stakes a claim for its author's promise as a legitimate, as opposed to a popular, poet: the mode, the imitations, the borrowings, the glosses all proclaim a serious and accomplished poet worthy of serious patronage. Edmund Spenser, we should recall, started his career in exactly the same way fifteen years earlier. The work has been notable in modern criticism (it had no subsequent edition in the Renaissance) for the theory, now largely discredited, that it reveals "a school of night" to which William Shakespeare supposedly responded in satiric portions of his *Love's Labour's Lost* (1598). Part of that theory makes Chapman the rival poet mentioned in Shakespeare's Sonnet 86.

Ovid's Banquet of Sense followed *The Shadow of Night* in 1595, the same year that Chapman joined the Admiral's Men, Philip Henslowe's company of actors playing at the Rose Theatre. In addition to the title poem of 117 nine-line stanzas, *Ovid's Banquet of Sense* includes some commendatory verses (one by Sir John Davies), the ten sonnets of "A Coronet for his Mistress Philosophy," "The Amorous Zodiac" (translated from the French poem by Gilles Durant, 1587), and "The Amorous Contention of Phillis and Flora," followed by some of its Latin original. The two translations are not by Chapman. The title poem depicts Ovid feasting each of his five senses as he watches Corinna in her bath. The poem is an extraordinary comic tour de force in the popular mode of Ovidian erotic poetry, and it remains a minimasterpiece, a reductio ad absurdum of the conventions of contemporary erotic poems. Chapman grafts onto the old trope of the banquet of sense all the possibilities of that fashionable mode: its eroticized Platonism, its faculty psychology, its innumerable strategies of seduction and pleas for mercy, its aggressive self-justifications. Ovid, even in the highest flights of his erotic fantasy, feasts on his own poetry. He gets little or nothing from Corinna. The poem was popular enough to see another edition as late as 1639, though its reputation in the twentieth century rests on viewing it as a masterful explication of Neoplatonic love and, in essence, a semiserious philosophical and consciously obscurantist poem. Such a view badly underestimates a poem that is in fact a burlesque.

Chapman's earliest drama, *The Blind Beggar of Alexandria*, was produced in 1596, the year after *Ovid's Banquet of Sense* appeared, and had been through at least twenty-two productions before it was published in 1598. Even though the play as printed is heavily cut, one can follow easily the machinations and wooings of Irus the beggar and some fine touches of social satire throughout.

Hero and Leander, one of the best-known poems of its era, appeared in 1598 as well and is the first poem in which Chapman directly courts a noble patron, in this case the wife of Sir Thomas Walsingham, a cousin of his better-known contemporary Sir Francis. Throughout his career, Chapman's quest for patronage would prove both painful and vain, but there could scarcely be a more propitious beginning. Though in his dedication he somewhat disingenuously calls his poem a trifle (and promises matter of

more substance later), we should recognize some claims to distinction. After all, he wryly notes, "He who shuns trifles must shun the world." Christopher Marlowe's portion of the poem had been an instant success and, in Abraham Fraunce's words, "in every man's mouth." Marlowe's 334-line poem, published early in 1598, was republished later the same year, now divided into two sestiads (after Hero's town Sestos), with four new sestiads by Chapman. Chapman's completion was published with Marlowe's fragment in all subsequent editions. The poem is based on the *Hero and Leander* of Musaeus, a fifth-century poet who may have written from Alexandria. The Greek text of his poem was one of the first published by the famous Aldine press of Venice in 1494. Musaeus's *Hero and Leander* is one of several late-Greek epic poems intentionally un-Homeric, often focusing on minor mythological figures, subjects, and themes distinctly unclassical. They often aim at high pathos in a poetic style at once intricate, hyperbolic, and even, on occasion, bombastic. The great Latin exemplar for the Renaissance was the enormously popular *Rape of Proserpina* of Claudian (circa 400). There were many editions to follow in the sixteenth century as well as adaptations of the poem by major poets all over Europe, including Hans Sachs. The adaptation by Marlowe and Chapman expands considerably upon the original (which both certainly knew), all the while observing its possibilities and suggestions. There are, for example, the characteristic epic similes, epic digressions in the tales of Mercury and Teras, battles or disputes with the gods, and jocular or satiric asides by the narrator-poet. Both poets preserve as well all the obsessions of their original: the focus on Hero's torch, the division between Sestos and Abydos, the manic insistence on secrecy, the elaborate manipulation of the imagery of light and dark and day and night, the compounding of paradox, especially in Hero being Venus's Nun. *Hero and Leander* is an exceptionally elaborate, brilliant, and often-comic story of the seduction of Hero by Leander, their marriage and its consummation, and their tragic deaths at the hands of the gods. The poem was tremendously popular, echoed in scores of contemporary works, and printed in at least seven editions by 1637. While Marlowe's portion has always been praised, Chapman's continuation has, in this century at least, been maligned for what has been taken to be its intrusive moral commentary. Yet such expansions, as other scholars see them, are both functional and appropriate to the original text. Chapman later translated Musaeus's *Hero and Leander* in 1616 and dedicated it to Inigo Jones. Unlike his earlier adaptation, Chapman's is one of the most judicious and accurate (as well as one of the shortest) of the several translations in the period. He clearly used the Greek of the Aldine text (1494 and many subsequent editions), frequently consulting the Latin translation that was published with it.

Chapman's most successful bid for noble patronage (and, as it turned out, the most unfortunate and bitter) began with his first translations of Homer in 1598: his *Seven Books of the Iliad*, translations in fourteeners of books 1, 2, and 7-11; and *Achilles Shield*, a partial translation of book 18 of the *Iliad* in decasyllabic couplets. Both were dedicated to the brilliant Robert Devereux, second Earl of Essex. Whether Chapman actually benefited from this work at the time we do not know. Essex might have been either pleased or embarrassed that the plight of Achilles in book 18 was made a direct analogy to his own circumstances in Chapman's dedicatory epistle. The rest of Chapman's *Iliad* was not to appear until 1609, with another, royal patron.

Chapman's attention turned almost exclusively to drama for the next ten years. *A Humorous Day's Mirth* was published in 1599, though it had been notably popular since 1597, when it was performed by the Admiral's Men, perhaps because it was one of the "new plays of humors," a comedy of humors.

Chapman left Henslowe's company sometime in 1600, a year marked as well by his imprisonment for debt at the hands of a notorious usurer, John Wolfall. Chapman joined the Children of the Chapel (the Children of St. Paul's), a company performing at the Blackfriars Theatre, and continued writing for this company until 1609. The company could scarcely have greater luck, for in 1603 or 1604 it produced Chapman's first and best-known tragedy, *Bussy D'Ambois*, which was published in 1607. It enjoyed a remarkable popularity well into the Restoration. Bussy, the colossally self-confident and fearless courtier, after having offended various powers at the French court, succeeds in becoming a favorite of King Henry III. He is undone, however, after a sexual intrigue with Tamyra, the count of Montsurry's wife. The duke of Guise and Montsurry plot against Bussy and, by stabbing and torturing Tamyra, succeed in luring him to his death. The play was clearly a smashing success, with five is-

Title page for the comic, erotic poem in which Ovid exercises each of his five senses while he watches a young woman bathing

sues or editions by 1657, a revival by Nathan Field for the Whitefriars in 1610, performances by the King's Men (Shakespeare's old company) in 1634 and 1638, and a notably successful rewrite by Thomas D'Urfey for the Theatre Royal in Drury Lane, published in 1691. Despite John Dryden's unappreciative remarks in the preface to his *Spanish Friar* (1681), the play has remained exceptionally popular into the twentieth century, having been published in a large number of editions.

The Children of St. Paul's also performed Chapman's now-lost *The Old Joiner of Aldgate* in February of 1603. From all evidence a farce based on contemporary gossip, the play is the first that got Chapman in trouble with local authorities (a relative commonplace for London playwrights). On this occasion he was interrogated in a slander suit but was not arrested. Chapman may also have been the "second Pen" mentioned in the preface to Ben Jonson's *Sejanus his Fall*, performed in 1603 and published in 1605. That "Pen" or hand is credited with "a good share" of Jonson's play. Henslowe's diary does in fact attribute to Chapman "ii actes of a Tragedie of Bengemens [that is, Jonson's] plotte."

Our first sure record of a performance of Chapman's play *All Fools* is on New Year's Day of 1605 at the Blackfriars. *All Fools* is a far more sophisticated, high comedy than Chapman's earlier plays in the genre. The lines glitter with wit, the characterization is fascinating, and the plot is masterfully handled, involving a whole series of intrigue and types: a jealous husband, a jealous father, a courtier, a wayward son, and Reynoldo the trickster. Chapman may have been pleased about the quiet success of *All Fools* in 1605, for while he had faced minor difficulties with the production of the *Old Joiner*, in 1603, he could never have forseen the storm that broke over *Eastward Ho* upon its publication and performance in 1605. A collaborative effort of Chapman, Ben Jonson, and John Marston, the play is a reply to Thomas Dekker and John Webster's *Westward Ho*, performed in 1604 and published in 1607. Both are London City comedies filled with character types and deceptions, as well as with contemporary news, ballads, songs, and plays. There are, for example, at least five allusions to *Hamlet* in *Eastward Ho*. The cause célèbre of the play, however, was a pointed gibe at the large number of Scots newly arrived in England (at James I's accession). The offending lines were immediately canceled from the first quarto, and Chapman and Jonson were imprisoned straightway. Apparently King James himself, according to Jonson's later testimony, had been told of the outrage and ordered the arrest. They were released some weeks later, after a whole series of letters and petitions. Though city comedies were extremely popular in the theater, the notoriety of *Eastward Ho*, its relation to *Westward Ho*, and its exceptional comedy made it an instant, and perhaps to its authors an unwelcome, hit. One response was another play by Dekker and Webster, *Northward Ho* (acted in late 1605 and published in 1607), in which Chapman is gently satirized as the genial scholar Bellamont, a man witty enough to help unravel a plot to discredit a friend's wife and to escape a

trick designed to make a fool of him. There were three editions of *Eastward Ho* in 1605, simultaneous with its production at Blackfriars. The play was revived—offending passage omitted, of course—for a 1614 production at Whitehall before Princess Elizabeth and King James himself. The play retained its popularity well into the late eighteenth century. Chapman followed *Eastward Ho* with two other comedies, *Monsieur D'Olive* (performed at Blackfriars in late 1604 or early 1605 and published in 1606) and *Sir Giles Goosecap* (performed in 1603, published in 1606). The plot of *Monsieur D'Olive*, which involves a series of benevolent deceptions by Vandome, and the subplot, centered on D'Olive (a scurrilous satirist and perfect burlesque of a courtier), never do meet in what must be described as an entertaining, though imperfect, comedy. The parody of courtliness in D'Olive has some fine touches, especially in his extended panegyric on tobacco in act 2.

Sir Giles Goosecap, published anonymously in 1606, is probably Chapman's. It is clearly a comedy of humors, where the plot is markedly secondary to the examination of such characters as Foulweather, Rudesby, and the foolish, if benign, Sir Giles himself. The main plot, adapted from the first three sections of Geoffrey Chaucer's *Troilus and Criseide*, focuses on Clarence, a studious and pure lover of Eugenia. The delay in publication of *Sir Giles Goosecap* is a likely result of censorship. Contemporary evidence strongly suggests that there were objections to the play and that the principal characters, especially Lady Furnivall, are satiric portraits of contemporary figures.

The Gentleman Usher, performed in 1601 or 1602 and published in 1606, is a play very different from Chapman's earlier efforts. With a typically complex plot, centered about Vincentio's love for Margaret (rewarded at the end), but with a pronounced attention to the dramatic possibilities of language, the play comes near to being a comedy of manners or, in the high pathos of some speeches, almost a tragicomedy. Stock comic characters remain, to be sure, as well as a series of standard deceptions. But acts 4 and 5 shift markedly to a comic/pathetic mode: the appearance of a real and dangerous villain, a real danger of death, the high pathos in the disfigurement of Margaret, and the final reconciliation. Although we have little evidence of the play's success, it does mark Chapman's first attempt at tragicomedy. The second is *The Widow's Tears*, composed circa 1605 and published in 1612. There are primarily two sets of lovers in the play,

Tharsalio, the cynical former servant who woos and wins his former mistress, Eudora, and Lysander, who puts his faithful wife, Cynthia, to cruel test of her fidelity. Cynthia does succumb to a seduction by her disguised husband, but, upon discovering his plot, turns the tables on him. This play shares with *The Gentlemen Usher* a focus on plot rather than (stock) character, avoids for the most part either satire or parody, and revels in incidents more appropriate to tragedy than comedy.

Chapman delayed the sequel to *Bussy D'Ambois* (*The Revenge of Bussy D'Ambois*) until 1610 or 1611, when it was produced at the new Whitefriars by Nathan Field's new company, the Queen's Revels. Chapman's second tragedy came four years after the singular success of *Bussy D'Ambois*: two plays combined as one, *The Conspiracy and Tragedy of Charles Duke of Byron*, composed in early 1608 and published the same year. The Byron plays mark a considerable departure from dramatic trappings of Senecan drama—the blood, revenge, grotesqueries, and ghosts—of the Bussy plays. The focus in the Byron plays is unremittingly on the hero and his brand of virtuous Marlovian virtu. While these plays interest us as a new direction in Chapman's tragedies, they also interest us for the furor they aroused. They were based on a recent controversy—the treason and execution of Charles de Gontant, Baron de Biron, courtier to Henry IV of Navarre. The French ambassador to court, Antoine Lefèvre de la Boderie, protested the production and arranged to have three of the actors jailed. Chapman apparently escaped and later sought refuge with Ludovick Stuart, Duke of Lennox. The offending scene, soon struck by the master of the revels, portrays the queen of France indelicately dressing down and boxing the ears of the king's mistress, Madame Henriette D'Entragues, Marquise de Verneuil. There is as well the interview between Byron and Queen Elizabeth in act 4 that also came under the hand of the censors. As a consequence, act 4 of the *Conspiracy*, where a report of the interview with the queen is now reported secondhand, is badly mangled, as are acts 1 and 2 of the *Tragedy*. The censors apparently felt comfortable in allowing only one scene of act 2 in the *Tragedy* to remain, the masque where Queen Marie de Médicis (as Chastity) and the king's mistress (appropriately playing Liberality) are reconciled. The *Conspiracy* traces the seduction of the proud and pliant Duke of Byron to a conspiracy against King Henry IV of Navarre and his ulti-

Title page for the first edition of Christopher Marlowe's popular poem on legendary lovers, completed by Chapman

mate capitulation to the king's power. The *Tragedy* finds Byron in yet another plot and again called to court to confess his treason. He first refuses, then appears to protest his innocence, convinced the king will never condemn one so valuable to the state. Act 5 wholly focuses on Byron, caught between Christian resignation and Herculean fury until he is finally executed.

The year 1609 seemed to promise the beginning of the end of Chapman's recurring money troubles. He had received a promise from the young Henry, Prince of Wales, of an annuity and the princely sum of three hundred pounds for his translation of Homer. He had revised his *Seven Books* of 1598 and added books 3, 4, 5, 6, and 12 for his *Homer Prince of Poets* (1609). This portion of *The Iliad* Chapman renders in a supple and innovative fourteen-syllable line, a verse form often taken as appropriate to the hexameter line of the classical epic by some Renaissance translators. His epistle dedicatory, partly a panegyric on Henry and partly a piece of literary criticism, is directed "To the High Borne Prince of Men, Henry." Here Chapman enunciates views common in contemporary literary criticism: the usefulness (nay, the necessity) of poetry to princes (especially the heroic poetry of Homer) and the request for the prince to protect and advance the sacred vocation of poets. This epistle is followed by another, "To the Reader." Both stand as a defense of poetry, the former more generalized, the latter very detailed. In the second, Chapman directly defends his native English as a language fully capable of catching the nuances of Homer's Greek, even superior to other modern languages. He defends as well his "Pariphrases," his expansions on the original in his own translation, as both judicious and necessary. Indeed, those who translate word-by-word are quite wrong because a translation must be guided by a perception of Homer's complete invention, the scope and direction of the epic as a whole. It is here that we may discover not only Chapman the translator, but Chapman the dramatist, taking as his guide the coherence of character and plot for his rendering of individual lines and words. The epistle concludes with a remarkably vivid and accomplished attack on his detractors.

Euthymiæ Raptus; or the Tears of Peace, also 1609, is likewise dedicated to Henry, beginning and ending with notable references to Chapman's Homer. The poem is of a piece with other "complaints" or lamentations of the period. Homer appears to the poet and introduces him to the allegorical figure Peace, whose tears are complaints about the degradation of Learning and the elevation of power and ambition in the world. This subject, about which Chapman wrote constantly in nearly all the prefaces and epistles to his works, might well stand as a constant thematic idea throughout his life and work.

Yet no thematic can account for Chapman's continued success on the popular stage. Even while finishing his translation of the *Iliad*, his *May Day* (1611) and *The Revenge of Bussy D'Ambois* (1613) were being produced in 1611. Both are in notable, popular modes. *The Revenge of Bussy D'Ambois* is Chapman's attempt at the venerable revenge tragedy, focusing on the character of Clermont D'Ambois, a reluctant avenger who avoids both fury and haste, ever mindful of the tension between private revenge and public law. There is, of course, the ghost of Bussy to de-

mand revenge, but Clermont is more comfortable in echoing Epictetus on the vanity of ambition and wealth than plotting deaths. He dies at the end not by the machinations of villains, but from grief at the loss of an ally and at the prospect of living in a world devoid of justice. *May Day* is a typical comedy of disguise and deception, multiple sets of lovers in multiple assignations, with the braggart soldier, the unapproachable lady, the bawdy maid (Temperance), the gull (Innocentio), and the witty intriguer (Lodovico). Chapman is consciously following the current hits of the day, providing not only a good deal of music and dance (even a masque) in the concluding act, but a large number of direct echoes from his contemporary playwrights.

Chapman entered *The Iliads of Homer* in the Stationers' Register in April 1611. Dedicated again to Prince Henry, this edition comprises all twenty-four books of the epic, including entirely new versions of books 1 and 2, some minor revisions of 3 to 12 (from the earlier editions), plus the new books, 13 to 24. Chapman added yet another "Preface to the Reader" (in prose) and a brief essay, "Of Homer." The latter is the typical and epideictic minibiography of most late-medieval or Renaissance translations. The preface is of a piece with his earlier preface of 1609: another defense of his paraphrases and/or circumlocutions on historical and critical grounds, a response to the charge that he translated Homer out of Latin solely and not his Greek, and a promise to go on to a translation of the *Odyssey*. For the first time the text appears with a full, critical apparatus: marginal glosses and comments throughout and ten commentaries ("Commentarius"). The commentaries are justifications of various renderings of the Greek and quibbles with earlier translators. The volume concludes with a brief prose comment and a prayer. This comment is notable for the astonishing claim that Chapman rendered the last twelve books of the *Iliad* in "lesse than fifteene weekes."

The volume appeared with an exceptionally handsome engraved title page and all the critical apparatus worthy of so great a poet and so beneficent a patron. Any of Chapman's expectations, however, were soon dashed at the death of Henry, Prince of Wales, in 1612 at the age of eighteen. Though Chapman was to dun the court with letters pleading for the rewards Henry had promised, nothing was forthcoming. Even the production of *The Memorable Masque* for the nuptials of Princess Elizabeth and Frederick V, Elector Pal-

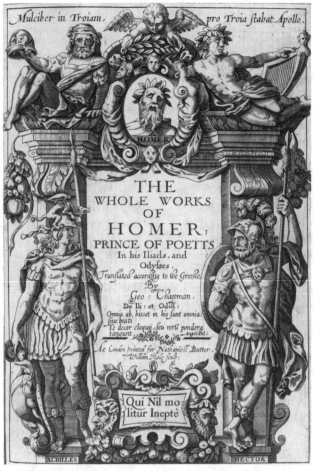

Title page, engraved by William Hole, for the first complete edition of Chapman's translations of Homer's epics
(Henry E. Huntington Library and Art Gallery)

atine, in 1613 would not avail. The masque was commissioned by the Middle Temple and Lincoln's Inn and performed before King James in February. It was designed by Inigo Jones and written by Chapman. The published version (also 1613) includes a prose account of the great procession to Whitehall, a description of the set, and some stage directions as well as the "argument" or plot of the piece: Honour, presented like a goddess, meets Plutus (Riches) who is reformed by his love of Honour. Capriccio, a man of wit, has a dialogue with Plutus before he presents his (rather clumsy) antemasque. The celebration follows with songs and dances, and the volume concludes with a hymn to Hymen and an epithalamion. It has been speculated that Chapman had a hand in several masques, especially late in his career. This speculation is based largely, perhaps, on the strength of Ben Jonson's testimony that besides himself, only Chapman "could make a masque." But *The Memorable Masque* is the only specimen we have.

Chapman's direct response to Prince Henry's death was his *Epicede or Funerall Song* in late 1612. The lament on Henry was vastly expanded when Chapman added to it, at line 354, an adaptation/translation of Angelo Poliziano's *Elegia sive Epicedion* (1546). Chapman's poem appears to have been the first in a steady stream of elegies by, among others, John Webster, Cyril Tourneur, John Donne, George Herbert, and John Heywood. The volume concludes with an extended description of the funeral itself. The loss of his patron did not deter Chapman from his project of publishing all of Homer in English. It did, however, send him in search of other patrons, where he discovered yet more misfortunes.

One of these attempts, perhaps, was Chapman's elegy on the death of William, Lord Russell, in 1613, *Eugenia: Or True Nobilities Trance* (1614). The poem is at once an elegy, a satiric complaint about the world, and a heroic poem. The sister of Fame, Eugenia, falls into a trance upon Russell's death, is revived by news of Russell's son and heir, and thence begins the four "vigils" or speeches. Another was undoubtedly *The Whole Works of Homer* (1616?), with the previously published *Iliads* (its unsold sheets included here) and the new translation of the twenty-four books of *The Odyssey* in decasyllabic couplets. In some copies there is a separate title page to *The Odyssey*, suggesting that part of the volume was published separately for special patrons or friends. It is certain, however, that books 13 to 24 are from the press of a different, and distinctly inferior, printer. It was entered in the Stationers' Register on 2 November 1614 and probably appeared sometime between 1614 and 1616. The Register also lists Chapman's *Odyssey* on that date, and it is likely that the first twelve books were printed as a New Year's gift for Robert Carr, Earl of Somerset, to whom the whole volume is dedicated. This epistle to Somerset, newly appointed lord chamberlain, includes perhaps Chapman's clearest statement on how he understood the two epics in distinctly moral terms:

> And that your Lordship may in his Face take view of his Mind, the first word of his *Iliads* is *menin*, wrath; the first word of his *Odysses*, *andra, Man*—contracting in either word his each worke's Proposition. In one, Predominant Perturbation; in the other, over-ruling Wisedome; in one, the Bodie's fervour and fashion of outward Fortitude to all possible height of Heroicall Action; in the other, the Mind's inward, constant and unconquerd Empire, unbroken, unalterd with any most insolent and tyrannous infliction.

The epistle is also notable for its explicit defense of poetry, where Chapman takes poetry as the soul of truth inhabiting a body of fiction. As such, poetry teaches not only the most profound and useful matters but always extols virtue and condemns vice. Some of these views appear again in the marginalia to the volume (though the commentaries disappear), where *apologiae* for certain renderings, often with abundant philological rationales, are mixed with moral readings of the passage in question. These glosses become very sparse in the final twelve books of *The Odyssey*.

Chapman's choice of ten-syllable couplets for his translation forces a far more involved syntax than did the fourteeners he championed as appropriate for the Homer of his *Iliads*. This form and the haphazard printing of books 13 to 24 often make for some difficult reading. Yet even

these defects and his sometimes radical departure from Homer's Greek (as well as from his favorite Latin text and commentary of Jean de Sponde [Spondanus]) do not finally destroy either the vigor or the originality of his work.

There can be little doubt that Chapman rushed to complete the volume and made special efforts to present it to Somerset. Chapman, unfortunately, could scarcely have made a worse choice to replace Henry as the recipient of his Homer. The unfortunate relationship between Somerset and Chapman began somewhat earlier in 1614 when Chapman, on 16 March, registered and then published his *Andromeda Liberata or the Nuptials of Perseus and Andromeda*. The poem is dedicated to Somerset and Lady Frances Howard and was intended to celebrate their marriage. Despite the fact that Chapman borrows liberally from Comes's *Mythologia*, from Marsilio Ficino, and from Plutarch for the poem, it is clear that the public took the poem as a very personal, contemporary allegory. In the poem Cepheus, profoundly disturbed by the appearance of a monstrous whale sent by Neptune to ravage his kingdom, consults an oracle. He discovers the curse can be removed if he exposes his daughter Andromeda to the monster. Cepheus complies and chains Andromeda to a rock. Perseus discovers her, falls in love, kills the monster, and marries her. Though Chapman is clear about some of the allegorical and mythological equivalents in the tale, many apparently saw a clear allusion to the sensational divorce proceedings brought by Lady Frances against her former husband, Robert Devereux, third Earl of Essex. Lady Frances, who testified that she was in fact a virgin and that the earl was impotent, won an annulment of the marriage in 1613. Three months later, Lady Frances married Somerset. The allegorical equivalents seemed plain: Somerset as Perseus had freed Frances as Andromeda from the rock Essex. Chapman immediately responded to the furor over his poem with *A Free and Offenseless Justification of Andromeda Liberata* (1614), a fascinating essay on the nature of allegory, which, of course, denied the public construction that brought so much notoriety to the poem. It is of some note to Chapman that matters for Somerset and Lady Frances only got worse. In 1615 it was discovered, and later proved in an extraordinary trial in 1616, that Lady Frances had arranged the murder of the go-between in her affair with Somerset, Thomas Overbury, the noted character writer. Though Frances confessed and Somerset maintained his innocence, both were convicted and sent to the Tower until 1622. Chapman remained faithful to Somerset, however, dedicating to him both his *Pro Vere* in 1622 and his concluding volume of Homer, *The Crown of All Homer's Works* around 1624. Between the Overbury affair and that last volume of Homer, Chapman published his translation of Hesiod's *Works and Days. The Georgicks of Hesiod* (1618) is replete with glosses, commendatory verses by Michael Drayton and Ben Jonson, and a dedication to Sir Francis Bacon. Chapman's text here is Philipp Melanchthon's Greek text of Hesiod (1532) as well as a Latin rendering by Spondanus (1606). Chapman returns to the ten-syllable couplets he used in his *Odyssey*.

The *Crown of All Homer's Works* effectively concludes Chapman's life as a public poet, and one may sense something profoundly elegiac in it. The volume includes the mock epic *Batrachomyomachia* (the battle of the frogs and mice), thirty-two Homeric hymns, sixteen miscellaneous poems, and, finally, Chapman's own apologia for the whole project with its justly famous first line, "The Worke that I was borne to doe is done."

Despite the fact that scholars sense some diminution of Chapman's powers in this his last volume of poetry, the translation of *Batrachomyomachia* is very deft and, if one may say, very English. The welter of Greek names for the frogs and mice are given in highly comic and contemporary renderings (as "Bacon-flitch gnawer"), and on almost every occasion Chapman finds English equivalents for the abundant Greek nouns. This is not the case in the *Hymns*, where decorum would demand a more reticent approach to Englishing. Throughout the volume there is a grace and clarity in his rhymed couplets in spite of the fact that he occasionally bungles the Greek.

Even a cursory survey of Chapman's poetry reveals his consistent preference for heroic verse both in his own English poems and in his translations (even in his sources, borrowings, and tragedies, it should be added). Even though some have seen in this a self-identification of a heroic Chapman with his poetic forebears in heroic poetry (indeed, the handsome title page of the *Batrachomyomachia* shows Chapman beneath a look-alike Homer), the better explanation might aim at two other causes: the search for patronage, and the humanist dogma that takes heroic poetry as the crown of a serious poetic vocation. Indeed, Chapman remained sensitive about this all his pro-

fessional life, especially since his heroic poetry required a thorough knowledge of Greek. His final apologia appears at the end of the volume in the elegant eighty-seven-line poem defending his ability against the scholars of the schools:

> And what's all their skill but vast varied reading?
> As if brode-beaten High-waies had the leading
> To Truths abstract, and narrow Path and Pit,
> Found in no walke of any worldly wit.
> And without Truth, all's only sleight of hand,
> Or our Law-learning in a Forraine land,
> Embroderie spent on Cobwebs, Braggart show,
> Of men that all things learn and nothing know.

There were two plays that remained to be published, though both were undoubtedly written and produced earlier, *Caesar and Pompey* of 1631 and *The Tragedy of Chabot* in 1639. For the former, the source of historical information is Plutarch's *Lives* (Shakespeare's favorite) and, occasionally, some of his *Moralia*. The hero was the perennial favorite, Cato, the heroic voice for proper and rational choice, and the action centers on the contest of Julius Caesar and Pompey for power. The real interest of the play occurs after the battle of Pharsalia, when Cato declares his preference for justice and a free death rather than tyranny and servitude. He stabs himself and, in a typically Jacobean turn, plucks out his entrails before anyone can save him. Caesar enters, condemns Pompey's murderers, and in a final paean to Cato's just life, orders a magnificent tomb to be erected.

The Tragedy of Chabot, written in collaboration with James Shirley, was licensed in 1635 (the year after Chapman's death) for production at the Phoenix Theatre in Drury Lane. Most would place its composition sometime between 1611 and 1625. Chabot, an absolutely just and loyal servant of Francis I, is accused of defrauding the treasury. His proud and uncompromising protestations of loyalty infuriate the king, who orders that Chabot be tried by Chancellor Poyet. The trial is outrageously manipulated, the charges fabricated, the conviction coerced, and the minor sentence altered. With the intercession of the queen, Francis calls Chabot to him and offers him a pardon. In an astonishing scene, Chabot heroically refuses and submits that he cannot accept a pardon for something he has not done. The king, repenting his test of his absolute authority on a subject whose true conscience is his own authority, convenes a second trial, in which the treachery of the first is revealed and Poyet dismissed. Chabot,

Title page, engraved by W. Pass, for the last of Chapman's Greek translations, depicting Chapman at the bottom of the page

cleared but stricken to the heart with the injustice of it all, dies.

There are in fact few of Chapman's plays that, according to evidence, were *not* popular. It was not uncommon for later publishers to attach Chapman's name to plays he never wrote, hoping to benefit from his fame. This accounts, in some cases, to several plays ascribed to Chapman that are not his: *Charlemagne or the Distracted Emperor, The Ball, The Tragedy of Alphonsus Emperor of Germany, The Revenge for Honour, Two Italian Gentlemen,* and *The Disguises.*

Chapman is likely to have written plays or collaborated in others we no longer have. Sometime after 1623 he may have been responsible, along with Richard Brome, for the now-lost *Christianetta.* Henslowe's diary has indications that Chapman's hand was involved in several plays now unknown: "The ylle of A Woman," "the

ffount of new facianes," "the world Rones A Whelles" or "all fooles but the foolle" (perhaps *All Fools*), and a "pastrall tragedie."

George Chapman died in May of 1634. Of the last twenty years of his life we know next to nothing. There have been suggestions of contributions to other masques or plays, but we have no evidence of them. We do know, however, that Inigo Jones (the most famous architect and stage designer of his time) designed a Roman monument for Chapman which was to bear the inscription, "Georgis Chapmanus, poeta Homericus, Philosophers verus, (etsi Christianus poeta)." He is buried in the churchyard of St. Giles in the Fields.

It is a matter of some note, in assessing Chapman's achievement, that nearly all modern commentators on his work have been essentially hostile to it: condemning him for his borrowings, for the supposed heterodox ethical or religious views in his fictions, and generally denouncing him for either conscious obscurity or simply bungling sense across the canon of his works. In almost all of these views, the works of Shakespeare and his other contemporaries are always the standard for comparison. The fact of Chapman's evident success argues quite a different story. He was recognized among his contemporaries as one of the best dramatists of the age, as an accomplished poet of striking powers in both popular and elite modes, and as a rare and accomplished scholar. The reputation of his Homer has survived any number of rivals (Alexander Pope not the least among them) even into our own century. Even though he was not successful in becoming financially comfortable, in choosing patrons, or even in marriage (his negotiations with a well-to-do widow came to naught), his work stands as equal to any number of his better-known contemporaries.

Bibliography:

Samuel A. Tannenbaum, *George Chapman, A Concise Bibliography* (New York: Samuel Tannenbaum, 1938).

Biography:

Jean Jacquot, *George Chapman, 1559-1634, sa vie sa poésie, son théâtre, sa pensée* (Paris: Les Belles Lettres, 1951).

References:

Hardin Craig, ed., *The Parrott Presentation Volume* (Princeton, N.J.: Princeton University Press, 1935);

Elizabeth Story Donno, Introduction to *Elizabethan Minor Epics*, edited by Donno (New York: Columbia University Press, 1963), pp. 1-20;

T. S. Eliot, *Selected Essays* (London: Faber & Faber, 1953);

Darryl J. Gless, "Chapman's Ironic Ovid," *English Literary Renaissance*, 9 (Winter 1979): 21-41;

D. J. Gordon, "The Renaissance Poet as Classicist: Chapman's *Hero and Leander*," in *The Renaissance Imagination*, edited by Stephen

Orgel (Berkeley: University of California Press, 1975), pp. 102-133;

John Huntington, "Condemnation and Pity in Chapman's *Hero and Leander*," *English Literary Renaissance*, 7 (Autumn 1977): 307-323;

Huntington, "Philosophical Seduction in Chapman, Davies, and Donne," *ELH*, 44 (Spring 1977): 40-59;

Huntington, "The Serious Trifle: Aphorisms in Chapman's *Hero and Leander*," *Studies in the Literary Imagination*, 11 (Spring 1978): 107-113;

William Keach, *Elizabethan Erotic Narratives* (New Brunswick, N.J.: Rutgers University Press, 1977);

Frank Kermode, "The Banquet of Sense," in *Shakespeare, Spenser, Donne* (London: Routledge & Kegan Paul, 1971), pp. 84-115;

C. S. Lewis, "Hero and Leander," in *Elizabethan Poetry*, edited by Paul J. Alpers (New York: Oxford University Press, 1967), pp. 235-250;

George de Forest Lord, *Homeric Renaissance: The Odyssey of George Chapman* (New Haven: Yale University Press, 1956);

Millar MacLure, *George Chapman: A Critical Study* (Toronto: University of Toronto Press, 1966);

Ennis Rees, *The Tragedies of George Chapman* (Cambridge, Mass.: Harvard University Press, 1954);

Franck Schoell, *Etudes Sur L'Humanisme Continental en Angleterre à la Fin de la Renaissance* (Paris: Champion, 1926);

James Smith, "George Chapman," *Scrutiny*, 3 (March 1935): 339-350; 4 (June 1935): 45-61;

Gerald Snare, *The Mystification of George Chapman* (Durham: Duke University Press, 1989);

Charlotte Spivack, *George Chapman* (New York: Twayne, 1967);

Algernon Charles Swinburne, *George Chapman, A Critical Essay* (London: Chatto & Windus, 1875);

Raymond B. Waddington, *The Mind's Empire: Myth and Narrative Form in George Chapman's Narrative Poems* (Baltimore: Johns Hopkins University Press, 1974).

Richard Corbett
(1582 - 28 July 1635)

Mary Arshagouni Papazian
Oakland University

BOOKS: *Certain Elegant Poems, written by Dr. Corbet, Bishop of Norwich* (London: Printed by R. Cotes for Andrew Crooke, 1647);

Poëtica Stromata or a Collection of Sundry Pieces in Poetry: Drawne by the known and approued Hand of R.C. (Holland?: 1648);

Poems written by the Right Reverend Dr. Richard Corbet Late Lord Bishop of Norwich, third editon, corrected and enlarged (London: Printed by J. C. for William Crook, 1672);

The Poems of Richard Corbett, Late Bishop of Oxford and of Norwich. The 4th edition, with considerable additions. To which are now added, "Oratio in funus Henrici principis," edited by Octavius Gilchrist (London: Longman, Hurst, Rees & Orme, 1807);

The Poems of Richard Corbett, edited by J. A. W. Bennett and H. R. Trevor-Roper (Oxford: Clarendon Press, 1955).

OTHER: "A Poeme Upon Tom Coriatts Crudities," in *Coryats Crudities. Hastily gobled vp in five Moneths travells in France, Savoy, Italy . . .*, by Thomas Coryat (London: Printed by W. Stansby for the author, 1611);

Justa Oxoniensium, includes an elegy on the death of Prince Henry by Corbett (London: Impensis Iohannis Bill, 1612);

Justa Funebria Ptolemæi Oxoniensis Thomæ Bodleii Equitis Avrati Celebrata in Academia Oxoniensi Mensis Martij 29. 1613, includes verse by Corbett (Oxford: Printed by Josephus Barnesius, 1613);

Sir Thomas Overbury, *Sir Thomas Ouerbury His Wife. With Addition of many new elegies vpon his vntimely and much lamented death*, includes two poems by Corbett (London: Printed by Edward Griffin for Lawrence Lisle, 1616);

Jacobi Ara ceu in Jacobi . . . Auspicatissimum Reditum in Angliam Academiae Oxoniensis Gratulatoria, includes verse by Corbett (Oxford: J. Lichfield & G. Wrench, 1617);

Academiae Oxoniensis Funebria Sacra memoriae reginae Annae dicata, includes verse by Corbett (Oxford: Johannes Lichfield & Jacobus Short, 1619);

Oxoniensis Academiae Parentalia. Sacratissimae memoriae Jacobi, regis, dicata, includes verse by Corbett (Oxford: J. Lichfield & G. Turner, 1625);

John Donne, *Poems by J.D.: With Elegies on the Authors Death*, includes verse by Corbett (London: Printed by M. F. for John Marriot, 1633);

Poems. By Francis Beaumont, Gent. Viz. The Hermaphrodite. The Remedie of Love. Elegies. Sonnets, with other poems, includes verse by Corbett (London: Printed by Richard Hodgkinson for W. W. & Laurence Blaikelocke, 1640);

George Herbert, ed., *Witts Recreations. Selected from the finest Fancies of Moderne Muses. With a thousand outlandish Proverbs*, includes verse by Corbett (London: Printed by R. Hodgkinson for Humphry Blumden, 1640);

Wit Restor'd in several Select Poems not formerly publish't, includes verse by Corbett (London: Printed for R. Pollard, N. Brooks, & T. Dring, 1658);

"Charge of Bishop Corbet Delivered at Norwich, April 29, 1634," in *Documents Relating to the History of St. Paul's Cathedral* (London: Camden Society, 1880), pp. 134-139.

Richard Corbett, Anglican bishop of Oxford and Norwich, was one of the most fashionable of the minor poets in the reigns of James I and Charles I. A friend of Ben Jonson, acquainted with John Donne; George Villiers, first Duke of Buckingham; and Archbishop William Laud, he was associated with Oxford University for more than thirty years, during which time he gained recognition for the many commendatory and memorial verses he wrote on the deaths of prominent contemporaries. He was also a well-known wit, satirist, bon vivant, and anti-Puritan, who was often criticized for his disposition to flatter the powerful and prominent but also admired for his good nature and conviviality. In his *History of the*

Richard Corbett; portrait by an unknown artist, painted after Corbett became Bishop of Norwich in 1632 (Christ Church, Oxford)

Worthies of England (1662) Thomas Fuller describes Corbett as "a high wit and most excellent poet; of a courteous carriage, and no destructive nature to any who offended him, counting himself plentifully repaid with a jest upon him." Despite Corbett's immense popularity as a poet in his own day, he has attracted very little modern critical attention.

Born in 1582 in Ewall, Surrey, Richard Corbett was the son of Vincent Corbett, also known as Vincent Poynter, a well-known gardener and horticulturist at Twickenham, upon whose death Ben Jonson wrote an epitaph (which is included in his *Underwoods*, 1640). Richard Corbett, Jonson, and Sir Hugh Platt (in his *Flora's Paradise*, 1608) make frequent mention of both Vincent Corbett's simple character and his skills in the gardens and orchards. Little is known about the poet's mother, Benet Corbett, who was eulogized for her simplicity and humility in an epitaph by

William Strode. The family may have been connected to the more important Moreton Corbett family in Shropshire, the arms with which Richard Corbett sealed his letters and ornamented his tomb.

Corbett obtained his early education at Westminster School, where, according to John Aubrey, he was described by a school friend as "a very handsome man, but something apt to abuse, and a coward." Corbett proceeded to Oxford University, first to Broadgates Hall (which later became Pembroke College) during the Lenten term, 1597-1598, and then to Christ Church the following year. He received his B.A. on 20 June 1602 and his M.A. on 9 June 1605, at which time, according to Anthony Wood, he was "esteemed one of the most celebrated wits in the university, as his poems, jests, romantic fancies and exploits, which he made and perform'd extempore, shew'd." Aubrey reports that as a student

Corbett "was very facetious, and a good fellowe," and tells of his love for drink and merriment: "One time he and some of his acquaintance being merry at Fryar Bacon's study (where was good liquor sold), they were drinking on the leads of the house, and one of the scholars was asleepe, and had a paire of good silke stockings on. Dr. Corbett (then M.A., if not B.D.) gott a paire of cizers and cutt them full of little holes, but when the other awaked, and percieved how and by whom he was abused, he did chastise him, and made him pay for them." Corbett remained associated with Christ Church in a variety of positions for the next thirty years.

Corbett's first poems of substance were written in 1609. His elegy on the death of Dr. Ravis, bishop of London, dean of Christ Church, Oxford, was composed when Corbett first entered the university. This poem was the first of his many commemorations on public figures, perhaps the basis for his later clerical advancement. Corbett celebrates Ravis's virtue as he laments beholding "the Body of my Lord, / Trodd under foote by vice that he abhorr'd" and hopes that "swift flightes of vertue haue apt ends." According to J. A. W. Bennett and H. R. Trevor-Roper, Corbett's modern editors, his writing continued with "a series of academic satires, congratulatory epistles, epigrams, pasquinades, and tavernpieces, always with a vein of humour in them and only once notoriously malicious," referring to his verses "Upon An Unhandsome Gentlewoman, who made Love unto him." This last poem is reminiscent of the witty, dramatic, and satiric qualities of the love elegies of his contemporary John Donne. In it the speaker refers to the unfortunate "unhandsome gentlewoman" as "that thing" and proclaims that "never sinne was of so high a rate, / But one nights hell with her might expiate."

In 1612, when Corbett was junior proctor in the university and senior student of Christ Church, he delivered funeral orations in Latin for both Prince Henry and Sir Thomas Bodley. In regard to Prince Henry, Corbett wrote the "In Quendam Anniversariorum Scriptorem," a poem which bears the mark of his customary wit and wordplay: "Thou leaue him captive; since / Soe vile a Price ne'er ransom'd such a Prince." In this poem Corbett satirizes Dr. Daniel Price for his stream of poems on the anniversary of Prince Henry's death and cries out for a cessation of Price's profaning verses: "Was't not enough *Nature* and *strength* were foes, / But thou must yearly *murther* him in Prose?" Corbett also joined with other Oxford colleagues to write and publish additional occasional verses and orations in both Latin and English which appeared in collections of funeral verses from 1612, on the death of Prince Henry, to 1625, on the death of King James I. Some of the elegies that Corbett wrote during these years, often with an eye toward obtaining patronage or professional preferment, include: "An Elegie vpon the Death of Sir Thomas Ouerbury Knight poysoned in the Tower" (written in 1613), "On the Lady Arabella" (written in 1615), "An Elegie on the late Lord William Haward Baron of Effingham, dead the tenth of December. 1615," "On Francis Beaumonts death" (written in 1616), "An Elegie upon the death of the Lady Haddington who dyed of the small Pox" (written in 1618), "An Elegy upon the death of Queene Anne" (written in 1619), and "An Elegie upon the death of his owne Father" (written in 1619).

Corbett was ordained deacon and priest on 26 March 1613 and received his doctor of divinity degree on 8 May 1617. According to Wood, "he became a most quaint preacher and therefore much followed by ingenious men." Nevertheless, Corbett's taste in jests and practical jokes, which earned him a reputation while a student, never left him, even after he became a doctor of divinity. According to Bennett and Trevor-Roper, Corbett was known as a fine amateur ballad singer who "distinguished himself by putting on the leather jacket of a professional balladist who had excited scant attention and drawing crowds to hear him singing ballads outside a tavern in Abingdon." Corbett's affinity for ballads and songs is found in the meters of his poetry. His best-known poem, "A Proper New Ballad intitled The Faeryes Farewell: or God-A-Mercy Will," the reader is instructed, should "be sung or whistled to the tune of *The Meddow Brow* by the learned; by the unlearned to the tune of Fortune"; and his poem "The Distracted Puritane" is called, in the earliest printed text, "An excellent new dittie to the tune of *Tom o'Bedlam*," which was popular during Corbett's Oxford days.

In preaching the Easter sermon at Christ Church in 1613, Corbett had aligned himself with the anti-Puritan Arminian party at Oxford, led by William Laud, later archbishop of Canterbury, and against the party of George Abbott, then archbishop of Canterbury. (In 1616 this association led to Corbett being recommended for election to King James's projected college of theological controversy at Chelsea.)

When the king visited Cambridge on 7 March 1615, Corbett was one of the few Oxford men to travel to Cambridge for the festivities. According to John Chamberlain, Corbett deported himself well during this visit. In Chamberlain's words, "I wold not have missed yt for that I see therby the partialitie of both sides, the Cambridge men pleasing and applauding themselves in all, and the Oxford men as fast condemning and detracting all that was don, wherin yet I commend Corbets modestie whiles he was there, who beeing seriously dealt withall by some frends to say what he thought, aunswered that he had left his malice and judgement at home, and came thether only to commend."

Corbett commemorated the king's visit with his playful and entertaining "A Certain Poem as it was presented in Latine by Divines and Others, before his Maiestye in Cambridge, by way of enterlude, stiled, Liber Novus de Adventu Regis ad Cantabrigiam, faithfully done into English, with Some liberall additions." In it Corbett betrays his love of ballads, songs, linguistic wit, and playful satire, particularly as he mocks the Puritan Emanuel College:

> But the pure house of *Emanuel*
> Would not be like proud *Jesabel*,
> Now shew her selfe before the King
> An Hypocrite, or *painted* thing.

Such anti-Puritan satire is a frequent theme in Corbett's poems. His playfulness can be seen in the irreverent yet humorous lines that satirize the shameful practice of dispensing degrees without merit: "Oft have I warn'd, (quoth he) our durt / That no silke stockins should be hurt; / . . . The King being gon from *Trinity*, / They made a scramble for Degree."

Around 1616 Corbett may have associated with the circle of scholars, lawyers, and poets (which included Ben Jonson) that gathered regularly at the Mermaid Tavern in London. Through this association, Corbett developed a coterie of important friends at court. These included Ben Jonson, Thomas Aylesbury, and Sir Francis Stuart, a relative of King James. The encounter in a tavern between Jonson and Corbett described in Nicholas Le Strange's *Merry Jests* may have been their first meeting: "Ben: Johnson was at a Taverne, and in comes Bishoppe Corbett (but not So then) into the next Room: Ben:

Johnson Calls for a quart of raw wine, gives it the Tapster, Sirrha says he, carry this to the Gentleman in the next chamber, and tell him I sacrifice my Service to him; the Fellow did so, and in those words; Friend, sayes Doctor Corbett, I thanke him for his love, but pr'ythee tell him from me hee's mistaken, for Sacrifices are allwayes Burnt." Jonson subsequently accepted the invitation of Corbett and other university wits to visit Oxford on his return from Scotland in 1619 and receive a degree.

Corbett wrote the first of many poetical flatteries in December 1615: an elegy on the death of Lord William Howard of Effingham, the son of Charles Howard, Earl of Nottingham, lord high admiral, who was connected to both Sir Francis Stuart and Sir Thomas Aylesbury. In the poem Corbett claims, somewhat unconvincingly, that "I did not know thee, Lord, nor do I striue / To winne accesse, or grace, with Lords aliue." He concludes, "Let others write for glory or reward, / Truth is well paid when she is sung and heard." But with the fall of the lord high admiral from power, Corbett shifted his attention to the new favorite, George Villiers, Earl, later Marquis, and, finally in 1623, Duke of Buckingham.

In 1618 Corbett took a tour of France, which he described humorously in "A letter sent from Doctor Corbet to Master Aile[s]bury, Decem.9.1618." In 1620 he was appointed prebendary of Bedminster Secunda Church, in Sarum, near Salisbury (which he resigned on 10 June 1631), as well as vicar of Cassington near Oxford, and vicar of Stewkley, Berkshire (which he held until his death). On 24 June 1620 he was made dean of Christ Church, after the death of Dr. William Goodwyn. Shortly thereafter, John Donne was made dean of St. Paul's Cathedral, a promotion that caused John Chamberlain to suggest in a letter to Sir Dudley Carleton the next year that "we are like to have our new Deane Dr. Dun at Paules, so as a pleasant companion saide that yf Ben Johnson might be made deane of Westminster, that place, Paules, and Christchurch, shold be furnished with three very pleasant poeticall deanes."

Corbett's reputation as a poet at the time of his installation as dean of Christ Church was partly due to his longest poem (508 lines). *Iter Boreale* (1647) celebrates Corbett's journey through the Midlands north of Oxford with Leonard Hutten, canon of Christ Church (whose daughter, Alice, he would later marry), and two other clergymen. The description of the journey and the many stops of the four clergymen is interspersed with satire, humor, and reflection on subjects ranging from Puritans and Papists to criticism of usurping kings, expressions of true hospitality, and commentary on contemporary theater. For example, as his party approached the town of Lutterworth, Corbett recorded his thoughts on the suffering caused by the zeal of both Puritans and Papists:

> Our next dayes stage was *Lutterworth*, a towne
> Not willing to be noted or sett downe
> By any Traveller; for, when w'had bin
> Through at both ends, wee could not finde an
>   Inne:
> Yet for the Church sake turne and light wee must,
> Hoping to see one dramme of *Wickliff's* dust;
> But wee found none: for underneath the pole
> Noe more rests of his body, then his soule.
> Abused Martyr! how hast thou bin torne
> By two wilde factions! first the *Papists* burne
> Thy bones for hate; the *Puritans* in zeale
> They sell thy marble and thy brasse they steale.

And, as they approached the town of Leicester, Corbett could not help but reflect on usurping kings and the source of kingly power:

> Is not th' usurping *Richard* buryed there,
> That *King* of hate, and therefore *Slave* of feare;
> Dragg'd from the fatall feild *Bosworth*, where hee
> Lost life, and, what he liv'd for; Cruelty?
> Search, find his name? but there is none: Oh Kings!
> Remember whence your power and vastnesse
>   springs;
> If not as *Richard* now, so shall you bee;
> Who hath no Tombe, but Scorne and memorye.

Iter Boreale was extremely popular in Corbett's day and may well have suggested Richard Brathwaite's "Drunken Barnabees Journal" and many others.

Early in his tenure as dean of Christ Church, Corbett became known for one rather unfortunate incident. In August 1621 Corbett as the recently appointed royal chaplain was selected to preach before King James, who was making a visit to Oxford and keeping court at Woodstock. As Bennett and Trevor-Roper explain, "the sermon proved a fiasco: for owing to his preoccupation with a ring which the king had evidently given him, and which he had tied to the strings of his band, the preacher lost the thread of his sermon and had to give up, thus becoming a standing joke in the university." This fiasco was immortalized in a poem, "On Oxford Schollers going to Woodstock to heare Dr. Corbet preach before the King," by an anonymous university wag,

that circulated in manuscript and was later published in *Wit Restor'd* in 1658.

Rather than be undone by this unfortunate incident, Corbett turned his attention back to the king's favorite, Buckingham, to whom he continued to write verses and epistles. For New Year's Day, 1621, he wrote "A New-Yeares Gift to my Lorde Duke of Buckingham," in which he flattered and praised Buckingham, who at that time was only a marquis, by calling him both a parent and a king:

> When I can pay my Parents, or my King,
> For life, or peace, or any dearer thing:
> Then, *Dearest Lord*, expect my debt to you
> Shall bee as truly paid, as it is due.

He offered Buckingham "Vertue and my love" and contrasted himself to those "that buy preferment without praying, / Begin with bribes, and finish with *betraying*." This was followed by "An answer to certaine propositions controverted atwixt us and the Papists," written around 1622 for Buckingham on points of religion. In 1623 Corbett wrote his ingratiating "Letter to the Duke of Buckingham, being with the Prince in Spaine." This "piece of servility" celebrating the controversial secret journey by Prince Charles and Buckingham to secure the unpopular, and ultimately unsuccessful, Spanish match was, according to Bennett and Trevor-Roper, "too much even for some of his former admirers, and in the Oxford taverns the Dean of Christ Church was roundly declared to have overreached himself, prostituting his reputation as the poet of the taphouse to his ambition as a courtier." Despite this criticism, Corbett was not deterred from seeking favor from Buckingham, and he continued to write him letters and verses.

Two of Corbett's longest and best-known poems are "A Proper New Ballad intituled The Faeryes Farewell" (probably written shortly after *Iter Boreale*) and "The Distracted Puritan" (written sometime between 1615 and 1626), both of which use the seemingly lighthearted qualities of the ballad songs to offer satire and criticism on contemporary Puritanism. In "The Faeryes Farewell" Corbett laments the passing of the fairies, whom he associates with Catholicism, and the onset of Puritanism. Yet his lament is also an implicit criticism of the fairies for having "lost command":

> Lament, lament, old Abbies,
>   The *Faries* lost Command:

> They did but change Priests *Babies*,
>   But some have changd your *Land*;
> And all your Children sprung from thence
>   Are now growne *Puritanes*:
> Who live as *Changelings* ever since
>   For love of your Demaines.

This witty lament on the passing of the old religion and its replacement by the new lapses in its conclusion into a comic compliment to William Chourne of Staffordshire, the servant of Corbett's friend Leonard Hutten, who had accompanied Corbett on his journey through the Midlands. Corbett's poem, "The Distracted Puritane," is reminiscent of the prose character sketches that were popular in his day in its presentation of a particular "type," as in the "Characters" of Sir Thomas Overbury (1614). Corbett's presentation of the speaker of the poem creates an attack on contemporary Puritanism that is similar to that found in "The Faeryes Farewell." The playfulness of Corbett's attack is evident in the speaker's opening comments on his seeming "madness":

> Am I madd, o noble Festus,
> When zeale and godly knowledge
> Have put mee in hope
> To deale with the Pope,
> As well as the best in the Colledge?
>   Boldly I preach, hate a Crosse, hate a Surplice,
>   Miters, Copes, and Rotchets:
>   Come heare mee pray nine times a day,
>   And fill your heads with Crotchets.

The mocking rhyme and meter and the use of a musical refrain in lines 6-9 add to the undermining satire of Puritanism that is the essence of this poem.

These poems are not only among Corbett's most popular, but they are also the only ones, particularly "The Faeryes Farewell," to have attracted significant modern critical commentary. For example, Cleanth Brooks turned to Corbett's "A Faeryes Farewell" in order to demonstrate the importance of using older historical and linguistic methodologies in New Criticism. In so doing, Brooks offers a new critical/historical reading of the poem in which he argues that Corbett's criticism of Puritanism is "more damning" than his criticism of Catholicism, for he claims that Corbett "identifies the rise of Protestantism, particularly in its Puritan manifestations, with commercialism and with a kind of materialism hostile to

all poetry, whether that of the older church or that of England's peasant folklore." M. E. Bradford later read the poem as "prescient" in its disparagement of Puritanism and as an example of Corbett's ability to "accomplish serious things in what, at first, appears to be a trifling fashion."

Around 1625 Corbett married Alice Hutten, the daughter of his friend and companion Leonard Hutten, who had traveled with him to the Midlands on the journey described in *Iter Boreale*. Jeramiel Terrent celebrated this union with a poem, "On Dr. Corbett's Marriage," which later appeared in *Wit Restor'd*. Alice and Richard Corbett had two children, a daughter, Alice, and a son, Vincent. It was for him that Corbett wrote one of his most affectionate poems, "To his sonne Vincent Corbett." Corbett speaks with that gentle, loving voice that one associates with Ben Jonson's well-known poem "On My First Son":

> What I shall leave thee none can tell,
> But all shall say I wish thee well:
> I wish thee (*Vin*), before all wealth,
> Both bodily and ghostly health.
> Nor too much wealth, nor wit, come to thee:
> Too much of either may undoe thee.
> I wish thee learning, not for show,
> But truly to instruct and know:
> Not such as Gentlemen require,
> To prate at Table, or at Fire.
> I wish thee all thy mothers graces,
> Thy fathers fortunes, and his places.
> I wish thee friends, and one at Court,
> Not to build up, but to support:
> To keepe thee, not in doing many
> Oppressions, but from suffering any.
> I wish thee peace in all thy wayes,
> Nor lazy nor contentious dayes;
> And when thy soule and body part,
> As innocent as now thou art.

Apparently, Corbett's son disappointed him later in his life. Aubrey recorded that the lad "went to schoole at Westminster with Ned Bagshawe—a very handsome youth, but he is run out of all and goes begging up and downe to gentlemen." Smallpox claimed Corbett's wife in April 1628, and she was buried at Westminster.

After his wife's death Corbett again approached Buckingham for favors. In his poem "Against the Opposing the Duke in Parliament, 1628" he stands fast by his patron, despite the growing controversy that surrounded Buckingham. In this poem Corbett supported William Laud and King Charles against opposing Puritans and parliamentarians by warning of the dangers of social anarchy, "When lower strive to gett the upper hand." While his verses stirred controversy, Corbett received his reward. On 30 July 1628, just a few months later, he was nominated to the bishopric of Oxford, though more for his connections than his qualifications. At the same time William Laud became bishop of London and assumed complete control of the English church. Despite Corbett's early support for Bishop Laud, Laud's enforcement of ecclesiastical discipline proved uncongenial to the convivial and fun-loving bishop of Oxford.

Little is known of Corbett's official activities while bishop of Oxford. According to Bennett and Trevor-Roper, "he carried out an episcopal visitation of the diocese in 1629; lost no time in recommending himself to Laud on Laud's election as Chancellor of the University; and generally distinguished himself by his advocacy of Laudian doctrines." In his sermons, letters, and religious addresses he took every opportunity to attack the Puritans, often with vulgar satire. Moreover, his literary output seems to have declined after his election to the bishopric in 1628. Indeed, his best-known poems after his promotion were elegies on the death of John Donne in 1631 and on the death of Gustavus Adolphus "on the field of Lützen" in 1632. In his "Epitaph on Doctor Donne, Deane of Pauls," written sometime between Donne's death on 31 March 1631 and Corbett's election as bishop of Norwich in April 1632, Corbett implicitly compares himself to Donne as he celebrates Donne's wit, learning, and many friends:

Hee that would write an Epitaph for thee,
And do it well, must first beginne to be
Such as thou wert; for, none can truly know
Thy worth, thy life, but he that hath liv'd so;
He must have wit to spare, and to hurle downe:
Enought, to keepe the gallants of the towne.
He must have learning plenty; both the Lawes,
Civill, and Common, to judge any cause;
Divinity great store, above the rest;
Not of the last Edition, but the best.
Hee must have language, travaile, all the Arts;
Judgement to use, or else he wants thy parts.
He must have friends the highest, able to do;
Such as *Mecænas*, and *Augustus* too.
He must have such a sicknesse, such a death;
Or else his vaine descriptions come beneath;
Who then shall write an Epitaph for thee,
He must be dead first, let' it alone for mee.

Corbett's "Small Remembrance of the great King of Sweden" is a brief poem of fourteen lines in which Corbett celebrates the strength and power of "the great Gustavus," describes England's disbelief at his sudden death, and asserts that Gustavus Adolphus lives on in his martial deeds like Gideon and Joshua: "Who can say Gideon yet, or Josua's dead, / Whilst their eternall deeds of armes are read?"

Despite the paucity of his poetic output during his years as bishop of Oxford, Corbett remained interested in poetry and versifying and continued to have a reputation as a poet. His two chaplains were William Strode, the university poet, and Thomas Lushington of Pembroke College. Both men went with him to Norwich in 1632 when he became bishop there. According to Aubrey, Corbett and Lushington were very close and "loved one another. The bishop sometimes would take the key of the wine-cellar, and he and his chaplaine would goe and lock themselves in and be merry." Corbett's reputed last words upon his death in 1635 were "Good night, Lushington."

When Corbett became bishop of Norwich, Laud granted the vacated diocese of Oxford tò the king's candidate, John Bancroft. Although Corbett was supposed to counter the Puritans at Norwich, in Puritan East Anglia, he merely satirized their excesses. Away from Oxford and from Laud, Corbett could afford to be tolerant.

Nevertheless, Corbett did attempt to carry out two of Laud's policies, the first to reduce the independent Walloon and Dutch congregations in the diocese and the second to aid in rebuilding St. Paul's Cathedral. Corbett advanced the campaign against foreign congregations in his diocese by sending a letter dated 26 December 1634 to the minister and elders of the Walloon congregation at Norwich. In the letter Corbett demanded that the congregation vacate the church it had been allowed to use since 1619. He also became very involved in fundraising for the rebuilding of St. Paul's Cathedral. According to the *Dictionary of National Biography*, he "preached before Charles I at Newmarket on 9 March 1634 and contributed 400*l*. to the rebuilding of St. Paul's in 1634." The effort to rebuild St. Paul's is also the subject of his speech delivered in Norwich Cathedral on 29 April 1634. In this "Charge," addressed to his "worthy Frinds and Brethren of the Cleargy" [*sic*], Corbett asserts with a seriousness of tone that seems at odds with much of his lighthearted verse and his convivial personality that because St. Paul's "hath spoken maney a one in our [behalf]; hee hath raysed our inward Temples, let us help requit him in his outward." He pronounces all in his audience "Debtors" to this church in desperate need of repair and exclaims that "if to Repaire Churchs bee to innovate, I am of that Religion."

While bishop of Norwich and thus separated from Oxford, Corbett wrote little poetry, perhaps only the epitaph on his mother, who died on 2 October 1634. In his "Certain tru[e] Woords spoken concerning one Benet Corbett after her death," Corbett praises his mother's simple virtue in the gentle tone of his earlier poem on the birth of his son. He begins, "Here, or not many feet from hence / The virtue lies call'd Patience," and ends with the simple thought that "She had one husband and one sonne; / Ask who they were, and thou hast done."

Corbett soon followed his mother to the grave. He died on 28 July 1635 and was buried in the choir of the cathedral church of Norwich. Twelve years later his poems were first collected and published, under the title *Certain Elegant Poems, written by Dr. Corbet, Bishop of Norwich* (1647). This collection was probably edited by John Donne, Jr., the son of the poet.

In addition to the poems that have with some certainty been attributed to Corbett by John Donne, Jr., and subsequent editors and scholars, many others have been attributed incorrectly to him over the years. One of these is *The Times' Whistle: or, A Newe Daunce of Seven Satires, and other Poems: Compiled by R. C., Gent*, a manuscript volume dated about 1600 in the library of Canterbury Cathedral. According to Sir Sidney Lee in the *Dictionary of National Biography*, it was "printed for the first time by J. M. Cowper for the Early English Text Society in 1871. Mr. Cowper suggested that the author—'R. C., Gent.'—was the bishop." There is no mention of *The Times' Whistle* in either Wood or Aubrey, and Bennett and Trevor-Roper similarly question its authenticity as part of the Corbett canon. In Lee's words, "Internal evidence gives some support to the theory, but the description of the author and the date of the collection destroy it."

Corbett enjoyed great popularity in his day as a wit, satirist, clergyman, anti-Puritan, and bon vivant—he was, after all, linked by Chamberlain to both Donne and Jonson. Today Corbett is known as a clergyman who, as a minor poet of some distinction and wit, wrote occasional verse, generally with an eye toward his own personal advancement, and who was better known for his easygoing life-style and convivial personality than for his verse. The editors of the *Times Literary Supplement* conclude a tribute to Corbett with, "Poets of greater poetic ease, longer sustentation, and more show of professionalism, belong to histories of literature, but not, like Corbett in his small way, to the facts, the indestructible material, of poetic living."

Biography:

J. E. V. Crofts, "A Life of Bishop Corbett, 1582-1635," in *Essays and Studies by Members of the English Association*, volume 10 (Oxford: Clarendon Press, 1924), pp. 61-96.

References:

J. A. W. Bennett and H. R. Trevor-Roper, Introduction to *The Poems of Richard Corbett* (Oxford: Clarendon Press, 1955), pp. xi-lxv;

M. E. Bradford, "The Prescience of Richard Corbett: Observations on 'The Fairies' Farewell,'" *Sewanee Review*, 81 (Spring 1973): 309-317;

Cleanth Brooks, "The New Criticism and Scholarship," in *Twentieth Century English*, edited by William S. Knickerbocker (New York: Philosophical Library, 1946), pp. 371-383;

Charles Carlton, *Archbishop William Laud* (London & New York: Routledge & Kegan Paul, 1987);

J. M. Cowper, ed., *The Times' Whistle: or, A Newe Daunce of Seven Satires, and other Poems: Compiled by R.C., Gent* (London: Published for the Early English Text Society by N. Trübner, 1871);

"Here's to Thee, Corbett," *Times Literary Supplement*, 8 July 1955, pp. 1-2;

H. F. Lippincott, ed., *"Merry Passages and Jeasts": A Manuscript Jestbook of Sir Nicholas Le Strange (1603-1655)* (Salzburg: Institut für Englische Sprache, 1974);

Norman Egbert McClure, ed., *The Letters of John Chamberlain*, 2 volumes (Philadelphia: American Philosophical Society, 1939);

Ted-Larry Pebworth and Claude J. Summers, "Recovering an Important Seventeenth-Century Poetical Miscellany: Cambridge Add. Ms 4138," *Cambridge Bibliographical Society, England. Transactions*, 7, no. 2 (1978): 156-169;

I. A. Shapiro, "The 'Mermaid Club,'" *Modern Language Review*, 45 (January 1950): 6-17; *Years Work in English Studies*, 36 (1955): 155.

Papers:

Manuscripts for Corbett's poems can be found in libraries in Great Britain and the United States. The British Library contains manuscripts in its Additional, Egerton, Harleian, Lansdowne, Sloane, and Stowe series; the manuscripts at the Bodleian Library, Oxford, are described in *A Summary Catalogue of Western Manuscripts*, 7 volumes (1895-1953); the Corpus Christi College, Oxford, manuscripts in H. O. Coxe's *Catalogue of the Manuscripts in the Oxford Colleges* (1972); and those of Cambridge in *A Catalogue of the Manuscripts Preserved in the Library of the University of Cambridge*, 5 volumes (1856-1867), and in M. R. James's *Descriptive Catalogue of the Manuscripts in the Library of St. John's College Cambridge* (1913) and his *Descriptive Catalogue of the Manuscripts in the Library of Trinity Hall* (1907). There are also manuscripts at Trinity College, Dublin. Many of the manuscripts now in America are described briefly in Seymour De Ricci's *Census of Medieval and Renaissance Manuscripts in the United States and Canada*, 3 volumes (1935-1940). Corbett manuscripts are also located at the Folger Shakespeare Library, Washington, D. C., and the Harvard College Library.

John Davies of Hereford
(1565? - 1618)

Helen B. Brooks
Stanford University

BOOKS: *Mirum in Modum; a glimpse of Gods glorie and the soules shape* (London: Printed by V. Simmes for William Aspley, 1602);

Microcosmos; the Discovery of the Little World, with the Government thereof (Oxford: Printed by Jos. Barnes, sold by John Barnes, London, 1603);

Wittes Pilgrimage, (by Poeticall Essaies) through a World of Amorous Sonnets, Soule-passions, and other Passages, diuine, philosophicall, morall, poeticall, and politicall (London: Printed by R. Bradock for John Browne, 1605?);

Bien Venu. Greate Britaines Welcome to Hir Greate Friendes, and Deere Brethren the Danes (London: Printed for Nathaniel Butter, 1606);

Summa Totalis or, All in All, and, the Same for Euer: Or, an addition to Mirum in Modum (London: Printed by William Jaggard, 1607);

The Holy Roode, or Christs Crosse: containing Christ Crucified, described in Speaking-picture (London: Printed by J. Windet for Nathaniel Butter, 1609);

Humours Heau'n on Earth: With the Ciuile Warres of Death and Fortune. As also the Triumph of Death: Or, The Picture of the Plague, according to the Life; as it was in Anno Domini 1603 (London: Printed by A. Islip, 1609);

The Scourge of Folly: Consisting of satyricall Epigramms, and others in Honor of many noble and worthy Persons of our Land. Together with a Pleasant (Though Discordant) Descant upon Most English Prouerbes: and others (London: Printed by E. Allde for Richard Redmer, 1611);

The Muses Sacrifice, or Divine Meditations (London: Printed by T. Snodham for G. Norton, 1612);

The Muses-Teares for the loss of their Hope; Heroick and Nere-too-much praised, Henry, Prince of Wales (London: Printed by G. Eld for John Wright, 1613);

A Select Second Husband for Sir Thomas Overburies Wife, now a Matchlesse Widow (London: Printed by Thomas Creede & Barnard Allsopp for John Marriott, 1616);

Wits Bedlam, Where is Had Whipping-Cheer to Cure the Mad (London: Printed by G. Eld, sold by J. Davies, 1617);

The Writing Schoolemaster, or the Anatomie of Faire Writing (London: Sold by R. Daniell, 1620?; sixth edition, enlarged, London: Printed for M. Sparke, 1631).

Edition: *The Complete Works of John Davies of Hereford*, 2 volumes, edited by Alexander B.

John Davies of Hereford (engraving by W. J. Alais)

Grosart, Chertsey Worthies' Library (Edinburgh: Printed for private circulation by T. & A. Constable, 1878).

OTHER: William Parry, *A new and large Discourse of the Travels of Sir A. Sherley, knight*, includes a commendatory poem by Davies (London: Printed by V. Simmes for F. Norton, 1601);

Thomas Dekker, *Lanthorne and Candle-light*, includes a commendatory poem by Davies (London: Printed by G. Eld for F. Busby, 1608);

John Guillim, *A Display of Heraldrie*, includes a commendatory poem by Davies (London: Printed by W. Hall, sold by R. Mab, 1610);

Thomas Coryate, *Coryats Crudities*, includes a commendatory poem by Davies (London: Printed by W. Stansby, 1611);

"An Eclogue between Yong Willy the Singer of his Natiue Pastorals, and Old Wernocke his Friend," in *The Shepheards Pipe*, by William Browne (London: Printed by N. Okes for George Norton, 1614);

William Browne, *Britannia's Pastorals. The Second Booke*, includes a commendatory poem by Da-

vies (London: Printed by T. Snodham for G. Norton, 1616);

Capt. John Smith, *A Description of New England*, includes a commendatory poem by Davies (London: Printed by H. Lownes for R. Clerke, 1616).

Regarded by many as "a lively witness" to one of the richest periods in English literature, John Davies of Hereford deserves attention primarily for what his poetry reveals about his literary contemporaries—including William Shakespeare, John Donne, and Ben Jonson—and about daily life in England. Although Davies's poetry has not brought him into the ranks of distinguished poets, at times his verse compares with the best. He excelled as a penman and writing master, a profession that brought him into contact with some of England's most distinguished literary and aristocratic figures.

Of Welsh descent, Davies was born in the city of Hereford about 1565 and adopted the designation "of Hereford" to distinguish himself from other eminent figures who shared his name, most notably the writer Sir John Davies. In *Microcosmos* (1603) Davies requests "the Cittie of Hereford" to grant him permission to use her name, "That one, with other, may keepe *both* from death." In *Wits Bedlam* (1617) Davies commits himself to bringing fame to his native city: "Thou gau'st me breath, and I will giue thee fame / By writing, in a double kind." Although biographical details of Davies's life are limited, it is known that Davies had two sisters, Margaret and Anne, and two brothers, James and Richard, both of whom were also writing masters. Information about Davies's education, however, remains uncertain. Some scholars believe that Davies attended Oxford University after completing Latin School in Hereford. In his 1970 biography of John Donne, R. C. Bald, who believes that Donne and Davies met at Oxford, indicates that Davies entered Queen's on 15 October 1585; but at least two of Davies's poems suggest that he was not a student at Oxford or at least that he did not earn a degree. These two sonnets, which were written in praise of Oxford and Magdalen College at Oxford and appended to *Microcosmos*, point to Davies's career as writing master at Oxford, where it seems that he had many students.

Davies was married three times. The date of his first marriage is not recorded, but it is known that his first wife, Mary Croft, daughter of Thomas Croft of Okley Parke, died on 1 January

1612, within approximately one year of their marriage, having borne his only child, a son named Sylvanus. She and the two other women he married were of high social rank. In July 1613 he married Dame Juliana Preston of St. Thomas, who died in May 1614. His will of 1618 indicates that he was married a third time, to a woman named Margaret. Davies's burial at the Church of St. Dunstan in London, which he requested in his will to be "as neere as convenientlie may be in the place where Mary my late wel-beloved wife lyeth," is recorded on 6 July 1618.

Penmanship, which appears to be Davies's earliest profession, accounts in large part for his associations with many of England's most aristocratic families, for in the Renaissance the writing master was still regarded as a man of learning in a generally illiterate world. It seems certain that he began teaching penmanship while living in London, traveling to Oxford to meet with his students, who would have studied penmanship as part of their university education. His pupils seem to have included members of the prominent Pembroke, Derby, Herbert, Percy, and Egerton families. If Davies did not know Donne at Oxford, the two poets may have met in the household of the Egertons; Donne served as secretary to Sir Thomas Egerton (later lord chancellor) between 1597 and 1602. An epigram in *The Scourge of Folly* (1611), addressed to "the no lesse ingenious then ingenuous Mr. John Dun," may provide evidence of Davies's acquaintance with the distinguished poet:

> DVNNE is the mouse (they say) and thou art
>   Dunne;
> But no dunne mouse thou art; yet art thou one
> That (like a mouse) in steepe high-waies dost
>   runne,
> To find foode for thy Muse to prey vpon.

The Muses Sacrifice (1612) supplies a second allusion to Donne in Davies's praise for Donne's "Of the Progress of the Soule: The Second Anniversary," along with, interestingly, a denunciation of Donne's extravagant conceits. But both poems show that Davies, indeed, enjoyed the same verbal play as the "monarch of wit."

It has been suggested that Davies also was employed by the Sidney family and knew Sir Philip Sidney personally, though Davies would have been only about twenty years old when Sidney died in 1586. Davies's dedication of *Mirum in Modum* (1602) to the poet's brother Sir Robert Sidney, the poet's nephew William Herbert, third

Earl of Pembroke, and William's cousin Edward Herbert of Montgomery (later Lord Herbert of Cherbury) suggests an acquaintance with these distinguished figures. Sidney's sister, Mary Herbert, Countess of Pembroke, also may have been an acquaintance and patroness of Davies. Expense accounts of Henry Percy, ninth Earl of Northumberland, show that Davies was in the service of the Percy family during the years 1607 and 1609-1610. Some of Davies's numerous dedications to illustrious personages may simply derive from the conventions of patronage. His sources of financial assistance, other than the Percy family, are uncertain. Although assessments and bequests in his will suggest that Davies did enjoy a modestly prosperous standard of living, in fact, lines near the end of *Microcosmos* suggest that Davies's life may at times have been a financial struggle. Regardless, it is certain that his skill did not go unrecognized: in his *History of the Worthies of England* (1662) Thomas Fuller called Davies "the greatest Master of the Pen that England in her age beheld." The accuracy of Fuller's assessment is borne out by Davies's appointment as master of penmanship to Prince Henry, eldest child of James I and Anne of Denmark, in 1605, while the prince was studying at Magdalen College. These lines from "To my much honored, and intirely beloued Patronesse, the most famous Universitie of Oxford," one of the two Oxford sonnets in *Microcosmos*, underscore Davies's success as a writing teacher:

> For like a *Lady* full of roialtie,
> Shee giues me *Crownes* for my *Charactery*:
> Her *Pupils* crowne me for directing *them*,
> Where like a *King* I liue, without a *Realme*;
> They praise my *precepts*, & my *Lessons* learne,
> So doth the *worse* the *better* governe.
> But *Oxford*, O I praise thy situation
> Passing *Pernassus*, *Muses'* habitation!

Moreover, Davies's treatise on writing, *The Writing Schoolemaster, or the Anatomie of Faire Writing* (circa 1620), was frequently republished during the seventeenth century.

According to Anthony Wood's *Athenæ Oxonienses* (1691-1692), Davies already had earned the reputation of being a "good poet" at Oxford, even though his first printed work, *Mirum in Modum* ("a glimpse of Gods glorie and the soules shape"), the first of his long didactic poems, did not appear until 1602, when he was about thirty-seven years old. Like Davies's second long didactic poem, *Microcosmos*, the first third of

Mirum in Modum presents a complete theory of Elizabethan faculty psychology, which follows closely the English translation (1586-1601) of Pierre de la Primaudaye's *L'Academie Françoise*. Davies, following the Scholastics of the High Middle Ages, concludes that "the Minde for God [is] her Gole." *Mirum in Modum* devotes one-third of its stanzas to a close verse paraphrase of approximately eleven chapters in the second part of la Primaudaye's treatise, outlining in detail the functions of the soul's faculties, the chief powers of which are understanding, will, and memory. The second part of Davies's poem continues its focus on the faculties of the soul, but with primary attention to the operation of reason and its abuse. The final third of the poem discourses on, among other things, contemplation and the attributes of God.

Microcosmos, the longest of Davies's three didactic poems, followed closely upon *Mirum in Modum*. Published in 1603 with a second edition in 1605, *Microcosmos*, like *Mirum in Modum*, is modeled on the Spenserian nine-line stanza and versifies theological and philosophical treatises focusing primarily on the behavior of the soul. Sir John Davies's poem *Nosce Teipsum* (1599), to which Davies of Hereford's three long poems (especially *Mirum in Modum* and *Summa Totalis*, 1607) seem to be indebted, also presents the highly conventional system of scholastic psychology.

With *Microcosmos* Davies was one of the first English writers of religious poetry to draw on the influential French Huguenot poet Guillaume de Salluste, Seigneur Du Bartas. King James and Queen Anne, to whom Davies dedicated *Microcosmos*, were patrons of Du Bartas, whose epic work on the Creation, *Semaines* (1578), is a celebration of Christian virtues over the classical paganism latent in Renaissance thought. Josuah Sylvester's English translation of Du Bartas's work (part of which first appeared in 1595) was completed in 1608. Davies wrote two commendatory poems on Sylvester's translation. In one, Davies harshly criticized poets who "abuse" the Christian Muse with secular poetry that celebrates "Their onely god, their guts, their beastly Belly, / To whom they offer all their slender Store." *Microcosmos* includes a defense of turning prose works into verse, with Davies's primary justifications being that words set to meter fall more delicately on the ear and that these more succinct, ennobling words are easier to remember. Like so much else of Davies's writing, these justifications have their origin in another source, George Puttenham's *The Arte of English Poesie* (1589). Moreover, the opening lines of *Microcosmos* resume the versification of la Primaudaye on the faculties of the soul found in *Mirum in Modum*, followed by passages derived from la Primaudaye on such subjects as love, beauty, humility, the emotions, and pride. Aristotle's *De Anima* is the ultimate source for faculty psychology, and Galen is the source for his physiology; yet beyond their debt to la Primaudaye, *Mirum in Modum* and *Microcosmos* are compendiums of countless popular works in English on the subject. The poems thus lose much in the way of original and unified works. In the last verse of *Summa Totalis* Davies expressly "confesses" his debt to other sources.

Still, *Microcosmos* includes much that is not from *The French Academie*, including Davies's own excursions on the soul, some satirical passages on the passions, and an extended digression on "Policie," or the proper conduct of princes. Although there were countless writings on this subject, Davies's somewhat cynical treatment of princes may reflect the influence of Machiavellian politics as it was interpreted in Innocent Gentillet's *Contra-Machiavel* (1576), which was translated into English by Simon Patericke in 1602. In *Microcosmos* Davies also included a full, if not richly poetic, account of English "Princes" from William the Conqueror to the beginning of the rule of James I, presented so that "by th' event of *Actions* past, wee shall / The *present*, and *future*, the better sway."

Appended to the already lengthy—and often tedious—poem is another poem, "An Extasie," which employs the medieval convention of the dream vision, but which in its metaphysical turns of mind deserves to be compared with John Donne's "The Extasie." Also in the same volume are a substantial number of commendatory sonnets addressed to such well-known personages as John Whitgift, Archbishop of Canterbury; the "beloued" Sir John Davies; the countess of Pembroke; and the earl of Northumberland.

Records indicate that by 1605 at the latest Davies had established his residence in London, and by 1608 he was living in the parish of St. Dunstan-in-the-West at which point he began to write voluminously. *Wittes Pilgrimage* (entered in the Stationers' Register on 27 September 1605) begins with a sequence of approximately one hundred love sonnets in Shakespearean form. Often cited as among Davies's best verse, these sonnets have as their principal subject earthly love. The majority

Title page for the 1611 volume in which Davies included epigrams and other poems addressed to fellow poets such as George Chapman, William Shakespeare, John Donne, and Ben Jonson

are dominated by the Petrarchan lover's lament, but a few are organized around elaborate metaphysical conceits. Sonnet 69 in particular draws on the geographical conceit popular with Donne, and sonnet 43—among Davies's best—is similar in some respects to more than one of Donne's:

> My mind to me a mighty Kingdom is;
> Which I possesse, but not enjoy in peace;
> For if I did, I were a King of This,
> But Loue, my right, doth force me to release
> If Thou (great Loue) vsurpe anothers Right
> Thou art a Tyrant; and thou must resolue
> By fight to keep, what Thou has got by fight;
> If so of force, Thou must thy force dissolue:
> For with Thy force thou canst not winne from me
> My Mind, vnlesse Her force Thou quite defeate;
> Which, if Thou do, it is the worse for thee;
> For, thou defeatest That, that makes thee Great:
>   Then, o be not too fell, but let that Shee
>   For, and by whom I liue, raign there with
>   Thee.

Despite similarities between the two poets, Davies's interest in extended poetic treatments of philosophical and theological subjects has discouraged some critics from seeing too close an alliance between the poetry of Davies and the Metaphysical poets. In *The Philosophical Poems of Henry More* (1931) Geoffrey Bullough points out that Donne and other poets of the Metaphysical school "were less truly 'philosophical' poets than many of their contemporaries," including Sir

John Davies, John Davies of Hereford, Josuah Sylvester, Phineas Fletcher, and Henry More.

One longer poem in *Wittes Pilgrimage*, "An amorous Colloqui twixt Dorus and Pamela," written in fifty-two four-line tetrameter stanzas and drawing the names of its personae from Sidney's *Arcadia* (1590), is largely an inconsequential poem. Yet, even though the poem suffers from excessive wordplay and moralizing, its verse possesses an energy and directness not often found elsewhere in Davies's writing, much of which is written in a pentameter line. Dorus moves to a metaphysical appeal to Pamela that has been compared to that of Donne's lover in "The Extasie" or Edward, Lord Herbert of Cherbury's in "An Ode upon a Question moved, Whether Love should continue for ever?" "An amorous Colloqui" is followed by "The picture of Formosity," a lengthy poem in which language of cartography is appropriated for a sensual—even licentious—description of feminine beauty, a somewhat common appropriation in Renaissance writing. In addition to the sonnet sequence, *Wittes Pilgrimage* includes forty-eight other sonnets on subjects such as "The Trinity illustrated by a three-square perspective Glasse" and "In praise of Poesie" and commendatory poems to such persons as Davies's "deere Friend" Nicholas Deeble, the countess of Pembroke, and William, Earl of Pembroke.

The visit to London in the summer of 1606 by Denmark's King Christian IV, brother of Queen Anne of England, inspired Davies's next work, *Bien Venu* (1606). Dedicated to the visiting king, the poem is one of two major occasional poems written by Davies. The second, *The Muses-Teares* (1613), was written upon the death of his former student Prince Henry in 1612. Davies's poem is a moving tribute to the prince. As early as 1603, Davies had dedicated to Prince Henry "Cambria," one of the prefatory poems to *Microcosmos*, in which Davies expresses his delight that once again there is a Prince of Wales.

Summa Totalis, the third of Davies's three long didactic poems, appeared in 1607. This poem, along with *Mirum in Modum* and *Microcosmos*, has earned Davies credit for being the only poet of his time to versify the teachings of systematic theology. *Summa Totalis*, which Davies described as "an addition to *Mirum in Modum*," continues his discourse on the nature of God in the language of scholastic theology. Following an extended discussion of the nature of God, the poem takes up the individual attributes of God:

his Eternity, Immutability, Power, and Knowledge. This third didactic treatise, like the discourse on the conduct of Princes in *Microcosmos*, includes a somewhat cynical view of the traditional notion of kingship, that is, of the king as God's vice-regent on earth, and as such is a model of godly virtue. This view, increasingly called into question following the publication of Niccolò Machiavelli's *The Prince* in 1532, surfaces in Davies's poem in its oblique reference to the reigns of Edward IV and Richard II:

> Kings of the Earth, seeme blessed in their Crownes;
> Yet, they but onely seeme, but are not so:
> Sith they sit reeling in their fastest Thrones,
> That eu'ry moment, threats their ouerthrow;
> Which makes them sit on thorns, through pierc'd
>   with wo,
> And, though all mortall Knees to them do bow
> Th' adore their Chairs, not them.

Here, as in so much of early-seventeenth-century literature, the nature of reality is problematized to suggest that appearance and reality may not at all be the same. It is generally agreed that *Summa Totalis* is more formally organized than its companion treatise *Mirum in Modum*, though moral digressions on sinfulness intrude in *Summa Totalis* as well as in the earlier poem. In fact, the human predilection for sinfulness weighed heavily on Davies's mind throughout his career. In *The Muses Sacrifice*, for example, Davies "Confesses" his belief that, apart from the soul, humans are nothing but "Dust, Clay, Durt, Dung," and that only God's loving grace can effect one's salvation. Much of Davies's verse is devoted to repeated praise of the simple life and the condemnation of the bodily passions.

The two volumes that include most of Davies's devotional poems are *The Holy Roode, or Christs Crosse* (1609) and *The Muses Sacrifice, or Divine Meditations* (1612). *The Holy Roode*, modeled chiefly on the meditative practices of Saint Bernard of Clairvaux, is an exhortation to the soul to dwell on the principal events in the life of Christ, from his birth to the Crucifixion and Resurrection. Whereas earlier symbolism in the Middle Ages surrounding the life of Christ is restrained, Davies's poem is a more personal and emotionally wrought mystical devotion, centering on the agony of the Crucifixion, a change in emphasis characteristic of late Renaissance religious art, stimulated in large part by the Counter-Reformation. *The Holy Roode* consists of a few religious sonnets and a lengthy poem on Christ's sufferings and death, in which the speaker in graphic—and at times overwrought—detail repeatedly urges the soul to "see," or picture Christ's unmerited suffering. The poem ends with a consolation to Mary and the aspiration of the soul.

The Muses Sacrifice, dedicated to the three "Patronesses of the Muses" (Lucy, Countess of Bedford; Mary, Countess of Pembroke; and Elizabeth, Lady Cary, wife of Sir Henry Cary), opens with a long, commendatory dedicatory epistle, which includes a lengthy discourse on the virtues of poetry. This epistle is prefatory to forty-one verse meditations, of which nearly half express the thoughts of a "Pensive Soul, groaning under the burden of sinne." Theocentric in its orientation, this volume focuses upon a theme popular with religious poets, the "desire of vnion with the giuer." The devotional sonnets thus celebrate the renunciation of the earthly love that marks the love sonnets in *Wittes Pilgrimage* for divine love, a Petrarchan development in Davies's writing that is apparent elsewhere in Renaissance poetry, most notably in the sonnets of Spenser, Sir Fulke Greville, and Donne. The subject matter of *The Muses Sacrifice* may have been derived in part from a book of devotions attributed to Saint Augustine: *A Pretious Booke of Heauenlie Meditations, Called a Priuate Talke of the Soule with God*, translated in 1581 by Thomas Rogers. Yet scholars have emphasized that in his meditations Davies could more readily create his own phrasing than he could in his earlier didactic, and largely derivative, philosophical poems. Still, in *The Muses Sacrifice* Davies discourages his readers from looking for originality. Instead, in typical Renaissance fashion, the poet claims,

> Here are no Nouels (which yee most desire)
>   nor ought unusuall; but, here shall you see
> What hath beene said of old, in new Attire,
>   with our Thoughts interlac'd; so, ours they be.

One reason for this conservatism, however, may be that Davies most likely was of a Roman Catholic family and ultimately became a Roman Catholic himself. The strongest evidence for Davies's religious affiliation comes from Arthur Wilson, whose comment was preserved by Francis Peck in his *Desiderata Curiosa* (1732-1735): "I could not write the Court and Chancerie hands. So my father left me for halfe a yeare (this was about 1611) with Mr. John Davies, in Fleet Street (the most famous writer of his time) to learne

those hands. Who being also a Papist, with his wife and familie, their example and often discourse gave growth to my opinions. . . ." Davies's commendatory lines to Sir Thomas More in "Paper's Complaint" also suggest his Catholic ties:

> Ah good Sir Thomas Moore, (Fame bee with thee)
> Thy Hand did blesse the English Historie,
> Or els (God knowes) it had beene as a Pray
> To brutish Barbarisme vntill this Day.

As any recusant poet would have known at the time, it was best to keep one's religious preference a private matter. Thus, it is often difficult to ascertain the precise nature of the Christian perspective of his works. *Triumph of Death*, the third poem in *Humours Heav'n on Earth* (1609), centers on the devastating effects of the 1603 plague in England, without a specific sectarian stance. Unlike the preceding two poems in the volume, *Triumph of Death* is not allegorical. Instead, it provides a relatively straightforward account of the plague, with the conventional attribution of plagues to divine punishment for sins. Dedicated to Dorothie and Lucy Percy, daughters of the earl of Northumberland—who are asked to "Looke on this Picture; so perceiue ye shall, / We fall like Leaues, in Autumne from the Tree"—the poem gives an extensive catalogue of the plague (though in a disorderly arrangement), including the physical symptoms of the disease, the flight of citizens—and the king—from London, the enormous loss of life, the distraught survivors, the imposed quarantine, and the general social disorder. This poem is one of the most readable of Davies's works, in part because of its almost Virgilian and Spenserian sensuousness of detail and its resistance to the verbal excesses that dominate much of Davies's other verse. Passages such as the following capture the essence of the plague-stricken London as Davies perceived it:

> For some (like Ghosts) would walk out in the night,
> The Citie glowing (furnace-like) with heate
> Of this contagion, to seeke if they might
> Fresh aire, where oft they died for want of meate,
> The Traueler that spied (perhaps his Sire)
> Another farre off comming towards him,
> Would flie, as from a flying flame of fire
> That would, if it be met, waste life and limbe.

The first poems in the volume, *Humours Heav'n on Earth* and *The Civile Warres of Death and Fortune*—both dedicated to another of Davies's distinguished pupils, Algernon, Lord Percy, son of the earl of Northumberland—are both allegorical works on relatively conventional topics. The first, more successful than the second, is a morality poem focused on three sinners—Poliphagus the Glutton, Epithymus the Leacher, and Hyselophronus the Proud. Its greatest appeal lies in its vivid Dantean descriptions of Hell:

> Here, Seas of boiling Lead their Bounds oreflow,
> To make a boundlesse deluge of annoy:
> The Sands whereof the Soules orewhelm'd with
> 　woe:
> Which though destroi'd, yet death cannot destroy:
> For, endlesse lords of death still life do giue
> To those that in that death there still do liue.

While there is no firm evidence that Davies belonged to a coterie of poets, the satirical epigrams and the poems addressed "To Worthy Persons" in *The Scourge of Folly* address contemporaries including Sir Philip Sidney, the earl of Northumberland, Shakespeare, John Donne, Ben Jonson, Inigo Jones, George Chapman, and Thomas Campion. According to Alexander B. Grosart, Davies quite likely joined in the great "feasts of the soul" at the Mermaid Tavern, one of the favorite meeting places for writers. Davies, in fact, was one of the fifty-four men, including Donne, Jonson, Sir Henry Goodyer, and Jones, who wrote panegyric poems for *Coryats Crudities* (1611). At about the same time Davies addressed poems to Thomas Coryate, Donne, Jonson, Jones, and others in the title section of *The Scourge of Folly* and in "To Worthy Persons." Several of the poems suggest a personal acquaintance with the individuals addressed. In his epigram to Coryate (number 44), for example, Davies implies a "company" of Wits:

> Thy presence (like the presence of the sunne)
> Doth cheare the place, thy beames do ouer-runne
> And makes the company that it possesses
> Swim in delight, though drownd in deep distresses:
> The strange meanders of thy Wits vagaries
> Do grauell all disputing in St. Maries
> (In Oxford call'd the Austines) nay, then all
> That logick learne or letters liberall.

Epigram 159, to "Our English Terence Mr. Will: Shake-speare," has been taken to show that Davies knew Shakespeare, but it also has provoked interest in its apparent failure to mention Shakespeare as a playwright. Instead, Davies comments on Shakespeare as an actor, although the

references to his acting are somewhat obscure. The epigrams in *The Scourge of Folly*, primarily satirical in their purpose, traverse a wide range of subjects and persons. Hans Heidrich divides Davies's satirical topics into three broad categories: 1) grievances, such as usury, extravagance, selling of offices, prostitution; 2) subjects of ridicule at the time, such as the uses of makeup, wearing of finery, tobacco, gambling; and 3) criticism of individual trades or professions, such as greedy lawyers, fraudulent clergy, obsequious courtiers, incompetent writing teachers, and crooked shopkeepers. Many of the epigrams, running from single couplets to forty-six-line poems, are addressed to fictitious persons who embody some reprehensible behavior, such as "Against the great Swearer Mezentius" and "Against Grillus his greedy gluttony." Most have been described as "weak imitations" of the work of other epigrammatic writers, such as John Donne, who, like himself, Davies claims in Epigram 97, "rightly" directed his satires against "none but monsters like to men." Whereas Donne is among the early writers of formal Juvenalian satire, which flourished in the 1590s, Davies has been credited, along with Sir John Harington, of introducing the popular epigrammatic form associated with the more witty and cynical Martial.

Although the thrust of "satyricall Epigramms" is indeed satiric, the tone is less earnest than Martial's. At least two of Davies's epigrams are addressed to Harington; one, Epigram 124, points to their similar aims, "To beare the burden of [the Muse's] merry song: / To make them sorry who the world abuse." *The Scourge of Folly* also includes commendatory sonnets and epigrams. One, Epigram 156, addressed to his "well-accomplish'd friend Mr. Ben. Johnson," reflects Davies's desire to stand in Jonson's favor. Other commendatory poems in the volume are addressed to individual students of Davies. Lines from Epigram 291, "To my deere friend and Pupill Mr. Henry Twiddy," offer words of encouragement to Davies's pupils:

> Looke to your head, your hand to me commit,
> And I will make it pumpe your head for witt
> For letters fiue that may (in letters faire),
> Lure to your hand bright angells through the aire
> Of your faire fame.

Writing in 1878, Grosart complained that biographers had not sufficiently investigated the multiple and suggestive references to poets and other distinguished figures in Davies's verse, especially

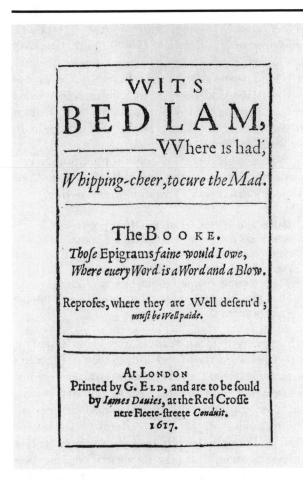

Title page for Davies's posthumously published book of poetry, including the epitaph in which he proclaims, "I lou'd the Muses, and sought by them / Long life in this life's shadow of a dreame"

in the volume that includes *The Scourge of Folly*, noting, for instance, the neglected poem to Sir Francis Bacon in "To Worthy Persons." Among Davies's other poems in this volume is a sonnet titled "The Flea." Although built on less elaborate a conceit than Donne's well-known poem of the same title, Davies's sonnet is remarkably similar to Donne's and thus provides for an interesting comparison.

Appended to *The Scourge of Folly* is a satire titled *Papers Complaint, compil'd in ruthfull Rimes Against the Paper-spoylers of these Times*, a 546-line poem in couplet form attacking current bad literature and regarded as original in its personification of paper. Lashing out at the abuses suffered by poor writers, Paper exclaims:

> Though I (immaculate) be white as Snow,
> (Which virgin Hue mine Innocence doth shew)
> Yet these remorceles Monsters on me piles
> A massy-heape of blockish senceles Stiles;

That I ne wot (God wot) which of the twaine
Do most torment me, heauy Shame, or Paine.

The poem is particularly valuable in its references to Shakespeare's *Venus and Adonis* (1593) and its popularity, as well as in its references to Thomas Nashe, Jonson, Thomas Dekker, and others. Early in the poem Davies alludes to Shakespeare, praising the "wit" in *Venus and Adonis* but criticizing the Bard's immorality, which may help to explain the absence of any mention of Shakespeares' plays in Davies's writing. *Papers Complaint* was republished in 1625, with a continuation by Abraham Holland, as *A Scourge for Paper-persecutors.*

Two years before his death Davies wrote a treatise on marriage, *A Select Second Husband for Sir Thomas Overburies Wife, now a Matchlesse Widow* (1616), appended to which are elegies on Overbury and a poem titled "Speculum Proditori." As the title of the principal poem implies, the subject matter is a consideration of the ideal husband, in imitation of Overbury, who had written of an ideal wife in his poem *A Wife* (1614). Davies's poem most likely was inspired by public interest in the scandal surrounding the murder of Overbury in 1613. The substance of the poem derives primarily from marriage-conduct books, which at the time were principally written by Puritans for the middle and lower classes, and is in part a versification of Henry Smith's sermon on marriage, published in a collection of Smith's sermons in 1611. *A Select Second Husband* is a valuable source of information on the English Renaissance social milieu. Davies's writing in general, in presenting a cross section of life in and around London, is marked by a realism and directness found in the works of first-ranked poets, perhaps most notably in Donne's.

Published the year after his death, *Wits Bedlam* includes poems on various subjects, including several epigrams on base sexual topics. An epitaph "upon a noted common lyer" is notable for the wordplay and punning characteristic of much of Davies's verse:

> Here lies Iack ap Iack: and wot yee why?
> A liue he still lyde; and dead still must lye:
> Who, in his life, lyde willingly still,
> but here in death, lies against his will.

It is generally accepted that Davies imitated the styles of writers such as Spenser, Sidney, Joseph Hall, and Donne; yet, as Grosart emphasized, "throughout in substance and workmanship, in matter and manner, in heavenly and earthly truths, in cadence and epithet, John Davies is himself.... His [is a] sturdy nonimitativeness.... Even in his epigrams and satirical poems the salt of wit is his own. His 'points' he himself selects. His vocabulary, if not marked by culture, is suggestive of considerable and out-o'-the-way reading."

A dichotomy nevertheless remains in Davies's poetry between the moralistic philosophical works and the witty, even ribald epigrams, such as those in *The Scourge of Folly*. Some of the unevenness and disparity of subject matter have been attributed to Davies's dual professions. The poems that Davies dedicated to the nobility and royalty he served as writing instructor are primarily didactic philosophical and theological verse in which he endeavored to combine his Christian beliefs with the thought of the ancients. At the same time it is clear that Davies also wrote to meet the demands of the marketplace, complaining in an introductory poem to *The Scourge of Folly*:

> The *Printer* praises me most vncessantly,
>   To make some *lines* to lash at *Lechery*:
> For that (sayth he) so rellish will the rest,
> That they will sell, and still be in request:
> For most men now (set on a merry Pin)
> Laugh to see others plagued for their sin.
>   *Then Reader, thinke when thou seest such a Straine,*
>   *Its for the* Lecher's *paine, and* Printers' *gaine.*

Although Davies's poetry includes much that would appeal to the court, we do not know if he profited from his writing. In the sixteen years between the first and last of his published poems, Davies seems to have exerted little influence on the writing of his contemporaries. The only direct evidence of his influence is in the names of allegorical figures in William Browne's *Britannia's Pastorals*. His reputation with his contemporaries may be inferred from the inclusion in Browne's *The Shepheards Pipe* (1614) of an eclogue by Davies ("An Eclogue between Yong Willy the Singer of his Natiue Pastorals, and Old Wernocke his Friend") and from the republication of eleven of his epigrams in *Wits Recreations: Selected from the Finest Fancies of the Modern Muses* (1640). Forty of his epigrams were included without attribution in Samuel Pick's *Festum Voluptatis* (1639). Davies was also called upon to contribute commendatory poems to works such as William Parry's *A new and large Discourse of the Travels of*

Sir A.[nthony] Sherley, knight (1601), Dekker's *Lanthorne and Candle-light* (1608), John Guillim's *A Display of Heraldrie* (1610), *Coryats Crudities* (1611), Browne's *Britannia's Pastorals. The Second Booke* (1616), and Capt. John Smith's *A Description of New England* (1616). Yet in his epitaph, written in the year of his death, Davies gives thought to his want of "Fame" (*Wits Bedlam*).

Although there were few contemporary references to his verse, the one in book 2, song 2, of Browne's *Britannia's Pastorals* is worth noting:

> *Davies* and *Wither*, by whose *Muses* power
> A *naturall* day to me seemes but an houre,
> And could I euer heare their learned layes,
> Ages would turne to artificiall dayes.
> These sweetly chanted to the *Queene of Waues*,
> She prais'd, and what she prais'd, no tongue depraues.

While many modern readers may grow impatient with Davies's verbose and didactic style, Browne's lines suggest that Davies's contemporaries were impressed not only by his commendatory poems but also by the breadth of his subject matter and the technique of his verse. Because Davies, as Charles Driscoll Murphy puts it, was not "truly a university man," he may be described best as a writer who "stood in an indeterminate place between two social and intellectual orders." In this view, perhaps, lies much that is of ongoing value in Davies's poetry: its rich and diverse commentary on the things that occupied the attention of many London citizens, whether aristocrats or commoners.

References:

Ruth L. Anderson, "A French Source for John Davies of Hereford's System of Psychology," *Philological Quarterly*, 6 (January 1927): 57-66;

Alexander B. Grosart, Introduction and notes to *John Davies of Hereford: The Complete Works*, 2 volumes, edited by Grosart, Chertsey Worthies' Library (Edinburgh: Printed for private circulation by T. & A. Constable, 1878);

Hans Heidrich, *John Davies of Hereford (1565?-1618) und sein Bild von Shakespeare's Umgebung* (Leipzig: Mayer & Müller, 1924);

R. B. McKerrow, "John Davies of Hereford (1565?-1618) und sein Bild von Shakespeare's Umgebung. Von Hans Heidrich. (Palaestra, 143.) Leipzig, 1924. Pp. vi.

124," *Review of English Studies*, 1 (April 1925): 242-244;

Charles Driscoll Murphy, "John Davies of Hereford," Ph.D. dissertation, Cornell University, 1940;

H. E. G. Rope, "John Davies of Hereford, Catholic and Rhymer," *Anglo-Welsh Review*, 11, no. 28 (1961): 20-36;

Jonathan Sawday, "Unattributed Manuscript Corrections to a Poem [*Mirum in Modum*] by John Davies of Hereford," *Notes and Queries*, new series 28 (February 1981): 40-41;

Howard H. Thompson, "A New Poem by John Davies of Hereford," *Ball State University Forum*, 9 (Spring 1968): 44-45.

Papers:

One of the two copies of the 1602 edition of *Mirum in Modum* at the British Library (1077.f.6[1]) includes corrections in the poet's own hand, which are not included in Alexander Grosart's edition of Davies's poetry. Examples of Davies's penmanship are preserved at Penshurst, the country seat of the Sidney family in Kent.

John Donne

(1572 - 31 March 1631)

A. J. Smith
University of Southampton

BOOKS: *Pseudo-Martyr* (London: Printed by W. Stansby for Walter Burre, 1610);

Conclaue Ignati (London, 1611); translated as *Ignatius his Conclaue* (London: Printed by N. O. for Richard More, 1611);

An anatomy of the World (London: Printed for Samuel Macham, 1611);

The Second Anniuersarie. Of The Progres of the Soule, published with *The First Anniuersarie. An Anatomie of the World* (London: Printed by M. Bradwood for S. Macham, 1612);

A Sermon Vpon The XV. Verse Of The XX. Chapter Of The Booke Of Ivdges (London: Printed by William Stansby for Thomas Jones, 1622);

A Sermon Vpon The VIII. Verse Of The I. Chapter of The Acts Of The Apostles (London: Printed by A. Mat for Thomas Jones, 1622);

Encænia. The Feast of Dedication. Celebrated At Lincolnes Inne, in a Sermon there vpon Ascension day, 1623 (London: Printed by Aug. Mat. for Thomas Jones, 1623);

Three Sermons Vpon Speciall Occasions (London: Printed for Thomas Jones, 1623);

Devotions Vpon Emergent Occasions (London: Printed by A. M. for Thomas Jones, 1624);

The First Sermon Preached To King Charles (London: Printed by A. M. for Thomas Jones, 1625);

Fovre Sermons Vpon Speciall Occasions (London: Printed for Thomas Jones, 1625);

A Sermon, Preached To The Kings Mtie. At Whitehall, 24. Febr. 1625 (London: Printed for Thomas Jones, 1626);

Five Sermons Vpon Speciall Occasions (London: Printed for Thomas Jones, 1626);

A Sermon Of Commemoration Of The Lady Dāuers (London: Printed by I. H. for Philemon Stephens & Christopher Meredith, 1627);

Deaths Dvell (London: Printed by Thomas Harper for Richard Redmer & Benjamin Fisher, 1632);

Ivvenilia (London: Printed by E. P. for Henry Seyle, 1633);

Poems (London: Printed by M. F. for John Marriot, 1633);

Six Sermons Vpon Severall Occasions (London: Printed by the Printers to the Universitie of Cambridge, sold by Nicholas Fussell & Humphrey Mosley, 1634);

John Donne circa 1595 (portrait by an unknown artist; Collection of the Marquess of Lothian, Newbattle Abbey)

Sapientia Clamitans (London: Printed by I. Haviland for R. Milbourne, 1638);

Wisdome crying out to Sinners (London: Printed by M. P. for John Stafford, 1639);

LXXX Sermons (London: Printed for Richard Royston & Richard Marriot, 1640);

ΒΙΑΘΑΝΑΤΟΣ *A Declaration of that Paradoxe, or Thesis that Selfe-homicide is not so Naturally Sinne, that it may never be otherwise* (London: Printed by John Dawson, 1647);

Essayes in Divinity (London: Printed by T. M. for Richard Marriot, 1651).

Editions: *Fifty Sermons* (London: Printed by Ja. Flesher for M. F. J. Marriot & R. Royston, 1649);

XXVI. Sermons (London: Printed by T. N. for James Magnes, 1660);

The Works of John Donne, D.D., Dean of Saint Pauls 1621-1631, With a memoir of his life, 6 volumes, edited by Henry Alford (London: John W. Parker, 1839);

The Poetical Works of Dr. John Donne, with a memoir, edited by James Russell Lowell (Boston: Little, Brown, 1855);

The Poems of John Donne, edited by E. K. Chambers (London: Lawrence & Bullen, 1896);

The Life and Letters of John Donne, 2 volumes, edited by Edmund Gosse (London: Heinemann, 1899);

The Love Poems of John Donne, edited by Charles Eliot Norton (Boston: Houghton, Mifflin, 1905);

The Poems of John Donne, edited by Herbert J. C. Grierson (Oxford: Clarendon Press, 1912);

Donne's Sermons: Selected Passages, edited, with an introduction, by Logan Pearsall Smith (Oxford: Clarendon Press, 1919);

Donne at about age eighteen. This engraving by William Marshall (possibly after a miniature by Nicholas Hilliard) was published in the 1635 edition of Donne's Poems.

The Poems of John Donne, edited by Hugh I'Anson Fausset (London & Toronto: Dent, 1931);

The Complete Poems of John Donne, edited by Roger E. Bennett (Chicago: Packard, 1942);

The Complete Poetry and Selected Prose of John Donne, edited by Charles M. Coffin (New York: Modern Library, 1952);

Essays in Divinity, edited by Evelyn M. Simpson (Oxford: Clarendon Press, 1952);

The Sermons of John Donne, 10 volumes, edited by George R. Potter and Simpson (Berkeley & Los Angeles: University of California Press, 1953-1962);

John Donne: The Anniversaries, edited by F. Manley (Baltimore: Johns Hopkins Press, 1963);

John Donne's Sermons on the Psalms and Gospels. With a Selection of Prayers and Meditations, edited by Simpson (Berkeley & Los Angeles: University of California Press, 1963);

The Complete Poetry of John Donne, edited by John

T. Shawcross (Garden City, N.Y.: Doubleday, 1967);

Donne's Prebend Sermons, edited by Janel M. Mueller (Cambridge, Mass.: Harvard University Press, 1971);

John Donne: The Complete English Poems, edited by A. J. Smith (Harmondsworth, U.K.: Penguin, 1971);

Devotions Upon Emergent Occasions, edited by Anthony Raspa (Montreal: McGill-Queen's University Press, 1975);

Biathanatos, edited by Ernest W. Sullivan II (Newark: University of Delaware Press / London: Associated University Presses, 1984);

John Donne, edited by John Carey (Oxford & New York: Oxford University Press, 1990).

John Donne's standing as a great English poet, and one of the greatest writers of English prose, is now assured. However, it has been confirmed only in the present century. The history of Donne's reputation is the most remarkable of any major writer in English; no other body of great poetry has fallen so far from favor for so long and been generally condemned as inept and crude. In Donne's own day his poetry was highly prized among the small circle of his admirers, who read it as it was circulated in manuscript, and in his later years he gained wide fame as a preacher. For some thirty years after his death successive editions of his verse stamped his powerful influence upon English poets. During the Restoration his writing went out of fashion and remained so for several centuries. Throughout the eighteenth century, and for much of the nineteenth century, he was little read and scarcely appreciated. Commentators followed Samuel Johnson in dismissing his work as no more than frigidly ingenious and metrically uncouth. Some scribbled notes by Samuel Taylor Coleridge in Charles Lamb's copy of Donne's poems make a testimony of admiration rare in the early nineteenth century. Robert Browning became a known (and wondered-at) enthusiast of Donne, but it was not until the end of the nineteenth century that Donne's poetry was eagerly taken up by a growing band of avant-garde readers and writers. His prose remained largely unnoticed until 1919.

In the first two decades of the twentieth century Donne's poetry was decisively rehabilitated. Its extraordinary appeal to modern readers throws light on the Modernist movement, as well as on our intuitive response to our own times. Donne may no longer be the cult figure he became in the 1920s and 1930s, when T. S. Eliot and William Butler Yeats, among others, discovered in his poetry the peculiar fusion of intellect and passion and the alert contemporariness which they aspired to in their own art. He is not a poet for all tastes and times; yet for many readers Donne remains what Ben Jonson judged him: "the first poet in the world in some things." His poems continue to engage the attention and challenge the experience of readers who come to him afresh. His high place in the pantheon of the English poets now seems secure.

Donne's love poetry was written nearly four hundred years ago; yet one reason for its appeal is that it speaks to us as directly and urgently as if we overhear a present confidence. For instance, a lover who is about to board ship for a long voyage turns back to share a last intimacy with his mistress: "Here take my picture" (*Elegy 5*). Two lovers who have turned their backs upon

Donne's father-in-law, Sir George More, who was angered by Donne's elopement with his daughter and tried to have the marriage annulled (Private Collection; from Derek Parker, John Donne and His World, *1975)*

a threatening world in "The Good Morrow" celebrate their discovery of a new world in each other:

> Let sea-discoverers to new worlds have gone,
> Let maps to others, worlds on worlds have shown,
> Let us possess one world, each hath one, and is one.

In "The Flea" an importunate lover points out a flea that has been sucking his mistress's blood and now jumps to suck his; he tries to prevent his mistress from crushing it:

> Oh stay, three lives in one flea spare,
> Where we almost, nay more than married are.
> This flea is you and I, and this
> Our marriage bed, and marriage temple is;
> Though parents grudge, and you, we' are met,
> And cloistered in these living walls of jet.

This poem moves forward as a kind of dramatic argument in which the chance discovery of the flea itself becomes the means by which they work out the true end of their love. The incessant play of a skeptical intelligence gives even these love poems the style of impassioned reasoning.

The poetry inhabits an exhilaratingly unpredictable world in which wariness and quick wits are at a premium. The more perilous the encounters of clandestine lovers, the greater zest they have for their pleasures, whether they seek to outwit the disapproving world, or a jealous husband, or a forbidding and deeply suspicious father, as in *Elegy 4*, "The Perfume":

> Though he had wont to search with glazed eyes,
> As though he came to kill a cockatrice,
> Though he have oft sworn, that he would remove
> Thy beauty's beauty, and food of our love,
> Hope of his goods, if I with thee were seen,
> Yet close and secret, as our souls, we have been.

Exploiting and being exploited are taken as conditions of nature, which we share on equal terms with the beasts of the jungle and the ocean. In "Metempsychosis" a whale and a holder of great office behave in precisely the same way:

> He hunts not fish, but as an officer,
> Stays in his court, as his own net, and there
> All suitors of all sorts themselves enthral;
> So on his back lies this whale wantoning,
> And in his gulf-like throat, sucks everything
>   That passeth near.

Donne characterizes our natural life in the world as a condition of flux and momentariness, which we may nonetheless turn to our advantage, as in "Woman's Constancy":

> Now thou hast loved me one whole day,
> Tomorrow when thou leav'st, what wilt thou say?
> . . . .
> Vain lunatic, against these 'scapes I could
>   Dispute, and conquer, if I would,
>   Which I abstain to do,
> For by tomorrow, I may think so too.

In such a predicament our judgment of the world around us can have no absolute force but may at best measure people's endeavors relative to each other, as Donne points out in "Metempsychosis":

> There's nothing simply good, nor ill alone,
> Of every quality comparison,
>   The only measure is, and judge, opinion.

The tension of the poetry comes from the pull of divergent impulses in the argument itself. In "A

Valediction: Of my Name in the Window," the lover's name scratched in his mistress's window ought to serve as a talisman to keep her chaste; but then, as he explains to her, it may instead be an unwilling witness to her infidelity:

> When thy inconsiderate hand
> Flings ope this casement, with my trembling name,
>   To look on one, whose wit or land,
>   New battery to thy heart may frame,
> Then think this name alive, and that thou thus
>   In it offend'st my Genius.

So complex or downright contradictory is our state that quite opposite possibilities must be allowed for within the scope of a single assertion, as in *Satire 3*: "Kind pity chokes my spleen; brave scorn forbids / Those tears to issue which swell my eye-lids."

The opening lines of *Satire 3* confront us with a bizarre medley of moral questions: Should the corrupted state of religion prompt our anger or our grief? What devotion do we owe to religion, and which religion may claim our devotion? May the pagan philosophers be saved before Christian believers? What obligation of piety do children owe to their fathers in return for their religious upbringing? Then we get a quick review of issues such as the participation of Englishmen in foreign wars, colonizing expeditions, the Spanish auto-da-fé, and brawls over women or honor in the London streets. The drift of Donne's argument holds all these concerns together and brings them to bear upon the divisions of Christendom that lead men to conclude that any worldly cause must be more worthy of their devotion than the pursuit of a true Christian life. The mode of reasoning is characteristic: Donne calls in a variety of circumstances, weighing one area of concern against another so that we may appraise the present claim in relation to a whole range of unlike possibilities: "Is not this excuse for mere contraries, / Equally strong; cannot both sides say so?" The movement of the poem amounts to a sifting of the relative claims on our devotion that commonly distract us from our absolute obligation to seek the truth.

Some of Donne's sharpest insights into erotic experience, as his insights into social motives, follow out his sense of the bodily prompting of our most compelling urges, which are thus wholly subject to the momentary state of the physical organism itself. In "Farewell to Love" the end

The cottage at Mitcham where Donne and his family lived from 1606 until 1611 (woodcut after a sketch by Richard Simpson). The house was demolished in 1840.

that lovers so passionately pursue loses its attraction at once when they have gained it:

> Being had, enjoying it decays:
>   And thence,
> What before pleased them all, takes but one sense,
>   And that so lamely, as it leaves behind
> A kind of sorrowing dullness to the mind.

Yet the poet never gives the impression of forcing a doctrine upon experience. On the contrary, his skepticism sums up his sense of the way the world works.

Donne's love poetry expresses a variety of amorous experiences that are often startlingly unlike each other, or even contradictory in their implications. In "The Anniversary" he is not just being inconsistent when he moves from a justification of frequent changes of partners to celebrate a mutual attachment that is simply not subject to time, alteration, appetite, or the sheer pull of other worldly enticements:

> All kings, and all their favourites,
>   All glory of honours, beauties, wits,
> The sun itself, which makes times, as they pass,
> Is elder by a year, now, than it was
> When thou and I first one another saw:
> All other things, to their destruction draw,
>   Only our love hath no decay;
> This, no tomorrow hath, nor yesterday,
> Running it never runs from us away,
> But truly keeps his first, last, everlasting day.

The triumph the lovers proclaim here defies the state of flux it affirms.

Some of Donne's finest love poems, such as "A Valediction: forbidding Mourning," prescribe the condition of a mutual attachment that time and distance cannot diminish:

> Dull sublunary lovers' love
>   (Whose soul is sense) cannot admit
> Absence, because it doth remove
>   Those things which elemented it.
>
> But we by a love, so much refined,
>   That our selves know not what it is,
> Inter-assured of the mind,
>   Care less, eyes, lips, and hands to miss.

Donne finds some striking images to define this state in which two people remain wholly one while they are separated. Their souls are not divided but expanded by the distance between them, "Like gold to airy thinness beat"; or they move in response to each other as the legs of twin compasses, whose fixed foot keeps the moving foot steadfast in its path:

> Such wilt thou be to me, who must
>   Like th' other foot obliquely run;
> Thy firmness makes my circle just,
>   And makes me end, where I begun.

A supple argument unfolds with lyric grace.

It must be borne in mind that the poems editors group together were not necessarily produced thus. Donne did not write for publication. No more than seven poems and a bit of another poem were published during his lifetime, and only two of these publications were authorized by him. The poems he released were passed around in manuscript and transcribed by his admirers singly or in gatherings. Some of these copies have survived. When the first printed edition of his poems was published in 1633, two years after his death, the haphazard arrangement of the poems gave no clue to the order of their composition. Many modern editions of the poetry impose categorical divisions that are unlikely to correspond to the order of writing, separating the love poetry from the satires and the religious poetry, the verse letters from the epithalamiums and funeral poems. No more than a handful of Donne's poems can be dated with certainty. The *Elegies* and *Satires* are likely to have been written in the early 1590s. "Metempsychosis" is dated 16 August 1601. The two memorial *Anniversaries* for the death of Elizabeth Drury were certainly written in 1611 and 1612; and the funeral elegy on

Prince Henry must have been written in 1612. The *Songs and Sonnets* were evidently not conceived as a single body of love verses and do not appear so in early manuscript collections. Donne may well have composed them at intervals and in unlike situations over some twenty years of his poetic career. Some of them may even have overlapped with his best-known religious poems, which are likely to have been written about 1609, before he took holy orders.

Poems so vividly individuated invite attention to the circumstances that shaped them. Yet we have no warrant to read Donne's poetry as a record of his life or the expression of his inner disquiets. Donne's career and personality are nonetheless arresting in themselves, and they cannot be kept wholly separate from the general thrust of his writing, for which they at least provide a living context. Donne was born in London between 24 January and 19 June 1572 into the precarious world of English recusant Catholicism, whose perils his family well knew. His father, John Donne, was an ironmonger. His mother, Elizabeth (Heywood) Donne, a lifelong Catholic, was the greatniece of the martyred Sir Thomas More. His uncle Jasper Heywood headed an underground Jesuit mission in England from 1581 to 1583 and, when he was caught, was imprisoned and then exiled; Donne's younger brother, Henry, died from the plague in 1593 while being held in Newgate Prison for harboring a seminary priest. Yet at some time in his young manhood Donne himself converted to Anglicanism and never went back on that reasoned decision. Though he was a tradesman, Donne's father claimed descent from the Herbert family, and his mother was the daughter of John Heywood, epigrammatist and author of interludes. Donne's father died in January 1576, and within six months Elizabeth Donne had married John Syminges, an Oxford-educated physician with a practice in London. In October 1584 Donne entered Hart Hall, Oxford, where he remained for about three years. Though no records of his attendance at Cambridge are extant, he may have gone on to study there as well and may have accompanied his uncle Jasper Heywood on a trip to Paris and Antwerp during this time. It is known that he entered Lincoln's Inn in May 1592, after at least a year of preliminary study at Thavies Inn, and was at least nominally a student of English law for two or more years. After sailing as a gentleman adventurer with the English expeditions to Cadiz and the Azores in 1596 and 1597, he entered the service of Sir Thomas Egerton, the lord keeper of England. As Egerton's highly valued secretary he developed the keen interest in statecraft and foreign affairs that he retained throughout his life.

His place in the Egerton household also brought him into acquaintance with Egerton's domestic circle. Egerton's brother-in-law was Sir George More, parliamentary representative for Surrey, whose family seat was Loseley House near Guildford in Surrey. More came up to London for an autumn sitting of Parliament in 1601, bringing with him his daughter Ann, then seventeen. Ann More and Donne may well have met and fallen in love during some earlier visit to the Egerton household; they were clandestinely married in December 1601 in a ceremony arranged with the help of a small group of Donne's friends. Some months elapsed before Donne dared to break the news to the girl's father, by letter, provoking a violent response. Donne and his helpful friends were briefly imprisoned, and More set out to get the marriage annulled, demanding that Egerton dismiss his amorous secretary.

The marriage was eventually upheld; indeed, More became reconciled to it and to his son-in-law, but Donne lost his job in 1602 and did not find regular employment again until he took holy orders more than twelve years later. Throughout his middle years he and his wife brought up an ever-increasing family with the aid of relatives, friends, and patrons, and on the uncertain income he could bring in by polemical hackwork and the like. His anxious attempts to gain secular employment in the queen's household in Ireland, or with the Virginia Company, all came to nothing, and he seized the opportunity to accompany Sir Robert Drury on a diplomatic mission in France in 1612. From these frustrated years came most of the verse letters, funeral poems, epithalamiums, and holy sonnets, as well as the prose treatises *Biathanatos* (1647), *Pseudo-Martyr* (1610), and *Ignatius his Conclave* (1611).

In the writing of Donne's middle years, skepticism darkened into a foreboding of imminent ruin. Such poems as the two memorial *Anniversaries* and "To the Countess of Salisbury" register an accelerating decline of our nature and condition in a cosmos that is itself disintegrating. In "The First Anniversary" the poet declares,

> mankind decays so soon,
> We' are scarce our fathers' shadows cast at noon.

Verse letter to Lettice Rich, Lady Carey, written by Donne while he was abroad with Sir Robert Drury in 1612 (Bodleian Library, Oxford, MS. Eng. poet. d. 197). This letter is the only extant manuscript for an English-language poem by Donne written in Donne's own hand.

Hence comes yt that yor Beauty woundy not harts
As others, wth prophane and sensuall dartz,
But as an Influence vertuous thoughts imparts.
But if such frindz by the' honor of yor sight
Grow capable of thys so great a light,
As to partake yor virtues and theyr might,
what must I thinke that Influence must doe,
when yt findz Sympathy and Matter too,
Vertu, and Beauty, of the same stuffe, as yow.
wch ys, yor noble worthy Sister; shee,
of whom if what in thys my extasy,
And Revelation of yow both, I see,
I should write here, As in short Galleryes
The master at the end large glasses eyes,
So to present the roome twice to or eye;
So I should giue thys letter length, and say
That wch I sayd of yow, there ys no way
from eyther, but by th'other, not to stray.
May therfore thys bee' inough to testify
my true Deuotion, free from flattery.
He that beleeus himselfe, doth never ly.

To the ffourable lady
the lady Carew.

. . . .
And freely men confess that this world's spent,
When in the planets, and the firmament
They seek so many new; they see that this
Is crumbled out again to his atomies.
'Tis all in pieces, all coherence gone.

Donne contends that at this late stage of creation we exhibit a pitiful falling off from the early state of humankind:

There is not now that mankind, which was then,
When as the sun, and man, did seem to strive,
(Joint tenants of the world) who should survive.
. . . .
Where is this mankind now? who lives to age,
Fit to be made Methusalem his page?
Alas, we scarce live long enough to try
Whether a true made clock run right, or lie.

Our attempts to know the world by means of our natural powers are inevitably misconceived. For we seek to order a degenerating cosmos with our decaying faculties and to impose a stable pattern upon a condition of continual flux that we cannot even adequately measure, as Donne claims in "The Second Anniversary":

And what essential joy canst thou expect
Here upon earth? what permanent effect
Of transitory causes? Dost thou love
Beauty? (and beauty worthiest is to move)
Poor cozened cozener, that she, and that thou,
Which did begin to love, are neither now;
You are both fluid, changed since yesterday;
Next day repairs, (but ill) last day's decay.
Nor are, (although the river keep the name)
Yesterday's waters, and today's the same.
So flows her face, and thine eyes, neither now
That saint, nor pilgrim, which your loving vow
Concerned, remains; but whilst you think you be
Constant, you'are hourly in inconstancy.

In this condition of gathering uncertainty the very latest of our so-called discoveries are likely to be the most unsettling, as shown in these lines from "The First Anniversary":

And new philosophy calls all in doubt,
The element of fire is quite put out;
The sun is lost, and th'earth, and no man's wit
Can well direct him where to look for it.

Yet Donne is not counseling despair here. On the contrary, the *Anniversaries* offer a sure way out of spiritual dilemma: "thou hast but one way, not to admit / The world's infection, to be

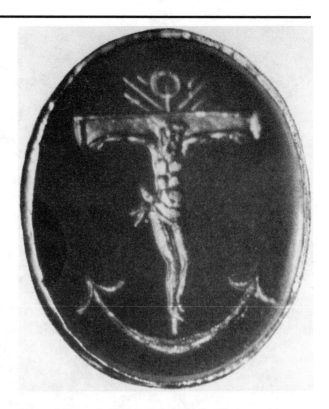

The seal Donne had made in 1615, when he began his career in the Church (Salisbury Cathedral Library)

none of it" ("The First Anniversary"). Moreover, the poems propose that a countering force is at work that resists the world's frantic rush toward its own ruin. Such amendment of corruption is the true purpose of our worldly being: "our business is, to rectify / Nature, to what she was" ("To Sir Edward Herbert, at Juliers"). But in the present state of the world, and ourselves, the task becomes heroic and calls for a singular resolution.

The verse letters and funeral poems celebrate those qualities of their subjects that stand against the general lapse toward chaos: "Be more than man, or thou'art less than an ant" ("The First Anniversary"). The foremost of these qualities must be innocence itself, for that is just the condition which Adam and Eve forfeited at the Fall. As an innocent person presents a pattern of our uncorrupted state, so an innocent death is an ambiguous event; for in itself it is no death at all; yet in its effects it reenacts the primal calamity. Elizabeth Drury's departure from the world left us dying but also better aware of our true state, as depicted in "The First Anniversary":

This world, in that great earthquake languished,
For in a common bath of tears it bled,
Which drew the strongest vital spirits out

> But succoured them with a perplexed doubt,
> Whether the world did lose, or gain in this.

With the loss of her preserving balm the world falls sick and dies, even putrefies, leaving the poet only the task of anatomizing it so as to demonstrate its corruption. Donne uncompromisingly carries this complex conceit of an innocent death right through the two anniversary poems for Elizabeth Drury, disregarding the practical disadvantage that he is thus led to attribute a great deal to a young girl he had not even met. Ben Jonson assured William Drummond "That Donne's *Anniversary* was profane and full of blasphemies," and said "That he told Mr. Donne, if it had been written of the Virgin Mary it had been something; to which he answered that he described *The Idea* of a woman and not as she was."

Donne does not seek to celebrate a uniquely miraculous nature or a transcendental virtue. He shows us how an innocent young girl effectively embodied in her own human nature the qualities that alone preserve the natural creation and why her death reenacts the withdrawal of those qualities from the world. He pointedly declines to take the girl for an emanation of the divine spirit, another Beatrice who rose above the flesh in her life and transcends the world finally in her death. On the contrary, Elizabeth Drury is celebrated for human excellences that are spiritually refined in themselves. She was a being in whom body and spirit were at one.

Most of the people Donne praised, alive or dead, were past the age of innocence. Yet the burden of the *Anniversary* poems is that Elizabeth Drury's death has shown us all how to resist the corrupting force of the world. A tried election of virtue is possible, though rarely achieved, which resists the common depravity of the Fall. Donne consoles a mourning woman with the conceit that she now incorporates her dead companion's virtues with her own, and has thus acquired the power to preserve both their beings from corruption: "You that are she and you, that's double she" ("To the Countess of Bedford"). He claims that a woman embodies all virtue in herself and sustains the world, so that "others' good reflects but back your light" ("To the Countess of Huntingdon"). He excoriates a blind world that unknowingly owes what little vitality it still retains to the virtue of a few moral prodigies who mediate Christ's own virtue, having the quasi-alchemic power to turn "Leaden and iron wills to good" and make "even sinful flesh like his" ("Resurrec-

Donne in 1616 (miniature by Isaac Oliver; Collection of Her Majesty the Queen, Windsor Castle)

tion, Imperfect"). Such virtuous beings rectify nature to what it was in their own bodies, so interfusing sense and spirit as to make an intelligent organism of the body itself, as depicted in "The Second Anniversary":

> we understood
> Her by her sight, her pure and eloquent blood
> Spoke in her cheeks, and so distinctly wrought,
> That one might almost say, her body thought.

These poems of Donne's middle years are less frequently read than the rest of his work, and they have struck readers as perversely obscure and odd. There is clearly some justification for that response, as seen in these lines from "The Second Anniversary":

> Immortal Maid, who though thy would'st refuse
> The name of mother, be unto my Muse
> A father, since her chaste ambition is,
> Yearly to bring forth such a child as this.

The poems flaunt their creator's unconcern with decorum to the point of shocking their readers. In his funeral poems Donne harps on decay and maggots, even venturing satiric asides as he contemplates bodily corruption: "Think thee a prince, who of themselves create / Worms which insensibly devour their state" ("The Second Anniversary"). He shows by the analogy of a beheaded man how it is that our dead world still appears to have life and movement ("The Second Anniversary"); he compares the soul in the newborn infant body with a "stubborn sullen anchorite" who sits "fixed to a pillar, or a grave / . . . / Bedded, and bathed in all his ordures" ("The Second Anniversary"); he develops in curious detail the conceit that virtuous men are clocks and that the late John Harrington, second Lord of Exton, was a public clock ("Obsequies to the Lord Harrington"). Such unsettling idiosyncrasy is too persistent to be merely wanton or sensational. It subverts our conventional proprieties in the interest of a radical order of truth.

Donne's reluctance to become a priest, as he was several times urged to do, does not argue a lack of faith. The religious poems he wrote years before he took orders dramatically suggest that his doubts concerned his own unworthiness, his sense that he could not possibly merit God's grace, as seen in these lines from *Divine Meditations 4*:

> Yet grace, if thou repent, thou canst not lack;
> But who shall give thee that grace to begin?
> Oh make thyself with holy mourning black,
> And red with blushing, as thou art with sin.

These *Divine Meditations*, or *Holy Sonnets*, make a universal drama of religious life, in which every moment may confront us with the final annulment of time: "What if this present were the world's last night?" (*Divine Meditations 13*). In *Divine Meditations 10* the prospect of a present entry upon eternity also calls for a showdown with ourselves and with the exemplary events that bring time and the timeless together in one order:

> Mark in my heart, O soul, where thou dost dwell,
> The picture of Christ crucified, and tell
> Whether that countenance can thee affright.

Christ's double nature, as God and man at once, assures his power to transform events in time; and it also confirms our power to outbrave our last enemy: "Death be not proud, though some have called thee / Mighty and dreadful, for, thou art not so." The ringing rhetoric sustains a mighty shout of defiance in *Divine Meditations 7*, proclaiming the possibility of a heroic triumph snatched from likely defeat:

> At the round earth's imagined corners, blow
> Your trumpets, angels, and arise, arise

> From death, you numberless infinities
> Of souls, and to your scattered bodies go.

Such a magnificent declamation gives our moral life the grandeur of a universal drama that is perpetually reenacted; it sets the trumpets blowing here and now to proclaim the sudden irruption of the Day of Judgment.

The poet is always fearfully aware that we cannot command such triumphs for ourselves, and that we may have part in them at all only by submitting ourselves to a course of repentance that will open us to God's grace at last. In *Divine Meditations 1* he states,

> But let them sleep, Lord, and me mourn a space,
> For, if above all these, my sins abound,
> 'Tis late to ask abundance of thy grace,
> When we are there; here on this lowly ground,
> Teach me how to repent.

The present moment may define us forever. We make our predicament immediate by imagining ourselves in mortal sickness, or at the point of final judgment, bringing ourselves sharply up against a reality that our daily lives obscure from us:

> I run to death, and death meets me as fast,
> And all my pleasures are like yesterday,
> I dare not move my dim eyes any way,
> Despair behind, and death before doth cast
> Such terror.

These *Divine Meditations* make self-recognition a necessary means to grace. They dramatize the spiritual dilemma of errant creatures who need God's grace in order that they may deserve it; for we must fall into sin and merit death even though our redemption is at hand; yet we cannot even begin to repent without grace. The poems open the sinner to God, imploring God's forceful intervention by the sinner's willing acknowledgment of the need for a drastic onslaught upon his present hardened state, as in *Divine Meditations 14*:

> Batter my heart, three-personed God; for, you
> As yet but knock, breathe, shine, and seek to mend;
> That I may rise, and stand, o'erthrow me, and bend
> Your force, to break, blow, burn, and make me
> new.

Anna

Georgij		More de		Filia
Roberti	{	Lothesley,	{	Soror:
Willelmj		Equit:		Nept:
Christophorj		Aurat:		proneft:

Fœminæ Lectissimæ, Dilectissimæqᵉ;
Coniugi charissimæ, castissimæqᵉ;
Matrj piissimæ, Indulgentissimæqᵉ;
XV annis in coniugio transactis,
vii post xii⁽ᵐ⁾partum (quorum vii superstant) dios
Ammani febre correpta,
(Quod hoc saxum farj iussit
Ipse, præ dolore Infans)
Maritus (miserrimum dictu) olim chara charus
Cineribus cineres spondet suos
Nouo matrimonio (annuat Deus) hoc loco sociandos.
Johannes Donne
Sacr: Theolog: profess:
Præfsit
Aᵒ xxxiiiᵒ Ætatis suæ et sui Iesu
(I) D C Xviiᵒ   231
Aug: xv.

Draft, in Donne's own hand, for the Latin epigraph he wrote for inscription on the monument to his wife, who died in childbirth on 15 August 1617 (Loseley MSS., Folger Shakespeare Library)

The force of the petition measures the dire extremity of his struggle with himself and with God's adversary. Donne pleads with God that he too has an interest in this contention for the sinner's soul: "Lest the world, flesh, yea Devil put thee out" (*Divine Meditations 17*). The drama brings home to the poet the enormity of his ingratitude to his Redeemer, confronting him bodily with the irony of Christ's self-humiliation for us. In *Divine Meditations 11* Donne wonders why the sinner should not suffer Christ's injuries in his own person:

> Spit in my face ye Jews, and pierce my side,
> Buffet, and scoff, scourge, and crucify me,
> For I have sinned, and sinned, and only he,
> Who could do no iniquity, hath died.

On the death of his wife in 1617 Donne's poetic response in *Divine Meditations 17* was movingly restrained and dignified:

> Since she whom I loved hath paid her last debt
> To nature, and to hers, and my good is dead,
> And her soul early into heaven ravished,
> Wholly in heavenly things my mind is set.

He turns his worldly loss to an occasion of final good in that he now finds only one sure way to be reunited with her. She becomes the means by which Christ woos his soul toward a remarriage in heaven: "But why should I beg more love, when as thou / Dost woo my soul for hers; offering all thine."

Donne's religious poems turn upon a paradox that is central to the hope for eternal life: Christ's sacrificing himself to save mankind. God's regimen is paradoxical, and in *Divine Meditations 13* Donne sees no impropriety in entreating Christ with the casuistry he had used on his "profane mistreses" when he assured them that only the ugly lack compassion:

> so I say to thee,
> To wicked spirits are horrid shapes assigned,
> This beauteous form assures a piteous mind.

In *Divine Meditations 18* he resolves his search for the true Church in a still bolder sexual paradox, petitioning Christ as a "kind husband" to betray his spouse to our view so that the poet's amorous soul may "court thy mild dove": "Who is most true, and pleasing to thee, then / When she'is embraced and open to most men." The apparent indecorum of making the true Church a whore and Christ her complaisant husband at least startles us into recognizing Christ's own catholicity. The paradox brings out a truth about Christ's Church that may well be shocking to those who uphold a sectarian exclusiveness.

Wit becomes the means by which the poet discovers the working of Providence in the casual traffic of the world. A journey westward from one friend's house to another over Easter 1613 brings home to Donne the general aberration of nature that prompts us to put pleasure before our due devotion to Christ. We ought to be heading east at Easter so as to contemplate and share Christ's suffering; and in summoning up that event to his mind's eye, he recognizes the shocking paradox of the ignominious death of God upon a Cross: "Could I behold those hands, which span the poles, / And turn all spheres at once, pierced with those holes?" ("Good Friday, 1613. Riding Westward"). An image of Christ's degradation is directly imposed upon an image of God's omnipotence. We see that the event itself has a double force, being at once the catastrophic consequence of our sin and the ultimate assurance of God's saving love. The poet's very journey west may be providential if it brings him to a penitent recognition of his present unworthiness to gaze directly upon Christ:

> O Saviour, as thou hang'st upon the tree;
> I turn my back to thee, but to receive
> Corrections, till thy mercies bid thee leave.
> O think me worth thine anger, punish me,
> Burn off my rusts, and my deformity,
> Restore thine image, so much, by thy grace,
> That thou mayest know me, and I'll turn my face.

A serious illness that Donne suffered in 1623 produced a still more startling poetic effect. In "Hymn to God, my God, in my Sickness" the poet presents his recumbent body as a flat map over which the doctors pore like navigators to discover some passage through present dangers to tranquil waters; and he ponders his own destination as if he himself is a vessel that may reach the desirable places of the world only by negotiating some painful straits:

> Is the Pacific Sea my home? Or are
>   The eastern riches? Is Jerusalem?
> Anyan, and Magellan, and Gibraltar,
>   All straits, and none but straits, are ways to
>   them.

John Donne, circa 1620 (from the school of Cornelius Janssen; Dyce Collection, Victoria and Albert Museum). This painting may be a copy of the portrait by an unknown artist in the Deanery of St. Paul's Cathedral.

By this self-questioning he brings himself to understand that his suffering may itself be a blessing, since he shares the condition of a world in which our ultimate bliss must be won through well-endured hardship. The physical symptoms of his illness become the signs of his salvation: "So, in his purple wrapped receive me Lord, / By these his thorns give me his other crown." The images that make him one with Christ in his suffering transform those pangs into reassurance. The flushed face of the fevered man replicates Christ's bloodied flesh, which is also the purple robe of Christ's saving dominion; the sufferer's spasms of pain become the thorns of Christ's crown, which is also a true crown of glory. By intertwining Christ's agony and loving power with the circumstances of his own desperate illness, Donne identifies the travails of a holy death with Christ's anguish on the Cross, making such a death a means to bliss. His witty conceit seeks to catch the working of Providence itself, which shapes our human accidents in the pattern of timeless truth.

In Donne's poetry, language may catch the presence of God in our human dealings. The pun on the poet's name in "A Hymn to God the Father" registers the distance that the poet's sins have put between himself and God, with new kinds of sin pressing forward as fast as God forgives those already confessed: "When thou hast done, thou hast not done, / For, I have more." Then the puns on "sun" and "Donne" resolve these sinful anxieties themselves:

> I have a sin of fear, that when I have spun
> 　My last thread, I shall perish on the shore;
> But swear by thy self, that at my death thy son
> 　Shall shine as he shines now, and heretofore;
> 　　And, having done that, thou hast done,
> 　　　I fear no more.

For this poet such coincidences of words and ideas are not mere accidents to be juggled with in jest. They mark precisely the working of Providence within the order of nature.

The transformation of Jack Donne the rake into the Reverend Dr. Donne, dean of St. Paul's Cathedral, no longer seems bizarre. To impose

The nave of Old St. Paul's Cathedral, of which Donne became dean in November 1621. The cathedral was destroyed by the Great Fire of London in 1666 (engraving by Wenceslaus Hollar, 1652).

such clear-cut categories upon a man's career may be to take too rigid a view of human nature. That the poet of the *Elegies* and *Songs and Sonnets* is also the author of the *Devotions* and the sermons need not indicate some profound spiritual upheaval. One reason for the appeal of Donne in modern times is that he confronts us with the complexity of our own natures.

Donne took holy orders in January 1615, having been persuaded by King James himself of his fitness for a ministry "to which he was, and appeared, very unwilling, apprehending it (such was his mistaking modesty) to be too weighty for his abilities." So writes his first biographer, Izaak Walton, who had known him well and often heard him preach. Once committed to the Church, Donne devoted himself to it totally, and his life thereafter becomes a record of incumbencies held and sermons preached.

His wife died in childbirth in 1617. He was elected dean of St. Paul's in November 1621, and he became the most celebrated cleric of his age, preaching frequently before the king at court as well as at St. Paul's and other churches. One hundred and sixty of his sermons have survived. The few religious poems he wrote after he became a priest show no falling off in imaginative power, yet the calling of his later years committed him to prose, and the artistry of his *Devotions* and sermons at least matches the artistry of his poems.

The magnificent prose of Donne's *Devotions* embodies a way of thinking that gives it both its character and its power. The impassioned development of a thought through metaphor sets up links and correspondences that are caught in the structure of the sentences themselves, as witnessed in this prayer, number 20 in *Devotions Upon Emergent Occasions*:

I am come by thy goodness, to the use of thine ordinary means for my *body*, to wash away those *peccant humours*, that endangered it. I have, O Lord, a *River* in my *body*, but a *Sea* in my *soul*, and a *Sea* swollen into the depth of a *Deluge*, above the *sea*. Thou hast raised up certain *hills* in me heretofore, by which I might have stood safe, from these *inundations* of *sin* . . . and to the *top* of all these *hills*, thou has brought me heretofore; but this *Deluge*, this *inundation*, is got above all my *Hills*; and I have sinned and sinned, and multiplied *sin* to *sin*, after all these thy assistances against *sin*, and where is there *water* enough to wash away this *Deluge*?

The highly dramatic counterpointing of the syntax follows out an elaborate pattern of understanding. This set of twenty-three *Devotions* presents a prime example of the attempt to find an eternal significance in the natural occurrences of the world, even such a down-to-earth proceeding as a forced evacuation of the bowels to relieve a physical malady.

Donne wrote his *Devotions* in his convalescence from a protracted bout of relapsing fever that brought him very near to death in November and December 1623. He plots in formal stages the day-to-day physical progress of the illness, discovering in it nothing less than a universal pattern of ruin and (as it turns out) recovery. By taking his own constitution for a little world that reproduces the economy of the larger world, he works out in elaborate detail the correspondence between his present predicament and the disordered state of nature. As his illness is no mere physical accident but the embodiment of a spiritual condition, so the whole of nature itself now decays in consequence of reiterated sin. At the very nadir of his being Donne contemplates the prospect of his imminent death, as well as the final ruination of the world, by occasion of the death of another human being whose funeral bell he hears tolling close at hand. The celebrated passage from number 17 in *Devotions Upon Emergent Occasions* gains power in its context:

> Perchance he for whom this *Bell* tolls, may be so ill, as that he knows not it *tolls* for him; And perchance I may think my self so much better than I am, as that they who are about me, and see my state, may have caused it to toll for me, and I know not that. The *Church* is *Catholic, universal,* so are all her *Actions; All* that she does, belongs to *all.* When she *baptizes a child,* that action concerns me . . . who bends not his *ear* to any *bell,* which upon any occasion rings? But who can remove it from that *bell,* which is passing a *piece of himself* out of this *world?* No Man is an *Island,* entire of it self; every man is a piece of the *Continent,* a part of the *main;* if a *Clod* be washed away by the *Sea, Europe* is the less, as well as if a *Promontory* were, as well as if a *Manor* of thy *friends,* or of *thine own* were; Any Man's *death* diminishes *me,* because I am involved in *Mankind;* And therefore never send to know for whom the *bell* tolls; It tolls for *thee.*

It is thus harrowingly brought home to him that his own predicament is not particular to himself but shared with the whole of nature. All funeral bells toll for us all, as well as for our dying world.

However, the sudden and unexpected remission of his fear also realizes a spiritual truth. A countermovement against the rush to ruin may save us and the world if we will sustain it in our lives. Christ's blood can counteract the seas of sin that threaten to inundate the world. In one man's extremity the universal design of Providential love discloses itself, and Donne's formal meditation on his sickness stands as a powerfully sustained feat of thinking that discovers the coherence of God's creation in the very fortuities that seem to deny it.

The publication in 1919 of *Donne's Sermons: Selected Passages,* edited by Logan Pearsall Smith, came as a revelation to its readers, not least those who had little taste for sermons. John Bailey, writing in the *Quarterly Review* (April 1920), found in these extracts "the very genius of oratory . . . a masterpiece of English prose." Sir Arthur Quiller-Couch, in *Studies in Literature* (1920), judged the sermons to include "the most magnificent prose ever uttered from an English pulpit, if not the most magnificent prose ever spoken in our tongue."

Donne's best-known sermon, *Deaths Duell* (1632), is his last one, which he preached at court just a month before he expired. He was already visibly dying, and this sermon is often taken to seal his long preoccupation with death. In fact it celebrates a triumph over death that is confirmed by the Resurrection of Christ. Donne draws out three distinct senses of his text from Psalm 68, "And unto God the Lord belong the issues Of death." God has power to bring about our deliverance *from* death; our deliverance *in* death (by his care for us in the hour and manner of our death); and our deliverance *by means of* death (through Christ's sacrifice of himself for us). By examining each of these senses in turn, Donne shows that they finally cohere in Christ's life. The sermon culminates in a meditation upon Christ's last hours and sufferings, inviting the reader to acquiesce in oneness with Christ's own condition, just because he is the second Adam, who redeems the sin of the first:

> There we leave you, in that blessed dependency, to hang upon him, that hangs upon the cross. There bathe in his tears, there suck at his wounds, and lie down in peace in his grave, till he vouchsafe you a Resurrection, and an ascension into that Kingdom which he hath purchased

Donne in his shroud, frontispiece to Deaths Duell *(1632), the sermon he preached a month before his death. This engraving by Martin Droeshout is after a drawing that was also the basis for the memorial statue of Donne in St. Paul's Cathedral.*

for you, with the inestimable price of his incorruptible blood.

Over a literary career of some forty years Donne moved from skeptical naturalism to a conviction of the shaping presence of the divine spirit in the natural creation. Yet his mature understanding did not contradict his earlier vision. He simply came to anticipate a Providential disposition in the restless whirl of the world. The amorous adventurer nurtured the dean of St. Paul's.

Letters:

Letters to Severall Persons of Honour, edited by John Donne, Jr. (London: Printed by J. Flesher for Richard Marriott, 1651); facsimile, introduction by M. Thomas Hester (Delmar, N.Y.: Scholars' Facsimiles & Reprints, 1977);

A Collection of Letters, Made by Sʳ Tobie Mathews,

Kt., edited by John Donne, Jr. (London: Printed for Henry Herringman, 1660).

Bibliographies:

Geoffrey Keynes, *A Bibliography of Dr. John Donne: Dean of St. Paul's*, fourth edition (Oxford: Clarendon Press, 1973);

John R. Roberts, *John Donne: An Annotated Bibliography of Modern Criticism, 1912-1967* (Columbia: University of Missouri Press, 1973);

A. J. Smith, ed., *John Donne: The Critical Heritage* (London & Boston: Routledge & Kegan Paul, 1975);

Roberts, *John Donne: An Annotated Bibliography of Modern Criticism, 1968-1978* (Columbia: University of Missouri Press, 1982).

Biographies:

Izaak Walton, *The Lives of Dr. John Donne, Sir*

Henry Wotton, Mr. Richard Hooker, Mr. George Herbert, and Robert Sanderson (London: Printed by Tho. Newcomb for Richard Marriott, 1670)—the *Life of Dr. John Donne* first appeared in the 1640 edition of Donne's *LXXX Sermons*;

Augustus Jessopp, *John Donne, Sometime Dean of St. Paul's A. D. 1621-1631* (London: Methuen, 1897);

Sir Edmund Gosse, *The Life and Letters of John Donne*, 2 volumes (London: Heinemann, 1899);

Hugh I'Anson Fausset, *John Donne: A Study in Discord* (London: Cape, 1924; New York: Harcourt, Brace, 1925);

R. C. Bald, *Donne and the Drurys* (Cambridge: Cambridge University Press, 1959);

Edward LeComte, *Grace to a Witty Sinner: A Life of John Donne* (New York: Walker, 1965);

Bald, *John Donne: A Life* (New York & Oxford: Oxford University Press, 1970).

References:

N. J. C. Andreasen, *John Donne: Conservative Revolutionary* (Princeton: Princeton University Press, 1967);

John Bailey, "The Sermons of a Poet," *Quarterly Review*, 463 (April 1920): 317-328;

R. C. Bald, *Donne's Influence in English Literature* (Morpeth, U.K.: St. John's College Press, 1932);

Joan Bennett, *Four Metaphysical Poets: Donne, Herbert, Vaughan, Crashaw* (Cambridge: Cambridge University Press, 1934);

Louis I. Bredvold, "The Naturalism of Donne in Relation to Some Renaissance Traditions," *Journal of English and Germanic Philology*, 22, no. 4 (1923): 471-502;

Douglas Bush, *English Literature in the Earlier Seventeenth Century, 1600-1660* (Oxford: Clarendon Press, 1945);

John Carey, *John Donne: Life, Mind and Art* (New York: Oxford University Press, 1981);

Dwight Cathcart, *Doubting Conscience: Donne and the Poetry of Moral Argument* (Ann Arbor: University of Michigan Press, 1975);

Charles Monroe Coffin, *John Donne and the New Philosophy* (New York: Columbia University Press, 1937);

Rosalie L. Colie, *Paradoxia Epidemica: The Renaissance Tradition of Paradox* (Princeton: Princeton University Press, 1966);

Patrick Cruttwell, *The Shakespearean Moment and Its Place in the Poetry of the 17th Century* (London: Chatto & Windus, 1954);

Joseph E. Duncan, *The Revival of Metaphysical Poetry: The History of a Style, 1800 to the Present* (Minneapolis: University of Minnesota Press, 1959);

T. S. Eliot, "The Metaphysical Poets," *Times Literary Supplement*, 20 October 1921, pp. 669-670;

William Empson, "Donne the Space Man," *Kenyon Review*, 19 (Summer 1957): 337-399;

Barbara Everett, *Donne: A London Poet* (London: Oxford University Press, 1972);

Anne Ferry, *All in War with Time: Love Poetry of Shakespeare, Donne, Jonson, Marvell* (Cambridge, Mass.: Harvard University Press, 1975);

Ferry, *The "Inward" Language: Sonnets of Wyatt, Sidney, Shakespeare, Donne* (Chicago: University of Chicago Press, 1983);

Peter Amadeus Fiore, ed., *Just So Much Honor: Essays Commemorating the Four-Hundredth Anniversary of the Birth of John Donne* (University Park: Pennsylvania State University Press, 1972);

Dennis Flynn, "Donne and the Ancient Catholic Nobility," *English Literary Renaissance*, 19 (Autumn 1989): 305-323;

Flynn, "Donne's Catholicism," *Recusant History*, 13 (April 1975): 1-17; (April 1976): 178-195;

Helen Gardner, ed., *John Donne: A Collection of Critical Essays* (Englewood Cliffs, N.J.: Prentice-Hall, 1962);

K. W. Gransden, *John Donne* (London & New York: Longmans, Green, 1954);

Donald L. Guss, *John Donne, Petrarchist* (Detroit: Wayne State University Press, 1966);

M. Thomas Hester, *Kinde Pitty and Brave Scorn: John Donne's Satyres* (Durham, N.C.: Duke University Press, 1982);

Hester and R. V. Young, Jr., eds., *John Donne Journal*, 1982- ;

Merritt Y. Hughes, "Kidnapping Donne," *University of California Publications in English*, 4 (1934): 61-89;

Richard E. Hughes, *The Progress of the Soul: The Interior Career of John Donne* (New York: William Morrow, 1968);

Clay Hunt, *Donne's Poetry: Essays in Literary Analysis* (New Haven: Yale University Press, 1954);

Robert S. Jackson, *John Donne's Christian Vocation* (Evanston, Ill.: Northwestern University Press, 1970);

Frank Kermode, "Dissociation of Sensibility," *Kenyon Review*, 19 (Spring 1957): 169-194;

F. R. Leavis, "The Influence of Donne on Modern Poetry," *Bookman*, 79 (March 1931): 346-347;

Pierre Legouis, *Donne the Craftsman* (Paris: Didier, 1928);

J. B. Leishman, *The Monarch of Wit: An Analytical and Comparative Study of the Poetry of John Donne* (London: Hutchinson University Library, 1951);

C. S. Lewis, *English Literature in the Sixteenth Century Excluding Drama* (Oxford: Clarendon Press, 1954);

Anthony Low, *Love's Architecture: Devotional Modes in Seventeenth-Century English Poetry* (New York: New York University Press, 1978);

M. M. Mahood, *Poetry and Humanism* (New Haven: Yale University Press, 1950);

Arthur F. Marotti, *John Donne, Coterie Poet* (Madison: University of Wisconsin Press, 1986);

Louis L. Martz, *The Poetry of Meditation: A Study in English Religious Literature of the Seventeenth Century* (New Haven: Yale University Press, 1954);

Marjorie Hope Nicolson, *The Breaking of the Circle: Studies in the Effect of the "New Science" upon Seventeenth Century Poetry* (Evanston, Ill.: Northwestern University Press, 1950);

David Novarr, *The Disinterred Muse: Donne's Texts and Contexts* (Ithaca, N.Y.: Cornell University Press, 1980);

Douglas L. Peterson, *The English Lyric from Wyatt to Donne* (Princeton: Princeton University Press, 1967);

Sir Arthur Quiller-Couch, *Studies in Literature* (Cambridge: Cambridge University Press, 1920), pp. 96-117;

John R. Roberts, ed., *Essential Articles for the Study of John Donne's Poetry* (Hamden, Conn.: Archon, 1975);

Murray Roston, *The Soul of Wit: A Study of John Donne* (Oxford: Clarendon Press, 1974);

Terry G. Sherwood, *Fulfilling the Circle: A Study of John Donne's Thought* (Toronto & Buffalo: University of Toronto Press, 1984);

Evelyn M. Simpson, *A Study of the Prose Works of John Donne* (Oxford: Clarendon Press, 1924);

Thomas O. Sloane, *Donne, Milton, and the End of Humanist Rhetoric* (Berkeley: University of California Press, 1985);

A. J. Smith, ed., *John Donne: Essays in Celebration* (London: Methuen, 1972);

Smith, *The Metaphysics of Love: Studies in Renaissance Love Poetry from Dante to Milton* (Cambridge & New York: Cambridge University Press, 1985);

James Smith, "On Metaphysical Poetry," *Scrutiny*, 2 (December 1933): 222-239;

Theodore Spencer, ed., *A Garland for John Donne, 1631-1931* (Cambridge, Mass.: Harvard University Press, 1931);

Arnold Stein, *John Donne's Lyrics: The Eloquence of Action* (Minneapolis: University of Minnesota Press, 1962);

Claude J. Summers and Ted-Larry Pebworth, eds., *The Eagle and the Dove: Reassessing John Donne* (Columbia: University of Missouri Press, 1986);

Edward W. Tayler, *Donne's Idea of a Woman: Structure and Meaning in "The Anniversaries"* (New York: Columbia University Press, 1991);

Rosemond Tuve, *Elizabethan and Metaphysical Imagery: Renaissance Poetic and Twentieth-Century Critics* (Chicago: University of Chicago Press, 1947);

Leonard Unger, *Donne's Poetry and Modern Criticism* (Chicago: Regnery, 1950);

Helen C. White, *The Metaphysical Poets: A Study in Religious Experience* (New York: Macmillan, 1936);

Baird W. Whitlock, "Donne's University Years," *English Studies*, 43 (February 1962): 1-20;

George Williamson, *The Donne Tradition: A Study in English Poetry from Donne to the Death of Cowley* (Cambridge, Mass.: Harvard University Press, 1930);

Yvor Winters, "The 16th Century Lyric in England: A Critical and Historical Reinterpretation," *Poetry*, 53 (February 1939): 258-272.

Papers:

With the exception of the *Anniversaries*, almost none of Donne's poems were published during his lifetime; only one poem survives in his holograph. The texts for all others derive from more than two hundred pieces of manuscript evidence, the majority of which are catalogued by Peter Beal in *Index to English Literary Manuscripts*, volume one (London: R. R. Bowker, 1980). A forthcoming project under the general editorship of Gary Stringer, *The Variorum Edition of the Poetry of John Donne*, aims to account for the complete textual and critical history of Donne's poems.

Michael Drayton

(1563 - December 1631)

Jean R. Brink
Arizona State University

BOOKS: *The Harmonie of the Church. Containing, The Spirituall Songes and holy Hymnes, of godly men* (London: Printed by T. Orwin for R. Jhones, 1591);

Idea. The Shepheards Garland, Fashioned in nine Eglogs. Rowlands Sacrifice to the Nine Muses (London: Printed by T. Orwin for T. Woodcocke, 1593); revised as *Poemes Lyrick and pastorall. Odes, Eglogs, The Man in the Moone* (London: Printed by R. Bradock for N. Ling & J. Flasket, 1606);

Peirs Gaueston. Earle of Cornwall. His life, death, and fortune (London: Printed by J. Roberts for N. Ling & John Busby, 1594?);

Ideas Mirrovr. Amovrs in qvatorzains (London: Printed by J. Roberts for N. Linge, 1594);

Matilda. The faire and chaste Daughter of the Lord Robert Fitzwater (London: Printed by J. Roberts for N. Ling & J. Busby, 1594);

Endimion and Phœbe. Ideas Latmvs (London: Printed by James Roberts for John Busbie, 1595);

Mortimeriados. The Lamentable ciuell warres of Edward the second and the Barrons (London: Printed by J. Roberts for Mathew Lownes, 1596); revised as *The Barrons Wars in the raigne of Edward the Second. With Englands Heroicall Epistles* (London: Printed by J. Roberts for N. Ling, 1603);

The Tragicall Legend of Robert, Duke of Normandy, With the Legend of Matilda the chast, daughter to the Lord Robert Fitzwater, poysoned by King Iohn. And the Legend of Piers Gaueston, the great Earle of Cornwall: and mighty fauorite of king Edward the second. By Michaell Drayton. The latter two, by him newly corrected and augmented (London: Printed by J. Roberts for N. Ling, 1596);

Englands Heroicall Epistles (London: Printed by J. Roberts for N. Ling, 1597); revised and enlarged edition [adds five new epistles and deletes dedications to William Parker, fourth Baron Monteagle, and Lord Henry Howard] (London: Printed by P. Short for N. Ling, 1598); revised and enlarged, with

Michael Drayton (portrait by an unknown artist; Dulwich College)

Idea [adds Geraldine's reply to Surrey, completing the twenty-four epistles] (London: Printed by J. Roberts for N. Ling, 1599); revised, with *Idea* [allusions to Robert Devereux, second Earl of Essex, are deleted, especially from the epistles of Richard II and Isabella; sonnets to James VI of Scotland and others appended] (London: Printed by J. Roberts for N. Ling, 1600); revised and enlarged, with *Idea* [epistles of Edward the Black Prince and Alice, Countess of Salisbury, added] (London: Printed by R. Roberts for N. Ling, 1602);

The first part OF the true and honorable historie, of the life of Sir John Old-castle, the good Lord Cobham, by Drayton, Richard Hathway, Anthony Munday, and Robert Wilson (London: Printed by V. Simmes for Thomas Pauier, 1600);

To the Maiestie of King James. A gratulatorie Poem (London: Printed by J. Roberts for T. Man & H. Lownes, 1603);

The Owle (London: Printed by E. Allde for E. White & N. Ling, 1604);

A Pæan Trivmphall. Composed for the Societie of the Goldsmiths of London (London: Printed by F. Kingston for J. Flasket, 1604);

Moyses in a Map of his Miracles (London: Printed by H. Lownes, sold by T. Man the younger, 1604);

Poems: by Michaell Draiton esquire (London: Printed by V. Simmes for N. Ling, 1605; revised edition, London: Printed by H. Ballard for J. Smethwicke, 1608);

The Legend of Great Cromwel (London: Printed by Felix Kyngston, sold by I. Flasket, 1607); republished as *The historie of the life and death of the lord Cromwell* (London: Printed by F. Kyngston for W. Welby, 1609);

Poly-Olbion (London: Printed by H. Lownes for M. Lownes, J. Browne, J. Helme & J. Busbie, 1612);

Poems by Michael Drayton Esqvyer (London: Printed by W. Stansby for J. Swethwicke, 1619);

The Second Part, or a continvance of Poly-Olbion (London: Printed by A. Mathewes for J. Marriott, J. Grismand & T. Dewe, 1622);

The Battaile of Agincovrt. Fovght by Henry the fift of that name, King of England, against the whole power of the French: vnder the Raigne of their Charles the sixt, Anno Dom. 1415. The Miseries of Queene Margarite, the infortunate Wife, of that most infortunate King Henry the sixt. Nimphidia, the Court of Fayrie. The Quest of Cinthia. The Shepheards Sirena. The Moone-Calfe. Elegies vpon Sundry Occasions (London: Printed by A. Mathewes for W. Lee, 1627);

The Muses Elizivm, Lately discouered, By a New Way Over Parnassvs. The passages therein, being the subiect of ten sundry Nymphalls, Leading three Diuine Poemes: Noahs Floud. Moses, his Birth and Miracles. David and Golia (London: Printed by Thomas Harper for John Waterson, 1630).

Editions: *Minor Poems of Michael Drayton*, edited by Cyril Brett (Oxford: Clarendon Press, 1907);

Poems of Michael Drayton, 2 volumes, edited by John Buxton (Cambridge, Mass.: Harvard University Press, 1953);

The Works of Michael Drayton, 5 volumes, volumes 1-4 edited by William Hebel, volume 5 edited by Hebel, Kathleen Tillotson, and Bernard H. Newdigate (Oxford: Printed at Shakespeare Head Press, and published by Basil Blackwell, 1931-1941; revised edition, 1961).

PLAY PRODUCTIONS: *The Famous Wars of Henry I and the Prince of Wales* (also known as *The Welshman's Prize*), by Drayton, Henry Chettle, and Thomas Dekker, London, Rose theater, March 1598;

Earl Goodwin and his Three Sons, parts 1 and 2, by Drayton, Chettle, Dekker, and Robert Wilson, London, Rose theater, spring 1598;

The Funeral of Richard Coeur-de-Lion, by Drayton, Chettle, Anthony Munday, and Wilson, London, Rose theater, June 1598;

Hannibal and Hermes, part 1 (also known as *Worse Afeard than Hurt*), by Drayton, Dekker, and Wilson, London, Rose theater, July 1598;

The Madman's Morris, by Drayton, Dekker, and Wilson, London, Rose theater, July 1598;

Pierce of Winchester, by Drayton, Dekker, and Wilson, London, Rose theater, July-August 1598;

Worse Afeard than Hurt (presumably part 2 of *Hannibal and Hermes*), by Drayton and Dekker, London, Rose theater, September 1598;

The Civil Wars of France, parts 1, 2, and 3, by Drayton and Dekker, London, Rose theater, autumn 1598;

Connan Prince of Cornwall, by Drayton and Dekker, London, Rose theater, October 1598;

Chance Medley, by Drayton, Chettle or Dekker, Munday, and Wilson, unknown theater, circa 1598;

Mother Redcap, by Drayton and Munday, London, Rose theater, circa 1598;

Pierce of Exton, by Drayton, Chettle, Dekker, and Wilson, unknown theater, circa 1598;

The first part of the true and honorable historie, of the life of Sir John Old-castle, the good Lord Cobham, by Drayton, Richard Hathway, Munday, and Wilson, London, unknown theater, Company of Earl of Nottingham, Lord High Admiral of England, 1599;

William Longsword, by Drayton and others, unknown theater, circa 1599;

Fair Constance of Rome, part 1, by Drayton, Dekker, Hathway, Munday, and Wilson, London, Rose theater, June 1600;

Fair Constance of Rome, part 2, by Drayton, Hathway, and others, unknown theater, 1600-1601;

Sir John Oldcastle, part 2, by Drayton, Hathway, Munday, and Wilson, unknown theater, 1600-1601;

Owen Tudor, by Drayton, Hathway, Munday, and Wilson, unknown theater, 1600-1601;

The Life and Rising of Cardinal Wolsey, by Drayton, Chettle, Munday, and Wentworth Smith, London, Fortune theater, August-November 1601;

Caesar's Fall, or the Two Shapes, by Drayton, Dekker, Thomas Middleton, Munday, and John Webster, London, Fortune theater, May 1602.

In late-seventeenth-century estimates of literary stature, Michael Drayton ranks only slightly below Sir Philip Sidney, Edmund Spenser, and Ben Jonson. Until the middle of the twentieth century, Drayton's position as an important minor poet seemed secure, but his lengthy historical poems did not lend themselves to the techniques of close reading popularized during the vogue of New Criticism in the 1940s and after. An intellectual heir of the humanists, Drayton believed in the tradition of *bonae litterae* and envisioned the poet as a spokesman for public values. He was born during the reign of Elizabeth but lived through the Jacobean and into the Caroline period. By the end of his life, the didactic verse and historical epics upon which Drayton had lavished so much care no longer commanded an audience. The division between poetry and history had broadened, and that breach had undermined the great humanist tradition and its assumption that epic poetry grounded in the history of a nation towered over all other genres. Drayton's own remarkable historical self-consciousness enabled him to understand and to record in his works the changes in the role of the poet that occurred during his lifetime.

Few documentary sources exist for the life of Michael Drayton, and even those that have survived and can be verified are not very revealing. He was born in the vicinity of Hartshill village, Mancetter parish, Warwickshire, early in 1563. His social status was inferior to that of William Shakespeare and well below that of Edmund Spenser or Samuel Daniel, both of whom obtained university degrees. Though early-twentieth-century editors and critics constructed a gentrified version of his life based on autobiographical anecdotes gleaned from his works, Drayton's origins were humble. Dedications, which he intended as bids for patronage, were interpreted literally as factual records of his social and literary milieu.

The anecdote used to construct Drayton's genteel background as page in the household of Sir Henry Goodyer the elder (1534-1595) occurs as an aside in a poem, which he published when he was sixty-four. In "Of Poets and Poesie" (1627), an elegy addressed to Henry Reynolds, Drayton reminisces about his youth, as "a proper goodly page," and reports that he asked his tutor "what strange kinde of men" poets were. His "milde Tutor" directs him in vintage Elizabethan fashion to Latin classics: *Mantuan*, Virgil's *Eclogues*, and *William Elderton*. Drayton's account of his education offers no particulars; his "milde Tutor" might be anyone from a clergyman who educated promising village children to the schoolmaster of a grammar school, but it was later interpreted as referring to a tutor employed by Sir Henry Goodyer or to Goodyer himself.

No seventeenth- or eighteenth-century biography mentions connections between Drayton and the Goodyers. However, in the late nineteenth century Drayton's allusion was interpreted as a reference to Sir Henry Goodyer and used to construct his privileged youth at Polesworth, Sir Henry's country manor. The first editor to interpret the "goodly page" reference as anything other than a literary allusion was John Payne Collier, who argued that Drayton was a page in the household of Sir Walter Devereux on the grounds that Drayton's first publication was dedicated in 1591 to Lady Jane Devereux, sister-in-law to Sir Walter. Collier is also the first biographer to mention a possible patronage relationship between Drayton and the Goodyers, but he dismisses any intimate connection on the grounds that nothing is heard of the Goodyer family in Drayton's work before 1597. Drayton's sheltered youth at Polesworth was invented by Oliver Elton in his 1895 *Introduction to Michael Drayton* and influenced all subsequent studies of Drayton. Elton writes: "By some chance, or through the brightness of his parts, Michael Drayton, while yet a little boy, was picked out and made a man of by a house of gentlefolk in the same countryside." Drayton's reference to a "milde Tutor" was even used to bestow a university degree upon him. The *Dictionary of National Biography* article

Drayton in 1599 (portrait by an unknown artist; National Portrait Gallery, London)

on Sir Henry Goodyer mentions that Drayton was assisted at the university by Sir Henry, but, in fact, there is no record of Michael Drayton's having received a university degree. The extant documentary evidence indicates that Drayton spent his youth not at Polesworth but in the household of Thomas Goodyer, Sir Henry's younger brother, and that he was employed not as a "goodly page" but as a servant.

The twentieth-century gentrification of Drayton has established the grounds for critical approaches to his work. Poems that do not fit the mild and inoffensive image constructed for Drayton have been overlooked or dismissed. His numerous assaults on title and privilege have been ignored because they do not ring true as the docile reflections of a "goodly page." Drayton was highly critical of the pro-Spanish foreign policy initiated by James I, and he despised the manners and morals of the Jacobean court. His contemporaries regarded him as honest and out-

spoken. His one surviving portrait depicts him as a satiric laureate: represented as wearing the traditional laurel wreath of the poet in the frontispiece to the 1619 folio edition of his works, he is portrayed as frowning in disapproval.

By 1590 Drayton had probably located in London. After publishing *The Harmonie of the Church*, verse translations from Old Testament prayers, in 1591, he experimented with a series of genres between 1591 and 1595, including the pastoral, the sonnet sequence, and the minor epic. His efforts in these genres were related, as repetition of "Idea" in the title of each poem suggests: *Idea. The Shepheards Garland* (1593), *Ideas Mirrour* (1594), *Endimion and Phœbe. Ideas Latmus* (1595). It is significant that not one of these early poems is dedicated to the Goodyers: *Idea. The Shepheards Garland*, pastoral eclogues modeled on Spenser's *Shepheardes Calender* (1579), is dedicated to Robert Dudley; *Peirs Gaveston* (1594?), an experiment with the historical complaint, is dedicated to Henry Cavendish; *Ideas Mirrour*, a sequence of fifty-one poems of three or four quatrains concluded by a couplet, is dedicated to Anthony Cooke. *Ideas Mirrour* also includes several allusions to Mary (Sidney) Herbert, Countess of Pembroke: she is called Pandora, the true patroness of poets, Minerva, goddess of the arts, and Meridianis, an anagram for Mary Sidney. *Matilda* (1594), a secular saint's life in which Matilda chooses death rather than dishonor at the hands of King John, and *Endimion and Phœbe*, a mythological narrative in couplets describing the fortunes of Endimion (Drayton), who falls in love with Phoebe (Lucy Harington), are dedicated to Lucy Harington, later Lucy Harington Russell, Countess of Bedford.

Drayton's 1593 pastoral, *Idea. The Shepheards Garland, Fashioned in nine Eglogs. Rowlands Sacrifice to the Nine Muses*, is organized as a poetic manifesto. The nine eclogues form a garland that will crown Drayton's "Idea" of poetry, while honoring the nine muses who preside over learning. To reinforce this circular structure, he pairs the first four eclogues with the last four so that, like a garland, they surround the apotheosis of poetry in the fifth. The fourth, fifth, and sixth eclogues function as the poetic core. The fourth eclogue, a pastoral elegy, laments the death of Elphin, Sir Philip Sidney, while the sixth praises the patronage of his sister, Mary Sidney Herbert, Countess of Pembroke.

The fifth eclogue begins with a dialogue in which Motto and Rowland discuss contemporary abuses of poetry. Drayton devotes the first sixty lines, nearly one-third of the fifth eclogue, to a scathing denunciation of how literary clientage can corrupt poetry. He is unmistakably hostile to distinctions of class. Those who brag of their lineage are described as "forgers of suppos'd Gentillitie / When he his great, great Grand-sires glory blases, / And paints out fictions in base coyned Phrases." This dialogue is followed by the apotheosis of the Idea of poetry. Poetry is the "stately Theater" upon which virtue plays a "princely part." Poetry's wisdom insures that the scenes played in England's "stately Theater" will be "pronounced by a Sage" and given immortality by "divinest Poets Arte." Drayton's images and diction emphasize the social function of poetry and its political importance.

While finishing the Idea poems, Drayton was also working on historical poems, which he at first described as tragical complaints and later called legends. In 1596 he published *Mor-*

timeriados, his first attempt at epic; his latest versions of *Peirs Gaveston* and *Matilda*; and his new complaint, *The Tragicall Legend of Robert, Duke of Normandy* (1596). All of these poems appeared with effusive dedications to Lucy, Countess of Bedford. The dedication in *Mortimeriados* is especially laudatory, praising the Haringtons, Lucy's family by birth, and the Bedfords, her family by marriage, and acknowledging her kinship with the Sidneys. Drayton concludes by promising that her name "shall lyve in steele-out-during rimes."

In 1596 Drayton had not yet arrived at a stable conception of either the complaint or the epic as a genre. For his third effort at the complaint he selected the historical figure Robert of Normandy, oldest son of William the Conqueror. Robert joined Godfrey of Bouillon on the First Crusade, leaving Normandy and England in his brother's hands. After his return Robert is blinded and imprisoned by his brother. The first version of *Robert, Duke of Normandy* was heavily embellished with rhetorical set speeches by Fame and Fortune, and Drayton republished equally ornate revised versions of *Peirs Gaveston*, to which he had added twenty-five new stanzas, and *Matilda*, to which he had added twenty-six. These early revisions and additions suggest how Drayton worked at the beginning of his career. He experimented with a particular genre or tradition and published the resulting poem. He continued to experiment and revise his published poems and then republished them later with new material. There are two or more versions for nearly all of Drayton's early works.

Drayton's promise is realized fully in *Englands Heroicall Epistles* (1597), a work suited to his rhetorical virtuosity. The poem consists of eighteen letters in rhymed couplets exchanged between couples who played important roles in English history. In 1598 and 1599 Drayton added to the collection, bringing the total number of epistles to twenty-four. Drayton's model was Ovid's *Heroides*, but he borrowed little from Ovid except the concept of a collection of verse epistles. Instead of imitating Ovid's thematic unity and subtle variations in tone, Drayton strives for contrast and generic variety. He also intended *Englands Heroicall Epistles* as a major bid for patronage. His earlier works had each contained one dedication, but this poem contains nine dedications, one for each set of epistles. He remains most interested in retaining the patronage of Lucy, Countess of Bedford, and her husband, Edward Russell, Earl of Bedford.

Englands Heroicall Epistles was the most popular of Drayton's works: five separate editions appeared between 1597 and 1602; in contrast, between 1596 and 1609 only one edition of Spenser's *Faerie Queene* (1590, 1596) was printed while *Englands Heroicall Epistles* went through seven editions. In these verse letters Drayton successfully interweaves fiction with history while contributing to a genre that had as yet attracted few English practitioners. *Englands Heroicall Epistles*, in addition, addressed themes of political importance to Drayton's audience. In the 1597 version each of the paired epistles involves at least one monarch, sometimes two. Moreover, each set of epistles after the first two concerns the deposition of a monarch (reigns of Edward II, Richard II, Henry VI) or a struggle over the succession. Drayton's additions to *Englands Heroicall Epistles* in 1598 and 1599 render the political thrust less obtrusive but by no means eliminate it.

In 1597 *Englands Heroicall Epistles* concluded with epistolary exchanges between Mary Tudor and Charles Brandon, and between Guilford Dudley and Lady Jane Grey; these two couples were ancestors of Edward Seymour, Lord Beauchamp, the Suffolk-Grey claimant to the English throne. Drayton's subject matter was politically very risky. Beauchamp, the son of Lady Catherine Grey Seymour, Countess of Hertford, had the advantage over James VI, King of Scotland, of having been born and brought up in England. There were also legal grounds for insisting on the primacy of the Suffolk-Grey claim. When Henry VIII had Parliament establish the Act of Succession, after his own children he put next in line the offspring of his younger sister, Mary Tudor, and her husband, Charles Brandon, Duke of Suffolk. Even though, according to primogeniture, the offspring of his older sister, Margaret Tudor, would have preceded the offspring of Mary Tudor, his ordering of the succession excluded Mary Stuart, Queen of Scots, and her son, James, from the throne until the Suffolk-Grey line had been exhausted.

Drayton may have inserted the exchange between Henry Howard, Earl of Surrey, and Lady Geraldine between the Brandon and Grey correspondence to soften the political implications. Nevertheless, the sequence still concluded with the tragic death of Lady Jane Grey and her husband, whom Drayton portrays as martyrs. Perhaps even more politically ill-advised than his treatment of the succession was Drayton's obvious support for Robert Devereux, second Earl of Essex. Sir John Hayward was sent to the tower for having prefaced his history of the reign of Henry IV with a dedication to Essex. The government interpreted Hayward's history as a cunning attempt to establish parallels between Richard II and Elizabeth, Henry IV and Essex, and to suggest the desirability of a popular uprising to put Essex on the throne. Even though Drayton made additions to *Englands Heroicall Epistles* in 1598 and 1599, it was not until 1600 that he engaged in a wholesale revision of the Richard II exchange, excising any passages that might relate the epistles to Essex. However, Drayton's revisions probably came too late for him to retain the patronage of the Bedfords. His lack of a patron may have prompted him to try his hand at writing for the professional theater in 1598. His success in handling English history in *Englands Heroicall Epistles* would have recommended him to the Admiral's Men as a likely collaborator on chronicle plays. From *Henslowes's Diary*, Philip Henslowe's book of receipts and record of payments for the company eventually known as the Admiral's Men, sponsored by Lord Charles Howard of Effingham, Lord High Admiral of England, one can reconstruct Drayton's career as a dramatist. He and his collaborators wrote twelve plays in the summer season of 1598, two in 1599, three in 1600, and one each in 1601 and 1602. Drayton may also have collaborated on *The London Prodigal* sometime between 1603 and 1605. Of these twenty or twenty-one plays, only the first part of *Sir John Oldcastle* (1600) was printed, and only it has survived.

In 1598, while Drayton was writing for the public theater, he appeared as a witness in the suit that Margaret Goodyer Saunders, the widow of Thomas Goodyer, brought against the Goodyers over her jointure and her son's inheritance. The proliferation of Henry Goodyers makes the case somewhat difficult to follow, but these legal documents establish that Drayton spent his early years as a domestic servant. It is significant that Drayton was called as a witness by Margaret Saunders in her suit against William Goodyer and his son, Sir Henry Goodyer the younger (1571-1627). Sir Henry Goodyer the elder, who owned Polesworth and had no sons, had considered making his younger brother, Thomas (whose son was also named Henry Goodyer after his uncle), his heir. After Thomas's death in 1585, Sir Henry changed his mind and instead made his other nephew, Sir Henry Goodyer the younger, the heir. In 1593, when

Engraved title page, depicting Albion "in Neptunes armes embras't," and portrait of Prince Henry, Britain's "best hope, and the world's delight," in the 1613 edition of Drayton's verse history and geography of Great Britain (engravings by William Hole)

Frances Goodyer had married her cousin Sir Henry Goodyer the younger, Sir Henry the elder bequeathed Polesworth to them. Sir Henry Goodyer the younger was the close friend of John Donne and a client of the countess of Bedford, who had acted as the godmother of the first child of Frances and Sir Henry the younger. The child was named Lucy after the countess, who later provided her dowry.

Drayton testified on 16 August 1598. His deposition, supplemented by other testimony, indicates that he served in the Collingham, Nottinghamshire, household for at least five years prior to Thomas's death in 1585; he probably joined the household in 1573 when the marriage between Thomas and Margaret Saunders took place. According to Drayton's testimony, just before his death Thomas told his wife Margaret to summon two servants "that be thy frendes that thou best lykest of" to be witnesses to his state-

ments about the Collingham lease. It is highly unlikely that Margaret would select Drayton as her witness to protect her interests against the Goodyer uncles if he had grown up in the bosom of the Polesworth family. In addition, since Collingham was located more than seventy miles away from Polesworth, visits cannot have been very frequent.

Both Drayton's master, Thomas Goodyer, and Sir Henry Goodyer the elder were dead before Drayton alluded to the Goodyers in his dedications. The sequence of dedications makes sense only if one assumes that Drayton was not intimately acquainted with any of these people. He appears to have hinted at and elaborated his Polesworth connections to enhance his eligibility as a literary client and particularly to consolidate his position with the countess of Bedford. Drayton had dedicated mythological and historical poetry to the countess in 1594, 1595, and

1596, and it is especially significant that he dedicated *Mortimeriados*, his first attempt at epic, to her in 1596.

Sometime prior to 1602 Drayton seems to have entered the service or won the patronage of Sir Walter Aston (1583-1639). When Aston was created a knight of the bath at the coronation of James I in 1603, Drayton acted as Aston's esquire. A year earlier Drayton had dedicated to Aston the as yet undedicated epistles of Edward the Black Prince and Alice, Countess of Salisbury, in *Englands Heroicall Epistles*. Sir Walter, whose father, Edward, had died in 1597, was a very wealthy man with estates in Stafford, Derby, Leicester, and Warwick counties and rents reputed to exceed ten thousand pounds a year. Drayton may have become acquainted with Aston through Warwickshire connections. Sir Walter's mother, Anne Aston, was the daughter of Sir Thomas Lucy, and Aston and his sisters were brought up at Charlecote, the Lucy estate. Through the Lucys, Aston was also a first cousin of Sir Henry Rainsford, for whom Drayton was to write a glowing and warm elegy in 1622. Rainsford also married Anne Goodyer after her father's death in 1595.

Drayton probably served Aston as a secretary or steward. He dedicated his 1619 folio to Aston, but he wrote no entertainments for the Aston family and only one polite verse epistle to Aston's wife, Gertrude Sadleir Aston. Moreover, in 1618 when Sir Henry Goodyer the younger was in debt and in danger of losing his property, Drayton acted as an agent in arranging a conveyance to protect the estate. Drayton probably acted on behalf of either Sir Henry Rainsford, Goodyer's brother-in-law, or Sir Walter Aston.

Prior to the conclusion of Elizabeth's reign, Drayton revised *Mortimeriados* as *The Barrons Wars* (1603). The result has met with mixed reactions among modern critics: John Buxton praises the economical language of *The Barrons Wars* highly, but Richard Hardin prefers the more romantic *Mortimeriados*. In 1603 Drayton welcomed James with a poem entitled *To the Majestie of King James*, and in 1604, probably also in hopes of gaining James's favor, he wrote the first of his divine poems, *Moyses in a Map of his Miracles*. James was known to enjoy theological debate and to favor biblical verse.

These bids for the king's patronage were unsuccessful: Drayton never received and never again sought favor from the Jacobean monarch. He addressed no verse to James after *A Pæan*

Triumphall (1604), entered in the Stationers' Register on 20 March; his long and imposing *Poly-Olbion* (1612) was dedicated first to Prince Henry and then to Prince Charles. His isolation from the court has been attributed to a social lapse. His biographer and editors describe him as naively violating decorum by failing to mourn Queen Elizabeth in *To the Majestie of King James*. This explanation for Drayton's failure to receive any favor from James is repeated by every scholar who discusses Drayton's relationship to the Jacobean court. The myth of Drayton's supposed error of taste in failing to mourn Elizabeth should be put to rest along with the fiction of his genteel upbringing. In *Englandes Mourning Garment* (1603) Henry Chettle reprimands a long list of poets for failing to mourn Elizabeth before welcoming James, including Samuel Daniel, William Warner, George Chapman, Ben Jonson, William Shakespeare, Thomas Lodge, Thomas Dekker, John Marston, and Henry Petowe. Daniel and Jonson were especially favored in the new reign, but quite a few poets received royal support of some kind.

By the time that James succeeded to the throne, Drayton had lost the favor of Lucy, Countess of Bedford. On 23 April 1603, when James was welcomed and entertained at the Harington family estate, Samuel Daniel's *A Panegyrike congratulatorie to the kings majestie* (1603) was presented to the king under Lucy's auspices. The title page to *A Panegyrike congratulatorie* states that Daniel personally delivered the poem to James. A few months later, Lucy arranged for Daniel to present his play *The Vision of the Twelve Goddesses* at Hampton Court on 8 January 1604. She also promoted Ben Jonson's efforts to gain recognition by the court. It must have been galling to Drayton that Lucy, whose patronage he had earlier enjoyed, was achieving prominence in the new court but ignoring him entirely.

Emphasis on the timing of Drayton's *To the Majestie of King James* has diverted attention from the text. If, in fact, James read this poem, he might well have been offended by Drayton's stern advice that he must banish from his court "the foole, the Pandar, and the Parasite." *To the Majestie of King James*, however, was not the only one of Drayton's poems that could have offended James. *The Owle*, a biting satire filled with topical allusions, was entered in the Stationers' Register on 8 February 1604 just prior to the triumphal entrance of the royal family into London on 15 March 1604. Drayton's public offering for the

Lux Haresbulla tibi (Warwici villa, tenebris,
Ante tuas Cunas, obsita) Prima fuit.
Arma, Viros, Veneres, Patriam modulamine dixti;
Te Patria resonant Arma, Viri, Veneres.

Portrait of Drayton at fifty, published in the 1619 edition of his Poems *(engraving by William Hole)*

royal entry, *A Pæan Triumphall*, perfunctorily praises the royal family but concentrates on a history of Drayton's sponsor, the Goldsmiths' Company. The first editions of *To the Majestie of King James* and *A Pæan Triumphall* were also the last. Contrary to his usual practice of reworking his poems, Drayton never reprinted either of these tributes to James in later collections of his poetry.

As Daniel and Jonson became increasingly favored literary figures at court, Drayton must have realized that he had little chance of regaining Lucy's favor, but he cannot have foreseen how powerful the countess would, in fact, become. Once he did understand that he would be ignored by the court, Drayton launched a breathtaking attack on Lucy, who after the queen had become the most prominent female figure of the court. In 1606 he reprinted *Idea. The Shepheards Garland* as *Poemes Lyrick and pastorall* with a new ver-

sion of the eighth eclogue. In it for the first time he identifies Anne Goodyer Rainsford as "Modest Idea, flowre of Womanhood, / That Rowland hath so highly Deifide." In the earlier versions of his Idea poems, he praised Mary Sidney Herbert, Countess of Pembroke, and Lucy, identifying them as Idea and celebrating them as ideal patrons.

Identification of Anne Goodyer as Idea is part of a calculated insult to Lucy. He retains an abbreviated version of his complimentary references to Mary Sidney, but Lucy is portrayed as Selena, a faithless patroness. Selena, whose name like Lucy's is associated with light, has deserted the faithful Rowland (Drayton) to favor Cerberon, a "beastly clowne," figuratively named after the three-headed dog who guards the gates to hell. In the concluding lines of his invective, Drayton consigns Lucy's name to oblivion, taking back his earlier dedications promising her immortality: "Let age sit soone and ugly on her brow, / No sheepheards praises living let her have / To her last end noe creature pay one vow / Nor flower be strew'd on her forgotten grave, / And to the last of all devouring tyme / Nere be her name remembred more in rime." Calling for "age" to make this reigning beauty old and ugly before her time, he curses Lucy to unhappiness while she lives and oblivion after she dies. When Drayton prepared a folio collection of his early work in 1619, he removed the passages attacking Selena, but to insure that Lucy's name would not be remembered in his rhymes, he eliminated all of the dedications and complimentary poems that he had addressed to her during the 1590s.

By 12 August 1607 Drayton joined a group that hoped to establish a company called Children of the King's Revels at Whitefriars. He was associated with Lordinge Barry, William Trevill, William Cooke, Edward Sibthorpe, and John Mason, all of whom became bound "jointly and severally" to Thomas Woodforde for the sum of £120. The Children of the Queen's Revels, for whom Samuel Daniel acted as licenser, had received royal protection under patent in 1604, and Drayton's company hoped to achieve a similar success. The Children of the King's Revels failed miserably; by 1609 Whitefriars was in the possession of the Children of the Queen's Revels, but a series of court cases concerning the Children of the King's Revels continued well into the seventeenth century.

In 1612 *Poly-Olbion*, Drayton's attempt to preserve in verse the history and geography of Great Britain, appeared with a dedication to James's heir, Prince Henry, who seemed to many the member of the royal family who most symbolized Elizabethan values. Drayton's bid for favor was successful, but fate intervened; Prince Henry died on 6 November 1612. Henry's household accounts record grants of pensions of twenty pounds to Joshua Sylvester for his translations and ten pounds to Drayton for *Poly-Olbion*, but the first part was not a popular success. The second part was completed in 1618, but Drayton did not find a publisher until 1622. While attempting to find a printer and bookseller, he began a correspondence in 1618 with the Scottish poet William Drummond of Hawthornden, asking Drummond to put him in touch with Andro Hart, the Edinburgh bookseller who had published Drummond's work. Although Drummond and Drayton never met, they corresponded intermittently until Drayton's death in 1631. After

THE
BATTAILE
OF
AGINCOVRT.

FOVGHT BY HENRY THE fift of that name, King of *England*, against the whole power of the *French*: vnder the Raigne of their CHARLES the sixt, *Anno Dom.* 1415.
The Miseries of Queene MARGARITE, the infortunate VVife, of that most infortunate King HENRY the sixt.
NIMPHIDIA, the Court of *Fayrie.*
The Quest of CINTHIA.
The Shepheards SIRENA.
The *Moone-Calfe.*
Elegies vpon sundry occasions.

By MICHAELL DRAYTON *Esquire.*

LONDON,
Printed for WILLIAM LEE, at the Turkes Head in Fleete-Streete, next to the Miter and Phænix.
1627.

Title page for the book that Drayton dedicated to "those Noblest of Gentlemen" of Great Britain, "who in these declining times, have yet in your brave bosomes the sparkes of that sprightly fire, of your couragious Ancestors"

Drayton's death, Drummond expressed interest in bringing out any manuscripts of *Poly-Olbion* that had survived and eloquently prophesied that its author would "live by all likelihead so long as . . . men speak English."

In the 1619 folio edition of his early poems, *Poems by Michael Drayton Esquyer*, Drayton published the final version of *Idea*, the sonnet sequence which he had begun in 1594 and repeatedly revised over the years. This final collection includes the sonnet "Since ther's no helpe, Come let us kisse and part," an acknowledged masterpiece. Although the 1619 folio is dedicated to Sir Walter Aston, Drayton's service with Aston may also have ended in 1619. King James had appointed Sir Walter as ambassador to Spain, charging him with negotiation of a Spanish Catholic marriage for Prince Charles. Drayton's elegies explicitly criticize James's foreign policy, but the poems, written around 1621, were not published until after James's death in 1625.

After the appearance of the second part of *Poly-Olbion*, in which Drayton pays tribute to Tixall, the Aston family estate, Drayton published two more collections of poetry. The collection entitled *The Battaile of Agincourt* (1627), Drayton's final and most successful epic, was comprehensively dedicated to those noble men who had the magnanimity of their courageous ancestors and who respected poetry. This collection also contains Drayton's troubling satire, *The Moone-Calfe*; his mock epic, *Nimphidia, the Court of Fayrie*; his other pastorals, *The Quest of Cinthia* and *The Shepheards Sirena*; and his verse epistles, *Elegies upon Sundry Occasions*. Among the elegies, he published a tribute to Sir Henry Rainsford, kinsman of Aston and husband of Anne Goodyer, who had died on 27 January 1622. In "Upon the Death of his Incomparable Friend, Sir Henry Raynsford Of Clifford" Drayton uses the death of Sir Henry as an emblem of human mortality and movingly describes him as "so fast a friend, so true a Patriot." Sir Henry's widow, Anne Goodyer Rainsford, is not mentioned in the funeral elegy. Ben Jonson wrote a prefatory tribute to the 1627 folio, calling Drayton's work "pure, and perfect *Poesy*" and celebrating him in images of the seven liberal arts and of "bright *Ideas*," language that Drayton himself might have used.

Drayton's final folio appeared in 1630 under the title of one of his finest poems, *The Muses Elizium*. This volume also included two new divine poems, *Noahs Floud* and *David and Golia*, and reprinted a poem published in 1604 under the new title, *Moses, his Birth and Miracles*. The collection is dedicated to Edward Sackville, fourth Earl of Dorset, the grandson of Thomas Sackville, first Earl of Dorset, author of the induction to the 1563 enlarged edition of *A Mirror for Magistrates*. In his dedication Drayton says that the constancy of Sackville's favors since they first began "have now made me one of your family, and I am become happy in the title to be called Yours." This heightened rhetoric, however, should not be interpreted literally, since there is no evidence that Drayton received any more patronage from Dorset than did other poets: Donne was his guest at Knole; Jonson praised his liberality; Robert Herrick approved of his talents as a literary critic.

The Muses Elizium contains Drayton's last critical statement on the craft of poetry. For England, which he portrays as an unhappy isle, he ironically selects the name Felicia (a Latin equivalent of the Greek pun used to render the title "Poly-Olbion" as "Happy Albion"). In *The Muses Elizium* Drayton retracts *Poly-Olbion*, his valiant effort to realize the humanist ideal of the poet as spokesman for public values. He may have deliberately left *Poly-Olbion* unfinished because he had concluded that epic poetry could no longer be written with conviction since heroic values had disappeared from life and art. *The Muses Elizium*, his last pastoral, forecasts that poets will turn to satire and romantic escape. However, the Orphic bard, the civilizer who embodies Drayton's ideal of the poet, cannot escape into a romantic world in which poetry becomes an end in itself. For Drayton, satire is preferable, and so he abandons his pastoral name Rowland and becomes the old Satyre, whom the muses favor because of his truthfulness. In *The Muses Elizium* Michael Drayton prophesies a bleak future for England and no future at all for the kind of poetry he had spent his life writing.

Drayton's truthfulness earned him the respect of his contemporaries even if it did not win him prosperity. Henry Peacham observed that "Honest Mr. *Michael Drayton* had about some five pounds lying by him at his death," and the final inventory of his estate was reported by his brother Edmund to be 24 pounds, 8s. 2d. The antiquary William Fulman, however, described his funeral as impressive: "He dyed at his lodging in Fleet Street . . . the Gentlemen of the Four Innes of Court and others of note about the Town, attended his body to Westminster, reaching in order by two and two, from his Lodging almost to Standbridge."

Bibliographies:

Alfred Harbage, *Annals of English Drama 975-1700* (Philadelphia: University of Pennsylvania Press / London: Oxford University Press, 1940); second edition, revised by Samuel Schoenbaum (Philadelphia: University of Pennsylvania Press, 1964);

Richard F. Hardin, "Michael Drayton," in *The Popular School*, edited by T. P. Logan and S. S. Smith (Lincoln: University of Nebraska Press, 1975), pp. 137-147;

Monument to Drayton in Westminster Abbey

James L. Harner, *Samuel Daniel and Michael Drayton: A Reference Guide* (Boston: G. K. Hall, 1980).

Biographies:

Kathleen Tillotson, "Drayton and the Gooderes," *Modern Language Review*, 35 (July 1940): 341-349;

Bernard Newdigate, *Michael Drayton and his Circle* (Oxford: Blackwell, 1941; revised, 1961);

Dick Taylor, "Drayton and the Countess of Bedford," *Studies in Philology*, 49 (April 1952): 214-228.

References:

Anne Barton, "Harking Back to Elizabeth: Ben Jonson and Caroline Nostalgia," *ELH*, 48 (Winter 1981): 706-731;

Jean R. Brink, *Michael Drayton Revisited* (Boston: Twayne, 1990);

Michael D. Bristol, "Structural Patterns in Two Elizabethan Pastorals," *Studies in English Literature*, 10 (Winter 1970): 33-48;

John Buxton, *A Tradition of Poetry* (New York: Macmillan, 1967);

Lilly B. Campbell, *Divine Poetry and Drama in Sixteenth-Century England* (Cambridge: University Press / Berkeley: University of California Press, 1959);

Campbell, "The Use of Historical Patterns in the Reign of Elizabeth," *Huntington Library Quarterly*, 1 (January 1938): 135-167;

Katherine D. Carter, "Drayton's Craftsmanship: The Encomium and the Blazon in *Englands Heroicall Epistles*," *Huntington Library Quarterly*, 38 (August 1975): 297-314;

Walter R. Davis, " 'Fantastickly I sing': Drayton's *Idea* of 1619," *Studies in Philology*, 66 (April 1969): 204-216;

M. J. Dickson, "William Trevell and the Whitefriars Theatre," *Review of English Studies*, 6 (July 1930): 309-312;

Margaret Dowling, "Further Notes on William Trevell," *Review of English Studies*, 6 (October 1930): 443-446;

Parker Duchemin, "Barbarous Ignorance and Base Detraction: The Struggles of Michael Drayton," *Albion*, 14 (Summer 1982): 118-138;

Duchemin, "*Poly-Olbion* and the Alexandrine Couplet," *Studies in Philology*, 77 (Spring 1980): 145-160;

Barbara C. Ewell, "*Drayton's Endimion and Phoebe*: An Allegory of Aesthetics," *Explorations in Renaissance Culture*, 7 (1981): 15-26;

Ewell, "Drayton's *Poly-Olbion*: England's Body Immortalized," *Studies in Philology*, 75 (Summer 1978): 297-315;

Ewell, "From Idea to Act: The New Aesthetics of Drayton's *Englands Heroicall Epistles*," *Journal of English and Germanic Philology*, 82 (October 1983): 515-525;

Ewell, "Unity and the Transformation of Drayton's Poetics in *Englands Heroicall Epistles*," *Modern Language Quarterly*, 44 (September 1983): 231-250;

Scott Giantvalley, "Barnfield, Drayton, and Marlowe: Homoeroticism and Homosexuality in Elizabethan Literature," *Pacific Coast Philology*, 16 (1981): 9-24;

Joan Grundy, " 'Brave Translunary Things,' " *Modern Language Review*, 59 (October 1964): 501-510;

Grundy, *The Spenserian Poets* (London: Edward Arnold, 1969);

Richard F. Hardin, *Michael Drayton and the Passing of Elizabethan England* (Lawrence: University of Kansas Press, 1973);

Richard Helgerson, *Self-Crowned Laureates* (Berkeley & Los Angeles: University of California Press, 1983);

Wyman Herendeen, *From Landscape to Literature: The River and the Myth of Geography* (Pittsburgh: Duquesne University Press, 1986);

Geoffrey G. Hiller, "Drayton's *Muses Elizium*: A New Way over Parnassus," *Review of English Studies*, 21 (February 1970): 1-13;

Clark Hulse, *Metamorphic Verse: The Elizabethan Minor Epic* (Princeton: Princeton University Press, 1981);

Anthony LaBranche, "Drayton's *The Barons Warres* and the Rhetoric of Historical Poetry," *Journal of English and Germanic Philology*, 62, no.1 (1963): 82-95;

LaBranche, "Poetry, History, and Oratory: The Renaissance Historical Poem," *Studies in English Literature*, 9 (Winter 1969): 1-19;

Barbara Lewalski, "Lucy, Countess of Bedford: Images of a Jacobean Courtier and Patroness," in *Politics of Discourse: The Literature and History of Seventeenth-Century England*, edited by Kevin Sharpe and Steven Zwicker (Berkeley: University of California Press, 1987), pp. 52-77;

David Norbrook, *Poetry and Politics in the English Renaissance* (London: Routledge & Kegan Paul, 1984);

William A. Oram, "*The Muses Elizium*: A Late Golden World," *Studies in Philology*, 75 (Late Winter 1978): 10-31;

Annabel Patterson, *Censorship and Interpretation: The Conditions of Writing and Reading in Early Modern England* (Madison: University of Wisconsin Press, 1985);

Vincent F. Petronella, "Double Ecstasy in Drayton's *Endimion and Phoebe*," *Studies in English Literature*, 24 (Winter 1984): 87-104;

Stella P. Redvard, "The Design of Nature in Drayton's *Poly-Olbion*," *Studies in English Literature*, 17 (Winter 1977): 105-117;

Joan Rees, "Hogs, Gulls, and Englishmen: Drayton and the Virginian Voyages," *Yearbook of English Studies*, 13 (1983): 20-31;

Kathleen Tillotson, "Drayton and Richard II: 1597-1600," *Review of English Studies*, 15 (April 1939): 172-179;

Tillotson, "Michael Drayton as a 'Historian' in the 'Legend of Cromwell,' " *Modern Language Review*, 34 (April 1939): 186-200;

Michael D. West, "Drayton's 'To the Virginian Voyage': From Heroic Pastoral to Mock-Heroic," *Renaissance Quarterly*, 24 (Winter 1971): 501-506.

Papers:

One autograph letter to William Drummond of Hawthornden on 22 November 1620 is preserved in the National Library of Scotland (MS 9931, f. 21). Copies of Drayton's poems also appear in manuscript verse miscellanies and song-books; for a complete listing, see Peter Beal, *Index of English Literary Manuscripts* (1980).

William Drummond of Hawthornden

(13 December 1585 - 4 December 1649)

Theresa M. DiPasquale
Florida International University

BOOKS: *Teares on the Death of Meliades* (Edinburgh: Printed by Andro Hart, 1613);

Poems (Edinburgh?, 1614?); revised as *Poems: Amorous, Funerall, Diuine, Pastorall, in Sonnets, Songs, Sextains, Madrigals* (Edinburgh: Printed by Andro Hart, 1616);

In Pious Memorie of The right Worthie and Vertuous Evphemia Kyninghame, Who In the Prime of Her Youth Died the 23. of Iulie, 1616 [half sheet] (Edinburgh: Printed by Andro Hart, 1617);

Forth Feasting. A Panegyricke to the Kings Most Excellent Majestie (Edinburgh: Printed by Andro Hart, 1617); slightly revised and republished in *The Mvses Welcome to the High and Mightie Prince Iames* (Edinburgh: Printed by Thomas Finalson, 1618);

A Midnights Trance: wherin is discoursed of death, the nature of soules, and estate of immortalitie (London: Printed by G. Purslow for J. Budge, 1619); revised and republished as *A Cypresse Grove* in *Flowres of Sion* (1623);

Flowres Of Sion. By William Drvmmond of Hawthorenedenne. To which is adjoyned his Cypresse Grove (Edinburgh?: Printed by the heirs of Andro Hart?, 1623; revised and enlarged edition, Edinburgh: Printed by the heirs of Andro Hart, 1630);

Auctarium Bibliothecae Edinburgenæ, sive Catalogus Librorum quos G. Drummondus d. (Edinburgh: Printed by the heirs of A. Hart, 1627);

The Entertainment of the High and Mighty Monarch Charles into His Auncient City of Edinburgh (Edinburgh: Printed by Iohn Wreittoun, 1633);

To the Exequies of the Honourable Sʳ. Antonye Alexander. Knight, &c. A Pastorall Elegie (Edinburgh: Printed in King James his College by George Anderson, 1638);

Polemo-Medinia Inter Vitarvam et Nebernam (Edinburgh?, between 1642 and 1650?); republished as *Polemo-Middinia. Carmen Macaronicum. Autore Gulielmo Drummundo, Scoto-*

Britanno (Oxford: E Theatro Sheldoniano, 1691);

The History of Scotland, from the Year 1423 until the Year 1542) (London: Printed by Henry Hills for Richard Tomlins and himself, 1655).

Editions: *Poems by That most Famous Wit, William Drvmmond of Hawthornden*, edited by Edward Phillips (London: Printed for Richard Tomlins, 1656); republished as *The most Elegant and Elabovrate Poems Of that Great Court-Wit, Mr William Drummond* (London: Printed for William Rands, 1659);

The Works of William Drummond, Of Hawthornden, edited by Bishop John Sage and Thomas Ruddiman (Edinburgh: Printed by James Watson, 1711);

The Poetical Works of William Drummond of Hawthornden With 'A Cypresse Grove,' 2 volumes, edited by L. E. Kastner (Edinburgh & London: Printed for the Scottish Text Society by W. Blackwood & Sons, 1913);

Conversations, in *Ben Jonson*, 22 volumes, edited by C. H. Herford and Percy Simpson (Oxford: Clarendon Press, 1925-1954); I: 128-178;

William Drummond of Hawthornden Poems and Prose, edited by Robert H. MacDonald, The Association for Scottish Literary Studies, 6 (Edinburgh & London: Scottish Academic Press, 1976)—includes the text of the "Memorialls."

OTHER: *Mavsolevm Or, The Choisest Flowres of the Epitaphs, written on the Death of the neuer-too-much lamented Prince Henrie*, includes two sonnets and a pyramid-shaped epitaph by Drummond (Edinburgh: Printed by A. Hart, 1613);

Sir William Alexander, *Doomes-Day, or, The Great Day of the Lords Ivdgement*, includes a commendatory poem by Drummond (Edinburgh: Printed by Andro Hart, 1614);

Sir Thomas Kellie, *Pallas armata, or Militarie Instructions for the Learned*, includes a commenda-

Portrait by an unknown artist, 1623 (from Robert H. MacDonald, ed., The Library of Drummond of
Hawthornden, *1971)*

tory poem by Drummond (Edinburgh: Printed by the heirs of A. Hart, 1627);

Sir William Moore, *The Trve Crvcifixe for True Catholickes*, includes a sonnet by Drummond (Edinburgh: Printed by J. Wreittoun, 1629).

William Drummond of Hawthornden was a Scotsman whose English poetry—elegant, sensuous, and fluid—established him in his time as Edinburgh's unofficial poet laureate. Tracing the extensive borrowings and derivations in his work, scholars have sometimes overemphasized Drummond's lack of originality; but his intertextual weavings have earned him literary admirers in every century, especially the nineteenth, when several new editions of his poetry were published. Charles Lamb ranks him with Christopher Marlowe, Michael Drayton, and Abra-

ham Cowley as one of the "sweetest" of poets. Although now remembered chiefly for the notes he took of his conversations with Ben Jonson, Drummond was never "sealed of the Tribe of Ben"; the Scotsman's poetry was too aureate and Petrarchan for Jonson's taste. Jonson was of the opinion—duly recorded by Drummond in his record of Jonson's "Informations and maners"—that the laird's verses "were all good . . . save that they smelled too much of the schooles and were not after the Fancie of the time."

Born 13 December 1585, the poet was the son of John Drummond, who became a laird through the purchase of the Hawthornden estate a few miles outside Edinburgh and was knighted upon James's succession to the English throne in 1603. The poet's mother, Susannah Fowler, was the sister of another Scottish poet, Queen Anne's

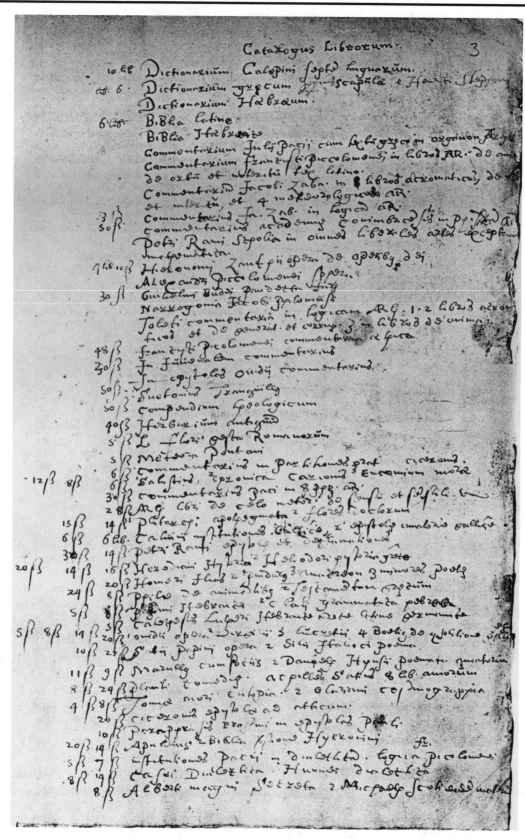

Pages from a rough-draft list of his books that Drummond made before 1611 and from his 1611 catalogue of his library
(Hawthornden Manuscripts, National Library of Scotland)

370

Table of Italian bookes
anno 1611.

Gierusalem conquistata
del Sigr: T. Tasso, of the edition
of Paris ————————— 2 ß Ing.
Gierusalem et prinlet at
with ——————————— 18 d. Ing.
Le sette giornate del S. T. Tasso — 20 d. Ing.
Rime et prose del Sigr: T. Tasso
foure Tomes ————————— 4 ß Ing.
Lettere familiares del S. T. Tasso — 10 ß fer
Orlando furioso di M. Lodouico
Ariosto ————————— 2 ß Ing.
Rime Di M. L. Ariosto — 18 d. Ing.
Gli asolim di M. pietro Bembo — 1 ß Ing.
Rime di M. pietro Bembo ——— 8 ß Fra.
iL Petrarcha ————————— 1 ß Ing.
Creatione del mondo del S. Gasparo
Murtola ————————— 2 ß Ing.
Rime di Iacomo Castellano — 18 d. Ing.
La comedia di Dante ———— 1 ß Ing.
Leone Hibreo ————————— 1 ß Ing.
~~iL~~ pastor fido Madrigali di Baptista
Guarini ————————— 1 ß Ing.

private secretary, William Fowler. Having attended the High School in Edinburgh and, in 1605, having earned his M. A. from the recently founded University of Edinburgh, Drummond set out for France to study law. The poet's eighteenth-century biographer claims that Drummond distinguished himself as a student; but the lists Drummond kept to record books "red be me" each year from 1606 through 1614 suggest that he devoted more time to belles lettres than to statutes and precedents. He listed only one law book—the *Institutes of Justinian*—as having been read during his time in France. In 1611, when he made an inventory of his books, he listed relatively few titles under the heading of law; many more are included in the categories of theology, philosophy, and poetry. At any rate, Drummond's training was never put to use. He returned to Scotland in late 1608, and, when his father died in 1610, he became laird of Hawthornden. The estate was quite modest but allowed him—after something of a legal scuffle with his mother—sufficient means to forego professional labors; he retired to his country home and probably never left Scotland again.

During the nine years he kept his lists, Drummond read more than 220 works in French, Italian, English, Spanish, Greek, and Hebrew. In 1606 he read 42 books, including 3 courtesy manuals, William Shakespeare's *Romeo and Juliet* (1599 edition), *Love's Labor's Lost* (1598), *A Midsummer Night's Dream* (1600), and *Lucrece* (1594), Sir Philip Sidney's *Arcadia* (1590), and Ludovico Ariosto's *Orlando Furioso* (1570 edition). Later lists include Edmund Spenser's *Amoretti and Epithalamion* (1592) and *The Faerie Queene* (1590, 1596), a second reading of the *Arcadia*, Giovanni Battista Guarini's *Pastor Fido* (1603 edition), Francis Bacon's *Essays* (1597-1625), and Jonson's *Epigrams* (possibly in a nonextant edition of 1612), as well as works by Thomas Campion, Samuel Daniel, François Rabelais, and Guillaume de Salluste, Seigneur du Bartas. Drummond's poetry showcases the influence of his voracious reading; Sidney and Spenser were his most important English models, while in French he borrowed much from Jean Passerat, Philippe Desportes, Pierre de Ronsard, and Pontus de Tyard. His favorites in Italian and Spanish were Giambattista Marini, Battista Guarini, Torquato Tasso, Garcilaso de la Vega, and Juan Boscán Almogaver.

Drummond's first publication was *Teares on the Death of Meliades* (1613), a pastoral elegy mourning Prince Henry. The death of King James's heir in 1612 was a shock to Britain and occasioned an outpouring of literary tributes; the quality of these funerary poems is generally unimpressive. Drummond's piece is an exception; though conventional, its language is rich, measured, and sometimes quietly magnificent. Like many of the poets who eulogized the prince, Drummond mourns the loss of one who might have been a Protestant warrior-saint; in a note on the title, Drummond explains that Henry jousted under the name Moeliades, which "in *Anagramme* maketh *Miles A DEO*" (Soldier of God). Thus, Drummond focuses in one passage upon the heroic potential of the prince. The martial theme does not, however, bring out the best in Drummond's talent; the poem's finest moments come later, in reflections upon the pain of bereavement.

L. E. Kastner notes Drummond's debt to Sidney, pointing out that the poem is modeled on an elegy from the *Arcadia*. Drummond does use some of Sidney's phrases and conceits, but his poem is not wholly derivative; even when he borrows, Drummond is able to work some distinctive changes upon his source materials. He delights in the prosopopoeia essential to pastoral elegy, and his lamenting Scottish rivers provide occasion for some Caledonian details: "Tweed *through her greene Mountaines cled with Flockes, / Did wound the* Ocean, *murmuring thy Death.*" The personifications are perhaps most beautiful in the poem's final section, where the prince is, like Scipio or Troilus, lifted up to a vantage point outside the celestial spheres; he is able to observe the vanities of the world,

> And in their turning Temples *to behold,*
> In siluer Robe the Moone, *the* Sunne *in Gold,*
> Like young Eye-speaking Louers *in a Dance,*
> With Majestie by Turnes retire, aduance.

The sight of God is consummate bliss, and the prince's soul can now "*rest saciate*" with the beatific vision. The sense of religious solemnity in the final section of the poem is typical of what David Masson calls Drummond's "metaphysical mood," his preoccupation with philosophical and theological immensities. Reflecting on the divine nature, the poet builds to a rare Neoplatonic conceit; God is

> Life *of all Liues,* Cause *of each other Cause,*
> The Spheare, *and* Center, *where the* Minde *doth pause:*
> Narcissus *of himselfe,* himselfe the Well,
> Louer, *and* Beautie, *that doth all excell.*

In addition to *Meliades*, Drummond's 1613 volume includes an epitaph in sonnet form and another in the shape of a pyramid. He contributed the two shorter poems—the sonnet having been carefully revised—along with another sonnet, to a 1613 collection of elegiac verse by various hands, and Drummond's four poems were published again in a so-called third edition of the elegy, dated 1614 (no second edition seems to have existed). Several of Drummond's works have rather complicated histories, as the details of their publication were often affected by private considerations. Many of the extant volumes are presentation copies, which differ from each other in appearance, having been printed on various kinds of paper or with different engravings and ornaments. Drummond probably took an active part in financing and overseeing the publication of his writings, which are tastefully and rather lavishly printed. He often circulated among friends copies of his poems printed on loose sheets, and in at least one case (that of the 1623 *Flowres of Sion*) he had specially printed and bound "some copies equalling the number of my friends and those to whom I am beholden."

In 1614 Drummond met Sir William Alexander of Menstrie (later first Earl of Stirling); the two became good friends, corresponding on a regular basis and addressing one another in verse by the pastoral names "Alexis" and "Damon." The poetry of Alexander plays a part in Drummond's next piece, a Petrarchan sonnet sequence. The speaker of Drummond's lyrics tells Alexis of how his beloved read Alexis's poetry aloud: "Her Voyce did sweeten here thy sugred Lines, / To which Winds, Trees, Beasts, Birds did lend their Eare." As Ronald D. S. Jack demonstrates, Drummond's sequence is indebted both to Alexander's *Aurora* and to *The Tarantula of Love*, a Petrarchan sequence by the poet's uncle, William Fowler.

Drummond's love sonnets were first published, along with a small collection called "VRANIA, or Spirituall Poems," in an undated volume. Titled simply *Poems*, this collection was bound with *Meliades* and miscellaneous *Madrigalls and Epigrammes*. Robert H. MacDonald concurs with Kastner's estimation that the volume was published in 1614, a date which would make the sequence too early to be an account of the poet's own love and bereavement, as was long assumed. The belief that Drummond's sequence was autobiographical stemmed from a memoir prefixed to the 1711 edition of Drummond's *Works* and attributed to one of its editors, Bishop John Sage:

> Love stole in upon him, and did intirely captivate his Heart: For he was on a sudden highly Enamour'd of a fine Beautiful young Lady, Daughter to Cuninghame of Barns.... He met with suitable Returns of chast Love from her ... but when the day for the Marriage was appointed ... she took a Fever, and was suddenly snatched away by it, to his great Grief and Sorrow.

The link between this romantic account and Drummond's sonnet sequence does not hold; for the lady Sage mentioned apparently died some years later. In 1617 Drummond published, on a loose half sheet, a sonnet titled *In Pious Memorie of The right Worthie and Vertuous Euphemia Kyninghame, Who In the Prime of Her Youth Died the 23. of Julie, 1616*. The claim that the lady thus lamented was Drummond's betrothed is itself called into question by the fact that, in the 1623 edition of *Flowres of Sion*, Drummond included the same sonnet with a dedication to the recently deceased Jane Drummond, Countess of Perth. The lady of Drummond's sonnet sequence is, at any rate, probably a mistress as fictional as any other celebrated in the verse of the day. Her name, Auristella (which sounds like a blatant fusion of Sidney's Stella and Alexander's Aurora), is mentioned only once; but like Laura, she enthralls her lover both *in vita* and *in morte*. The first part of Drummond's sequence tells of his enamorment, the second of his bereavement. If this arrangement did spring from sad experience, Drummond seems to have made the most of it: he is recorded—again by Sage—as having claimed "that he was the first in the Isle that did celebrate a mistress dead, and Englished the madrigal." The first part includes fifty-four sonnets, ten madrigals, two sestinas, and two longer lyrics designated "songs" but including more narrative than the sonnets. The second part has thirteen sonnets, two songs, and five madrigals.

Many of the poems in the sequence are translations or close adaptations of works by Continental and English writers. Kastner's notes carefully document Drummond's borrowings, which reflect the poet's conservative opinions on the doctrine of imitation. In an undated letter to a friend, the Latinist Arthur Johnston, Drummond objects to the efforts of poets who have attempted the "reformation" of poetry and have

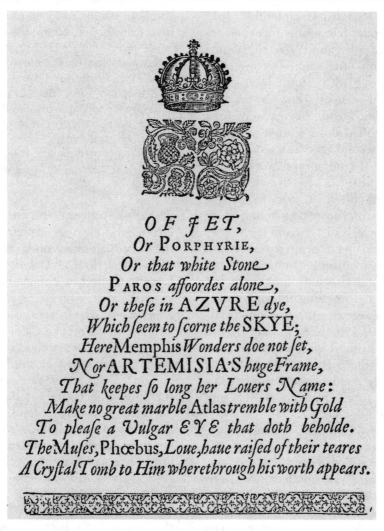

OF ÆT,
Or PORPHYRIE,
Or that white Stone
PAROS affoordes alone,
Or these in AZVRE dye,
Which seem to scorne the SKYE;
Here Memphis Wonders doe not set,
Nor ARTEMISIA'S huge Frame,
That keepes so long her Louers Name:
Make no great marble Atlas tremble with Gold
To please a Vulgar EYE that doth beholde.
The Muses, Phœbus, Loue, haue raised of their teares
A Cryſtal Tomb to Him wherethrough his worth appears.

The pyramid poem Drummond published with Teares on the Death of Meliades, *his elegy for Prince Henry, who had jousted under the name "Moeliades," an anagram for "Miles a Deo," or "Soldier of God" (reproduced from the so-called third edition, 1614)*

"endevured to abstracte her to Metaphysicall Ideas, and Scholasticall Quiddityes":

> Neither doe I thinke that a good piece of poesie, which Homer, Virgill, Ovid, Petrach, Bartas, Ronsard, Boscan, Garcilasso (if they were alife, and had that langage) could not understand, and reach the sense of the writer.... What is not like the ancientes and conforme to those Rules which hath beene agreed unto by all tymes, maye (indeed) be some thing like unto poesie, but it is no more Poesie than a Monster is a Man. Monsteres breed admiration at the first, but have ever some strange loathsomnesse in them at last.

It is not clear whether Drummond was inspired to this outburst by the work of the English metaphysicals or (as Kastner speculates) by the innovations of François de Malherbe in France. In notes made circa 1615, Drummond asserted that Petrarch is "By Consent of the whole Senate of Poets," the finest love poet, though he has been surpassed in some things by Sidney and Alexander. Considering writers of less thoroughly Petrarchan love poetry, loosely categorized as "Anacreontick Lyricks," Drummond avers that "*Donne* ... is Second to none." But his work, Drummond feels, cannot be compared to Alexander's or Sidney's since they chose "diverse Paths; the one flying swift, but low; the other, like the Eagle, surpassing the clouds." His overblown estimate of Alexander perhaps shows a friend's bias; but in his choice of models for the Auristella sequence, Drummond demonstrates a well-developed literary taste and an instinct for selecting materials suited to his talent.

He manages to combine or modify borrowed ingredients in such a way as to give his poems a flavor of their own; but the components remain indisputably conventional. In the opening sonnet the speaker tells of how his past dabbling in amatory lyric led him "to praise a perfect Red and White" before he experienced the pain of love. He omits none of the requisite oxymora and employs many familiar Petrarchan conceits; but the most striking characteristic of the lyrics is their rich sensuality. The poems are thick with pearl and ivory; the atmosphere is filled with sobbing birdsong and stirred by breezes which play upon his beloved's lips, "*Kissing sometimes these purple Ports of Death.*"

After the first eleven sonnets comes a lengthy semi-allegorical song describing how the lover first saw his beloved and her companions bathing. His rapturous gazing is interrupted when a majestic woman bursts upon the scene, sweeps the ladies into her chariot, and carries them off to the "Fort of Chastitie." The song is saturated with Sidneyan language, and the river scene is based on a song from book 2 of the *Arcadia*. Several of the sonnets in the first part also show a mastery of one of Sidney's favorite patterns, in which twelve lines of conventional wisdom are suddenly reversed by love's stubborn irrationality. Like Astrophil, the lover of Drummond's sequence chides himself for failing to seize opportunity when he finds the lady sleeping and decides that he "who liues in Loue can neuer bee too bolde." After that, he makes one attempt at a carpe diem poem; but he never aspires to the impudence of Astrophil's sophistical arguments, and his suit makes little or no progress. In the second song he waits amid the beauty of a garden where Auristella is to meet him, but she never arrives; echoing Friar Lawrence's somewhat uncanny image from *Romeo and Juliet* (II. iii), he stands alone to watch the rising sun:

> Phoebus *in his Chaire*
> *Ensaffroning Sea and Aire,*
> *Makes vanish euery Starre:*
> Night *like a Drunkard reeles*
> *Beyond the Hills to shunne his flaming Wheeles.*

In the sonnets concluding the first part, it becomes clear that his beloved has gone away.

The second part begins in a frenzy of apostrophes: "Of mortall Glorie ô soone darkned Raye! / O posting Ioyes of Man! . . . / O fond Desires!" The speaker's lady is dead, and his poetry becomes self-consciously otherworldly. In a poem

based on a madrigal by Guarini, for example, Drummond alters the Italian's comparison of life to a feather in order to call it a glimmering "*Bubble blowen vp in the Aire, / By sporting Childrens Breath*":

> *And though it sometime seeme of its owne Might*
> *(Like to an Eye of gold) to be fix'd there,*
> *And firme to houer in that emptie Hight,*
> *That only is because it is so light,*
> *But in that Pompe it doth not long appeare;*
> *For euen when most admir'd, it in a Thought*
> *As swell'd from nothing, doth dissolue in nought.*

In the songs of the second part the speaker questions the natural beauty he praised so vividly in the first. The lover's pastoral paradise is blasted by winter, and "*Hilles stand with Clouds like Mourners, vail'd in Blacke.*" At the end of the sequence, the lady appears to her lover and preaches a Neoplatonic homily: he who relies only upon his senses is like one dwelling beneath the seas; he "*Can not beleeue that here be Temples, Towres, / Which goe beyond his Caues and dampish Bowres.*" It is no surprise, given the lady's message, that the sonnet sequence is bound together with "Urania," a brief collection of religious meditations on such subjects as the ephemerality of earthly life, the evil of the present time, and the redeeming work of Christ; the last piece is a song which decries human sinfulness but begs God's mercy, since "*Lesse are our Faults farre farre than is thy Loue.*"

A revised edition of *Poems*, published in 1616, has the expanded title *Poems: Amorous, Funerall, Divine, Pastorall, in Sonnets, Songs, Sextains, Madrigals*. Clearly Drummond was experimenting with various genres, presenting in one volume the best of his work to date. The title page identifies the author as "W.D. the Author of the Teares on the Death of Moeliades," and as in the earlier edition of *Poems*, the love poems and religious lyrics are bound together with that elegy and a separate collection of *Madrigalls and Epigrammes*. The added madrigals, like those which appear in the sequence proper, are charming translations and variations on common conceits. In rendering Marini's poem on a milk maid, for example, Drummond finds a rhyme worthy of Robert Herrick: "*Among that strained Moysture (rare Delight!) / Her Hand seem'd Milke in Milke, it was so white.*" The epigrams, however, are in general some of Drummond's least distinguished efforts. Some, like "Alcons Kisse," in which a lover's fiery passion is quenched by his be-

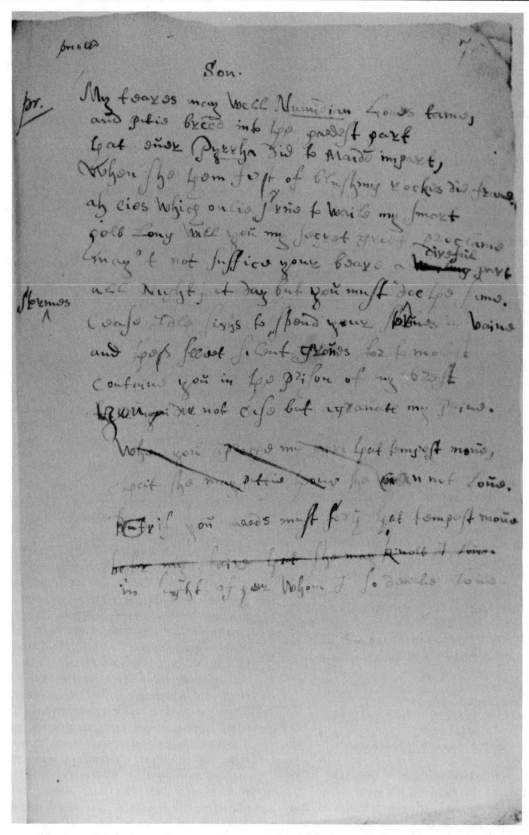

Manuscript, in Drummond's hand, for one of the sonnets he included in his 1614(?) Poems (National Library of Scotland, MS. 2062, folio 70)

loved's runny nose, are considerably more nauseating than funny.

In 1617 King James visited Scotland, and Drummond published another occasional poem in heroic couplets: *Forth Feasting. A Panegyricke to the Kings Most Excellent Majestie.* The speaker of the poem is the River Forth, who welcomes the return of the Scottish-born monarch. Awakened from sleep by the sounds of rejoicing, Forth asks the reason for the tumult: "Then is it true what long I wish'd in vaine? / That my much-louing PRINCE is come againe?" She declares a "Holie-day" and calls all the waters of Scotland to join in celebration:

> *Nesse* smoaking-Sulphure, *Leaue* with Mountaines
> crown'd,
> Strange *Loumound* for his floting Isles renown'd:
> The irish *Rian*, *Ken*, the siluer *Aire*,
> The snakie *Dun*, the *Ore* with Rushie Haire,
> The Chrystall-streaming *Nid*, lowd-bellowing *Clyd*,
> *Tweed* which no more our Kingdomes shall deuide.

Turning to the king, Forth bids him welcome:

> To Virgins Flowres, to sunne-burnt Earth the
> Raine,
> To Mariners faire Winds amidst the Maine:
> Coole Shades to Pilgrimes, which hote Glances
> burne,
> Please not so much, to vs as Thy Returne.

The river goes on to praise the king as a hunter and as a student of astronomy, philosophy, and all the arts which make him a wise ruler. He is a great poet, and he has ruled Scotland's "People fierce" by the strength of his good example; in ages to come, no ancient monarch will be esteemed as highly as James, for the king's fame is now celebrated in the New World.

The river begs that James's visit may endure; but it is only a matter of time until Forth must lose the king to another. In a remarkable passage, she adopts the accents of a mistress spurned, imagining James's return to "*Isis*," the Thames:

> Now when (by *Honour* drawne) thou shalt away
> To Her alreadie jelous of thy Stay,
> When in Her amourous Armes Shee doth Thee
> fold,
> And dries thy Dewie Haires with Hers of Gold,
> Much questioning of Thy Fare, much of Thy Sport,
> Much of Thine Absence, Long, how e're so short,
> And chides (perhaps) Thy Comming to the North,
> Loathe not to thinke on Thy much-louing FORTH.

In *Teares on the Death of Meliades* Drummond had called the Scottish river Prince Henry's nurse and recorded her "*hoarse Plaint*" at the news of his passing; in *Forth Feasting* the river finds a voice, but her experience—and her suffering—remain very specifically female. It is ironic, then, that the most distinctive aspect of Drummond's personification should have been lost upon an admirer of the poem; in his elegy on the death of Drummond, the poet's friend George Lauder misremembered the very poem he praised so highly:

> And how did he from black *Benlowmond* bring
> Old Father *Forth*, to *Feast* his Lord and King?
> . . . .
> And to his Prince a *Panegyrick* sung,
> That *Mantua*'s Muse, and *Ascra*'s both had hung
> Their Heads for shame, his Heavenly Strains to
> hear.

Lauder's implied comparison of his friend to Virgil and Hesiod is typical elegiac excess, but Drummond's work was praised during his lifetime as well. His acquaintances were particularly moved by his evocations of melancholy. In a commendatory sonnet published with the second impression of the 1616 edition of *Poems*, Alexander wrote of how much he enjoyed reading his friend's poetry when he himself was sad:

> Then thou so sweetly *Sorrow* makes to sing,
> And troubled Passions dost so well accord,
> That more *Delight* thine *Anguish* doth afford,
> Than others *Ioyes* can Satisfaction bring.

Another of Drummond's friends, Mary Oxlie of Morpet, said that in *Meliades* the Orphean magic of Drummond's muse made all of nature mourn with him. From Drayton, in his metrical epistle "On Poets and Poesy," Drummond earned more modest praise; the Englishman commended both Alexander

> And my deare *Drummond*, to whom much I owe
> For his much love, and proud I was to know,
> His poesie, for which two worthy men,
> I *Menstry* still shall love, and *Hauthorne-den*.

As is clear from these lines, Drayton's respect for Drummond's work was entwined with personal regard. He first wrote to the laird of Hawthornden in 1618, seemingly to introduce a friend traveling in Scotland, and Drummond responded with two rhapsodic letters praising Drayton's works. Thus was launched an affectionate correspon-

Engraved portrait of Drummond inserted in the Bodleian Library copy of Drummond's 1614(?) Poems

dence which continued, though the two never met, until Drayton's death in 1631.

Drummond's admiration of other writers' work is expressed in various commendatory verses he composed; poems by him are prefixed to such volumes as the 1614 version of Alexander's *Doomes-Day* and Thomas Kellie's military manual, *Pallas armata* (1627). In praise of *The Trve Crvcifixe for True Catholickes* (1629), a polemical work by William Moore, Drummond wrote a sonnet pirating images from John Donne's poem "The Crosse." One of Drummond's most interesting poems of praise was, however, not published during his lifetime. Celebrating the writing of Lady Mary Wroth, Hawthornden declares that she and her uncle Sir Philip Sidney have described almost every kind of passion; however, one "and that most rare remaines / Not told by you, but to be proud by me." He has fallen in love, he explains, with her "speaking portrait drawn with liuing lines"; her poetry has sparked an emotion which "may (as begune) last without sight, / And by degrees contemplatively grow."

Of all Drummond's literary acquaintances the most famous was Ben Jonson, whom he met when the English poet walked to Scotland in 1618. Jonson stayed at Hawthornden from the end of the year into early January 1619. How

they were introduced is not clear; perhaps Jonson read the original edition of *Forth Feasting* or saw a slightly revised version in a 1618 collection, *The Muses Welcome*. At any rate, they spoke of the piece during his visit, for the Scotsman recorded Jonson's admission that, despite his reservations about Drummond's poetry, "he wished to please the King, that piece of Forth-Feasting had been his owne."

Jonson proved, of course, a voluble guest; and Drummond's notes on the English poet's pronouncements reveal something of the Scotsman's own character. Anxious to purge his verse of northern dialect, Drummond asked his visitor to clarify some points of grammar; and Jonson took every opportunity to advise the milder-tempered Scotsman on other subjects: "He recommended to my reading Quintilian (who (he said) would tell me the faults of my Verses as if he had Lived with me)." Jonson also offered the personal criticism "that I was too good and simple, and that oft a mans modestie, made a fool of his witt." Whatever Jonson may have thought, the laird of Hawthornden made a few mildly scathing judgments of his own. After recording Jonson's opinions of Petrarch, Guarini, and Ronsard, Drummond quietly observed that "all this was to no purpose, for he neither doeth understand French nor Italianne." Drummond's summary account of Jonson's character is deservedly famous:

> He is a great lover and praiser of himself, a contemner and Scorner of others, given rather to losse a friend, than a Jest, jealous of every word and action of those about him (especiallie after drink) which is one of the Elements jn which he liveth). . . . he is passionatelie kynde and angry, careless either to gaine or keep, Vindicative, but, if he be well answered, at himself.

The Scot clearly felt that he had been able to give Jonson the answer he deserved once or twice; but he remained cordial, and after the great man's departure the two corresponded briefly, as Drummond undertook to send Jonson various bits of historical and geographical information to be used in a play or poem about Scotland.

The notes on Jonson show that Drummond's interests were not exclusively grave and scholarly. He had a taste for clever anagrams and bawdy anecdotes, and took as much interest in Jonson's off-color comments as in his literary judgments. He records, for example, Jonson's theories on female companionship: "he thought the use of a maide, nothing jn comparison to the wantoness of a wyfe & would neuer have ane other Mistress." Drummond would not have been shocked with such talk; though he remained unmarried until the age of forty-five, he took a mistress during his thirties and, between 1625 and 1628, fathered three illegitimate children. He recorded their births and deaths (only one survived infancy), along with a detailed record of his own sicknesses and injuries over the years, in a list of "Memorialls."

"The moneth of November 1620," he notes there, "was fatall to mee by a sort of pleurisie on my right side which continued eight weeks." The disease inspired Drummond to write his own epitaph; in a sonnet to his friend Alexander, he asks that "Alexis" will, when he dies,

> graue this short Remembrance on my Graue.
> Heere *Damon* lyes, whose Songes did some-time
> grace
> The murmuring *Eske*, may Roses shade the place.

This sonnet was published—along with *A Cypresse Grove*, his prose treatise on death—in *Flowres of Sion*. The volume includes most of the poems previously published in the "Urania" collection, as well as some new religious pieces: sonnets, madrigals, longer hymns, and an incomplete poem on the Apocalypse. In moving from erotic to divine love, Drummond seems to have had in mind poetic as well as spiritual exaltation. MacDonald quotes a revealing passage from the poet's notebooks, in which he sketched an outline for a eulogy on himself:

> Δρουμμονδος . . . describing earthly Beautye and love . . . left all other of the Muses of Albion behind him . . . Now writing of heavenlye beauty and love and praising the eternal king of this universe he hath over-runne and out-matched himselfe . . . If Albions language were by tyme to perish it . . . should be preserved by thes . . . noble poems.

Though he never finished it, Drummond may thus have intended "The Shadow of Ivdgement" to be his greatest achievement; it is his lengthiest poem (ending abruptly in the midst of line 458) and demonstrates that he had some ability as a narrative poet. Echoing du Bartas's *Semaine* (1578) and Ronsard's "Hymne de la Justice," Drummond presents allegorical representations of figures such as Truth and Nature, who petition that the evils of the world may be put to an end. God unleashes on creation three haglike furies who vividly embody the biblical scourges of war, famine, and plague. The remainder of the fragment, however, involves rather stilted descriptions of wicked and godly men responding to the cataclysm.

Many of the sonnets in *Flowres of Sion* focus on the life of Christ and the saints. The best is a memorable piece on John, "The last and greatest Herauld of Heauens King." The imagery of the sonnet subtly evokes John the Baptist's hunger for the nourishment which the son of Mary would provide: "His food was Blossomes, and what yong doth spring, / With Honey that from virgine Hiues distil'd." Imagining the saint's "hollow Eyes" surveying the wilderness, Drummond paints a bleak portrait of his prophetic ministry:

> There burst he foorth; All yee, whose Hopes
> relye
> On GOD, with mee amidst these Desarts mourne,
> Repent, repent, and from olde errours turne.
> Who listned to his voyce, obey'd his crye?
> Onelie the Ecchoes which hee made relent,
> Rung from their Marble Caues, repent, repent.

Less dark and pessimistic are the hymns. Drummond's terza-rima poem on the Passion is a rendering of a piece in that meter by Jacopo Sannazaro. Drummond's melancholy muse is particularly well suited to the descriptions of nature mourning for the Redeemer:

> *And, cutting from her Browes her Tresses bright,*
> *The Moone doth keepe her Lords sad Obsequies,*
> *Impearling with her Tears this Robe of Night.*

The other hymns celebrate the Resurrection, the Ascension, "True Happinesse," and God as "the Fairest Faire." Two of these—the Ascension poem and the hymn of happiness—have unusual stanzas (of eight and six lines, respectively), which combine trimeter and pentameter; both have been compared to the unprecedented stanza of John Milton's "Nativity Ode," written in 1629.

The question of whether Milton was an admirer of Drummond's work has been much discussed. Milton would have appreciated the Scotsman's prosodic skills; and despite Drummond's Royalism, the tenor of several of his pieces would have appealed to the English poet. In his *History of Scotland* (1655) Drummond puts into the mouth of a sixteenth-century noble an eloquent argument for religious tolerance; and his poetry—especially the "Hymne of the Fairest Faire"—often resonates with a sense of the di-

Portrait of James I in Forth Feasting, *the poem Drummond wrote to celebrate the king's 1617 visit to Scotland*

vine not unlike Milton's own. In his edition of *Paradise Lost*, Alastair Fowler compares the opening of book 3, with lines from Drummond's hymn:

> O most holie One,
> Vnprocreat'd Father, euer-procreat'd Sonne,
> Ghost breath'd from both, you were, are, aye shall bee
> (Most blessed) Three in One, and One in Three,
> Vncomprehensible by reachlesse Hight,
> And vnperceiued by excessiue Light.

Later in the same poem, a beautifully enjambed couplet on the joys of Eden rings, despite the bondage of rhyme, with a Miltonic sentiment. Addressing God, the poet cries, "O Ioy of Ioyes! with our first Parents Thou / To commune then didst daigne, as Friends doe now." Another connection between Milton and Drummond is the fact that Milton's nephew, Edward Phillips, edited a posthumous collection of the Scotsman's poetry in 1656. David Masson, who wrote biogra-

phies of both Milton and Drummond, speculates in his account of the edition that "phrases about Drummond from Milton's own mouth were worked by Phillips into his prose preface." Phillips could not deny that Drummond "hath not had the good fortune to be so generally famed abroad as many others, perhaps of less esteem," but he declared the poet "a genius the most polite and verdant that ever the Scottish nation produced," and asserted that he had been outdone by "neither Tasso, nor Guarini, . . . nor even the choicest of our English Poets."

Despite the relatively limited circulation of his poetry, Drummond was not without honor in his own country. He proudly recorded in his "Memorialls" the various communities which made him a burgess, noting that, when that title was conferred upon him by Edinburgh in 1626, there was a "Ticket given mee in gold letteres." The city council may have honored Drummond in this way at least in part because of his generous donation—recorded that year and carried out in 1627—of some five hundred volumes to the University of Edinburgh Library. The poet had printed, for presentation with the books, a Latin catalogue to which he prefixed a preface, also in Latin, celebrating the value of books and libraries. In 1628, and again in 1630, Drummond contributed additional volumes.

Of the many books Drummond gave the library, the copy of his own *Flowres Of Sion* is particularly interesting. Many individual lines of text have been pasted over, presumably by the poet himself, with slips of paper on which are printed revised versions of the lines in a typeface resembling that of the surrounding text. The new readings are in most cases those which Drummond chose to adopt in the 1630 edition. He was always a careful reviser, but the fastidious changes he made between editions were not always well advised. Where the original reading shows an inspired talent, the altered version often makes painfully clear that the laird of Hawthornden was a man with just a bit more leisure time than poetic genius.

Nor was all of his energy spent on literary pursuits; in 1627 Drummond was granted a patent for some fantastic inventions. Presumably, none of his plans went beyond the sketchy descriptions included in the patent, but he proposed to build sixteen machines, including several automatic weapons, a tank-like *"Thundering Chariot,"* and a perpetual motion device. A more realistic pursuit was his rebuilding of Hawthornden house, which was completed in 1638. The renovations may have been prompted by the needs of a growing household, for in 1632 he had married Elizabeth Logan and started a family. Of their nine children, only three survived him.

When King Charles made plans for his official coronation visit to Scotland, the city of Edinburgh called upon Drummond to plan a ceremonial pageant. During a sickness of five weeks in February-March 1629, the poet prepared a script—combining passages in prose, Latin mottoes, descriptions of sets and costumes, and lyrics to be recited by persons representing Caledonia, the Muses, Endymion, and various mythological divinities. The king's visit to Scotland was long delayed, however, and the triumphal entry into Edinburgh did not take place until 15 June 1633; the text of *The Entertainment of the High and Mighty Monarch Charles* was published that year. In light of the events which were soon to unfold

in Britain, the lines spoken by Jove have a particularly ironic ring:

> Thou shalt turne Clients to the force of law,
> Thou armes shalt brandish for thine owne defence,
> Wrongs to repell, and guard weake innocence[.]
> . . . .
> All overcome, at last thy selfe orecome,
> Thou shalt make passion yield to reasons doome:
> For smiles of fortune shall not raise thy mind,
> Nor dismall most disasters turne declin'd[.]

The Olympian voices a devout Royalist's desires, and in the years that followed, Drummond never completely abandoned his hopes that Charles would prevail and maintain peace; but the ruler's inability to protect those faithful to the crown sorely tried Drummond's loyalties. Many of the unpublished prose treatises which he wrote during the reign of Charles are concerned, in one way or another, with the institution of monarchy. Around 1633 he began his *History of Scotland*; in 1638 he wrote "Irene," arguing that Scotland should respond with grateful obedience to King Charles's concessions in the autumn of that year. Neither these pieces, nor any of the other treatises, addresses, and letters Drummond wrote during the 1630s and 1640s, were published during his lifetime; but many of them were no doubt circulated in and around Edinburgh.

He was to publish only one more poem—a pastoral elegy on the death of William Alexander's son Anthony. This 1638 piece, like the *Entertainment*, appeared anonymously. The laird of Hawthornden had clearly turned away from the pursuit of poetic laurels in order to contribute his wisdom to the state in a time of increasingly turbulent politics. The educated gentry had, he felt, an obligation to serve as advisers to the monarch and examples to the people. Despite the gravity with which he approached that obligation, however, Drummond was becoming more and more disillusioned. The unpublished verses he wrote during his later years express his exasperation, and they are unlike any of the pieces he put into print. Some have the sarcastic, highly topical feel of traditional Scots *flyting*; his lines "On the isle of Rhe," for example, play upon the Scots pronunciation of "duke" and the kind of cannon called a "drake" to criticize the military failures of George Villiers, first Duke of Buckingham: if he would "haue better lucke" the king must "Send forth some Drakes, and keep at home the Ducke." Other pieces, such as his four-line epigram on the death of the politician John Pym, bristle with the sort of wit Jonson would have enjoyed: when the Parliamentarian enters the gates of Hell, he asks where he is and a devil answers: "This is the lower howse."

Sometime around the spring of 1639, Drummond was finally pressured into signing the Presbyterian party's National Covenant; his verses on the subject are particularly bitter:

> Giue me a thousand couenants, I'll subscriue
> Them all, and more, if more yee can contriue
> Of rage and malice; and let eurye one
> Blake treason beare, not bare Rebellione.
> I'll not be mockt, hist, plunder'd, banist hence
> For more yeeres standing for a . . . prince.
> . . . .
> I'll not die Martire for any mortall thing,
> It's enough to be confessour for a king.

Whatever word was intended to fill the blank space before "prince," Drummond was clearly angry with Charles. Even so, he continued until the end of his life to write satirical and polemical prose defending an essentially Royalist stance.

During his later years, in spite of the violence and unrest plaguing Britain, the poet did perhaps manage some lightheartedness; if it is by Drummond, as his editors conjecture, the macaronic *Polemo-Medinia* is evidence that Drummond never lost his somewhat pedantic sense of humor. The poem, first published in an undated edition sometime between 1642 and 1650 (and again under Drummond's name in 1691), tells of a dispute between two Fifeshire communities about which should have the right of way on a certain stretch of road. A great battle ensues when the muck carts of Scotstarvet—led by the Amazonian personification "Vitarva"—are challenged by the folk of Newbarns under their leader, the alarming "Neberna furens." The combatants, named in epic catalogue, include such titans as "Willie Dick, heavi-arstus homo," and the action reaches its climax when one of the Vitarvian warriors is pierced by a Nebernian girl's sewing needle. As the narrator proclaims: "O qualis hurlie burlie fuit!"

The hurly-burly of the times was, however, all too real; and it must have taken its toll on the aging laird. Charles I was executed in January 1649, and on 4 December of that year Drummond's son recorded in the "Memorialls" that his father had "dyed of a sort of gravell." In epitaphs on two acquaintances who preceded him to the grave during 1649, Drummond marks the fact that they "dyed with our Monarchie and State." To the poet, Britain without her prince was but a corpse.

Drummond's brother-in-law and friend John Scot of Scotstarvet was probably responsible for the 1655 publication of his *History of Scotland*, which was bound together with several of the political treatises, some of Drummond's private correspondence, and *A Cypresse Grove*. Scotstarvet probably also provided Edward Phillips with the copy texts from which he prepared the 1656 edition of *Poems by That most Famous Wit, William Drvmmond of Hawthornden*. The first edition of Drummond's *Works*, complete with its introductory memoir by Bishop Sage, appeared in 1711. The renewed interest in his writings was no doubt due to the admiration which a remnant of put-upon Scottish Episcopalians had for Drummond's conservative prose. The notes on Jonson were abridged in the 1711 edition of Drummond's works and first published in their entirety by the Society of Antiquaries of Scotland in *Archaeologia Scotica* (volume 4, 1833). Both Kastner's edition and French Rowe Fogle's study include selections of previously unpublished poems from the Hawthornden manuscripts.

Even during his lifetime, Drummond's audience was not large; he portrayed himself as a man in love with solitude, content to dwell "Farre from the madding Worldlings hoarse Discords." But as the echo of this line in Thomas Gray's *Elegy written in a Country Church-Yard* (1751) suggests, Drummond's poetry may have worked its quiet influence on his successors.

Biographies:
"The Life of William Drummond of Hawthornden," attributed to Bishop John Sage, in *The Works of William Drummond, Of Hawthornden*, edited by Sage and Thomas Ruddiman (Edinburgh: Printed by James Watson, 1711), pp. i-xi;

David Masson, *Drummond of Hawthornden: The Story of His Life and Writings* (London: Macmillan, 1873).

References:
David W. Atkinson, "The Religious Voices of Drummond of Hawthornden," in *Studies in Scottish Literature 21*, edited by G. Ross Roy (Columbia: Department of English, University of South Carolina, 1986), pp. 197-209;

Robert Cummings, "Drummond's *Forth Feasting*: A Panegyric for King James in Scotland," *Seventeenth Century*, 2 (January 1987): 1-18;

H. Neville Davies, "Milton's Nativity Ode and Drummond's 'An Hymne of the Ascension,'" *Scottish Literary Journal: A Review of Studies in Scottish Language and Literature*, 12 (May 1985): 5-23;

French Rowe Fogle, *A Critical Study of William Drummond of Hawthornden* (New York: King's Crown Press, Columbia University, 1952);

Ronald D. S. Jack, "Drummond of Hawthornden: the Major Scottish Sources," *Studies in Scottish Literature*, 6 (July 1968): 36-46;

Jack, *The Italian Influence on Scottish Literature* (Edinburgh: Edinburgh University Press, 1972);

Jack, "Petrarch in English and Scottish Renaissance Literature," *Modern Language Review*, 71 (October 1976): 801-811;

Jack, ed., *The History of Scottish Literature, I: Origins to 1660 (Medieval and Renaissance)*, general editor Cairns Craig (Aberdeen: Aberdeen University Press, 1988);

Robert H. MacDonald, "Drummond of Hawthornden, Miss Euphemia Kyninghame, and the 'Poems,'" *Modern Language Review*, 60 (October 1965): 494-499;

MacDonald, ed., *The Library of Drummond of Hawthornden* (Edinburgh: Edinburgh University Press, 1971);

David Masson, *The Life of Milton Narrated in Connexion with the Political, Ecclesiastical, and Literary History of His Time*, volume 5 (London: Macmillan, 1877);

Edwin Morgan, "Gavin Douglas and William Drummond as Translators," in *Bards and Makars: Scottish Language and Literature: Medieval and Renaissance*, edited by Adam J. Aitken, Matthew P. McDiarmid, and Derick S. Thomson (Glasgow: University of Glasgow Press, 1977), pp. 194-200;

Sibyl Lutz Severance, " 'Some Other Figure': The Vision of Change in *Flowres of Sion*, 1623," in *Spenser Studies: A Renaissance Poetry Annual*, volume 2, edited by Patrick Cullen and Thomas P. Roche, Jr. (Pittsburgh: University of Pittsburgh Press, 1981), pp. 217-225;

Ruth C. Wallerstein, "The Style of Drummond of Hawthornden in its Relation to His Translations," *PMLA*, 48 (December 1933): 1090-1107;

Wolfgang Weiß, "The Theme and Structure of Drummond of Hawthornden's Sonnet Sequence," *Scottish Studies*, 4, *Scottish Language and Literature, Medieval and Renaissance*, edited by Dietrich Strauss and Horst W. Drescher (Frankfurt am Main, Bern & New York: Peter Lang, 1986), pp. 459-466.

Papers:

The Hawthornden Manuscripts, bound into fifteen volumes, are owned by the Society of Antiquaries of Scotland and deposited at the National Library of Scotland in Edinburgh. Drummond's original manuscript of his conversations with Jonson has not survived, but a transcript made by Sir Robert Sibbald (1641-1722) is preserved in the same library among the Sibbald manuscripts (MS. 33. 3. 19, fols. 25-31).

Giles Fletcher the Younger

(1585 or 1586 - 1623)

Frank S. Kastor
Wichita State University

BOOKS: *Christs Victorie, and Triumph in Heaven, and Earth, over, and after death* (Cambridge: Printed by C. Legge, 1610);

The Reward of the Faithfull (London: Printed by B. Alsop for B. Fisher, 1623).

Editions: *Complete Poems of Giles Fletcher*, edited by Alexander B. Grosart (London: Chatto & Windus, 1876);

Giles and Phineas Fletcher: Poetical Works, 2 volumes, edited by Frederick S. Boas (Cambridge: Cambridge University Press, 1908, 1909).

OTHER: "A Canto Upon the Death of Eliza," in *Sorrowes Ioy. Or, A Lamentation for our late deceased Soveraigne Elizabeth, with a triumph for the prosperous succession of our gratious King, James* (Cambridge: Printed by J. Legat, printer to the University of Cambridge, 1603);

"In fatum sumi & beatissimi Principis Henrici" and "Carmen Sepulchrale," in *Epicedium Cantabrigiense, In obitum immaturum, semperque deflendum, Henrici, Illustrissimi Principis Walliae* (Cambridge: Printed by C. Legge, 1612); second printing, adds English poems, including "Upon the most lamented departure of the right hopefull, and blessed Prince Henrie Prince of Wales," by Fletcher (Cambridge: Printed by C. Legge, 1612).

Since his own day, Giles Fletcher the younger has been known as a member of an illustrious family of poets: his father, Giles, Elizabethan poet, courtier, and ambassador; his elder brother, Phineas, Cambridge fellow, poet, and priest; his cousin John, poet, dramatist, and collaborator with Francis Beaumont and others in many popular Jacobean plays. At Cambridge University, where he spent fifteen years (1603-1618), he was known for his important role in an active literary coterie, the "School of the Fletchers," and as the author of a successful heroic poem, *Christs Victorie, and Triumph in Heaven, and Earth* (1610),

which influenced, among others, John Milton. Subsequently, literary historians have related his work to Milton as well as to Edmund Spenser, who influenced Fletcher's poetry. He has been described as a bridge between Spenser and Milton, as a Spenserian poet, and as an early baroque religious poet. Interest in Giles Fletcher has been unusually mercurial over the centuries.

In his *History of the Worthies of England* (1662) Thomas Fuller recorded that Giles Fletcher the younger was born in London to "Giles Fletcher, doctor in law, and ambassador into Russia." His mother, Joan, was one of the Sheafes of Cranbrook, Kent, the Fletcher family seat. The third child and the second son, Giles was born sometime between the Novembers of 1585 and 1586, while his father was in London as a member of Parliament. The family appears to have divided its time between London and Cranbrook.

After studying at Westminster School, London, Giles joined his brother Phineas at Cambridge, entering Trinity College in late 1602 or early 1603. A scholarship in 1605 and a B.A. degree in 1606 were followed by a fellowship at Trinity in 1608. In 1603 poems by both brothers were selected for inclusion in a university anthology commemorating the death of Queen Elizabeth. The paradox stated in the full title of the volume clearly suggests an avoidance of public grief in a nation that was also welcoming a new king: *Sorrowes Joy. Or, A Lamentation for our late deceased Soveraigne Elizabeth, with a triumph for the prosperous succession of our gratious King, James.* In Fletcher's poem the nymphs, who "were woont to daunce & leape," were weeping over "Elizaes death" until "A sheapheard [James I] drove his flocke by chance that way / & made the nymph to dance that mourned yesterday."

"A Canto Upon the Death of Eliza" is a formal song (canto) of lament sung by a mythological figure, Ocyroe, the water nymph with prophetic powers described in Ovid's *Metamorphoses*. In Fletcher's poem she sits on a nonspecified

"The Nativity" and "The Baptism"; engravings by George Yate in the 1640 edition of Christs Victorie, and Triumph in Heaven, and Earth

rock, surrounded by nymphs, next to an unnamed pastoral stream. The same ideal pastoral world and mode of writing were common in Elizabethan literature; Spenser's *Shepheardes Calender* (1579) and Sir Philip Sidney's *Arcadia* (1590) both appear to have influenced Fletcher generally and this poem especially.

Along with mythological figures and allusions, the relationship of music and poetry is fundamental to "A Canto Upon the Death of Eliza," as it is in the typical well-made Elizabethan poem. (A few years later in "At A Solemn Music" Milton would refer to those "Sphere-born harmonious sisters, Voice and Verse.") Fletcher also employs the pastoral devices of personification and pathetic fallacy as Ocyroe evokes parts of nature—flowers, streams, trees, birds— soliciting their feelings. Highly rhetorical and elaborate description forms the stylistic center of the poem, which for all its conceptual thinness shows considerable skill:

Tell me ye velvet headed violets
That fringe the crooked banke with gawdie blewe,

So let with comely grace your prettie frets
Be spread, so let a thousand *Zephyrs* sue
To kisse your willing heads, that seeme t'eschew
    Their wanton touch with maiden modestie,
    So let the silver dewe but lightly lie
Like little watrie world within your azure skie.

Characterized throughout by such lovely, musical language, reminiscent of poems by Sidney, John Lyly, Michael Drayton, and Spenser, this graceful piece of Elizabethan verse seems an appropriate tribute to "our late deceased Soveraigne Elizabeth."

During the years 1603-1610, the two Fletcher brothers were the nucleus of a literary coterie which slowly grew around them at Cambridge. At first the group included two musician-poets, John and Thomas Tomkins, as well as Samuel Woodford and perhaps Giles Fletcher the elder. Later, Francis Quarles, Edward Benlowes, Izaac Walton, and perhaps Abraham Cowley joined their circle. The major achievement of this period of Giles's career was the publication by Cambridge University Press of his most significant work, *Christs Victorie, and Triumph*, a sacred, heroic poem, or epyllion, in four books. Not only did this poem become the basis of his subsequent reputation as a poet, it also proved significant in the literary history of the century. It powerfully yet economically presented Giles's claims for "prophane Poetrie to deale with divine and heavenly matters" (in "To the Reader").

Renaissance idealism about poetry, perhaps best expressed in English by Sidney's *Defence of Poesie* (1595), found a thoroughly religious commitment in the seventeenth century. To make that commitment, the poet had to escape from the traditionally close relationship of court and poetry, but seemingly few sixteenth-century poets could or would. Sidney, who best represents the ideal courtly Elizabethan poet, wrote mainly secular poetry. While Spenser had included religious material in his work (pastorally, allegorically, or eclectically mixed with secular material), he neither identified himself as a religious poet nor suggested for himself the role of *vates* (sacred or prophetic poet). Giles and Phineas Fletcher, John Milton, George Herbert, Richard Crashaw (to some extent), and John Bunyan were among those poets of the seventeenth century who identified themselves with that role and intentionally separated themselves from the court, from the clergy, or from both.

In "To the Reader" of *Christs Victorie, and Triumph*, Giles—like Sidney—argues on the basis of Aristotle, Horace, and Plato that poetry forms a more lofty and effective education than philosophy, history, and music, but he departs from Sidney's emphasis on secular poetry and focuses on divine poetry, referring to David and other sacred poets: Gregory of Nazianzus; Basil; Juvencus; Prosper; Prudentius; Sedulius Scottus; Nonnus; Jacopo Sannazaro; Guillaume de Salluste, Seigneur Du Bartas; Edmund Spenser; and King James. Giles also mentions "divine Poems of the Genealogie, Miracles, Parables, Passion of Christ" as well as "hymnes, and Psalmes, and spirituall songs." Of particular note are his remarks about Sannazaro, Du Bartas, and Spenser: "*Sanazar*, the late-living Image, and happy imitator of *Virgil*, bestowing ten years upon a song, onely to celebrat that one day when Christ was borne unto us on earth, & we (a happie change) unto God in heav'n: thrice-honour'd *Bartas*, & our (I know no other name more glorious then his own) Mr. *Edmund Spencer* (two blessed

Soules).... " Fletcher's debt to these poets (and Virgil) appears notable in *Christs Victorie, and Triumph* and suggests distinct approaches to the poem for readers and critics.

The "divine and heroical matters" of Fletcher's poem are indicated first in its full title—*Christs Victorie, and Triumph in Heaven, and Earth, over, and after death*—and then in the opening announcement of the epic subject:

> How God, and Man did both embrace each other,
> Met in one person, heav'n, and earth did kiss,
> And how a Virgin did become a Mother,
> And bare that Sonne, who the worlds Father is,
> And Maker of his mother, and how Bliss
>   Descended from the bosome of the High,
>   To cloathe himselfe in naked miserie,
> Sayling at length to heav'n, in earth, triumphantly,
>
> Is the first flame, wherewith my whiter Muse
> Doth burne in heavenly love, such love to tell[.]

Although this passage is glossed with a marginal note ("The Argument propounded in generall: Our Redemption by Christ"), many readers have been puzzled by Fletcher's treatment of his subject, as well as by the general structure of the work. The two main parts of the poem, the "Victorie" and the "Triumph" of Christ, are composed of two books each: "Christs Victorie in Heaven" (book 1) presents a debate between Mercy and Justice and ends with a brief description of Christ's Birth; "Christs Victorie on Earth" (book 2) deals with the Temptation of Christ by Satan in the Wilderness; "Christs Triumph over Death" (book 3) treats the Crucifixion; "Christs Triumph after Death" (book 4) presents the Resurrection and Ascension.

Fletcher's twenty-two-hundred-line poem includes few details of Christ's life and ministry but much seemingly extraneous material: for example, allegorical discussions in heaven about the Fall of Adam and Eve, wars of angels, Satan's apostasy in heaven, his evil seduction of man in the Garden of Eden, the creation of the cosmos, the nature of the physical universe, and a lengthy description of the heavenly city of God. Yet *Christs Victorie* emanates from a tradition practiced by writers mentioned in "To the Reader." Du Bartas's *Semaines*, completely translated into English by 1608 by Josuah Sylvester, was probably the most influential literary work of its time. A version of the Christian story of divine history, this twenty-three-thousand-line allegorical epic deals with the six days of creation. Other works in this

"The Temptation in the Wilderness" and "The Crucifixion"; engravings by George Yate in the 1640 edition of Christs Victorie, and Triumph in Heaven, and Earth

tradition include Prudentius's *Psychomachia*, which presents the struggle of good and evil as an epic war, and his *Harmartigenia*, which deals with episodes of scriptural history; Sedulius's *Carmen Paschale*, a version of the same story in five books; and Spenser's "A Hymn of Heavenly Love," a version in 1,753 lines.

Christs Victorie, and Triumph* is another version of the Christian story of divine history, and John Milton, who was familiar with Fletcher's poem, followed in the same tradition with *Paradise Lost* (1667) and *Paradise Regained* (1671). Thus the relationship between the two poets goes beyond the fact that Milton borrowed from Fletcher's poem. Milton's "On the Morning of Christ's Nativity" (written in 1629) bears a close relationship to the nativity descriptions in *Christs Victorie, and Triumph* (book 1), and *Paradise Regained* is even more similar to book 2.

Fletcher's poem is structured around four episodes from Christ's life: Nativity, Temptation, Passion, and Resurrection. Each of these events—

celebrated as part of the great victory of Christ over Satan, Sin, and Death—is at the center of one book. Around each is woven a vast panoply of Christian history and beliefs. Unlike most earlier Christian works in this tradition, Giles's poem is distinctly Christocentric. It could be viewed, therefore, as a *Christiad*, an English version of Vida's *Christiados* (1527), a Latin epic in six books.

Set in heaven among saints and angels, the first book, "Christs Victorie in Heaven," centers on a debate between personifications of Justice and Mercy over fallen man. Mercy pleads for guilty man with "the musique of her voice." "Not . . . deafe and blind," but "a Virgin of austere regard," Justice—carrying a sword amid a retinue of allegorical personages—indicts "wicked, unjust, and impure man" and calls for punishment. The climax of this book is Mercy's narration and celebration of Christ's first victory, his Nativity, described appropriately in heaven, where it was conceived. In response to Mercy's speech, God the Father and the angelic armies disavow "Their former rage [at Justice's indictment], and all to Mercie b[ow'd]."

Book 1 is static rather than dramatic, producing a sense of timeless significance, of emblematic celebration. To focus attention on themes and qualities rather than on events and characters, Fletcher employed the technical device of the *figure*. Mercy, who dominates book 1, is a *figure* especially rich in meanings. She is a "fairie Idea," who cannot be described because she is a Platonic Ideal: the absolute, perfect Idea of mercy, who exists only in God's mind. All particular instances of mercy are only imperfect versions of her. Her beauties must be described by *analogy* to physical things, for she exists on an abstract level. Her garments, depicting the whole Created Cosmos, symbolize her closeness to God the Creator and her permeation of the entire universe. Like Love, Justice, Wisdom, and Faith, she represents a segment of the mind of God the Father, but she also represents the Son. In short, Mercy is a character, an act, a theme, a value, a quality, a theological principle, a mystery of faith, an Ideal, a symbol. The art of book 1 is not the art of realistic representation but the art of the emblem, figure, and allegory. Description and rhetorical embellishments are important corollaries of its style.

Book 2, "Christs Victorie on Earth," is much more straightforward and narrative than book 1, and it deals with its principal event, the Temptation of Christ, directly and exclusively. Modern readers may find it difficult to view Christ's temptation in the wilderness as having as much importance as his Passion and Crucifixion, but Giles was not alone among his contemporaries in placing theological and literary emphasis on that event. They embraced the idea of Christ as the second Adam who had demonstrated that man could overcome the temptations of Satan.

Renaissance literature reflects the views of an age passionately concerned with trial and temptation. The Calvinists particularly focused on the subject. Trial and temptation are central to Spenser's *Faerie Queene* and most of Milton's prose and poetry. Milton equated the regaining of Paradise with Christ's victory in the wilderness rather than at Calvary. In *Areopagitica* (1644) he wrote: "I can not praise a fugitive and cloistered virtue, unexercised and unbreathed, that never sallies out and sees her adversary, but slinks out of the race where that immortal garland is to be run for, not without dust and heat. Assuredly we bring not innocence into the world, we bring impurity much rather: that which purifies us is trial, and trial is by what is contrary." That paragraph concludes, in fact, with a comment that applies directly to book 2 of Fletcher's poem: "which was the reason why our sage and serious poet Spenser, whom I dare be known to think a better teacher than Scotus or Aquinas, describing true temperance under the person of Guyon, brings him in with his palmer through the cave of Mammon and the bower of earthly bliss, that he might see and know, and yet abstain." Milton refers to a passage in Spenser's *Faerie Queene* (book 2) that is probably the source for the Cave of Despaire and Bower of Vaine Delight in book 2 of *Christs Victorie, and Triumph*; in fact book 2 is reminiscent of Spenser's *Faerie Queene* in episodes, allegory, action, place, style, verse texture, and even the pace of the narrative, which relies on description rather than characterization or drama. For critics who see Giles Fletcher as a literary bridge from Spenser to Milton, "Christs Victorie on Earth" provides a concrete link from *The Faerie Queene* to *Paradise Regained*.

Book 3, "Christs Triumph Over Death," celebrates the Passion and Crucifixion, without describing them as events. The poet's own voice dominates the poem just as a priest's dominates the liturgy. Lacking narrative movement, this book has the rational structure of a sermon in which scriptural details and themes concerning the Passion are used as motifs. All the rhetorical devices work toward the goal of persuading the reader to share the poet's response to the Passion, and the voice which carries the reader is that of the *vates* (literally as well as figuratively). Book 4, even less narrative than book 3, brings the poem to its thematic and rhetorical climax in the triumphant "Beatific Vision."

Although *Christs Victorie, and Triumph* is unquestionably eclectic in composition, art, and craft, it is unified by its style. Fletcher could be describing the basis of his own poetic technique in the "heav'nly Eloquence" of the figure Mercy:

> As melting hony, dropping from the combe,
> So still the words, that spring between thy lipps,
> Thy lippes, whear smiling sweetnesse keepes her
>   home,
> And heav'nly Eloquence pure manna sipps,
> He that his pen but in that fountaine dipps,
>   How nimbly will the golden phrases flie,
>   And shed forth streames of choycest rhetorie
> Welling celestiall torrents out of poësie?

Indeed, "the golden phrases . . . / . . . shed forth streames of choycest rhetorie, / Welling celestiall torrents" in *Christs Victorie, and Triumph*. In an age of great stylists, Fletcher demonstrated one of the most self-consciously rhetorical styles. Mercy's persuasive power is based on a single feature—her words. Fletcher describes this feature through a series of elaborate, overlapping conceits concerning liquid, each developing as an enlargement on the one before it: *melting, sips, fountain, streams, wells, torrents*. Additional adornments include anadiplosis and alliteration.

In this stanza particulars are elaborated into complex, highly controlled patterns. Through analogies Fletcher develops a single detail, "the words," into an elaborate symbol of the whole, Mercy's persuasive powers. This passage exemplifies his manner of celebrating Christ throughout the poem. He starts with the four structural events as pillars and develops them ornately, extensively, even fantastically through devices of rhetoric, raising an elaborate poetic structure, a baroque cathedral in words, to the greater glory of God.

Critical response to *Christs Victorie, and Triumph* over the centuries has been diverse. Extant seventeenth-century responses, like those of Thomas Fuller and William Winstanley, tend to be general and positive. Neoclassical critics, who cared little for religious poets, largely ignored Giles Fletcher and his *Christs Victorie, and Triumph*. In the nineteenth century, however, the work received considerable attention, mostly affirmative. In his *Lives of the Sacred Poets* (1834), Robert Willmott, for example, found large flaws in *Christs Victorie, and Triumph* but acknowledged beauty in parts: "It has not the lustre of one great luminous whole, unbroken in the purity of its splendour; its brilliancy is dazzling, but fragmentary." Comparing *Christs Victorie, and Triumph* with Milton's *Paradise Regained*, however, Willmott was more affirmative: "In Scriptural simplicity of conception, and in calm and sustained dignity of tone, the palm of superiority must be awarded to Milton; while in fertility of fancy, earnestness of devotion, and melody of expression, Fletcher may be said to stand, at least, upon an equality with him." Ezekiel Sanford, editor of *The Works of the British Poets* (1819-1822), commented on "a tone of enthusiasm peculiarly solemn"; Robert Southey said that *Christs Victorie, and Triumph* "will preserve his name while there is any praise." An anonymous reviewer of an 1835 edition of the poem remarked, "The page is sprin-

kled all over like a field of violets. The verse moves along stately and liquid, freighted with close thought and earnest moral sense." The Reverend R. Cattermole, an editor of the thirty-volume *Sacred Classics* (1834-1836), called *Christ's Victorie, and Triumph* "a work of extraordinary merit and interest."

The most audible critic of Fletcher and his poem during the nineteenth century was clearly his editor Alexander B. Grosart. Grosart is unmistakably zealous about establishing Giles Fletcher's true place among the "worthies." Grosart's "Memorial Introduction" exhibits his characteristic enthusiasm, unrestrained appreciation, and personal tastes:

> The intensity of the Poet's own Love and Faith, Hope and Graciousness lies over his Poem—like a bar of sunlight—as one has seen such shattering itself in dazzling glory against a heath-purpled mountain-side. In unexpected turns, in equally unexpected places, you are reminded that you have no mere Singer working artistically but a "Saint"—in the Biblical not Medieval meaning—pouring out the glad Worship of his whole nature—a nature rich of faculty in itself and enriched with celestial riches.

Twentieth-century critics (mirroring twentieth-century critical trends in general) have expressed more negative views. In *A History of English Poetry* (1903), W. J. Courthope found fault in Fletcher's "impersonations," complaining that "He mixes his abstractions with real personages." Courthope disliked Giles's "astonishing want of judgement in [describing] Christ with 'snowie cheekes' " ("the luxuriousness of Marini") as well as his "passion for coining new words." H. E. Cory in his lengthy discussion of Spenser, the Fletchers, and Milton (1912) is usually negative, but he occasionally rises to the kind of mixed reaction that is reflected in Douglas Bush's comment in *Mythology and the Renaissance Tradition in English Poetry* (1932) that *Christs Victorie* is an "uneven but often beautiful work." In *The Spenserian Poets* (1969), however, Joan Grundy, one of the most recent critics to deal at length with Giles Fletcher, is strongly favorable, minimizing the "Spenserianism" in his work: "*Christs Victorie, and Triumph* is, formally, a very fluid work, almost druidical in its capacity to flow from one literary form to another. Thus although there are Spenserian echoes throughout, the second book is the only one extensively to adopt Spenser's Method." Like Grosart, she emphasizes the intensity and

"The Apotheosis"; engraving by George Yate in Christs Victorie, and Triumph in Heaven, and Earth

sense of rapture in the poem, which describes Christ's triumph and a joyous New Jerusalem, "one of the most sustained passages of poetic rapture to be found anywhere," and finding "most of it, magnificent."

Most often in the twentieth century the work has been discussed in relation to its place in the literary history of the period. In this context Frank Warnke calls *Christs Victorie* one of "the three most significant epic or quasi-epic poems between *The Faerie Queene* and *Paradise Lost*. Of these, Fletcher's work strikes the modern reader as the most accessible." Warnke, Grundy, M. M. Mahood, and others also relate the poem to baroque art and literature. In his *Poetry and Humanism* (1950), Mahood points out, "Like every Baroque work of devotional art, Fletcher's poem directs the impulses of humanism to the end of faith." William B. Hunter, Jr., who reminds readers of Spenser's extensive influence on "English poetry until well into the reign of Charles" and of Fletcher's part in the Spenserian tradition,

notes that modern criticism has not been kind to the English Spenserians.

In an age noted for its many excellent minor poets, however, Giles Fletcher's *Christs Victorie, and Triumph* reveals a poet with impressive skills. As a heroic celebration of Christ in an essentially nonnarrative, nonrepresentational mode, the poem reveals a striking spirit of dedication and seriousness of purpose. When rhetoric and emotion correspond, the poetry comes alive. When the link between the two is weak, the poem seems too conceptualized or too embellished: sheer excessive artifice and rhetorical filler replace substance; sensuous strings of sound replace sense; ornamentation obfuscates the subject.

The death of Prince Henry in 1612, like that of Elizabeth earlier, produced yet another poetic response from the university literary community. Fletcher contributed two Latin poems to *Epicedium Cantabrigiense* (1612), a collection of memorial poems in foreign and classical tongues.

For the second printing, which added a section of English poems, he produced his English poem "Upon the most lamented departure of the right hopefull, and blessed Prince Henrie Prince of Wales." The poem memorializes Henry by suggesting his importance to the cultural and emotional life of England in past, present, and future, as well as his importance to Heaven's plan and its relation to England. Like Fletcher's earlier "A Canto Upon the Death of Eliza," this poem is written in twelve stanzas of rhyme royal, but this time Fletcher omitted the final alexandrine. Despite this formal similarity, the two poems represent different poetic styles and literary periods. The memorial to Prince Henry is a fine poem by a mature poet, written in tough, tight verse, with economy of language, intense feeling, and effectively striking metaphors. The conceits and wit, which should remind readers of Donne and George Herbert, point to changing literary tastes in the early seventeenth century.

In May 1615 Fletcher's patron, Doctor Thomas Nevile, master of Trinity College and dean of Canterbury, died. Giles had dedicated *Christs Victorie, and Triumph* to Nevile. Soon after Nevile's death Fletcher left Cambridge, but within a year he had secured new patronage and embarked on a new career. According to the Fletcher family records, Sir Roger Townshend and his uncle, Sir Francis Bacon, "presented Mr. Gyles Fletcher of Trin: Coll: Camb. to the rectory of Helmingsham in Suffolk," the living from which they owned. Giles returned to Trinity College in 1618 and remained long enough to complete a degree of bachelor of divinity in 1619. The next year he married Anne Purland and became a rector of the country church at Alderton,

Suffolk. After a period of ill health and hardship, he died in 1623, the year of publication of his final work, a book of devotional prose, *The Reward of the Faithfull*. The title forms a fitting epitaph for Giles Fletcher the younger, whom Thomas Fuller called,

> one equally beloved of the Muses and the Graces, having a sanctified wit; witness his worthy poem, intituled 'Christ's Victory,' made by him being but bachelor of arts, discovering the piety of a saint, and the divinity of a doctor. He afterward applied himself to school divinity (cross to the grain of his genius as some conceive), and attained to good skill therein. When he preached at Saint Mary's his prayer before his sermon usually consisted of one entire allegory, not driven, but led on, most proper in all particulars.

References:

H. E. Cory, "Spenser, The School of the Fletchers, and Milton," *University of California Publications in Modern Philology*, 2, no. 5 (1912): 311-373;

R. J. Fehrenback, "The Marriage and Last Years of Giles Fletcher, the Younger," *Modern Philology*, 83 (May 1986): 395-398;

Thomas Fuller, *History of the Worthies of England*, 3 volumes, edited by P. Austin Nutall (London: T. Tegg, 1840);

Joan Grundy, *The Spenserian Poets* (London: Arnold, 1969);

William B. Hunter, Jr., Introduction to *The English Spenserians*, edited by Hunter (Salt Lake City, Utah: University of Utah Press, 1977), pp. 9-13;

Frank S. Kastor, *Giles and Phineas Fletcher* (Boston: Twayne, 1978).

Phineas Fletcher
(April 1582 - 1650)

Frank S. Kastor
Wichita State University

BOOKS: *Locustæ, vel pietas Jesuitica* (Cambridge: Printed by T. & J. Buck, printers to the University of Cambridge, 1627);

Brittain's Ida. Written by that Renowned Poët, Edmond Spencer (London: Printed by N. Okes for T. Walkley, 1628);

Sicelides a piscatory, as it hath been acted (London: J. Norton for William Sheares, 1631);

Joy in Tribulation. Or, Consolations for Afflicted Spirits (London: Printed by J. Beale for J. Boler, 1632);

The Way to Blessednes, A Treatise or Commentary on the First Psalme (London: Printed by J. Dawson for J. Boler, 1632);

The Purple Island, or the Isle of Man: Together with Piscatorie Eclogs and Other Poeticall Miscellanies (Cambridge: Printed by T. Buck & R. Daniel, printers to the University of Cambridge, 1633);

Sylva Poetica, by Phineas Fletcher, and *De literis antiquæ Britanniæ*, by Giles Fletcher the elder (Cambridge: Printed by T. Buck & R. Daniel, printers to the University of Cambridge, 1633);

A Fathers Testament (London: Printed by R. White for Henry Mortlock, 1670).

Editions: *The Poems of Phineas Fletcher*, 4 volumes, edited by Alexander B. Grosart (Blackburn: C. Tiplady, 1869);

Phineas Fletcher. Selected Poetry, Orinda Booklets, no. 6 (Cottingham: J. R. Tutin, 1904);

The Spenser of his Age, being Selected Poetry from the Works of Phineas Fletcher, edited by Walter Jerrold (Cottingham: J. R. Tutin, 1905);

Giles and Phineas Fletcher: Poetical Works, 2 volumes, edited by Frederick S. Boas (Cambridge: Cambridge University Press, 1908, 1909);

Venus & Anchises (Brittain's Ida) and Other Poems, edited by Ethel Seaton (London: Oxford University Press, 1926).

Phineas Fletcher was a distinct literary presence in the first half of the seventeenth century: "This learned person, Son and Brother to two ingenious Poets [Giles Fletcher the elder and the younger] himself the third, not second to either . . . ," wrote William Winstanley in *The Lives of the most Famous English Poets* (1687), where he devoted more space to "Phineas Fletcher . . . poet and philosopher" than to John Milton, George Herbert, or John Donne. Further evidence of Fletcher's reputation and influence comes from many sources in the seventeenth century: Izaak Walton complimented him highly; Francis Quarles described him as "The Spencer [*sic*] of this age"; Thomas Fuller included a biography of him in *The History of the Worthies of England* (1662). Influenced by Edmund Spenser, Phineas Fletcher, the nucleus of "The School of the Fletchers," wrote both prolifically and diversely, influencing in his own century not only Milton but also Quarles, Walton, Richard Crashaw, Joseph Beaumont, Owen Feltham, perhaps Abraham Cowley, and others afterward.

The son of Giles Fletcher the elder and his wife, Joan Sheafe, Phineas Fletcher was born and baptized in April 1582 at the Fletcher family seat in Cranbrook, Kent. He spent his boyhood in Cranbrook and London, where his father's career took him often, but his rural home remained central to his poetic consciousness, perhaps because his mother's family, the Sheafes, resided there. Like his father, he attended Eton and went on to King's College, Cambridge. In 1600 Phineas was elected scholar there, beginning an academic career which lasted fifteen years. He earned a bachelor of arts degree in 1604, became a master of arts in 1608, and was ordained in 1611, the same year in which he was granted a bachelor of divinity and a fellowship.

In late 1612, however, he took an extended leave of more than a year and a half from the college. He returned to residency in 1614 and produced his play *Sicelides* there in 1615, but shortly after the performance he ended his university ca-

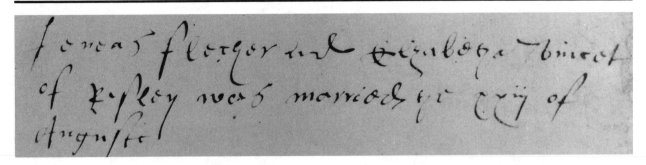

Entry for Fletcher's marriage in the parish register of Wilne, Derbyshire

reer. For the next five years he probably lived with Sir Henry Willoughby and his family at Risley Hall, Derbyshire, perhaps as chaplain. He married Elizabeth Vincent on 23 August 1615 at nearby Wilne, Derbyshire. In 1621 he became rector of the church at Hilgay, Norfolk (the living from which was owned by Willoughby), a position that he held for the rest of his life.

Fletcher, who wrote throughout most of his sixty-eight years, left behind a body of work larger than that of nearly any of his contemporaries; his works include three volumes of religious prose, an epic, an epyllion, a drama, several medium-length verse narratives, pastoral eclogues, verse epistles, epithalamia, hymns, psalms, translations, various songs, occasional pieces, lyrics, and devotional poems. In size, scope, and variety his canon rivals those of Spenser and Milton, the two literary giants to whom he is most often compared.

Fletcher, like Spenser, modeled himself on Virgil. Like both of these great poets, he began his career by writing pastorals and ended with epics. As Fletcher wrote in an early pastoral poem, "To my beloved Thenot," the "Two shepherds I adore with humble love" were Corydon of Virgil's *Bucolics* and Colin Clout of Spenser's *Shepheardes Calender* (1579). In Fletcher's earliest surviving poem, a pastoral, the singing shepherd is called Coridon.

The pastoral world may have offered an idealized natural world of universal truth to the Renaissance poet, but it also offered him the opportunity to disguise personal commentary as the song of a lowly shepherd. At Cambridge the young Phineas Fletcher was mainly concerned with the social aspects of pastoralism. His life, his friends, and his sense of being a poet are the subjects of his pastoral verses. Cambridge dominated his life and his poetry from about 1600 until 1615. The Cam River, the center of his pastoral setting, and the "oaten reed," symbolizing the pas-

toral poet, played the same roles for Fletcher as the river Mincius and the "reed" had for Virgil.

At Cambridge Phineas Fletcher was at the center of a literary group of relatives and friends, some of whom can be identified as the pastoral figures who people Fletcher's poems of this period. He was especially close to his brother Giles (Chromis), and their father, with whose role as a poet Phineas strongly identified, is Thelgon in the poems. Phineas's closest friend, John Tomkins, the organist of King's College and later of St. Paul's, London, became Thomalin in the pastorals. (Tomkins's brother, composer-musician Thomas Tomkins, was also a friend.) William Cappell, either a fellow student or Phineas's student, is Willy. Edmund Cook is the friend addressed as E. C., and William Woodford is probably Dorius. At first Phineas called himself Coridan, then he became Myrtil, Thirsil, and briefly Algon. Since he wrote under only one pseudonym at a time, they help to date his poems.

After borrowing the name Coridon from Virgil for his earliest pastorals, Fletcher took the name Myrtil (1603-1606), which had for him a special association with love and water, from a character in one of his father's pastorals. The name Thirsil, his main pastoral pseudonym for many years, was given to Phineas by his first lady love (called Fusca in his poems) in about 1606-1608. Fusca was from the other world of Phineas's poetry and life: Kent (especially Cranbrook, Brenchly's Hill, the Medway River, Ide Hill, and Hollingbourn). This region of his birth was peopled not only by the Sheafes but also by relatives such as the Pownalls (his aunt and cousins) and the Robarts (his cousins), as well as friends such as Elizabeth, Lady Culpeper of Hollingbourn, her daughter Elizabeth (possibly Fusca), and Elizabeth Irby. These friends, whom Phineas visited during vacations and to whom he wrote regularly, became part of his pastoral coterie, and

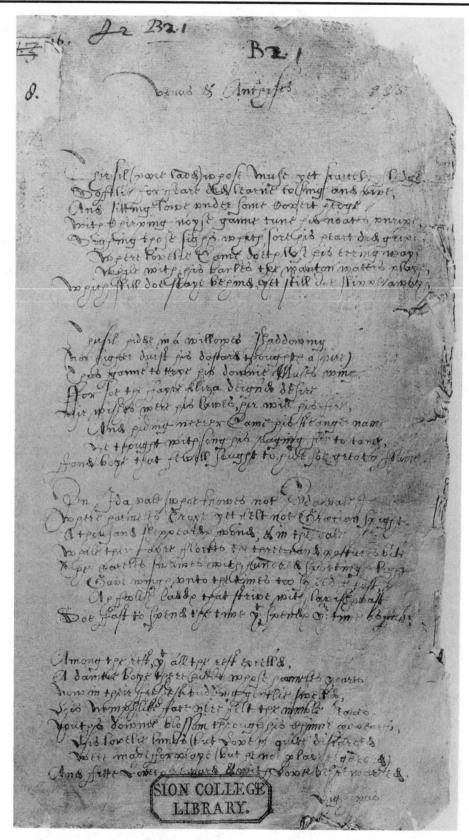

First page of Venus & Anchises *in the manuscript that establishes Fletcher's authorship of the poem, which was attributed to Edmund Spenser when it was published as* Brittain's Ida *in 1628 (Sion College Library, Cambridge; Latin Mss. Arc. L.40. 2/L.40.f. 235)*

Kent became an extension of Cambridge in his English pastoral poems, published as *Poeticall Miscellanies* in 1633, and his Latin *Sylva Poetica*, published in the same year.

Also published in 1633 was Fletcher's *Piscatorie Eclogs*, mostly written between 1606 and 1614 and undoubtedly meant to be his major pastoral work, his equivalent to Virgil's *Bucolics* or Spenser's *Shepheardes Calender*. Piscatory poetry forms a small but distinct part of the pastoral tradition. Although Theocritus had included some fisherboys among his shepherds, Jacopo Sannazaro's piscatory eclogues (1526) undoubtedly influenced Fletcher more. This piscatory type of pastorialism has its own Christian associations, symbols, and meanings.

Fletcher's *Piscatorie Eclogs*, like the *Bucolics* and *The Shepheardes Calender*, has an important biographical dimension. The seven eclogues are structured in loose chronological order by biographical events rather than by the date of their composition: 1) his father's career; 2) his father's departure from Cambridge; 3) Phineas's youthful loves; 4) his ministry; 5) love and marriage; 6) friendships; 7) his career change from university poet to poet-priest.

During his pastoral period Fletcher was also writing narrative poetry. *Venus & Anchises*, which may be his most extraordinary poem, was published in 1628 by Thomas Walkley as *Brittain's Ida*. Though Walkley attributed the poem to "*that Renowned Poët, Edmond Spencer* [*sic*]," Spenser scholars since the eighteenth century have rejected Spenser's authorship. Alexander B. Grosart first identified the poem as Phineas Fletcher's in 1869. In 1909 Frederick S. Boas devoted six pages to arguing for Fletcher's authorship by quoting extensive parallel passages from other Fletcher poems. Conclusive proof was provided in the 1920s, when Ethel Seaton found in the Library of Sion College, Cambridge, a manuscript that includes *Venus & Anchises* and six other poems by Phineas Fletcher.

Set in Ida Vale before the Greeks' siege of Troy, the story of *Venus & Anchises* is simple. One of the shepherd boys there, young, innocent Anchises, "A dainty playfellow for naked love," thinks neither of the "thousand maidens" who are pursuing him nor of sweet music and delights of song. He thinks only of hunting. Hunting one day, he finds "faire *Venus* grove," a veritable "Garden of delight" in which the sleeping Venus lies "halfe naked." Awaking, she thinks he is her beloved Adonis; then she realizes her error

but detains and loves Anchises. Though he falls in love with her, she must cajole him into confessing his feelings. After they consummate their love, he tells the world of their bliss, but jealous Jove hears about it and angrily sends his thunder down on Anchises, "Blasting his splendent face, and all his beauty swarted."

In the manuscript version of the poem the sixty-one eight-line stanzas (*ababbccc*) have no subdivisions. The published version, which lacks four stanzas, is divided into six cantos, each headed by a one-quatrain argument. Characterization is of little importance, while the description includes some notable extended word pictures, such as the Garden of Delight (nine stanzas including a love song) and Venus (thirteen stanzas). The Garden of Delight stanzas may be compared to the description in his brother Giles's *Christs Victorie, and Triumph* (1610) of the "Garden of Vaine Delight," which was influenced by Spenser's picture of the Bower of Bliss in *The Faerie Queene* (1590). Although Venus and her love song resemble Panglorie in Giles's poem and Spenser's Acrasia, Phineas's description of Venus depicts each part of her loveliness more systematically, creating more of an atmosphere of general sensuousness. This technique, also used effectively by Spenser and Milton, is appropriate for *Venus & Anchises*, where atmosphere is more important than character, setting, or plot. The pacing is also matched to the subject; the poem meanders like a languid stream where lovers might dally.

Among English Renaissance narrative love poems inspired by Ovid's *Metamorphoses* and *Amores*, *Venus & Anchises* must be rated high; it is comparable to Christopher Marlowe's *Hero and Leander* (1598) and William Shakespeare's *Venus and Adonis* (1593) in pace, lightness of touch, stylistic quality, and narrative skill. This poem may be Phineas Fletcher's finest work, but the early misattribution and uncertainty about its authorship, as well as the adulterated version that was published, have led to its virtual obscurity.

Around 1611 Fletcher completed a draft of *Locustæ, vel pietas Jesuitica* (1627), a narrative poem in Latin about the Gunpowder Plot, the bungled plan of Guy Fawkes and at least eight confederates to blow up the House of Parliament, murdering its members and James I, on 5 November 1605. Guy Fawkes Day had already become by act of Parliament "an annual and constant memorial of that day." In 1611 Fletcher first dedicated *Locustæ* to his father's friend James Montagu,

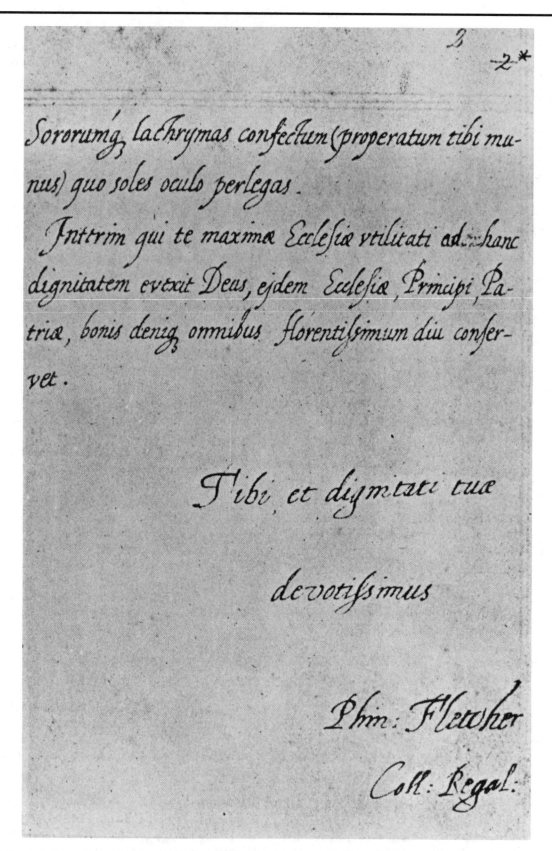

Part of the dedication to James Montagu, bishop of Bath and Wells, in the earliest of three surviving manuscripts, all in Fletcher's hand, for Locustæ, vel Pietas Jesuitica, *titled* Pietas Jesuitica *in the first two versions, both dating from 1611 (British Library, Sloane Mss. 444)*

Iesuitica

3

Qoin etiam sacri vulgata Scientia scripti
Invenit Superos terris, et luce corusca
Dissoluit tenebras, noctemq excussit inertem.
Et nunc illa qvidem, gentes emensa supremas,
Imperium terris æqvat, cæloq profundo.
Crescit in immensum pietas, finesq recusat
Relligionis amor; fugit Ignorantia, lucis
Impatiens, fugit Impietas, arcusq pudendos
Nuda Superstitio, et nunqvam non devius Error
Nunc etiam gentes multa olim nocte sepultas,
Virginiam nostras, umbræ, tot sæcula sedes,
Aggreditur; mox et manes, Stygiasq paludes
Tranabit, vix hunc nobis Acheronta relinqvet
At nos læthæo, per tuta silentia, somno
Sternimur interea, et media iam luce supini

Ster-

Page from the manuscript for the second version of Locustæ, *dedicated to Prince Henry (present location unknown; from Frederick S. Boas, ed.,* Giles and Phineas Fletcher: Poetical Works, *1908)*

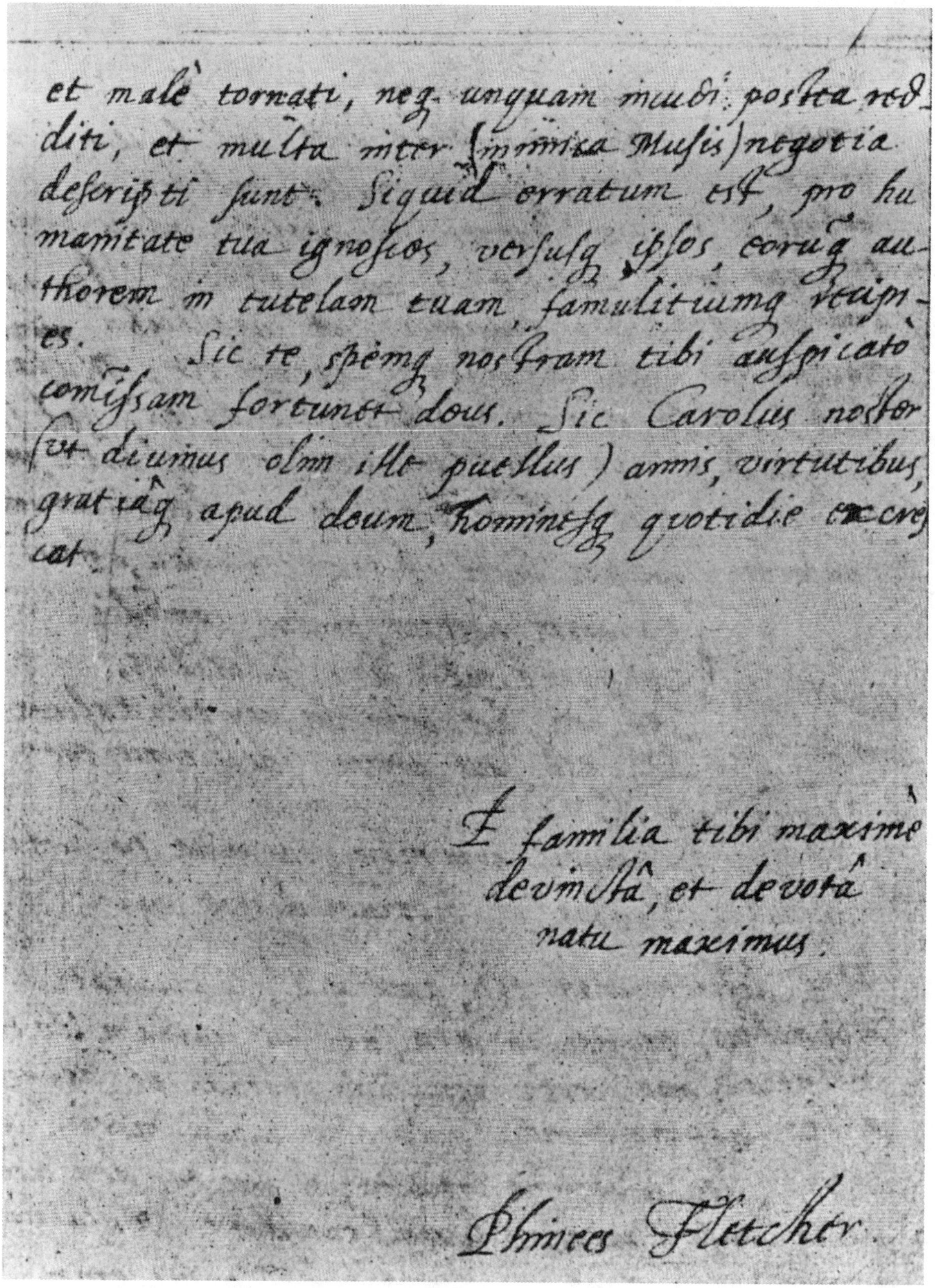

et malè tornati, neq. unquam incudi postea red-
diti, et multa inter (inimica Musis) negotia
descripti sunt. Siquid erratum est, pro hu-
manitate tua ignoscos, versusq ipsos, eorủg au-
thorem in tutelam tuam, famulitiủmq recipi-
es.   Sic te, spémq nostram tibi auspicatò
comissam fortunet deus. Sic Carolus noster
(ut divinus olim ille puellus) annis, virtutibus,
gratiàq apud deum, hominẻsq quotidie excres-
cat.

E familia tibi maxime
devinctâ, et devotâ
natu maximus.

Phinees Fletcher.

Part of the dedication to Thomas Murray in the manuscript for the third version of Locustæ, *written between 1612 and 1621*
(British Library, Harleian Mss. 3196)

bishop of Bath and Wells; but later in the same year he rededicated it to Prince Henry. After Henry's death in 1612, the poem was expanded, revised, and dedicated to Prince Charles and his tutor Thomas Murray. In 1627 it was published in Cambridge with a dedication to Sir Roger Townshend, patron of Giles Fletcher the younger. With it was published *The Locusts or Apollyonists*, which was dedicated to Mary, Lady Townshend. This English poem, customarily referred to as *Apollyonists*, is an expanded, paraphrastic version of *Locustæ*; its date of composition is unknown.

Like Milton's several Latin poems about the same subject, the *Apollyonists* presents the Gunpowder Plot as a Roman Catholic conspiracy against Protestant England. Forming a larger theological and narrative framework for the poem is the continuous battle of God with Satan and his forces. The poem thus relates not only to Milton's Latin epic "In Quintum Novembris" (1626) and his *Paradise Lost* (1667), but also to Giles Fletcher's *Christs Victorie, and Triumph*.

A heroic poem or epyllion of 5 cantos, 240 stanzas (rhymed *abababccc*), 1800 lines, the *Apollyonists* is more narrative and heroic than *Christs Victorie, and Triumph*. In the *Apollyonists* Phineas Fletcher presents the Gunpowder Plot as yet another episode in the eternal war between heaven and hell, the central conflict in the Christian view of history. Unlike large parts of *Christs Victorie, and Triumph* and most of *The Faerie Queene*, in both of which allegory is pervasive and central, the action in the *Apollyonists* is presented directly, with allegory playing a rare and merely decorative role. The *Apollyonists* is *not* a Spenserian poem. Directly religious and historical rather than allegorical and emblematic, tightly structured rather than diffuse, it moves sharply away from *The Faerie Queene* and strikingly toward *Paradise Lost*—for which it stands as a direct, influential precursor.

The *Apollyonists* is what Milton would call a "brief" epic (like "the book of Job" or his own *Paradise Regained*, 1671). Its tone is lofty; its style is epical; its narrative voice is that of the *vates*:

Teache me thy groome, here dull'd in fenny mire,
In these sweet layes, oh teach me beare a part:
Oh thou dread Spirit shed thy heavenly fire,
Thy holy flame into this frozen heart:
Teach thou my creeping Muse to heaven aspire,
Learne my rude brest, learne me that sacred art,
    Which once thou taught'st thy Israels
    shepheard-King:

O raise my soft veine to high thundering;
Tune thou my lofty song, thy glory would I
    sing.

Decorum as understood by a Renaissance writer necessitated that a poem to God's glory be a "lofty song." Like his brother Giles, Phineas employed rhetoric to create an appropriate, "high thundering" style. Relying on parallelism—varying aspects of isocolon, parison, paromoion—he also used many figures of speech, especially paradox, sententiae, and epic simile. The final alexandrine of each stanza is regularly "rhetorical": "Sleep's but a shorter death, death's but a longer sleep" (I. 6); "In proud, but dangerous gold: in silke, but restless bed" (I. 7); "For her he longs to live, with her he longs to die" (I. 13). These strong last lines also effectively strengthen the prosody.

Fletcher's epic is flawed, however. In cantos 3 and 4 the review of church and contemporary history is excessively long and redundant, and the style too often becomes journalistic. Fletcher's anti-Catholicism, which appears nowhere else in his work, is clearly a product of the occasion for this poem, but most modern readers will probably find his views excessive. Still, the *Apollyonists* may well seem a more impressive treatment of the Gunpowder Plot than Milton's "In Quintum Novembris"; and the fact that both Milton and John Oldham borrowed so much from this poem is itself a considerable testament.

About 1606-1608 Phineas began his most ambitious literary project, *The Purple Island* (1633). During the Renaissance the epic was held to be the most difficult and demanding type of poetry, the epitome of literary art, and inevitably the product of the poet's ripest years. It had been, for example, the final, crowning achievement in the literary careers of Homer, Virgil, Spenser, Torquato Tasso, Ludovico Ariosto, and Guillaume de Salluste, Sieur Du Bartas.

For a novice poet to write an epic poem was unprecedented. Fletcher's decision to do so while in his twenties reveals how fanciful his daydreams could be in this period—and how profound was his commitment to literature. Given his devotion to the pastoral during these same years, his decision to combine pastoral and heroic modes in a long narrative poem is understandable—at least as understandable as his making the narrator of *The Purple Island* "The Kentish lad that lately taught / His oaten reed the trumpets silver sound, / Young Thirsilis" and including some of his beloved friends as characters. By 1610, when his brother Giles described this work in progress, the main design and some parts, including the final scene, had been written. Internal evidence, including topical references and stylistic features, indicates, however, that Phineas continued to work on the poem until it was published in 1633.

The subject of *The Purple Island* is Man, treated allegorically as an island. By the end of the poem, the island is also a metaphor, a figure, and a complex symbol for Man. The pastoral world forms only a framework for the story that Thirsil tells to his fellow shepherds. Thirsil is a shepherd in both classical and Christian senses: "Great Prince of Shepherds, thou who late didst deigne / To lodge thy self within this wretched breast / . . . / Guide thou my hand, grace thou my artless quill: / So shall I first begin, so last shall end my will." The voice of the *vates*— literally a poet-priest before the poem was completed—is as unmistakable in *The Purple Island* as it is in *Christs Victorie, and Triumph*. Much larger and more ambitious than his brother's poem, Phineas's epic comprises five thousand lines in seven-line stanzas rhymed *ababccc*. Like the epics of Virgil and Spenser, *The Purple Island* is divided into twelve parts or cantos.

The work covers three large areas of Man: the external, physical anatomy; the internal, moral-mental-spiritual anatomy; and the war of virtues and vices. As in the *Apollyonists* and *Christs Victorie and Triumph*, the divine history of the conflict between God and Satan over man is an important unifying aspect, here providing a background against which the Isle of Man allegory is developed. As the only plot and action in the work, the Christian story provides something of a "higher Argument" for the epic.

Canto 1, an introduction or proem, establishes the subject, the type of poem, the literary precedents (both pastoral and heroic) and religious dimensions, as well as introducing the narrator and the other shepherds. Like all the cantos in the poem, canto 2 begins in the pastoral mode. Then Thirsil narrates the effects of the Fall upon Man, who is a "glorious image" of Christ. Stanzas 5-46, the remainder of the canto, are devoted to an extended, allegorical description of Man's physical anatomy. To make clear the relation between the human anatomy and the topography of the island, Fletcher wrote long, detailed glosses. For example, the "foundation," described in the poem as "rock" and "earth," is identified in a marginal note as "bones" and "cartilage." Streams, rivers, fountains, and trenches are glossed as blood, veins, arteries, and nerves.

The Isle of Man is divided into three "Metropolies," or governing regions (Belly, Brest, and Head), which serve as the main anatomical subdivisions in the rest of the poem. Canto 2 concludes with a detailed anatomy of the Belly or digestive system. Canto 3 describes features of island topography corresponding to aspects of the liver, the spleen, the kidneys, the uterus, and the generative organs, treating with modesty "those parts, which best are undescri'd.

Canto 4 moves to "th' Isles Heart-Cities," where the topography represents ribs, breast, muscles of respiration, diaphragm, lungs (including larynx, epiglottis, cartilage), and the heart. In canto 5, replete with classical mythology, the head is anatomized: "divided into the Citie, and suburbs; the brain within the wall of the skull, and the face without."

Canto 6 describes Adam, Eve, and their Fall from Eden, providing a transition to canto 7, which begins Thirsil's description of the internal, moral-religious anatomy of the island. Introducing the theme that happiness and success are not to be found on earth, the canto presents Satan's companions and qualities as allegorical personifications, including the Flesh, Adultery, Jealousie, Fornication, Sodomie, Lasciviousnesse, Idolatrie, Witchcraft, Heresie, Hypocrisie, Superstition, Hatred, Variance, Emulation, Wrath, Strife, Sedition, Murder, and Drunkennesse. These worldly sins are luridly portrayed in the fashion of late Medieval and early Renaissance theological allegory. In canto 8 Cosmos, the son of Satan, represents "the world or Mammon," whose battle companions are moral or ethical Vices, including Fearfulness, Foolhardiness, Arrogance, Prodigalitie, Covetousness, Feeblemindednesse, Ambition, Flatterie, Baseness of Minde, Morositie, Mad Laughter, Rusticitie, and Impudence.

Canto 9 provides allegorical portraits of theological Virtues—Spirit, Knowledge, Contemplation, Care, Humilitie, Obedience, Faith, Meditation, Penitence, Hope, Promise, Love, Remembrance, and Gratitude—and also "A lovely Swain . . . *Loves* twin," the Son of God, who is described at length. In canto 10 Thirsil describes moral and ethical Virtues, such as Peaceablenesse, Fortitude, Long Suffering, Courtesie, Temperance, Chastitie, and Modestie.

War breaks out in canto 11: "These mighty Heroes [Virtues] . . . / . . . / Glitt'ring in arms . . .

Title page and dedication in the volume that includes Fletcher's allegorical treatment of man's physical and spiritual being as the geography and inhabitants of an island

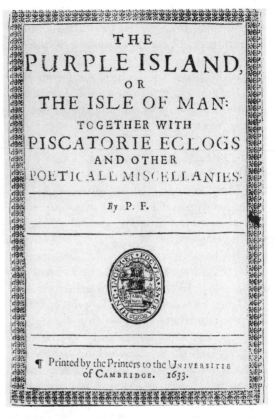

THE
PURPLE ISLAND,
OR
THE ISLE OF MAN:
TOGETHER WITH
PISCATORIE ECLOGS
AND OTHER
POETICALL MISCELLANIES.

By P. F.

Printed by the Printers to the UNIVERSITIE
of CAMBRIDGE. 1633.

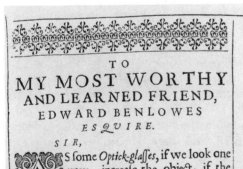

TO
MY MOST WORTHY
AND LEARNED FRIEND,
EDWARD BENLOWES
ESQUIRE.

SIR,

AS some *Optick-glasses*, if we look one way, increase the object; if the other, lessen the quantity: Such is an *Eye* that looks through *Affection*; It doubles any good, and extenuates what is amisse. Pardon me, *Sir*, for speaking plain truth; such is that eye whereby you have viewed these raw *Essayes* of my very unripe yeares, and almost childehood. How unseasonable are *Blossomes* in *Autumne!* (unlesse perhaps in this age, where are more flowers then fruit) I am entring upon my *Winter*, and yet these *Blooms* of my first *Spring* must now shew themselves to our *ripe wits*, which certainly will give them no other entertainment but derision. For my self, I cannot account that worthy of your *Patronage*, which comes forth so short of my *Desires,*

¶ 3

sires, thereby meriting no other light then the fire. But since you please to have them see more *Day* then their credit can well endure, marvel not if they flie under your *Shadow*, to cover them from the piercing eye of this very curious (yet more censorious) age. In letting them abroad I desire onely to testifie, how much I preferre your desires before mine own, and how much I owe to *You* more then *any other*: This if they witnesse for me, it is all their service I require. *Sir*, I leave them to your *tuition*, and entreat you to *love him* who will contend with you in nothing but to *out-love you*, and would be *known* to the world by no other *Name*, then

Your true friend,

P. F.

Hilgay. *May* 1. 1633.

To

/ Stood at the Castle gate, now ready bent / To sally out, and meet the enemies [Vices]." In canto 12 the Thunderer, "Like a Thousand Sunnes," comes out to battle; "The *KING* of Kings, & *LORD* of Lords" blasts the Dragon, and ends the war. The Dragon is imprisoned; the Prince of the Isle from "long imprisonment" comes out of the castle to "meet the Victour."

The Purple Island is easily one of the most unusual poems in English; it also may be one of the most eclectic and uneven. The superficial pastoralism, for example, seems to be present in the poem mainly because of Fletcher's preoccupation with pastoral poetry during the period when he began writing this epic.

His debt to Virgil and Spenser, his models during this period, is mentioned three times in *The Purple Island*, which also acknowledges the influence of Giles Fletcher's *Christs Victorie, and Triumph*. The two brothers were writing these two long poems at the same time, and internal evidence suggests that they were working closely together. In *The Purple Island* Phineas calls himself and his brother "two joyn'd in one, or one disjoyn'd in two." That closeness is reflected in their poems, each of which exhibits a strong sense of the poet as *vates* singing "Sacred Song" and includes cross-references to the other's poem. They even may have thought of their poems as parts of a larger, single work.

The two works certainly share another feature, allegory. Three writers that Giles mentions in *Christs Victorie, and Triumph*—Spenser, Du Bartas, and Prudentius—use allegory in the same way as Phineas does in *The Purple Island*. The allegorical war of Virtues and Vices within man, the subject of Prudentius's *Psychomachia*, is employed for similar moral, ethical, and theological ends in *The Faerie Queene* and *The Purple Island*.

The allegory of physical man as a purple island in cantos 2-5, however, distinguishes *The Purple Island* from other epics. These cantos, which form a nearly separate (and separable) section, read like science turned into literature. The long, involved marginal glosses reveal Fletcher's knowledge of human anatomy. A. B. Langdale concluded that Fletcher had derived some of the information in his glosses "from Aristotle, Galen, and Greece; from Ingrassias, Italy, and the sixteenth century; from Vicary; from John Caius and Gonville and Caius dissectors"; yet Langdale believes that he must also have had firsthand knowledge of human dissections: "Nothing intervened between the cadaver and the poet, and his writing was a reporting of what he had seen with his own eyes." Langdale is the only critic who has argued that the scientific part of *The Purple Island* is not only the most valuable part of the poem but also the high point of Fletcher's career, arguing that cantos 2-5 "rescue him from the slough of the commonplace and set him upon the high plain where he walks, humbly as was his wont, with Sir Francis Bacon, Galileo Galilei, William Harvey, and the other soldiers of science who warred against holy edicts, superstitions, lethargies, and all that vagrant rout." Since these four cantos are the sole example of Fletcher's "scientific" interests or knowledge, Langdale's inclusion of him among the "soldiers of science" seems excessive. Moreover, these cantos demonstrate how incompatible science and literature can be.

Combining science and literature in this fashion was a serious artistic and aesthetic error. Cantos 2-5 are dull, static, and often distasteful. They are also extraneous to the rest of the poem because the parts of the body play no direct role in the conflict and warfare described in cantos 6-12. In fact, all the parts of *The Purple Island* are dissonant. The blood and organs of the anatomy theater are hardly suitable subjects for a pastoral idyll, with its shepherds, flocks, and rural "ditties." Both these elements contrast with the heroic, valorous combat of medieval knights who are personified Virtues and Vices, or with the Christian mythological devils and angels. The pastoral pipes of peace ill support the epic trumpets of war. The science lessons in cantos 2-5, the interminable gallery of personified abstractions in cantos 6-10, and the epic battles in cantos 11 and 12 never coalesce.

Negative reactions to this poem have been nearly universal. Reviewing the criticism on this poem over the centuries, R. G. Baldwin concluded that it was considered "a curiosity, a literary eccentric to be exclaimed about, deplored, or chuckled at as the spirit moves." The poem has been called "bizarre," "strange," "ugly and arid," and "fantastic." In *England's Antiphon* (1868) George MacDonald exclaimed, "Of all the strange poems in existence, surely this is the strangest!" Comparing the Fletcher brothers' poems in *The Works of the British Poets* (1819-1823), Ezekiel Sanford wrote that Phineas had "a livelier fancy" but a "worse taste" than Giles, explaining that Phineas "lavished on a bad subject the graces and ingenuity that would have made a fine poem on a good design." Even Henry Headley, whose remarks in his *Select Beau-*

ties of Ancient English Poetry (1787) qualify him as a Fletcher apologist, says that in these cantos "the reader forgets the poet, and is sickened with the anatomist." He adds, however, that despite this "material error in judgement ... *ample amends* are made in what follows."

Unfortunately, most other readers seem not to proceed beyond canto 5. Headley is quite correct; cantos 6-12 are much stronger, more consistent, and much more impressive, alone forming a integral poem. In fact, the anatomical cantos may not have been part of the original design but may have been added around 1614-1615, when Fletcher returned briefly to Cambridge. These anatomical verses may have been written to impress his brother's patron, the science-minded Sir Francis Bacon. At any event, this "science" section is the main reason for the failure of the poem. After such mitigating circumstances as youth, naiveté, and immature judgement have been considered, the poem is still an instructive but monumental failure.

Fletcher's play *Sicelides* (1631) is better written than *The Purple Island*, but it has received less attention than the epic. Fletcher's return to residence at King's College between 16 December 1614 and 25 March 1615 was related to the royal visit to Cambridge of King James and his company, which included Prince Charles and John Donne. During this visitation, which took place on 7-11 March 1615, various colleges staged debates, disputations, feastings, and plays. Given the honor of presenting the final play on the last evening before some two thousand people (including eminent representatives of academe, church, and state), King's College performed *Sicelides* by Phineas Fletcher. Unfortunately the king and his whole party were forced to leave for London earlier than they had planned on the evening of 11 March, apparently missing the performance and depriving Fletcher of what might have been his greatest moment of literary recognition.

Related to both private and public Elizabethan and Jacobean plays, *Sicelides* is certainly reminiscent of the pastoral plays that the University Wits wrote for private performances at their colleges during the 1570s and 1580s; yet their combination of idealized types from the pastoral world of books with low-life realism spread to the public stage and never entirely left it. George Peele's *Arraignment of Paris* (staged in 1584), John Lyly's *Endimion* (staged in 1588), Robert Greene's *Friar Bacon and Friar Bungay* (produced circa 1588-1591), and William Shakespeare's *Love's Labors*

Lost (produced no later than 1599) are all indebted to the university tradition. Giles Fletcher the elder probably knew Lyly at court, and Phineas could easily have seen a performance of *Endimion* in London or Cambridge. Thus, it is not surprising that *Sicelides* bears some similarity to *Endimion*. Although Lyly relates his lovers more directly to levels of Platonic love and to court personages, both plays present three groups of lovers representing three worlds of love, dealing simultaneously with idealized love sentiments, romantic infatuation, and ribald low comedy.

Such multiple plots are common in Elizabethan and Jacobean dramas. The high romantic comedy of Shakespeare and his contemporaries was often tinged or infused with pastoralism, just as it often mixed higher-class characters speaking verse with low-life social types who spoke prose, and placed them in faraway settings (Fletcher's play is set in Sicily). While the piscatory element in *Sicelides* is unusual, his use of farce is part of the standard formula. This sort of play, popular in the 1580s and 1590s, had a notable revival around 1605-1615. For example, Shakespeare's *Pericles* and *The Faithful Shepherdess* by Phineas's cousin John Fletcher were both produced for the first time around 1608. *Philaster* by John Fletcher and Francis Beaumont followed in 1609, and Shakespeare's *Cymbeline*, *The Winter's Tale*, and *The Tempest* all premiered by about 1611.

With *Sicelides* Phineas could either have been returning to a type of play popular in his youth or trying to place himself among the fashionable dramatists of the London theater. In either event, it fits within the dramatic tradition of the years 1575-1615, during which the plays put on at the universities, at the Inns of Court, at the court, and on the great London public stages cannot be always clearly distinguished.

Sicelides was written for an educated, worldly audience; its wit, humor, and puns are consistently sophisticated, urbane, and racy. Yet the play is not without weakness. The dialogues, especially in act 1, tend to be overly rhetorical, long, and self-consciously stylized. Most of the characters are recognizable Elizabethan types: the wily servant, the nondescript romantic leads, even a Caliban creature (Orke). It has some good low-comedy scenes, but little seems original or unusual. Except for the piscatory paraphernalia, the play seems like another example of a common type of Elizabethan-Jacobean play. Yet overall it is a more-than-competent piece of stagecraft.

Arms of Edward Benlowes and Phineas Fletcher, with an inscription by Fletcher, in a copy of The Purple Island *presented to Benlowes (present location unknown; from Frederick S. Boas, ed.,* Giles and Phineas Fletcher: Poetical Works, *1908)*

The play also offers further evidence of the growing diversity and breadth of Phineas Fletcher's talents and accomplishments, and he was certainly disappointed when King James and the royal company left Cambridge before witnessing its performance. After his own departure from Cambridge two weeks later, he wrote in a verse epistle to his friend John Tompkins:

> Since then to other streams I must betake me,
> And spitefull *Chame* of all ha's quite bereft me;
> Since Muses selves (false Muses) will forsake me,
> And but this *Nothing*, nothing els is left me;
> Take thou my love, and keep it still in store;
> That given, *Nothing* now remaineth more.

Phineas's life changed almost totally in 1615, when he was thirty-three. Cambridge and Kent had been his world, the setting for his aspirations as well as the source of his poetic inspiration. He left them for a poor chaplaincy in the country home of the Willoughbys, farming gentry in a remote area of Derbyshire. He seems to have found compensation, however, in the congeniality of the Willougbys, in his marriage to Elizabeth Vincent in 1615, in the eight children born to them over the next twenty years, and in his duties as rector at Hilgay, Norfolk, which he performed from 1621 until his death in 1650.

He clearly adjusted to his new situation, which marked a new development in his writing. During the next twenty years of his life (1615-1635), his literary productivity exceeded that of even his prolific Cambridge years. He continued work on *The Purple Island*, as well as *Locustæ* and its English version, *Apollyonists*. He also continued to write short poems, producing a sizable body of impressive short works that were published as "Poeticall Miscellanies" with *The Purple Is-*

land. In addition, he produced two religious books: *The Way to Blessednes, A Treatise or Commentary on the First Psalme* (1632), dedicated to his patron, Sir Henry Willoughby, Baronet, and *Joy in Tribulation. Or Consolations for Afflicted Spirits* (1632), a work of 339 pages, which was dedicated to "His most Honorable Cousin, Sir Walter Robarts, Knight and Baronet and his Gracious Lady," of Kent, for whose marriage many years before he had written "An Hymen." He may also have begun writing *A Fathers Testament*, a third long book of religious prose, published posthumously in 1670.

Once he moved to Hilgay, Norfolk, in 1621 he was only about twenty miles from Cambridge and was closer to Alderton, Suffolk, where his brother Giles was performing his duties as rector. At Hilgay he also found new literary friends. They included Francis Quarles, who wrote glowing dedicatory verse to *The Purple Island*, calling Fletcher "The Spencer [*sic*] of this age." In his *Emblems* (1635) Quarles included the figure of a globe on which only four place-names are inscribed. Phineas's Hilgay is one of them. Another friend, Izaak Walton, wrote in his *Compleat Angler* (1653) of "Phineas Fletcher, an excellent divine, and an excellent angler; and the author of excellent Piscatory Eclogues, in which you shall see the picture of this good man's mind: and I wish mine to be like it."

The most important literary friend of Fletcher's Hilgay period was Edward Benlowes, twenty years Fletcher's junior. Benlowes was also a friend and patron to Quarles and other Cambridge writers. As Langdale notes, "during the exact years when Fletcher was friendly with Benlowes, the presses of London and Cambridge commenced to publish his works, one after another, in a steady stream. . . . " In dedicating the volume that includes *The Purple Island* to Benlowes, Fletcher thanked him for his encouragement but protested, "For my self, I cannot account that worthy of your *Patronage*, which comes forth so short of my *Desires*. . . . In letting them abroad I desire onely to testifie, how much I preferre your desires before mine own, and how much I owe to *You* more then *any other*."

The composition date for Fletcher's posthumously published prose work is uncertain. *A Fathers Testament. Written long since for the benefit of the particular Relations of the Author . . . And now made Publick at the desire of Friends*, which presents religious-moral advice and Christian "instruction," includes ten original poems: "The Vanity

of Possessions," "The Search after God," "The Beatific Vision," "The Passage Perilous," "The Divine Lover," "The Divine Offer," "Israel's Yoke," "God's Image in Man," "The Light of Lights," and "The Transfiguration of Man." Most of these products of Fletcher's maturity make use of rhetorical questions to produce prayerlike internal dialogues. The effect is sometimes startling, as in these lines from "The Divine Lover":

> Me Lord? can'st thou mispend
> One work, misplace one look on me?
>   Call'st me thy Love, thy Friend?
>   Can this poor soul the object be
> Of these love-glances, those life-kindling eyes?
> What? I the Center of thy arms embraces?
>   Of all thy labour I the prize?
>   Love never mocks, Truth never lies.
> Oh how I quake: Hope fear, fear hope displaces:
> I would, but cannot hope: such wondrous love
>   amazes.

The poems in *A Fathers Testament*, probably his last, form a peaceful end to a long, diverse, and prolific poetic career, speaking with a personal but dignified poetic voice in the love and service of God.

For a hundred or so years after Fletcher's death his reputation declined, along with those of other religious poets, including Milton, Donne, Herbert, and Giles Fletcher the younger. Thomas Percy's *Reliques of Ancient English Poetry* (1765) marks the beginning of a new wave of interest in earlier poetry in general, and Phineas Fletcher's poetry found a new audience. *Piscatory Eclogues, with other Poetical Miscellanies*, published in Edinburgh in 1771, was the first edition of his poetry to appear since 1633. In 1783 *The Purple Island or the Isle of Man, an Allegorical poem by Phineas Fletcher, esteemed the Spenser of his Age to which is added Christs Victorie and Triumph, A poem in four parts by Giles Fletcher* was published in London.

A few years later Henry Headley included poems by both brothers and a biographical sketch of them in his *Selected Beauties of Ancient English Poetry* (1787). In a supplement to this collection Headley focused extensive critical attention on Phineas's poetry, concluding: "It is to his honour that Milton read and imitated him, as every attentive reader of both poets must soon discover. He is eminently entitled to a very high rank among our old English classics." Throughout the nineteenth century, the Fletchers' poetry appeared with notable regularity in anthologies and various editions, both with and without commentary. The judgments of critics varied widely, and although *The Purple Island* usually received a negative response, Phineas's work was generally praised. In his edition of Phineas Fletcher's complete poems Grosart presented the most superlative and extensive, but least balanced, criticism. Yet over the centuries Fletcher's work has always found devotees, from contemporaries such as Benlowes and Quarles to Headley, Grosart, and, in the twentieth century, Boas and Langdale.

Twentieth-century scholars tend to classify Phineas Fletcher's poetry with such literary-historical clichés as "Spenserian," "of the school of Spenser," or a bridge between Spenser and Milton. Yet Joan Grundy concludes in *The Spenserian Poets* (1969), "No snap judgement on the Fletchers is therefore possible. They are both, but especially Phineas, more complicated than at first appears. . . . In the models they choose to follow, they are quite bewilderingly eclectic."

Most modern studies treat the Fletcher brothers' poetry as essentially interchangeable. Since they did work together for at least five years, it is not surprising that similarities exist. They are most alike as *vates* burning with a grand Christian vision of cosmic unity and producing English epic poetry in the new baroque fashion. This poetry was their most original and most influential (with Milton especially) contribution to English literary history. This description fairly well characterizes Giles's entire poetic canon, however, Phineas's work was much more diverse.

Phineas's writings have aspects completely lacking in Giles's, including a Virgilian pattern, a distinct pastoral mode, an autobiographical dimension, and the eroticism of *Venus & Anchises* and several lyrical love poems. He called upon many Muses (Chamus, Venus, Urania, Love, Science, God) whereas Giles devoted himself to one "sacred Muse." As a poet Giles appears serious, dedicated, introverted, inspired but humorless, a slow, careful worker. Phineas seems enthusiastic, mercurial (even childlike at times), exuberantly prolific but short on critical judgement, a poet of diverse moods. Giles's body of poetry, much smaller and more consistent in quality than his brother's, is easier to appreciate, and in general, it has been so appreciated in this century. Phineas's poetry, which is more impressive in its variety than Giles's, has not been properly examined or evaluated.

A study of the existing critical response reveals that through the centuries *The Purple Island*

has detracted significantly from his overall standing. Anthologies have tended too often to include selections mostly from *The Purple Island*, his least representative work. Yet, as Langdale notes,

> Despite its weaknesses, there are many reasons why Fletcher's poetry has been and will be read. . . . There is a manly vigor about all these poems which has been overlooked and which should recommend *The Apollyonists*, particularly, to more readers.

Unfortunately, no edition comprises all of his poetical work, and his three books of religious prose are largely unavailable. Until a complete, scholarly edition of his works appears, it will be difficult for most readers to evaluate his whole canon. In size and variety it rivals Spenser's and Milton's, but, unlike theirs, his writing is too radically uneven to allow either easy classification or simple evaluation.

References:

R. G. Baldwin, "Phineas Fletcher: His Modern Readers and His Renaissance Ideas," *Philological Quarterly*, 10 (October 1961): 462-475;

H. E. Cory, "Spenser, The School of the Fletchers, and Milton," *University of California Publications in Modern Philology*, 2, no. 5 (1912): 311-373;

Joan Grundy, *The Spenserian Poets* (London: Arnold, 1969);

William B. Hunter, Jr., Introduction to poems by Phineas Fletcher, in *The English Spenserians*, edited by Hunter (Salt Lake City: University of Utah Press, 1977), pp. 311-315;

Frank S. Kastor, *Giles and Phineas Fletcher* (Boston: Twayne, 1978);

A. B. Langdale, *Phineas Fletcher: Man of Letters, Science, and Divinity* (New York: Columbia University Press, 1937).

Papers:

A manuscript including *Venus & Anchises* and six other poems by Fletcher is in the Library of Sion College, Cambridge. Of three extant manuscripts for *Locustæ*—all in Fletcher's hand—the earliest is probably one titled "Pietas Jesuitica" at the British Library (Sloane Mss. 444); another manuscript, with the same title and dedicated to Henry, Prince of Wales, was once in the collection of Bertram Dobell; the third is at the British Library (Harleian Mss. 3196).

Joseph Hall

(1 July 1574 - 8 September 1656)

Ronald Corthell
Kent State University

BOOKS: *Virgidemiarum conteyninge Sixe Bookes. First three Bookes, of Tooth-lesse Satyrs* (London: Printed by T. Creede for R. Dexter, 1597);

Virgidemiarum. The three last bookes. Of Byting Satyres (London: Printed by R. Bradocke for R. Dexter, 1598);

The Kings Prophecie: or Weeping Joy (London: Printed by T. Creede for S. Waterson, 1603);

Meditations and Vowes, Divine and Morall. Devided into two bookes (London: Printed by H. Lownes for J. Porter, 1605);

Mundus Alter et Idem (Frankfurt: Ap. hæreds A. de Rinialme [London: Printed by H. Lownes], 1605); translated by John Healey as *The Discovery of a New World* (London: Printed by Ed. Blount and W. Barrett, 1609);

Meditations and Vowes, Divine and Morall: A third century (London: Printed by Humfrey Lownes for John Porter, 1606);

Heaven upon Earth: Or, Of True Peace and Tranquillitie of Minde (London: Printed by J. Windet for J. Porter, 1606);

The Arte of Divine Meditation (London: Printed by H. Lownes for S. Macham & M. Cooke, 1606);

Holy Observations. Lib. I. Also Some fewe of Davids Psalmes Metaphrased, for a taste of the Rest (London: Printed by H. Lownes for S. Macham, 1607);

Characters of Vertues and Vices (London: Printed by M. Bradwood for E. Edgar & S. Macham, 1608);

Epistles, 3 volumes (London: Printed by A. H. for E. Edgar & S. Macham, 1608-1611);

Salomans Divine Artes, of 1. Ethickes, 2. Politickes, 3. Oeconomicks. That is, the gouernment of 1. Behaviovr, 2. Common-wealth, 3. Familie. Drawn into method, out of his Prouerbs & Ecclesiastes. With An open and plaine paraphrase, vpon the Song of Songs (London: Printed by H. Lownes for E. Edgar & S. Macham, 1609);

Joseph Hall

The Peace of Rome. Proclaimed to All the world, by cardinall Bellarmine, and the casuist Navarre. Gathered out of their writings in their own words. Whereto is prefixed A Serious Disswasive from Poperie (London: Printed by J. Windet for J. Legate, 1609);

A Common Apologie of the Chvrch of England: Against the vniust Challenges of the ouer iust sect, commonly caled Brownists (London: Printed by W. Stansby for S. Macham, 1610);

Polemices Sacræ Pars Prior: Roma Irreconciliabilis (London: Printed by A. Hatfield, 1611);

Contemplations upon the Principall Passages of the Holie Storie, 8 volumes; volume 1 (London:

Printed by M. Bradwood for S. Macham, 1612); volume 2 (London: Printed by H. Lownes for S. Macham, 1614); volume 3 (London: Printed by H. Lownes & Eliot's Court Press for N. Butter & W. Butler, 1615); volume 4 (London: Printed by E. Griffin for H. Fetherstone, 1618); volume 5 (London: Printed by E. Griffin for N. Butter, 1620); volume 6 (London: Printed by J. Haviland for N. Butter, 1622); volume 7 (London: Printed by J. Haviland for H. Fetherstone, 1623); volume 8 (London: Printed by M. Flesher for N. Butter, 1626);

Quo Vadis? A Iust Censure of Travell as it is commonly undertaken by the Gentlemen of our Nation (London: Printed by E. Griffin for N. Butter, 1617);

The Honor of the Married Clergie, Maintayned Against the malicious Challenges of C. E. Masse-Priest (London: Printed by W. Stansby for H. Fetherstone, 1620);

The Works of Joseph Hall (London: Printed by J. Haviland, M. Flesher & J. Beale for T. Pavier, M. Flesher & J. Haviland, 1625; enlarged edition, London: Printed by M. Flesher, J. Haviland, & J. Beale, 1628);

The Second Tome. Contemplations upon the History of the New Testament (London: Printed by M. Flesher, 1628); enlarged as *The Second Tome: Containing The Contemplations upon the History of the New Testament, now complete: Together with Divers Treatises not hitherto reduced to the greater Volume: And, Some others never till now Published* (London: Printed by M. Flesher for N. Butter, 1634);

The Olde Religion (London: Printed by W. Stansby for N. Butter & R. Hawkings, 1628);

An Answer to Pope Urban His Inurbanitie, translated by B. S. (London: Printed by W. Jones for N. Bourne, 1629);

The Reconciler: An Epistle Pacificatorie of the seeming—differences of opinion concerning the truenesse and visibility of the Roman Church (London: Printed by M. Flesher for N. Butter, 1629);

Occasionall Meditations, 2 volumes, meditations 1-91 (London: Printed by B. Alsop & T. Fawcet for N. Butter, 1630); meditations 1-140 (London: Printed by W. Stansby for N. Butter, 1631);

A Plaine and Familiar Explication (by way of Paraphrase) of all the hard Texts of the whole Divine Scripture of the Old and New Testament (London: Printed by Miles Flesher for N. Butter, 1633);

Propositione Catholicæ (London: Printed by M. Flesher, 1633);

Αυτοσχεδιασματα. *Vel, Meditatiunculae Subitaneae* (London: Printed by N. Butter, 1635);

The Remedy of Prophanesse. Or, Of the true sight and feare of the Almighty (London: Printed by T. Harper for N. Butter, 1637);

Certaine Irrefragable Propositions worthy of Serious Consideration (London: Printed by M. Flesher for N. Butter, 1639);

An Humble Remonstrance to the High Court of Parliament (London: Printed by M. Flesher for N. Butter, 1640);

Christian Moderation (London: Printed by M. Flesher and sold by N. Butter, 1640);

Episcopacie by Divine Right (London: Printed by R. Badger for N. Butter, 1640);

A Defence of the Humble Remonstrance, Against the frivolous and false exceptions of Smectymnvvs (London: Printed for Nathaniel Butter, 1641);

A Short Answer to the Tedious Vindication of Smectymnvvs (London: Printed for Nathaniel Butter, 1641);

A Letter Lately sent by A Reverend Bishop from the Tower, to A private Friend (London, 1642);

The lawfulness and unlawfulnes of an Oath or Covenant (Oxford: Printed by Leonard Lichfield, 1643);

The Devout Soul, or, Rules of Heavenly Devotion, Also, the Free Prisoner, or The Comfort of Restraint (London: Printed by M. Flesher for Nat. Butter, 1644);

The Peace-Maker (London: Printed by M. Flesher for Nat. Butter, 1645);

The Remedy of Discontentment. Or a Treatise of Contentation (London: Printed by M. F. for Nat. Butter, 1645);

The Balme of Gilead; Or, Comforts for the Distressed, Both Morall and Divine (London: Printed by Nat. Butter, 1646);

Christ Mysticall; or The Blessed union of Christ and his Members. Also, An Holy Rapture ... Also, The Christian laid forth in his whole Disposition and Carriage (London: Printed by M. Flesher and sold by William Hope, Gabriel Beadle & Nathaniel Webbe, 1647);

Satans Fiery Darts Quenched, or, Temptations Repelled (London: Printed by M. F. for N. Butter, sold by N. Brooks, 1647);

Pax Terris (London, 1648);

Select Thoughts, one century. Also, The Breathings of the Devout Soul (London: Printed by J. L. for

N. B., sold by Nich. Bourn, George Latham, Phil Stevens & Gabriel Bedell, 1648);

Χειροθεσια. *Or The Apostolique Institution of Imposition of Hands, for Confirmation, revived* (London: Printed by J. G. for Nathanael Butter, 1649);

Resolutions and Decisions of Divers Practicall Cases of Conscience (London: Printed by M. F. for Nath. Butter, sold by Humphrey Mosley, Abel Roper & John Sweeting, 1649);

The Revelation Unrevealed (London: Printed by R. L. for John Bisse, 1650);

Susurrium cum Deo soliloqvies, or, Holy Self-Conferences of the Devout Soul upon sundry choice occasions: with humble addresses to the throne of grace: Together with The Souls Farewell to Earth, and Approaches to Heaven (London: Printed by Will. Hunt and sold by George Lathum, Jr., 1651);

The Great Mysterie of Godliness, Laid forth by way of affectuous and feeling Meditations. Also, The Invisible World, Discovered to spiritual Eyes, and Reduced to usefull Meditation (London: Printed for John Place, 1652);

Holy Raptures: or, Pathetical Meditations of the Love of Christ (London: Printed by E. C. for John Sweeting, 1652);

The Holy Order; or Fraternity of the Mourners in Sion. Whereunto is added, Songs in the Night: or, Cheerfulnesse under Affliction (London: Printed by J. G. for Nath. Brooke, 1654);

The Shaking of the Olive-Tree, The Remaining Works of that incomparable Prelate Joseph Hall, D. D. late Lord Bishop of Norwich. With Some Specialities of Divine Providence in his Life. Noted by His own Hand. Together with His Hard Measure: Written also by Himself (London: Printed by J. Cadwel for J. Crooke, 1660);

Divers Treatises, Written upon severall Occasions, By Joseph Hall late Bishop of Norwich, The Third Tome (London: Printed by R. H. J. G. & W. H. and sold by J. Williams, J. Sweeting, Nath. Brook & J. Place, 1662).

Editions: *The Works of the right reverend father in God Joseph Hall, D.D.*, 10 volumes, edited by Josiah Pratt (London: Printed by C. Whittingham for Williams & Smith, 1808);

Works, 12 volumes, edited by Peter Hall (Oxford: D. A. Talboys, 1837-1839);

The Works of the Right Reverend Joseph Hall, 10 volumes, edited by Philip Wynter (Oxford: University Press, 1863);

The Discovery of a New World, translated by John Healey, edited by Huntington Brown (Cambridge, Mass.: Harvard University Press, 1937);

Heaven upon Earth, and Characters of Vertues and Vices, edited by Rudolf Kirk (New Brunswick, N.J.: Rutgers University Press, 1948);

The Collected Poems of Joseph Hall, Bishop of Exeter and Norwich, edited by Arnold Davenport (Liverpool: Liverpool University Press, 1949);

Another world and yet the same: Bishop Joseph Hall's Mundus Alter et Idem, edited and translated by John Millar Wands (New Haven: Yale University Press, 1981);

Bishop Joseph Hall and Protestant Meditation in Seventeenth-Century England: A Study with the Texts of The Arte of Divine Meditation (1606) *and* Occasional Meditations (1633), edited by Frank Livingstone Huntley (Binghamton: Medieval & Renaissance Texts & Studies, 1981).

Joseph Hall is an excellent example of a major minor: a writer of importance and influence in his own day who has survived largely as a "background" figure in literary history. Hall's long and productive career as writer and divine spanned one of the most eventful periods of English literary, political, and ecclesiastical history. A century after his death, he was still renowned enough to be called "the famous Dr. Joseph Hall" by Laurence Sterne in *Tristram Shandy* (1759-1767); today Hall is known to specialists and remembered for his naturalizations into English of formal verse satire and the Theophrastan character sketch, *Characters of Vertues and Vices* (1608). His devotional prose, however, may prove to be his most enduring contribution to English poetry, as it has been much studied in recent scholarship on religious verse of the period. Hall's controversial pamphlets played an important role in defining the Church of England's position in ecclesiastical debates that preceded the civil war. He was involved in one way or another with some of the greatest literary names of the period. He was attacked by John Marston in Marston's satires; he was apparently a good friend of John Donne and wrote poetic prefaces to Donne's *Anniversaries* (1611, 1612); he was famously attacked by John Milton in a pamphlet war of the early 1640s; and during his last years in Norwich he was the friend and patient of Sir Thomas Browne. As this list suggests, Hall's career can be seen as an index to changing relationships between political, religious, and literary practices of late Tudor and early Stuart England.

That career also exemplifies the considerable upward mobility available during this period to talented young men not of gentle birth. Born at Bristow Park near Ashby de la Zouch in Leicestershire, where his father, John, served as bailiff of Henry Hastings, third Earl of Huntingdon, Joseph Hall grew up to become bishop of Exeter in 1627. As suggested by the title of his autobiography, "Observations of Some Specialities of Divine Providence" (1660), Hall followed convention in attributing his success to God's hand, but his character and achievements owed much to his mother (Winifride), his teachers, and his patrons. Hall himself compared his mother's influence to that of Monica on Saint Augustine, and while this claim may also be partly explained by autobiographical convention, Winifride's Calvinistic brand of piety was part of an environment of Ashby Puritanism that had a powerful effect on Hall's outlook later in life. The third earl of Huntington had founded the Ashby Grammar School and was involved in the establishment at Cambridge University of the Puritan-leaning Emmanuel College. Anthony Gilby, spiritual counselor to Hall's mother, was a hard-line Calvinist preacher and Marian exile who had a major role in setting the Ashby Grammar School curriculum. Joseph was marked very early for the ministry by his parents and at fifteen entered Emmanuel College, where he was tutored by Gilby's son, Nathanael. Emmanuel had been founded with a particular view to producing a Protestant clergy learned in theology, and very early in its history it became identified (by Queen Elizabeth among others) as a Puritan college. Given the sobriety and religiosity of his upbringing and environment, Hall's emergence as a poet while at the university looks even more impressive. Despite Emmanuel's apparently deserved reputation for seriousness (it graduated a large number of New England Puritans), Hall seems to have enjoyed himself thoroughly. He was highly regarded in his college and was elected fellow in 1595. His particular gift was in oratory; he was elected to the university lectureship in rhetoric for two successive terms and was remembered for his disputations, including a brilliant speech on the decline of the world mentioned by Thomas Fuller in his *History of the Worthies of England* (1662): "Yet, in some sort, his position confuteth his position, the wit and quickness whereof did argue an increase rather than a

Title page for Hall's Latin prose satire about a Cambridge scholar traveling in Antarctica

decay of parts in this latter age." In Hall's "Observations of Some Specialities of Divine Providence," he comments on his turn from secular to religious pursuits: "but finding that well-applauded work somewhat out of my way, not without a secret blame of myself for so much excursion, I finally gave up that task . . . and betook myself to those serious studies which might fit me for that high calling whereunto I was destined."

That Hall's early interest in worldly matters was real and not just a convention of the autobiographical form is demonstrated by his two volumes of formal verse satires, the *Virgidemiae* published in 1597 and 1598 while he was still a fellow at Cambridge. Hall had a reputation for brilliance at Cambridge, but the pious parents and teachers back in Leicestershire must have been surprised by this showy literary debut in which Hall proclaimed himself the "first English satirist." More than forty years later Bishop

Hall's Puritan opponents in ecclesiastical controversy would remind their readers that this leading voice of the establishment had once been an upstart Cambridge poet; while such dredging up of the opponent's past is a regular feature of controversial writing, the Puritan attacks perhaps also recall some of the stir created by the poet of Emmanuel (an unlikely nursery of poets) back in the late 1590s.

The poems are very smart, very much the product of a university fellow observing from the happy confines of academe some of the latest developments on the literary and social scene. Hall's claim to be the first English satirist has some merit. Thomas Lodge had attempted verse satires in the Roman vein in *A fig for Momus* (1595), and John Donne was writing but not publishing his satires before Hall's book appeared, but *Virgidemiae* was the first book-length publication that attempted in English an imitation of formal verse satire in the Juvenalian style. Some poems in *Virgidemiae* appeared to attack real persons and so provoked great interest and a host of imitations, including John Marston's *Metamorphosis of Pigmalions Image. And Certaine Satyres* (1598) which includes an entire satire devoted to attacking Hall's literary opinions. Marston's *Scourge of Villanie*, published later that year, includes more attacks on Hall and accuses him of pasting a satirical epigram on Marston into copies of *The Metamorphosis of Pigmalions Image*. Hall, who praised the "low Sayle" and "hye Happiness" of "an Academicke life," had succeeded in stirring up the London literati. A fad for epigram and satire ensued. The poetic mudslinging became so intense over the next year that the printing of satires was prohibited, and an assortment of satiric and erotic books (Hall's excepted) was burned in 1599.

Like most Elizabethan verse satirists, Hall places great emphasis on the satiric persona. A distinctive feature of his self-presentation is a literary self-consciousness that unfolds into a moral and social criticism. *Virgidemiarum*, the title of his collection, is a rare word meaning "a harvest of rods," by which Hall signals his corrective aim and also his departure from pastoral (identified with the preagricultural Golden Age), conventionally the beginning poet's genre. Indeed, the entire project is in the Spenserian tradition of literary debut in which literary and social criticism mesh with the presentation of a new poetic voice.

Virgidemiae appeared in two volumes: volume one, published in 1597, comprises three

books of what Hall termed "Tooth-lesse Satyrs"—"poeticall," "academicall," and "morall." This volume was followed in 1598 by a collection of three books of "Byting Satyres" on a variety of social themes. Forty years later in the heat of ecclesiastical controversy, Milton would twit Hall for his concept of "toothless" satire: "For if it bite neither the persons nor the vices, how is it a Satyr, and if it bite either, how is it toothlesse, so that toothlesse Satyrs are as much as if he had said toothlesse teeth." Hall explained in the first of the "biting" satires that "Those toothlesse *Toyes* that dropt out by mis-hap, / Bee but as lightning to a thunder-clap," and since he had made a similar claim in an epilogue to the toothless satires, it would appear that he was aiming for an effect of contrast between the two installments. The first three books would deal with follies, the last three with crimes, and the style would be appropriate to the subject matter. In the first three books Hall is no Elizabethan satyr-satirist; the poems are written in carefully balanced couplets and lack the moral hysteria of the rough-edged, "cankered muse" of Marston. The biting satires are longer, more vehement, and more difficult poems; but even the sharper style is marked by regular couplets, a characteristic that perhaps helps explain the admiration of Alexander Pope, who, according to John Nichols in his *Literary Anecdotes of the Eighteenth Century* (1812-1816), "esteemed them the best poetry and truest satire in the English language."

In the first three books the "poeticall" interests of the satirist stand out. In "His Defiance to Envie," a prefatory poem that was imitated by Marston and others in their collections, Hall considers the options available to the beginning poet, disclaiming any laureate ambition of trying his hand at epic or romance. He will instead "such lowly Satyres" sing as not to provoke the envy of his readers. In making this choice, however, Hall must acknowledge the Renaissance tradition of pastoral as the genre for beginning poets. He hints that he has written pastorals for a coterie of readers—"Speake ye attentive swaynes that heard me late"—but that his efforts cannot compare with Edmund Spenser's pastorals: "At *Colins* feete I throw my yeelding reed." More than admiration of Spenser seems operative here, however. As the rest of *Virgidemiae* makes clear, Hall is troubled by the idea of the literary career and by such related issues as the nature and function of poetry. The beginning poet's decision not to write pastoral is based also upon his feeling that pastoral perspectives, while sharing some features of satire (a lowly style, rude speaker, and "inside" literary and political references), must be skewed in order to convey a true image of the times. Instead of the pastoral reed, then, Hall takes up the satirist's rod, the "virga" of his title.

The nine poems of book 1 offer a genre-by-genre critique of contemporary literature in which "Th'eternall Legends" of Spenser's "Faery Muse" stand out as a standard of excellence. Besides Edmund Spenser there are clear references to Sir Philip Sidney, Robert Greene, Thomas Nashe, and Christopher Marlowe's *Tamberlaine* (1590), but Hall's quite successful strategy was generally to provoke literary gossip by hinting at contemporaries without identifying them. Hall's treatment of the current scene is also reinforced by an implicit set of neoclassical literary principles: his attacks on tragicomedy, heroic poetry, the complaint, classical metrics in English, "love-sicke" poets, and religious verse are informed by such critical precepts as genre, decorum, verisimilitude, and the unities. The most interesting of these poems is the satire on the theater, where Hall scores against the actors, the playwrights, the plays, and the audiences. The playhouse is for Hall an image of social disorder. In writing about and performing the career of Tamburlaine, playwrights and actors literally imitate and encourage others to imitate that "high-aspiring swaine." The snobbish satirist is clearly disturbed by the identification of the base and unruly audience with the misrule of the clowns in tragicomedy:

> Now, least such frightfull showes of Fortunes fall,
> And bloody Tyrants rage, should chance appall
> The dead stroke audience, mids the silent rout
> Comes leaping in a selfe-misformed lout,
> And laughes, and grins, and frames his Mimik face,
> And iustles straight into the Princes place.
> Then doth the *Theatre Eccho* all aloud,
> With gladsome noyse of that applauding croud.

This conservative ethos pervades the other five books of *Virgidemiae*, which include poems on what we now recognize as commonplace objects of Elizabethan satire: lawyers, doctors, astrologers, fops and upstart gentlemen, the nouveaux riches, and the decay of hospitality. The first satire in book 3, a nicely crafted poem contrasting the Golden Age of simplicity to modern sophistication, constructs a standard for life lived in accord with nature—"The kings pavilion, was the grassy greene, / Under safe shelter of the shadie treene"—and uses Hall's old theme of *mundus senescit* as a refrain: "Then farewell fayrest age, the worlds best daies, / Thriving in ill, as it in age decaies."

The three books of biting satires contain Hall's most ambitious work as a poet. The opening satire of book 4 displays Hall's denser, learned style; Hall crams his poem with classical echoes in a reply to critics who "upbraid these open rimes of mine / With blindfold *Aquines* [Juvenal], or darke *Venusine* [Horace]." In this very obscure tirade the satirist enjoys thinking of his readers struggling with the text:

> Yet when hee hath my crabbed Pamphlet red
> As oftentimes as PHILLIP hath beene dead,
> Bids all the Furies haunt each peevish line
> That thus have rackt their friendly readers eyne.

What disturbs him is the prospect of readers missing his moral indictments of them: "Should I endure these curses and dispight / While no mans eare should glow at what I write?" The second satire in book 4 is of interest in its attack on the father who "drudges all he can, / To make his eldest son a Gentleman." The upstart's attempts to rise by studying the law and "courtly carriage" are contrasted with the career plan that Hall's own parents had for him:

> Fooles, they may feed with words & live by ayre,
> That climbe to honour by the Pulpits stayre:
> Sit seaven yeares pining in an Anchores cheyre,
> To win some patched shreds of *Minivere*,
> And seven more plod at a Patrons tayle,
> To get a gelded Chappels cheaper sale.

After presenting an overview of social problems, the sixth satire of book 4 proposes a retreat to the ivory tower: "Mong'st all these sturs of discontented strife, / Oh let me lead an Academicke life."

Perhaps the most daring poem of the entire collection, and one that reflects the intense Puritanism of his college, is Hall's attack on Romish pageants, where the burlesque treatment of the Catholic Mass could have been construed as a blast against residual Romanism in the Church of England. The poem opens predictably in Rome, where "*Caesars* throne is turn'd to *Peters* chayre," but in the "sportfull" depiction of Catholic ritual, Hall displays the questionable taste and spitefulness of all great satirists:

The whiles the likerous Priest spits every trice
With longing for his morning Sacrifice,
Which he reres up quite perpendiculare,
That in the mid-Church doth spite the *Chancels*
    fare,
Beating their emptie mawes that would be fed,
With the scant morsels of the *Sacrists* bread.

Hall's literary, moral, and social concerns are finely woven together in book 6, an imitation of J. C. Scaliger's *Teretismata* (*Poemata*, 1574), which ironically recants the satiric project and celebrates the poetaster Labeo, bard of the new decadent age. Reversing the decline and fall topos, Hall gives up satire because the times call for praise, not blame. The true poet of the age is Labeo, whose education as an epic poet is recounted in the last portion of the satire. The satirist, on the other hand, muses on his failure to earn "a Poets name." His litany of neglected geniuses recalls Cuddie's complaint in Spenser's "October" eclogue, and his review of already threadbare themes anticipates Milton's search for an epic subject:

No man his threshold better knowes, than I
Brutes first arivall, and first victory,
Saint *Georges* Sorrell, or his crosse of blood,
Arthurs round board, or *Caledonian* wood,
Or holy battels of bold *Charlemaine*,
What were his knights did *Salems* siege maintaine;
How the mad Rivall of fayre *Angelice*
Was Phisick't from the new-found *Paradice*.

The satirist's hesitancy is contrasted with the proliferation of inferior writing: "ech man hath a Muse appropriate, / And she like to some eareboar'd slave / Must play and sing when, and what he would have!" Against such poetasters Hall ironically upholds the model laureate career of Labeo, who first "in hy startups walk't the pastured plaines" as a pastoral poet, and now "reaches right . . . / The true straynes of *Heroicke* Poesie." As usual, Hall provides a standard that exposes the satiric target: Labeo "names the spirit of *Astrophel*" and "knows the grace of that new elegance, / Which sweet *Philisides* fetch't of late from *France*." Labeo's perversion of the true ends of poetry is exemplified in Hall's mock-blazon of the laureate's mistress as a defiled source of inspiration:

Her chin like *Pindus* or *Pernassus* hill
Where down descends th'oreflowing stream doth fil
The well of her fayre mouth. Ech hath his praise.
Who would not but wed Poets now a daies!

Hall's distinction as a satirist, then, derives from his use of Elizabethan ambivalence about poetry as a stratagem for attacking literary abuses in the poetical satires and, in the later books, the moral and social disorders imitated by this literature. If Hall tends to disparage the literary life, he nonetheless expresses his moral and social values in the terms of Sidney's poetics. Spenser had begun his literary career by celebrating Elizabeth; in *Virgidemiae*, "Th'eternall *Legends* of thy *Faery Muse*"—not the Fairy Queen—evoke young Joseph Hall's warmest praise.

Virgidemiae signaled a movement in literary history, but no sooner did Hall announce his arrival on the literary scene than he took his conventional leave of it, saying farewell to poetry in a "Post-script" after having "shaked handes with all her retinue." However, Hall's literary activities at Cambridge probably continued; there is good evidence for believing that he helped write the so-called "Parnassus plays," which dealt with academic life and contemporary literature in much the way *Virgidemiae* did, and he was probably also working on his prose satire *Mundus Alter et Idem* (1605). The three Parnassus plays, *The Pilgrimage to Parnassus* and two plays together called *The Return from Parnassus*, follow the careers of two poetically-inclined Cambridge students as they move from the university to London. The plays contain many close parallels to *Virgidemiae* and an attack on Marston that, in light of Marston's subsequent attack on Hall, suggests that Marston at least thought Hall was the author. *Mundus Alter et Idem*, a satirical imaginary voyage in the Lucianic tradition, recounts the travels in Antarctica of the Cambridge scholar Mercurius Brittannicus, who visits the kingdoms of Crapulia (land of gluttons), Viraginia (land of Amazons), Moronia (land of fools), and Lavernia (land of thieves). The book is a *satura* or mixture, experimental like the verse satires, and attacks with exaggerated learning the follies and crimes suggested by the kingdoms while mocking the genre of travel literature itself. It was not published until 1605, surreptitiously in London with a false "Frankfurt" imprint and a preface by Hall's friend William Knight claiming that Hall opposed publication. Although this imprint may have been a ploy to evade the edict that almost committed his *Virgidemiae* to flames in 1599, the reasons for Hall's caution probably had more to do with his situation and interests in 1605, as he was beginning to publish his work on meditation. The book was translated into racy English by John Healey in

The Scale of Meditation of an Author,
ancient, but namelesse.

* Degrees of Preparation.

1 Question. } What I { thinke.
should thinke.

2 Excussion. { A repelling of what I should not
thinke.

3 Choice,
or } Of what most { necessarie.
Election. expedient.
comely.

* Degrees of proceeding in the
vnderstanding.

4 Commemoration. { An actuall thinking vpon the
matter elected.

5 Consideration. { A redoubled Commemoration of
the same, till it be fully knowne.

6 Attention. { A fixed and earnest consideration
whereby it is fastned in the minde.

7 Explanation. { A clearing of the thing considered
by similitudes.

8 Tractation. { An extending the thing considered
to other points, where all questi-
ons of doubts are discussed.

9 Dijudication. { An estimation of the worth of the
thing thus handled.

10 Causation. { A confirmation of the estimation
thus made.

11 Rumination, { A sad and serious Meditation of all
the former, till it may worke vp-
on the affections.

From hence to the degrees of
affection.

A guide to systematic meditation that Hall developed in The Arte of Divine Meditation, *a book that has been recognized as an important contribution to "Protestant poetics" (reproduced from a 1621 edition of Hall's works)*

1609 as *The Discovery of a New World.*

After *Virgidemiae* Hall's poetry was limited to occasional verse and translations of some psalms. He had been ordained near the end of his fellowship on 14 December 1600 and, after hesitating to accept a headmastership of a newly founded school, was offered and gladly accepted the rectory of Hawstead in Suffolk. His relationship to his Hawstead benefactors, Sir Robert and Lady Anne Drury, has literary significance: Hall would eventually write the two prefatory poems to Donne's *Anniversaries* which eulogized the Drurys' daughter Elizabeth, who died at age fourteen. It may be that Hall first met Donne at Hawstead, since Donne's sister Anne was married to William Lyly, who was a close friend of Sir Robert Drury's. Hall's situation at Hawstead was uneasy from the start; he suspected Anne's husband of prejudicing Drury against him in advance and regarded Lyly's death from the plague as one of the "specialities" of Providence in his career. More-

over, he was constantly at odds with Sir Robert over his salary, being "forced to write books to buy books." Despite his difficulties, Hall married Elizabeth Winiffe and began a family while in Hawstead. The Halls would have two daughters and six sons; four of their sons eventually following their father into the clergy. Hall left the Drurys in 1607, having sought and obtained the better position of chaplain to the household of Baron Edward Denny and rector of the abbey church of Waltham Holy Cross in Essex.

Hall had come to Lord Denny's attention partly because of the books he wrote during his years of service to the Drurys, books quite different from *Mundus Alter et Idem.* In 1605 he published *Meditations and Vowes, Divine and Morall,* the first of many devotional books that he issued steadily until the end of his life. These works are part of a literature of devotion that includes the poetry of George Herbert, Henry Vaughan, and Thomas Traherne. Although the *Meditations and*

Vowes are primarily ethical calisthenics, brief essays for focusing the conscience, they introduce two developments in Hall as a writer: the curt aphoristic style that became his trademark, and his promotion of a type of religious writing that addressed the individual on a more personal level than did the sermons he was preaching three times a week at Hawstead. Hall's interest in devotional writing may have been galvanized by his trip to Europe in 1605 with Lady Drury's brother, Sir Edmund Bacon; Hall was fiercely anti-Catholic but felt that Protestantism needed to catch up to the great devotional theories and practices of Catholic Europe. Upon his return he wrote a theoretical work on the subject, *The Arte of Divine Meditation* (1606), which has in recent years been recognized as a major contribution to English "Protestant poetics." The book is a clear, direct, and engaging guide to meditation, which Hall defines as "nothing else but a bending of the mind upon some spiritual object, through divers forms of discourse, until our thoughts come to an issue." He distinguishes two types of meditation, "extemporal" and "deliberate," but emphasizes that both aim at "the enkindling of our love of God." Extemporal meditation is "occasioned by outward occurences offered to the mind"; deliberate meditation is "wrought out of our own heart." Hall would have considered his *Meditations and Vowes* extemporal; they consist mainly of brief reflections on commonplaces or proverbs that move in a clipped, Senecan style through the three faculties of memory, intellect, and will. But his major contributions in the extemporal vein were published in 1630 and 1631 as *Occasionall Meditations*, spiritual reflections on the "book of creatures" (nature), from the heavens to boys playing jacks, from a dog barking to a spider in the window. In *The Arte of Divine Meditation*, however, the bulk of the discourse is devoted to a description of the deliberate type of meditation, since "Of extemporal meditation there may be much use, no rule." Deliberate meditation, although systematic, is also a highly flexible form. Hall writes that he has "endeavored . . . to prescribe a method of meditation, not upon so strict terms of necessity that whosoever goeth not my way erreth. Divers paths lead oft-times to the same end, and every man aboundeth in his own sense." Hall places considerable weight on being free of worldly thoughts and, following biblical examples, on solitude; otherwise he allows for great variety in the circumstances and subject matter of meditation. The meditation itself has two major movements: "It begins in the understanding, endeth in the affection; it begins in the brain, descends to the heart; begins on earth, ascends to heaven, not suddenly but by certain stairs and degrees till we come to the highest." Fearing that earlier meditative scales might discourage the ordinary devout Christian, Hall required of his reader "only a deep and firm consideration of the thing propounded, which shall be done if we follow it in our discourse through all, or the principal of those places which natural reason doth afford us." The intellectual stage of meditation proceeds by describing the topic, determining its causes and effects, and comparing and contrasting it to other topics. Once this "difficult and knotty part of meditation" is completed, the meditator is ready for the more important stage of responding emotionally to the topic. Scholars have disputed the question of the Catholic or Protestant sources of Hall's theory. The currently prevailing view is that Hall was part of a developing Protestant tradition of meditation that saw Scripture as the key to meaning and method, and that included a particular emphasis on application to the self. The difficulty of identifying sources testifies to the skill with which Hall synthesizes a range of devotional influences; the treatise is a masterpiece of exposition cum persuasion.

At Hawstead, Hall also became interested in Neostoicism. His first publication in this field was *Heaven upon Earth* (1606), wherein Hall employed his Senecan prose style in the service of the Stoic topic of tranquility of mind. A sentence from his dedication exemplifies the style and the thesis of this work: "I have undertaken a great taske . . . wherein I have followed Seneca, and gone beyond him; followed him as a Philosopher, gone beyond him as a Christian, as a Divine." The entire work unfolds in this manner, each section of the treatise bifurcated like one of its balanced antithetical sentences. This was a style of sententiousness that would earn Hall favor at the court of James I and the title of "our Christian Seneca."

Hall's *Meditations and Vowes* had been enthusiastically received at the court of Prince Henry, where Hall was invited to preach in 1607. His two sermons were enough to make him one of the prince's chaplains. At about the same time Providence struck again in the form of Lord Denny's offer. Hall settled at Waltham, twelve miles from London, for the next twenty years. His next work, dedicated to Denny and Denny's son-in-law James, Lord Hay, was brilliantly crafted to meet with success at the Jacobean court. In the *Characters of Vertues and Vices* (1608) Hall once again presented himself as a literary innovator and once again started a short-lived vogue now best known through the works of others (Sir Thomas Overbury's "Characters" appended to his poem *A Wife* in 1614 and John Earle's *Microcosmography* of 1628). As in *Heaven upon Earth*, in the *Characters* Hall claims to have "trod" the path of an ancient model, "but with an higher and wider step." This time the original was Theophrastus's *Characters*, particularly the scholarly edition, Latin translation, and commentary by Isaac Casaubon (1592), the famous scholar much admired by James I. In this book Hall skillfully combines the proverbial style much affected by James with the Renaissance theory of literature as a "speaking picture" which leads the reader to love virtue and detest vice. Like *Virgidemiae*, Hall's *Characters* adapts an ancient form to a modern purpose.

Hall's new patrons were well connected, and he had the talent to make the most of them. At Waltham he preached three times a week, saw to the spiritual needs of the large Denny family, tended to his own family, and continued to produce books at an impressive rate. It should be noted in passing that his sermons were important enough to be included as one of the five styles surveyed by Abraham Wright in his preaching manual, *Five Sermons in Five Several Styles* (1656). His poetic work of this period is limited to translations of some psalms (1607), and occasional verse, including the prefatory poems to Donne's two *Anniversaries* and a short elegy on the death of Prince Henry (1612). The two prefaces, "To the Praise of the Dead, and the Anatomy" and "The Harbinger to the Progress," are excellent guides to reading the *Anniversaries*. In the first preface Hall, like Donne, shows little personal interest in the dead Elizabeth Drury and focuses instead on promoting the poetic virtuosity of Donne and the symbolic significance of the girl:

> thou the subject of this well-born thought,
> Thrice noble maid, couldst not have found nor
>   sought
> A fitter time to yield to thy sad fate,
> Than whiles this spirit lives, that can relate
> Thy worth so well to our last nephews eyne,
> That they shall wonder both at his and thine.

"The Harbinger to the Progress" is perhaps more tasteful in its double praise of the girl's spiritual progress and Donne's imitation of her in verse; Hall's praise of Donne here sounds more like spiritual counsel for his friend, the courtier poet:

> Yet still thou vow'st her more; and every year
> Mak'st a new progress, while thou wanderest here;
> Still upwards mount; and let thy maker's praise
> Honour thy Laura, and adorn thy lays.

Some fewe of Davids Psalmes Metaphrased (1607) is a competent effort at a metrical version of the Psalms, a project attempted by many poets of the period, including Spenser, Sidney, and Milton.

Early in the Waltham period Hall dedicated to Prince Henry yet another genre experiment, the first of his three volumes of *Epistles* (1608-1611), and again there is the familiar preface in which he claims to introduce "a new fashion of discourse, by epistles; new to our language, usual to others." Hall characterized these compositions as a familiar form of writing by which "we do but talk with our friends by our pen and express ourselves no whit less easily, somewhat more digestedly." But Hall's letters read more like lectures; they have little in common with the familiar letters of Donne or James Howell and much with Seneca's weighty *Epistulae Morales*. When they do address personal matters, they are hardly informal. The first letter of the collection is one of the most interesting, a letter written to and attacking a former classmate, Jacob Wadsworth, for his conversion to Catholicism; in this letter the English satirist is reborn as Hall revels in reducing the rituals of Catholicism to clownish absurdity. While two-thirds of the *Epistles* deal with such unpromising religious topics as "the estate of a true, but weak Christian," there are also discourses on divorce, dueling, Hall's 1607 translation of the Psalms, clerical marriage, and an interesting letter to John Smith and John Robinson, leaders of the Separatists and founders of Plymouth Colony.

As his epistles on Roman Catholicism and separatism suggest, Hall became active in religious controversy at this time. By writing against both positions, Hall felt he was constructing a middle way that most Church of Englanders could live with. His attitude toward Catholicism was not always that of the biting satirist; by seventeenth-century standards he was a moderate, and by the time of his most considered anti-Roman tract, *The Olde Religion* (1628), Hall was suspected of Romish sympathizing by some Puritans. A sign of things to come, Hall was much harsher with the

*Letter from Hall to his friend James Calthrop (Pierpont
Morgan Library)*

Separatists in *A Common Apologie of the Church of England* against the Brownists (1610).

Hall seems to have been divided in his spiritual interests and in some respects mirrors the split personality of the Church of England with its Calvinist theology and episcopal form of government. He was a major writer in the ecclesiastical controversies that racked the first half of the seventeenth century in England, and he showed great skill as a rhetorician and logician in these works. Yet he also declared repeatedly his belief that inner devotional life was the core of religion. While he was learning the trade of controversialist, he was also working on his meditations. The *Occasionall Meditations* were probably composed over a long period of time that began with *The Arte of Divine Meditation*. Along with *The Arte*, they have been considered an influence on the great religious poets of the century. In addition to his work on the "book of creatures," Hall also produced throughout this period meditations on the "book of scriptures," his eight volumes of *Contemplations upon the Principall Passages of the Holie Storie* (1612-1626). Hall, like many seventeenth-century Protestants, regarded the reading of Scripture as an act of meditation, and his work in this vein deserves more consideration for, among other things, what it can tell us about Protestant reader response to the Bible. Hall's method in these books is to wrap highly dramatic incidents from Scripture with his own details of setting, character, and speech in order to produce a heartfelt and thoughtful response in the individual Christian reader. If his character analyses and emotionalism often seem forced, they also have something in common with the meditative poetry of Donne.

Hall's reputation as a churchman and writer resulted in King James three times selecting him for foreign missions, the most important being the international Synod of Dort in Holland in 1618, convened to settle a dispute over Arminianism. Although Hall fell ill after only two months at the synod, he was remembered for a sermon which used Ecclesiastes, one of James's favorite biblical texts, to recommend that each side abandon its hard theological line and join in a return to Scripture for an answer. This was a role Hall felt he was playing in his controversial writing, as suggested by titles such as "Via Media," written in 1624 and published in the 1660 collection, and *The Reconciler* (1629), and he was, through the rest of his career as a controversialist, ac-

cused of Romanism by the Puritans and Puritanism by the High Church Laudians.

Hall was made bishop of Exeter in 1627 and was best known during this period of his life as a defender of prelacy. His most important statement in the controversy over episcopacy was probably his first, *Episcopacie by Divine Right* (1640), but it was his *A Defence of the Humble Remonstrance* (1641) that started an exchange with the so-called Smectymnuans (a name devised from the initials of five Puritan divines) and eventually drew Milton into the trench warfare. Hall's misfortune as a controversialist is to be remembered primarily as the object of Milton's ad hominem attacks in *Animadversions upon the Remonstrant's Defense against Smectymnuus* (1641) and *Apology for Smectymnuus* (1642). Hall began this controversy by appealing again for moderation and reasonableness on both sides, but as the attacks continued his responses became clogged with learning and hair-splitting logic. If Milton is vituperative and obscure, Hall is boring. For the student of Hall's poetry, the most interesting aspect of Milton's attack is his attempt to undercut Hall the bishop with Hall the writer; Milton consistently portrays Hall as a flashy, proud, self-dramatizing figure who uses his rhetorical skills to advance his career—not an unusual argument to make against a member of the establishment.

This member of the establishment did spend time in prison. Hall was made bishop of Norwich in November 1641, but he was delayed from assuming this post because of trouble from the Puritan-dominated Parliament. Earlier that year in July, he had been impeached by a Parliament intent on abolishing episcopal control of government. On 30 December, Hall, Archbishop William Laud, and eleven other bishops were arrested for high treason and sent to the Tower of London. There Hall wrote "prison works" of the sort we generally associate with Puritans, "Observations of Some Specialities of Divine Providence" and *A Letter Lately sent by A Reverend Bishop from the Tower* (1642). Released after five months, Hall moved to Norwich, but his troubles with the Puritans were not over. In 1643 Hall was deprived of his bishopric by the Act of Sequestration and five years later was evicted from his house; he moved to Higham, where he continued to preach and even to ordain. These hardships are recounted in *Hard Measure* (1660), a sequel to the autobiography begun in prison. In these final years Hall returned to his first love, meditative writing, and also ventured into casu-

The true Picture of the Right Reuerend father in God
Ioseph Hall Bishop of Norwich. Samuell. Waker 16

Portrait engraved after Hall's death

istry, another important genre of seventeenth-century religious writing that focused on the inner life of the believer.

In *English Literature in the Earlier Seventeenth Century 1600-1660* (1962) Douglas Bush calls Hall "that inevitable pioneer" because of his innovations in verse satire, the character sketch, meditation, and the epistle. The satires and the meditative works are currently regarded as the most important of these experiments. Some scholars have attempted to reconcile this apparent contradiction in Hall's career, but perhaps it should be allowed to stand. The first English satirist presented himself as a new voice but also as a moralist out of step with the new age. The poems are informed both by solid classical learning and by a lively interest in contemporary life and (especially) literature. In his middle years he rose at least partly by means of a mastery of courtly style, yet he also promoted the cultivation of a personal spirituality which we perhaps too readily associate with those who opposed him. In

a sense, Hall's career was a continual negotiation between the Puritanism in which he was raised and the Royalism by which he advanced. A bishop who spent time in the Tower, he reminds us that his was the time of "the world turned upside down."

Biographies:

John Jones, *Bishop Hall, His Life and Times* (London: L. B. Seeley, 1826);

George Lewis, *A Life of Joseph Hall, D. D.* (London: Hodder & Stoughton, 1886);

Tom Fleming Kinlock, *The Life and Works of Joseph Hall, 1574-1656* (London: Staples Press, 1951).

References:

R. C. Bald, *Donne and the Drurys* (Cambridge: Cambridge University Press, 1959);

Benjamin Boyce, *The Theophrastan Character in England to 1642* (Cambridge, Mass.: Harvard University Press, 1947);

Audrey Chew, "Joseph Hall and John Milton," *Journal of English Literary History*, 17 (December 1950): 274-295;

Chew, "Joseph Hall and Neo-Stoicism," *PMLA*, 65 (December 1950): 1130-1145;

Wendell Clausen, "The Beginnings of English Character-Writing in the Early Seventeenth Century," *Philological Quarterly*, 25 (January 1946): 32-45;

Ronald J. Corthell, "Beginning as a Satirist: Joseph Hall's *Virgidemiarum Six Bookes*," *Studies in English Literature 1500-1900*, 23 (Winter 1983): 47-60;

Corthell, "Joseph Hall and Protestant Meditation," *Texas Studies in Literature and Language*, 20 (1978): 367-385;

Corthell, "Joseph Hall's *Characters of Vertues and Vices*: A 'Novum Repertum,' " *Studies in Philology*, 76 (January 1979): 28-35;

Harold Fisch, "Bishop Hall's Meditations," *Review of English Studies*, 25 (1949): 210-221;

Fisch, "The Limits of Hall's Senecanism," *Proceedings of the Leeds Philosophical Society*, 6 (1950): 453-463;

Frank Livingstone Huntley, *Bishop Joseph Hall 1574-1656: A Biographical and Critical Study* (Cambridge: D. S. Brewer, 1979);

Huntley, "Joseph Hall, John Marston, and *The Returne from Parnassus*," in *Illustrious Evidence: Approaches to English Literature of the Early Seventeenth Century*, edited by Earl Miner (Berkeley & Los Angeles: University of California Press, 1975), pp. 3-22;

Ejner J. Jensen, "Hall and Marston: The Role of the Satirist," *Satire Newsletter*, 4 (Spring 1967): 72-83;

U. Milo Kaufmann, The Pilgrim's Progress *and Traditions in Puritan Meditation* (New Haven: Yale University Press, 1966);

Alvin Kernan, *The Cankered Muse: Satire of the English Renaissance* (New Haven: Yale University Press, 1959);

Rudolf Kirk, "A Seventeenth-Century Controversy: Extremism vs. Moderation," *Texas Studies in Literature and Language*, 9 (1967): 5-35;

Thomas Kranidas, "Style and Rectitude in Seventeenth-Century Prose: Hall, Smectymnuus, and Milton," *Huntington Library Quarterly*, 46 (Summer 1983): 237-269;

Claude Lacassagne, "La Satire Religieuse dans *Mundus Alter et Idem* de Joseph Hall," *Recherches Anglaises et Americaines*, 4 (1971): 141-156;

Louis Lecocq, *La Satire en Angleterre de 1588 a 1603* (Paris: Didier, 1969);

Barbara Lewalski, Donne's Anniversaries *and the Poetry of Praise: The Creation of a Symbolic Mode* (Princeton: Princeton University Press, 1973);

Lewalski, *Protestant Poetics and the Seventeenth-Century Religious Lyric* (Princeton: Princeton University Press, 1979);

Louis Martz, *The Poetry of Meditation: A Study in English Religious Literature of the Seventeenth Century*, revised edition (New Haven: Yale University Press, 1962);

Richard McCabe, "The Form and Methods of Milton's *Animadversions upon the Remonstrants Defence against Smectymnuus*," *English Language Notes*, 18 (June 1981): 266-272;

McCabe, *Joseph Hall: A Study in Satire and Meditation* (Oxford: Clarendon Press, 1982);

Gerhard Muller-Schwefe, "Joseph Hall's *Characters of Vertues and Vices*: Notes toward a Revaluation," *Texas Studies in Literature and Language*, 14 (1972): 235-251;

John Peter, *Complaint and Satire in Early English Literature* (Oxford: Clarendon Press, 1956);

Sanford M. Salyer, "Hall's Satires and the Harvey-Nashe Controversy," *Studies in Philology*, 25 (April 1928): 149-170;

Raman Selden, *English Verse Satire, 1590-1750* (London: Allen & Unwin, 1978);

Philip A. Smith, "Bishop Hall, 'Our English Seneca,' " *PMLA*, 63 (December 1948): 1191-1204;

Arnold Stein, "Joseph Hall's Imitation of Juvenal," *Modern Language Review*, 43 (July 1948): 315-322;

Gardner Stout, "Sterne's Borrowings from Bishop Joseph Hall's *Quo Vadis?*," *English Language Notes*, 2 (March 1965): 196-200;

Florence S. Teager, "Patronage of Joseph Hall and John Donne," *Philological Quarterly*, 15 (October 1936): 408-413;

Leonard D. Tourney, *Joseph Hall* (Boston: Twayne, 1979);

Tourney, "Joseph Hall and the *Anniversaries*," *Papers on Language and Literature*, 13 (Winter 1977): 25-34;

John Millar Wands, "The Early Printing History of Joseph Hall's *Mundus Alter et Idem*," *Publications of the Bibliographical Society of America*, 74, no. 1 (1980): 1-12;

George Williamson, *The Senecan Amble: A Study in Prose Form from Bacon to Collier* (Chicago: University of Chicago Press, 1951).

Edward, Lord Herbert of Cherbury

(3 March 1583 - 1? August 1648)

Mary Norton
Western Carolina University

BOOKS: *De Veritate Provt Distingvitvr A Revelatione, A Verisimili, A Possibili, Et A Falso* (Paris, 1624; London: Per A. Matthaeum, 1633); third edition, revised and enlarged, with *De Causis Errorum* and *De Religione Laici* (London, 1645);

De Causis Errorum: Una Cum tractatu de Religione Laici (London, 1645; facsimile, Stuttgart-Bad Cannstatt: Frommann, 1966);

The Life and Raigne of King Henry the Eighth. Written By the Right Honourable Edward, Lord Herbert of Cherbury (London: Printed by E. G. for Thomas Whitaker, 1649);

Expeditio In Ream Insulam, Authore Edovardo Domino Herbert (London: Prostant apud Humphredum Moseley, 1656);

De Religione Gentilium errorumque apud eos causis (Amsterdam: Printed by John & Peter Blaeu, 1663); translated by W. Lewis as *The Antient Religion of the Gentiles, and Causes of their Errors Consider'd* (London: Printed for John Nutt, 1705);

Occasional Verses of Edward Lord Herbert, Baron of Cherbury and Castle-Island. Deceased in August, 1648 (London: Printed by T. R. for Thomas Dring, 1665);

The Life of Edward Herbert of Cherbury Written by Himself (Strawberry Hill, 1764);

A Dialogue Between a Tutor and his Pupil (London: Printed for W. Bathoe, 1768; facsimiles: Stuttgart-Bad Cannstatt: Frommann, 1971; New York & London: Garland, 1979).

Editions: *The History of King Henry VIII*, in volume 2 of *A Complete History of England*, edited by John Hughes (London: printed for B. Aylmer, 1706; revised, London: Printed for R. Bonwicke, 1719);

The Expedition to the Isle of Rhé [Expeditio In Ream Insulam] (London: Printed by Whittingham & Wilkins, 1860);

Autobiography of Edward Lord Herbert of Cherbury. The History of England under Henry VIII (London: Alexander Murray, 1872);

Edward, Lord Herbert of Cherbury (portrait attributed to W. Larkin; National Portrait Gallery, London)

The Autobiography of Edward, Lord Herbert of Cherbury, edited, with a continuation of the Life, by Sidney L. Lee (London: Nimmo, 1886; New York: Scribner & Welford, 1886; revised edition, London: Routledge / New York: Dutton, 1906);

The Poems, English & Latin, of Edward, Lord Herbert of Cherbury, edited by G. C. Moore Smith (Oxford: Clarendon Press, 1923);

De Veritate, translated by Meyrick H. Carré (Bristol: Published for the University of Bristol by W. Arrowsmith, 1937);

Lord Herbert of Cherbury's De Religione Laici, edited and translated by Harold R. Hutcheson (New Haven: Yale University Press / London: Oxford University Press, 1944);

The Life of Edward, First Lord Herbert of Cherbury, written by J. M. Shuttleworth (London, New York & Toronto: Oxford University Press, 1976).

OTHER: "Elegy for the Prince," in *Lachrymæ Lachrymarum,* enlarged edition edited by Josuah Sylvester (London: Printed by H. Lownes, 1613).

Widely recognized as an influential philosopher because of his seminal tract on deism, *De Veritate* (1624), Edward Herbert has nevertheless remained a poet known primarily by association: as the older brother of poet-divine George Herbert and as an imitator of John Donne's secular Metaphysical poetry. Critics disagree about the merit of Edward Herbert's poetry, some troubled by its sometimes perplexing syntax and peculiar diction, others by its impersonal abstractness and lack of engaging imagery. Indeed, Herbert at times appears more concerned with metaphysics than with aesthetics. G. C. Moore Smith, editor of the standard edition (1923) of Herbert's poetry, disagrees, however, and steadfastly contends that "in poetic feeling and art, Edward Herbert soars above his brother George." Admittedly, the corpus of Herbert's poetry includes works of uneven quality, but Herbert's persistently abstract and philosophical mode, with individualistic and often iconoclastic perspectives, gives his poetry a distinct voice amid the Metaphysical poets of the seventeenth century.

Most of the poems in *Occasional Verses* (published posthumously by Herbert's brother Henry in 1665) do not, for instance, make use of the standard poetic devices of Metaphysical poetry—the "objective correlative" or arresting conceits, such as Donne employs; instead, Herbert's poetry relies on a more abstract vocabulary to convey philosophical contemplations on the nature of politics, death, love, beauty, and truth. Herbert frequently uses form to imitate content, and thus the difficulties of Herbert's poetic voice and style derive from the complexities he attempts to signify: abstract and intricate perceptions and a sensitivity to the implications of experience. A calculatingly deliberate artificer, he manipulates stanzaic patterns and rhyme schemes to accommodate the meaning of a poem and also as devices that can, in themselves, connote additional meaning: structure is tenor as well as vehicle.

The unusual abundance of information about activities in Herbert's life up to 1624 comes from his own *Autobiography* (written circa 1643-1648), which is distinguished by moments of quasi-inflated truth. The pervasive egotism of the work, inseparable from its robust celebration of the self and accomplishments, is best read with the tolerant understanding that Herbert was creating memoirs intended to bring esteem to his family and his family name. He is fashioning the persona of "the public" Lord Herbert, the handsome and debonair lover, the accomplished courtier, the diligent ambassador, designed for the admiration and emulation of posterity. The *Autobiography* recounts very little of Herbert's vast intellectual, spiritual, and artistic activity, that being reserved for the genres of poetry and the philosophical treatise.

Born on 3 March 1583 at Eyton on Severn, Edward Herbert was the eldest of the ten children of Richard Herbert, Esquire, of Montgomery Castle, and Magdalen Newport, daughter of Sir Richard Newport. The *Autobiography* depicts a quite precocious toddler, shy and astoundingly introspective, whose first inquiry was, "how I came into this world?" As the son of aristocracy, his childhood education came from a private tutor, and in May 1596, at the age of thirteen, he entered University College at Oxford as a gentleman commoner. In the same year, Herbert's father died.

Through an arranged marriage, on 28 February 1599, Herbert wed his cousin Mary Herbert, daughter and heir to Sir William Herbert of St. Juliens, who had enforced the stipulation that Mary marry a man of identical surname to receive her inheritance. In the same year, Edward's mother moved her entire family to Oxford, apparently to assist in Edward's education and social advancement. Yet, soon thereafter, in 1600, the Herberts left Oxford and relocated in London, where Edward continued his studies, teaching himself French, Italian, and Spanish, with the goal of becoming "a citizen of the world." Possessing musical talent as well, he became an accomplished lutenist and composed nine respectable works for the instrument. His mother, well respected for her gracious hospitality and honored by both John Donne and Izaak Walton for her generous spirit, also introduced young Edward to some of the leading intelligentsia and artists of the day, including the historian William Camden and the musician William Byrd. Perhaps most significant, however, was that during this time in London between 1600 and 1608 Herbert developed an enduring friendship with John Donne, and

Ruins of Herbert's birthplace, at Eyton, Shropshire, as depicted in an 1816 issue of the Gentleman's Magazine

the two exchanged correspondence and poetry until Donne's death in 1631. Herbert is the addressee of one of Donne's finest verse epistles; Herbert wrote the earnest "Elegy for Doctor Dunn" celebrating their friendship and praising Donne's verse.

While in London, Herbert was granted an audience at Queen Elizabeth's court, and according to the *Autobiography*, the aged queen "looked attentively upon me and swearing again her Ordinary oath said, It is a pitty he was married so young and thereupon gave me her hand to kiss twice, both tymes gently clapping me on the Cheeke." Rather than devote himself to the endeavors of the court, however, Herbert pursued his studies until he came of age in 1603 and then, like other ambitious young men, went to court to display his loyalty to the newly crowned King James, who bestowed upon him the Order of the Bath. In 1605 he was made sheriff of Montgomeryshire, and residing in the rustic countryside there, his "beloved studies" still took precedence over court life.

The year 1608 became important in the philosophical and artistic development of Edward Herbert because it was then that he, now proficient in many languages, left his wife and four children to travel the Continent with Aurelian

Townshend. His marriage had evidently been adequately happy, and he boasts of his ten years of fidelity, but foreign travel was, he contended, a requisite part of his education. Critics generally agree that, while abroad, he was introduced to new forms of theology and religious conduct that would inform and empower his later philosophical and poetic work. While he was in France, Herbert became acquainted with Henri, Duc de Montmorency, leader of "The Politiques," a group of liberal intellectuals that believed a strong central monarchy and religious toleration would ensure justice and peace. The exposure to such ideas led to the composition of Herbert's first works of poetry, and his association with Montmorency had other, though secondary, advantages as well; when the duke moved from his castle at Merlou to Chantilly, he allowed Herbert the use of his horses and his forest for hunting, and, at Merlou, Herbert polished his social and military graces. In his *Autobiography* he describes himself as a dark and handsome young man, instigating duels over small points of honor, enamoring women, and living the enviable life of the accomplished and privileged courtier.

The new experiences during this Continental journey evidently generated or stimulated Herbert's creative interests: "Parted Souls" (written in 1608) is Herbert's first known poem, marking the occasion of his leaving England and his feelings about leaving, presumably, his wife. The peremptory, yet sympathetic, tone conveys the separation as necessary and inevitable, but because the lover compares himself to a departing (dying) soul, the parting is rendered a form of death, which "unto us must be freedom and rest." In many respects, the poem recalls Donne's "A Valediction: forbidding mourning" and "The Legacie," as well as other poems of departure such as Thomas Carew's "To My Mistress in Absence" and Richard Lovelace's "To Lucasta, Going Beyond Seas." An obviously Platonic conception of love in Herbert's poem foreshadows his later, more mature and more commanding, poems, "To His Mistress for Her True Picture" and "Ode Upon a Question Moved Whether Love Should Continue Forever."

The remaining poems of 1608 concern Herbert's public and social reflections; he wrote two satires in 1608 and the playful lyrics "Madrigal" and "Another." "The State progress of Ill," composed in August 1608 at the Montmorency estate at Merlou, is the first of two 1608 satires and is perhaps most responsible for afflicting Herbert with the unfortunate reputation for obscurity. Composed of heavily elliptical, heavily enjambed couplets, its political and philosophical arguments are indeed labyrinthine. The poem's broad philosophical interest is with authority and liberty, specifically the relation of government to human freedom, and it examines the forces within the individual and the forces imposed upon the individual that have brought about the progressive loss of freedom and equality. The double entendres in the title ("state" as both a condition and a political body, and "progress" as both motion and a royal excursion) reveal the forward but meandering movement of evil and corruption ("Ill") throughout political history. Though it shows numerous similarities to Donne's 1601 poem, "Metempsychosis: The Progresses of the Soul," Herbert's poem stands consistently and boldly political.

The second, and less intricate, satire of 1608, "Of Travellers: (*from*) Paris," is addressed to Ben Jonson and exhibits the tenor of some of Jonson's later vituperative epigrams (1616) about arrogant and self-serving courtiers, "On Something That Walks Somewhere" and "On Don Surly." Those travelers to France who were transformed into affected dandies also echo Sir Politic Would-be from Jonson's *Volpone* (1607). Most im-

portant, such preoccupation with integrity and decency in public and private conduct in the two 1608 satires is characteristic of Herbert's regard for the abstract, and profoundly meaningful, implications of actions, events, and behavior.

Himself displaying the requisite abilities of a truly cultured gentleman, Herbert wrote several poems that incorporate musical structures and techniques. John Hoey has read Herbert's first, "Madrigal," as a debate, each stanza offering "provisional solutions," then "new proposals," about "how to love best," but its style is more musically playful than dryly forensic. Rather, like a madrigal, it braids together contrapuntal and polyphonic voices. There is a great sense of "play," a metaphysical delight in playing with ideas and perspectives about love within this dynamically musical context; Herbert again, typically, uses form and style to amplify content. It is not surprising that the Pre-Raphaelite Algernon Swinburne, himself a superb stylist, was apparently much taken with this poem, exclaiming, "How lovely in feeling, and how near excellence in expression is the Madrigal ['How should I love my best']." Herbert's "Another" (that is, another madrigal) also orchestrates musical rhythms, balancing the cadence of varied line lengths with the measured rhyme scheme of *aabccbdeedff*. This poem joins form with meaning to enact the philosophical argument: ideas separated by line breaks are unified by rhyme, just as the poem argues that distance between material things (the bodies of lovers) does not necessitate spiritual separation because of the unifying, transcendental power of love.

These early poems primarily address some of the immediate concerns of Herbert's personal life, which would become, however, increasingly social. After nearly eight months at Merlou, Herbert returned to Paris and, as he reported in his *Autobiography*, lived for a time with the "incomparable scholar Isaac Casaubon." In January 1609 Herbert traveled back to England and was received by King James and Queen Anne. Surely James's own learning and artistic sensibilities must have appealed to Herbert. The most notable poem of this year, "Epitaph Caecil. Boulstr.," Herbert's first elegiac poem, marks the death, on 4 August 1609, of Cecilia Boulstred, a kinswoman of one of Donne's closest friends, Lucy, Countess of Bedford. Herbert's poem invites comparison with Donne's "Elegie on Mris Boulstred." Herbert's abstract contemplation about the relationship among death, sin, and virtue limits itself, how-

Herbert circa 1610-1614 (portrait by Isaac Oliver; Powis Castle Collection)

ever, to the specific person of Cecilia, and this early poem includes seeds of Herbert's later Platonism and Neoplatonic preoccupation with the relationship of the soul and body. It also includes one of those particularly penetrating concrete images with which Herbert occasionally surprises: "Methinks Death like one laughing lyes, / Shewing his teeth, shutting his eyes. . . ." The stanzaic pattern is typically purposeful, the final "triumphant" stanza of couplets signaling the victorious resolution of the poem.

The poems of the next decade illustrate Herbert's evolving philosophical and artistic interests, which he somehow found time to pursue amid his almost frenetic activity. He served as Merioneth's member of Parliament in 1610, but in June or July left England once more to serve as one of four thousand English troops on the side of the Protestants aiding Prince Philip William of Orange in his attempt to capture the city of Juliers (Jülich) in Holland. The *Autobiography* portrays not only a valiant soldier, but one who, when he returned to London, was exceptionally

popular among even the highest ladies of court, a few allegedly falling in love with him after merely seeing his portrait.

The less boisterous years of 1611 to 1614 were spent in England, where Herbert divided his time between the court and his family. His poetry of this time reveals his increasing involvement in social and political affairs. On 6 November 1612, when Henry, Prince of Wales, died, Herbert mourned his death in his earthy yet political "Elegy for the Prince," one of the few poems published in his lifetime, in a 1613 collection by Josuah Sylvester, *Lachrymæ Lachrymarum*. Herbert's elegy explores the question of what the world will do without Henry's rule, or what the people (the body politic) will do without the soul (the ruler). Beginning with a treatment of earthly anxieties, the poem ascends to Platonic considerations, concluding with images of the prince's immortal place in his people's memories.

When the Juliers dispute revived in 1614, Herbert returned to the Low Countries, where he participated in the brief military action be-

167

tween the Spanish and the Dutch (he prevented the destruction of a monastery). He left when a peace was negotiated in November 1614 and traveled through Germany to Italy (Venice, Florence, Rome) where he remained two years. He attended lectures at the University of Padua, and in Rome he visited the English Catholic College, where he perceived the ecclesiastical suppression of individualism as the antithesis of the political and religious toleration he himself supported and espoused. Significantly, he also became acquainted with a group of philosophers, Lucillo Vanini in particular, who advocated forms of deism, a belief in a God who should be worshipped, but a rejection of orthodox, organized religious creed.

Herbert's poetry of this year does not reflect much of his diverse political or philosophical activity, however; instead, he wrote the lovely lyrics "Ditty in imitation of the Spanish" and "Tears, flow no more." "Tears, flow no more" combines traditional Petrarchan themes and images with a complex logical structure. The first stanza—addressed in apostrophe to tears, not the lover—is in the form of a series of commands that attempt to control the uncontrollable ("if you needs must flow"), and the poem shows a struggle for power between falling tears and the poet wishing them quelled. Yet the final stanza once again admits what seems to be inevitable for the unrequited Petrarchan lover: that the tears still flow, sighs still blow, fires still burn. Inquiring (not demanding) why the lover's sighs should not serve the purpose of ending his pain, the poem concludes with a question that admits a surrender to love's authority. Typical of Herbert's poems, the focus is less on the concrete imagery than on the philosophical and metaphysical concepts they imply, and these are enhanced by its style. A predominance of soft consonant sounds combined with the abundance of long *O* sounds is reinforced by the melodious *aabcbc* rhyme scheme of the three six-line stanzas; it is obvious why the poem has been acclaimed for its "haunting music."

Though such poetry concentrates on personal emotions and relationships, Herbert was in fact occupied with contemporary politics, and, given his animosity toward the Church, it is not surprising that in 1615 he responded to the request of Charles Emanuel I, Duke of Savoy, to conduct four thousand Protestant troops from Languedoc to Piedmont to fight against Catholic Spain. When Herbert arrived at Lyons, however,

he was promptly, though briefly, imprisoned because raising of troops by outsiders had been prohibited by Queen Marie de Médicis of France. He soon returned to England but was afflicted with what was probably malaria, ailing, he wrote, for "a year and an half without intermission, and a year and an half longer at Spring and Fall." On days he was not entirely bedridden he could do little but read.

In 1617, perhaps motivated by his own illness, he wrote the moving and extraordinary poem "Elegy over a Tomb," a contemplation of death directed at the tomb (not the person) of an unknown young lady; numerous critics have noted that its unusual force comes from the qualities of a love lyric it possesses. The first five stanzas are a series of questions seeking knowledge about what becomes of Beauty after a beautiful person dies. In addition to the grief caused by death itself, the loss of beauty itself causes lament. Thus, the answer to the overriding question simultaneously offers the consolation for the woman's death, not the typical consolation of the Christian afterlife, but reassurance of the symbiotic relationship between life and earth, between destruction and creation: "Had not your beauties giv'n this second birth / To Heaven and Earth?"

The poem is also significant for its deistic underpinnings; while Herbert's work on *De Veritate* did not commence until 1619, this poem manifests evidence of his developing thought, as is apparent in the final stanza, with its repetitive demand for independent revelation, a primary tenet of deistic philosophy:

> Tell us, for Oracles must still ascend,
>   For those that crave them at your tomb:
> Tell us, where are those beauties now become,
>   And what they now intend:
> Tell us, alas, that cannot tell our grief,
>   Or hope relief.

The "Oracles" are the agent from which the poet seeks knowledge, and this emphasis on private revelation is predicated on the deistic belief that truth can be received rationally, emotionally, sensuously, and intuitively. In *De Veritate*, Herbert would assert his lack of interest in "truths of faith"; visions presented in scripture, for example, should not constitute prescience: "what is received by others as revelation must be accounted not revelation but tradition or history."

His work on the treatise and his poetic creativity were not in the least interrupted when he was appointed British ambassador to France in

1619. His friendship with Sir George Villiers, Marquis (later first Duke) of Buckingham, probably helped secure him the diplomatic assignment, an important post he was surprised to acquire. He set out on 13 May 1619 for France, Thomas Carew among his official attendants. Herbert's activities would side him with the Protestant—or at least anti-Catholic—cause in the 1619 dispute over Bohemia, which marked the beginning of the Thirty Years War. His first ambassadorial term came to an end in 1621, however, because of a quarrel with Charles d'Albert, Duc de Luynes, a favorite of Louis XIII, principally over the issue of the "pacification" of the Huguenots. Luynes died suddenly while Herbert was back in England, and Herbert was returned to his post in 1622.

The first three years of Herbert's ambassadorship were enormously creative and productive despite the demands of his position. When Herbert's life was most active and tumultuous, his writing was most fruitful, as if the vitality of his life nourished his mind and artistic sensibility. During the summer of 1620, for example, he revisited the Montmorency castle at Merlou and wrote one of his most celebrated poems, "Sonnet" ("You well compacted Groves, whose light and shade"). It is a focused encomium (not a broad encomium of estate, such as Jonson's "To Penhurst" or Carew's "To Saxham") venerating the Montmorency forest as the nexus of earthly, sensual beauty and universal harmony. Herbert praises an Aristotelian "golden mean" with exaltation upon the grand knowledge and power of nature. Evoking all five senses, the warm and lush texture of the description also suggests Herbert's experimentation with the poetic techniques of the Italian poet Giambattista Marino, who happened to have been in Paris from 1615 to 1624. Marino's influence can be noted primarily in the quality of *la meraviglia* an exotic, luxuriant, and colorful imagery:

> Upon a Greene embroidering through each Glade
> 　An Airy Silver, and a Sunny Gold,
> 　　So cloath the poorest they do behold
> Themselves, in riches which can never fade[.]

Equally notable is the sestet's implications of a preconscious, self-perpetuating sensibility. The structure of the poem, however, is unusually conventional for Herbert, with its Petrarchan octave (*abba abba*) and a Spenserian sestet (*cdcdee*).

Between the writing of his "Sonnet" and 1624, Herbert wrote five poems forming a constellation, and perhaps a logical sequence. The three sonnets "To Her Face," "To Her Body," "To Her Mind" unarguably form a sequence. Hoey contends that these poems seem to be amplifications of aspects of "A Description," evidently also written sometime before 1624. Although these poems do not have external sequentiality (except for their printing order), G. C. Moore Smith has convincingly argued that "Love's End" forms the conclusion to the sequence.

"A Description" offers a useful context for the other poems as it is a Platonic variation of the *blazon*, an extended catalogue of a lady's anatomy; but in Herbert's poem, each tangible part of the lady incarnates some cosmic entity. The particular not only suggests but embodies the universal; the corporeal substance possesses ethereal essence. The final stanza equates the lady's goodness with beauty but accentuates her conscious control over her own essence. The poem is often compared to Donne's "Love's Progress," to Carew's "Love's Complement," and to stanzas 10 and 11 of Edmund Spenser's "Epithalamium."

A combination of Platonic and Christian elements can be found also in the sonnet "To Her Face," wherein the lady's face manifests a purity so absolute that it precludes even original sin: "Sure *Adam* sinn'd not in that spotless Face." The lady is at once associated with prelapsarian perfection and the Platonic ideal of beauty and goodness. What she arouses in the poet is, therefore, no profane sort of love but an intellectual and spiritual apprehension of perfection. The diction of the poem suggests the subtle and coercive (though not sinister) subjection of the poet: the lady's face has an "*influence*" that "*inclines* the Will," and "*moves* the Sense" that she alone "constrain'st" (forces, compels, obliges); that "kindles" desires, "inspires" the mind and soul, and will be "dazling" the eye that beholds her. Thus, the lady's face is "Fatal": decreed by destiny. The poet apparently had no choice but to "gaze" in "wonder and amaze." Additionally, the deductive logic of the typical sonnet form has been purposefully inverted: Herbert's sonnet begins with the conclusion, the sestet (*ababba*) preceding the octave (*cdcdefef*).

Such subversion of the male will is also suggested by the next poem in the sequence, "To her Body," in which the body of the woman is described not in sensual terms, but in terms of its authority, its "fix'd Majesty": "State sits inthroned

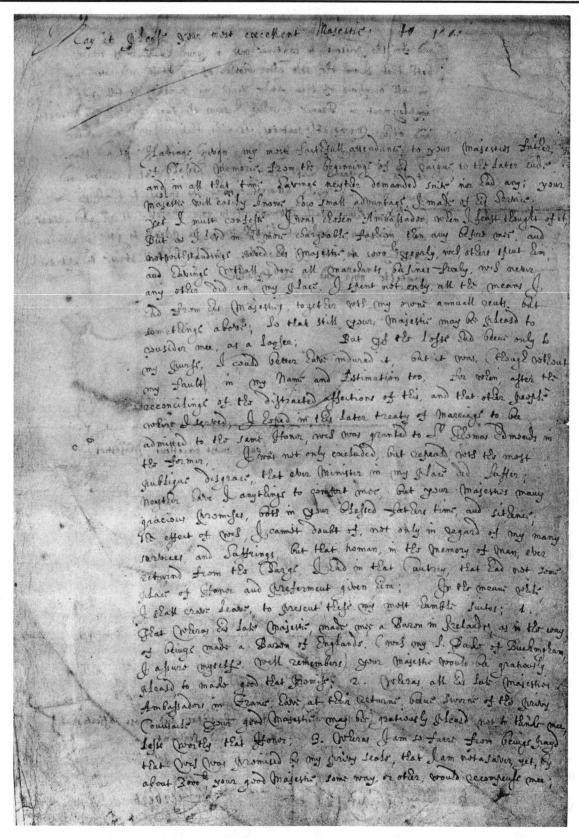

First page of a letter from Herbert to Charles I, written 8 May 1626 (private collection; lent to the Pierpont Morgan Library)

in thee, / Divulging forth her Laws in the fair Book / Of thy Commandements. . . ." The political and biblical metaphors elevate her body to ordained, ineluctable domination ("which none mistook, / That ever humbly came therein to see / Their own unworthiness . . ."). Her body is praised, above all, for its proportion and symmetry as the embodiment of cosmic harmony. As in "A Description," both the substance and the ethereal essence of the woman imply Platonic and Christian perfection.

The Platonic ascension of contemplation from the face and mind to the body results in the understanding of perfection, and so consummate is this lady's mind that language is inadequate to represent it; the poet consequently surrenders his attempt:

> Then pardon me that Rapture do profess,
>   At thy outside, that want, for what I see,
> Description, if here amaz'd I cesse
> Thus—

Herbert may be stretching the limits of poetic good taste, but the use of one word for an entire line indicates his persistent, though not always successful, application of style to imitate meaning and intention. The poem further represents the culmination of the imagery and themes of the first two sonnets: the intertextuality existing among all three poems signals this the penultimate sonnet in the sequence.

The initial apostrophes in each of the sonnets unify the sequence further, serving the dual purpose of describing not only the woman's features, but the lover's state of mind. "Fatal Aspect!," "Regardful Presence!," and "Exalted Mind!" are all concurrently descriptive and self-referential. "Aspect" may be considered a noun signifying the lady's countenance or appearance and may also function as a verb indicating the action and way the poet perceives her. "Regardful" describes the lady's body as worthy of regard as well as it represents the lover as observant and heeding. "Exalted" denotes the elevated status of the lady's mind, but the word also portrays the impassioned, rapturously excited lover. This deliberate merging of the lover and the beloved dramatizes a psychological force of empathy not usually accentuated in a Platonic relationship.

"Love's End" offers a dramatic and emotional dimension that the philosophical contemplations of the previous poems in the sequence do not. The lover begins with a peremptory an-

nouncement, "Thus ends my love," but it is not the end of love that "grieves [him] most" because endings and the pain of endings themselves have end. He is most troubled "that I am set / free, worse then deny'd." As in "To Her Body," a relationship between freedom and bondage of the will or of the heart, respectively, is suggested and is resolved with the poet removing from the temple of his mind the object of worship which had evidently held him: "there only rests but to unpaint / Her form in my mind, that so dispossest / It be a Temple, but without a Saint." This concluding poem indicates the existence of a physical affair in which the lover-persona had invested his emotional love as well as his Neoplatonic meditations.

During these immensely fruitful first years as ambassador to France, and probably in 1621, Herbert composed yet another sequence, which extols what he terms "black" beauty as superior to pale beauty. The five poems of the sequence— "To Mrs. Diana Cecyll," "To Her Eyes," "To Her Hair," "Sonnet of Black Beauty," and "Another Sonnet to Black Itself"—evolve from a long poetic tradition in praise of *blackness*, beginning with Dionysius the Areopagite and extending to Shakespeare's sonnets. It is not insignificant that Herbert himself had dark hair and beard; his *Autobiography* describes his father also as "black-haired and bearded as all my ancestors on his side are said to have been."

The first poem of the "Black Beauty" sequence, "To Mrs. Diana Cecyll," addresses this notorious beauty of Herbert's day, and the first stanza calls attention to the rejection of the standard Petrarchan Laura-figure of pale beauty ("of Milk, or Snow") in order to praise instead the gentle, sweet, yet still powerful and awe-inspiring, refracted light that emanates from the rising sun or a diamond.

The second stanza reiterates his rejection of the standard, "vulgar" poetic glorification of light hair, and praises Mrs. Cecyll's as "reverend black." Stanza 3 compliments the interrelationships, as well as independence, of her "parts" for their perfection and harmony. The final stanza proclaims that Diana Cecyll not only represents the Platonic ideal of beauty but is, paradoxically, the tangible manifestation of it: one need "ascend no higher."

In the same vein, the next poem, "To Her Eyes," asserts the Neoplatonic concept that the eyes reveal the state of the soul, itself a reflection of God, and makes a claim for divinity at the end of the poem, suggestively, in line 33, a number associated with the life of Christ.

Likewise "To Her Hair," the longest and most technically complicated of the poems, builds on the ideas of the first two poems, again asserting the superiority of blackness and claiming that common "white" light blinds lovers to the superior, true beauty of blackness, a superior light which requires a superior insight to perceive. The sequence thus incorporates a Platonic ascension itself, commencing with contemplation of the concrete, beautiful Lady Cecyll and rising to reflection on the abstract concept of beauty, black beauty in particular. In "Sonnet of Black Beauty" the poet restates the superiority of black beauty based on its constancy, which renders it virtuous; and he continuously, even arrogantly, emphasizes that human ineptitude blinds one to recognizing such preeminence. According to Douglas Runnels, the fifth poem in the sequence "presents the reader with the *quintessence* of 'Black itself,'" as it recapitulates the contentions of the previous poems of the sequence in the succinct form of a unified sonnet.

At this time Herbert also remained hard at work on his *De Veritate*, which he completed in June 1623. He was encouraged by Hugo Grotius and Daniel Tilenus to publish the work, and in his *Autobiography*, Herbert also claims motivation from a divine sign, "a loud though gentle noise . . . from the heaven" in answer to his prayer for reassurance. He had *De Veritate* printed in 1624 in Paris, at his own expense. Herbert's philosophical and poetic achievements from these years in France do not reflect the turbulent politics of his ambassadorship, abruptly ended in 1624 because of his candid opinions about James I's policies and strategies toward matrimonial alliances in Europe, which Herbert foresaw as failures. When Herbert returned to England, he found himself deeply in debt, his salary never having been fully paid, though he was awarded the Irish peerage of Castle Island (County Kerry). The next years were neither productive nor happy ones, but on 7 May 1629 he was raised to English peerage as first Baron Herbert of Cherbury.

Herbert did continue to write poetry, and sometime before 1631 wrote four poems about color as it represents beauty. He does not equivocate his claims for the absolute superiority of blackness, but esteems the beauty in other colors and the colors of other beauties, such diversity of opinion attesting to his recognition of the immense plurality of beauty itself. His "The Brown Beauty"

Edward, Lord Herbert of Cherbury (artist unknown; Powis Castle Collection)

praises the combination of black and white as the perfection of balance, claiming brown "dignify'd" because it represents neither extreme.

The sensual "La Gialetta Gallante, or, The Sun-burn'd Exotique Beauty" praises a luscious, earthy, and tropical beauty, much preferable to the English paleness of "our Lovers." He admires the native quality of the woman, whose "Gold shew like som Copper-mine," such natural sensuality also implied in the provocative images of fruit, "cordial to both sight and taste."

The two "Green-sickness" poems, "Though the pale white within your cheek compos'd" and "From thy pale look, while angry Love doth seem," rather unexpectedly praise paleness (apparently caused by "green-sickness," or chlorosis, a form of anemia that affected young women) for the innocence it connotes. The poems celebrate the beauty of pale purity with images of virginity and lilies that eclipse the mature "blush" of roses.

Consistent with his praise of dark beauty in the four "color" poems, "nut brown" is acclaimed "the loveliest color which the flesh doth crown" in "To His Mistress for Her True Picture." The main concern of the poem, however, is not with color but with the correlation between physical darkness and light, and between spiritual ignorance and the illumination of understanding. This poetic contemplation of Death offers some of Herbert's most distinctive and memorable imagery, often rendered through his application of deistic principles. The poem insists on private revelation and is not content to accept the standard depiction and interpretations of Death which he views as confused with its mere effect: the rotting and decay of "Flesh beauty" in the grave. Rather than denigration or even defiance, Death is given the role of the ultimate controlling force in life ("Death, my lifes Mistress, and the soveraign Queen / Of all that ever breath'd"), and the poet beckons Death not to remain mysterious, shrouded in darkness, but to show herself "A day-star of the light" with the ability to elucidate life and give it justice and meaning. Death is elevated, therefore, to the role of the savior, "the true Guide," because full apprehension of Death, a "true picture," brings knowledge, thus liberty, thus peace. The poem also raises the question of the power of art and its relevance to reality when it asks, "Can pictures have more life / Then the original?"; this question implicitly recognizes the power of any cultural artifact ("pictures" of death) to shape an individual's spiritual perceptions. This iconoclastic poem extols independence of thought and belief; and the Platonic desire to escape from the "bodies Prison" in order to achieve absolute understanding is emphasized for its ability to effect individual freedom.

Herbert's enduring concern with the freedom of the will, with an autonomous spirituality, underlies much of his poetry, but can perhaps best be seen in "An Ode upon a Question moved, Whether Love should continue for ever?" This poem has attracted the most, and the most positive, critical response to Herbert's poetry, with Robert Ellrodt proclaiming that it "bears comparison with the most beautiful poems in English literature." Patterned after Donne's "The Extasie," but without Donne's entangled paradoxes, Herbert's ode is a pastoral dialogue between two lovers, Melander ("the dark one") and Celinda ("pretty blind one" or "little heavenly [fair bright] one"). In their sweet repose in the garden, Celinda raises the question as to what becomes of love after one dies. She thinks it must certainly die with the body but has difficulty understanding why; Melander's Neoplatonic answer emphasizes the difference between corporeal love and superlunary love, which is truest because it emanates from the One. Love, he says, will be made eternal and perfect, as will joy and

virtue, and the body will also be resurrected in Heaven. "Equal love" can make souls immortal, and so the poem concludes with the "silent peace" of the lovers who have been becalmed by their inspired knowledge of the benignity and purposefulness of existence.

Herbert devoted most of the 1630s to writing prose works, both political (*The Expedition to the Isle of Rhé*, 1656) and historical (*The Life and Reign of King Henry the Eighth*, 1649), and he published the first London edition of *De Veritate* in 1633. His wife, Mary, died in 1634. During this decade Herbert did not produce much poetry, but the middle poem in a sequence of five Platonic love poems is dated 1639. Many critics have read this sequence as intimately autobiographical.

The first "Platonic Love" comprises five stanzas, each consisting of two tercets, the first of which sets up an assertion that the second affirms with additional considerations. The poem defines Platonic love as absolute passion experienced within the soul, so that physical love is simultaneously subjugated and elevated to the ethereal. The lover urges his lady "to appear" and not deny him her mere physical presence.

"Platonic Love II" is twice the length of the first poem, expounding upon the basic tenets of Platonic love. The first two stanzas reject sensual love as "sport but for the Idle Boy" who "love[s] not Woman, but the sex." Stanzas 3 and 4 further establish the dichotomy between physical love and spiritual love and reveal love's ascent toward the spiritual realm. Stanzas 5 and 6 express the advantages of spiritual love, one being the absence of earthly anxieties such as fears over inconstancy. Stanzas 7 and 8 depict the results of the spiritual union of souls as the complete and harmonious coalescing of wills and desires such that bestows the greatest happiness. The final two stanzas present the consequence of this union in the mutual "increase" of their mutual love, knowing no "bounds of growth." Such love is intimated to be infinite and beyond even a celestial state; the lovers may ultimately even "incline" further and higher so that "They would, besides what Heaven doth dispense, / Have their contents they in each other find."

The middle poem in the sequence, "The IDEA, Made of Alnwick in his Expedition to Scotland with the Army, 1639," was written while Herbert was encamped with King Charles I's forces, to which he had been summoned, at Alnwick in the fight against the Scots in the first of the Bishops' Wars. This was the last time he would

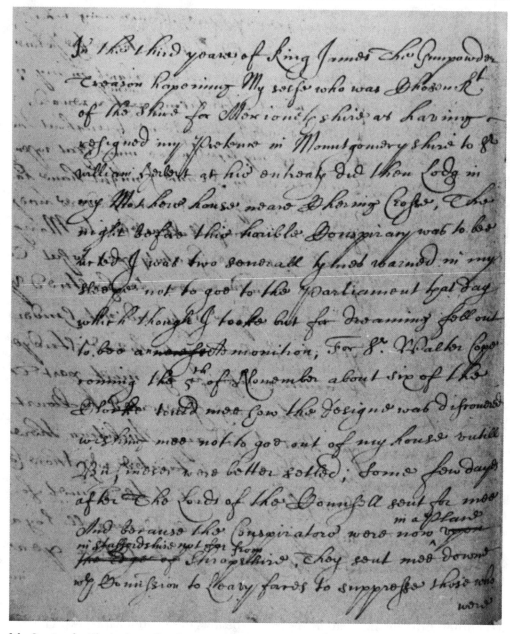

Description of the Gunpowder Plot in the earlier of two extant manuscripts for Herbert's autobiography. This first manuscript is a transcription by Herbert's secretary, Rowland Evans, with corrections by Herbert (Powis Mss., National Library of Wales).

openly support the monarchy, and by this point in his life, he was not much given to the vainglorious activities of his younger days as a soldier, traveler, and errant lover. The poem, does, however, deal with separation from a lover. It has been read variously by critics, Eugene Hill finding it amusing and erotic, Mario Rossi finding it nothing more than a "philosophical song of impotence." Yet it can conclusively be perceived as concerned with the inherent contradictions of emphasis and negation of the role of physical beauty in Platonic love. This paradox is indicated

by the lover's play with the relation between fair and foul, and "idea" as both a tangible configuration and an indication of the Platonic prototype.

"Platonic Love III" fuses elements of Petrarchanism, Platonism, and Christianity. The diffident tone foregrounds the disconsolate Petrarchan lover, one "manacled" by the inescapable yet unfulfilled love, but one who has succumbed to adore from afar and has surrendered control to the beloved in the affair, for there is, evidently, no hope for reciprocation. The final poem in the sequence, "An appeal to his hopes not to fail him," displays similar themes, although the self-abasement is more extreme, and the Petrarchanism surpasses the Platonic concerns with its recurring insistence "that none could love her more."

While Herbert's support of King Charles in 1639 was his last show of overt sympathy with the monarchy, neither would he side with parliamentary forces during the Civil War. He tried to remain neutral, retreating to his castle in Montgomery, and when, in September 1644, parliamentary troops descended upon him there, he quickly and quietly surrendered the castle.

Herbert moved to London in October, apparently in ill health and supported only by a meager stipend from the parliamentarians; his poem "October 14, 1664" (the date is the manuscript reading, but obviously an error) poignantly contemplates the dualities and paradoxes of existence: Time both kindles and devours life; grief both destroys and saves an individual. Strongly deistic, this dramatic soliloquy reasserts his long-held claims for the validity of individual spirituality over established religious dogma. Another solemnly introspective poem, the mood set by the image of the gentle, solitary light of a candle reaching ever-upward, "A Meditation upon his Wax-Candle burning out" shows a man, no longer the young gallant, surveying his life. The poem seeks to reconcile the reality of the past with the reality of the present, and the candle is used as a corporeal object toward which the poet's thoughts are directed, as well as a metaphor for time, which he had already recognized in "October 14, 1644" as a force that paradoxically perpetuates and denies the continuation of life. The poem concludes with a rejection of the resurrection of the body.

Near the end of his life, he devoted much time to expressing his philosophical convictions; in 1645, he published a third edition of *De Veritate*, to which he added *De Religione Laici* and *De Causis Errorum*, both of which forcefully reiterate and expand the arguments of *De Veritate*. Evidently during the 1640s he also wrote *A Dialogue Between a Tutor and his Pupil* (1768), a powerful polemic advancing deism and disparaging Christianity for its institutional corruptions, and *De Religione Gentilium* (1663), which places deism in a historical context. His work on his *Autobiography* began in 1643, but the work would remain unfinished.

When Herbert was dying at his house in Queen Street in early August 1648, Archbishop James Ussher, lord primate of Ireland, was summoned to give him the last rites; yet Ussher ultimately refused to anoint him because Herbert professed only that the sacrament might do him some good and certainly would "do him no harm." Thus, turning his head, he died. His body is buried in the Church of St. Giles-in-the-Fields; the Latin inscription on his gravestone, apparently by his friend Philip, Lord Stanhope, commemorates him as the author of *De Veritate*.

The poetry of Edward, Lord Herbert of Cherbury, evolved its own distinctive, personalized voice, one that would transcend the mere imitation of the poetic techniques of Donne and Marino, as well as the fashionable Neoplatonic conventions that some of his own early poetry displayed. His voice was different from those of other Metaphysical Poets because it dignified emotions and experiences by examining them for what they could reveal about Truth, for their intrinsic metaphysical worth. The diversity of topics that occasioned Herbert's verse—music, women, love, death, color, beauty—has implied to some that Herbert was writing poetry simply because it was fashionable to do so. Yet his traditional place as a minor poet whose work is occasionally anthologized is currently being questioned by those who would elevate him to major status for the consistently philosophical depth of his poetry. His technical virtuosity, especially evident in his diverse stanzaic patterns, further reflects an integrated, synthetic relationship between his poetry and his complex thought. Above all, Lord Herbert's poetry reveals his deep commitment to the personal revelation of Truth, which he believed the individual had the capacity to discover and understand through the noble art of poetry.

Letters:

Herbert Correspondence, The Sixteenth and Seventeenth Century Letters of the Herberts of Chirbury, edited by W. J. Smith (Cardiff: University of Wales Press, 1963).

Bibliography:

J. M. Shuttleworth, "Edward, Lord Herbert of Cherbury (1583-1648): A Preliminary, Annotated Checklist of Works by and about Him," *National Library of Wales Journal*, 20 (1977): 151-168.

Biography:

John Butler, *Lord Herbert of Chirbury (1582-1648):*

An Intellectual Biography (Lewiston, N.Y.: Edwin Mellen Press, 1990).

References:

R. D. Bedford, *The Defense of Truth: Herbert of Cherbury and the Seventeenth Century* (Manchester, U.K.: Manchester University Press, 1979);

Robert Ellrodt, *Les Poètes métaphysiques anglais*, 3 volumes (Paris: Jose Corti, 1960);

D. H. Fordyce and T. M. Knox, "The Library of Jesus College, Oxford, with an appendix on the books bequeathed thereto by Lord Herbert of Cherbury," *Proceedings and Papers of the Oxford Bibliographical Society*, 5, part 2 (1937): 53-115;

Catherine A. Hébert, "The Platonic Love Poetry of Lord Herbert of Cherbury," *Ball State University Forum*, 11 (Autumn 1970): 46-50;

Eugene Hill, *Edward, Lord Herbert of Cherbury* (Boston: Twayne, 1987);

John Hoey, "A Study of Lord Herbert of Cherbury's Poetry," *Renaissance and Modern Studies*, 14 (1970): 69-89;

Don A. Keister, "Donne and Herbert of Cherbury: An Exchange of Verses," *Modern Language Quarterly*, 8 (December 1947): 430-434;

Mary Ellen Rickey, "Rhymecraft in Edward and George Herbert," *Journal of English and Germanic Philology*, 57 (1958): 502-511;

Mario Rossi, *La Vita, le opere, i tempi de Edoardo di Chirbury*, 3 volumes (Florence: G. C. Sansoni, 1947);

Douglas Runnels, "A Study of the English Poetry of Edward, Lord Herbert of Cherbury," Ph.D dissertation, University of Chicago, 1969;

Frank J. Warnke, "This Metaphysick Lord: A Study of the Poetry of Herbert of Cherbury," Ph.D dissertation, Columbia University, 1954;

Basil Willey, *The Seventeenth Century Background: Studies in the Thought of the Age in Relation to Poetry and Religion* (London: Chatto & Windus, 1934), pp. 119-132;

Gordon Williams, "Spiritual Love and Sexual Death in Edward Herbert's Poetry," *Language and Literature*, 2 (1974): 16-31.

Papers:

The main collection of Herbert's papers, previously held at Powis Castle, Welshpool, is now in the National Library of Wales. This collection includes *Religio Laici*, an unpublished manuscript for a work independent from *De Causis Errorum: Una Cum tractatu de Religione Laici* (1645) and probably written between 1624 and 1645. A small number of the Powis manuscripts are in the Powis Public Record Office, and a few have been sold to university collections. A manuscript (BL Add. MS 37157) which appears to be Edward Herbert's own collection of his poems, dated 1630, is at the British Library.

John Hoskyns

(1 March 1566 - 27 August 1638)

Gary R. Grund
Rhode Island College

WORKS: "Ph. Sidnæi Peplus," in *Peplvs. Illvs-trissimi Viri D. Philippi Sidnæi Svpremis Honoribvs Dicatvs*, edited by J. Lloyd (Oxford: Printed by J. Barnesius, 1587);

Oxoniensivm στεναγμὸς, Siué, Carmina ab Oxoniensibus conscipta, in obitum illustrissimi Herois, D. Christophori Hattoni Militis, summi totius Angliae, nec non Academiæ Oxoniensis Cancellarii, includes a poem by Hoskyns (Oxford: Printed by J. Barnesius, 1592);

William Gager, *Vlysses Redux. Tragoedia Nova*, includes three commendatory verses by Hoskyns (Oxford: Printed by J. Barnesius, 1592);

"Absence," in *A Poetical Rapsody*, edited by Francis Davison (London: V. Simmes for J. Baily, 1602);

Oxoniensis Academiæ Funebre Officium in memoriam Elizabethæ, nvper Angliæ, Franciæ, & Hiberniæ Reginæ, includes a poem by Hoskyns (Oxford: Printed by J. Barnesius, 1603);

Academiæ Oxoniensis Pietas Erga Serenissimum et Potentissimum Iacobum Angliae Scotjae Franciae & Hiberniae Regem, includes a poem by Hoskyns (Oxford: Printed by J. Barnesius, 1603);

Inscription on the north wall of New College Cloisters, Oxford, in *Remaines of a Greater Worke, Concerning Britaine*, by William Camden (London: Printed by G. Eld for S. Waterson, 1605);

John Owen, *Epigrammatum Joannis Owen Cambro-Britanni, Oxoniensis libri tres*, third edition, includes two epigrams by Hoskyns (London: Printed by H. Lownes for S. Waterson, 1607);

Rowland Vaughan, *Most Approved, and Long Experienced VVater-VVorkes. Containing, The manner of Winter and Summer-drowning of Medow and Pasture, by the aduantage of the least, River, Brooke, Fount, or Water-prill adiacent*, includes commendatory verse by Hoskyns (London: Printed by G. Eld, 1610);

Thomas Coryate, *Coryats Crudities. Hastily gobled up in five Moneths trauells*, includes nonsense verse by Hoskyns with two measures of music added (London: Printed by W. Stansby for the author, 1611);

"Sir Henry Wotton, and Serjeant Hoskins, riding on the way," in *Reliquiae Wottonianae*, (London: Printed by Thomas Maxey for R. Marriot, G. Bedel, & T. Garthwait, 1651);

"On a young Gentlewoman," in *Musarum Deliciæ: or, The Muses Recreation. Conteining Severall Select Pieces of Sportive Wit*, by John Mennes and James Smith (London: Printed for Henry Herringman, 1655);

Epitaphs in *The Dr. Farmer Chetham MS.* [MS. Chetham 8012] *being a Commonplace-Book in the Chetham Library*, edited by Alexander B. Grosart, volumes 89 and 90 of *Publications of the Chetham Society* (Manchester, 1873);

Andrew Clark, ed., *Brief Lives*, by John Aubrey, 2 volumes, includes poems by Hoskyns (Oxford: Clarendon Press, 1898).

Edition: *The Life, Letters, and Writings of John Hoskyns: 1566-1638*, edited by Louise Brown Osborn (New Haven: Yale University Press/ London: Oxford University Press, 1937).

Although he left no published work of prose—despite the fact that Ben Jonson called him "father" (" 'twas he that polished me") and that Sir Walter Ralegh had him review his style while a fellow prisoner in the Tower—John Hoskyns was a man revered in his time for the soundness of his rhetorical advice and his wit. Similarly, his verse—though scattered about the countryside on gravestones, etched on college cloister walls, or embedded in a host of literary miscellanies—helped shape the design of poetry in the early seventeenth century. "There were few or none that published books of poetry," wrote Anthony Wood in his *Athenæ Oxoniensis* (1691, 1692), "but did celebrate his memory in them . . . and fewer but did lay them at his feet for approbation before they went to the press."

Miniature of John Hoskyns by artist John Hoskins with Hoskyns's self-portrait on the back
(Collection of Walter Scott, ninth Duke of Buccleuch)

Hoskyns was one of those enigmatic characters from the Renaissance who knew everybody. At Winchester School he met John Owen, later the chief Latin epigrammatist of England. At New College, Oxford, he knew Sir Henry Wotton and Sir Philip Sidney, was a drinking companion of Jonson, and a friend to John Donne, John Selden, and Samuel Daniel. His poetical work was long ascribed to the Donne canon and, according to H. J. C. Grierson, is "a not uninteresting link between the manner of Sidney and the Elizabethans and of Donne and the 'Metaphysicals.'" If his English poetry smells of the coterie—it is usually nonsense verse directed to his closest friends—it does possess an undeniable vigor. His Latin writing, more distant now surely, earned him John Aubrey's praise as "the best Latin epitaphs of his time," and even modern readers must be impressed with his minting of the Latin verb, *Fleetstreetare*. In what may seem at first a strange clutter of verses, Hoskyns's poetry exhibits his clever humor and good sense; he himself confessed during his imprisonment that he "had rather dy with witt then live without it." If his is not an entirely new voice, it is surely a novel one.

John Hoskyns was born on 1 March 1566 in the small village of Mouncton, now called Mon-

nington-upon-Wye, in Hereford. He was the second of the seven sons of John and Margery, and, though not much is known about the family, their name indicates Welsh extraction. Sent to the Latin grammar school at Westminster, but "not speeding there," according to Aubrey, Hoskyns was transferred to Winchester College on 15 December 1579. At the age of nineteen he proceeded to New College, Oxford, where he matriculated as a *plebii filius*, or son of a commoner. On 6 May 1588 he was admitted bachelor of arts, receiving the degree in 1589, and on 26 February 1592 he was licensed master of arts. At this time he was selected to perform the part of *terrae filius*, or university buffoon, and, presumably, to burlesque some tenets of Scholastic philosophy. Hoskyns plunged headlong and "propter dicteria maledica sub persona Terrae filii" (on account of some abusive remarks as *terrae filii*) was forced to resign his fellowship and leave the university. He then appears to have taken a teaching post at Ilchester in Somersetshire where he compiled a Greek lexicon as far as the letter *Mu*. After a year in the isolation of Ilchester, Hoskyns was admitted to the Middle Temple in London on 13 March 1593 to study law. He would remain at this Inn of Court for the next thirty years and, according to Aubrey, "He wore good cloathes, and kept good company. . . . At his first comeing to London he gott acquainted with undersecretaries at court, where he was often usefull to them in writing their Latin letters." This was a time of great literary and social activity for Hoskyns. On 2 May 1600 he was called to the bar. He married Benedicta ("Bennet") Bourne on 1 August 1601. The Hoskyns would have two children: a son, Bennet, and a daughter, Benedicta. On 19 March 1604, Hoskyns took his seat in Parliament for the city of Hereford. By 5 April 1614 he was elected to sit in James I's second Parliament, but on 7 June the same jeu d'esprit that Hoskyns displayed at Oxford got him sent to the Tower for his seditious arguments against the king's subsidies to the Scots. During his yearlong confinement he met Ralegh, and, upon his release on 8 June 1615, Hoskyns determined to avoid further official displeasure. Consequently, in June 1621 he was appointed judge in Wales for the district of Carmarthen, Pembroke, and Cardigan, and on 26 June 1623 he was raised to serjeant-at-law for Herefordshire. After the death of his wife on 6 October 1625, he married his stepdaughter Elizabeth Bourne on 10 December 1627 and returned to Parliament until 1629. Thereafter, he retired to Hereford where he died on 27 August 1638. Aubrey gives a memorable account: "Not many moneths before his death (being at the assizes or sessions at Hereford) a massive countrey fellowe trod on his toe, which caused a gangrene which was the cause of his death."

Throughout his life Hoskyns was known for his ingenuity and his wit. His poetry—with the important exception of his contributions to *Peplus*, the memorial volume dedicated to Sidney (1587)—bears witness to his personal charm. His random inclusions in Francis Davison's *Poetical Rapsody* (1602), William Camden's *Remaines of a Greater Worke* (1605), and Thomas Coryate's *Crudities* (1611) as well as the substantial number of poems still in manuscript testify more to his friendships and breadth of personal contacts that to any divine calling. His verse, then, can be conveniently arranged according to the rubric of his life: the poems written at Winchester and at Oxford, those in London, and those at home in Hereford.

There can be no doubt that Hoskyns, like most men of his time, began writing poetry in Latin as an exercise at school; in fact, this was an established method, especially preached by Desiderius Erasmus, of instructing boys in the

Latin language. Two poems which date from his apprenticeship at Winchester testify to Hoskyns's early abilities and exhibit what were to be his major stylistic concerns throughout his career as a poet.

Of the first, Aubrey wrote that "The Latin verses in the quadrangle at Winton Colledge, at the cocks where the boyes wash their hands, were of his making, where there is the picture of a good servant, with hind's feet." The poem is a delightful, if adolescent, attempt to emblemize a half-human, half-animal figure. The meter is a ponderous hexameter with the young poet packing as many cases, moods, and idioms into the verse as possible. The final effect, naturally enough, is heavy-handed: "Accinctus gladio, clypeo munitus, et inde / Vel se vel Dominum quo tueatur, habet" (Girt with a sword, a shield for defense, from there he'll protect both himself and his Master). His efforts to produce the chiasmus of the first line as well as the complex syntax of the second line stem from his early fascination with the devices of rhetoric familiar to every Renaissance schoolboy.

More significant, perhaps, is Hoskyns's praise of Justus Lipsius in the second early poem from his days at Winchester. The verses entitled "In Syllabam *Cos*; in Pentecost Dom. in Scola Wintoniensi" furnish an interesting commentary on the study of Lipsius at Winchester during Hoskyns's stay there. His later reliance on Lipsius for the organization of his study on the *ars dictaminis*, or art of letter writing, included in his prose work, *Directions For Speech and Style*, written circa 1599, was probably a product of his Winchester days. It is clear from the poem that as early as the 1580s Lipsius was regarded as a teacher of specifically anti-Ciceronian rhetoric:

> Tu deleta reples mutili vestigia verbi,
>> Et rara est apicem, quae tibi blatta rapit.
> Arte tua sensusque redit chartaeque per aequor
>> Litera naufragio Sparsa priore coit

> (You restore the lost traces of maimed words, words so obsolete that they make your blood run cold. But through your art sense returns and the scattered writings, adrift in a sea of paper, are joined again).

These are strong phrases for Hoskyns to use—"mutili . . . verbi," "naufragio . . . priore." They permit us to understand that we are in the midst of a great debate on the quality of Lipsian reform, a program designed to substitute perspicuity and brevity for Cicero's ponderous, circuitous figures of rhetoric. To the charge that Lip had altered what Cicero said, Hoskyns responded for the Flemish scholar: "Verum ego de veteri codice muto nihil" (Truly, I change nothing that I find in an ancient manuscript). It is with this assurance that Hoskyns dedicates his future to studying Lipsius's writings and asks, "Da mihi Laetitias Lipsi, Da Juste Lepores" (Give me your Joys, Lipsius; give me your delights, Justus). Some years would pass before he returned to his ardor for Lipsius in writing the *Directions For Speech and Style*. In the meantime an event occurred while Hoskyns was at Oxford in 1586 which had a profound effect on his sympathies: the death of Sir Philip Sidney.

Sidney's death was commemorated by countless elegies and memorials, probably the most famous being Edmund Spenser's "Astrophel." It was as a student at Oxford that Hoskyns was introduced to Sidney, so it is understandable that his poems lamenting Sidney's death should be contained in a volume composed exclusively by New College men. This volume, *Peplus*, is a quarto of fifty-four pages dedicated to Henry Herbert, second Earl of Pembroke. The title is an allusion to the spurious *Peplus* of Aristotle, a commemoration of the heroes who fell at Troy. It was, in other words, a title fit to commemorate the universal sorrow which England felt for the death of Sidney, its noblest hero. Hoskyns's contributions amount to more than nine hundred lines and are a testimony to his enduring respect for Sidney.

The poems themselves are more sophisticated attempts at Latin verse than his earlier writings. They are, of course, elegiac in tone and meter. His poems range from the traditional elegiac distich to such uncommon meters as the iambic dimeter acatalectic and the iambic trimeter. The final effect is, unfortunately, rather common: "*Sidnæus, Sidnæus*, & hoc bis nomine dicto / Plura locuturæ comprimit ora dolor" (*Sidney! Sidney!* and having said it twice, by so much more does sorrow stop my mouth from speaking). As one might almost expect, Sidney's death compels the poet to form such words as "*Sidnæus*," "virtus *Sidneïa*," and the like. So, also, "Philip" and "Sidney" become more than names; the opposition, therefore, at the battle of Zutphen is not between the enemy and England but between "*Belgica*" or "*Hispanus*" and "*Philippus*." As every classical hero was fully to be remembered by the deeds of his descendants, so it must be with Sidney: "Senserat Alcides, Alcidæ senserat hæres; / Sensit

Phyllirides, Phylliridæqué puer" (Hercules had felt this [fate], and so did his descendants. Philip [Sidney] felt it, too, as will his). Moments of deep and honest emotion are rare—the pathetic fallacy is constantly invoked, further distancing author and reader—but a few moving passages still appear: "Quæ siturus eram, cùm narratura dolorem, / Tu tace, ait. Tacui. Sic priore illa refert" (Whatever might be set down when this sorrow is spoken of, be still, he says. I am still. That is all that matters). But all too often Hoskyns relies on the effects of rhetoric to stimulate emotion. His reliance on such figures as oxymoron, praeteritio, and chiasmus only tend to dull the emotion which he means to arouse. Such examples are manifold: "Mors grauis nimis, ah, nimis grauis mors" (Death, so profound and beyond measure, ah, beyond measure so profound is death), or

Ita vos nihil, *Philippi*
Nisi nomen hoc in orbe,
Et in orbe nil celebre
Nisi nomen hoc *Philippi*.

Thus, nothing can more honor your family, Sir Philip, unless your name is on earth, and on earth there is nothing more honorable than this name of Sir Philip.

Combined with this use of rhetorical devices is Hoskyns's fascination with postclassical vocabulary; his models are more often Seneca and Martial than Horace or Virgil. His interest in these writers, an interest encouraged by Lipsius, was shared by many of his contemporaries. Thus, it was at this same time that the vogue for epigrams was widespread in England. Hoskyns's friend John Owen, who also contributed poems to *Peplus*, was known by his fellow poets as the chief Latin epigrammatist in England. Statements by Lipsius, Sir Thomas Ryves ("Rivius"), and Daniel Heinsius on the virtues of the minor contemporaries of Tacitus and Seneca also help us understand why such writers enjoyed favor in the later Renaissance: why Valerius Maximus and Velleius Paterculus, for example, are so often quoted by Ben Jonson, Michel Eyquem de Montaigne, and Sir Thomas Browne.

In his vocabulary in *Peplus*, Hoskyns repeatedly reverts to participial constructions or relies on the conjugations of obscure deponent verbs to express simple thoughts or approximate his grief: "Quæ siturus eram, cùm narratura dolorem" or his "Quam quærendo petis,

Page from a manuscript for Directions For Speech and Style, *written circa 1599 (British Library, Ms. Harley 4604)* quamqué tacendo cupis" (As you seek to gain, so you wish to be silent). The qualities of sound in these participles contribute greatly to the elegiac tone of the verse, but their preponderance makes the sorrow seem artificial. They are often used almost playfully by Hoskyns when, for instance, he juggles the various tenses of verbs over the course of a few lines: "tollit . . . tulit . . . et laturus" (all forms of *tollo*; I raise up), "capiscor . . . capturus sum" (from *capio*: I take hold of), and so on.

It is difficult for the modern reader to appreciate such writing. It was certainly easier for Hoskyns himself to write more humorous poetry, judging from the opinions of his contemporaries. Nevertheless, his Latin poetry is peculiarly representative of his own time. His early desire to write down his thoughts in the Latin language is evocative of the training the schools provided. The public schools were the real source and cause of the existence of Anglo-Latin poetry as an active branch of English literature, as Leicester Bradner observed long ago. In the main, volumes like *Peplus* were conventional exhibitions of proficiency in the learned languages as well as occasional elegies. It is further interesting to note in his contributions to the volume the frequency of references to Sidney's then unpublished *Arcadia* (written about 1583-1584, published 1590). The reference to "Philisides," meaning Sidney, is matched also by sporadic references to *Astrophel and Stella* (written circa 1582, published 1591). Throughout the volume as a whole, Owen, Hoskyns, and others all refer to Sidney as "*stellati pastoris.*" The intensity of Hoskyns's regard for Sidney in *Peplus* blossomed years later when he drew on the *Arcadia* as a standard of prose style in the *Directions For Speech and Style*.

Unfortunately, by virtue of more than four centuries, modern readers can never fully appreciate Hoskyns's commitment to Latin verse. Some other more serious epitaphs in Latin consistently recur to the method of *Peplus*; they attempt to be witty, rhetorical, and syntactically complex. However, it is with such lines as

> Hic jacet Egremundus Rarus,
> Tuendis paradoxis clarus
> Mortuus est, ut hic apparet:
> At si loqui posset, hoc negaret

> (Here lies Egremond Rare,
> Distinguished for defending paradoxes.
> He's dead, as here appears,
> But if he could speak, he'd deny it)

that one may begin to approach the manner of Hoskyns's English poetry:

> Here lyeth the bodie of Hugh Poache
> Bellied like a herringe headed like a Roache
> God of his mercy send him his grace
> For he never had heare, growe one his face.

There is a pleasing sense of wit in such poems, a sense only partially apparent in Hoskyns's Latin poems. The English poems are more satirical, certainly, less studied, more fluid, and decidedly cosmopolitan.

Hoskyns wrote epitaphs throughout his life, but by far the greatest period of activity occurred after he was admitted to the Middle Temple in 1593 and began the acquaintances and friendships for which he is largely remembered. It was during this period, too, that he composed serious poems in English—most of them anonymously and still in manuscript. Hoskyns's dependence on his wit for poetic structure remained intact in these poems. His interest in artifice extended from an easy, semihumorous faith in verbal trickery, such as puns, rhetorical flourishes, and verbal jesting to a more intellectualized system of logical and poetical antithesis. The common denominator, early and late, however, hinged on the applicability of artifice itself. In some of his earlier compositions there exists the conventional Elizabethan sense of wit, a sarcasm at times—the "city" man's mockery of country virtue, and so on—all written to entertain a coterie of readers. In his "Song vppon a bellowes mender," for example, one finds a characteristic attempt at punning: "Hee that made bellowes could not make breath," or an even more typical

> She was younge slender and prettye
> and died a Mayde, mor's the pittye.

As he continues to write, Hoskyns only slowly begins to vary the formula, to extend his subjects beyond urbane consideration. For example,

> If life be time that here is spent
> and time on earth be cast away
> Who so his time hath here mispent
> hath hastned his owne dying day
> So it doth proue a killing crime
> to massacre our living time.

The structure here is a simple quatrain and couplet. The rhyming pattern, *ababcc*, usually indicates a stave of six, one of Matthew Arnold's favorite forms and best illustrated by William Wordworth's "I Wandered Lonely as a Cloud." Instead of the fluidity common to this format, Hoskyns's meter is all too obviously iambic tetrameter made ponderous by an overwhelming use of monosyllables. In a further variation, Hoskyns chooses to use the couplet in an unusual way as an aphoristic or interpretive unit; the rest of the stanza seems too short to support such epigrammatic pointedness. One can, thus, understand his necessity to make the quatrain as strictly logical as it is: to act as a base from which a sententious couplet would not stand out. It does not seem to work, however. The implied conditional if/then/therefore construction of these six lines is met by a similar thematic parallel of "spent"/"mispent"/"hastned." Somehow, though, the couplet still sounds bathetic; perhaps the redundancy of "killing" and "massacre" is to blame. Nonetheless, the arresting vocabulary employed here, reminiscent of Metaphysical verse, and the witty contrast in the couplet between life and death are traits which will reappear with regularity in Hoskyns's poems.

A more interesting, if less inventive, poem is his "On Dreames." Here Hoskyns consciously employs the ballad stanza—iambic tetrameter, rhyming *abab*. The subject is a conventional one: the poet laments that dreams, and not he, can be present in his mistress's mind. It begins with a pleasing onomatopoeic quality: "Yo^u nimble dreams wth cob webb winges," but ends with a confusing conglomerate of monosyllables:

> O that yo^u would [me] once preferr
>   to bee in place of one of yo^u
> that I might goe to visitt her
>   and shee might sweare here dreame was true.

All through the poem antitheses abound: "wth much adoe and little paine," "most busie in their ease," among others. In his prose *Directions For Speech and Style*, Hoskyns defines antithesis as a figure, "respecting the contrarieties of things . . . fit to set forth a copious style. This figure serues much for amplificac$\tilde{o}$n." The figure served Hoskyns abundantly well in his verse as one of his other poems, "Loue is a fooolish melancholie," makes clear. As the title would suggest, Hoskyns makes another suit to Petrarchanism as he did in "On Dreames": "I will not loue and yet I will." The artificial mood, posture, and diction continue in "The Dying Louer." In this rather

long poem Hoskyns catalogues the various afflictions and diseases which the lover suffers upon being spurned by his beloved. Despite its length, the poem breaks down into small units because it overflows with apostrophes, a process of dissolution further emphasized by the heroic-couplet structure. Combined with all this are Hoskyns's typical statements of antitheses, of illogic:

> her Smiles were Loue's darts & her frowns were
>   thine
> I'ue Seen her mix a Sad look wth a Sweete
> Then Life & death All Ioyes All torments meete
> like twilight as her Louer could not Say
> whether his feares brought night or hopes brought
>   day.

The only progression that the poet seems to be making in lines like these is toward an increased use of imagery. As Rosemond Tuve observed, the expectation in such lines as these is the experience of a greater intellectual pleasure, because simultaneously some truth is conveyed and a relatedness is seen. Hoskyns says as much when discussing metaphor in the *Directions For Speech and Style*: "a *Metaphor* is pleasant because it enricheth o^r knowledge wth two things at once wth the truth and wth simillitude." By expressing a thing "with more light and better note," Hoskyns hoped to achieve a fit characterization of the grieved lover. He lacks the unified metaphysic of Donne, choosing not to make a logic of the illogic, so to speak, but to dwell on the devices of illogicality for the effects they create.

But in his most successful poem, "Absence," long ascribed to Donne, Hoskyns unites the various modes of his earlier writing. The argument of the poem, he tells us in a subtitle, is simply "That time and absence proves / Rather helps than hurts to loues." This antithetical core fortunately needs no elaborate or witty explication by the poet. Instead, it is simply given. The poem proceeds lyrically with Hoskyns's stressed syllables less weighted emotionally or vocally than before:

> Absence heare my protestation
>   Against thy strengthe
>   Distance and lengthe,
> Doe what thou canst for alteration:
>   For harts of truest mettall
>   Absence doth joyne, and time doth settle.

In the four stanzas of the poem, Hoskyns's meter moves from the opening tetrameter to dimeters,

Letter from Hoskyns to his wife, written on 23 November 1614, while he was imprisoned in the Tower of London for speaking against the king's subsidies to "the Scots who consumed both king and kingdom in insolency and all kind of riot" (from Louise Brown Osborn, ed., The Life, Letters, and Writings of John Hoskyns, 1566-1638, *1937)* and finally back to a four-beat iambic line which includes a pregnant extra syllable. The effect of such writing is to frame each of the stanzas as composite units with a lack of wordplay or lyrical artificiality. As a conscious artist, Hoskyns forces us to see the relatedness of time and absence to love; we watch the intellect at work. The "strong lines" of the poem—its compacted syntax, its intellection, its arresting language ("My Sences . . . / . . . / Like rich men that take pleasure / In hidinge more then handling treasure")—are often softened by the logic of the poem which approaches sincere pathos:

> By absence this good means I gaine
>   That I can catch her
>   Where none can watch her
> In some close corner of my braine:
>   There I embrace and there kiss her,
>   And so enjoye her, and so misse her.

Hoskyns's able handling of this concluding stanza in long, delicate vowels and elongated sibilants, combined with pathetic monosyllables, brings the reader back to a similar lament in *Peplus*: "*Tu tace, ait. Tacui.*" But in "Absence" there is no dallying with language or polysyllabic complexity. The final couplet expresses the simplest of emotional statements

Near the end of his life Hoskyns was forced to leave the lodgings in the Middle Temple that he had occupied for thirty years as a judge and serjeant-at-law in the Welsh circuit; yet he continued to compose. He acquired a country seat at Morehampton where, according to Aubrey, Hoskyns inscribed the walls with Latin verses. At the gatehouse he also drew a picture of the man who made the fires and in the garden a sketch of Adam the gardener with his rake, spade, and waterpot in hand, and wrote beside them Latin distiches. He also buried his first wife and his stepson, for both of whom he composed the epitaphs. His last poem was written in 1638, the year of his death. This poem, too, is an epitaph which looks back with some regret and yet forward with a sense of hope:

> Years sixty six, I have with vigour Past,
> But Death, my Daily Thought, is come at last;
> My sayings, writings, Deeds, of trifeling Play,
> Lett endless Silence, in her Bosom lay:
> Be my wrong Dealings, by my Heir redres't,

> That no complaint, my Ashes may molest:
> And what's to God, from a vile spendthrift, due,
>
> To Christ, for Payment { with his Blood, I sue. / in my name,

It is somehow typical that Hoskyns should have ended his last verses with an example of the rhetorical figure of "parenthesis" as an aid in illustration.

If Hoskyns ever approached Parnassus, he did so as a passerby. His cleverness in the turn of a thought, his suitability for any occasion, and his subtle honesty of feeling are qualities at once individual and yet highly representative of his time. His merits were small compared to the greater poets and prose writers of his age. His education and his personal contacts, however, brought him close to the centers of artistic importance in early-seventeenth-century England and gave him the stimulus to compose both verse and prose.

References:
Leicester Bradner, *Musae Anglicanae: A History of Anglo-Latin Poetry 1500-1925* (New York: Modern Language Association, 1940);
Herbert J. C. Grierson, ed., *Donne's Poetical Works*, 2 volumes (Oxford: Oxford University Press, 1912), II: lvii;
Gary R. Grund, *John Hoskyns, Elizabethan Rhetoric, and the Development of English Prose* (New York: Garland, 1987), pp. 199-219;
Rosemond Tuve, *Elizabethan and Metaphysical Imagery* (Chicago: University of Chicago Press, 1947), pp. 40-41, 66-67, 120-124, and 204-205.

Papers:
Hoskyns's poetic materials are scattered in many manuscript collections throughout England, but mainly located at the British Library; the Bodleian Library, Oxford; Lambeth Palace; and Hatfield House. The manuscripts of his correspondence, most in Hoskyns's own hand, are preserved in the muniment room of Sizergh Castle, Kendal, Westmorland. Other artifacts, including a delightful miniature of Hoskyns attributed to the artist John Hoskins, are in the possession of Canon Sir Edwyn Clement Hoskyns, Baronet, and Walter Scott, ninth Duke of Buccleuch.

Ben Jonson

(11 June 1572? - August 1637)

Robert C. Evans
Auburn University at Montgomery

See also the Jonson entry in *DLB 62: Elizabethan Dramatists*.

BOOKS: *The Comicall Satyre of Every Man out of His Humor* (London: Printed by Adam Islip for William Holme, 1600);

Every Man in His Humor (London: Printed by Simon Stafford for Walter Burre, 1601);

The Fountaine of Selfe-Love. Or Cynthias Revells (London: Printed by Richard Read for Walter Burre, 1601);

Poetaster or the Arraignment (London: Printed by Richard Braddock for Matthew Lownes, 1602);

B. Jon: His Part of King James His Royall and Magnificent Entertainement through His Honourable Cittie of London, Thurseday the 15. of March. 1603 . . . Also, A Briefe Panegyre of His Maiesties First and Well Auspicated Entrance to His High Court of Parliament, on Monday, the 19. of the Same Moneth. With Other Additions (London: Printed by Valentine Simmes and George Eld for Edward Blount, 1604);

Seianus His Fall (London: Printed by George Eld for Thomas Thorpe, 1605);

Eastward Hoe, by Jonson, George Chapman, and John Marston (London: Printed by George Eld for William Aspley, 1605);

Hymenaei: or The Solemnities of Masque, and Barriers (London: Printed by Valentine Simmes for Thomas Thorpe, 1606);

Ben: Jonson His Volpone or the Foxe (London: Printed by George Eld for Thomas Thorpe, 1607);

The Characters of Two Royall Masques. The One of Blacknesse, the Other of Beautie. . . . The Description of the Masque. With the Nuptial Songs. Celebrating the Happy Marriage of Iohn, Lord Ramsey, Vicount Hadington, with the Lady Elizabeth Ratcliffe (London: Printed by George Eld for Thomas Thorpe, 1608);

Ben: Jonson, His Case is Altered (London: Printed by Nicholas Okes for Bartholomew Sutton, 1609);

Ben Jonson (portrait by an unknown artist; National Portrait Gallery, London)

The Masque of Queenes Celebrated from the House of Fame (London: Printed by Nicholas Okes for Richard Bonion & Henry Wally, 1609);

Catiline His Conspiracy (London: Printed by William Stansby? for Walter Burre, 1611);

The Alchemist (London: Printed by Thomas Snodham, for Walter Burre & sold by John Stepneth, 1612);

The Workes of Benjamin Jonson (London: Printed by William Stansby, 1616)—comprises *Every Man in His Humour, Every Man out of His Humour, Cynthia's Revels, Poetaster, Sejanus, Volpone, Epicoene, The Alchemist, Catiline, Epigrams, The Forrest, The King's Coronation Entertainment, A Panegyre, The Entertainment at Althorp, The Entertainment at Highgate, The Entertainment of the Two Kings at Theobalds, An*

Entertainment of the King and Queen at Theobalds, The Masque of Blackness, The Masque of Beauty, Hymenaei, The Haddington Masque, The Masque of Queens, Prince Henry's Barriers, Oberon the Fairy Prince, Love Freed From Ignorance and Folly, Love Restored, A Challenge at Tilt, The Irish Masque, Mercury Vindicated from the Alchemists, The Golden Age Restored;

Lovers Made Men. A Masque (London, 1617);

Epicoene, or The Silent Woman. A Comoedie (London: Printed by William Stansby & sold by John Browne, 1620);

The Masque of Augures. With Several Antimasques (London, 1621);

Time Vindicated to Himselfe and to His Honors (London, 1623);

Neptunes Triumph for the Returne of Albion, A Masque 1623 (London, 1624);

The Fortunate Isles and Their Union. A Masque 1624 (London, 1625);

Love's Triumph through Callipolis. A Masque, by Jonson and Inigo Jones (London: Printed by John Norton, Jr., for Thomas Walkley, 1630);

Chloridia, Rites to Chloris and Her Nymphs (London: Printed for Thomas Walkley, 1631);

Bartholomew Fayre. The Divell Is an Asse. The Staple of Newes (volume 2 of Jonson's works) (London: Printed by John Beale for Robert Allot, 1631);

The New Inne. Or, The Light Heart (London: Printed by Thomas Harper for Thomas Alchorne, 1631);

Ben: Jonson's Execration against Vulcan. With Divers Epigrams (London: Printed by John Okes for John Benson & Andrew Crooke, 1640);

Q. Horatius Flaccus: Horatius Flaccus: His Art of Poetry. Englished by Ben: Jonson. With Other Workes of the Author, Never Printed Before (London: Printed by John Okes for John Benson, 1640);

The Workes of Benjamin Jonson, volume 1 (London: Printed by Richard Bishop & sold by A. Crooke, 1640)—a reprint of *The Workes of Benjamin Jonson* (1616); volumes 2-3 (London: Printed for Richard Meighen & Thomas Walkley, 1640)—comprises the sheets of the 1631 works (volume 2) together with *The Magnetic Lady, A Tale of a Tub, The Sad Shepherd, The Fall of Mortimer, Christmas His Masque, Lovers Made Men, The Vision of Delight, Pleasure Reconciled to Virtue, For the Honour of Wales, News from the New World Discovered in the Moon, The Gypsies Meta-* morphosed, *The Masque of Augurs, Time Vindicated, Neptune's Triumph, Pan's Anniversary, The Masque of Owls, The Fortunate Isles, Love's Triumph through Callipolis, Chloridia, The Entertainment at Welbeck, Love's Welcome at Bolsover, The Underwood, Horace, His Art of Poetry, The English Grammar, Discoveries* (volume 3) (London: Printed by John Dawson, Jr., for Thomas Walkley, 1640).

Editions: *Ben Jonson*, 11 volumes, edited by C. H. Herford and Percy and Evelyn Simpson (Oxford: Clarendon Press, 1925-1952)—comprises *A Tale of a Tub, The Case is Altered, Every Man in His Humour* (original and revised texts), *Every Man out of His Humour, In Memoriam: Charles Harold Herford, Cynthia's Revels, Poetaster, Sejanus, Eastward Ho, Volpone, Epicoene, The Alchemist, Catiline, Bartholomew Fair, The Devil is an Ass, The Staple of News, The New Inn, The Magnetic Lady, The Sad Shepherd, The Fall of Mortimer, Masques and Entertainments, The Poems, The Prose Works*;

Ben Jonson, edited by Ian Donaldson (Oxford & New York: Oxford University Press, 1985).

PLAY PRODUCTIONS: See *DLB 62*.

Although Ben Jonson is still best known as a dramatist, his significance as a poet is hard to overestimate. His influence helped transform English verse. His "plain style" made him a crucial figure in a central tradition, but his deceptively complex works reward close reading. Sophisticated, self-conscious, and strongly influenced by the Greek and Roman classics, his writing nonetheless rarely seems foreign or artificial. His vigorous and colloquial style exemplifies both wide reading and a deep interest in "reality." He moved as comfortably through books as through London's streets and taverns—a man of learning who never lost touch with life. A social poet especially concerned with ethics, he wrote lasting poems that also vividly reflect their era.

Jonson achieved much despite early disadvantages. Notes taken by his friend William Drummond of Hawthornden in 1618-1619 reveal that Jonson's father had "Losed all his estate under Queen Marie, [and,] having been cast jn prison and forfaitted, at last turn'd Minister." Jonson was "born a moneth after his fathers decease," during Queen Elizabeth's reign, apparently sometime between May 1572 and January 1573—probably on 11 June 1572, in or near London. His mother later married a bricklayer, apparently a highly practical man. Drummond wrote that Jonson remembered having been "brought up poorly, putt to school by a friend . . . after taken from it, and put to ane other Craft . . . which he could not endure." His time at Westminster School under the great intellectual William Camden made a lasting impact. Jonson later praised Camden in his *Epigrams* (1616) as the "most reuerend head, to whom I owe / All that I am in arts, all that I know." Since most boys at Westminster went on to university, the break in Jonson's schooling (so he could be, Drummond guessed, "a Wright or Bricklayer") must have been keenly disappointing. Neither he nor his later antagonists ever forgot his early experience as a manual laborer.

After serving in the Low Countries (where, Drummond reports, Jonson "Killed ane Enimie" and took his weapons), Jonson returned to England and "his wonted studies." On 14 November 1594, he married Anne Lewis (whom he described to Drummond as "a shrew yet honest"); from this marriage at least four children were born. He became both an actor and a playwright, thus supporting himself through his valued "studies." By July 1597 he was employed as a writer by Philip Henslowe, the theatrical entrepreneur. Later that summer, however, he was jailed for collaborating with Thomas Nashe on *The Isle of Dogs*, which was described in a Privy Council report as "lewd," "seditious & sclandrous." From August to October Jonson and two actors were imprisoned, but this did not seem to dampen his enthusiasm for the stage. Henslowe recorded repeated payments and loans, and by 1598 Jonson's writing was being praised.

The autumn of 1598 was momentous. September probably saw the performance of *Every Man in His Humour*—the first play Jonson valued enough to preserve. Jonson told Drummond that during the same month, in a duel with an actor, he "Killed his adversarie, which had hurt him jn the arme & whose sword was 10 Inches Longer than his, for the which he was Emprissoned and almost at the Gallowes." He escaped execution only by proving he could read a biblical verse in Latin. Drummond records that while Jonson was jailed, he was converted to Catholicism "by trust of a priest who Visited him jn Prison," where Jonson was both spied upon and interrogated. He never lost his contempt for spies, whom he compared in Epigram 59, "On Spies," to candles that first "Stinke" and then "are throwne away." His

treatment may have resulted from his newfound religion. In any case, his decision to embrace Catholicism, a creed officially scorned in Protestant England, suggests an independent mind and spirit.

His first datable poem (collected as *Ungathered Verse* 1 by C. H. Herford and Percy Simpson in *Ben Jonson*, 1925-1952), written around 1598, commends a Catholic author, Thomas Palmer, and already suggests Jonson's persona and values. He signs himself "gent" and praises his subject's gravity, skill, and "rich labors" while professing his own weakness and "wonder." This, like the early "Ode to James Earle of Desmond" (*Underwood* 25), is one of several poems that seem a bit too rapturous, and in fact the ode was later mocked by rivals. However, these poems indicate the lofty ideals communicated more effectively in such other works as his lengthy "Epistle To Elizabeth Countesse of Rutland" (*Forest* 12), presented as a New Year's gift in January 1600—his first datable poem to seem so utterly Jonsonian.

Jonson's "plain style" was neither artless nor utterly clear; instead, it avoids both sublimity and vulgarity. It was meant to communicate, to have an effect, and it gives his poetry a directness, practicality, seriousness, and force that loftier, lower, or more complicated phrasing would obscure. Its tone is often forthright, its emphasis ethical and didactic, although Jonson generally rejects priggish preaching. He mocked cant and jargon and usually avoids them himself. He chiefly praises and blames, often in the same poem. He sought to understand and judge, to distinguish and discriminate. Whether exacting or generous, his judgments were meant to seem objective, not personal. As social poetry, his works often display a civilized urbanity and decorum partly influenced by classical example. His ferocious satire complemented his idealism. Through praise he sought to inspire, through mockery to shame. He hoped to inculcate virtue and discourage vice. His poems display many emotions and rhetorical stances, but most also display a distinct personality and clear values. Jonson prizes reason, cherishes friendship, endorses merit, admires self-control, and disdains hypocrisy, greed, stupidity, and pride.

Jonson's characteristic tone is more self-confident than self-questioning; he scrutinizes others more often than himself, yet at times he does examine himself searchingly. He also could poke fun at himself when not poking fun at—or simply poking at—others, and his poems often min-

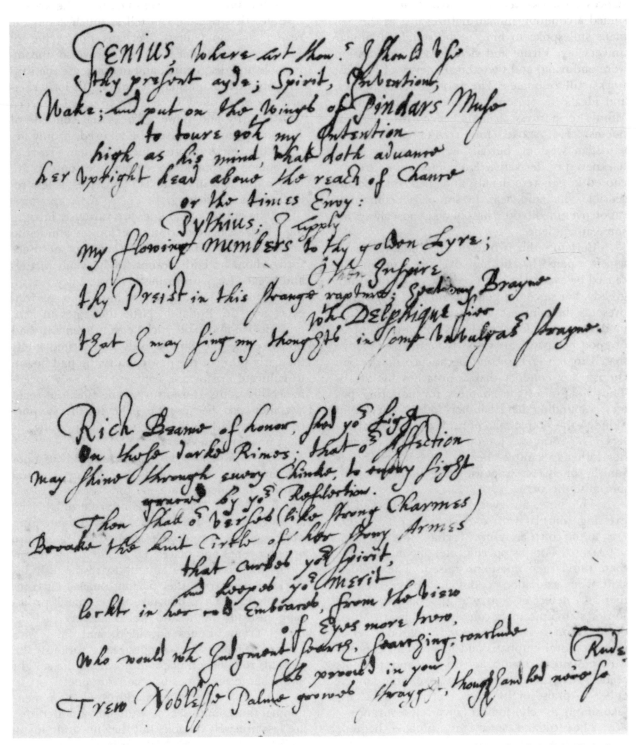

First page of Jonson's manuscript for "Ode to James Earle of Desmond," written circa 1600 (Christ Church College, Oxford)

gle ethical seriousness with verbal wit. Although often responsive to particular persons or circumstances, his works were meant to be timeless. He assumed a common human nature; just as the Romans still spoke to him, so he sought a similar universality. Virtue and vice, reason and passion were enduring, and the ethical energy of his best works still resonates. The fools, foibles, heroes, and ideals he presents do not seem unfamiliar. Moral seriousness ballasts even his slightest poems. He spoke for traditional classical-Christian wisdom, but his writings rarely seem hackneyed or derivative. His compositions are anchored in concrete details, and their voice seems sensible, vital, and clear. Jonson prized communication over meditation; his poems almost always assume an audience.

Certainly this is true of the Rutland epistle, which opens by ticking off the corruptions caused by avarice at court. People of all ranks are greedy, but since the poet has no gold to give, he presents the countess with a poem. Condemning modern materialism, he looks to past examples of good behavior; his vision is more conservative than Utopian. Yet present decadence makes him cherish any conduct that approaches his ideals. Thus he praises the countess for honoring poetry, reminding her that her father—Sir Philip Sidney—was both a man of rank and a man of letters. The countess, Jonson is sure, will emulate her father's example. Beauty, blood, and riches vanish; "onely *Poets*, rapt with rage diuine," can immortalize the virtuous.

This note, however, is instantly checked by pressing concern with a rival "verser . . . / (Or *Poet*, in the court account)." Perhaps this was Samuel Daniel, but his specific identity matters less than the larger questions raised. The sudden shift from exaltation to disdain can be seen either as a defect or simply as an example of how Jonson's circumstances complicated his art. Much depends on what is expected. Jonson's verse, with its moral emphasis and its constant concern with judgment, invites assessment, and Jonson's readers (like the poet himself) have often tended either to praise or to blame. Yet it seems a mistake simply to echo Jonson's own self-assurance.

The Rutland epistle is valuable because both it and reactions to it are so typical. Its very "imperfections" are fascinating, as when Jonson asserts that he does not envy the rival poet, but that his rival envies him. How does one respond? By taking the claim at face value? By dismissing it? By turning away, embarrassed? Or by recogniz-

ing it as a particularly intriguing moment in a poem whose motives are both highly complex and quite human? However one reacts, the work illustrates that reading can tell as much about the reader as about texts. Perhaps one value of Jonson's verse is that it can still prove so uncomfortable and disquieting, and in this sense the Rutland epistle is exquisitely disturbing. Its lofty rhetoric is conditioned by a very practical concern with security and power. The social contexts of Jonson's poems can rarely be ignored, if only because the works so often mention them. To read the poems in context, to see how the contexts are fully implicated in the texts themselves, is less reductive than enriching.

The epistle's final lines are variously intriguing. Addressing one countess, Jonson alludes to another—Lucy Harrington, Countess of Bedford, whom he both praises for heavenly virtues and tweaks for patronizing his rival. Lucy was already one of his own most important patronesses, and the Rutland epistle illustrates in general how important such encouragement had now become and how actively he solicited it. By the early years of the new century, he had begun to cultivate aristocratic contacts, not only to enhance his status and ensure some financial security, but also because he believed that a poet could best influence society by influencing its most powerful members.

The epistle also shows Jonson's pride as a poetic innovator who could domesticate classical genres, producing unusual or "strange *poems*, which, as yet, / Had not their forme touch'd by an English wit." He sought to make contemporary poetry as respectable as the great literature of other times and places. By alluding to and imitating the classics, he sought to distinguish his works sharply from the "tickling rimes, / Or common places, filch'd, that take these times," promising instead "high, and noble matter, such as flies / From braines entranc'd, and fill'd with extasies." These lines suggest how seriously he took his role, how much and how early he sought to discharge the duties of a laureate poet.

Jonson's other poems addressed to or mentioning the countesses of Rutland and Bedford are less precisely datable, but they illustrate many aspects of his persona and self-image. Thus Epigram 79 to Lady Rutland proclaims that "*Poets* are far rarer births then kings," but then turns apparent self-praise into skillful commendation of the countess and her father, Sir Philip Sidney. It is interesting to note how much this short poem assumes (even if only whimsically) the existence of competition and rivalry: poets compete with kings, and earlier and later poets compete with Sidney. The *destinies* feel challenged by Sidney's genius and so deny him a son, and then *Nature* retaliates against the *destinies* by giving Sidney a talented daughter. Everyone and everything seeks to outdo, outcreate, the others. Even Sidney, if alive to view his daughter's verse, "would burne, or better farre his booke." The poem suggests how tightly Jonson linked creation with emulation.

Competition of a different sort is implied in another poem probably addressed to the countess of Rutland, *Underwood* 50, which praises its subject for a wisdom that allows her to "conquer rumour, and triumph on spight" by shunning even the "suspition" of bad behavior, especially when vices have grown so "fruitfull." Apparently the countess's husband was traveling when the poem was written, and the poet defends her against any imputation of unfaithfulness. He claims that "when the rest of Ladyes view" her many virtues, "It will be shame for them, if they have none." The poem is utterly Jonsonian, not only in what it says but in the kinds of questions it raises. It both praises and blames; it exalts morality and learning, offering both the countess and (implicitly) the poet as good examples. Its rhetoric is lofty, but the poem's very existence suggests the complicated social context from which so many of Jonson's works emerged. If the countess's virtue was so obvious, one wonders why she or the poet needed to worry about "rumour" or "spight." This poem, like many others, implies that Jonson's patrons also had to compete, and that the poet could serve as a valuable ally. Yet the poet could play patrons off against each other—as he does, to some extent, in the final part of the Rutland epistle, where he mentions Lucy, and as he does again in a short poem to Lucy herself, Epigram 84, that reminds her of an unfulfilled promise she made after telling her of another patron who had broken a similar promise. The implication is clear, but the tone is playful. Jonson's subtlety is both social and aesthetic.

Similar subtlety appears in Epigram 94, "To Lucy, Countess of Bedford," enclosed with copies she probably requested of John Donne's satires. The poem shows the kinds of contacts (both with aristocrats and with other writers) that Jonson had begun to develop. He later told Drummond that he considered Donne "the first poet jn the World jn some things." He felt that Donne had

"written all his best pieces err he was 25 years old" (that is, before the turn of the century), and he knew some of Donne's verse "by Heart." As always with Jonson, however, praise was balanced by criticism; indeed, his critical faculty guaranteed the worth of his commendations. At one point he remarked that "Done for not keeping of accent deserved hanging," and he also predicted that "Done himself for not being understood would perish." Such comments reveal much about Jonson's own poetic ideals. They help explain his attention to both metrics and matter, to rhythm and clarity. Certainly Epigram 94 is one of his clearest and best-shaped poems. Its circular structure is apt, since it praises the countess as simultaneously "The *Muses* euening, as their morning-starre," punning on her first name while complimenting her interest in Donne. Although she lives at court, where "the matter" of satire "is bred," her willingness to read attacks on vice testifies to her own goodness. Of course, all this praise of Lucy—for her friendship, love of good verse, and devotion to virtue—reflects back on Jonson. Whatever their subjects, the poems usually tell us something about their author, especially about Jonson's ideals and how he wished to be perceived.

By the beginning of the new century, then, Jonson had begun to achieve the kind of recognition and encouragement he sought as a public poet. In 1599 he wrote an epitaph on Margaret Ratcliffe (Epigram 40), who had been very close to Queen Elizabeth. *Every Man Out of His Humour*, acted both at the Globe theater and at court sometime late in 1599, demonstrated how daring an innovator Jonson could be—how determined he was to make an original mark even while endorsing traditional values. Although similar in title to *Every Man in His Humour*, performed in 1598, *Every Man Out of His Humour* differs radically in construction; it suggests Jonson's determination to challenge both himself and his audience. Sometimes, however, he crossed the line: the play's original ending was criticized (and deleted) for daring to praise the queen by impersonating her onstage. This and other slips emphasize how tactful Jonson needed to be in pursuing favor. However, his interest in impressing Elizabeth and in both reflecting and affecting behavior at court is suggested again by *Cynthia's Revels*, staged in 1600, which satirizes self-love and foolishness while celebrating the virtue of true nobles and worthy poets.

Like many of Jonson's early dramas, *Cynthia's Revels* is extremely self-conscious and invites attention to its own author and artistry. It and the two plays preceding it were indebted to a fashion for satire so strong in the late 1590s that the authorities sought to suppress it. Biting moralism could easily mask personal invective or social dissent. In any case, satire seems to have been particularly popular with the young men (such as Donne) who lived and studied at the Inns of Court—men who were often destined to play important social and political roles, and men with whom Jonson seems to have been especially close. Years later he dedicated *Every Man Out of His Humour* to his friends at the Inns, and his links there and at court suggest the kind of company and status he had begun to enjoy. In 1599 John Weever had already praised his rich style and "wondrous gallant spirit," and Jonson's notoriety is attested by the many excerpts printed in Robert Allott's *Englands Parnassus* (1600), an anthology of "The choysest Flowers of our Moderne Poets." *Ungathered Verse* 2, his commendatory poem for Nicholas Breton's *Melancholike Humours* (1600), suggests Jonson's own interest in satirizing abnormal psychology, but it also shows that his public approval was now sought and valued. This is suggested also by his contributions to Robert Chester's *Loves Martyr*, published in 1601. Those poems display his command of different genres and his range of tones, from the learnedly clever and amusing (*Forest* 10) to the cryptically epigrammatic (*Ungathered Verse* 4), from exuberantly exaggerated praise (*Ungathered Verse* 5), to didactic and reflective moralism (*Forest* 11). He had begun to make his mark with a style and personality far from shy and retiring.

Jonson could provoke admiration as well as scorn—often from the same people. Weever, who had recently praised Jonson's "gallant spirit," in 1601 mocked his alleged greed and insincerity, calling him "one of those that if a man can finde in his purse to giue them presently, they can find in their hearts to loue him euerlastingly"; few, he charged, were "coriuals with [Jonson] in the loue of siluer." Weever in turn was answered by Breton, whom Jonson had recently praised, and Jonson himself gibed at Weever in Epigram 18. However, the most important and defining literary battle of Jonson's life also began around this time—the so-called poetomachia with John Marston and Thomas Dekker. Its exact causes and chronology are hard to trace, but over many months Jonson gave as good as he got. Jonson's *Poetaster*,

a dramatic satire staged in 1601, attempted both to answer Marston's *What You Will*, staged earlier that year, and to preempt *Satiromastix*, a stinging assault mainly written by Dekker, first performed in autumn 1601. An underrated play, *Poetaster* characteristically reflects on the purposes of poets and the functions of poetry. Particularly interesting is its presentation of the Roman poets Ovid, Virgil, and Horace as well as their various patrons.

Although Jonson clearly identified with Horace, in doing so he only gave his antagonists further ammunition. *Satiromastix* taxes him for arrogance, hypocrisy, lame writing, false friendship, avarice, and assorted other faults, including popery, murder, humble origins, and bad skin. Such feuds may seem irrelevant or even embarrassing today, but they must have seemed extremely important to those involved in Jonson's time. They suggest much about the milieu in which Jonson lived and wrote, but they also involved larger principles. Jonson was always greatly concerned with proper interpretation; he held readers, other writers, and himself to the same high standards. Many of his *Epigrams* concern writing and reading, and indeed the first three poems explicitly address the poet's reader, book, and bookseller. Epigram 1, a lone couplet, epitomizes the concise resonance of much of his poetry. By urging his reader, "Pray thee, take care," he both supplicates and warns: for Jonson, reading always involved judgment, not only by but *of* the reader. Misreading abuses both writer and text while also disclosing the reader's own shortcomings. Reading involves self-discovery and self-revelation as well as risks and obligations. Our chief obligation is "to vnderstand"—always a key verb for Jonson, suggesting an integration of mind and emotion, empathy and assessment.

Epigram 2 is typically self-conscious about its own genre, audience, and potential competition. Jonson makes clear that in writing epigrams he meets the distinctive requirements of an ancient form, of which most of his contemporaries know nothing. He forswears writing that is "bold, licentious, full of gall," rejecting interest in "the worlds loose laughter, or vaine gaze," and concluding that "He that departs with his owne honesty / For vulgar praise, doth it too dearely buy." All these are characteristic notes, particularly the emphasis on self-respect and honesty. Here again Jonson depicts himself as an artistic innovator whose distinction involves reviving ancient standards. Each of the first three *Epigrams* echoes Martial, an immensely influential predecessor. Jonson often expected his works to be read in the light of literary tradition, and his poems gain greater resonance when such echoes are perceived. Even a poem as apparently rooted in contemporary life as Epigram 3 is informed by classical example.

Although the first three *Epigrams* may have been among the last written, since they assume a book-length collection, their qualities exemplify the writing Jonson already was doing in the early 1600s. Moreover, they epitomize the uneasy relations with his audience and other writers already apparent by then. Although most of the *Epigrams* are impossible to date precisely, their attitudes toward the poet, his readers, and other writers are consistent with the stances and persona Jonson had adopted by the time of the poetomachia. Epigram 9, for instance, proclaims that Jonson honors virtue, not rank. As if to reinforce the point, Epigram 10 curtly dismisses an unnamed "Lord Ignorant" for disdaining the poet. Epigram 17, "To the Learned Critick," professes the poet's eagerness to submit his work to such a reader's "sole censure hye," while the next poem expresses contempt for ignorant readers who compare Jonson's epigrams to those of untalented contemporaries. Juxtapositions like these typify the whole collection's structure, emphasizing virtue and wisdom by setting them next to examples of foolishness and vice.

That Jonson could be generous in praising other writers is evident from Epigram 23, which celebrates John Donne for his "earely" (or precocious) "wit," praising his "language, letters, arts, best life, / Which might with halfe mankind maintayne a strife." Donne exemplifies the integration of morality and artistry that Jonson sought to emulate and encourage. The obverse is apparent in Epigram 49, one of the poems defending Jonson's work against criticism from poetasters. A corrupt mind, he implies, cannot produce a worthy poem. Nor can it judge one: Epigram 52 rejects the "weake applause" of an auditor whose attempt to seem discriminating displays his folly while imperfectly concealing his spite. The next poem, Epigram 53, attacks plagiarism and self-commendation—two vices of which Jonson himself often stood accused. Like many of his satirical poems, this one seems as intriguing for the interpretive questions it raises as for the confident judgments it makes.

Epigram 53 may have been aimed at Marston, and many of Jonson's satires may have had specific targets. Although he often claimed to satirize vice, not persons, *Poetaster* alone shows how easily this distinction could be blurred. Much the same is suggested by Epigram 54, which also mentions one risk of blatant personal satire. A lawyer, Chev'ril, threatens action against the poet's "libells," but Jonson, of course, turns the tables, accusing Chev'ril himself of petulance. The poem is typical in its effective brevity and disdain for lawyers. In Jonson's eyes, lawyers, like poets, were obliged to use language and learning to promote public good; too often, however, they corrupted those gifts in the pursuit of self-interest. Indeed, rampant self-interest is the common vice of most of the malefactors Jonson assaults. For example, his attack "On Poet-Ape," Epigram 56, condemns another plagiarist, suggesting again a highly competitive literary milieu in which wit had become a kind of property, worth stealing and protecting. (On this point, see also Epigrams 81, 100, and 112.) The poem implies that a plagiarist insults his audience as much as his victims; here as elsewhere, Jonson suggests that his satire simply voices common sense, and that anyone who fails to agree is a fool. Like many of his works, this poem not only judges its target but intimidates its readers.

The importance of an intelligent audience is emphasized again in "To Groome Ideot," Epigram 58. This poem's abrupt syntax, colloquial tone, direct diction, and allusion to very specific circumstances all suggest an actual encounter, although there is, of course, no way to know this for certain. Still, Jonson's convincing verisimilitude exemplifies his talent. The epigram mocks "Ideot" for attempting to exploit public reading of the poet's works for self-display. By smiling and laughing inappropriately, "Ideot" reveals that even the most apparently spontaneous behavior can be mannered and self-conscious. Ironically, he and the poet share a similar concern with their public reception; both were necessarily performers, and lampooning "Ideot's" display becomes, in turn, part of Jonson's. This is one of many poems in which clear distinctions between satirist and target seem to blur on closer examination—a sign not of Jonson's failure but of the complexities embedded, perhaps, in any social use of language. Jonson often seems to use words with serene self-confidence, but even a poem so apparently simple and straightforward raises intriguing questions when examined with a slightly skeptical eye. The point is not to question Jonson's "sincerity," but to suggest how his seem-

Lucy, Countess of Bedford, the patron Jonson praised as "a learned, and a manly soule," possessed of "each softest vertue"

ingly uncomplicated poems exemplify the complex drama and political contention implicit in even the "simplest" aspects of human life.

Issues of power were certainly central to the poetomachia, which perhaps involved Epigram 68, "On Play-wright." Jonson later told Drummond that he once "beate Marston and took his pistoll," and the epigram chides its target in similar terms. Yet despite Jonson's physical pugnacity, most of his attacks were verbal. Certainly this is true of the stinging poem, "To Court-ling," Epigram 72, a poem that claims an indifference to criticism that its very existence belies. Typically, a courtling's power was more derivative than personal: it was as a "chamber-critick . . . / At MAD-AMES table" that he could be a threat. Here as in the Rutland epistle, the power of the poet's rivals—like the poet's own power—depended on the endorsement of others, including patrons. Jonson's social position was quite typical in its double insecurity, since he was vulnerable both to hos-

tile antagonists and to indifferent superiors.

The aftermath of the poetomachia was unpleasant. *Poetaster* offended others besides Dekker and Marston; prosecution was threatened in 1601, and Jonson's defiant apology for the work, an "Apologetical Dialogue," only created greater hostility. Dejected, he abandoned comedy, eventually producing *Sejanus* (1605), a tragedy about a corrupt Roman favorite. This was probably first staged in 1603, an important year. Elizabeth's death in March meant the accession of James I, the king who most promoted Jonson's career. The poet was commissioned to write his first aristocratic entertainment to welcome James's wife, Anne of Denmark, and son, Prince Henry, on their journey south from Scotland. This commission was followed by many others, and within a few years he had become the preeminent writer of masques at court. Yet his good fortune was not unblemished. *Sejanus* provoked Henry Howard, Earl of Northampton, to accuse him of popery and treason, and in 1603 he also lost his first-born son, Ben, to the plague. This death elicited one of his best poems, Epigram 45, "On my First Sonne," in which he tries to come to terms with a loss he obviously felt deeply. The poem's power derives from tension between clear pain and attempted consolation. In another fine poem, Epigram 120, Jonson had already mourned the loss, in 1602, of the child actor Solomon Pavy, but the phrasing of that poem is more clever, less intense. Epigram 22, of uncertain date, records the death of his daughter, Mary, and numerous other works display his mastery of the epitaph and of elegiac conventions (Epigrams 27, 32, 33, 40, 124; *Underwood* 12, 16, 35, 60, 63, 83, 84; *Ungathered Verse* 9, 22, 25, 26, 28, 31). Such poems commemorate embodied ideals as much as specific individuals. Jonson speaks to the living as much as he speaks of the dead; he celebrates virtue more than he laments mortality. Like his poems extolling friends, his poems on death provide an important context for his satires. They openly endorse the same values the satires defend through attack. Informed both by Christian faith and by Stoic rationality, the epitaphs and elegies suggest the positive core at the center of Jonson's worldview. Many reveal, as well, another facet of his talent as a social or public poet. In most of these poems Jonson speaks not only for himself but for the shared ideals of his community.

This role as public poet was one he could increasingly practice after the accession of King James. He was selected, for instance, to help celebrate the coronation in March 1604 by writing speeches of greeting. The "Panegyre," commemorating James's opening of Parliament, is richly resonant, epitomizing many of his most enduring political ideals. In politics as in all spheres, Jonson emphasized the importance of moderation and personal virtue. The commonwealth could flourish only if its members—especially the monarch and aristocrats—took their ethical responsibilities seriously, and Jonson felt that the poet was obliged to advise and encourage them to do so. They, in turn, could demonstrate their virtue by encouraging virtuous poets. By working together, writers and aristocrats could promote the community's well-being. Jonson seems, by and large, to have genuinely admired James. Both men prided themselves on their intellectual prowess; both shared lofty views of their social roles; yet both could be refreshingly and even crudely un-

buttoned. They combined earthy humor and high ideals, and many charges aimed at the king (that he took himself too seriously, failed to practice what he preached, and was insufficiently self-critical and excessively inflexible) have also been aimed at the poet. Jonson himself sometimes faulted James, but on the whole he seems to have considered the king well-intentioned, and the fact that his career flourished under James suggests something about the king's regard.

Jonson would have claimed that his praise was meant to teach; the ideal king he extols was an ideal James should emulate. Instruction through delight was a dictum at least as ancient as Horace, whose views on poetry Jonson clearly respected. (He twice translated the *Ars Poetica* [1640] and wrote a lost commentary on it.) Epigram 4, for instance, praises James as both the "best of Kings" and "best of *Poets*," but it also implies that although James no longer has much time to write, he can still encourage poetry by showing "grace" to Jonson. Epigram 5, probably from 1604, celebrates James as a "priest" who marries Scotland and England, while Epigram 35, perhaps written at around the same time, praises him for ruling "by example, more than sway." This note is typical: the king's "manners draw, more than thy powers constraine." Such praise holds him to an exacting moral standard, and when Jonson alleges in Epigram 36 that James "cannot flatter'd bee," he at once compliments and challenges. When James was rumored to have been stabbed in March 1606, Jonson acted as public spokesman to celebrate the rumor's falsity (Epigram 51), while Epigram 64, probably written in May 1608, extols the king's wisdom in rewarding virtue. Similar praise is offered in Epigram 67, and although Jonson was clearly aware that the king was not perfect, their relations seem to have been rooted in a basic mutual regard.

It is true that *Eastward Ho*, a play on which Jonson collaborated with George Chapman and John Marston perhaps in early 1605, ruffled feathers at court. A well-connected Scot complained of some anti-Scottish satire during an unlicensed summer performance, and apparently even the king took offense. The authors were imprisoned and threatened with physical punishment. Surviving letters to aristocrats show that Jonson vehemently pleaded his innocence, attacked his accusers, and asked to be examined. Eventually he was released, and nothing much seems to have come of this incident. January 1605 had already seen the performance of Jonson's first royal masque, *The Masque of Blackness*, and his letters suggest how well-connected he had by now become at court. He probably owed his release, in part, to the intervention of his correspondents, who included such influential aristocrats as Esmé Stuart, Lord D'Aubigny, himself a Scot and a kinsman to the king. Jonson in fact may have been lodging in Aubigny's house at this time; he later told Drummond that he resided there (and away from his wife) for five years, although dating his stay precisely is difficult. In any case, in an undated poem (Epigram 127), he professes deep thanks for Aubigny's support. Such poems, along with his letters, suggest how important his aristocratic connections were now becoming.

That he enjoyed such connections despite his Catholicism seems worth stressing. Not all Catholics were persecuted subversives. The Gunpowder Plot, a notorious attempt by Catholic dissidents to blow up the king and ruling elite in Parliament, was foiled on 4 November 1605. In October Jonson had actually dined with some conspirators, but after the plot's discovery the government employed him to contact a sympathetic priest. In a letter to Robert Cecil, Earl of Salisbury, and James's most important deputy, Jonson offered to serve with "all readynesse." The fact that he was thus trusted so soon after *Eastward Ho* suggests that his loyalty was not in doubt, and Epigram 60, "To William Lord Mounteagle," extols the lord who revealed the conspiracy. On 26 April, before Easter Sunday, it is true, Jonson faced charges in Consistory Court of promoting Catholicism, failing to attend Anglican services, and refusing Anglican communion. He denied the first two charges and promised to take communion if certain scruples could be satisfied. In any event, little seems to have resulted from these charges. He apparently remained a Catholic for several more years.

During this period his prominence continued to grow. *Hymenaei* was performed in January 1606 to commemorate a marriage intended to heal the rifts between two court factions (the marriage of Robert Devereaux, third Earl of Essex, to Lady Frances Howard), and July saw the performance of an entertainment written to celebrate a visit by James and Christian IV of Denmark to Theobalds, the estate of Cecil. Cecil, a master politician, had by now become one of Jonson's most important patrons; *Hymenaei* had directly served his interests, and over the next few years he commissioned other entertainments. Jon-

son in turn praised Cecil in several poems that illustrate the complexity of his writing for patrons. Epigram 43, for instance, perhaps written to celebrate Cecil's creation, in May 1605, as earl of Salisbury, opens by bluntly asking, "What need hast thou of me? or of my *Muse?*" The rest of the poem, of course, implies precisely the poet's usefulness. Cecil's power and personality had won him contempt and envy, and although Jonson identifies Cecil's "foes" with those of England, reference to their "hate" would have reminded the earl of his many enemies at home. Here as elsewhere, Jonson plays on his patrons' insecurities; their positions were in some ways as uncertain as his. Thus he disclaims any self-serving or "seruile flatterie," and in Epigram 64, written to celebrate Cecil's appointment in May 1608 as lord treasurer, Jonson distinguishes himself from those lured by the earl's new power. Instead, he typically praises a time when "good mens vertues them to honors bring, / And not to dangers," and he commends James for promoting Cecil. Similarly, in Epigram 63 he praises Cecil for having risen through "vertue," not "fortune," and he extols the "iudgement of the king" that shines in the earl.

At some point, however, Jonson seems to have developed misgivings. Years after the earl was dead and disgraced, the poet complained to Drummond about Cecil's snobbery, and he also more bitingly remarked that "Salisbury never cared for any man longer [than] he could make use of him." The well-known poem "To my Muse," Epigram 65, may have been written with Cecil in mind. There Jonson repents his "most fierce idolatrie" to "a worthlesse lord." Such service, he claimed, would win a man only "the times long grudge, the courts ill will; / And, reconcil'd, keepe him suspected still. / Make him loose all his friends; and, which is worse, / Almost all wayes, to any better course." There were, it seems, risks as well as benefits to associating with a man as powerful as Cecil. From now on, Jonson vows, he intends to "write / Things manly, and not smelling parasite," but this declaration is soon modified by the claim that "Who e're is rais'd, / For worth he has not, He is tax'd, not prais'd." This was a standard defense: if an object of celebration failed to live up to the poet's praise, that was the object's fault, not the poet's, and what had been written as praise then functioned as implicit satire. Such claims never prevented Jonson's enemies from charging him with flattery, and the poems to Cecil illustrate in partic-

Robert Cecil, Earl of Salisbury, one of the patrons Jonson celebrated in his Epigrams
(portrait by Renold Elstrack; British Museum)

ularly interesting ways how a fuller understanding of his social circumstances can highlight the artistic complexities of his works. Such understanding suggests the tensions and ambivalences, subtleties and ambiguities often implicit in his poems. Jonson told Drummond that "He never esteemed of a man for the name of a Lord," but his works reflect neither complete autonomy nor total subservience. All his poems can be seen as both performances and negotiations. This view can help restore some sense of their original energy and vitality and can help prevent treatment of them either as insincere flattery or as inert restatements of pious clichés.

Poems to superiors comprise many of Jonson's works. All reveal different aspects of his complex role as a social poet. He seems to have been highly aware that any poem addressed to a superior might seem calculated or insincere, and such poems are interesting partly for the ways

they wrestle with this problem. Epigram 67, for instance, addressed to Thomas Howard, Earl of Suffolk, begins by announcing that "Since men haue left to doe praise-worthy things, / Most thinke all praises flatteries." Jonson thus instantly challenges anyone who would question his motives, and, as in various other poems, he quickly moves to act as a spokesman for virtue. His own praise merely articulates the esteem felt for Suffolk by God, the king, and the people. Similarly, while praising the "weigh'd iudgements" of Lord Chancellor Thomas Egerton in Epigram 74, Jonson displays his own: the poem carefully marshals evidence before pronouncing its verdict, so that its very syntax pays tribute to the jurist. The well-known poem "To William Earle of Pembroke" (Epigram 102) depicts William Herbert as a representative of all good men and as an opponent and target of the vicious. Jonson thus allies himself and his patron to higher principles, and the qualities and courage he praises in the earl of Pembroke reflect his own. Moreover, by highlighting Herbert's vulnerability, the poet implies his own usefulness as an ally.

The epigram to Pembroke, Sir Philip Sidney's nephew, is one of many poems Jonson wrote to members of the extended Sidney family. These poems help reveal the range of his genres, themes, and tones. Thus Epigram 103, "To Mary Lady Wroth" (Sidney's niece), claims that identifying her as a Sidney is praise enough. By commending her he commends the entire family, and the assertion that his "praise is plaine" only highlights his subtle artistry. Another poem to Mary, Epigram 105, at once underplays and displays his inventiveness. Epigram 114 to Mary's sister, Mistress Philip Sidney (named after her uncle), effectively raises many possible explanations of this Philip's worth, then judiciously leaves all the possibilities open. In a complex birthday ode to their brother, Sir William Sidney (*Forest* 14), Jonson acts as a kind of tutelary spirit, urging the youth to live up to his family's heritage; here as in so many other poems, celebration serves as a pretext for moral advice. The same is true of the lengthy poem to Sir Robert Wroth (*Forest* 3), Mary's husband, which turns praise of Wroth's attachment to his country estate into a basis for wide-ranging ethical reflection. The poem indicts the corruptions of city and court, condemning various kinds of malice and pride and finally invoking God to authorize the Stoic ideals it commends.

Perhaps his best poem for the Sidneys, however, is "To Penshurst" (*Forest* 2), addressed to the country house of Sir Robert Sidney, Sir Philip's brother and William's father. Few other poems illustrate so well so many of Jonson's tones and talents. Addressing the estate itself, he achieves greater aesthetic distance than in his comparable poem to Sir Robert Wroth. Penshurst, ancient and rather modest, is contrasted with the gaudy, self-indulgent palaces then being built by such men as Cecil. Those houses arouse envy, whereas Penshurst (Jonson claims) evokes reverence and respect. The poem's centripetal structure moves in from the outer grounds to the gardens to the house itself, and then to its guests and inhabitants. In the process Jonson conjures up an entire world and worldview rooted in hierarchy, harmony, selfless service, and love. Both house and poem reconcile apparent opposites, including male and female, youth and age, classical and Christian, peasant and aristocrat, service and

affection, nature and culture, indulgence and moderation, spontaneity and order, the physical and the spiritual, the humorous and the serious, sexuality and virtue, and many others. Penshurst seems almost Edenic, a kind of earthly paradise where all receive their due, including their due respect. Each inhabitant and guest—including the poet—is quite literally at home. The estate and poem resonate with vitality, serenity, and good humor, and the Christian god stands at the top of the harmonious hierarchy Jonson describes and extols.

Although this is probably how Jonson intended the poem to be read, other approaches highlight its different facets. For instance, archetypal critics might emphasize how the poem exploits the mythic patterns in human thought. Penshurst is a great mother, fruitful and provident. Natural, human, and divine coalesce in this sacred center; the poem appeals to deep instincts and desires, to a hunger for order and purpose, to a need to see time as meaningful, not pointless or chaotic. Conversely, a psychoanalytic critic might argue that the poem reflects and projects Jonson's own psychic needs. The boy whose father died before the boy's birth finds a true home. The poet who struggled for acceptance is fed and honored by the Sidneys. The former bricklayer now associates with aristocrats and kings; the grown child of the city extols a country paradise. The competitor for patronage enjoys security and reward; the father who lost two children becomes part of an extended family. The man who often lashed out in anger celebrates serenity and love.

Marxists, who stress economic explanations and class conflicts, might see the work as defending a dying elite threatened by monied social climbers. The poem (they might contend) mystifies or romanticizes the relations it depicts, undervaluing labor and obscuring tensions between the Sidneys and their dependents. At the same time, they might argue, the poem inadvertently anticipates a new system that prizes individual merit or worth over birth. Thus the poem might be seen as both conservative and corrosive, implicitly undermining the very life-style it extols. Feminists, on the other hand, might stress its views of women and other females, arguing that it helps legitimize a male-centered worldview by presenting women as subservient—as mothers, wives, and tame domestics. The poem would thus illustrate the ways males both dominate and depend on females, whose roles they define and control.

Deconstructors, scanning for contradictions, might argue that the natural world the poem praises is itself infected by the corrupt civilization it ostensibly rejects. Whereas formalists would emphasize the poem's harmonies, deconstructors might argue that those harmonies are inevitably unstable and uncertain. Similarly, "new historicists" might point to the poem's complex expression of power relations. However, while a Marxist might emphasize class struggle, a "new historicist" might instead stress individual competition, showing how this poem that attacks self-interest nonetheless helps Jonson and the Sidneys compete. Because of its length and complexity, "To Penshurst" lends itself particularly well to a variety of critical approaches, but what is true of this poem is equally true of others: The "meaning" of Jonson's poems will depend greatly on what is asked of them. The different possible readings the poem can elicit suggest that much of Jonson's poetry may be more complex and ambiguous, less plain and simple, than is often assumed.

Jonson's poems to the Sidneys exemplify the many tones and techniques he could employ in addressing patrons, and they also suggest how gratifying the support of patrons could prove. Of course, not all were as encouraging as Pembroke, whom Jonson admired and who started giving the poet twenty pounds each year to buy books. Well before the end of James's first decade of rule, Jonson seems to have grown uneasy with Cecil, but Cecil was hardly the only superior he came to distrust. He seems to have become increasingly disgruntled with the countess of Bedford, and despite his long poem praising Robert Wroth, he later called him "a Jealous husband." The earl of Rutland apparently resented his own lady's links to Jonson, and Jonson reported that Sir Walter Ralegh, with whom he had various connections, "esteemed more of fame than conscience." Jonson even seems to have questioned the king's tastes in poetry and his skills in reading it aloud, and, of course, he considered the earl of Northampton—responsible for the accusations concerning *Sejanus*—his "mortall enimie." He noted the vanities and deceptions of Elizabeth's court, and his attacks on unnamed corrupt courtiers or morally deficient superiors fill the pages of the *Epigrams*. In the crisp Epigram 10, "To my lord Ignorant," two curt lines exact revenge on a superior who had called Jonson a "*Poet*, as a terme of shame." By refusing to name him, Jonson inflicts some punishment, as if the

aristocrat were too insignificant to mention. However, printing his name might also have seemed libelous, and part of the irony of the work is that in reading the poem aloud, Jonson probably did identify its target. Thus the poem derived part of its immediate social effectiveness from the same kind of utterance it derides.

Many other poems indict unworthy superiors. Epigram 11, for instance, attacks a courtier identified in the title only as "some-thing, that walkes some-where." At first the title suggests that Jonson is refusing his target even the dignity of being identified as human, but it soon evolves that the poem additionally reflects the essential nullity or deadness of its subject. Other poems also attack figures of rank or status, although one can never be sure in any given instance whether Jonson had a particular person in mind. (See, for example, Epigrams 15, 19, 20, 25, 26, 28, 29, 46, 47, 48, 50, 62, 65, 73.) Moreover, many of Jonson's other works contain incidental gibes at persons of social standing. The detailed descriptions offered by his satirical poems frequently suggest that the portraits were meant to be recognizable, but the amount of detail may simply demonstrate his artistic skill. Besides, even if particular targets were originally aimed at, Jonson knew that such poems would survive only if they voiced ethical judgments not confined to a specific person, place, or time.

One poem definitely written before the late summer of 1609 was in fact specifically targeted. This is the ferocious "Epigram on The Court Pucell" (*Underwood* 49). Playing on the double meaning of "Pucell" (virgin/whore), Jonson attacks an unnamed woman of status and her coterie of sycophants. Few other poems so memorably suggest the prostitution of social relations at court, and Jonson's opening couplet seems deliberately defiant: "Do's the Court-Pucell then so censure me, / And thinkes I dare not her? let the world see." Years later he revealed that his target had been Cecilia Bulstrode, a relative and friend of the countess of Bedford; but he also mentioned that the poem had been "stollen out of his pocket by a Gentleman who drank him drousie & given Mistress Boulstraid, which brought him great displeasur." Apparently he had never intended her actually to see it. Because it was recited publicly by Jonson but not published until years after his death, its satire was all the more stinging by being deniable. The "displeasur" he experienced may have been a temporary loss of favor with Lucy. In any case, without

Drummond's anecdote, one might simply assume that the poem was aimed at general vice instead of a specific person. It is hardly an indictment of Jonson to suggest that many of his satires may have been prompted by real persons and circumstances, and in fact the vitality of his satiric writing may derive partly from its real links to his own life.

When Bulstrode died at twenty-five on 4 August 1609, Jonson was asked to write an epitaph. He did (*Ungathered Verse* 9), and critics ever since have tried to explain the divergent tones of Jonson's two poems about Bulstrode. The possibility that he may have had a sincere change of heart is complicated by the fact that he was still reading his satire to Drummond—and identifying its target—almost a decade after Bulstrode's death. It seems most sensible to assume that in the epitaph Jonson was discharging the conventional duty of saying the appropriate thing. Both satire and epitaph celebrate virtue, albeit by different means, and celebrating virtue is finally what Jonson's poetry is all about. The Bulstrode episode only suggests how complex that task could sometimes be.

By the time Bulstrode died in 1609, Jonson had firmly established his status and genius. He had written court masques in 1606, 1608, and 1609, and in 1606 his comic masterpiece, *Volpone*, had been acted at the Globe theater. Another great play, *Epicoene*, was probably staged in 1609, and was followed in 1610 by still another artistic triumph, *The Alchemist*. These comedies are among the best in English, but they were succeeded in 1611 by a tragedy—*Catiline*—that proved tragic mainly in its hostile reception. The play *is* defensible, and later it was often cited respectfully, but the derision it first provoked must have reminded Jonson of earlier humiliations. Indeed, in the period following the production of *Catiline*, he may have felt that he was living a bad dream. Cecil, the patron by whom he eventually felt betrayed, died in early 1612, and was widely vilified even before he ceased breathing. Prince Henry, the heir who had taken an interest in Jonson's work, died suddenly later that fall. The patronage of the Sidneys may have offered some consolation in the aftermath of *Catiline* (evidence suggests that "To Penshurst" may have been written sometime in the first half of 1612), but a poem to Lady Katherine, wife of Lord Aubigny, written sometime between 1609 and early 1612 (*Forest* 13), recalls the early Rutland epistle in its sense of embattled insecurity. Jonson claims that

he is reported to be "dangerous / By arts, and practise of the vicious, / Such as suspect them-selues, and thinke it fit / For their owne cap'tall crimes, t[o]'indite my wit." He feels "forsooke / Of *Fortune*" and notes that sincere compliments are derided as flatteries, "So both the prais'd, and praisers suffer." All these notes are characteristic, but that hardly means that they were conventional. Admittedly Jonson often echoes previous poets (including himself), but his echoes can suggest much about his perception of his own feelings and circumstances. His poetry can be called derivative only in the most superficial sense.

If Jonson in fact felt insecure at this time, that may have been due as much to frustration with such rivals as Inigo Jones as to frustration with such patrons as Cecil. Jones was as talented in his own fields (architecture and design) as Jonson was in his, and it was partly this mutual talent that made them uneasy collaborators on the masques at court. Exactly when relations became strained cannot be determined; Jonson publicly noted Jones's contributions to their first four collaborations, although even here there may be hints of annoyance. For instance, a note to *Hymenaei* (1606) expresses a desire to avoid any imputation of "an ignorant neglect." Similarly, a note to *The Masque of Queenes* (1609) professes to "willingly acknowledge" Jones, "since it is a vertue, planted in good natures, that what respects they wish to obtayne fruictfully from others, they will giue ingenuously themselves." In fact, it may have been each man's clear sense of his own professional dignity that led to their conflict. Jonson saw poetry as the soul of masques; the ephemeral physical properties were mere "*bodies*" or "*carkasses*." Although both men shared similar assumptions about the didactic purposes of art, tensions between such strong personalities were probably inevitable.

Evidence of a rift may be contained in two bitter satires from the *Epigrams* volume. Epigram 115, "On the Townes honest Man," attacks its target as a self-promoting hypocrite, a cowardly flatterer and backbiter who is his "owne fames architect." Similarly, Epigram 129, "To Mime" expresses frustration with Mime's widespread social acceptance, although it ends by claiming that Mime's supposed friends actually regard him with contempt. If this were entirely true, of course, or if Jones's viciousness was as widely recognized as Epigram 115 contends, there would have been little reason for Jonson's assaults. It was precisely the social acceptance achieved by fig-

Penshurst Place, country house of Sir Robert Sidney and subject of Jonson's "To Penshurst"

ures such as Jones that seems to have bothered and threatened Jonson, and his satires often express derision while implying uneasiness. Such tensions contribute to the works' artistic complexity and psychological interest, and it seems a mistake to ignore such complications, either by dismissing the works as embarrassing or by simply taking sides. Rivalry seems to have been as important to Jonson as his relations with superiors. Both kinds of relations suggest the extent to which he and all persons are caught up in relations of power.

Various comments suggest tense relations with other contemporary writers. In addition to his feud with Dekker and Marston, Jonson also told Drummond that Samuel "Daniel was at Jealousies with him," that Michael "Drayton feared him, and he esteemed not of him," that "Francis Bea[u]mont loved too much himself & his own verses," that "Sir W[illiam] Alexander was not half Kinde unto him & neglected him because a friend to Drayton," that Gervase Markham was "a base fellow" and that "such were [John] Day and [Thomas] Mid[d]leton." The list could go on, but it should be balanced by the equally plentiful evidence that Jonson admired, and was admired by, many talented contemporaries. For instance,

he could quote others' verses from memory, and he told Drummond that "Sr John Roe loved him," that "Sir R. Aiton loved him dearly," that George "Chapman and [John] Fletcher were loved of him," and that "of all stiles he loved most to be named honest, and hath of that ane hundreth letters so naming him." Drummond's own assessment seems sensibly balanced. He considered Jonson "passionately kynde and angry, carelesse either to gaine or keep, Vindicative, but if he be well answered, at himself." Much evidence suggests that both Jonson and his works were at least as complex as these words imply.

Jonson's capacity for friendship was one of his most attractive traits, and he celebrates that ideal in many memorable poems. Friendship could provide an alternative to relations with superiors and competitors, and Jonson seems to have treasured true friendship, despite Drummond's opinion that he was "a great lover and praiser of himself, a contemner and Scorner of others, given rather to losse a friend, than a Jest." Certainly his friendships, like most human relations, must have been complicated at times, and certainly the poems on friendship often prove more complex than they seem at first. Just as certainly, however, those poems are among his best and most characteristic works. His celebration of his old teacher William Camden in Epigram 14, for instance, is typical in both stance and tone. Jonson not only expresses personal regard but also speaks for a much larger public that must similarly acknowledge Camden's merit. Merit, in fact, is at the center of Jonson's conception of friendship: only the truly good—or rather, only those who genuinely aspire to goodness—can truly be friends. Friends love each other's virtues, and the links between well-intentioned friends preserve and nourish civil society. Friendship for Jonson was rarely a private affair: it epitomized all that was best in the life of any healthy culture. It is no exaggeration when Jonson speaks of the "pietie" he feels toward Camden.

Jonson's praise of friends, like his praise in general, often reflects upon himself. This is hardly surprising, since any praise of virtue may imply one's own recognition or possession of it. This reflexiveness especially characterizes his commendatory poems on other writers or artists, such as the poem to Donne (Epigram 23); or the intriguingly clever praise of Francis Beaumont answering Beaumont's own praise of Jonson (Epigram 55); or the commemoration of Edward Allen (Epigram 89), which ends by noting how fitting it is that an actor "who did giue / So many *Poets* life, by one should liue." One thinks, too, of the poem commending the translator Sir Henry Saville (Epigram 95) that extols him as a man "That dares nor write things false, nor hide things true." Similarly, a poem to Sir Edward Herbert (Epigram 106) celebrates his "learning," "wit," "valour," "iudgement," self-respect, and "pietie to God, and friends," while two poems to Sir Clement Edmonds (Epigrams 110, 111) praise him as both a writer and a man. Sir Thomas Overbury (who later "turn'd [Jonson's] mortall enimie") is praised for bringing "letters, and humanitie" to the court (Epigram 113), while Benjamin Rudyerd is extolled in Epigram 121 for his "better studies," in Epigram 122 for his "wise simplicitie," and in Epigram 123 for his skills as both a "writer" and a "iudge" of writing. In these and in such poems as Epigrams 130-132, Jonson praises friends not only for their creativity but for their exemplary virtue.

Perhaps his most memorable celebration of friendship, however, is Epigram 101, "Inviting a friend to Supper." Charmingly serious and humorously thoughtful, it begins by humbly inviting a "graue" gentleman to the poet's "poore house"—"Not that we thinke vs worthy such a ghest, / But that your worth will dignifie our feast, / With those that come." The poem epitomizes the dignity, gravity, and worth it praises; it enacts and thus helps perpetuate the good manners and civility on which society ultimately depends. Lists and catalogues are favorite devices of Jonson's poetry, but after elaborately detailing the various foods he hopes to provide, he admits his willingness to "lye," and "tell you of more . . . so you will come." The poem implies that the dinner's success will depend less on the food than on the mutual respect the host and guests will display. Both mind and body will be satisfied; wine will be consumed, but not to excess; and the conversation will be free, innocent, and "mirthfull." Spies—the opposite of friends—will not be present, and "No simple word" will "affright / The libertie, that wee'll enioy to night." The poem celebrates serenity and relaxation, but it ends by reminding us that any respite from uneasiness can be only temporary, that the world of spies and competition, of distrust and vice, can be escaped only for a time. It is precisely this that makes friendship for Jonson so precious, so appealing, but also so tinged with complex emotion.

As "Inviting a friend to Supper" demonstrates, vice is never far from Jonson's mind, even in a work that celebrates its absence. Many of the *Epigrams*—the nondramatic poems by which he must have won his initial fame as a wit—excoriate various kinds of fools and knaves. His quick and clever sarcasm shows him at his satiric best, emulating the phrasing, techniques, and themes of such forebears as Martial, but always achieving a decidedly fresh and contemporary tone. Here as in the major comedies, Jonson indicts dupes, deceivers, and the self-deceived. His pungent humor underscores his moral seriousness; his scorn for corruption is informed by his ethical ideals. The poems mock pride (Epigram 6), whoring (Epigram 7), bribery and injustice (Epigram 8), fraud and lechery (Epigram 12), medical incompetence (Epigram 13), pompous clothing (Epigram 15), belligerence and cowardice (Epigram 16), literal and figurative stink (Epigrams 19 and 20), false piety (Epigram 21), vile manners (Epigram 24), voluptuousness (Epigram 25), imagined adultery (Epigram 26), arrogance and pretense (Epigram 28), dishonor (Epigram 29), usury (Epigram 31), impudence (Epigram 38), cuckoldry (Epigram 39), greed (Epigram 41), marital discord (Epigram 42), materialism (Epigram 44), avarice (Epigrams 46 and 47), affectation and timidity (Epigram 48), obsession with the physical (Epigram 50), bawdry and usury (Epigram 57), unnatural birth-control (Epigram 62), obsession with sex (Epigram 69), neglect of debts (Epigram 73), puritanism (Epigram 75), undue self-concern (Epigram 77), ironic self-display (Epigram 78), plagiarism (Epigram 81), mutual exploitation (Epigram 82), feminine sins (Epigram 83), cheating (Epigram 87), foreign affectations (Epigram 88), sexual rapacity (Epigram 90), political intrigue (Epigram 92), ambition and gaudy dress (Epigram 97), boasting (Epigram 107), whoring (Epigram 117), and gluttony and lechery (Epigram 118). Significantly, the *Epigrams* volume ends with a mock-heroic poem (Epigram 133) that whimsically emphasizes all manner of physical corruption, underscoring the importance of the spiritual, immaterial values celebrated in the commendatory epigrams—values noticeable by their absence in the satires. Although the satirical epigrams attack a wide range of vices, common to nearly all the failings they assault is excess—a failure of moderation and proper balance. Paradoxically, Jonson's poetry derives much of its own vigor, energy, and verve from its implied endorsements of constancy, prudence, and reason.

By 1612, when Jonson had written most of his *Epigrams*, he had achieved unprecedented success, but his life was also undergoing major changes. Sometime around 1610 he apparently satisfied his earlier scruples and returned to the Anglican church. He later told Drummond that "at his first communion jn token of true Reconciliation, he drank out all the full cup of wyne," but religion seems not to have been as important to his writing as it was, for instance, to Donne's. Given his longtime Catholicism, his relative silence on religious topics is not surprising, but even after his reconversion he seems to have written comparatively little on religious themes. He considered himself a sincere and convinced Christian, and Christian values obviously underlie many if not most of his works. However, religion is more often alluded to than dwelt upon, and Drummond regarded Jonson as being "for any religion as being versed jn both." Apparently, after 1610, he chose rather to stress the points of contact between Catholics and Protestants than to emphasize their differences, just as he seems to have had little trouble reconciling his Christianity with classical philosophy, especially Stoicism. He seems to have been first and foremost a defender of reason, and he seems to have considered Chris-

tianity eminently reasonable. Nonetheless, his tone in addressing God is sometimes urgent, as in his poem "To Heaven" (*Forest* 15), which offers one of our few extended glimpses into his religious thinking.

Thanks to his interest in religion, there is evidence of Jonson's presence in Paris in September 1612. There he attended a debate on Catholic and Protestant theology, but his chief purpose seems to have been to act as a governor to the young son of Sir Walter Ralegh. Drummond noted that

> this Youth being knavishly jnclyned ... caused [Jonson] to be Drunken & dead drunk, so that he knew not wher he was, therafter laid him on a Carr which he made to be Drawen by Pioners through the streets, at every corner showing his Governour streetched out & telling them that was a more Lively jmage of ye Crucifix then any they had, at which Sporte young Raughlies mother delyghted much (saying his father young was so jnclined) though the father abhorred it.

The elder Ralegh, imprisoned since 1603, had lately been composing a massive *History of the World* (1614) on which Jonson, among others, was employed. The poet claimed to have "written a peice to him of ye punick warr which [Ralegh] altered and set in his booke." This is only one example of Jonson's interest in history; another is his poem (*Underwood* 24) which prefaced Ralegh's work when it was published in 1614, a poem that echoes Cicero in calling history "The light of Truth, and life of Memorie."

Clearly Jonson saw his own vocation as similar to the historian's, a point obvious from another poem from 1614 praising John Selden (*Underwood* 14). This poem, typically, celebrates not only a friend and friendship but also the courage and acuity essential to all good writing. Jonson writes interestingly of the complexities of praise—the conflict one could feel when asked to assess a friend's work, the mistakes one could make when passing any public judgment. He admits that he has "too oft preferr'd / Men past their termes, and prais'd some names too much," but he contends that it was "with purpose to have made them such." His praise is hortatory: its function is to inspire as much as to commend, to obligate as much as to reward. Although he admits to having sometimes been "deceiv'd," he now claims to "turne a sharper eye / Upon my selfe, and aske to whom? and why? / And what I write? and vexe it many dayes / Before men get a verse: much

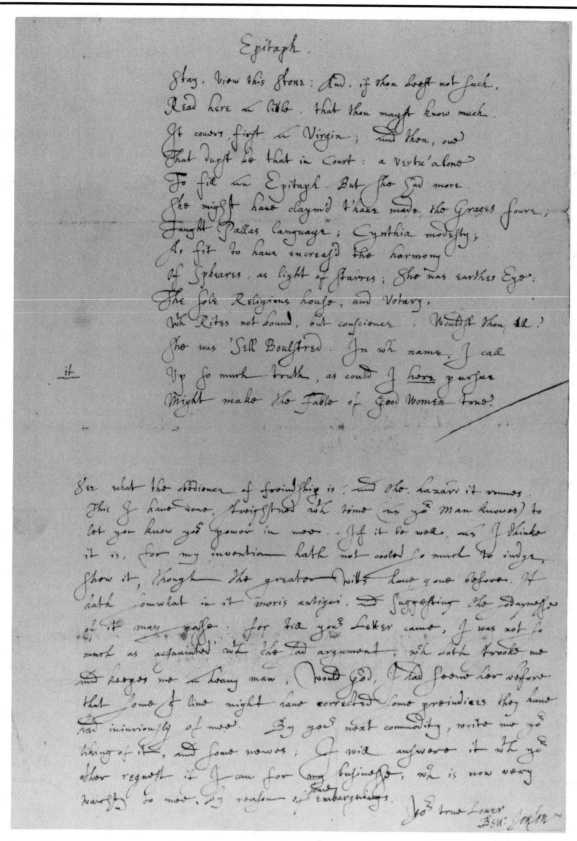

Page from a letter to George Garrard, in which Jonson included his epitaph on Cecilia Bulstrode (Lowell Autograph Collection, Houghton Library, Harvard University)

lesse a Praise." Selden, of course, passes muster, and the qualities he admired in Selden and in Selden's work were qualities he also sought to attain. The poem is completely typical in its style, techniques, themes, structure, and tone, exhibiting all the directness and subtlety, all the plainness and complexity, all the self-conscious deliberation and selfless idealism one associates with Jonson's best and most characteristic works.

By the time the poem to Selden appeared, Jonson had long been home. He had witnessed the accidental burning of the Globe theater on 29 June 1613, and by the end of that year he had resumed writing courtly entertainments. More significantly, by the fall of 1614 he had also resumed writing plays, producing *Bartholomew Fair*, one of his most original and memorable comedies. This was followed during the next two years by more masques and another comedy, *The Devil Is an Ass* in 1616. By this time Jonson could look back on nearly two decades of steady, innovative writing and unusual social prominence. His status was doubly acknowledged in 1616 when James awarded him one hundred marks per year for life and when his massive folio *Workes* was published. No volume like it had ever appeared before in England; it was the physical testimony to the change Jonson had helped effect in the public standing of poets. Although he had apparently planned to publish his *Epigrams* as early as 1612 (and may in fact have done so), the poems, plays, and masques printed in the *Workes*, combined with his pension, suggested that by 1616 (coincidentally the year of Shakespeare's death), he had become his nation's unofficial poet laureate.

This did not shield him, of course, from all misfortune; if anything, it made him more conspicuous. He later told Drummond that he had been "accused" for personal satire detected in *The Devil Is an Ass*, and that the king had "desyred him to conceal it." Moreover, when *Pleasure Reconciled to Virtue*—now considered one of his best masques—was first performed in January 1618, it was widely attacked; even the king expressed disappointment. The work's poetry was condemned, and one courtier said that Jonson "should retourne to his ould trade of bricke laying." Twenty years of achievement had not erased the stigma of his background—a fact he could never forget. When he decided to walk to Scotland later that year, he was accused of doing so "for profit," and he told Drummond that he suspected that the poetaster John Taylor had been dispatched on a similar journey "to scorn him."

Whatever Jonson's motives, his visit to Scotland provided one of the best biographical records—Drummond's transcriptions of their conversations in late 1618 and early 1619. Drummond's Jonson is not unblemished, and scholars have often made excuses for the poet or denigrated his host. Yet it should hardly be surprising us that Jonson was human, and instead of being embarrassed, we should perhaps be glad to have so colorful and untouched a portrait of a great poet in something like his full complexity.

Drummond's notes offer many insights into Jonson's views of poetry and other poets. For instance, he called couplets the best sort of verses; other forms could seem "forced." Although unafraid to experiment (see *Forest* 14, for example), Jonson believed that style should serve sense, not obscure it. In fact, he reported that "he wrott all his [poetry] first jn prose," as Camden had taught him. Decorum, or appropriateness, was also important; he criticized many poets for making "every man speak as well as themselves"—a comment that helps explain his interest in dialect and jargon, especially in drama. He told Drummond that reading Quintilian "would tell me the faults of my Verses as if he had Lived with me," specifying that books 6-8 "were not only to be read but altogither digested." He memorably remarked "That Shaksperr wanted Arte"—one of several assessments of others that help define his own ideals. He said that some of Drummond's poems "smelled too much of ye schooles"—a statement balancing the one on Shakespeare by indicating that the art Jonson prized required skill but should also seem natural and unstrained.

In addition to their literary value, the *Conversations* also provide many interesting glimpses of Jonson's life and personality. One memorable event concerned a vision of his young son, whose death he had mourned in Epigram 45. Not long before the boy died in 1603, the poet imagined seeing him "w^t ye Marke of a bloodie crosse on his forehead." Amazed, he prayed, only to learn shortly in "letters from his wife of ye death of yt Boy jn ye plague." The boy had "appeared to him . . . of a Manlie shape & of yt Grouth that he thinks he shall be at the resurrection." Also interesting is his report that when it seemed Jonson might be executed for his involvement with *Eastward Ho*, performed in 1605, his "old Mother" claimed to have prepared him poison, and to prove "that she was no churle she told she minded first to have Drunk of it herself." Another time, Jonson admitted that "jn his youth" he had been "given to Venerie" (sexual promiscuity), and that he "thought the use of a maide, nothing jn comparison to ye wantoness of a wyfe & would never haue ane other Mistress." Drummond notes that Jonson once deceived a woman by dressing up as "ane old Astrologer . . . jn a Longe Gowne & a whyte beard," and the poet famously told his host that "he heth consumed a whole night jn lying looking to his great toe, about which he hath seen tartars & turks Romans and Carthaginions feight in his imagination." Comments like these again suggest the complex traits also visible in his works—his profundity and playfulness, his seriousness and imaginative intensity.

Drummond considered Jonson "a great lover and praiser of himself, a contemner and scorner of others, . . . jealous of every word and action of those about him (especiallie after drink) which is one of the Elements jn which he liveth) a dissembler of ill parts which raigne jn him, a bragger of some good that he wanteth." Surely it would not have been easy to have Jonson as a houseguest for weeks at a time. Drummond's harsh assessment can be corroborated from many other sources, but so can his comments about Jonson's playfulness, good humor, and capacity for love and generosity. It was Drummond himself, after all, who noted that Sir John Roe "died jn [Jonson's] armes" and that the poet paid for his funeral, and it was he who reported Jonson's willingness to "destroy" many of his own poems for the chance to have written one by Robert Southwell that he particularly admired. The notes alone suggest Drummond's personal regard for Jonson, and John Taylor remarked that in Scotland Jonson was "among Noblemen and Gentlemen that knowe his true worth, and their owne honours, where with much respectiue loue he is worthily entertained." The picture of Jonson that emerges from the *Conversations* is surely complicated, but it is, perhaps, all the more valuable for that reason.

Jonson's own whimsical self-portrait, sent to Drummond, describes a man of "Six and forty yeares," with a "hundred of Gray haires," a "Mountaine belly," and a "rockye face." Although his skin had been mocked years earlier, apparently as a youth he was lean. Now middle-aged, he weighed well over two hundred pounds. By his own testimony, he fluctuated between 250 and 270 pounds. However, he enjoyed joking about his appearance, and he does so in several late poems (most memorably in *Underwood* 52). His physical shortcomings provide much of the humor in his important sequence of ten lyrics, "A Celebration of Charis" (*Underwood* 2). Most of these seem to have been written during the second decade of James's reign. Like many of Jonson's works, they deal with body and soul, flesh and spirit, the material and ethereal, the real and the ideal, but these poems are especially concerned with love. Jonson himself had already attempted to explain "Why I write not of Love" (*Forest* 1), and the biographer John Aubrey later noted a lady's comment that "B. J. never writes of Love, or if he does, does it not naturally." In fact, however, he did write of love, especially in the masques and later plays, and love is a theme of many lyrics collected in *Underwood*.

The themes and attitudes expressed in the love poems vary greatly, as do their forms and devices. "A Celebration of Charis" is notoriously complex, and critics have disagreed significantly about its tones and meanings. It centers on old "Ben's" courtship of a younger woman, although links to Jonson's life seem less certain than his desire to experiment with conventions. The short lines and tripping rhythms give the lyrics charming energy; the tone is by turns playful and thoughtful, serious and silly, parodic and biting, and Jonson reveals a capacity for humor and lyricism worth remembering when reading his more lofty, satiric, or prosaic verse. The poems show a gift for poetic storytelling, although the outcome of this story seems deliberately unclear. The poet's own attitudes are ambiguous, but it is clear that the sequence must have been as much fun to write as it is to read.

The same humor seems characteristic of many of his poems on love, which vary widely in mood and manner. *Underwood* 3 is a pastoral dialogue; *Underwood* 4 is an impassioned song. In *Underwood* 5, a woman defends women, while *Underwood* 6 justifies feminine inconstancy. *Underwood* 7 describes "A Nymphs Passion," whereas *Underwood* 8 discusses love and death. *Underwood* 9 mocks Jonson's physique, *Underwood* 10 attacks jealousy, and *Underwood* 11 recounts an erotic dream. *Underwood* 18 describes the uncertainties of love, while *Underwood* 19 describes feminine beauty and celebrates marriage, just as beauty and ideal love are extolled in *Underwood* 22. *Underwood* 27 reveals Jonson's familiarity with the works of past love poets, while *Underwood* 36 is one of many poems describing the traits of Cupid. *Underwood* 38, 40, and 41 are love elegies so much in Donne's witty style that some readers have wondered who really wrote them, while *Underwood* 42 is utterly characteristic of Jonson in mixing idealism and biting satire. Finally, in *Underwood* 56, addressed "To my Lady Covell," Jonson describes himself as being "fat and old, / Laden with Bellie," a man who "doth hardly approach / His friends, but to breake Chaires, or cracke a Coach."

By the time he returned to England in 1619, he was becoming a weighty figure in other ways. With the help of Pembroke, who was chancellor of Oxford University, Jonson was made an honorary M.A., and his absence at court had apparently been "regretted." His resumption of masque writing led George Villiers, Earl of Buckingham (and James's favorite), to commission *The Gypsies Metamorphosed* in 1621. This was performed three times, and for it Jonson received one hundred pounds—far more than his yearly pension. He was a rumored candidate for the Royal Academy then being discussed, and by autumn 1621 he was being considered for a knighthood. In October he was nominated to receive the reversion of the office of master of the revels. This post would have allowed him to supervise dramatists and their manuscripts if he had lived long enough to receive it, but the warrant alone suggests the trust, esteem, and influence he now enjoyed at court.

Jonson knew, however, how slippery good fortune could prove. His own career had shown this, and 1621 provided another example in the fall of Sir Francis Bacon. By January, when Jonson composed *Underwood* 51 in his honor, Bacon was lord chancellor and baron Verulam, and would soon be viscount St. Albans. Jonson calls for "a deep-crown'd-Bowle, that I may sing / In raysing him the wisdome of my King," but parliamentary critics soon charged Bacon with corruption, and by autumn his career lay in ruins. Nor was Jonson's own fortune completely firm. In the summer of 1623 he felt excluded from plans to welcome Prince Charles's intended Spanish bride, the Infanta, to England, particularly since Jones, his old rival, had been given a prominent role. His bitterness boiled over in *Underwood* 47, "An Epistle answering to one that asked to be Sealed of the Tribe of Ben." Jonson attacks corrupt but prosperous courtiers and other men-about-town, vowing to "Live to that point I will, for which I am man, / And dwell as in my Center, as I can, / Still looking to, and ever loving heaven; / With reverence using all the gifts then[ce] given."

This ideal of disciplined self-containment was central to his thinking but difficult to achieve; he could rarely ignore the need to compete, however much he disdained it. In the "Tribe of Ben" epistle as in other poems, friendship offers an alternative to competition, and it is in fact a major theme of the *Underwood* collection. It figures prominently, for instance, in *Underwood* 15, written to persuade a friend to war. Although Jonson generally endorsed James's pacifism, war is here depicted as the opposite of "vitious ease," rousing "Mans buried honour." In fact, the poem satirizes corruption far more than it glorifies war; it catalogues Jonson's many social convictions, concluding that he "Who falls for love of God, shall rise a Starre." *Underwood* 17 defines ideal friendship by proclaiming that "Nothing there / Is done for gaine: If 't be, 'tis not sincere," while *Underwood* 26 counsels a "High-spirited friend" about the virtue of self-control. *Underwood* 37 admits that virtue is difficult to achieve, and also describes the obligations and balance friendship entails. *Underwood* 45 similarly declares that " 'Tis vertue alone, or nothing, that knits friends" and stresses the need to inspect potential friends closely. As Jonson aged, friendship seems to have become even more important to him, and some of his best later poems celebrate its joys while defining its demands. True friends provided a standard against which patrons and rivals, like those in the "Tribe of Ben" epistle, could be judged.

Not long after writing that bitter poem, Jonson suffered another blow: in autumn 1623 his house burned. The fire destroyed many of his manuscripts and books, but it also provoked one of his best and liveliest poems, "An Execration upon Vulcan," god of fire (*Underwood* 43). The poem shows Jonson at his stoic best, facing misfortune with astonishing good humor, but it also provides a very useful record of his literary activities in the years before the blaze. He claims he had written, for instance, a treatise on poetry, an English grammar, a poem about his trip to Scotland, a history of Henry V, and twenty-four years' worth of notes from his extensive reading. The grammar was rewritten, but the rest remains lost. If the notes taken from his reading were anything like his later prose *Discoveries* (1640), they would have been exceptionally interesting, and the loss of his criticism, narrative verse, and history is lamentable. Yet the "execration" wastes little time lamenting. By turns boisterous, funny, and satiric, Jonson uses the poem to champion his various ideals in a tone that turns apparent tragedy into a personal and artistic triumph. Like the well-known "Fit of Rime against Rime" (*Underwood* 29), this poem highlights the good-spirited playfulness of much of his best writing.

A different tone is audible in the two famous tributes to William Shakespeare that preface the posthumous 1623 folio (*Ungathered Verse* 25, 26). Although Jonson said that he "lov'd" Shakespeare "on this side Idolatry," he did not always find his friend's writings flawless. *Ungathered Verse* 26 calls him the "Soule of the Age" yet also declares that "He was not of an age, but for all time!" But the work also stresses the labor and discipline (not just natural genius) great poetry required, and it praises Shakespeare's "well torned, and true-filed lines." It was Shakespeare's artistry as much as his native gifts that allowed him to impress "*Eliza*, and our *Iames*," and Jonson's poem commemorates both his friend's life and art and their shared history.

One part of that history would soon end. King James, under whom Jonson's career had flourished, died on 27 March 1625 and was succeeded by his son Charles, more polished but more distant. Jonson seems to have respected both men, but he must have wondered how the transition might affect him, and he could not have been encouraged when Buckingham, still the favorite, engineered the dismissal of John Williams—James's protegé, Jonson's patron, Pembroke's ally, and Bacon's successor as Lord Keeper. *Underwood* 61 laments his fall; it depicts the court as a place where "whisper'd Counsells, and those only thrive," and it bemoans the contemporary "flood" of "riot, and consumption." Williams, despite his fall, is described as the "Favorite of God"—perhaps a jibe at Buckingham, whose enormous power had long aroused misgivings. When Buckingham was assassinated in 1628 by John Felton, Jonson was suspected of writing "To his confined friend Mr Felton," a poem which praised the deed. Jonson denied upon "his christianity & hope of salvation" having written or even copied the verses, and he claimed to regard them with "detestation." In any case, it would hardly have been surprising if, by 1625, he had come to share the widespread distrust of Buckingham, whose influence on Charles many considered pernicious. With the death of James, Jonson's own prominence at court began to wane. For whatever reasons, masque commissions ceased for several years, and by February 1626

the aging poet had returned to the public stage with a new comedy, *The Staple of News*.

Jonson now relied increasingly on plays to support himself. Such works as *The New Inn* (staged in early 1629), *The Magnetic Lady* (staged in autumn 1632), and *A Tale of a Tub* (staged in May 1633) are not among his best, although each has its merits and defenders. Yet audience reaction was mixed at best, and *The New Inn* was widely attacked. One critic even mocked the paralyzing stroke Jonson had suffered in 1628, and in an angry "Ode to himselfe," the poet vowed once more to "leave the lothed stage," promising instead to sing "The glories of thy *King*, / His zeal to *God*, and his just awe o'er men." But another poem, appended to *The New Inn*, suggested disappointment in Charles's patronage and may have prompted the gift of one hundred pounds for which he thanked the king in *Underwood* 62. Many of the late poems celebrate the royal family and important courtiers (*Underwood* 63-67, 72-79, 82), and by the start of the 1630s Jonson seems to have regained some of his old standing. On 26 March 1630 his annuity was increased to one hundred pounds, and masques or entertainments were commissioned in 1631, 1633, and 1634.

Perhaps the best of Jonson's later poems is his ode celebrating two young friends, Sir Lucius Cary and Sir Henry Morison (*Underwood* 70). Morison died in 1629, and Jonson's poem meditates not only on friendship—always one of his central concerns—but on the goals of art and life. Imitating Pindar, the poem is both complex and ambitious, intimate and revealing. Jonson celebrates a good life as if it were a good poem—"ample, full, and round, / In weight, in measure, number, sound," contending that "In small proportions, we just beautie see: / And in short measures, life may perfect bee." He disarmingly alludes to his own "feares" and "miseries" and to his recent embarrassments "on the Stage," as if he meant to remind himself, as much as his readers, of the values life should exemplify. He anticipates his own death and extols the virtue of Cary and Morison, whose "*Friendship*, in deed, was written, not in words: / And with the heart not pen." Yet his own poem, of course, resolves the tensions these lines imply: written with both heart and pen, it functions both as deed and words, manifesting the very virtue it praises.

This Cary-Morison ode is only one of a variety of challenging poems Jonson wrote in his final decade. It would be wrong to think of these

Portrait of Jonson engraved by Robert Vaughan no later than 1627

years as a period of total decline. The various poems on members of the royal family are interesting in their own ways, as are the poems addressed to such important later patrons as William Cavendish, Earl of Newcastle, or Richard Weston, the controversial earl of Portland. Moreover, the lengthy "Epithalamion" written to celebrate the marriage of Portland's son (*Underwood* 75) is more complex and intriguing than has often been recognized. The same might be said of the fragmentary sequence "Eupheme" (*Underwood* 84), written to commemorate Venetia Digby, the deceased wife of Sir Kenelm Digby, Jonson's patron and friend. Ambitious in their own ways are the lively invectives the poet directed against his old antagonist Inigo Jones (*Ungathered Verse* 34-36); these and other works from his last ten years show that he had not lost his touch for ferocious satire. The sting of these poems derives in

part from Jonson's recognition that Jones was now ascendant, and in one of his last datable poems, published in 1635, Jonson wonders whether he will even any longer "be heard" (*Ungathered Verse* 42). Yet the commendatory poem in which he raises this question shows that his opinion was still valued, and the poem itself is utterly typical in its commitment to "*Truth*," in its satirical verve, and in its professions of careful judgment. Clearly Jonson was still valued by many readers, and following his death on 16 August 1637, he was escorted to his grave in Westminster Abbey by a crowd that included "all or the greatest part of the nobilitie and gentry then in town." (Although 6 August 1637 was long regarded to be the date of Jonson's death, Wayne H. Phelps has concluded, "Ben Jonson appears to have died about the middle of August 1637, rather than the beginning of that month.") Within a year a volume of elegies, *Jonsonus Virbius* (1638), had been issued to celebrate his memory; in content and style, these poems testify to the force of his personality and literary influence.

The writings Jonson left behind included not only his many poems, plays, masques, and entertainments, but also a collection of prose notes entitled *Timber: or Discoveries* (1640). Often derived from his voluminous reading, these notes offer many insights into his thinking about poetry and its social contexts. This is especially true of the work's concluding section, in which Jonson follows Aristotle in claiming that the purpose of poetry is to express human life "in fit measure, numbers, and harmony." A poem "is the worke of the Poet; the end, and fruit of his labour, and studye. *Poesy* is his skill, or Crafte of making." It is "the Queene of Arts: which had her Originall from heaven"; it has been found in all nations "that profess'd Civility." The study of poetry "offers to mankinde a certaine rule, and Patterne of living well, and happily," since "it nourisheth, and instructeth our Youth; delights our Age; adornes our prosperity; comforts our Adversity; entertaines us at home; keepes us company abroad, travailes with us; . . . insomuch as the wisest and best learned have thought her the absolute Mistresse of manners, and neerest of kin to Vertue." Poetry is "a dulcet, and gentle *Philosophy*, which leades on, and guides us by the hand to Action, with a ravishing delight, and incredible Sweetnes." Poetic talent is formed "by nature, by exercise, by imitation, by Studie," and the poet, "as by a divine Instinct . . . utters somewhat above a mortall mouth." Yet the poet must be disciplined; he must "bring all to the forge, and file, againe; tourne it a newe." He must imitate the best of his predecessors, but not in any slavish fashion. Rather, he must "draw forth out of the best, and choisest flowers, with the Bee, and turne all into Honey, worke it into one relish, and savour: ... observe, how the best writers have imitated, and follow them.... Hee must read many; but, ever the best, and choisest: those, that can teach him any thing, hee must ever account his masters, and reverence."

Words like these, and the work in which they are embedded, offer clear evidence of Jonson's poetic ideals, but those ideals are also implicit in nearly everything he wrote and in the life he tried to lead. The *Discoveries* show how seriously Jonson took poetry, but his whole career suggests the same. Thanks to that career, poets and poetry attained a higher stature in English public life than perhaps at any point before. Jonson was above all a social poet; he tried to use his art to transform his society, but in the process he helped transform the purpose and social standing of his art.

Bibliographies:

Samuel A. Tannenbaum, *Ben Jonson: A Concise Bibliography* (New York: Privately printed, 1938) and Samuel A. Tannenbaum and Dorothy R. Tannenbaum, *Supplement to a Concise Bibliography of Ben Jonson* (New York: Privately printed, 1947); both republished as volume 4 of *Elizabethan Bibliographies* (Port Washington, N.Y.: Kennikat Press, 1967);

D. Heywood Brock and James M. Welsh, *Ben Jonson: A Quadricentennial Bibliography, 1947-1972* (Metuchen, N.J.: Scarecrow, 1974);

James Hogg, *Recent Research on Ben Jonson* (Salzburg, Austria: Institut für Englische Sprache und Literatur, 1978);

Walter D. Lehrman, Delores J. Sarafinski, and Elizabeth Savage, *The Plays of Ben Jonson: A Reference Guide* (Boston: G. K. Hall, 1980);

David C. Judkins, *The Nondramatic Works of Ben Jonson: A Reference Guide* (Boston: G. K. Hall, 1982).

Biographies:

Marchette Chute, *Ben Jonson of Westminster* (New York: Dutton, 1953);

Rosalind Miles, *Ben Jonson: His Life and Work* (London & New York: Routledge & Kegan Paul, 1986);

David Riggs, *Ben Jonson: A Life* (Cambridge, Mass. & London: Harvard University Press, 1989).

References:

Eckhard Auberlen, *The Commonwealth of Wit: The Writer's Image and His Strategies of Self-Representation in Elizabethan Literature* (Tübingen: Gunter Narr Verlag, 1984);

J. B. Bamborough, *Ben Jonson* (London: Hutchinson, 1970);

Jonas A. Barish, ed., *Ben Jonson: A Collection of Critical Essays* (Englewood Cliffs, N.J.: Prentice-Hall, 1963);

Anne Barton, *Ben Jonson, Dramatist* (Cambridge: Cambridge University Press, 1984);

L. A. Beaurline, "Ben Jonson and the Illusion of Completeness," *PMLA*, 84 (1969): 51-59;

Gerald Eades Bentley, *Shakespeare and Jonson. Their Reputations in the Seventeenth Century Compared*, 2 volumes (Chicago: University of Chicago Press, 1945);

William Blissett, Julian Patrick, and R. W. Van Fossen, eds., *A Celebration of Ben Jonson* (Toronto: University of Toronto Press, 1973);

J. F. Bradley and J. Q. Adams, *The Jonson Allusion-Book, 1597-1700* (New Haven: Yale University Press, 1922);

Jennifer Brady, " 'Beware the Poet': Authority and Judgment in Jonson's *Epigrammes*," *Studies in English Literature*, 23 (Winter 1983): 95-112;

William E. Cain, "The Place of the Poet in Jonson's 'To Penshurst' and 'To my Muse,' " *Criticism*, 21 (Winter 1979): 34-48;

Cain, "Self and Others in Two Poems by Ben Jonson," *Studies in Philology*, 80 (Spring 1983): 163-182;

Paul M. Cubeta, "Ben Jonson's Religious Lyrics," *Journal of English and Germanic Philology*, 62 (1963): 96-110;

Richard Dutton, *Ben Jonson: To the First Folio* (Cambridge: Cambridge University Press, 1983);

Robert C. Evans, *Ben Jonson and the Poetics of Patronage* (Lewisburg, Pa.: Bucknell University Press, 1989);

Evans, *Jonson, Lipsius, and the Politics of Renaissance Stoicism* (Wakefield, N.H.: Longwood, 1992);

Anne Ferry, *All in War with Time: Love Poetry of Shakespeare, Donne, Jonson, Marvell* (Cambridge: Harvard University Press, 1975);

Richard Finkelstein, "Ben Jonson's Ciceronian Rhetoric of Friendship," *Journal of Medieval and Renaissance Studies*, 16 (Spring 1986): 103-124;

Stanley Fish, "Authors-Readers: Jonson's Community of the Same," *Representations*, no. 7 (Summer 1984): 26-58;

Alastair Fowler, "The Silva Tradition and Jonson's *The Forrest*," in *Poetic Traditions of the English Renaissance*, edited by Maynard Mack and George DeForest Lord (New Haven: Yale University Press, 1982);

Harris Friedberg, "Ben Jonson's Poetry: Pastoral, Georgic, Epigram," *English Literary Renaissance*, 4 (Winter 1974): 111-135;

Judith K. Gardiner, *Craftsmanship in Context: The Development of Ben Jonson's Poetry* (The Hague: Mouton, 1975);

Thomas M. Greene, "Ben Jonson and the Centered Self," *Studies in English Literature*, 10 (Spring 1970): 325-348;

Greene, *The Light in Troy: Imitation and Discovery in Renaissance Poetry* (New Haven: Yale University Press, 1982);

Achsah Guibbory, "The Poet as Mythmaker: Ben Jonson's Poetry of Praise," *Clio*, 5 (Spring 1976): 315-329;

Richard Helgerson, *Self-Crowned Laureates: Spenser, Jonson, Milton, and the Literary System* (Berkeley: University of California Press, 1983);

W. H. Herendeen, "Like a Circle Bounded in Itself: Jonson, Camden, and the Strategies of Praise," *Journal of Medieval and Renaissance Studies*, 11 (Fall 1981): 137-167;

G. R. Hibbard, "The Country House Poem of the Seventeenth Century," *Journal of the Warburg and Courtauld Institute*, 19 (1956): 159-174;

George Burke Johnston, *Ben Jonson: Poet* (New York: Columbia University Press, 1945);

Jonathan Z. Kamholtz, "Ben Jonson's *Epigrammes* and Poetic Occasions," *Studies in English Literature*, 23 (Winter 1983): 77-94;

Kamholtz, "Ben Jonson's Green World: Structure and Imaginative Unity in *The Forest*," *Studies in Philology*, 78 (Spring 1978): 170-193;

W. David Kay, "The Christian Wisdom of Ben Jonson's 'On My First Sonne,'" *Studies in English Literature*, 11 (Winter 1971): 125-136;

William R. Keast, ed., *Seventeenth Century English Poetry: Modern Essays in Criticism*, revised edition (London: Oxford University Press, 1971);

Joseph John Kelly, "Ben Jonson's Politics," *Renaissance and Reformation*, new series 7 (August 1983): 192-215;

William Kerrigan, "Ben Jonson Full of Shame and Scorn," *Studies in the Literary Imagination*, 6 (April 1973): 199-217.

Alexander Leggatt, *Ben Jonson: His Vision and His Art* (London: Methuen, 1981);

John Lemly, "Masks and Self-Portraits in Jonson's Late Poetry," *English Literary History*, 44 (Summer 1977): 248-266;

Joseph Loewenstein, "The Jonsonian Corpulence: or, The Poet as Mouthpiece," *English Literary History*, 53 (Fall 1986): 491-518;

Hugh Maclean, ed., *Ben Jonson and the Cavalier Poets* (New York: Norton, 1974);

Arthur F. Marotti, "All About Jonson's Poetry," *English Literary History*, 39 (June 1972): 208-237;

Katharine Eisaman Maus, *Ben Jonson and the Roman Frame of Mind* (Princeton: Princeton University Press, 1984);

William A. McClung, *The Country House in English Renaissance Poetry* (Berkeley: University of California Press, 1977);

David McPherson, *Ben Jonson's Library and Marginalia: An Annotated Catalogue: Texts and Studies, 1974*, special issue of *Studies in Philology*, 71 (December 1974);

Earl Miner, *The Cavalier Mode from Jonson to Cotton* (Princeton: Princeton University Press, 1971);

Richard Newton, *Foundations of Ben Jonson's Poetic Style: Epigrammes and The Forest* (New York: Garland, 1988);

J. G. Nichols, *The Poetry of Ben Jonson* (New York: Barnes & Noble, 1969);

David Norbrook, *Poetry and Politics in the English Renaissance* (London: Routledge & Kegan Paul, 1984);

George Parfitt, *Ben Jonson: Public Poet and Private Man* (London: Dent, 1976);

Edward B. Patridge, "Jonson's *Epigrammes*: The Named and the Nameless," *Studies in the Literary Imagination*, 6 (April 1973): 153-198;

Annabel Patterson, *Censorship and Interpretation: The Conditions of Writing and Reading in Early Modern England* (Madison: University of Wisconsin Press, 1984);

E. Pearlman, "Ben Jonson: An Anatomy," *English Literary Renaissance*, 9 (Autumn 1979); 364-394;

Richard S. Peterson, *Imitation and Praise in the Poems of Ben Jonson* (New Haven: Yale University Press, 1981);

Wayne H. Phelps, "The Date of Ben Jonson's Death," *Notes and Queries*, 27 (April 1980): 146-149;

G. W. Pigman III, "Suppressed Grief in Jonson's Funeral Poetry," *English Literary Renaissance*, 13 (Spring 1983): 203-220;

J. C. A. Rathmell, "Jonson, Lord Lisle, and Penshurst," *English Literary Renaissance*, 1 (Autumn 1971): 250-260;

James A. Riddell, "The Arrangement of Ben Jonson's *Epigrammes*," *Studies in English Literature*, 27 (Winter 1987): 53-70;

Isabel Rivers, *The Poetry of Conservatism, 1600-1745: A Study of Poets and Public Affairs from Jonson to Pope* (Cambridge: Rivers Press, 1973);

George E. Rowe, *Distinguishing Jonson: Imitation, Rivalry, and the Direction of a Dramatic Career* (Lincoln: University of Nebraska Press, 1988);

Bruce R. Smith, "Ben Jonson's *Epigrammes*: Portrait-Gallery, Theater, Commonwealth," *Studies in English Literature*, 14 (Winter 1974): 91-109;

Claude J. Summers and Ted-Larry Pebworth, *Ben Jonson* (Boston: Twayne, 1979);

Summers and Pebworth, eds., *Classic and Cavalier: Essays on Jonson and the Sons of Ben* (Pittsburgh: University of Pittsburgh Press, 1982);

Summers and Pebworth, eds., *"The Muses Common- weale": Poetry and Politics in the Seventeenth Century"* (Columbia: University of Missouri Press, 1988);

Joseph Summers, *The Heirs of Donne and Jonson* (London: Oxford University Press, 1970);

Wesley Trimpi, *Ben Jonson's Poems: A Study in the Plain Style* (Stanford, Cal.: Stanford University Press, 1962);

Sara J. van den Berg, *The Action of Ben Jonson's Poetry* (Newark: University of Delaware Press, 1987);

Lawrence Venuti, "Why Jonson Wrote Not of Love," *Journal of Medieval and Renaissance Studies*, 12 (Fall 1982): 195-220;

Don E. Wayne, *Penshurst: The Semiotics of Place and the Poetics of History* (Madison: University of Wisconsin Press, 1984);

Wayne, "Poetry and Power in Ben Jonson's *Epigrammes*: The Naming of 'Facts' or the Figuring of Social Relations," *Renaissance and Modern Studies*, 23 (1979): 79-103;

Robert Wiltenburg, *Ben Jonson and Self-Love: The Subtlest Maze of All* (Columbia: University of Missouri Press, 1990);

Jack D. Winner, "Ben Jonson's *Epigrammes* and the Conventions of Formal Verse Satire," *Studies in English Literature*, 23 (Winter 1983): 61-76;

R. V. Young, Jr., "Style and Structure in Jonson's *Epigrammes*," *Criticism*, 17 (Summer 1975): 201-222.

Aemilia Lanyer

(January 1569 - April 1645)

Susanne Woods
Franklin and Marshall College

BOOK: *Salve Deus Rex Judæorum* (London: Printed by Valentine Simmes for Richard Bonian, 1611).

Edition: *The Poems of Aemilia Lanyer*, edited by Susanne Woods (New York: Oxford University Press, 1992).

Aemilia Lanyer was the first woman writing in English to produce a substantial volume of poetry designed to be printed and to attract patronage. The volume comprises a series of poems to individual patrons, two short prose dedications, the title poem on Christ's Passion (viewed entirely from a female perspective), and the first country-house poem printed in English, "The Description of Cooke-ham," which precedes the publication of Ben Jonson's "To Penshurst" by five years. Lanyer's poetry shows evidence of a practiced skill. The volume is also arguably the first genuinely feminist publication in England: all of its dedicatees are women, the poem on the Passion specifically argues the virtues of women as opposed to the vices of men, and Lanyer's own authorial voice is assured and unapologetic.

She was baptized Aemilia Bassano on 27 January 1569, daughter of court musician Baptist Bassano, whose will describes him as a "native of Venice," and Margaret Johnson, his common-law wife. Though her father died when she was seven, Aemilia grew up with access to Elizabethan court circles, and spent some of her early years in the household of Susan Bertie, Countess of Kent. By the time Aemilia's mother died, Aemilia, who was eighteen, was sufficiently in court favor to attract the attention of Henry Carey, first Lord Hunsdon, Queen Elizabeth's lord chamberlain, whose mistress she remained for several years. Despite the forty-five-year age difference, Lanyer looked back on her time with Hunsdon with great fondness, and apparently resented being married off to Alphonso Lanyer, a court musician, when she became pregnant by the lord chamberlain in 1592. Her son, Henry, was born early in the following year. A daughter

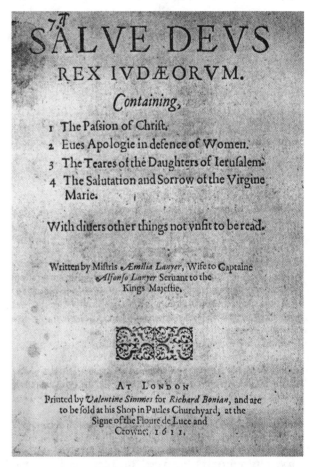

Title page for Lanyer's only book, whose title, she said, "was delivered unto me in sleepe many yeares before I had any intent to write in this maner"

by Alphonso, Odillya, was born in December 1598, but lived only ten months.

Astrologer Simon Forman, whom Lanyer visited several times during 1597, recorded in his diary that Lanyer was concerned about her husband's prospects for a knighthood or other advancement (he was a soldier on an expedition with Robert Devereux, second Earl of Essex, during her visits to Forman); that she was subject to miscarriages; that she had enjoyed the good favor of Queen Elizabeth and missed her days at court; and that Forman found her attractive. In fact, he made an effort to have sexual relations with her, and, although she was friendly, she apparently did not allow him to consummate the relationship. The only extant physical description of her comes from Forman, and it is hardly a full portrait: "she hath a wart or mole," he wrote, "in the pit of the throat or near it." The modern historian A. L. Rowse, who misreads some of Forman's diaries, argues from them and from Lanyer's association with the lord chamberlain that Lanyer was William Shakespeare's "dark lady," assuming that her Italian background gave her a dark complexion and that her flirtations with Forman showed her to be a loose woman. Although the world of middle-class artistic servants of the court was not large, and Lanyer, as the lord chamberlain's mistress, may well have encountered some of the Lord Chamberlain's Men (the theatrical troupe that included Shakespeare), there is no evidence that she knew Shakespeare.

Central to Lanyer's published work are her associations with Margaret, Countess of Cumberland, whom Lanyer claimed as her principal inspiration and patron, and Margaret's daughter, Lady Anne Clifford. "The Description of Cookeham" celebrates a sojourn Lanyer enjoyed with these ladies at a country place then in the possession of Margaret's brother, William Russell of Thornhaugh, and praises its extensive grounds as a lost paradise for a learned and religious female community. The details and exact date of the visit are obscure, but it occurred sometime during the first decade of the seventeenth century, and Lanyer credits the visits and the countess with inspiring her to write religious verse.

Lanyer's volume of poems, *Salve Deus Rex Judæorum*, has no discernible early reception history, although the survival of versions in which some of the dedicatory poems have been omitted argues care in targeting her readership. One such volume was apparently given by the countess of Cumberland to Prince Henry, heir apparent to the throne, and another was given by Alphonso Lanyer to Thomas Jones, Archbishop of Dublin, with whom he had served in Ireland. The book did not make Aemilia Lanyer's fortune. After Alphonso died in 1613, she found herself in protracted legal battles with his relatives over the income from a hay-and-grain patent he had received from King James in 1604. From 1617 to 1619 she ran a school in the wealthy London suburb of St. Giles in the Fields, where she sought "to teach and educate the children of di-

vers persons of worth and understanding," but she lost the lease to the building she was using, and there is no evidence that she attempted to teach again, nor is anything more known about what she taught or whom.

Lanyer spent her later years near her son's family. Henry, who had become a court flautist, married Joyce Mansfield in 1623 and had two children, Mary, born in 1627, and Henry, born in 1630. After Alphonso's death in 1613, Aemilia Lanyer continued to pursue rights to the hay-and-grain patent on behalf of herself and later her grandchildren. She was listed as a "pensioner," a designation indicating a steady income. In her seventy-six years she had seen most of the reigns of Elizabeth I (1558-1603) and Charles I (1625-1649), as well as all of the intervening reign of James I (1603-1625).

A middle-class woman of no fortune, Lanyer nonetheless enjoyed the attention of some important Elizabethans—the queen, Lord Hunsdon, the countess of Kent, and the countess of Cumberland. Both the entries from Forman's diaries and Lanyer's own poetry suggest that she was a woman of considerable intelligence and spirit. Although James's reign offered the Lanyers some financial security through Alphonso's patent, it was not a reign sympathetic to women, particularly women who spoke out publicly. It is impossible to know whether Lanyer received any substantial patronage from her remarkable book of poetry, but the evidence of her legal battles strongly suggests that she did not. Whether or not she continued to write, she apparently never attempted publication again.

Salve Deus Rex Judæorum, Lanyer's only book, was entered into the Stationers' Register on 2 October 1610 and published in 1611, the same year as the King James version of the Bible; John Donne's *First Anniversary*; several printings and reprintings of quarto plays by Shakespeare, Ben Jonson, and Christopher Marlowe; George Chapman's translation of Homer's *Iliad*; and the first collected edition of Edmund Spenser's works.

There are nine extant copies of the *Salve Deus*, five of which are complete or nearly so. They begin with eleven dedicatory pieces, nine in verse and two in prose, each of which celebrates in some fashion the achievements and community of women: "To the Queenes most Excellent Majestie" (to James's consort, Anne of Denmark); "To the Lady Elizabeths Grace" (to Princess Elizabeth Stuart); "To all vertuous Ladies in generall"; "To the Ladie Arabella" (to Arabella Stuart, James's perceived rival for the throne—a poem missing from three of the four incomplete volumes); "To the Ladie Susan, Countess Dowager of Kent, and daughter to the Duchesse of Suffolke"; "The Authors Dreame to the Ladie Marie, the Countesse Dowager of Pembrooke" (Mary Sidney, Countess of Pembroke, sister of Sir Philip Sidney, and a recognized author in her own right); "To the Ladie Lucie, Countesse of Bedford"; "To the Ladie Margaret Countesse Dowager of Cumberland" (in prose; Lanyer's principal dedicatee); "To the Ladie Katherine Countesse of Suffolke"; "To the Ladie Anne, Countesse of Dorcet" (Margaret's daughter, at the time fighting to inherit her late father's lands); "To the Vertuous Reader" (in prose).

This unapologetic creation of a community of good women for whom another woman is the spokesperson and eternizer is unusual and possibly unique in early-seventeenth-century England. During the sixteenth century Englishwomen found voices through the contradictory injunctions of Protestantism, which reasserted the traditional expectation of womanly silence and subservience but also affirmed the supremacy of individual conscience, even in women, to which God could speak directly and, in theory, allow exceptions to the general rule of silence. So the popular Protestant tract, Robert Cleaver's *A Godlie Forme of Household Government* (1598), allows a wife some authority over children and servants but demands full obedience to her husband. She must be "dutifull, faithfull, and loving" to him and silent if she disagrees with him. Yet women were increasingly free to translate religious works and write of their own religious experience, even to the extent of producing religious verse. The certification of her husband's name on the title page—where she is identified as "wife to Captaine Alfonso Lanyer"—gives Lanyer authority to speak outside the household, and her religious topic is broadly decorous.

Yet her work is different from its predecessors. Although Mary Sidney, Countess of Pembroke, had written in praise of Queen Elizabeth, and a great many male poets had dedicated work to the queen and such important patronesses as the countess of Pembroke and Lucy, Countess of Bedford, there is no other work of sustained and exclusive dedication to women patrons. Further, the central poem, the "Salve Deus" itself, has no generic predecessor among English women poets. The first identifiable woman religious poet writing in English was probably Anne Lok, who appended a poetic meditation on the fifty-first Psalm to her translation from the French of John Calvin's *Sermons upon the Songe that Ezechias made after he had bene sicke* (1560). The most important Elizabethan woman poet is certainly the countess of Pembroke, with her 107 psalm translations completing the sequence begun by her brother, Sir Philip Sidney. The countess's complex and sophisticated lyric versions of Psalms 44-150 were widely circulated in manuscript, and admired by Donne and Jonson, as well as Lanyer. Apart from these English psalm translations, there was one other notable work of religious verse written before Lanyer's: Elizabeth Melvill, Lady Culros, published *Ane Godlie Dreame* in Edinburgh in 1603. This dream allegory breaks the commitment to "translation" that English women's verse carried, but its intense focus on a single conscience sidesteps the issue of authority. By contrast, Lanyer's religious poem claims biblical and historical authority, and grants the viewpoint of women as much or greater authenticity as that of men.

Each of the three sections in the book has some generic connection with contemporary writing, though the connections are in many cases as distracting as they are illuminating.

The dedicatory poems situate Lanyer among the increasing number of professional poets who sought support through patronage. It was still usual for high-born writers to avoid the self-advertising "stigma of print," but it was acceptable for middle-class writers to claim attention—and assistance—by blazoning their patrons' virtues in verse. The patronage system was an early step in the professionalization of literature, but its economic impetus received social and intellectual force by claiming to reflect classical models and ideals. The classical epideictic tradition saw the poetry of praise as a means of affirming social and cultural values. Renaissance poets invoked that tradition and used it to enhance the value of their own role as definers of, as well as speakers for, their society.

It was the expected ritual for the lower-born poet to acknowledge unworthiness in speaking to his social betters, and to request and at the same time claim the forgiveness that sends the grace of worthiness to the poet from the exalted subject of his verse. By acknowledging social distance the poet bridges it, and by expressing humility the poet receives the grace of excellence. This is precisely what Lanyer does in her dedicatory

Margaret Russell, Countess of Cumberland, and her daughter, Anne Clifford, Countess of Dorset, Lanyer's principal patrons (left: portrait by an unknown artist; National Portrait Gallery, London; right: portrait attributed to Larkin; Collection of Lord Sackville)

verses, though her stance is complicated by her status as a woman as well as a commoner. It leads her to claim a special identity with her dedicatees, and to allow their dignity and high birth to assert the dignity and merit of all women. By collapsing her unworthiness as a woman into the general unworthiness all poets must acknowledge in their dedications to the high born, she renders the happenstance of gender as visible—and as ultimately inconsequential—as the male poet's happenstance of birth.

While the dedicatory poems provide Lanyer's principal authority for publishing her verse, her central topic, Christ's Passion, provides another authority. If women are not expected to write, they are expected to experience the joy and power of conversion and cannot be enjoined from expressing what God has spoken to them. Lanyer claims that her full conversion to Christ resulted from the influence of her main dedicatee, the countess dowager of Cumberland, and that other women had a godly influence on her, including the countess dowager of Kent (in whose household she had resided as an unrepentant young

woman), Queen Anne (through her godly example), and the countess of Pembroke (through her psalms).

The title poem, "Salve Deus Rex Judæorum" (Hail God, King of the Jews), is a subtle and complex work of 1,840 lines in ottava-rima, iambic-pentameter stanzas. For a woman to write authoritatively on so sacred a subject is unusual, but for her to revise fifteen hundred years of traditional commentary in the process is unheard of. A useful contrast may be made between Lanyer's "Salve Deus" and Queen Catherine Parr's *The Lamentacion of a Sinner* (1547), which set a model for women writing on religious matters. It includes some commentary on biblical texts, arguing a Protestant position on justification by faith among other things, but makes no challenge to the primacy of men. By contrast, the "Salve Deus" starts with personal references and has a strong polemical thrust, attacking the vanity and blindness of men and justifying women's right to be free of masculine subjugation. Many of the arguments are put in the voice of Pilate's wife, who, according to the Bible, warned her husband to have "nothing to do with that just man," Jesus (Matt. 27.19). Lanyer expands that brief warning, which Pilate ignores, into a lengthy "apologie," or defense and explanation, for Eve. Then she moves so seamlessly from the argument back to the narrative that it is difficult to tell where the voice of Pilate's wife ends and the voice of the narrator continues. Lanyer's confidence in a general female point of view makes the diffusion of narrative boundary appropriate.

"Salve Deus" begins with a short tribute to the late Queen Elizabeth I and moves to a lengthy and meditative dedication of the work to the countess dowager of Cumberland. Lanyer acknowledges that this poem is not "Those praisefull lines of that delightful place, / Which you commaunded me," possibly the celebration of Cookeham, but is instead a praise of Christ's "almightie love," which comforts the worthy countess in her unhappiness. The references to Margaret's unhappiness are probably to her alienation from her late husband, George Clifford, third Earl of Cumberland, and the legal battles with his relatives that followed his death in 1605. She championed the claims of her daughter, Cumberland's only heir, Anne Clifford, but King James and the court bureaucracy were willing only to negotiate cash settlements that were well short of Anne's full legal claim to the various Cumberland lands and titles. These offers both Margaret and Anne refused to accept, assuring the alienation and suffering that Lanyer chronicles in this poem and in "The Description of Cooke-ham." Lanyer offers Margaret the story of Christ's Passion as a comfort and assurance of God's love in the face of these worldly tribulations.

The version of the Passion Lanyer describes follows closely Matthew 26.30-28.10, the only version which includes the warning of Pilate's wife. She also borrows freely from other Gospels, taking references to women wherever they appear. (See Mark 14.26-16.11, Luke 22.39-24.12, and John 18.1-20.18.) Lanyer's version is woman centered throughout, chronicling female virtues and suffering as part of her strategy for comforting and praising the countess of Cumberland. Within that context, however, the story is a richly imagined version of the most central events of the Christian faith.

The Passion, or suffering, of Jesus Christ is the story that brings into vivid focus the basic elements of Christian theology. Lanyer retells the powerful story of Jesus' last night and day, meditating and expanding on the events from a distinctly female point of view. The story proper begins at line 330; Jesus' first action appears in line 333, when he "to *Mount Olives* went, though sore afraid." In Renaissance numerology 333 is a figure for the trinitarian God and a version of the number nine, which was thought to express God's self-contained perfection. Although Lanyer does not appear to work numerology into the poem throughout, as some of her contemporaries apparently did (Spenser's *Epithalamion*, published in 1595, is a famous example), it is possible that she deliberately chose to begin the action at this line.

Lines 330-480 tell the story of Jesus' retirement with his disciples to the Garden of Gethsemane on the Mount of Olives, where he prayed in a very human agony while his disciples, whom he urged to watch with him, could not keep themselves from falling asleep. Lines 481-632 describe the arrival of Judas and the soldiers of the high priest, Judas's betrayal of Jesus, Peter's attack on one of the soldiers, Jesus' rebuke of violence, and the frightened dispersal of the disciples. Lines 633-744 tell of the soldiers leading Jesus to the high priest, Caiaphas, who demands to know if Jesus is the Son of God. Jesus makes an affirmative though somewhat ambiguous answer, and Caiaphas determines to send him to Pontius Pilate, the only one with the authority to order an execution. The last two of these stanzas describe the remorse and suicide of Judas.

Line 745 begins the story of Jesus' appearance before Pilate and includes the words of Pilate's wife, with her apology for Eve, in lines 753-912. Sometime before line 912 the narrative voice seems to merge with that of Pilate's wife, but at line 913 the attention turns to the fears of Pilate, at which point the narrative voice again takes full control. Pilate is convinced of Jesus' innocence, but he nonetheless gives in to the crowd and orders the death. In the three stanzas of lines 945-968 Jesus begins his walk to Mount Calvary, the site of his execution, a procession interrupted narratively by "The teares of the daughters of Jerusalem" (lines 969-1008). This becomes another opportunity to extol the pious virtues of the women as opposed to the murderous men on the scene. Immediately after the praise of the daughters of Jerusalem comes "The sorrow of the virgin Marie" (lines 1009-1040), which in turn is followed by the story of Mary's annunciation and the centrality of her role in redemption (lines 1041-1135). The stanza at lines 1137-1144 tells of Simon of Cyrene being compelled to help carry Christ's cross in the last part of the route to Calvary.

The Crucifixion scene presented in lines 1145-1264 has two interesting additions to the original. The first is the visual focus on the crucified Christ: "His joynts dis-joynted, and his legges hang downe / His alabaster breast, his bloody side . . ." (lines 1161-1162). Imagining the visual scene of the Crucifixion had long been a pious Christian exercise, though more encouraged in the Catholic than in the Protestant tradition. Focusing the female gaze on the male body is not a usual pious exercise, however, and that female gaze is underscored by Lanyer's second addition to the Crucifixion scene. At this point in the poem Lanyer turns "To my Ladie of Cumberland" to comment: "This with the eie of Faith thou maist behold, / Deere spouse of Christ, and more than I can write" (lines 1169-1170). Although the church as a whole (and each individual soul) was conventionally referred to as the "spouse" of Christ, here the countess is brought into the story personally and specifically. She is placed firmly at the foot of the cross and presented as Christ's particular spouse, who truly sees ("with the eie of Faith") the dying body of her beloved: "His count'nance pale, yet still continues sweet, / His blessed blood watring his pierced feet" (lines 1175-1176).

The conclusion of the Crucifixion section in lines 1265-1268 is even more remarkable, since the pictures of Christ's Crucifixion and its saving grace, the disruption of the world and the overthrow of tyranny, are all portrayed as a gift from the poet to the countess:

> Which [Christ] I present (deare Lady) to your view,
> Upon the crosse depriv'd of life or breath,
> To judge if ever Lover were so true,
> To yeeld himselfe unto such shamefull death[.]

Though in the conventional diction of patronage and piety, these verses make redemption the poet's vision and gift, and the power of Christ's sacrifice subject to the judgment of the countess of Cumberland.

Lines 1274-1288 tell of Christ's burial, and present one good man—Joseph of Arimathea— who takes the body to the tomb. At lines 1289-1296 the women come to embalm the body, but find no one in the tomb:

> For he is rize from Death t'Eternall Life,
> And now those pretious oyntments he desires

> Are brought unto him, by his faithfull Wife
> The holy Church; who in those rich attires,
> Of Patience, Love, Long suffring, Voide of strife,
> Humbly presents those oyntments he requires:
> The oyles of Mercie, Charitie, and Faith,
> Shee onely gives that which no other hath.

The Church and the individual soul (whether of a man or a woman) were both conventionally treated as female and as the bride of Christ, but this language also echoes and anticipates the language with which Lanyer has described and will continue to describe the countess of Cumberland. The countess becomes the whole Church.

In lines 1297-1320 Lanyer turns the reader's gaze on the body of the risen Christ, fashioning her richly sensuous language after that of the Song of Solomon:

> His lips like skarlet threeds, yet much more sweet
> Than is the sweetest hony dropping dew,
> Or hony combes, where all the Bees do meet:
> . . . .
> His lips, like Lillies, dropping downe pure
>   mirrhe,
> Whose love, before all worlds we doe preferre.

The next stanza (lines 1321-1328) confirms the countess as a living shrine for Lanyer's sensuous vision of Christ, and as the ultimate true spouse of that Christ:

> in your heart I leave
> His perfect picture, where it still shall stand,
> Deeply engraved in that holy shrine,
> Environed with Love and Thoughtes divine.

The last five hundred lines of the poem interweave the significance of Christ's redemption with praise for the many virtues, particularly heroic faithfulness, that the countess possesses. As the early dedication to the countess catalogues the weaknesses of outward beauty in contrast to her inner virtue, so this last section of the poem catalogues biblical heroines and other symbols of purity and faithfulness (including "Great *Alexander*" and Cleopatra), and finds the countess far worthier of praise. In the midst of this paean, at lines 1457-1461, Lanyer asserts her poetic vocation and portrays herself quite literally as born to praise the great countess:

> And knowe, when first into this world I came,
> This charge was giv'n me by th'Eternall powres,
> Th'everlasting Trophie of thy fame,

To build and decke it with the sweetest flowres
That virtue yeelds . . . [.]

The catalogue concludes with an extensive comparison between the countess and the Queen of Sheba, who sought the wisdom of Solomon. Folded in the comparison are a vision of the apocalypse (lines 1649-1672) and a baroque description of the blood of Christ (lines 1729-1738):

Sweet holy rivers, pure celestiall springs,
Proceeding from the fountaine of our life;
Sweet sugred currents that salvation brings,
Cleare christall streames, puring all sinne and
    strife,
Faire floods, where soules do bathe their snow-
    white wings,
Before they flie to true eternall life:
    Sweet Nectar and Ambrosia, food of Saints,
    Which whoso tasteth, never after faints.

This hony dropping dew of holy love,
Sweet milke, wherewith we weaklings are
    restored [.]

Lanyer's extended transformation of the image of Christ's blood is not characteristic of Jacobean poetics, but is an early indicator of a richly sensuous biblical poetry that we usually associate with that later master of baroque religious imagery Thomas Crashaw. While they have little else in common, both poets spent their lives surrounded by music.

"The Description of Cooke-ham" is the last poem in the volume. Its 1611 publication predates by five years the poem usually cited as the first in a tradition of country-house poems in seventeenth-century England, Ben Jonson's "To Penshurst," which first appeared as the second poem in the "Forrest" section of his *Workes* (1616). Editors usually assume that Jonson's poem was written sometime before late 1612, since a reference to "King *James* . . . With his brave sonne, the Prince" is generally taken to refer to the king in company with Prince Henry, who died in November of that year. It is possible that "To Penshurst" was written before "The Description of Cooke-ham," but Lanyer's poem is without question the first to appear in print.

Lanyer's poem suggests that she was aware of country-house poems by Horace and Martial, and that she was writing in the Augustan tradition of contrasting an idyllic natural order with a fallen human civilization—themes which Jonson, Thomas Carew, Robert Herrick, and Andrew Mar-

vell variously exploit in their later reflections of classical models. More to the point, however, is her exploitation of the natural order as a mirror of human feeling, a device firmly grounded in the pastoral tradition and its English representations.

"The Description of Cooke-ham" is a moving valediction to the pleasures of a noble country estate. The poet memorializes an environment of sweet companionship that she claims to have shared with the countess of Cumberland and her daughter, Anne Clifford, a companionship reflected by the natural world. The poem's 210 lines are roughly divided into an introductory farewell (lines 1-10); an invocation to the countess to contemplate the past beauty of the setting and its responsiveness to her presence (lines 11-74); a reflection on the natural world of Cookeham as an image of God (lines 75-92); a praise of Anne Clifford (lines 93-102); a diatribe against fortune, which has exiled all three from Cookeham (lines 103-126); a portrait of Cookeham's grief at their departure, symbolized by the move through autumn to winter (lines 127-146); a description of the countess's gracious leave-taking, centrally figured by her kiss on the great oak tree, which kiss the poet claims to have stolen from the oak (lines 147-176); a reprise of nature's mourning (lines 177-204); and the poet's concluding farewell (lines 205-210).

Lanyer's conclusion implies that the poem was commissioned by the countess ("Wherein I have perform'd her noble hest"), and therefore asserts itself as a professional work in a longstanding tradition of poet as memorializer of great places, persons, and deeds. Cookeham's epithet, "that delightfull place," recalls both the classical *locus amoenus* and the Christian Eden, both worlds where the natural order reflects social and spiritual harmony. But the imperfections of the larger world, signified by "fortune" and "occasions," conspire to send the countess, Anne, and the poet away from the place and from each other. The poet loses the rich companionship of her social superiors, but in the process she creates a poem that eternizes the place and its former inhabitants, including herself. Despite the poem's melancholy topic, it therefore concludes the volume with an unmistakable and unabashed claim for the poet's classical role as a participant in the social order she celebrates. There would be no similar audacity by a woman writing in English for at least another generation, when Katherine Philips and Margaret, Duchess of Newcastle, made their different claims for public attention.

The coda to Lanyer's volume is designed to erase any lingering doubt about her poetic authority. In a short prose note "To the doubtfull Reader" she assures us that the title *Salve Deus Rex Judæorum* came to her in a dream "many yeares before I had any intent to write" the story of the Passion of Christ. After she had written her poem, she remembered the dream, "and thinking it a significant token, that I was appointed to perform this Worke, I gave the very same words I received in sleepe as the fittest Title I could devise for this Booke." Her claim of a godly vocation is very much part of seventeenth-century Protestant poetics, but it remains the only fully articulated example of such a claim by a woman.

The verse throughout Lanyer's book is iambic pentameter, although the forms vary from the quatrains of "The Authours Dreame" and the couplets of "The Description of Cooke-ham," to ottava rima in the poem to Anne Clifford and the "Salve Deus," to the six- or seven-line stanzas considered appropriate for serious English poetry from Geoffrey Chaucer forward. By standards of its period, the quality of the verse is generally high, which suggests that Lanyer was a practiced poet. We have as yet no evidence of existing examples of her work other than what is in *Salve Deus Rex Judæorum*.

References:

Elaine Beilin, "The Feminization of Praise: Aemilia Lanyer," in her *Redeeming Eve: Women Writers of the English Renaissance* (Princeton: Princeton University Press, 1987), pp. 177-207;

Barbara K. Lewalski, "Imagining Female Community: Aemilia Lanyer's Poems," in her *Writing Women in Jacobean England* (Cambridge, Mass.: Harvard University Press, forthcoming 1993);

Lewalski, "The Lady of the Country-House Poem," in *The Fashioning and Functioning of the British Country House*, edited by Gervase Jackson-Stops, Gordon J. Schochet, Lena Cowen Orlin, and Elisabeth Blair Mac-Dougall (Washington, D.C.: National Gallery of Art, 1989), pp. 261-275;

Lewalski, "Of God and Good Women: The Poems of Aemilia Lanyer," in *Silent but for the Word: Tudor Women as Patrons, Translators, and Writers of Religious Works*, edited by Margaret P. Hannay (Kent, Ohio: Kent State University Press, 1985), pp. 203-224;

Lewalski, "Re-writing Patriarchy and Patronage: Margaret Clifford, Anne Clifford, and Aemilia Lanyer," *Yearbook of English Studies*, 21 (1991), pp. 87-106;

A. L. Rowse, Introduction to *The Poems of Shakespeare's Dark Lady: Salve Deus Rex Judæorum*, edited by Rowse (London: Cape, 1978);

Rowse, *Simon Forman: Sex and Society in Shakespeare's Age* (London: Weidenfeld & Nicolson, 1974), pp. 96-117;

Wendy Wall, "Our Bodies/Our Texts?: Renaissance Women and the Problem of Publication," in *Anxious Power*, edited by Carol J. Singley and S. E. Sweeny (Albany: State University of New York Press, forthcoming 1993).

John Owen

(1564 - 1622)

Edmund Miller
C. W. Post Campus, Long Island University

BOOKS: *Epigrammatum Libri Tres* [Books I-III] (London: Printed by John Windet for Simon Waterson, 1606);

Epigrammatum Liber Singularis [Book IV] (London: Printed by Humphrey Lownes for Simon Waterson, 1607);

Epigrammatum Libri Tres [Books V-VII] (London: Printed by Nicholas Okes for Simon Waterson, 1612);

Epigrammatum Libri Tres [Books VIII-X] (London: Printed by Nicholas Okes for Simon Waterson, 1612);

Epigrammatum Libri Decem [Books I-X] (London: Printed by Nicholas Okes for Simon Waterson, 1622).

Editions: *Ioannis Audoeni Epigrammatum Libri I-III*, edited by John R. C. Martyn (Leiden: Brill, 1976);

Ioannis Audoeni Epigrammatum Libri IV-X, edited by Martyn (Leiden: Brill, 1978).

Translations into English: *Epigrams of that Most Wittie and Worthie Epigrammatist Mr John Owen*, translated by John Vicars (London: Printed by W. Stansby for T. Smethwicke, 1619);

"John Owen: Certaine Epigrams Out of His First Foure Bookes," translated by Robert Hayman, part 2 of *Quodlibet Lately Come Over from New Britaniola New Found-Land* (London: Printed by Eliz. All-de & F. Kingston for R. Michell, 1628);

The Latine Epigrams of John Owen, translated by Thomas Harvey (London: Printed by R. White for N. Simons & T. Sawbridge, 1677);

Owen's Epigrams and Other Echoes of Paris, translated by Mary Kent Davey Babcock (New York: Parnassus, 1931).

Latin composition was still commonplace in the seventeenth century, John Donne, George Herbert, Richard Crashaw, and John Milton being among the major poets who wrote substantial works in this language to stand beside their works in English. But John Owen was among the last writers to use Latin as a primary vehicle for the composition of poetry (another such writer in the British Isles was George Buchanan, 1506-1582). For both sharpness of wit and ingenuity of style, Owen is one of the foremost writers ever to compose Latin epigrams, and in the seventeenth century he was certainly the most famous of the poets working in that language. Indeed in his own age he was the best-known poet of the British Isles, his work having been widely disseminated abroad and translated into several vernacular languages. Part of his success is undoubtedly due to a fashionable taste for epigrammatic satire and the prestige still accorded the language in which he wrote, but in an age in which anyone with the smattering of an education could read Latin fluently, his success was also firmly grounded in the excellence of his verse. He clarified for his age an understanding of the epigram as a form distinct from the lyric. He did not write general-purpose poetry or amatory verse such as might have taken Ovid or Catullus for a model. Instead his poetry shows the clear purpose of making a satiric, moralistic, or devotional point with calculated wit. Indeed he changed the perception of the age with regard to the meaning of the term *epigram*, and he was paid the compliment of not only having his work republished extensively on the Continent but having it imitated widely as well. Despite Owen's demonstrable debt to the Roman poet Martial in both form and substance, the imitators in their uninspired slavishness show how clear is Owen's special mastery of the form.

John Owen, the third son of Thomas and Jane Morris Owen, was born on his father's estate of Plas dû, in Llanarmon, Caernarvonshire, Wales, in 1564. He attended Winchester School and New College, Oxford, where he was a fellow. Having received the degree of B.C.L. on 2 May 1590, he spent an additional year in Oxford but left in 1591 to teach school at Trelech, Monmouthshire. Within a few years he had become

John Owen (engraving from the 1650 Amsterdam edition of Owen's Epigrammatum; *courtesy of Duke University Library)*

headmaster of King Henry VIII's School, Warwick.

It was only after settling in this post that he began writing the Latin epigrams which form his entire literary output and for which he was to become so celebrated, his earliest being one on Queen Elizabeth's chief minister William Cecil, Lord Burghley, dated 1596. Perhaps a sensitivity to the cadences of language deriving from the fact that his native language was Welsh, combined with his experience as a schoolmaster and headmaster, brought him to a full understanding of the opportunities for the exercise of wit afforded by the epigram as a literary mode. Whatever the stimulus, he produced the whole substantial body of his work in a short period of time.

Adopting Ioannes Audoenus as the Latinized version of his name, he published his work serially in four volumes (1606, 1607, and two in 1612) with each volume subdivided into three books except the second, which comprises only one. (John J. Enck has clarified the bibliographic history of these editions.) Owen's success led to imitation, since a spurious eleventh book of epigrams, *Monosticha* (numbered V of XI in collections that include it), apparently written in the previous century by Michele Verino, was added to the 1633 London edition and had been included in Continental editions as early as 1620. Despite this publication history, Owen's 1,514 epigrams are essentially one work and have been republished and translated as such ever since. With greater consis-

Title page for one of the many Continental editions of Owen's epigrams (courtesy of Duke University Library)

tency than Martial himself, Owen made the elegiac couplet his only stanza form, and all the epigrams are but a few couplets in length.

Owen provided authority for dividing his work into three broad categories since he said of it, "in libris tria verba meis celebrantur, Ad, In, De; / De docet, Ad dignos laudat, et In lacerat" (three words recur in my books, *To, In,* and *Of: Of* instructs, *To* praises worthies, and *In* attacks). Since there is perhaps more instruction and less attack to Owen's epigrams than this division might suggest, a more convenient grouping would be into these three large categories: conventional wry generalizations about life, satiric observations on specific targets, and devotional exercises. In epigrams of the first two sorts (which both instruct and satirize), Martial is Owen's clearly acknowl-

edged master. The devotional epigrams have no specific classical model.

In the conventional, general epigrams Owen was merely bringing to stylistic perfection the schoolboy exercises of the preceding millennium. Especially in light of their frequent allusion to the commonplaces of academic life, Owen's epigrams of this sort may be seen as the culmination of the whole of medieval and Renaissance education, the purpose of which was the acquisition of facile Latin style. As Martial was the master of the genre, it is no surprise to find him providing Owen not only with general guidelines and standards but often with specific subjects and treatments. Owen wrote epigrams on such familiar topics as the inconstancy of women, the poverty of authors, the venality of lawyers, the degeneracy of nobles, the flattery of courtiers, the incompetency of physicians, the uxoriousness of husbands, and the blindness of cuckolds. As Leicester Bradner points out, his attacks seldom have any underlying bitterness. These lines on the ambitions of courtiers illustrate both Owen's gentle mockery and his concise wordplay:

> Nil distant labor atque labos, nihil arbor et arbos:
>   idem honor et honos: qui rapit ergo, sapit.

> (Work and works keep not apart,
>   Anymore than a tree does from other trees.
> The same thing ought to go for honor and
>   honors:
>   He who carries off the one ought to savor
>   the other.)

In his epigrams directed at specific targets, Own also takes Martial as his guide. Yet, as with the confessedly general epigrams, Owen presents these with a universalizing perspective, eschewing personalities. Bradner has suggested that one of the reasons for Owen's immediate fame may well have been that he remained more accessible than other epigrammatists of the day, whose arcane allusions may have lost them the wider audience Owen enjoyed. Indeed some of these less successful epigrammatists are also derivative of Martial in their specific content, with only the names changed. Where Owen parts company with Martial is in the bite of his wit. While Martial has a Juvenalian thrust, Owen's taste is for gentler Horatian mockery, and he has none of Martial's erotic coarseness. Subjects are more often celebrated than criticized, and often the subject's predicament is the occasion for a witty observation about life that makes no judgment on culpability for the predicament. Institutions such as Winchester School, Oxford University, and the Bodleian Library are among those celebrated. Members of the royal family receive particularly generous praise. Books honored include Sir Philip Sidney's *Arcadia* (1590), Sir Thomas Overbury's "Characters" (1614), and Joseph Hall's *Meditations* (1605, 1606). Other literary figures noted include Edward, Lord Herbert of Cherbury; Michel Eyquem de Montaigne; Sir Henry Wotton; Sir John Harington; John Hoskins; and Samuel Daniel. "Thomas Morus" (Thomas More) may be taken as typical of this group of epigrams:

> Quid de se fieret, meditans in carcere Morus,
>   Inspicit urinam; nil ibi triste videt.

Urinam Regis potius lustrasset; in illa
   Vidisset mortis turbida signa suæ.

In John R. C. Martyn's translation, this epigram reads:

> More, wondering in prison what fate was in store
>   for him,
>   Inspected his urine. He saw nothing sinister
>   there.
> He should rather have examined the King's urine;
>   In it he would have seen turbid signs of his
>   own death.

Despite Owen's Protestantism (jibes against Roman Catholics in other poems caused a wealthy uncle to disinherit him), this poem takes no side in the historical dispute. Owen's characteristic wordplay is illustrated by his using the prosaic "Inspicit" to refer to More's inspection of his own urine but the epic "lustrasset" to refer to the hypothetical scrutiny of the king's urine. Martyn points out that the harsh music of the second line neatly contrasts with the matter-of-fact nature of a medical examination. The point as a whole indicates Owen's sharp sense of irony and his quick wit in reading contemporary events.

There is no counterpart in Martial to the devotional epigram, and in this mode Owen is something of an innovator. He is fond of biblical subjects, and his moralizing tone is conventional and explicit. Yet he manages to make these poems fresh with his wit and his terse closure. A typical poem is "Ad Hebræos" (To the Jews):

> Relligio lex vestra; fides at nostra vocatur;
>   Vos bene non vultis credere; nos, facere.

> (Ritual is your law while ours is known as faith;
> It is not good for you to give credence to exterior
>   things;
>   It is for us to make interior things.)

Owen's genius is, however, expressed in stylistic ingenuity, not subject matter. In 1941 J. Henry Jones pointed out that Owen's "fondness for assonance and word-play" have "no parallel elsewhere in Latin" literature. His ability to ring as many as five anagrammatic changes on a sequence of letters was perhaps particularly appropriate to the author of traditional exercises in a dead language. But he has more substantive wordplay as well in his pointed use of antithesis, ambiguity, and more sophisticated of schemes of repetition such as antimetabole, epanalepsis, anadiplosis, epistrophe, and anaphora.

Owen seems to have given up writing after the publication of the second of his 1612 volumes. In retirement as in his active life, he lived simply—on patronage rather than from the sale of books, something not remarkably remunerative for authors in his age. He died in London late in 1622 and is buried in St. Paul's Cathedral.

His international reputation was sustained for a long time, particularly in Germany, where he had his greatest influence on subsequent poetry. At present he is little read. His epigrams have not even been included in several recent anthologies of neo-Latin poetry, perhaps because modern taste in poetry is so decidedly for the lyric.

Bibliographies:

John J. Enck, "John Owen's *Epigrammata*," *Harvard Library Bulletin*, 3 (1949): 431-434;

P. N. Poole-Wilson, "The Best-Seller Abroad: The Continental Editions of John Owen," in *Theatrum Orbis Librorum: Liber Amicorum Presented to Nico Israel on the Occasion of His Seventieth Birthday*, edited by Ton Croiset van Uchelen, Koert van der Horst, and Günter Schilder (Utrecht: Hes Publishers, 1989), pp. 242-249.

References:

F. T. J. B., "Translation from John Owen etc.," *Notes and Queries*, 2 (7 December 1850): 460-461;

Edward (von Blomberg) Bensly, "John Owen and Archbishop Williams," *Notes and Queries*, tenth series 2 (20 August 1904): 146;

Bensly, "John Owen the Epigrammatist," *Notes and Queries*, tenth series 11 (9 January 1909): 21-22;

Bensly, "Robert Burton, John Barclay, and John Owen," in *The Cambridge History of English Literature*, 15 volumes, edited by A. W. Ward and A. R. Waller (Cambridge: Cambridge University Press, 1907-1927), IV: 242-267;

Leicester Bradner, *Musæ Anglicanæ: A History of Anglo-Latin Poetry 1500-1925* (New York: Modern Language Association of America / London: Oxford University Press, 1940);

Charles Clay Doyle, "The Hair and Beard of Thomas More: With Special Reference to the Play *Sir Thomas More* and an Epigram by John Owen," *Moreana: Bulletin Thomas More*, 18, no. 71-72 (1981): 5-14;

Doyle, "Thomas More and the Epigrams of John Owen: A Reference and an Analog," *Thomas More Gazette* [*Moreana*, no. 67-68], 2 (1980): 39-42;

J. Henry Jones, "John Owen, *Cambro-Britannus*," in *Transactions of the Honourable Society of Cymmrodorion* (London, 1940), pp. 130-143;

Jones, "John Owen the Epigrammatist," *Greece and Rome*, 10 (February 1941): 65-73;

Ian Laurenson, "A Pasquinade for John Owen," *Notes and Queries*, new series 26 (October 1979): 403-405;

John R. C. Martyn, "John Owen and Tudor Patronage: A Prosopographical Analysis of Owen's Epigrams," *Humanistica Louvaniensia: Journal of Neo-Latin Studies*, 28 (1979): 250-257;

Martyn, "John Owen on Thomas More," *Moreana: Bulletin Thomas More*, 13, no. 50 (1976): 73-77;

Martyn, "Notables amongst the Unknown in Owen's Epigrams," *Notes and Queries*, 28 (1981): 521-522;

Clarence Miller, Review of *Ioannis Audoeni Epigrammatum Libri I-III*, edited by Martyn, *Moreana: Bulletin Thomas More*, 14, no. 54 (1977): 95-100;

Gilbert Waterhouse, *The Literary Relations of England and Germany in the Seventeenth Century* (Cambridge: Cambridge University Press, 1914);

Frederick Adam Wright and Thomas Alan Sinclair, *A History of Later Latin Literature: From the Middle of the Fourth to the End of the Seventeenth Century* (New York: Macmillan, 1931).

Samuel Rowlands
(circa 1570 - 1630)

Frederick Waage
East Tennessee State University

BOOKS: *The Betraying of Christ. Iudas in despaire* (London: Printed by Adam Islip, 1598);

The Letting of Hvmovrs Blood in the Head-Vaine (London: Printed by W. White for W. Ferbrand, 1600); revised as *Hvmors Ordinarie: Where a man may be verie merrie and exceeding well used for his Sixe-pence* (London: Printed for W. Ferbrand, 1605?);

'Tis Merrie when Gossips meete (London: Printed by W. White, sold by G. Loftus, 1602);

Ave Cæsar. God Save the King. The Joyfull Ecchoes of Loyall English Hârtes, Entertayning His Majestie's Late Arivall in England (London: Printed by W. White for W. Ferbrand & G. Loftus, 1603);

Looke to it: For, Ile Stabbe ye (London: Printed by E. Allde for W. Ferbrand & G. Loftus, 1604);

Humors Antiqve Faces: Drawne in proportion to his Seuerall Antique Jestures (London: Printed by E. Allde for Henry Rockett, 1605);

Hell's Broke Loose (London: Printed by W. White, sold by G. Loftus, 1605);

A Theater of Delightfull Recreation (London: Printed by R. Field for A. Johnson, 1605);

A Terrible Battell betweene the two consumers of the whole World: Time, and Death (London: Printed by W. Jaggard for John Deane, 1606?);

Diogines Lanthorne (London: Printed by E. Allde for Thomas Archer, 1607);

Democritus, or Doctor Merry-man his Medicines, against Melancholy Humors (London: Printed by W. Jaggard for J. Deane, 1607); republished as *Doctor Merrie-man: or, Nothing but Mirth* (London: Printed for John Deane, 1609);

The Famous Historie of Guy, Earle of Warwick (London: Printed by E. Allde for W. Ferbrand, 1607);

Hvmors Looking Glasse (London: Printed by E. Allde for W. Ferbrand, 1608);

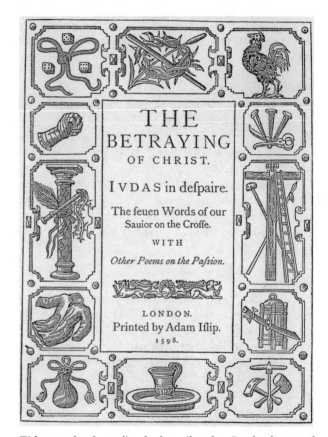

Title page for the earliest book attributed to Rowlands, one of five volumes of religious poetry written during a career largely devoted to verse satire

A Whole Crew of Kind Gossips, All Met to be Merry (London: Printed by W. Jaggard for J. Deane, 1609);

The Knave of Clubbes (London: Printed by E. Allde for W. Ferbrand, 1609)—second edition of *A Merry Meeting, or 'Tis Merry When Knaves Meet* (nonextant, 1600);

The Knave of Harts (London: Printed by T. Snodham, sold by G. Loftus, 1612);

More Knaues Yet? The Knaues of Spades and Diamonds (London: Printed by E. Allde for J. Tap, 1613);

Sir Thomas Overbury, or The Poysoned Knights Complaint [broadside] (London: Printed by G. Eld for J. White, 1614?);

A Fooles Bolt is soone shott (London: Printed by E. Allde for G. Loftus, 1614);

The Melancholie Knight (London: Printed by R. Blower, sold by G. Loftus, 1615);

The Bride (London: Printed by W. Jones for T. Pavier, 1617);

A Sacred Memorie of the Miracles wrought by our Lord and Savior, Iesus Christ (London: Printed by Bernard Alsop, 1618);

The Night-Raven (London: Printed by G. Eld for J. Deane & T. Baily, 1620);

A Paire of Spy-Knaves (London: Printed by G. Purslowe, 1620?);

Good Newes and Bad Newes (London: Printed by G. Purslowe for H. Bell, 1622);

Heavens Glory, Seeke It. Earts Vanitie, Flye It. Hells Horror Fere It (London: Printed by T. Cotes for M. Sparke, 1628).

Editions: *The Letting of Humours Blood in the Head Vaine*, edited by Walter Scott (Edinburgh: Printed by James Ballantyne for William Blackwood, 1814);

The Four Knaves: A Series of Satirical Tracts, edited by Edward F. Rimbault (London: Printed for the Percy Society, 1843);

Collected Poems of Samuel Rowlands, 2 volumes, edited by Edmund Gosse (Glasgow: Hunterian Club, 1880);

Uncollected Poems by Samuel Rowlands, introduction by Frederick Waage (Gainesville: Scholars' Facsimiles & Reprints, 1970).

Samuel Rowlands was one of the most consistent and imaginative of the early Stuart pamphleteers. Sarah Dickson, in "The 'Humours' of Samuel Rowlands" (1950), one of the few articles devoted to him, considered him "the most undeservedly neglected of Jacobean writers." This statement is still true more than forty years later, even though this author of twenty-six known works between 1598 and 1628, some republished in multiple editions up to the Restoration, played a significant role in the Jacobean literary world as satirist and devotional writer.

Edmund Gosse, in his introduction to his edition of Rowlands's works, gave as much information on his life as is known 110 years later: nothing is known, except what can be inferred from his works themselves. Rowlands seems to have lived all his life in London, to have had no university background, and to have had intimate contact with lower- and middle-class London life. He seems to have been a moderate Puritan, with an aversion to extremism of either "left" or "right" which threatened social order. He was more sympathetic to, and understanding of, women than many of his male literary contemporaries. He had strong literary opinions, often condemning "courtly" amorous versifying. Most of his comments on the theater are negative; yet he betrays familiarity with—and the ability to satirize—both drama and courtly verse. He shows familiarity with the Bible and, if not with the classics, at least with the conventions of classical satire and epigram as practiced by their Renaissance imitators.

Rowlands's career has a contrapuntal rhythm. His first known work is a conventional verse meditation on scripture, and in 1605, 1606, 1618, and 1628 he published other religious verse and prose. The majority of his works, however, are collections of verse satires and satiric "characters" emphasizing and often reveling in profane knavery and roguery.

Rowlands's first known work was published in 1598 as *The Betraying of Christ. Judas in despaire. The Seven Words of our Savior on the Cross. With other Poems on the Passion.* Its dedication launches what would become his persistent criticism of the current "art of Poesie" for its devotion to love's follies and fooleries rather than divine matters. "The Betraying of Christ" is a sequence of poems in iambic-pentameter sextets (which would become his favorite verse form), tinged with Spenserian neo-archaism, moving from Christ's betrayal in the Garden of Gethsemane to his interment. "Judas in Despair" is the betrayer's penitent complaint, evoking Old and New Testament incidents before ranting on to suicide. The "Seven Words" poems are formed as meditations on "Deus meus, Deus Meus, ut quid me dereliquisti?" and other exclamations of Christ from the cross. Two lesser poems, "The Death of Death . . . " and "The Wonders at Christ's Death," precede the final long poem on Christ's deposition and burial.

Two years later, in a remarkable leap of faithlessness, Rowlands took advantage of the vogue for satiric drama and verse during Elizabeth's last years to write his most notorious book, which garnered the only known documentary reference to him outside his own works. Because of the edict against satires issued by John Whitgift, bishop of London, on 1 June 1599, all extant copies of *The Letting of Humours Blood in the Head-Vaine* (1600) and *A Merry Meeting, or 'Tis Merry when Knaves*

HVMORS
ORDINARIE,
Where a man may be
*verie merrie, and excee-
ding vvell vsed for his
Sixe-Pence*

At London,
Printed for William Firebrand, *and are to
be sold at his shop in Popeshead Pallace, right
over against the Tauerne doore.*

Title page for the slightly revised version of The Letting of Humours Blood, *which was ordered burned by the Court of the Stationers' Company on 26 October 1600*

Meet (a possible source of Rowlands's *'Tis Merrie when Gossips meete*, 1602, or a previous version of his *The Knave of Clubbes*, 1609) were ordered destroyed by the Court of the Stationers' Company on 26 October 1600; some copies of the first survived, but none of the second is extant. These works seem to have been persecuted less for specific content than as part of an ecclesiastical campaign against satire in general. In any case, *The Letting of Humours Blood* was republished under the new reign, only slightly altered, as *Humors Ordinarie* (1605?).

The Letting of Humours Blood as it survives seems unthreatening. In fact, its introduction bewails current social sins spurred by humor and fashion, such as epicureanism and pride. The introduction is followed by an address to poets encouraging them to write against "bastard humours" rather than wasting talent on drama and love poetry. The body of the work consists of thirty-seven epigrams, mainly in couplets, ranging from a quatrain to twenty-five lines, followed

by seven longer "satires" in couplets. Like those in Rowlands's later works, most of the epigrams are "characters" of urban types engaged in negative social behavior, such as smoking, dicing, and prostitution. The best of them are dramatic monologues. In thus displaying the humourous behavior of young single males Rowlands seems inspired, despite his scorn for drama, by the Jonsonian comedy of humours. The satires extend the same material, in more detail and more vividly, in accomplished dramatic monologues. The final satire evokes two future Rowlands personae, Heraclitus and Democritus, as types of mourning and laughing commentators on the vices of Troynovant (London).

At one time a prose pamphlet of 1602, *Greenes Ghost Haunting Conie-Catchers*, was attributed to Rowlands, and it is included in the 1880 collection. This attribution no longer seems credible: there is no such extended prose in his other works, and he seems less interested in the kind of underworld exposés so successfully purveyed by Robert Greene, Thomas Dekker, and others. Therefore, Rowlands's third extant work seems to be the witty and empathetic *'Tis Merrie when Gossips meete* (1602), a trialogue between a wife, a widow, and a fifteen-year-old maid carried on over wine at a tavern. *'Tis Merrie when Gossips meete* has two later "sequels," *A Whole Crew of Kind Gossips* (1609) and *The Bride* (1617), all three semidramatic discussions of domestic relationships.

After evoking Geoffrey Chaucer's Tabard Inn as its prototype, *'Tis Merrie when Gossips meete* launches into an ingenious prose dialogue between a gentleman and a bookseller's apprentice. Referring to pamphlets by Greene and Thomas Nashe, this dialogue ends with the gentleman's purchase of *'Tis Merrie when Gossips meete*, and he begins reading its dedication to "all merry London Gentlewomen," which follows. In the trialogue proper the gossips meet by chance at the tavern door, and the widow leads the others to a private room, where they engage in "girl talk" and order one pint after another. The main topic of the meeting is which of them has the best life, but many others are covered as the women's inebriation grows: red-haired and black-bearded men, the proper marriage time for the maid, the evils of tobacco, the meaning of dreams. After many pints they leave, but not before the widow has caused a commotion by drunkenly teasing the vintner.

Satire is not, however, Rowlands's only chord. When the death of Queen Elizabeth and accession of James were respectively bewailed and celebrated in a great literary outpouring, Rowlands contributed a short poem in sextets, *Ave Cæsar. God Save the King* (1603). It displays much of the imagery conventionally associated with the new reign: James, as the sun, appears from the clouds; Elizabeth's death is analogized to that of Saul; James's London entry is likened to those of Henry II, Richard I, and Henry V. Classical divinities are invoked to bless his progress, in particular the Muses, since James is "our famous Kingly *Poet*." The poem is symmetrical, with beginning and ending stanzas on Elizabeth's death and James's entrance, and a central epitaph on Elizabeth, written in italicized couplets.

Looke to it: For, Ile Stabbe ye (1604) has a "character" orientation. Each of its short satiric poems has a titular social type: "Wealthy Citizens," "Greedy Usurer." In an introduction Rowlands explains his governing conceit: the fashion among humourous urban males of finding a reason to "give the stab" to others. The author reverses this threat, introducing Death—in effect the speaker in each poem—who at the end threatens the characterized type with "I'll Stab You." Death's first victims are "Tyrant Kings," and he works down the scale to pseudorespectable citizens and finally to disreputable enemies of society such as panders and adulterers. These short satires are followed by a long poem in couplets wherein Death proclaims general threats of destruction to all evildoers. The pamphlet ends with "Death's Epitaph, upon Every Man's Grave."

Rowlands was prolific in 1605, publishing four works: *Humors Ordinarie, Humors Antique* [Antic] *Faces, Hell's Broke Loose,* and *A Theater of Delightfull Recreation.* Rowlands's revision of *The Letting of Humours Blood,* retitled *Humors Ordinarie,* is set in the framing metaphor of book/world/tavern, as a temple of inebriation to which the host "Satir" welcomes the reader. The Chaucerian author urges his readers both to condemn the sinful tavern frequenters and to enjoy the mirth they provide. A good example of this double standard (unchanged from *The Letting of Humours Blood*) might well have disgruntled the bishop of London: a vicar's flock follows him everywhere, so when he leaves an alehouse swearing he will not set foot there again because the female tavern keeper will not let him "carouse," she loses most of her trade. When she relents and invites him back, he is too moral to break his oath, so he has his parishioners "carry him to drink."

Published anonymously, *Humors Antique Faces* might be considered an earlier version of *Humors Looking Glasse* (1608), depending on weight given to the nine epigrams that appear in both volumes. Most of its poems are satiric epigrams, with a prologue creating the framing device of Oberon at night charging the speaker to "scourge the humors of this age." Its final poem does tribute to Proteus, the archetypal Antic, "mad, melancholy, drunk, and variable."

Hell's Broke Loose is a new departure for Rowlands, a trip into controversial terrain. In a careful address to the reader, he relates his tragic protagonist, John of Leyden, to other sectarian rebels since biblical times who have tried to overthrow Christian orthodoxy and establish theocratic states—usually communitarian dictatorships. The most emphasized of these are Jack Straw, John Ball, and other leaders of the Peasants' Revolt of 1381. Since *Hell's Broke Loose* was entered in the Stationers' Register on 29 January 1605, its reference to the Gunpowder Plot of November 1605 is problematic. Its emphasis on the legitimacy of "God's Anointed" suggests a strong endorsement of the new Jacobean reign and anxiety over popish or Puritan efforts to undermine it.

The poem itself, in sextets, is directly titled "The Life and Death of John of Leyden," introduced by the conceit of a dream vision, in which John's mangled corpse speaks to the dreamer. Using Genesis to argue that God meant all property to be held in common, John inspires his tradesmen cohorts to attack the city of Munster. In the second section Tom Mynter preaches this doctrine, and undergoes a symbolic rechristening. In the third the rebellion gains many boors and clowns as converts, formulating an absurd "Twelve Articles of Christian Liberty." Next, the rebels invade and sack the city. The final section describes the siege of Munster by the duke of Saxony, and the capture, torture, and death of the rebels. Unfortunately, by turning the actual Anabaptist "kingdom of a thousand years" (1534-1536) into an object of ridicule, Rowlands tends to discredit its use as a cautionary tale for his own England.

"A Theater of Divine Recreation" is the original Stationers' Register title of *A Theater of Delightfull Recreation,* one of Rowlands's leaps into piety. The work falls into three sections: the usual introductory matter, including an invocation of the Muses; versified incidents from the

Old Testament as counterparts to those from the New; and miscellaneous divine poems. The tone of all is penitential and confessional. Most interesting is his prefatory retraction, renouncing his profane works by name, starting with *The Letting of Humours Blood*, and denouncing "profane poets." Much of the verse focuses on the wages of sin and the remorse of the unrepentant. The final poem arraigns the entire world at "Gods general sessions." Given this emphasis, it is interesting that all but three of Rowlands's later works are the kind of satires he denounces here.

Yet what is apparently his next piece is in harmony with *A Theater of Delightfull Recreation*. Written in sextets, *A Terrible Battell betweene the two consumers of the whole World: Time, and Death* (1606?) is a poetic dialogue with a "dance of death" vision and the tone of late-medieval moral allegory. Death is the executioner of villains, as he is in *Looke to it: For, Ile Stabbe ye*, and he recounts his visits in the company of Time to various evil types, such as misers and usurers. One interesting victim is a poet who is guilty of excessive devotion to love and the hypocritical praise of women. Death eventually becomes angry at Time's boastfulness. They fall to railing and mockery but eventually make peace and go off to deal with the thousands more waiting at the point of death.

Rowlands's most productive period as a satirist might be considered 1607 to 1618, the year in which his next devotional work was published; some of his works published during this time went into multiple editions, and his verse demonstrates confidence and ingenuity. In 1607 he published *Diogines Lanthorne*, which was in its eighth edition by 1634. Its prologue, illustrated by the title-page woodcut, evokes the philosopher Diogenes searching Athens for an honest man. The text consists of Diogenes' first-person complaint, in prose, against the usual city sins, such as cruelty and usury, followed by a series of Aesopian moral fables versified mainly in rhyming trimeter and quatrimeter. These two sections are separated by an address in couplets, presumably from the author to Diogenes, pointing out all the city sinners Diogenes missed on his search.

Democritus, or Doctor Merry-man his Medicines, against Melancholy Humors was also published in 1607, and republished in 1609 as *Doctor Merrieman: or, Nothing but Mirth*, running through six more editions by 1627. Most of its humorous anecdotes, versified in couplets, describe the gulling of "fools"—country fellows, idle fellows, clowns,

and the like. The fools are victimized generally by witty verbal repostes; for example an aging widower, grotesquely caricatured physically, tries to woo a fifteen-year-old maid, and gets the reply "You shall not thatch my new House with old straw." By contrast, the most ambitious poem in the collection is a haughty, boasting monologue of a courtesan, describing all the tricks she plays on fools to get their money.

The apparent first edition of Rowlands's longest-lived work, republished through the Restoration, occurred also in 1607. *The Famous Historie of Guy, Earle of Warwick* retells in verse a hoary medieval romance originating as early as the twelfth century and popular through the nineteenth. Rowlands's epistle to "the Noble English Nation" expresses a deep source of this popularity: Guy is a truly English hero, not one borrowed from traditions of other nations. Rowlands's version is divided into twelve cantos of iambic-pentameter sextets, and ornamented with appealingly naive woodcuts. Rowlands's Guy goes to perform exploits on the Continent to win the hand of the fair Phaelice. After two adventurous expeditions he succeeds, marries the lady, but then gets religion: "I have done nothing for to purchase Grace / But spend my time about a lady's face." He leaves for Jerusalem, returns unrecognized as an anchorite, and summons his abandoned lady only on his deathbed. The penitential emphasis of this tale must have appealed particularly to Rowlands, who was often contemptuous of romance.

Humors Looking Glasse (1608) is an epigram collection closely allied with *Humors Antique Faces*, and perhaps first published prior to it, although no earlier edition is extant. The important words are *antic* and *mirror*, and in his address to the reader Rowlands compares his pages with the barber's mirror in which clients can examine their trims and (punningly) "how they are reformed by him." The humours included are commonplaces, treated in several different verse forms, from sextets to poulter's measure, and diverse applications of first- and third-person point of view.

Rowlands's second "domestic dialogue," *A Whole Crew of Kind Gossips, All Met to be Merry*, was published in 1609. Unlike that of its predecessor, its theme is the battle of the sexes. Rowlands dedicates it to the maidens of London, telling them that it will reveal all the nasty tricks wives play on their husbands, to dissuade them from such behavior when they themselves are wed. Be-

Title page and illustrations from the 1682 edition of Rowlands's best-known poem, which was popular throughout the seventeenth century

fore the wives' stories begin though, the husbands break in choricly, vowing to wait out with patience their wives' damning self-revelations. Each gossip in turn boastfully confesses her husband's bad humours and her reciprocal techniques of husband abuse. For example, one gossip takes the Wife of Bath as her model: when her husband hit her, "with my very fist / I did bepommel him until he pissed." In the second half of the pamphlet the accused husbands defend themselves in the same order and "give their wives the lie," the burden of their defenses being that they are goaded to any unseemly behavior only by their wives' shrewish ways, which they bear with heroic patience.

Rowlands's next three works are "knave" pamphlets named after the four playing-card suits. *The Knave of Clubbes* (1609) was followed by *The Knave of Harts* (1612) and *More Knaves Yet? The Knaves of Spades and Diamonds* (1613). At one time Rowlands was considered the author of an intervening work—*Martin Mark-all, Beadle of Bridewell, His Defence and Answere to the Belman of London* (1610), which attacks Thomas Dekker's celebrated rogue pamphlet of 1608; but since the time of A. V. Judges's influential anthology *The Elizabethan Underworld* (1930), the attribution to Rowlands has been discredited. *The Knave of Clubbes* is probably a new edition of *A Merry Meeting, or 'Tis Merry when Knaves Meet*, ordered burned in 1600. In its new guise it is dedicated to Fustis, Knave of Clubs, who practices all the city sins and here anatomizes all the knaves that are his followers. An interesting example is "Master Makeshift" the "needy poet," who, starving and invited to dine in a tavern by some good fellows, manages to steal all the money they have laid out for food and drink. Rowlands's promise of sequels was first fulfilled by *The Knave of Harts*, which includes the versified characters of some sixteen knaves "marching in order," and a subsequent farrago of anecdotes, conceits, and epigrams. Prominent is a complaint by the Knave of Hearts against the playing-card makers who portray the knaves in ridiculous Frenchified attire on the faces of their cards, supplicating them to dress these knaves in current fashions.

More Knaves Yet? is dedicated to fools and madmen; the two new knaves also announce the failure of the supplication to card makers previously mentioned, and refer to the title-page woodcut for *More Knaves Yet?*, in which the printer has kindly modernized their attire. The Knave of Diamonds's part is about the sea, and very short,

since apparently Rowlands did not know many sea stories. The Knave of Spades, however, digs up much of Rowlands's familiar urban terrain of usurers and coxcombs.

One of Rowlands's most interesting works is the broadside *Sir Thomas Overbury, or The Poysoned Knights Complaint*, probably published in 1614, the year that Overbury's celebrated poem *A Wife* was published posthumously. Overbury was notorious as the victim of poison administered to him while he was a prisoner in the Tower of London, through the machinations of Robert Carr, Earl of Somerset, and his mistress, the divorced Frances Howard, Countess of Essex, whose marriage Overbury opposed. When the plot was unraveled, Overbury gained posthumous popularity, and Somerset and the countess popular hatred. Headed by a dramatic woodcut, Rowlands's *Complaint* bewails the poisoning in strong and sober couplets, with Overbury likening himself to the two murdered princes and other victims of injustice.

A dramatic title-page woodcut of a man in jester's garb aiming a crossbow directly at the reader introduces *A Fooles Bolt is soone shott* (1614). The poems, in couplets, consist of the usual mildly humorous stories, many of which involve fools as victims of tricks. "Shooting their bolts" figures their failure to anticipate their antagonists' tricks. One poem is about the fools' bolts of counterfeit poets, criticized in particular for writing the sort of pointed satiric epigrams that Rowlands himself composes.

Considered by some Rowlands's most original work, *The Melancholie Knight* (1615) is a lengthy dramatic monologue spoken by a knight afflicted physically (as his picture, with folded arms and slouching hat, on the title page indicates) and spiritually with fashionable melancholy. The poem is introduced by a speaker's recounted dream vision of the knight moping in a tavern. The knight then uncases his complex and ludicrous thoughts to the speaker. He complains about everything: the degeneracy of the present, his debts and lack of money, the tricksters and rogues who get rich while he stays honest and poor. He boasts about the morality and hospitality of his household and even quotes the nutritionally enlightened poem posted in his entry hall. He elaborately rationalizes his cowardice as hatred of war and confesses his plots to gain his rich father-in-law's inheritance and to cheat his tenants. Intermittently, while criticizing tobacco, he calls for another pipe. He admires old chival-

Title pages for the poems in which Rowlands anatomizes various sorts of "knaves"

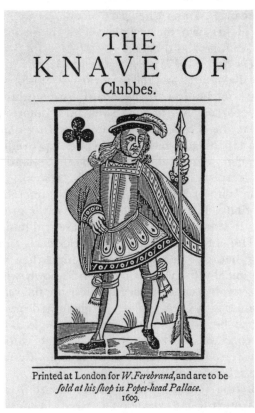

ric romances, and recites part of one, as well as some of his own melancholy verses to Fortune, Lady Pecunia, and others.

The Bride (1617) is the last of Rowlands's "domestic dialogues," and the most earnest. It is probably a contribution to the heated print controversy sparked by Joseph Swetnam's notorious *Araignment of Lewde, Idle, Froward, and Unconstant Women* (1615), to which three replies, apparently by women, were published in 1617. Rowlands's bride is spirited, arguing through "reason," as did the Wife of Bath, that marriage is preferable to virginity. Like her prototype, she gives great weight to God's injunction to "increase and multiply." Her interlocutors are the bridesmaids preparing her for her wedding. Though they all argue initially for virginity, the bride slowly wins them over, her clinching argument being the realistic one that it is easy to get pregnant and much better to be pregnant married than single. The bride concludes with a lecture on the eight duties of a wife, but the piety of this formula cannot erase the vitality of the preceding argument.

In the following year was published Rowlands's next-to-last devotional piece, *A Sacred Memorie of the Miracles wrought by our Lord and Savior, Jesus Christ*. Rowlands addresses it to all witches, necromancers, and other of Satan's representatives on earth, contrasting their counterfeit wonders to the true power of miracles; and then to all true Christians, warning them of Satan's representatives. Each of the subsequent poems recounts a particular miracle; each is referenced to scripture and prefaced by an emblematic woodcut. Hard upon this holy work came Rowlands's *The Night-Raven* (1620), reveling in the dark side. The raven tells of the nefarious activities of the night: "Were I not black, as all crows be / I should even blush at things I see." Though the raven concludes with a chastening call to repentance by the "usurpers of the night's dark hours," these usurpers, especially the "night Swaggerer" and "The Roaring-Boy and his Punk," are exuberantly full of life, providing some of Rowlands's best word portraits. Of special note is "Mistaking in the Dark," which alludes to the night tricks in Chaucer's "Miller's Tale."

The early 1620s saw the last of Rowlands's knaves and rogues. *A Paire of Spy-Knaves* (date uncertain) exists in only one imperfect copy. It begins with a complaint against the world and the immorality of the time, which it illustrates with characters of fools and knaves, many of which recapitulate other pieces in this vein. *Good Newes*

and Bad Newes (1622) has these two personified on the title page, one in black pantaloons, the other in white. The author bewails the prominence of newsmongering and rumormongering, in which good and bad news are mingled. He proposes to separate them, and the poems that follow have two parts each: the first, under the heading "Good News," tells a tale of an individual's good fortune; but when the page is turned, its sequel, headed "Bad News," recounts the ill-fortune which this same protagonist incurs. The collection concludes with a series of unrelated epigrams.

Six years separate this work from the last one attributable to Samuel Rowlands. *Heavens Glory* (1628) is a thick volume of Christian exhortation, verses, and prayers, ornamented by an elaborate title page. "To the Reader" is signed "Samuell Rowland," but the book is published by Michael Sparke, a prolific religious writer, and some of its poems and prayers appear in Sparke's best-selling *Crumms of Comfort* (1627). It seems likely that Rowlands himself wrote only the first half of the book, the prose discussions of "Heaven's Glory," "Earth's Vanity," and "Hell's Torments," with their associated verses.

Rowlands seems to have attracted the most critical notice in the nineteenth century, when Sir Walter Scott, Edward Rimbault, and Edmund Gosse edited his works, finding him "curious" and of interest, but generally disapproving of the milieus he wrote about. Most twentieth-century references are to him as a prolific "popular" writer, but do not involve detailed critical estimation. The length and consistency of his career, his mastery of urban satire and social commentary, and the unreconciled tension between his "profane" and devotional works make his significance to his literary moment belie his contemporary status.

References:

Sarah Dickson, "The 'Humours' of Samuel Rowlands," *Papers of the Bibliographical Society of America*, 44 (1950): 101-118;

A. V. Judges, Notes to *Martin Markall*, in *The Elizabethan Underworld*, edited by Judges (London: Routledge, 1930), pp. 514-517;

Glenn C. Rogers, Jr., "Three Poems by Samuel Rowlands: A Critical Edition of *Tis Merry When Gossips Meet, A Whole Crew of Kind Gossips*, and *The Bride*," Ph.D. dissertation, University of North Carolina, 1974.

George Sandys

(2 March 1578 - March 1644)

Deborah Rubin
Nassau Community College, State University of New York

See also the Sandys entry in *DLB 24: American Colonial Writers, 1606-1734.*

BOOKS: *A Relation of a Iourney begun An: Dom: 1610. Fovre Bookes Containing a description of the Turkish Empire, of Ægypt, of the Holy Land, of the Remote parts of Italy, and Ilands adioyning* (London: Printed for W: Barrett, 1615);

The First Five Bookes of Ovids Metamorphosis, translated by Sandys (London: Printed for William Barrett, 1621);

Ovid's Metamorphosis Englished by G. S. (London: Printed by William Stansby, 1626);

Ovids Metamorphosis Englished, Mythologiz'd, and Represented in Figures. An Essay to the Translation of Virgil's Æneis (Oxford: Printed by John Lichfield, 1632; facsimile edition, New York, Garland, 1976);

A Paraphrase Vpon the Psalmes of David and Vpon the Hymnes Dispersed throughout the Old and New Testaments (London: Printed by John Legatt, 1636);

A Paraphrase Vpon the Divine Poems (London: Printed by John Legatt, 1638 [i.e., 1637]);

Christs Passion. A Tragedie. With Annotations, Sandys's translation of Hugo Grotius's *Christus patiens* (London: Printed by John Legatt, 1640);

A Paraphrase Vpon the Song of Solomon (London: Printed by John Legatt, 1641).

Editions: *The Poetical Works of George Sandys,* 2 volumes, edited by Richard Hooper (London: John Russell Smith, 1872); republished as *George Sandys: The Poetical Works,* 2 volumes (Hildesheim, Germany: Georg Olms Verlagsbuchhandlung, 1968);

Ovid's metamorphosis Englished, Mythologized, and Represented in Figures, edited by Karl K. Hulley and Stanley T. Vandersall (Lincoln: University of Nebraska Press, 1970).

George Sandys—praised in his own century for his verse translation of and commentary on

George Sandys, 1632 (portrait by Cornelius Janssen; Graythwaite Hall, North Lancashire)

Ovid's *Metamorphoses,* his metrical paraphrases of Old Testament psalms and songs, and his travel accounts—is in the twentieth century known best to scholars of English prosody, translation, and mythography. His poetry is still read by students of the heroic couplet, who see in Sandys an anticipation of the mature "closed" form achieved by Restoration poets such as John Dryden. Some of his biblical paraphrases live on in hymnals, set to the music of Henry Lawes and others. His encyclopedic commentary on the text of the *Metamorphoses* remains of interest to historians of mythography, the tradition of interpreting ancient myths for later, disbelieving readers.

In a broader cultural sense, Sandys's claim that part of his translation of Ovid was "bred in the New-World" (composed in Jamestown, where he served as treasurer of the Virginia Company) is important to historians of the early colonies and of American literature. Recent studies of the European representation of non-Western peoples seem likely to further enhance Sandys's reputation as a pioneering humanist traveler and as an interpreter of the "other." His accounts of the Levant and his anecdotal references to the peoples, landscape, and lore of the New World are a valuable resource for those who wish to understand the attitudes of a cultured, tolerant, and curious Englishman towards the non-Christian worlds of classical literature, the Middle East, and the precolonial Americas.

George Sandys, born on 2 March 1578, was the youngest of nine children born to Edwin Sandys (1516?-1588) and his second wife, Cicely Wilford Sandys (died 1611). Edwin Sandys, a highly educated man with roots in the country gentry of Lancashire, studied divinity at Cambridge University and was subsequently exiled on the Continent for his religious views. He returned after the death of Queen Mary in 1558 to rise rapidly within the Church of England and be named archbishop of York in 1576. His principled stand for Protestantism and his propensity to engage in ecclesiastical quarrels may have influenced his son George in his selection of moralizing, dogmatic Christian commentaries for his *Ovids Metamorphosis Englished, Mythologiz'd, and Represented in Figures* (1632). The father also provided a model as a biblical translator, having participated in the translation of the Bishops' Bible (1568). Cicely Wilford Sandys was descended from a prominent Kentish family; little else is known about her life.

Of George Sandys's brothers, three were knighted and the second, Sir Edwin (1561-1629) had a distinguished career in the House of Commons, taking particular interest in colonial affairs, as would George after him. He was a member of the East India Company and took an active role in the Virginia Company, where he fought for greater independence from the Crown, helping to establish the first representative assembly in the British colonies in North America.

George may have begun his education when he was seven in York at St. Peter's. In 1589, at the age of eleven, he entered Oxford University

along with his brother Henry, and on 23 October 1596 he was admitted to the Middle Temple to study law. About this time, according to Richard Beale Davis, he married Elizabeth Norton under pressure from his family, who had contracted for the marriage as early as December 1584 in order to consolidate some lands. The marriage was apparently unhappy, the couple separated by 1606, and by 1609 Elizabeth's family was attempting to recover some of her properties. George's departure for the Holy Land in 1610 marks the end of his formative years and his married life and the beginning of his career as a writer.

He was not the first member of his family to make an educational tour abroad and write about it. Sir Edwin, his brother, had toured France, Italy, and Germany and in 1599 composed *Europae Speculum* (first published as *A Relation of the State of Religion*, 1605), a discussion of religion and manners in western Europe. As in much else, George seems to have followed in the footsteps of this older brother; however, his distinctive qualities as an observer, stylist, and humanist are apparent in the journal he published of his travels. *A Relation of a Journey begun An: Dom: 1610* chronicles Sandys's travels to Italy, the islands of the Aegean, Turkey, Egypt, and the Holy Land, an itinerary that hints at Sandys's interest in ancient history, classical literature, and human society in all of its diversity. While Sir Edwin's book focuses on contemporary politico-religious issues, George's work constitutes a meditation on the relation between ancient civilizations and seventeenth-century Christendom. The decline of great empires of the past, the encroaching threat of Islam, and the frailty of human achievements are the themes of his work.

Where Sandys focuses on contemporary culture, however, he reveals the broad-ranging curiosity of an anthropologist/archaeologist and the taste for observation of a naturalist. He describes many aspects of the lives of the people he encounters, including their material culture, architecture, and customs and folklore; and he describes the more remarkable features of the land, its flora and fauna.

The narrative of *A Relation of a Journey* is written in prose, but substantial portions of the work consist of quotations from classical and Renaissance Latin poets followed by Sandys's verse translations. These poetic interludes are more than ornaments appended to the central text; they are integral to its style and meaning. Jonathan Haynes argues that they contribute to an ele-

Sandys's parents, Edwin and Cicely Wilford. Edwin Sandys became archbishop of York in 1576 and participated in the translation of the Bishops' Bible (National Portrait Gallery, London)

vated rhetorical mode in which Sandys evokes great lost civilizations viewed in ruins: "As instruments for description the Latin and Neo-Latin poetry Sandys uses exceeds anything possible in his prose in its formality, its pomp, its heightened imagery and diction, as well as its closer connections with the mythological tradition." Sandys's abundant quotations from Virgil, Lucretius, Horace, Martial, and Ovid, among others, form an anthology of extracts from the greatest Latin poets. Placed as they are within his narrative, they add a dimension of mythological allusion, poetic diction, and historical reference to what might otherwise be a conventional Renaissance travel guide.

Sandys's English translations of these extracts already show his serious concern with prosody and the art of translation. His heroic couplets are notable for the vivid strength, concision, fidelity to Latin syntactic structures, and controlled experimentation with enjambed lines that characterize his later *Metamorphosis*. In the five years between the beginning of his travels and the publication of *A Relation of a Journey*, Sandys must have devoted considerable time to evolving a metrical form suitable for translation from diverse Latin meters and to polishing his verse. At the time he began the project, the most distinguished English models were Arthur Golding's

translation of the *Metamorphoses* (1565,1567) and George Chapman's of the *Iliad* (1611), both written in fourteeners. Chapman abandoned these awkward heptameter couplets in favor of pentameter couplets when he published his translation of the *Odyssey* (1616?), but by that time Sandys had also published his *Relation of a Journey*. His choice of the heroic couplet thus appears to have been an independent one, and he continued to explore the potential of the form throughout his life as a translator. The large number of quotations from the *Metamorphoses* to be found in *A Relation of a Journey* suggest as well that Sandys was already immersing himself in the text so central to the Renaissance imagination. Many of these passages appear in the complete translation of the *Metamorphoses* that followed in 1626.

Sandys's *Relation of a Journey*, graced by carefully chosen engravings, found immediate favor in England and on the Continent. It was reprinted in England eight times within the century, and translated into Dutch and German. As Haynes notes, the influence of *A Relation of a Journey* can be traced in the works of Francis Bacon, Robert Burton, Thomas Browne, Abraham Cowley, Thomas Fuller, Ben Jonson, and John Milton; one hundred years later it was still a classic in the eyes of Samuel Johnson, who recom-

Engraved title page for the first edition of Sandys's travel journal, which examines the relationship between ancient civilizations and seventeenth-century Christendom

mended it to a young clergyman as educational reading.

In the nine years following George Sandys's tour of the Levant, his activities are documented primarily in the records of the London-based Virginia and Bermuda companies, established to promote colonization. Continuing legal proceedings regarding the properties of his estranged wife provide the only glimpse we have of his personal life. We may assume that he spent considerable time living in the households of various relatives, and that he was on close terms with several of his brothers, who included him in their colonial ventures.

Sir Edwin Sandys had been active in the Virginia Company from its inception in 1609, consolidating his position by enrolling as many family members as possible as voting shareholders. In a 1612 charter, George is listed as a company stock-

holder. During the next six years, as a crisis of leadership emerged within the company and as Sir Edwin struggled to enact reforms and to wrest control from the treasurer, Sir Thomas Smith, George appears to have devoted much of his time to the company's business. By the spring of 1619 he was proposed by his brother's faction as treasurer of the Bermuda Company—which had now split off from the Virginia Company. While he declined to be considered, this proposal serves as evidence, according to Davis, of George's administrative skills and practical experience.

From 1619 to 1621, Sir Edwin served as treasurer of the Virginia Company and was successful in seeing Sir Francis Wyatt, the candidate of the Sandys faction, elected resident governor of Virginia in 1621. George began serving on two Virginia Company committees within three weeks after Wyatt's election, and in the same year George was elected the first resident treasurer of the company. Previous treasurers, occupying the highest position within the company, had left direct supervision of the colony to the governor. However, the company's inability to collect revenues and to bring about reforms such as the diversification of the plantation economy had compelled it to construct a more responsive administrative structure. George, as the first resident treasurer, was charged with receiving rents, implementing the company's directives, and providing company investors in London with information on local conditions in the colony.

Before embarking for Virginia, Sandys arranged for the publication of the second edition of his *Relation of a Journey*, and saw through the press an edition of *The First Five Bookes of Ovids Metamorphosis* (1621). He left England on 1 August 1621 with an established reputation as poet, travel writer, and translator as well as administrator. He took with him to Virginia a staff of household servants, twenty-five colonists to settle his personal lands, several Italian glassmakers destined to establish a "furnace" for the manufacturing of glass and beads, and his copy of *The Metamorphoses*, which he continued to translate on the voyage to the New World. He and his contemporaries saw this passage as a significant event for English literature as well as commerce. Michael Drayton, in his poem "To Master George Sandys, Treasurer for the English Colony in Virginia," wrote of his expectations:

And (worthy GEORGE) by industry and use,
Let's see what lines *Virginia* will produce;
Goe on with OVID, as you have begunne,
With the first five Bookes; let your numbers run
Glib as the former, so shall it live long,
And doe much honour to the *English* tongue.

Sandys himself, in his preface to the 1632 edition of the *Metamorphoses*, was to characterize the work as "a double Stranger: Sprung from the Stocke of the ancient Romanes; but bred in the New-World."

Sandys and his party arrived at Jamestown in October 1621. During his first six months in Virginia, despite his own sickness, the death of many settlers, and inadequate supplies, Sandys oversaw beginning work on a glassworks, iron works, and water mill; in addition, he furthered plans to establish silk, wine, and cotton industries and to diversify food crops. On 22 March 1622, however, his hopes were overturned when the set-

tlement was attacked by local Indian tribes, who killed over 300 people, including six members of the council, and destroyed the iron works. Sandys's role in the colony's equally bloody response is commemorated in a broadside ballad that begins:

Stout Master George Sandys upon a night
    did bravely venture forth
And mong'st the Savage murtherers
    did forme a deede of worth

When the Virginia Company responded to news of the massacre by censuring its representatives in Virginia, Sandys, in letters to friends and relatives, criticized the administration of the colony previous to his arrival and listed the factors that had prevented effective changes. When King James established a committee to investigate the Virginia and Bermuda companies after the massacre, Sandys's private letters were publicly disclosed.

During the remainder of his tenure in Virginia, Sandys resumed his efforts to collect revenues and to diversify the colony's economy and industries. He sat as well in the Virginia General Assembly, the Council of State, and the Council-Court. In the time free from official duties, he completed his translation of the *Metamorphoses* (published in 1626 after his return to England) and documented the natural history of Virginia's land and inhabitants. These seemingly unrelated projects were united in his later, annotated edition of the *Metamorphoses* (1632), where Sandys draws upon his personal experiences in the New World to enrich his compendium of traditional Ovidian commentaries.

After the dissolution of the Virginia Company and the reversion of the colony to royal control, Sandys returned to England late in the summer of 1625 to resume his career as a writer and to enter the service of Charles I, who succeeded to the throne early the next year. The 1626 edition of the fifteen books of the *Metamorphoses* was dedicated to the new king, who granted Sandys a royal patent for the work. Six years later, Sandys published a sumptuous folio edition, *Ovid's Metamorphosis Englished, Mythologiz'd, and Represented in Figures* on which his fame as a writer largely rests. This lavishly produced volume, described by Davis as "one of the handsome books of English Renaissance printing," contains a revised version of the 1626 translation, an erudite and massively researched commentary on the text, and specially commissioned copperplate engravings ("figures") prefacing each book.

Sandys's achievement in the 1632 edition is threefold. As a poet, his anticipation of neoclassical balance and restraint in the heroic couplet places him in the English prosodic tradition culminating with John Dryden, and Alexander Pope. As a translator, he provided a model of tactful, unobtrusive, Latinate diction and syntax, a break from the Elizabethan exuberance of Golding or the impassioned intensity of Chapman. As a commentator working at the end of a long tradition, he produced a masterpiece of encyclopedic mythography.

An "amateur" poet and a member of the circle of Lucius Cary, Lord Falkland, at Great Tew, Sandys is more notable in his relationship to English literary tradition than as an independent artist. He carefully studied the works of his contemporaries and predecessors, and, through his translation, influenced major poets over a span of two centuries. Jonson and Milton read him, and Sandys's Ovid with commentaries appears to have been used widely in English grammar schools. Although Dryden criticized Sandys's translation in some respects, in the preface to his *Fables Ancient and Modern* (1700) he described Sandys as "the Ingenious and Learned *Sandys*, the best Versifier of the former Age." The Augustans in general learned much from Sandys's diction, and Keats relied on his English Ovid.

What distinguishes Sandys's poetry from that of earlier English translators and original poets is a concern with balance, clarity, and decorum, qualities congenial in a translator of Ovid. Compared with Golding's breathless narratives or the tortuous arguments of the Metaphysical poets, Sandys's syntax is relaxed in its flow and rational in the relationship between rhetoric and meter. Lighter punctuation, lighter caesurae, and frequent end-stopped lines permit a new integrity of line and couplet. This, combined with the compactness forced upon Sandys by his attempt to translate Ovid line for line, opens the way for his exploitation of parallelism and antithesis, the hallmarks of the "closed" heroic couplet. Inspired by Ovid, Sandys pays close attention to the placement of words so that conceptual relationships are revealed:

So Lambs from Wolves, Harts fly from Lyons so;
So from the Eagle springs the trembling Dove:
They, from their deaths: but my pursuite is Love.

The exact parallel of the half-lines "Lambs from Wolves" and "Harts . . . from Lyons"; the reversed and extended parallel in line 530, where the predator now precedes the prey; and the antithesis in line 531 between harts or doves fleeing death and the nymph Daphne fleeing love illustrates the neatness, variety, and clarity of Sandys's verse. Intricate shapes of thought—equations, comparisons, cause and effect, analogies, ironic conjunctions—are given a physical counterpart in balanced words and phrases framed in metrically balanced lines. Sandys's selective use of alliteration—often across the caesura—strengthens these effects, offering natural correspondences springing from words themselves that echo the ordered structures of thought and meter.

As a translator, Sandys assumed a place in a rich Renaissance tradition that had its roots in the recovery of classical texts and in the Protestant dissemination of the Bible in the vernacular. Translation was regarded as a central cultural activity, a major literary form, and a subject worthy of critical study. When, in his dedication to *Examen Poeticum* (1693), Dryden comments on Sandys's Ovid, he disparages it for being pedantic, unnatural, and devoid of poetry. His serious consideration of Sandys's work, however, demonstrates its importance in the literary genealogy running from Chapman to Sandys and finally to Dryden and other Augustans.

The dilemma of translators is that they cannot re-create the original in its totality; they must sacrifice some part of the original meaning and search for an inadequate equivalent of its style and feeling within the resources of another language. Temperamentally a cautious, responsible, unobtrusive writer, Sandys chose fidelity to Ovid's Latin over an artist's self-expression. While Dryden is a better poet than Sandys, he is also, in his translations, more willing to impose contemporary and personal values upon the matter he is translating, and to expand upon the original in the process. Sandys, in contrast, is scrupulous in his focus on the Latin, molding the English language to the utmost to reflect the line and couplet units, rhetorical units, syntactical structures, and vocabulary of Ovid's poem. His goal is a transparent style in which the Latin shines through the English.

Sandys attempts to translate Ovid line by line and phrase by phrase, and since Latin is a far more economical language, he is compelled to condense the English, drawing upon the ellip-

Engraved title page and the illustration for book 3 of Sandys's 1632 edition of the Metamorphoses. *Sandys translated the work in Virginia and drew upon his experiences there to enrich the commentaries.*

tic potential of the language but also introducing Latin devices not entirely natural to English. His strategies include inversion of normal word order; imitation of Latin syntactical forms; and use of Latinate vocabulary, often with Latin meanings not customary in the English cognates. This policy results in some lines of great spareness and allusive beauty, others of quaint Latinity, and still others that are almost unintelligible. A generation later, Milton employs similar Latinate devices in *Paradise Lost* (1667), lending a sense of epic dignity and ambiguous semantic depth to his own poem, and demonstrating the influence of the tradition of classical translation on native English verse.

Accompanying each book of the *Metamorphoses*, Sandys's 1632 edition provides a prose mythographical commentary on Ovid's text suitable for "the ordinary Reader." Written in a vigorous, clear style with verse translations of all classical quotations, this compendium of received opinions on the *Metamorphoses* combined with Sandys's original additions represents the culmination of a tradition extending back more than a

thousand years. Such commentaries typically provided defenses of Greek, Latin, and Middle Eastern myth in later ages when belief in the Gods and mythic events had waned. With the customary emphasis on pleasure and profit, Sandys employs a variety of strategies to salvage great classical literature through reinterpretation, typically claiming to find hidden tales of historical figures (euhemerism), wisdom concerning the forces of nature, and moral observations on human nature.

Sandys's commentary is characterized by its inclusivity and toleration of divergent opinions. He cites or refers to approximately two hundred authorities spanning twenty-five centuries—poets; historians; philosophers; writers on science and technology, medicine, and astrology; Church Fathers and other theologians; and Renaissance humanists, among others. From his sources, he selects a panoply of interpretations, often inconsistent and incompatible in their premises. Sandys himself emphasizes the importance of diversity in his dedication, "To the Reader," where he explains, "In the Muthologie I haue rather followed (as fuller of delight and more vsefull) the varietie of mens seuerall conceptions, where they are not ouer-strained, then curiously examined their exact proprietie."

While many passages reflect the harsh morality and misogyny of earlier models, others—often influenced by Bacon—illustrate contemporary Renaissance wisdom on political power, advice to the courtier on how to survive. Most original, however, are those passages where Sandys brings to his commentary firsthand accounts of the New World. These demonstrate the merging of early modern experience with an ancient tradition, and the rapid creation of new folklore in the process. Responding to Ovid's account of the Lycian peasants turned frogs, Sandys writes:

> These were sent as a plague to the *Aegyptians* . . . and now not a little infest *Virginia* in Summer: called *Powhatans* hounds by the *English*, of their continuall yelping.

More fancifully, relying on a secondhand report, Sandys updates ancient travel lore, setting an old story in a new location. Reporting the existence of a miraculous herb with the power to unlock doors and release prisoners, Sandys writes:

> And I knew a fellow, who six or seaven yeares had beene a slave to the *Spanjard* in the *West-Indies*, who with desperate oaths would averre, how such an hearb was common in those countries; insomuch as the shackles would often unbolt, and fall from the feet of the horses, as they fed in the pastures.

This blend of a humanist's careful observation, an adventurer's democratic use of informants, a traveler's credulous belief in the wonders of foreign lands, and a scholar's knowledge of the classics makes Sandys's commentary of exceptional interest.

Sandys's 1632 Ovid was reprinted seven times in the seventeenth century and continued to be an important text into the nineteenth century. Used in many grammar schools, Sandys's verses served as models of English prosody and as an introduction to Ovid for generations of later poets and general readers. "Sandys's Ghost," by Alexander Pope, testifies to the vitality of his translation in 1717, and a hundred years later, John Keats turned to Sandys's Ovid as background for his mythological poems. With access to new translations and with radical changes in prosody, twentieth-century readers for the most

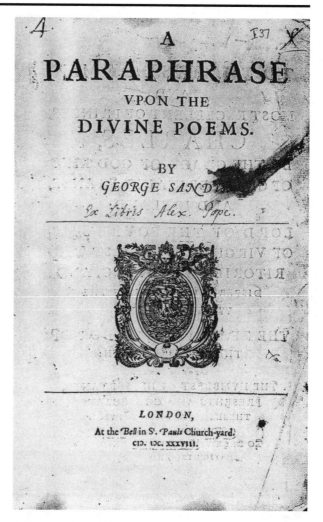

Title page for Alexander Pope's copy of the second edition (1637) of one of Sandys's devotional works (Sotheby's auction catalogue, sale number 2006, 19 July 1990)

part read Sandys's Ovid for its historical interest, although the verse and commentaries still give pleasure.

In the remaining years of his life, Sandys continued to pursue his court career, his interests in the Virginia Colony, and his vocation as a poet-translator. Soon after his return from Virginia, according to Davis, he probably became a Gentleman of the Privy Chamber, and he continued to solicit the favor of Charles I through dedications in his subsequent publications. He remained active as well in matters relating to Virginia until as late as 1641. During the 1630s, he was intimately involved in the circle at Great Tew. This group included the best poets of the age, along with scholars and theologians, providing Sandys with an ideal community in which to pursue his varied interests.

As the poet grew older and England moved toward civil war, it is not surprising that Sandys took an increasing interest in religion. After the Ovid, all of his major works are devotional in focus. In 1636 he published *A Paraphrase Upon the Psalmes of David and Upon the Hymnes Dispersed throughout the Old and New Testaments*; in 1637, *A Paraphrase Upon the Divine Poems*; in 1640, *Christ's Passion*; and in 1641, *A Paraphrase Upon the Song of Solomon*. *Christ's Passion* is a translation of a 1608 Latin play by Hugo Grotius, the Dutch jurist and statesman. The other three volumes are "paraphrases," or loose translations from the Old and New Testaments. The first work includes 150 psalms and hymns drawn from Exodus, Deuteronomy, Judges, I and II Samuel, Isaiah, Jonah, Habakkuk, and Luke, and it contains as well one of Sandys's few original poems, "Deo Opt. Max," written in praise of God and as a summation of the poet's life. The second work, an enlargement of the first, includes as well translations of the Book of Job and excerpts from Ecclesiastes and Jeremiah.

The composition of poetry on religious themes and the translation of sacred texts were both important literary activities in the English Renaissance. In moving from secular to sacred concerns in his last years, Sandys gave his life a traditional closure, much as John Donne had done. As noted earlier, however, his early books also reflect spiritual concerns—*A Relation of a Journey*, in the final object of the journey and in the underlying themes, and *Ovids Metamorphosis*, in the strain of Christian moralizing commentary that Sandys juxtaposes to Ovid's sophisticated and cynical poem.

Perhaps because of the devotional nature of his later works, Sandys's approach to the art of translation is quite different than in his Ovid. These are indeed paraphrases, following the content of the original, but enlarging upon it and fundamentally altering its style to suit another audience. While Sandys strove to match Ovid in line, phrase, and even cognate words, subordinating his own personality and poetic talent to Ovid's, in his paraphrases he largely abandons the densely balanced syntax and concrete imagery of the Hebrew for a more literal, prolix, expository voice. This new voice is especially evident where he employs heroic couplets, whose iambic pentameter lines are too short to accommodate Latin hexameters or elegiacs but too long, apparently, to preserve the feeling of the Hebrew verses. For exam-

ple, the opening lines of the Book of Job in the King James version read as follows:

> There was a man in the land of Uz, whose name was Job; and that man was perfect and upright, and one that feared God, and eschewed evil.

In Sandys's paraphrase this passage becomes,

> In Hus, a land which near the sun's uprise,
> And northern confines of Sabaea, lies,
> A great example of perfection reign'd;
> His name was Job, his soul with guilt unstain'd.

Where Sandys explores stanzaic forms with variable line lengths he is more successful in capturing qualities of the original, but the tone is still altered. For example, Psalm 38 in the King James version begins,

> O Lord, rebuke me not in thy wrath: neither chasten me in thy hot displeasure.
> For thine arrows stick fast in me, and thy hand presseth me sore.

The passage in Sandys's paraphrase reads,

> Not in thy wrath against me rise,
>   Nor in Thy fury, Lord, chastise:
>   Thy arrows wound,
>   Nail to the ground,
>   Thy Hand upon me lies.

The King James version has an urgency and syntactic clarity that Sandys cannot match.

Sandys's paraphrases offer the reader a mediated experience of the biblical texts, adjusted to seventeenth-century devotional and literary conventions. The rhythms lend themselves to musical settings as hymns, and the paraphrases anticipate Dryden's translations in their muting of emotional extremity and their explanatory tone. Some of Sandys's more successful stanzaic poems are reminiscent of George Herbert's *Temple* (1633) in their use of ebbing and flowing lines to trace subtle inflections of mood.

The dedicatory poems adorning Sandys's later volumes bear witness to the poet's reputation among his literary contemporaries. Contributors to *A Paraphrase Upon the Divine Poems* included Lord Falkland, Henry King, Sidney Godolphin, Thomas Carew, and Edmund ("Edward") Waller. This edition also includes Henry Lawes's musical settings to the psalms, designated on the title page as "for private Devotion." *Christ's Passion*, a closet drama written by a

Boxley Church, Kent, where Sandys was buried on 7 March 1634. A monument was erected for the first time in 1848 (from Richard Beale Davis, George Sandys, Poet-Adventurer *[1955])*

controversial Protestant exile, interested Sandys's friends at Great Tew chiefly because of the author's theological views, and probably had a more limited audience.

In the next generation, Dryden viewed Sandys's verse and practice of translation as skillful but old-fashioned, and, after Sandys's Ovid ceased to be the standard grammar-school text, the poet's readership dwindled. Twentieth-century interest in Sandys focuses on his travel book, which remains an important document of the *mentalité* of the age, and his commentaries on Ovid, the culmination of a long and rich tradition. Some of Sandys's psalms, with Lawes's settings, are still to be found in hymnals.

George Sandys died in March 1644. He is buried at Boxley Abbey in Kent, near the estate of the Wyatt family with whom he had maintained close ties since his return from Virginia. Above the date of his burial, 7 March 1644, the parish register reads, *"Poetarum Anglorum sui saeculi facile princeps"* (Certainly the master among English poets in his age). Unlike some English Renaissance poets—Donne and Herbert above all—who have been rediscovered in this century and whose writings appeal to modern and post-modern critics and readers, Sandys's reputation appears to be rooted firmly in his century. Living in the last age when one could be at the same time a scholar, poet, adventurer, courtier, administrator, and deeply religious man, he shaped his life around those things most highly valued in his time. His life and work have most meaning today in the context of the culture that informed them.

Letters:

Susan Myra Kingsbury, ed. *The Records of the Virginia Company of London*, 4 volumes (Washington, D.C.: U.S. Government Printing Office, 1906-1935).

Bibliographies:

Richard Beale Davis, "Early editions of George Sandys's 'Ovid': The Circumstances of Production," *Papers of the Bibliographical Society of America*, 35 (October, November, December 1941): 255-276;

Davis, "Two New Manuscript Items for a George Sandys Bibliography," *Papers of the Bibliographical Society of America*, 37 (Third Quarter 1943): 215-222;

Davis, "George Sandys and Two 'Uncollected' Poems," *Huntington Library Quarterly*, 12 (November 1948): 105-111;

Fredson Bowers and Richard Beale Davis, *George Sandys: A Bibliographical Catalogue of Printed Editions in England to 1700* (New York: New York Public Library, 1950);

Davis, "Sandys' *Song of Solomon*: Its Manuscript Versions and Their Circulation," *Papers of the Bibliographical Society of America*, 50 (Fourth Quarter 1956): 328-341.

Biography:

Richard Beale Davis, *George Sandys, Poet Adventurer: A Study in Anglo-American Culture in the Seventeenth Century* (London: Bodley Head/ New York: Columbia University Press, 1955).

References:

Robert R. Cawley, "Burton, Bacon, and Sandys," *Modern Language Notes*, 56 (April 1941): 271-273;

Richard Beale Davis, "America in George Sandys' 'Ovid,' " *William and Mary Quarterly*, third series 4 (July 1947): 297-304;

Davis, "Volumes from George Sandys's Library Now in America," *The Virginia Magazine of History and Biography*, 65 (October 1957): 448-457;

Christopher Grose, *Ovid's Metamorphoses: An Index to the 1632 Commentary of George Sandys*, Humana Civilitas: Studies and Sources Relating to the Middle Ages and the Renaissance, 7 (Malibu, Cal.: U.C.L.A. Center for Medieval and Renaissance Studies-Urdena Publications, 1981);

C. B. Hardman, "Marvell's 'Bermudas' and Sandys's *Psalms*," *Review of English Studies*, new series 32 (February 1981): 64-67;

Jonathan Haynes, *The Humanist as Traveler: George Sandys's Relation of a Journey begun An. Dom. 1610* (Rutherford, N. J.: Fairleigh Dickinson University Press, 1986);

Albert C. Labriola, "The Titans and the Giants: *Paradise Lost* and the Tradition of the Renaissance Ovid," *Milton Quarterly*, 12 (March 1978): 9-16;

Lee T. Pearcy, *The Mediated Muse: English Translations of Ovid, 1560-1700* (Hamden, Conn.: Archon, 1984);

Marie A. Powles, "Dramatic Significance of the 'Figures' Prefacing Each Book of Sandys' Translation of Ovid's *Metamorphosis*," *University of Dayton Review*, 10 (Summer 1974): 39-45;

Deborah Rubin, *Ovid's Metamorphoses Englished: George Sandys as Translator and Mythographer* (New York: Garland, 1985);

Rubin, "Sandys, Ovid, and Female Chastity: The Encyclopedic Mythographer as Moralist," in *The Mythographic Art: Classical Fable and the Rise of the Vernacular in Early France and England*, edited by Jane Chance (Gainesville: University of Florida Press, 1990);

Karl Eugene Schmutzler, "George Sandys' Paraphrases on the Psalms and the Tradition of Metrical Psalmody: an Annotated Edition of Fifty Selected Psalms, with Critical and Biographical Introduction," Ph.D. dissertation, Ohio State University, 1956;

Ruth C. Wallerstein, "The Development of the Rhetoric and Metre of the Heroic Couplet, Especially in 1625-1645," *PMLA*, 50 (March 1935): 166-209.

Papers:

The Richard Beale Davis papers at the library of the University of Virginia in Charlottesville, and the Alexander McElwain papers at the Houghton Library at Harvard University represent these scholars' research materials on George Sandys. Both include notes and correspondence about Sandys; Davis's papers include as well photocopies of original documents, many from the British Public Record Office, and reprints of secondary materials on Sandys.

Josuah Sylvester

(1562 or 1563 - 28 September 1618)

Frances M. Malpezzi
Arkansas State University

BOOKS: *A Canticle of the Victorie Obteined by the French King, Henrie the Fourth. At Yvry*, by Guillaume de Salluste, Sieur Du Bartas, translated by Sylvester (London: Printed by Richard Yardley, 1590);

The Triumph of Faith. The Sacrifice of Isaac. The Shipwracke of Jonas, by Du Bartas, translated by Sylvester (London: Printed by Richard Yardley & Peter Short, 1592);

Monodia (London: Printed by Peter Short, 1594);

The Profit of Imprisonment. A Paradox, by Odet de La Noue, translated by Sylvester (London: Printed by Peter Short for Edward Blunt, 1594);

The Second Weeke or Childhood of the World, by Du Bartas, translated by Sylvester (London: Printed by Peter Short, 1598);

The Miracle of the Peace in Fraunce. Celebrated by the Ghost of the Divine Du Bartas, by Jean Du Nesme, translated by Sylvester (London: Printed by Richard Bradocke for John Browne, 1599);

Bartas his Devine Weekes and Workes, translated by Sylvester (London: Printed by Humfrey Lownes, 1605; facsimile, Gainesville: Scholars' Facsimiles & Reprints, 1965);

Tetrastika. Or The Quadrains of Guy de Faur, Lord of Pibrac, translated by Sylvester (London: Printed by Humfrey Lownes, 1605);

I Posthumus Bartas. The Third Day of his Second Weeke, translated by Sylvester (London: Printed by Humfrey Lownes, 1606);

II. Posthumus Bartas. The Fore-noone of the Fourth Day of his Second Week, translated by Sylvester (London: Printed by Humfrey Lownes, 1607);

Automachia, or the Self-Conflict of a Christian, by George Goodwin, translated by Sylvester (London: Printed by Melchisedec Bradwood for Edward Blount, 1607);

Bartas his Devine Weekes and Workes [first complete edition], translated by Sylvester (London: Printed by Humfrey Lownes, 1608);

Lachrimæ Lachrimarum (London: Printed by Humfrey Lownes, 1612); enlarged, with works by Sylvester and others, as *Lachrymae Lachrymarum* (London: Printed by Humfrey Lownes, 1613);

The Parliament of Vertues Royal (London: Printed by Humfrey Lownes, 1614);

St. Lewis; the King (London: Printed by Humfrey Lownes, 1615);

The Second Session of the Parliament of Vertues Reall (London: Printed by Humfrey Lownes, 1616);

Tobacco Battered; & the Pipes Shattered (London: Printed by Humfrey Lownes, 1617);

The Maidens Blush: or, Joseph, by Girolamo Fracastoro, translated by Sylvester (London: Printed by Humfrey Lownes, 1620);

The Wood-mans Bear (London: Printed by Thomas Jones & Laurence Chapman, 1620);

Du Bartas his Divine Weekes and Workes with a Compleate Collection of all the Other . . . Workes Translated and Written by . . . Josuah Sylvester Gent. (London: Printed by Humfrey Lownes, 1621; enlarged edition, London: Printed by Robert Young, 1633; enlarged again, 1641);

Panthea: or, Divine Wishes and Meditations, revised by James Martin (London: Printed by G. Purslowe for F. Coules, 1630).

Editions: *The Complete Works of Joshuah Sylvester*, 2 volumes, edited by Alexander B. Grosart, Chertsey Worthies' Library (Edinburgh: Printed for private circulation by T. & A. Constable, 1880);

The Divine Weeks of Josuah Sylvester, edited by Theron Wilber Haight (Waukesha, Wis.: H. M. Youmans, 1908);

The Divine Weeks and Works of Guillaume de Saluste Sieur Du Bartas, 2 volumes, edited by Susan Snyder (Oxford: Clarendon Press, 1979).

OTHER: Pierre Matthieu, "A Panegyre.—The Tropheis," translated by Sylvester, in *The Heroyk Life and Deplorable Death of Henry the*

Josuah Sylvester (engraving by Cornelius van Dalen the Elder, from the 1633 edition of Sylvester's works)

Fourth, by Matthieu, translated by Edward Grimeston (London: Printed by G. Eld, 1612).

The contemporary renown and the subsequent literary reputation of Josuah Sylvester have been inextricably tied to that of Guillaume de Salluste, Sieur Du Bartas, the French Huguenot poet whose works Sylvester translated. During the Renaissance, Du Bartas was not only lauded in his own country but received almost universal renown, primarily for his hexameral *La Semaine ou Création du monde* (1578) and its sequel, *La Seconde Semaine* (1584). The *Semaines* were provided with an extensive commentary written between 1581 and 1601 by the Calvinist clergyman Simon Goulart. They underwent numerous contemporary editions (forty-two for *La Semaine* and twenty-nine for *La Seconde Semaine*) and were

widely translated. Du Bartas was especially admired in Great Britain. While Sylvester's translations are the most extensive and the most significant, published in numerous editions through 1641, some writings by Du Bartas were translated by Sir Philip Sidney and Thomas Churchyard (works now lost), as well as by King James, John Eliot, William Lisle, Thomas Lodge, Thomas Winter, Robert Barret, and Josiah Burchett. Du Bartas's visit to England and to the court of his admirer James VI of Scotland in 1587 surely helped secure his reputation there. Du Bartas's works, known primarily through Sylvester's translations, received widespread acclaim, were praised by major literary figures in England, and were quoted, borrowed from, and alluded to by great writers at least through the eighteenth century, but his reputation has waned considerably since then. Although Sylvester wrote original poetry and translated other works from both French and Latin, his place in literary history has been primarily preserved through his role as the English conduit to a French poet who long ago fell from favor. Critical studies of Sylvester have placed him in the context of the French influence on English literature and the role of divine poetry in the period. Criticism also focuses on his translation of Du Bartas as a source for lines and images of other writers (Edmund Spenser, William Shakespeare, Michael Drayton, John Donne, John Milton, Andrew Marvell, and Alexander Pope, for example).

Details of Sylvester's life are somewhat sketchy. Born in Kent in 1562 or 1563—possibly the son of Robert Sylvester, a clothier of London, or Thomas Silvester, a clothier of Burford, Oxfordshire—Josuah Sylvester was brought up by his maternal uncle, William Plumbe. One of the most significant and formative events of his childhood was his enrollment at about nine or ten in the Southampton grammar school of Hadrianus Saravia, a Belgian Protestant divine. The school specialized in French-language instruction, and boys who lapsed into English were punished. Sylvester remained there approximately three years before venturing into a commercial career in the cloth trade, an endeavor which probably began in 1576 with an apprenticeship to the Society of Merchant Adventurers. During his mercantile career he most likely divided his time between England and the Low Countries.

Literature was clearly his avocation. His first publication in 1590 was a translation of Du Bartas's poem celebrating the victory of Henry of Navarre at Ivry. This introduction to Du Bartas's works was to play a crucial role in shaping Sylvester's literary aspirations. While continuing his career in the cloth trade, he worked on translations and published his efforts. In 1600 or 1601 he gave up the cloth trade, and for a time he was employed by William Essex, probably as a tutor to his sons, in Lambourn, Berkshire. The move allowed Sylvester more time for his literary pursuits. The accession of James VI of Scotland in 1603 to the English throne as James I encouraged Sylvester to seek patronage from this admirer and translator of Du Bartas. James's son Prince Henry, who shared an interest with Sylvester in translating the quatrains of the French moralist Guy Du Faur de Pibrac, awarded him a pension of twenty pounds a year, which was paid from 1608 until Henry's death in 1612, an occasion of great disappointment for Sylvester and

the subject of his elegy *Lachrimæ Lachrimarum* (1612). Possibly married in 1608 or 1609 and with children to support, Sylvester encountered financial difficulties in the ensuing years, but he never gave up his commitment to literature. He did receive gifts from Henry's siblings, Charles and Elizabeth, and may have been a clerk in Parliament. In 1617, if not earlier, he left England and accepted a secretaryship with the Merchant Adventurers in Middelburg, Zeeland, where he died on 28 September 1618.

In his original compositions and in his translations, Sylvester seems to have shared the aesthetic which Du Bartas articulated in *L'Uranie*. His works are primarily influenced by Urania, the muse of divine poetry, and he had clearly accepted her advice to merge mirth with instruction. Both Du Bartas and Sylvester share what Anne Lake Prescott has termed "an aesthetics of levitation," a focus on poetry which is morally and spiritually uplifting. Throughout his works Sylvester sings the praises of God, lauds exemplary models of virtue and Christian heroism, and castigates the vices of his age.

Though not published until 1620, two years after his death, one of Sylvester's earliest original poems (possibly composed about 1595), *The Woodmans Bear*, is unlike his other works in subject matter. Generally regarded as an autobiographical poem because of the association of sylvan/Sylvester/woodman, the work has been read by Alexander B. Grosart, Susan Snyder, Franklin B. Williams, Jr., and others as detailing an unhappily concluded amatory relationship. The speaker of the poem observes a sorrowing woodman who is implored to relate his story to a Forest Queen. After a long immunity to love, the woodman at last becomes Cupid's victim when that god of love assumes the form of a beautiful she bear. The compassionate queen sends her nymphs to Diana's fount to procure an herb that will heal the woodman and relieve his distress. Praised by Grosart as superior to much love verse by Sylvester's contemporaries, the poem is generally seen as interesting only in terms of what it can reveal about Sylvester's life, with most attention devoted to trying to identify the lady (often assumed to be a girl named Ursula) and to establishing biographical details of Sylvester's early years. This conventional story of a thwarted Cupid transforming himself to snare a new victim—as well as the consequent suffering of the lover—however, suggests that this poem might be something more or other than a simple autobio-

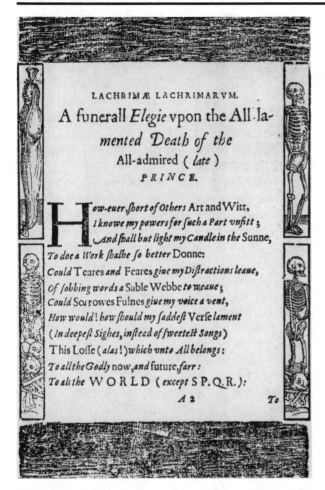

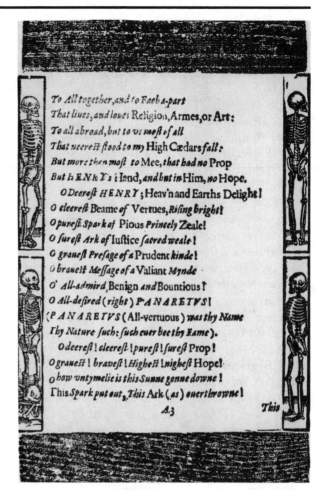

Opening pages from the 1612 edition of Sylvester's elegy on Prince Henry, who shared Sylvester's interest in the quatrains of Guy Du Faur de Pibrac

graphical account of unrequited love. Surely another line of inquiry might well be the relationship of the poem to moralizations of Ovid's *Metamorphoses*.

Although Sylvester's early literary endeavors—*The Wood-mans Bear*; *Monodia*, his 1594 elegy for Dame Helen Branch, the aunt of his friend Robert Nicholson; the posthumously printed lyrics and epistles to Arctoa—were original compositions, his forte was the art of translation and his long-term project the translation of the poetry of Du Bartas. Sylvester began his publishing career in 1590 with what was probably Du Bartas's last work before his death, *Cantique de la Victoire*, celebrating the 14 March 1590 triumph of the Protestant king, Henry of Navarre, at Ivry. Sylvester's next publication (1592) was a translation of the Huguenot poet's *Le Triomfe de la Foy* and fragments from his *Seconde Semaine*. Sylvester continued piecemeal translations of Du Bartas's epic work and in 1598 published additional parts

from *La Seconde Semaine*. Then in 1605 Sylvester published *Bartas his Devine Weekes and Workes*. Dedicated to James I (as part of his campaign to gain royal patronage), this edition was a complete translation of *La Semaine* and included all of *La Seconde Semaine* that had been published at the time of Du Bartas's death. In 1606 and 1607 Sylvester published translations of material by Du Bartas that had appeared in France posthumously, the third and fourth days of *La Seconde Semaine*. The 1608 edition of *Bartas his Devine Weekes and Workes* includes all the earlier material plus translations of more sections of *La Seconde Semaine*. Sylvester published another edition of this volume in 1611 and republished it in 1613. After his death editions of his collected works appeared in 1620 and 1621. The final contemporary printing of Sylvester's translation was in Robert Young's 1641 edition of Sylvester's complete works, *Du Bartas his Divine Weekes and Workes with a Compleate Collection of all the Other most delightful*

Workes Translated and written by the famous Philomusus Josuah Sylvester Gent. This extensive publishing history testifies to the popularity of the material as well as to Sylvester's commitment to making the works of Du Bartas accessible to an English audience. Translating the *Semaines* was no small endeavor. The work runs more than twenty thousand lines, and with Sylvester's additions the translation is even lengthier. Moreover, its encyclopedic nature would test any translator's general knowledge.

Epic in scope and based on the first two books of Genesis, as well as commentaries on it, *La Premiere Semaine* is in the hexameral tradition of accounts of the days of Creation. While Saint Basil's *Hexaemeron* in the fourth century is the earliest known Christian work to center on Creation, the genre was especially popular during the Renaissance. Burton O. Kurth sees the *Divine Weeks* as the prototype of the Renaissance hexameral epic. *The First Week* focuses on the days of Creation, beginning with Chaos and ending with the Sabbath. Informed by the Book of Creation tradition—the belief that God is manifest in his works—and replete with detail about God's magnificent handiwork, *The First Week* provides an astounding compendium of commonplace beliefs about religion, science, and nature as it draws not only on the hexameral tradition but that of the medieval encyclopedia. The unfinished *Second Week* has an even greater plan. Based on the conclusion of Saint Augustine's *City of God* (written 413-427), Du Bartas's sequel was to give us a view of the history of man from the Fall through the end of time. The seven days were each to be further divided into four parts. Four days (sixteen parts) were finished before Du Bartas died.

Sylvester is generally noted for his accuracy in translation, his early grounding in French standing him in good stead. Because he believed in the divine inspiration of poetry, he had great respect for the original and was faithful to it. He was even loyal to what are often deemed eccentricities of Du Bartas's style—the compound epithet and onomatopoeic duplication of syllables, for instance. Sylvester clearly distinguished his own emendations to the text through the use of italics. Most scholars—including Sidney Lee, Vagn Lundgaard Simonsen, Anne Prescott, and Burton Kurth—cite Sylvester as being more detailed and concrete in his translation. Snyder notes that Sylvester's drive to explain and specify lengthened the 20,738-line original to 22,889 lines. Sylvester also particularized the work for his English

readers as he expanded his text. He replaced French references with local references to create a decidedly English atmosphere for his audience. For example, he substituted English place names for French and replaced French history with English history. Nearly all critics agree that Sylvester is much more aggressively Protestant than the relatively tolerant Du Bartas. Sylvester's translation is marked with an anti-Catholic fervor absent from the original.

While the numerous editions document the popularity and significance of Sylvester's translation, source studies attest to its contemporary influence. Sylvester's translation of Du Bartas is seen as a source for many writers in both content and form. Called one of the major influences on John Milton's prosody, and a major influence in establishing the heroic couplet as the appropriate form for the epic, Sylvester's *Divine Weeks* was also a persuasive force in Abraham Cowley's choice of the couplet in *Davideis* (1656) as well as an influence on John Dryden's choice of the couplet for his translation (1697) of the *Aeneid*. Dryden's *Religio Laici* (1682) and his *Hind and the Panther* (1687) invite comparison to Sylvester's translation of Du Bartas, which could well have been a major factor in the diction of writings about nature in the eighteenth century. In fact, ties to Sylvester abound also in the works of Samuel Daniel, John Davies of Hereford, Joseph Hall, Edmund Spenser, William Shakespeare, Michael Drayton, George Chapman, John Donne, Andrew Marvell, and Alexander Pope.

Although the *Divine Weeks*, because of their sheer volume and epic scope, represent Sylvester's most significant achievement, a nonetheless crucial poem in Sylvester's canon is *L'Uranie*, a translation of a poem by Du Bartas first published in *La Muse Chretienne* (1574). Important because it provides such a clear sense of a shared Du Bartasian/Sylvestrian aesthetic, the poem dramatizes the conversion experience and education of its poet-protagonist through the intercession of the muse Urania. Nine-voiced Urania exhorts the poet to accept her as a guide. The poet-protagonist is compared to a pilgrim who has lost his way; his earlier poems, sinful and base, have prostituted his muse. Through them he has flattered the unworthy and sung the praises of wanton love. Urania abjures this poetic, warning him he will damn himself and spiritually harm his readers because poetry is able to imprint the good or evil of the poet on the reader. Acknowledging God to be the source of all poet-

Engraved title page for the 1641 edition of Sylvester's works

ry, Urania articulates the conventional Neoplatonic belief in poetry as a divine fury. Kindled by this fury, the soul ravished by God must lead others to the divine. Divinely inspired, a conduit of the Holy Ghost, the poet must help others achieve harmony with God and thus earn his reward—not an earthly crown of laurel but a heavenly crown that never fades. In the course of the poem, the speaker has been edified, has learned his obligations to God, neighbor, and self. *L'Uranie* presents the creed of a Christian poet, delineating what and why he should write. It provides a compendium of beliefs about the role of Christian art and the responsibilities of the Christian artist, beliefs shared by many in Sylvester's society and echoed by later writers. The beliefs provided the shaping force in Sylvester's choice of subject matter throughout his career. For Sylvester literature was much more than an avocation;

it was a divine calling. That is why he continued his work translating and writing even when pressed by the burdens of his career and by increasing financial difficulties.

The aesthetics of Urania are put into practice in other works translated by Sylvester, including some by Du Bartas. In addition to the ponderous *Semaines*, Sylvester translated various of Du Bartas's briefer poems that had clear spiritual import. In *The Triumph of Faith*, a dream arising from the gates of horn (the source of true visions), the speaker sees the triumphal procession of the sacred virgin Faith. With unpainted face, a body full of eyes that pierce heaven to see the divine, sweet tongues that praise God, mighty wings to ascend to heaven, and a crown of unwithering roses from Honor's tree, Faith is attended by the handmaidens Truth, Courage, Constancy, Patience, Charity, Repentance, and Humility. Before Faith proceeds her antithesis, a woman who (like Spenser's false Fidessa) seems fair, but a closer look reveals her to be (Duessa-like) most foul. Disguising her deformity behind masks and cloaks, her tongues blaspheming God, her eyes seeing only at night and blind to the light of day, her Icarian wings raising her in pride before her fall, she has in her train a countless host of sinners beginning with Cain. The speaker, after cataloguing those who have warred against Christ, prays to be released from that throng and in canto 3 lauds the champions of Faith, a list that includes prophets and martyrs and concludes with Mary, the mother of Christ. Canto 4 describes the tables carried in the procession that depict the victories of Faith. When the dreamer wakes from his vision, he realizes the evil of the times, a view that threatens the stability of his own faith. He does not, however, give in to despair, but recognizes the Satanic forces at work to stop the triumphant victory of Faith. The work ends on an apocalyptic note, as the speaker awaits the Last Judgment, when the goats will be separated from the lambs and the triumphal procession he envisioned will be a reality. He prays that Reason will direct his Faith while he awaits the Second Coming.

A translation of *La Judit* (1574), Sylvester's *Bethulains Rescue* (1614) is also a quintessential Du Bartasian poem. Based on the apocryphal story of Judith and Holofernes, Du Bartas's work was first translated into English by Thomas Hudson in 1608. Sylvester's version takes its title from Bethulia, the home of Judith and the town besieged by Holofernes. This epic, which begins in medias res with the Jews deciding to resist the aggression of Holofernes, celebrates the heroism of the widow Judith, who decapitates the evil Holofernes and enables the Jews to defeat a now-leaderless enemy army. E. M. W. Tillyard, who sees the realism of this minor epic as a possible model for Cowley's *Davideis*, also believes Sylvester excels in social commentary as he explores the weaknesses of the unregenerate.

While translating Du Bartas's works represents Sylvester's most prominent and most extensive efforts in that field, he also translated other writings, from both French and Latin, which would have pleased the Christian muse. In 1594 he published a translation of Odet de La Noue's *Paradoxe* (1588) as *The Profit of Imprisonment. A Paradox* and in 1599 sonnets from Jean Du Nesme. Then in 1605 he published his translations of Guy Du Faur de Pibrac, the work that helped Syl-

vester to gain Prince Henry's patronage. Pibrac's 126 quatrains of decasyllabic verses were regarded as a basic code of wisdom and gentlemanly conduct. In his dedication to Henry, Sylvester notes that he intends the work to reiterate the rules of state, religious lessons, and precepts the prince has already learned from his father. In 1607 Sylvester published a translation, *Automachia, or the Self-Conflict of a Christian*, from the Latin of George Goodwin. In Virgilian overtones the poem sings not of the siege of Troy but of the warring dualities within the self. In 1612 and 1616 he published translations of works by Pierre Matthieu, and in 1620 he published *The Maidens Blush: or, Joseph*, a translation of an incomplete Latin epic by the poet, humanist, and physician Girolamo Fracastoro, best known for his long Latin poem on syphilis and for a scientific treatise about the microbic origin of contagious diseases. With the death of Henry in 1612, Sylvester had turned to others in the royal family for patronage. *The Maidens Blush: or, Joseph* is not only dedicated to Charles, but includes an invocation to him in which Sylvester asks for help on his sacred voyage and points to Joseph as a prophetic model of Charles's princely virtues.

Just as Sylvester's translations focused on moral and devout works, so most of his original compositions could be said to have been inspired by Urania. *Lachrimæ Lachrimarum*, published in 1612 and augmented with works by Sylvester and others in 1613, is Sylvester's elegy for Prince Henry. Eulogizing Henry as a pattern of virtue and, with what obviously has special bearing on their relationship, the reward of arts, Sylvester begins with a conventional acknowledgment of his unworthiness to his task. He delineates the grief Henry's death has caused—for his parents, for the world, and especially for the poet himself, since Henry was his sustaining prop, his hope. Then Sylvester treats the death of Henry as the judgment of God on the people of England. He delineates the faults of various groups—clergy, nobles, magistrates, gentry, courtiers, lawyers, purveyors. He sees parallels with the death of Josiah for the sins of Israel, the death of Edward for England's sin, and Henry's death. Then he exhorts the sinful to pray for the safety of the sovereign, to shield James, Anne, Charles, and Elizabeth that their lives might not be given in retribution for the evil in the land. England's loss at Henry's death is Henry's gain: he has wed his savior and traded his earthly crown for one far greater. Through emphasizing Henry's sacrificial bargain,

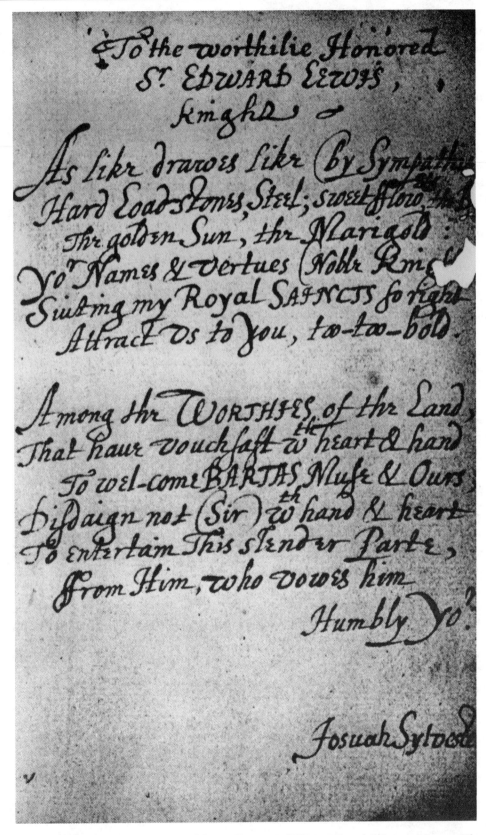

Inscription by Sylvester bound in a copy of his Parliament of Vertues Royal *(Pierpont Morgan Library)*

the poem not only underscores the retribution for sin, calling for a moral reform of England, but also illustrates the eternal reward of those, like Henry, who are dedicated to the virtuous life.

With another original poem, *Tobacco Battered* (1617), Sylvester joined an array of writers dealing with the controversial tobacco issue. Sylvester's position against the weed he saw antithetical to God's herb of grace was sure to have pleased King James, whose own *Counter-blaste to Tobacco* (1604) placed him in the forefront of antitobacco writers. Sylvester places his topic in the context of the corruption of the Fall as he examines the use and abuse of tobacco. Comparing tobacco to a gun which shoots homeward instead of forward, he outlines its deleterious physical and spiritual effects. As he questions whether both Indians and Christians might have benefited had the New World never been discovered, he engages in some of the biting satire for which he has been noted.

Once the darling of his age, lauded by a range of greats from Gabriel Harvey to Anne Bradstreet, Josuah Sylvester is often ignored or held in low regard today. The very qualities of his work which made him so popular in his time are often cited as the reasons for the decline in his reputation. The criticism that does exist has tended to regard Sylvester's work as a quarry to be mined for sources for more prominent writers—finding allusions to Sylvester in Shakespeare, Donne, Milton, Marvell, or Pope, or looking to Sylvester as a model for the prosody of various writers. Yet Sylvester's work should be seriously considered in its own right, especially in a critical age so concerned with a decidedly Protestant poetics in England and the continuation of such tradition in early America. While Sylvester appropriated Continental materials, his translations transformed them into English works. His emendations and additions to Du Bartas's *Semaines* are examples of the way he has transmuted the original. Not only did he substitute En-glish locales and English history for French and add concrete examples, but he also added a section on the Gunpowder Plot (1605), an example of his increased Protestantization of an already Protestant work. Because Sylvester was so popular in his time and because he clearly exerted an influence then and beyond, critics concerned with a Protestant English tradition would do well to look closely at his works—both his translations and his original compositions.

References:

W. B. Hunter, Jr., "The Sources of Milton's Prosody," *Philological Quarterly*, 28 (October 1949): 125-144;

Katherine Jackson, "Sylvester's 'Du Bartas,'" *Sewanee Review*, 16 (April 1908): 316-326;

Burton O. Kurth, *Milton and Christian Heroism: Biblical Epic Themes and Forms in Seventeenth-Century England* (Hamden, Conn.: Archon Books, 1966);

Sidney Lee, *The French Renaissance in England: An Account of the Literary Relations of England and France in the Sixteenth Century* (Oxford: Clarendon Press, 1910);

James L. Potter, "Sylvester's Shaped Sonnets," *Notes & Queries*, eleventh series 202 (September 1957): 405-406;

Anne Lake Prescott, *French Poets and the English Renaissance: Studies in Fame and Transformation* (New Haven: Yale University Press, 1978), pp. 167-234;

Vagn Lundgaard Simonsen, "Josuah Sylvester's English Translation of Du Bartas' 'La Premiere Sepmaine,'" *Orbis Litterarum*, 8 (1950): 259-285;

E. M. W. Tillyard, *The English Epic and Its Background* (New York: Oxford University Press, 1954), pp. 351-355;

Alfred Horatio Upham, *The French Influence in English Literature* (New York: Columbia University Press, 1908), pp. 145-218;

Franklin B. Williams, Jr., "The Bear Facts about Joshua Sylvester, The Woodman," *English Language Notes*, 9 (December 1971): 90-98.

John Taylor

(24 August 1577 or 1578 - December 1653)

Patricia Panek

SELECTED BOOKS: *The Scvller, Rowing from Tiber to Thames* (London: Printed by E. Allde, sold by N. Butter, 1612; facsimile, Amsterdam: Theatrvm Orbis Terrarvm / New York: Da Capo Press, 1970); revised and enlarged as *Taylors Water-Worke* (London: Printed by T. Snodham for N. Butter, 1614);

Great Britaine, All in Blacke (London: Printed by E. Allde for J. Wright, 1612);

Laugh and Be Fat: or, A Commentary Upon the Odcombyan Banket (London: Printed by W. Hall for H. Gosson, 1612?);

Heavens Blessing, and Earths Ioy (London: Printed by E. Allde for J. Hunt and H. Gosson, sold by J. Wright, 1613);

Odcombs Complaint (London: Printed by G. Eld for W. Burre, 1613);

The Eighth Wonder of the World (London: Printed by N. Okes, 1613);

The Nipping or Snipping of Abvses (London: Printed by E. Griffin for N. Butter, 1614);

The Pennyles Pilgrimage, or the Money-lesse Perambulation, of J. Taylor. From London to Edenborovgh (London: Printed by E. All-de, at the charges of the author, 1618);

Mr. Thomas Coriat to his friends in England sendeth greeting (London: Printed by J. Beale, 1618);

A Kicksey Winsey (London: Printed by N. Okes for M. Walbanck, 1619); revised and enlarged as *The Scourge of Basenesse* (London: Printed by N. Okes for M. Walbancke, 1624);

Taylor his Travels; From the Citty of London in England, to the Citty of Prague in Bohemia (London: Printed by N. Okes for H. Gosson, sold by E. Wright, 1620);

The Praise, Antiquity, and Commodity, of Beggery, Beggers, and Begging (London: Printed by E. Allde for H. Gosson, sold by E. Wright, 1621);

Taylor's Motto. Et Habeo, Et Careo, Et Curo (London: Printed by E. Allde for J. Trundle and H. Gosson, 1621);

John Taylor the "Water Poet" (portrait by an unknown artist; Bodleian Library, Oxford)

A Common Whore with all these Graces Grac'd (London: Printed by E. Allde for H. Gosson, 1622);

An Arrant Thiefe (London: Printed by E. All-de for H. Gosson, 1622);

Sir Gregory Nonsence His Newes from No Place (London: Printed by N. Okes, 1700 [i.e., 1622]);

The Praise and Vertue of a Iayle, and Iaylers (London: Printed by J. Haviland for R. Badger, 1623);

Taylors Pastorall (London: Printed by G. Purslowe for H. Gosson, 1624);

The Praise, of Cleane Linnen (London: Printed by E. All-de for H. Gosson, 1624);

A Bawd (London: Printed by A. Mathewes for H. Gosson, 1624?);

The Fearefull Summer, Or Londons Calamity (Oxford: Printed by J. Lichfield and W. Turner, 1625);

A Dog of War (London, 1628?);

All the Workes Of John Taylor The Water-Poet (London: Printed by J. Beale, Eliz. Allde & B. Alsop & T. Fawcet for J. Boler, 1630; facsimile, Menston, Yorkshire & London: Scolar Press, 1973);

The Olde, Old, Very Olde Man or the Age and Long Life of Thomas Par (London: Printed by A. Mathewes for H. Gosson, 1635);

A Swarme of Sectaries, and Schismatiques (London, 1641);

A Reply as true as Steele (London, 1641);

A Pedlar And A Romish Priest (London, 1641);

Mad Fashions, Od Fashions, All out of Fashions (London: Printed by J. Hammond for T. Banks, 1642);

A full and compleat Answer against the Writer of a late Volume set forth, entitled A Tale in a Tub (London: Printed for F. Cowles, T. Bates & T. Banks, 1642);

A Plea for Prerogative (London: Printed for T. Bankes, 1642);

Mad Verse, Sad Verse, Glad Verse and Bad Verse (Oxford: Printed by L. Lichfield, 1644);

Aqva-Mvsae (Oxford: Printed by L. Lichfield, 1645);

John Taylors Wandering to see the Wonders of the West (London, 1649);

A Short Relation Of A Long Iourney (London, 1652);

The Certain Travailes of an uncertain Journey (London, 1653).

Edition: *Works of John Taylor the Water Poet Not Included in the Folio Volume of 1630*, Publications of the Spenser Society, nos. 7, 14, 19, 21, and 25 (Manchester: Spenser Society, 1870-1878; 4 volumes, New York: Burt Franklin, 1967).

John Taylor the "Water Poet," a Thames waterman, was prompted by a facility for extemporaneous verse to venture into print in 1612. His ensuing career as a published poet spanned four decades and encompassed the genres of travel literature, parody, history, and satire. Taylor's poetic work does not fit neatly into the categories of seventeenth-century English poetry. Unable to compete with the classicism of poets such as Ben Jonson and unwilling to attempt the artificial style of the Metaphysical and lyrical poets, he chose instead to write simply about everyday life.

Although his poetry occasionally strays into modes associated with the professional poet (elegies, epithalamia, and sonnets), these instances are rare. His most typical works focus on a single theme, are written in rhymed couplets of irregular meter, and are narrative and often humorous in tone. Taylor's poetry was directed to a broad cross section of the reading public, particularly reflecting topics of interest and concern to the London middle class. By eschewing conventional modes and topics, he distanced himself from poets of his time and drew from the native English satiric tradition. Taylor's formal works, particularly those influenced by George Wither, show that he was more than capable of handling traditional styles of poetry. The unconventional form and content he adopted in his mature poetry reflect his characteristic, satiric style.

John Taylor was born on 24 August in 1577 or 1578 in St. Owen's parish in the city of Gloucester. His father was a chirurgeon, and Taylor mentions several brothers in his works. He attended St. Owen's parish grammar school under the tutelage of a Master Greene. Taylor showed an early facility for verse: he relates in an anecdote that he and several classmates were punished for writing a poem about the schoolmaster's drunken exploits. When he reached the Accidence in his curriculum, he was unable to master the Latin grammar and so ended his formal education. He was apprenticed to a waterman in London, where he ferried passengers across the Thames to the Bankside theaters. Acquainted with actors, he may be connected with the "John Tayller, Owermaker" who witnessed a document for Philip Henslowe on 8 April 1595. After being pressed into the Royal Navy and serving on seven voyages in Elizabeth I's reign (including the siege of Cadiz in 1596 and the Islands expedition in 1597), he returned to the waterman's trade. Taylor was also collector of wines for the Tower of London, a post he held intermittently until 1622. According to Taylor's own account he served as a waterman in the household of King James I, was several times voted ruler of the company of watermen, and often represented the guild as spokesman in legal disputes and at the royal court. He owned three businesses in his lifetime: a victualing house in Oxford and public houses in Southwark and Covent Garden. Taylor was married twice. He married his first wife in his "yonger wooing dayes," most likely in London. Their marriage was happy but childless; Taylor praised her constancy in *Taylor's Motto* (1621) and said, "*I care* to keepe my wife in that degree, / As that she alwayes might my equall be." She died in London circa 1643. Of Taylor's second wife, Alice, little is known except that she survived him by several years, dying in London on 30 January 1657.

Taylor's first published work was *The Sculler, Rowing from Tiber to Thames* (1612), a "hotchpotch, or Gallimawfry of Sonnets, Satyres, and Epigrams." The title page includes a woodcut of Taylor rowing his scull or wherry on the Thames. The prefatory matter of this work reveals that Taylor was already known to other writers; Nicholas Breton and Samuel Rowlands contributed dedicatory verses, and Taylor praises his "deere respected friend Mr. Beniamin Iohnson." In "The Author in his owne defence," Taylor indicates that critics were already claiming that he stole his lines, apparently unable to believe that someone with so little formal education could write poetry. Taylor castigates his critics and offers his lines to

You worthy fauorites of wisdomes lore,
Onely your favors doth my Muse implore:
If your good stomackes these harsh lines digest,
I careles bid a rush for all the rest.
My lines first parents (be they good or ill)
Was my vnlearned braine, and barren quill.

Epigrams in *The Sculler* are divided into satires of "Romish" vices (Tiber) and "British" vices or virtues (Thames). The "Romish" epigrams are anti-Catholic rhetoric, arguing against Jesuit doctrine, undoubtedly written to please Taylor's employer Sir William Waad, Lieutenant of the Tower, to whom the work is dedicated. The "British" epigrams are light in tone and similar to "jest-book" anecdotes, less biting than Jonson's and Donne's but portraying similar character types and perhaps specific individuals at court.

One of the serious poems in this work, "Pastorall Equiuocks, or a Shepheards complaint," is written from the point of view of a shepherd who has been rejected by his lover:

No Castle, Fort, no Rampier, or strong Hold,
But Loue will enter without Law or Leaue;
For where affections force hath taken hold,
There lawles loue will such impression leaue,
That Gods, nor men, nor fier, earth, water, winde,
From Loues straight lawes can neither turne nor wind.

Typical pastoral pleasures are mentioned only in the sense that the hero no longer enjoys them;

the poem ends with his death of a broken heart. Taylor uses identical words for his rhyme scheme, playing on their different meanings to achieve an interesting effect.

The Sculler was sufficiently popular to encourage Taylor's pursuit of a literary career, and a revised and enlarged edition was published in 1614 as *Taylors Water-Worke*. The high proportion of traditional verse forms (sonnets, epigrams) in this work as well as the dedicatory material from established poets suggest that Taylor hoped initially to be considered a serious poet.

A satirical jab in *The Sculler*, aimed at the eccentric travel writer Thomas Coryate, sparked a dispute that increased Taylor's notoriety at court. In 1611 Coryate had printed several popular pamphlets boasting extravagant dedicatory verses from established poets. Many of the contributors were friends of Coryate and ridiculed him in print in a bantering way. Taylor's remarks were intended to be taken in the same vein. He refers to Coryate as "a Wooll-packe, cramd with Greeke" and mocks his reputation at court:

The choysest wits would neuer so adore me;
Nor like so many Lackies runne before me:
But honest Tom, I enuy not thy state,
There's nothing in thee worthy of my hate.

Coryate took umbrage at the poem and swore revenge. Taylor responded with *Laugh and Be Fat: or, A Commentary Upon the Odcombyan Banket* (1612?), a parody of *Coryats Crudities* (1611). Coryate angrily appealed to King James I, who settled the dispute by having copies of *Laugh and Be Fat* burned. *Laugh and Be Fat* also offended many of the established poets, as Taylor's parody included parodies of their dedicatory verses. Although Taylor respected their poetic talents, he ridiculed them for associating with Coryate, who he considered to be a pompous fool. Taylor avenged himself with *Odcombs Complaint* (1613), a humorous elegy on Coryate's supposed drowning, and *The Eighth Wonder of the World* (1613), in which Coryate is miraculously rescued from death and hell. His final parody of Coryate, *Mr. Thomas Coriat to his friends in England* (1618), mimics Coryate's grandiloquent letter-writing style and is so convincing that it has sometimes been mistaken for Coryate's own work. The Coryate incidents brought Taylor into the limelight at court, amusing the king and courtiers, but his standing with established poets suffered. This may have strengthened his resolve to succeed as a poet on his own terms.

Two of Taylor's pamphlets show his involvement with the royal family at this time. Taylor's first elegy, *Great Britaine, All in Blacke* (1612), was written in response to the untimely death of Prince Henry on 6 November 1612. Taylor was present at the court, as evidenced by his registration of the work with the Stationers' Company the day after Henry's death and a full week before any other elegies were entered. At the time, Taylor was assisting in preparations for the marriage of the king's daughter Elizabeth and Frederick, Elector Palatine. Taylor participated in the Thames water pageant feting the couple's wedding and described the celebrations in verse and prose in *Heavens Blessing, and Earths Joy* (1613). Both pamphlets were likely to have had a wide circulation due to the importance of the events involved.

The poet George Wither was less fortunate in his dealings with the royal family. His satire *Abuses Stript, and Whipt* (1613), considered overly critical of the government, was suppressed and Wither was imprisoned in the Marshalsea. Taylor was Wither's friend and admired his satires; he was particularly impressed by Wither's claim that he would flatter no one in his honest depiction of vices of the age. Taylor adopted this stance in his satires as well, but treats his subjects with a tolerance and humor that are lacking in Wither's defiant attitude. Taylor's *The Nipping or Snipping of Abuses* (1614) is a mix of humorous and serious sonnets, epigrams, and satires. It was intended as a display of Taylor's poetic skill and includes some of his best poetry written on traditional themes. The pamphlet's dedications to royalty and courtiers and frequent references to Wither's imprisonment suggest that it was meant to draw attention to Wither's plight and secure him a pardon. The clearest reference to Wither, and also the finest poem in the collection, is "Loues labyrinth," in which Taylor visits a "shady, darke, vnhaunted desart groue" (Marshalsea prison), in which a "man cast downe by Fate" (Wither) grieves his loss of favor:

> Oh you immortall, high Imperious pow'rs,
> Haue you in your resistlesse doomes decreed,
> To blast with spight, & scorne my pleasant houres,
> To starue my hopes, and my despaire to feed?
> Once more let me attaine those sunshine showres:
> Whereby my withered ioyes againe may breed.
> If gods no comfort to my cares apply,
> My comfort is, I know the way to dye.

The doomed man bequeaths his faults to the gods as personified by the planets and carves a farewell sonnet on a tree. It is clear that the captive, "mad with loue" (that is, for his sovereign), is in despair until he can regain royal favor.

In addition to the influence of Wither, a native English poetic tradition is also evident in the "Skeltonicall salutation" introducing the work (written in the rapid rhyming style of John Skelton) and "The Authours description of a Poet and Poesie, with an Apology in defence of Naturall English Poetry," perhaps inspired by Philip Sidney's *Defence of Poesie* (1595). Taylor's "Apology" defies the notion that English poetry is inferior to poetry based on classical models:

> In what strange tongue did *Virgils* Muse commerce?
> What language wast that *Ouid* wrote his verse?
> Thou sayst 't was Latin: why I say so too,
> In no tongue else they any thing could doo:
> . . . .
> Why may not then an English man, I pray;
> In his owne language write as erst did they?
> Yet must we suit our phrases to their shapes,
> And in their imitations be their Apes.

Taylor singles out Sidney and Wither as model English poets and again defends his own work from critics who accuse him of plagiarism or scorn his lack of education:

> But wherefore doe I take a Schollers part,
> That haue no ground or Axioms of Art,
> That am in Poesie an artlesse creature,
> That haue no learning but the booke of Nature;
> No Academicall Poeticke straines,
> But home-spun medley of my mottley braines?
> . . . .
> Now in my owne defence once more I'l say,
> Their too rash iudgements too much runne astray,
> That, 'cause my name is *Taylor*, I doe theeue it,
> I hope their wisdomes will no more beleeue it:
> Nor let my want of learning be the cause,
> I should be bitten with blacke enuies iawes:
> For whose'r by nature is not a Poet,
> By rules of Art he neuer well can show it.
> . . . .
> A Poet needs must be a Poet borne,
> Or else his Art procures his greater scorne.

The Nipping or Snipping of Abuses marks a turning point in Taylor's career. His defense of nonclassical models and his claim to be "a Poet borne" were not sufficient to silence his critics, who still did not accept him as a serious poet, so he decided on nontraditional subject matter and style as ways of making his mark. There are few instances of traditional verse forms, such as sonnets, in his works after 1614. Taylor's characteristic narrative poems written in rhymed couplets developed during this period, and a trip to Germany in 1616 inaugurated a new career as a writer of travel literature. Taylor's journeys were often "adventures upon returns," combining wagering with publication subscription. After publishing a bill outlining the conditions, Taylor collected signatures from those wishing to wager on the journey's successful completion. When Taylor returned, the descriptive pamphlets (often in verse) would be printed and delivered for payment. Taylor was an early practitioner of publication by subscription, though he reserved its use for accounts of his wagering journeys; it became a common method of financing publications later in the century. During his lifetime, Taylor traveled to Germany, Bohemia, Scotland, Wales, and most of the counties of England. His travels allowed him to extend his readership beyond the greater London area and resulted in his becoming a much-recognized figure. As travel literature his pamphlets offer little topographical description, but they faithfully record tidbits of local history and items of interest to Londoners.

The broadening of experience occasioned by his travels may have given Taylor the idea for another nontraditional series of poems. Taylor's "praise" pamphlets are satires, mock-heroic depictions of the lower stratum of urban society (beggars, whores, bawds, and thieves). Taylor uses his persuasive powers to convince his readers of the antiquity (and implied nobility) of such professions and the ways in which such persons are better off than their wealthier, more respectable neighbors. The first of these pamphlets, *The Praise, Antiquity, and Commodity, of Beggery* (1621), depicts the pleasures of beggars in a pastoral vein:

> A Begger euery way is *Adams* Son,
> For in a Garden *Adam* first begun:
> And so a Begger euen from his birth,
> Doth make his Garden the whole entire Earth.
> The fields of Corne doth yeeld him straw & bread,
> To Feed and Lodge, and Hat to hide his head:
> And in the stead of cut-throat slaughtering shambles,
> Each hedge allows him Berryes from the brambles.
> . . . .
> His musicke waytes on him in euery bush,
> The Mauis, Bulfinch, Blackbird and the Thrush:
> . . . .

> These feather'd Fidlers sing, and leape, and play,
> The Begger takes delight, and God doth pay.

This earthly paradise is not devoid of sharp social satire. Taylor relates an anecdote about a noble, compassionate lord who kept a "well furnish'd Table" to feed the beggars at his gate: "For 'tis within the power of mighty men, / To make fiue hundred Beggers, and feed Ten." The lord, confounded by the number of beggars asking for relief, asks his fool for advice; the fool recommends hanging them all. Shocked, the lord reminds the fool that the beggars are Christians and deserve better treatment:

> Tush (said the Foole) they are but beggers tho,
> And thou canst spare them, therefore let them goe:
> If thou wilt doe, as thou hast done before,
> Thou canst in one yeere make as many more.

Taylor's mock-heroic praise pamphlets of lowly subjects show the influence of earlier prose works such as Thomas Nashe's *Nashes Lenten Stuffe* (1599) and Thomas Dekker's *The Belman of London* (1608), works that also flaunt their anti-establishment stance and defiance of current literary canons.

George Wither reappears as an influence on Taylor in 1621. Wither had written *Wither's Motto* (1621), a personal manifesto in verse expressing his political opinions in the motto "Nec Habeo, Nec Careo, Nec Curo" (Nor Have I, Nor Want I, Nor Care I). Taylor registered his own *Taylor's Motto. Et Habeo, Et Careo, Et Curo* (I Have, I Want, I Care) on 18 June two days after, before Wither's pamphlet was approved for publication. In *Taylor's Motto*, Taylor's firmly stated opinions on religion, poetry, government, and other themes are a rare specimen of his personal reflections on life. He praises his wife, describing a marriage soundly based on trust; he regrets his lack of children; and he expresses his humble belief in God. Wither's influence on Taylor reappeared in 1645, when his alliance with Parliamentarian forces turned Taylor's admiration to dismay; Wither's *Campo-Musae* (1643) was answered by Taylor's Royalist *Aqua-Musae* (1645).

After *Taylor's Motto*, Taylor's determination to pursue nontraditional poetry and his identification with his London readership continued in *Taylors Pastorall* (1624). His previous treatments of a pastoral theme (*The Sculler* and *Praise of Beggery*) did not fit the classical mold, as the first was a love lyric only incidentally connected with shepherds, and the second was an urban satire em-

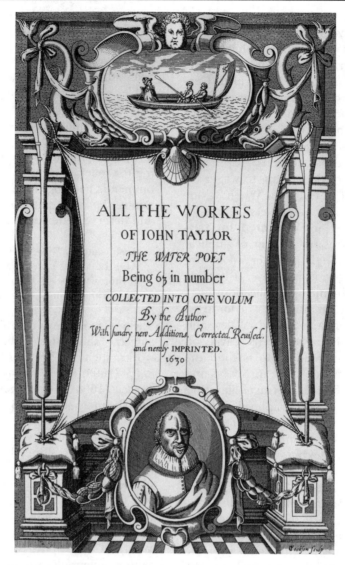

Engraved title page for the folio edition that collects most of Taylor's work. Insets depict scullers rowing a passenger on the Thames and a portrait of Taylor based on a painting at Watermen's Hall in London.

ploying pastoral description. Here Taylor muses that though "VIRGIL, OVID, MANTVAN, *and many of our learned English and Scottish Poets*" had written pastorals, "*yet for all their paines, diligent search and collections, my weake capacitie can finde matter enough to make an honest Pamphlet out of what they haue ouerseene, neglected, or made slight account of.*" Instead of using classical models, Taylor relates biblical stories of shepherds and discusses the use of the sheep or lamb as a religious symbol. The many uses of products from sheep (food, parchment, wool, leather) are documented, showing their necessity to life and, symbolically, the omnipresence of the divine in the ordinary. The pamphlet also praises London guilds connected with clothmaking, particularly the Drapers' guild; Tay-

lor even lists in prose all lord mayors of London who had been drapers, with their charitable deeds to the city. The overall treatment is similar to Taylor's praise pamphlets except it is more serious than satirical, emphasizing values of industry, faith, and civic pride that would have appealed to Londoners. Instead of glorifying Arcadian swains, Taylor's witty pastoral portrays shepherds in the practical context of their spiritual and commercial importance, firmly grounded in reality.

Also in 1624 Taylor wrote *The Praise, of Cleane Linnen*, another praise pamphlet that returns to his mock-heroic style. Dedicated to a laundress at the Inns of Court, the poem describes the uses of cloth literally from the cradle to the grave: "Our Corps first Couer, at our naked birth: / And our last garment when we turne to Earth." Taylor's wry humor evident throughout this work is exemplified in the depiction of a dinner table as a battlefield:

> Though raging hunger make the Stomacke wroth,
> 'Tis halfe asswag'd by laying of the Cloth.
> For in the warres of eating 'tis the vse,
> A Table cloth is hungers flagge of Truce:
> Whilst in the fight the Napkins are your friends,
> And wait vpon you, at your fingers ends.

He commends the work of laundresses, instructing his readers to treat them with respect. The laundress is compared to a kingfisher, which was said to spread its plumage only in good weather:

> So doth a *Laundresse*, when the Sun doth hide
> His head, when skyes weepe raine and thunder chide,
> When powting, lowring, slauering sleete & snow,
> From foggy Austers blustring iawes doth blow,
> Then shee in moody melancholy sittes,
> And sighing, vents her griefe by girds and fittes:
> Her liquid *Linnen* piteous pickl'd lyes,
> For which shee lowres and powts as doth the skies,
> But when bright *Phoebus* makes *Aurora* blush,
> And roabes the welkin with a purple flush,
> When mourning cloudes haue wasted all their teares,
> And welcome weather faire and dry appeares,
> Then to the hedge amaine the *Laundresse* ambles,
> In weeds of pennance clothing bryers and brambles.

Cleane Linnen represents the mature poetic style of Taylor's comic praise pamphlets. His use of colorful description and figures of speech, which came naturally to him in prose, became integrated into his poetry in these works.

The crowning achievement, and perhaps also the swan song, of Taylor's poetic career was his 1630 publication, *All the Workes Of John Taylor The Water-Poet*. This folio edition of most of Taylor's prose and poetic works reflects his desire to be taken seriously as a poet and writer. Folio editions were still an expensive novelty; the only others previous to 1630 were Ben Jonson's *Workes* (1616) and the First Folio of William Shakespeare (1623). Like Jonson, Taylor took responsibility for the volume's arrangement and content, making numerous corrections and revisions. Production of a definitive folio text was a way to legitimize and preserve his works. The folio's publication shows that Taylor's works were popular enough to guarantee sale of the volume and that his admirers included persons of moderate wealth.

Taylor was ill when the work was in press, and he may have thought it would be his last work. The volume begins and ends with religious pamphlets, which may underscore that assumption. The "Epistle Dedicatory" preceding the texts is satirical but more jaded in tone than Taylor's other satires. Dedicated to "The World," it is both a satire of the world's faults and an ironic farewell. "You neuer fauored me," Taylor writes, ". . . all that I craue of thee liuing, is a graue when I am dead." He asks the world a favor: prevent his readers from being persuaded that the volume was not written by him, "for opinion doth worke much in such cases." Obviously, Taylor was still defending himself against detractors; of this work, he says, "were it nameless, I am perswaded that it would passe more blamelesse." Nevertheless, he entrusts the world with his book, declaring, "I am wearie of you and it, and take leaue to leaue you."

Taylor continues to emphasize the nontraditional nature of his work by referring to his status as a waterman/poet. He includes the nickname "Water-Poet" in the folio's title, written on the engraved title page across a sail suspended from two sculler's oars. Insets depict scullers rowing a passenger on the Thames and a portrait of Taylor based on a painting at Watermen's Hall in London. He reflects on this distinction in the dedication: "knowing my selfe for two conditions to haue no fellow; first, in beeing a Sculler; secondly a Water-Poet; of the last of which, there is and shall bee no more I hope."

Although he survived his illness, the folio was a formal farewell to his poetry. The majority of Taylor's works written after 1630 are in prose, for reasons hinted at in the dedication. He was tired of fighting for acceptance as a poet; prose writers were not subject to assumed prerequisites of rank or education. Taylor also asks the world for good clothes, "because I haue occasion to speake with great men, and without good cloathes (like a golden sheath to a leaden blade) there is no admittance." This may indicate Taylor's high rank in the Watermen's guild at this time, borne out by the portrait predating the folio. He was also increasingly concerned with the political and religious issues, which occupy the bulk of his remaining writings in verse and prose. His political and religious satires supporting the Royalists during the English Civil War, in fact, were particularly successful and much imitated. His Royalist sympathies, however, made it too dangerous for him to remain in London at the outbreak of the English Civil War. He followed King Charles I to Oxford, where he was treated well by the king's court and the university scholars. During his tenancy there he ran a victualing house and was overseer of a commission to clear the Thames of debris to allow passage of needed supplies to the new capital. King Charles made him a yeoman of the guard in recognition of his years of service to the Crown.

Taylor returned to London in 1647 and ran a public house called the Crown, located in Phoenix Alley in Covent Garden. When King Charles was beheaded, Taylor changed his sign to the Mourning Crown. Commonwealth authorities were displeased, so he changed the sign to the Poet's Head, displaying his own portrait with verse couplets. Forced to curb his political satire under the Commonwealth, Taylor renewed his "adventures upon returns" for income. Despite his advancing age (he was in his seventies), Taylor journeyed to Cornwall, Wales, and the east coast of England, often on foot. Taylor's last "adventure upon returns" and last pamphlet, *The Certain Travailes of an uncertain Journey* (1653), sums up his view of poetry and life:

Some men do travell in their contemplations,
In reading Histories and strange Relations:
Some few do travell in the wayes Divine,
Some wander wildly with the Muses nine;
For every man would be a Poet gladly,
Although he write and Rime but badly madly.
Sometimes the wits and tongues do, most unfit,
Travell, when tongues do run before the wit.
But if they both keep company together,
Delight and profit is in both, or eyther.

Thus, despite his unlikely beginnings, Taylor did succeed in establishing himself as a popular poet of his time, finding both "delight and profit" in his career. He died at about the age of seventy-five in early December of 1653, leaving no will, and his burial was recorded in the parish register of St. Martin's-in-the-Fields on 5 December 1653.

John Taylor progressed from grammar-school dropout to noted writer, from humble waterman to national celebrity; it is therefore small wonder that such an unusual career would elicit disparate responses. The popularity of his pamphlets shows his ability to capture the interest of a diverse reading public. In Ben Jonson's *Timber: or Discoveries* (1640), Jonson's comment on Taylor

and that public was "Nay, if it were put to the question of the water-rhymer's works, against Spenser's; I doubt not, but they would find more suffrages; because the most favour common vices, out of a prerogative the vulgar have, to lose their judgements, and like that which is naught." Jonson was also quoted by William Drummond in his Conversations as saying that King James preferred Taylor's verses. John Aubrey, who met Taylor in Oxford in 1643, wrote in his *Brief Lives* (1813), "He was very facetious and diverting company; and for stories and lively telling them, few could out-doe him." Aubrey reported that Josias Howe, an Oxford M.A. and companion of Taylor's at the university, claimed that he could choose six verses of Taylor's "as good as you will find in any other." Near the end of Taylor's life, and after his death, he had few outspoken supporters, of course, for such expressions would have been politically dangerous. The pamphlet *Sportive Wit*, containing two fond epitaphs on Taylor, was withheld until 1656, three years after Taylor's death. The address to the readers mentions that the pamphlet had "passed the Verdict of a Grand Jury" after being "too severely dealt withall." The political climate of the Commonwealth prevented Taylor from freely publishing his satires during his later career and also led to suppression of reprints of his works after his death. Had he lived to see the Restoration, his position as a Royalist and former servant of the royal household might have restored him to favor at court, and certainly would have ended suppression of his pamphlets. Gradually his work slipped into obscurity, until the rarity of his pamphlets sparked the interest of antiquarians. Robert Southey included him in his *Lives of the Uneducated Poets* (1831), and Charles Hindley reprinted a selection of Taylor's works in *The Old Book Collector's Miscellany* (1871-1873). The scarcity of modern editions still contributes to his neglect.

Taylor's work can best be compared with two contemporary prose writers. Though Taylor's wit does not have the sparkle of Thomas Nashe's, he has the same love of language and was influenced by the comic viewpoint of such works as Nashe's *Lenten Stuff*. Like his friend Thomas Dekker, Taylor saw the world through the eyes of urban London and shared a delight in characters and details to be found in everyday life. His combination of satiric description with personal warmth also has much in common with the style of these writers.

Assessment of Taylor's contribution to poetry is a more difficult task. Critics from his own lifetime to the present have complained of Taylor's poor education and waterman's rank. Then, as now, Taylor challenged perceptions of a poet's status in society and clashed with his era's expectation that a poet should be an educated aristocrat. His poetic career also developed in a different fashion than the norm. He refused to rely on patronage for income, feeling that his satires would thereby be free from undue influence and prefering the "honest" labor of a waterman. Rather than working his way up from obscurity to recognition, Taylor was popular with and accepted by the royal court from the outset of his career, suffering decline when the king and court were abolished. Despite having a large readership that was socially and geographically diverse, Taylor seems never to have been accepted as a poet by the literary community at large. His respect for these poets and personal choice not to compete with them led to his experimentation with informal poetry. Although he cannot be said to have had a direct influence on other poets, Taylor's innovations include some of the earliest nonsense verse in English and unromanticized depictions of ordinary life, both elements of much later schools of poetry. He also championed poetry written in English, especially poetry that departed from classical models. His formal works show that he was not devoid of poetic talent in conventional modes, but his informal poems, particularly his satires and praise pamphlets, created the style that made his mark. Taylor's strongest claim to posterity as a poet may simply be his willingness to test the boundaries of poetic convention.

Bibliography:

R. B. Dow, "The Life and Times of John Taylor the Water Poet," M.A. thesis, Harvard University, 1930.

Biographies:

R. B. Dow, "The Life and Times of John Taylor the Water Poet," M.A. thesis, Harvard University, 1930;

John Aubrey, *Brief Lives*, edited by Richard Barber (Woodbridge, Suffolk: Boydell Press, 1982), pp. 298-299.

References:

Edward Arber, ed., *A Transcript of the Registers of the Company of Stationers of London: 1554-1640 A.D.*, 5 volumes (London: Privately printed, 1875-1894; facsimile, London: Peter Smith, 1967);

Sandra Clark, *The Elizabethan Pamphleteers: Popular Moralistic Pamphlets 1580-1640* (London: Athlone Press, 1983);

Wallace Notestein, *Four Worthies* (London: Cape, 1956);

George Parfitt, ed., *Ben Jonson: The Complete Poems* (New York & London: Penguin, 1988);

Marjorie Rushforth, "Two John Taylor Manuscripts at Leonard Lichfield's Press," *Library*, 11, fourth series (September 1930): 179-192.

Papers:

Two manuscript verses by Taylor are among the papers of the Earl De La Warr, Baron Buckhurst, and autograph manuscripts of *The Causes Of The Diseases And Distempers Of This Kingdom* and *Aqua-Musae* (1645) are in the Bodleian Library.

Aurelian Townshend
(by 1583 - circa 1651)

Julie W. Yen

California State University, Sacramento

BOOKS: *Albions Triumph. Personated in a Maske at Court. By the Kings Maiestie and his Lords. The Sunday after Twelfe Night. 1631* (London: Printed by Aug. Mathewes for Robert Allet, 1631 [i.e., 1632]);

Tempe Restord. A Masque. Presented by the Queene, and foureteene Ladies, to the Kings Maiestie at Whitehall on Shrove-Tuesday. 1631 (London: Printed by A. M. for Robert Allet & George Baker, 1631 [i.e., 1632]).

Editions: *Aurelian Townshend's Poems and Masks*, edited by E. K. Chambers (Oxford: Clarendon Press, 1912);

The Poems and Masques of Aurelian Townshend: With Music by Henry Lawes and William Webb, edited by Cedric C. Brown (Reading, U.K.: Whiteknights Press, 1983).

PLAY PRODUCTIONS: *Albions Triumph*, London, Whitehall, 8 January 1632;

Tempe Restord, London, Whitehall, 14 February 1632.

Aurelian Townshend is known today for two court masques and a small collection of graceful poems. He led a relatively obscure life, except for a brief period of success in 1631, when the contentious relationship between Ben Jonson and Inigo Jones finally erupted in a quarrel that resulted in Jonson's dismissal, leaving the position of court masque writer vacant. Asked to step in and provide the next season's court entertainment for Charles I and Henrietta Maria, Townshend composed *Albions Triumph* and *Tempe Restord*. Apart from the masques, Townshend also wrote about twenty poems for the court audience. He was one of the last of John Donne's followers, at a time when the metaphysical style was beginning to lose its popularity. In contrast to the vigorous wit of Donne's poetry, Townshend's forte is sophisticated gallantry. The wedding of "manly gallantry and wit" central to his works, then, might well derive from his dual commitment to the lyric and the masque—a wedding of

styles that is nowhere more evident than in his mastery of the genre of the compliment to a lady.

This emphasis on the art of courtesy in his writings reflects in some ways his family origins. Under the Tudors, the Townshend family had risen to some importance in society through the legal profession. Aurelian was the son of John Townshend and his wife, Anne Catlin, of West Dereham, Norfolk. The precise date of his birth is unknown, but he must have been born by the year 1583, because in the will of Thomas Townshend, yeoman, of Crymplesham in Norfolk, dated 12 December 1583, he and a sister Fanceline are left a legacy of thirty pounds. In 1600 he came to the attention of Sir Robert Cecil (later first Earl of Salisbury), who noticed his good breeding, beautiful handwriting, and knowledge of French and Italian. To train him for his son William's service, Cecil sent Townshend to the Continent, first to Paris for a year, then on to Venice. During three years abroad, Townshend wrote Cecil seven letters, profusely expressing gratitude for Cecil's patronage and also revealing young Townshend's naiveté. In October 1602 in Florence, Townshend met an Englishman, Sir Anthony Sherley, who borrowed two hundred scudi of Cecil's money from Townshend and then promptly abandoned him. With the help of one of Donne's friends, Basil Brooke, Townshend was able to secure a loan from an English merchant; but later when he sent the merchant a bill of exchange on Lord Cecil, his patron refused to honor it. It is not known if the merchant ever got his money back, but Townshend was immediately summoned back to England. On his way home he met with a series of misfortunes that further depleted his funds. He injured his ankle and then became seriously ill at Nancy, France, where he exhausted all his resources, so that he had to borrow more money from friends to continue on his journey. (From these events, it seems clear that the 12 February 1603 entry in John Manningham's diary, which claims that "Ben John-

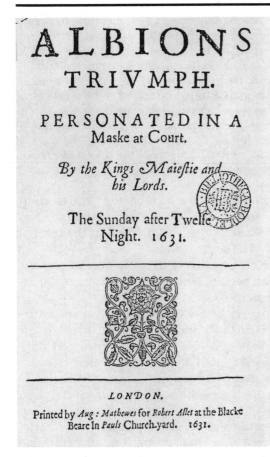

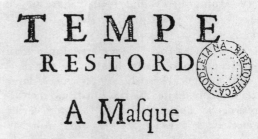

Title pages for the masques Townshend wrote after he replaced Ben Jonson as Inigo Jones's collaborator on entertainments for the court of Charles I and his queen, Henrietta Maria

son the poet nowe lives upon one Townesend and scornes the world," cannot, as is often supposed, refer to the poet Aurelian Townshend.)

Townshend's best-known poem, "Victorious Beauty," is addressed to Catherine Howard, Countess of Salisbury, William Cecil's wife, but there is no concrete evidence that Townshend actually entered the service of William, who succeeded his father, Robert Cecil, as second Earl of Salisbury in 1612. In 1608, the year William and Catherine were married, Townshend was traveling on the Continent, this time in the train of Sir Edward Herbert, later Lord Herbert of Cherbury. It is likely, however, that Townshend was given a second chance with the older Cecil; for Townshend is described as being in sole attendance on Cecil, by then lord treasurer, at his deathbed on 24 May 1612.

After this date there are no records of Townshend's life for the next twenty years. During this period, he was married and set up house in St. Giles, Cripplegate. His house in the Barbi-

can was close to the estate of John Egerton, first Earl of Bridgewater, and he had some connections with the earl. A copy of *Albions Triumph* preserved in the Huntington Library is a presentation copy from the poet to the earl of Bridgewater, and the Bridgewater children took part in the later masque *Tempe Restord*. When Frances, Countess of Bridgewater, died on 11 March 1636, Townshend composed "A Funerall Elegie" in her memory.

Townshend's wife was Anne Wythies of Copgrave, Yorkshire, widow of William Agborough who had died and left her with a son, Robert, who later adopted Townshend's name. Townshend also had five children of his own: George, Mary, James, Herbert, and Frances. Herbert died in infancy. Mary grew up to be a celebrated beauty with a considerable reputation at court, as the mistress (at age sixteen) of Charles Louis, Elector Palatine, and, sometime before her marriage at the age of twenty, as the mistress of Edward Sackville, fourth Earl of Dorset. A much-quoted account, attributed to Philip Herbert,

Earl of Montgomery and fourth Earl of Pembroke, describes Townshend in 1642 as

a poore & pocky Poett, but a marryed man & an howsekeeper in Barbican, hard by ye now Earl of Bridgewaters. Hee hath a very fine & fayer daughter, Mrs. to the Palsgrave first, and then afterwards ye noble Count of Dorset, a Priuy councelour & a Knight of ye Garter. Aurelian would bee glad to sell an 100 verses now at sixepence a piece, 50 shillings an 100 verses.

Little else is known about Townshend's life, although two accounts of his litigious activities suggest that he outgrew his early naiveté. He petitioned the courts for the wardship of Philippa Ivatt, the lunatic widow of Thomas Ivatt, searcher, of London, and was successful on 3 June 1629, thereby gaining control of her estate. In March 1643 he appealed to the House of Lords for protection when he was threatened with arrest for debt to a silkman by the name of Tulley, for merchandise ordered on behalf of Lewis Boyle, Lord Kinalmeakey. Pleading that he was a servant of the king and that he did not personally owe Tulley any money, Townshend was successful in his suit.

The exact date of Townshend's death is uncertain. He may have left England after the fall of Oxford, the last stronghold of the Royalists, in June 1646, going with Prince Rupert to France or Prince Maurice to The Hague. The discovery of a fragment of an elegy that Townshend wrote on the death of Charles I in 1649 (quoted by Vita Sackville-West in *Knowle and the Sackvilles*, 1922) establishes that he was alive in that year. He is now believed to be the "Townshend" whose "A Dialogue: Amyntas, ho!" appears as a commendatory verse in Clement Barksdale's *Nympha Liberthris: or the Cotswold Muse*, published in 1651. There is no evidence of his survival after that year.

Townshend's earliest success came in 1631 when Jonson was dismissed from his post as court masque composer. On the title page of *Love's Triumph through Callipolis*, a masque presented to the king on 9 January 1631, Jonson had put his name before that of the set designer, architect Inigo Jones, who was enraged by Jonson's presumption. In a 12 January 1632 letter to Sir Thomas Puckering, John Pory gave an account of the incident:

The last Sunday at night the Kinges masque was acted in the banquetting house, the

Queens being suspended till another time, by reason of a sorenes which fell into one of her delicate eyes. The Inventer or Poet of this masque was Mr. Aurelian Townshend sometimes towards the lord Treasurer Salisbury, Ben Jonson being for this time discarded, by reason of the predominant power of his Antagonist Innigo Jones, who this time tweluemoneth was angry with him for putting his owne name before his in the title-page, which Ben Jonson made the subject of a bitter Satyr or twoe against Innigo.

Townshend may have secured the post of court masque writer with the help of Edmund Taverner, with whom he had traveled in the train of Edward Herbert. Taverner was secretary to Philip Herbert, first Earl of Montgomery, the lord chamberlain, whose duties included the arrangement of court entertainments.

However he got the position, Townshend responded to the opportunity by composing the king's masque, *Albions Triumph*, performed on 8 January 1632 (1631 by the ecclesiastical calendar then in use). The masque presents Charles as Albanactus, a new Roman emperor, and Queen Henrietta Maria as the goddess Alba, personification of virtue and beauty. In the masque, Charles is first seen in a royal procession, an expression of his political power, then in a religious setting where he is sanctified as a sacred monarch, and finally in a scene wherein he is joined with his goddess-queen who "embraces him, and makes him Copartner of her Diety." This transformation of the royal couple into "*Hymens Twin* the Mary-Charles" gave symbolic form to Charles's arrogant perception of himself, which was later manifested in his disregard of Parliament and his years of prerogative rule. This construction of himself and his queen united in an image of a divine hermaphrodite flattered Charles's illusion of his absolute power and self-sufficiency. But the symbol was even more significant as an expression of a contemporary political reality. After the royal favorite George Villiers, first Duke of Buckingham, was murdered in 1628, Henrietta Maria had taken his place as Charles's main adviser; what was represented by the created vision in the masque actually extended into the real world.

As Stephen Orgel points out, the Caroline masque is mainly "about sight and knowledge, or about the relation of the mind to the external world." This concern with vision is evident at the beginning of *Albions Triumph*, which opens with a Platonic dialogue between two representatives of the commonwealth, Publius and Platonicus, who

Inigo Jones's preliminary sketch and final design for the costume of Roman Emperor Albanactus, the character representing Charles I in Albions Triumph *(from Stephen Orgel and Roy Strong,* Inigo Jones: The Theatre of the Stuart Court, *1973)*

debate the relative value of seeing with the physical eye and seeing with the mind's eye. Publius enters after having exerted great effort to brave the crowds to see the emperor Albanactus pass in his triumph. Platonicus, on the other hand, has stayed home in his study and claims to have seen and understood more: Publius can offer only a detailed description of the outward public show of the procession, whereas Platonicus, as he explains, has seen the inner ideal virtues of the emperor with his mind's eye:

> for a supplement to thy lame Story, Know, I have seene this brave ALBANACTUS CAESAR, seene him with the eyes of understanding, vew'd all his Actions, look't into his Mind, which I finde armed with so many morall vertues that he dayly Conquers a world of Vices, which are wild Beasts indeede.

The queen's masque, *Tempe Restord*, was pre-

sented on 14 February. Like *Albions Triumph*, it is concerned with the relation between sight and knowledge, and with the celebration of the ideal union of the royal couple. A young man lured by Circe becomes her slave, is transformed by her into a lion after a lovers' quarrel, and is then restored to his former shape after she becomes remorseful. As soon as he is returned to his human shape, the young man takes the first opportunity to run away from Tempe, Circe's vale of pleasure. Upon his escape he comes into the presence of the king. The sight of the king and the apprehension of his heroic virtues sets the young man free and empowers him to resist Circe, who has followed him to the king's court. As the young man explains, he is awed by the king's presence and inspired by the good that the monarch represents to forsake vice and seek virtue, while Circe "dares not come but in a maske" and appears before the king's throne on bended knee. Furthermore, the sight of the virtuous king has made the young man realize that his enslavement by Circe has been caused by his own weakness and willing complicity:

> Tis not her Rod, her Philters, nor her Herbes,
> (Though strong in Magicke) that can bound mens
>   minds
> And make them Prisoners, where there is no wall:
> It is consent that makes a perfect Slave. . . .

The queen then appears as the personification of divine beauty, descending from the sky in a gem-studded gold chariot, the most difficult "Ingining" Inigo Jones had ever designed. Like the heroic qualities of the king, the queen's beauty is to be read as an agency of good, for as Jones explains in "The Allegory" at the end of the masque, "Corporeall Beauty, consisting in simetry, colour, and certaine unexpressable Graces, shining in the Queenes Majestie, may draw us to the contemplation of the Beauty of the soule, unto which it hath Analogy." The influence of the queen's divine beauty, combined with the heroic virtue of the king, finally persuades Circe to give up her usurpation of Tempe and restore it to the Muses. Once again, the royal couple is united in an image that represents power and the values of the court.

The court masque, written for a celebratory occasion and full of complicated private allegories, can by its very nature be unattractive to twentieth-century eyes. Moreover, the most important parts of the masque were the dance, the music, the spectacle, and the architecture, rather than the verse, which merely served as a vehicle to convey the flattering fictions created by the poets to celebrate courtly ideals. Today we have lost the music and the carefully choreographed dances that were the major components of the masques, but we still have many of the elaborate designs that Inigo Jones drew for the sets and costumes. Twentieth-century audiences should therefore be able to understand what the master designer meant when he said of *Tempe Restord*, "these shows are nothing else but pictures with light and motion." In fact, the masque provides important insights on the way the court was perceived at the time. As each masque moved toward the culminating moment when the masquers led the spectators into a prepared formal dance, the magic of the spectacle eliminated the difference between fiction and reality. Indeed, in Townshend's two contributions to the genre one can sense his effort to create what Orgel has called "a kind of mimetic magic, as if

by the sheer force of poetry and spectacle incipient war and dissolution could be metamorphosed into harmony and peace."

Townshend's chief strength as a poet, however, lay in composing short lyrics. His graceful verse, with regular rhythms and simple stanzaic forms, was easily set to music. Out of the nineteen love poems that have been attributed to him, seven were set to music by Henry Lawes, and one by William Webb. None is more representative of his skill than "Victorious Beauty." It begins with the speaker dutifully paying the lady elaborate compliments, focusing on the familiar Petrarchan topos of the power of her eyes to captivate and harm. Instead of merely heaping hyperbole upon hyperbole in exaggerated praise of the lady, the speaker suddenly surprises his audience by revealing the fact that his heart comes already armed with a "former love":

> Victorious beauty, though your eyes
>   Are able to subdue an hoste,
> And therefore are unlike to boast
>   The taking of a little prize,
>   Do not a single heart despise.
>
> It came alone, but yet so armed
>   With former love, I durst have sworne
> That where a privy coat was worne,
>   With characters of beauty charmed,
>   Thereby it might have scapt unharmed.

Although the armor of his lady's love finally fails to protect him from the powerful charms of the "victorious beauty," the speaker does not thereby lose faith in his mistress's beauty:

> Thy conquest in regard of me
>   Alas was small, but in respect
> Of her that did my love protect,
>   Were it divulg'd, deserv'd to be
>   Recorded for a Victory,
>
> And such a one, as some that view
>   her lovely face perhaps may say,
> Though you have stolne my heart away,
>   If all your servants prove not true,
>   May steal a heart or two from you.

The speaker admits that he has been conquered, but is still confident that his own mistress is lovely enough to steal some of the "victorious beauty's" earlier conquests in return, if some of her servants prove to be unfaithful, just as he has proven unfaithful to his mistress. In this graceful encomium, Townshend is urbane and elegant. His tone is modest ("Thy conquest in regard of me / Alas was small"), but not overly obsequious.

Inigo Jones's costume designs for Divine Beauty (the character representing Henrietta Maria) and her attendant Stars in Tempe Restord *(from Stephen Orgel and Roy Strong,* Inigo Jones: The Theatre of the Stuart Court, *1973)*

In fact, it is even a little jocular, exhibiting the kind of self-mocking distance that Astrophil achieves in some of his sonnets to Stella. But perhaps the overall achievement of the poem is the masterful control of tone; as Cedric C. Brown notes, "In this kind of delicacy, Townshend seems both an individual poetic voice and also a representative of the more refined manners of the Caroline court."

On one occasion, after having been admitted into court to hear Queen Henrietta Maria sing, Townshend wrote a poem to commemorate the event. "On hearing her Majesty sing" plays on the familiar Renaissance topos of hearing a beautiful woman perform. The lyric presents no surprises in terms of profound ideas, but its charm lies in the grace with which it offers praise for the virtues and talents of the queen:

> I have been in Heav'n, I thinke,
> For I heard an Angell sing
> Notes my thirsty ears did drinke;
> Never any earthly thing
> Sung so true, so sweet, so cleer,
> I was then in Heav'n, not heere.

The simplicity of the monosyllabic adjectives *true, sweet,* and *clear* persuasively equates the beauty of the queen's voice with her angelic nature; the commonplace idea that the speaker has been transported to heaven, moreover, invites members of the audience to identify with the speaker's experience and compare it to similar pleasurable events in their own lives.

The short lyric "Your smiles are not" is another poem written in praise of a lady, and it also uses the familiar images of heaven and earth as aids for comparison:

> Your smiles are not as other womens bee
> Only the drawing of the mouth awrye,
> For breasts and cheekes and forehead wee may see,
> Parts wanting motion, all stand smiling by.
>> Heaven hath noe mouth, and yet is sayd to smile
>>> After your style;
>> Noe more hath Earth, yet that smyles too,
>>> Just as you doe.

In this poem Townshend compares the lady's smiles to those of heaven and earth. Heaven and earth have no mouth, but they are said to smile in the "style" of the lady, for the lady's smile is not merely a "drawing of the mouth awrye," but it is a combination of smiling "breasts and cheekes and forehead," parts of the body which, like heaven and earth, do not move, yet "all stand smiling by." This poem, according to E. K. Chambers, was probably written for Lady Judith May, second wife of Sir Humphrey May, who became vice-chamberlain of the king's household in 1629. Lady May was at one time "suspected for too much Familiarity" with an actor, Nathaniel Field, and Townshend was probably aware of her alleged indiscretions.

Aside from his poetic compliments to court ladies, Townshend also wrote some beautiful poems in the pastoral mode. "A Dialogue betwixt Time and a Pilgrime" is often included in anthologies of seventeenth-century poetry, and. T. S. Eliot lamented its omission from Herbert J. C. Grierson's historically significant *Metaphysical Lyrics & Poems of the Seventeenth Century* (1921). In its metaphysical evocation of the themes of death and mutability, Townshend's poem reminds us of Andrew Marvell's mower poems and curiously unresolved dialogues. In Townshend's dialogue, a pilgrim who is also a young man in love encounters the allegorical figure of Father Time mowing grass in a field:

> *Pilgrim:* Aged man, that mowes these fields.
> *Time:*   Pilgrime speak, what is thy will?
> *Pilgrim:* Whose soile is this that such sweet Pasture
>   yields?
>   Or who art thou, whose Foot stands never
>   still?
>   Or where am I? *Time:* In love.
> *Pilgrim:*   Yes and below, and round about,
>   Wherein all sorts of flow'rs are growing,
>   Which as the early Spring puts out,
>   Time falls as fast a mowing.

The pilgrim asks Time to pass his scythe through his thread of life before his mistress's, but Time refuses to answer his narcissistic request, replying that he obeys only the laws of Fate. The poem ends with neither Old Man Time nor the pilgrim having the last word, but a choral response introduced only at the conclusion of the dialogue: "Then happy those whom Fate, that is the stronger, / Together twists their threads, and yet draws hers the longer." The chorus affirms the happy fate of young men whose lives will be inextricably joined with those of their mistresses, and yet be finally spared the pain of bereavement, but it does not tell us whether that is to be the pilgrim's fate.

In a poem addressed to his daughter Mary, which subtly alludes to her early liaisons with the elector palatine and the earl of Dorset, Townshend again evokes the ideas of change and death, repeating the image of the scythe of time that is indifferent to the flowers of youth and beauty:

> Let not thy beauty make thee proud
>> Though Princes doe adore thee,
> Since tyme and sickness were alow'd
>> To mow such flowrs before thee.

This poem, moreover, is noteworthy for its dramatic first lines, which are reminiscent of Donne's powerful opening arguments. Though the context of Townshend's poem is counsel to his daughter against vanity, rather then self-examination in a religious meditation, his choice of diction and rhetorical style remind us of Donne's "Death, be not proud." Using the same simple but strong language that evokes images of the fall of excessive pride in greatness, Townshend successfully appropriates Donne's metaphors and makes them his own.

Some of Townshend's other attempts to imitate Donne, however, are not as effective. *A Paradox*, one of his longer love poems, begins with a Donnean opening that proposes a problem which engages the interest of the reader:

> There is no Lover, hee or shee,
> That ever was or can bee false.
> 'Tis passion or symplicitye
> Or some Apostata, that calls
> Those Votaries, those dead folkes, soe;
>> For if wee goe
> To vowes, to prayes, to paines, to all
> The penuryes monasticall,
>> Noe bare-foote man,
> Rock Hermytt, or Carthusian,
> Can in a course of life survive
> More stricte or more contemplative.

Like many of Donne's love poems, Townshend's *Paradox* uses religious imagery in an attempt to convey the mysteries of secular love. But Donne's original images of martyrs and purifying fires, saints and canonization, which he uses to such powerful effect throughout his *Songs and Sonnets*, abound so profusely in this one poem of Townshend's that they lose whatever imagistic force they may have had and merely seem excessive and confusing:

> What desperate challendger is hee
> Before hee vanishe in his Flame,
> What ere his paines or patience bee,

> That dares assume a Martyrs name;
> For all the waye he goes, hee's none
>> Till he bee gone.
> 'Tis deathe, not dyinge, that must doe
> This right to them and Lovers too;
>> Which they approve
> That make and marre the Lawes of Love;
> Yet better cheape can none acquire
> This crowne of thornes, that robe of Fyre.

In this stanza the wit in the pun " 'Tis deathe, not dyinge," playing on the fertile innuendoes in the popular Renaissance euphemism of saying "to die" in place of "to engage in the sexual act" is quite lost, the phrase being hidden in the middle of the stanza. Moreover, to apprehend the sense of the argument, the reader has to work hard to make the connection between the image of the martyr in the beginning of the stanza and the images of the crown of thorns and the robe of fire at its end. Even the wit in the paradox offered at the end of the poem seems too weak to sustain the burden of the images and arguments that the reader has had to go through: " 'Tis much to dye, 'tis more to finde / Two of my minde." This conclusion seems unsatisfying because it offers neither a resolution to the problem proposed at the outset nor possible further questions for the reader to ask. But although Townshend's *Paradox* may lack the beauty and intelligence of Donne's poems, he occupies a secure niche in the history of English poetry: he is master of the social gesture of courtly compliment to a lady, and his voice adds a distinct nuance to the metaphysical style.

Apart from these delicately crafted lyrics, Townshend's poetic range also included a rowdy drinking song, "Bacchus, I-acchus," written for the revival of William Cartwright's tragicomedy *The Royal Slave* (1639):

> Bacchus, I-acchus, fill our braines
> As well as bowles with sprightly straines.
>> Let souldiers fight for paye or praise,
>> And mony be the Mysers wish;
>> Poore Schollers study all their dayes,
>> And Gluttons glorye in their dish.
> 'Tis wyne, pure wyne, revives sad soules,
> Therefore give us the Cheere in boles.
> . . . .
> Bacchus, I-acchus, & c.
>> Some have the Tissike, some the Rhume,
>> Some have the Palsye, some the Gout,
>> Some swell with fatt, and some consume,
>> But they are sound that drinke all out.
> 'Tis wyne, pure wyne, & c.

Although again, the contexts are different, in his diction and even syntax, Townshend here recalls the speaker in Donne's "Canonization" who exclaims impatiently:

> For God's sake hold your tongue, and let me love,
>   Or chide my palsy, or my gout,
> . . . .
>   . . . what you will. . . .
>   So you will let me love.

Donne's speaker wants to be allowed to love, whereas Townshend's speaker wants to be allowed to drink in peace; but both speakers want the world to leave them alone and go about its daily business. Donne's speaker insists that a man can love in spite of old age and diseases, and Townshend's speaker asserts that drinking cures all: "they are sound that drinke all out." Once again, Townshend appears to have successfully reworked some Donnean ideas.

Although *Albions Triumph* and *Tempe Restord* were successful and he apparently got along well with Inigo Jones, Townshend was not engaged to write any more masques for the court. Benefiting from the experience of his predecessor, he put Jones's name before his own at the beginning of *Albions Triumph* and took care to stress the amicability of their working relations:

> The King and Queenes Majesty having signified their pleasure to have a new Maske this New yeare, Master *Inigo Jones* and I were employed in the Invention. And we agreed the subject of it should be a Triumphe in ALBIPOLIS the chiefe City of ALBION, the Triumpher ALBANACTUS, and ALBA this Ilands Goddesse.

Also, at the end of *Tempe Restord* Townshend is carefully modest, claiming responsibility only for the verses of the masque and giving credit for all the rest of the spectacle to Jones:

> All the Verses were written by Mr *Aurelian Townesend.* The subject and Allegory of the Masque, with the descriptions, and Apparatus of the Sceanes, were invented by *Inigo Jones,* Surveyor of his Majesties worke.

Perhaps Townshend's masques never approached the vision of Jonson's late works, or the breadth and depth of his friend Thomas Carew's *Coelum Britannicum* (1634), but they were well appreciated by his court audience and fellow poets. Carew described the capacity of Townshend's

masques to "dispence / Knowledge and pleasure, to the soule, and sense":

> The stories curious web, the Masculine stile,
> The subtile sence, did Time and sleepe beguile,
> Pinnion'd and charm'd they stood to gaze upon
> Th'Angellike formes, gestures, and motion,
> To heare those ravishing sounds that did dispence
> Knowledge and pleasure, to the soule, and sense.

For his contemporaries Townshend's work evidently achieved the dual goals of literature, to teach and to delight. In his influential 1921 essay on the metaphysical poets T. S. Eliot described Townshend's poetry as a "faint, pleasing tinkle" at the end of the metaphysical period, but today it seems clear that Townshend's work can no longer be dismissed so lightly. We must learn to appreciate his work once again. While Townshend's poems may not contain rigorously worked out conceits in the manner of the poets writing in the earlier part of the century, the distinctive nuances of grace and delicacy that he contributes to the metaphysical style reminds us that the "metaphysical" school of poetry in fact includes many poets writing in radically various styles, and that a poet capable of the exquisite grace and gallant charms of Townshend merits our fuller attention.

References:
Raymond A. Anselment, "Thomas Carew and the 'Harmlesse Pastimes' of Caroline Peace," *Philological Quarterly*, 62 (Spring 1983): 201-219;

Gerald Eades Bentley, *The Jacobean and Caroline Stage Plays and Playwrights*, 7 volumes (Oxford: Clarendon Press, 1941-1968), V: 1226-1231;

Jennifer Chibnall, "'To that secure fix'd state': The Function of the Caroline Masque Form," in *The Court Masque*, edited by David Lindley (Manchester: Manchester University Press, 1984), pp. 78-93;

T. S. Eliot, "The Metaphysical Poets," in *Selected Prose of T. S. Eliot*, edited by Frank Kermode (London: Faber & Faber, 1975), pp. 59-67;

Suzanne Gossett, "'Man-maid, begone!': Women in Masques," *English Literary Renaissance*, 18 (Winter 1988): 96-113;

Allardyce Nicoll, *Stuart Masques and the Renaissance Stage* (London: Harrap, 1937), pp. 88-94;

Stephen Orgel and Roy Strong, *Inigo Jones: The Theatre of the Stuart Court, Including the complete designs for productions at court for the most part in the collection of the Duke of Devonshire together with their texts and historical documentation*, 2 volumes (London: Sotheby Parke Bernet / Berkeley: University of California Press, 1973), I: 59-63, 452-477, 479-503;

Paulina Palmer, "Thomas Carew's Reference to 'The Shepherd's Paradise,'" *Notes and Queries*, new series 13 (August 1966): 303-304;

Michael P. Parker, "Annotating Aurelian," *John Donne Journal: Studies in the Age of Donne*, 6, no. 1 (1987): 159-161;

G. C. Moore Smith, "Aurelian Townshend," *Modern Language Review*, 12 (October 1917): 422-427;

Smith, "Aurelian Townshend," *Times Literary Supplement*, 23 October 1924, p. 667;

Erica Veevers, "*Albions Triumph*: A Further Corrected State of the Text," *Library: A Quarterly Review of Bibliography*, fifth series 16 (December 1961): 294-299;

Veevers, "A Masque Fragment by Aurelian Townshend," *Notes and Queries*, new series 12 (September 1965): 343-345.

Papers:

Manuscript transcriptions of Aurelian Townshend's poems are preserved in Renaissance commonplace books at the British Library; the Bodleian Library; Worcester College, Oxford; St. John's College, Cambridge; Trinity College, Dublin; the Paris Conservatoire; and the Huntington Library, San Marino, California. Seven letters from Townshend to Lord Cecil are preserved in the archives at Hatfield, England.

George Wither

(1588 - 2 May 1667)

James Doelman
Centre for Reformation and Renaissance Studies, University of Toronto

BOOKS: *Prince Henries Obsequies* (London: Printed by Edward Allde for A. Johnson, 1612);

Abuses Stript, and Whipt (London: Printed by G. Eld for F. Burton, 1613);

Epithalamia (London: Printed by F. Kingston for E. Marchant, 1612 [i.e., 1613]);

A Satyre: Dedicated to His Most Excellent Majestie (London: Printed by Thomas Snodham for G. Norton, 1614);

The Shepheards Hunting (London: Printed by T. Snodham for G. Norton, 1615);

Fidelia (London: Printed by Nicolas Okes, 1615);

A Preparation to the Psalter (London: Printed by Nicolas Okes, 1619);

Exercises upon the First Psalme (London: Printed by Edward Griffin for J. Harrison, 1620);

The Workes of Master George Wither (London: Printed by John Beale for Thomas Walkley, 1620);

The Songs of the Old Testament, tr. into English measures (London: Printed by T. Snodham, 1621);

Wither's Motto. Nec habeo, nec careo, nec curo (London: Printed by A. Mathewes, 1621);

Faire-Virtue, the Mistresse of Phil'Arete (London: Printed by A. Mathewes for John J. Grismand, 1622);

Juvenilia (London: Printed by T. Snodham for J. Budge, 1622);

Cantica Sacra (London: Printed by A. Mathewes, 1623?);

The Hymnes and Songs of the Church (London: Printed by J. Bill for G. Wither, 1623);

The Schollers Purgatory, discovered in the Stationers Common-wealth (London: Printed by G. Wood for the Honest Stationers, 1624);

Britain's Remembrancer (London: Sold by J. Grismond, 1628);

The Psalmes of David translated into Lyrick-Verse (Netherlands [Amsterdam?]): Cornelis Gerrits van Breughel, 1632);

A Collection of Emblemes, Ancient and Moderne (London: Printed by A. Mathewes for R. Allot, 1635; facsimile, Publications of the Renaissance English Text Society, 5-6 (Columbia,

George Wither (engraving by John Payne, in Wither's Collection of Emblemes *[1635])*

S.C.: University of South Carolina Press, 1975);

Halelujah, or Britans Second Remembrancer (London: Printed by I. L. for Andrew Hebb, 1641);

Mercurius Rusticus, or, A Countrey Messenger (London: 1643);

Campo-Musæ, or the Field-Musings of Captain George Wither (London: Printed by R. Austin & A. Coe, 1643);

Reasons Humbly Offered in Justification of an Order Granted to the Major George Wither (London, 1643);

Se Defendendo, a Shield, and Shaft, against Detraction (London, 1643);

The Speech without Doore (London, 1644);

Two Incomparable Generalissimos of the world (London: Printed for James Butler, 1644);

Letters of Advice, Touching the Choice of Knights and Burgesses (London: Printed by Robert Austin, 1644);

Vox Pacifica (London: Printed by Robert Austin, 1645);

Justitiarius Justificatus, the Justice justified (London: 1646);

To the Most honourable the Lords and Commons in Parliament assembled (London: 1646);

What Peace to the Wicked? (London, 1646);

Opobalsamum Anglicanum (London, 1646);

Carmen Expostulatorium (London, 1647);

The Tired Petitioner (London, 1647?);

Amygdala Britannica, Almonds for Parrets (London, 1647);

The Doubtfull Almanack, or a very suspitious Presage of great Calamities yet to ensue (London, 1647?);

Major Wither's Disclaimer (London: Printed by R. Austin, 1647);

Prosopopœia Britannica, Britans Genius, or Good-Angel, personated (London: Printed by R. Austin, 1648);

Articles Presented Against This Parliament (London, 1648);

A Single Si Qvis, and a Quadruple Qvere (London, 1648);

Carmen-Ternarium Semi-Cynicum (London, 1648?);

An Allarum from Heaven (London: Printed for G. Wharton, 1649);

Carmen Eucharisticon (London: Printed by Robert Austin, 1649);

Respublica Anglicana (London: Printed by F. Leach for G. Thompson, 1650);

Three Grains of Spirituall Frankincense, Infused into Three Hymns of Praise (London: Printed by R. Austin, 1651);

The British Appeals with God's Mercifull Replies, on behalf of the Commonwealth of England (London: Printed for the author, sold by Nathaniel Brooks, 1651);

A Timelie Cavtion (London: Printed by John Clowes, 1652);

Westrow Revived, A Funerall Poem without Fiction (London: Printed by F. Neile, 1653);

The dark Lantern, Containing A dim Discoverie, in Riddles, Parables, and semi-Riddles, intermixt with Cautions, Remembrances and Predicitions, as they were promiscuously and immethodically represented to their Author, in his Solitary Musings, the third of November 1652. about Midnight. Whereunto is annexed, A Poem, Concerning A Perpetuall Parliament (London: Printed by R. Austin, sold by Richard Lowndes, 1653);

The Protector (London: Printed by J. C., 1655);

Vaticinivm Cavsvale (London: Printed for T. Ratcliffe & E. Mottershed, 1655);

Boni ominis Votum (London: Printed for John Hardesty, 1656);

A Suddain Flash (London: Printed for John Saywell, 1657);

The Petition, and Narrative of Geo. Wither, Esq; (London, 1658 or 1659);

Salt upon Salt (London: Printed for L. Chapman, 1659);

Epistolium-Vagum-Prosa-Metricum (London, 1659);

A Cordial Confection (London: Printed by James Cottrel, 1659);

Furor-Poeticus (i.e.) Propheticus, a Poetick-Phrensie (London: Printed by James Cottrel, 1660);

Fides-Anglicana (London, 1660);

Speculum Speculativum, or, a Considering-Glass (London, 1660);

Joco-Serio (London, 1661?);

A Triple Paradox (London: Printed for the author, 1661);

An Improvement of Imprisonment, Disgrace, Poverty, into Real Freedom; Honest Reputation; Perdurable Riches (London: 1661);

The Prisoners Plea (London, 1661);

A Declaration of Major George Wither (London: Printed for S. Jones, 1662);

A Proclamation in the Name of our King of Kings (London, 1662);

Verses Intended to the King's Majesty (London, 1662);

Paralellogrammaton (London, 1662);

Tuba-Pacifica (London: Printed for the author, 1664);

Meditations upon the Lords Prayer (London, 1665);

A Memorandum to London (London, 1665);

Ecchoes from the Sixth Trumpet (London, 1666);

Vaticinia Poetica (London: Sold by Edward Blackmore, 1666);

Three Private Meditations (London, 1666);

Sighs for the Pitchers (London, 1666);

Vox et Lacrimæ Anglorum (London, 1668);

Fragmenta Prophetica (London, 1669);

Divine Poems (by way of Paraphrase) on the Ten Commandments (London: Printed by T. S., sold by R. Janeway, 1688).

Editions: *Miscellaneous Works of George Wither,* Publications of the Spenser Society, nos. 12-13, 16, 18, 22 and 24 (Manchester: C. E. Simms, 1872-1878; 6 volumes, New York: Burt Franklin, 1967);

Britain's Remembrancer, Publications of the Spenser Society, nos. 28-29 (Manchester: C. E. Simms, 1880; 1 volume, New York: Burt Franklin, 1967);

The Poetry of George Wither, 2 volumes, edited by Frank Sidgick (London: A. H. Bullen, 1902);

The History of the Pestilence (1625), edited by J. Milton French (Cambridge: Harvard University Press, 1932);

The English Spenserians: The Poetry of Giles Fletcher, George Wither, Michael Drayton, Phineas Fletcher, and Henry More, edited by William B. Hunter, Jr. (Salt Lake City: University of Utah Press, 1977).

OTHER: Nemesius, *The Nature of Man,* translated by Wither (London: Printed by M. Flesher for H. Taunton, 1636);

Vox Vulgi, edited by W. Dunn Macray, Anecdota Bodleiana: Gleanings from Bodleian Mss., 2 (Oxford: James Parker, 1880).

The reputation and stature of George Wither, poet and pamphleteer, has varied widely, both in his own lifetime and in the centuries that have followed. His outspoken and topical approach attracted many readers in his own time and has rendered him difficult, and at times tedious, for readers less familiar with the politics and events of the seventeenth century. He deserves to be read and discussed for his widespread popularity in his own time and for his lifelong commitment to writing as his chief profession. He also illustrates well the problems inherent in attempting to categorize writers of the early Stuart and Interregnum periods into either the Royalist or opposition camp.

George Wither was born in 1588 to George and Mary Wither in the village of Bentworth, Hampshire. The poet's brother James grew up to be mayor of Basingstoke. After early education under Ralph Starkey, a near relative, and John Greaves, a local schoolmaster, Wither went to Magdalen College, Oxford, in 1603 when he was fifteen. He studied for a few years but left disgruntled without taking a degree. Between 1606 and 1611 Wither's movements are not altogether clear, although he did spend some of that time in Ireland, probably in a military capacity under Sir Thomas Ridgway. Throughout his life he would exhibit a strong sympaty for the Protestant settlers of Ireland. On 8 July 1615 Wither entered Lincoln's Inn, but while he made some use of his legal training in the 1640s and 1650s, his chief vocation throughout his life was that of poet. A reputation in his early life for philandering gave way to marriage to Elizabeth Emerton sometime in the late 1620s or early 1630s.

Nearly all of Wither's poetry and prose is closely bound up with the events of both his own

*Engraved title page for Wither's 1628 work in which a recent outbreak of bubonic plague
is presented as God's judgment upon England*

life and society at large. He held that the poet's role was one of public service; it involved serving the "common weal" at all times, though in a variety of ways. Most often for Wither, this service took the form of advising and cajoling both the people and their rulers. He did not shy away from dealing with controversy; as William Winstanley wrote in *Lives of the most famous English Poets* (1687), Wither was "one who loved to fish in troubled waters." Frequently, Wither presented himself as a savior or prophet to the nation, but one who, like other prophets, was unappreciated in his own land and time. His personal misfortunes, therefore, are the subjects of many of his works, for they confirm that he was chosen by God to play this important, if unappreciated, role. In his early years this role of public poet was presented in the shape of the laureate career, like that of Virgil and Edmund Spenser. After 1625 this public role was more often expressed in the terms of a prophet who warned England in the way that the Old Testament prophets had warned Israel. However, through the 1640s some continued to describe him as "Poet Laureate," and Wither himself seemed intent on bringing together the two views of his office. He attempted this in spite of the inherent conflict between the two roles: the poet laureate was a servant of the crown, but the biblical prophet generally stood apart from it in order to admonish and criticize.

Ironically, Wither, so insistent on writing public poetry, appears the most self-possessed and personal of English Renaissance poets. Much of his poetry is taken up with self-explanation and justification. Wither often alludes to the rough and simple nature of his verse; early in his career he is most likely to apologize for it; later he presents it as a mark of simple honesty. Loosely structured rhyming decasyllabic couplets were his usual verse form throughout his career. In shorter works these may be replaced by rhyming tetrameter.

Wither's earliest poetry, which included secular love poetry, never reached print; we know of it only from a list compiled by the poet himself in *Fides-Anglicana* (1660). Wither presents two different works, *Prince Henries Obsequies* (1612) and *Abuses Stript, and Whipt* (1613) as his first entry into the public realm. *Prince Henries Obsequies* was certainly published in late 1612; the earliest surviving edition of *Abuses Stript, and Whipt* is from 1613, but there is evidence to suggest an earlier edition had been published. Whichever was first, the poems perform the same function: to introduce an important new poet on the scene. In *Prince Henries Obsequies* the poet laments the passing of Prince Henry on 6 November 1612. Prince Henry was heir to the English throne and the hope of many poets, especially ones who tended toward militant Protestantism. This poem marks the beginning of Wither's complex relationship with the English royal family: up until even the late 1640s he enthusiastically celebrated the English Crown and hoped for royal patronage but was repeatedly frustrated by what he perceived as the malice of the king's councilors. His willingness to attack such men brought Wither repeatedly into trouble. Such was the case with *Abuses Stript, and Whipt* in which he assailed various vices directly and indirectly attacked such figures as Henry Howard, Earl of Northampton. In regards to this and his other satires, Wither claimed that his audience read too much into the work: if they saw resemblances to real people, they had not been intended. However, his frequent disavowals seem only to have encouraged readers all the more, and the rumors of personal attacks probably brought about the numerous editions of the work.

For Wither, the writing of satire is consistent with the panegyric verse he wrote in *Prince*

Henries Obsequies and *Epithalamia* (1613): they are different means to the same end, of helping men and women distinguish between vice and virtue. In *Epithalamia* he extolled the virtues of the royal couple Princess Elizabeth and Count Frederick, Elector Palatine, who were married on St. Valentine's Day 1613. While his work, in a flood of similar works, was little noticed by the public, Wither was later to claim that he enjoyed the patronage of Elizabeth.

The offence caused by *Abuses Stript, and Whipt* led to Wither's imprisonment in the Marshalsea from late March to 26 July 1614. Out of this situation Wither brought forth two new works: *A Satyre: Dedicated to His Most Excellent Majestie* (1614) and *The Shepheards Hunting* (1615). The former defends and explains his intent in writing and publishing *Abuses Stript, and Whipt*; he claims that his only regret is that he was so cautious in his criticism. The latter, a group of five eclogues, transforms, although rather inconsistently, the Marshalsea into a pastoral setting. In them Wither, as represented by the shepherd Roget (in the later editions named Philarete), is consoled and encouraged by friends, two of whom can be identified as the poets William Browne of Tavistock and Christopher Brooke. Eclogues 4 and 5 of this work had been published earlier as appendices to Browne's *Shepheards Pipe* (1614). *The Shepheards Hunting* is in the pastoral tradition of Spenser's *Colin Clouts comes home againe* (1595) and continues the castigation of vice begun in *Abuses Stript, and Whipt*. Also appearing in 1615 was the collection of love poetry entitled *Fidelia*, most of which was probably written many years earlier.

Frequently in these five early works Wither alludes to a time when he will turn from his "young *Rusticitie*" to poetic work of greater importance and more serious intent. He most frequently hints that this future work may be of a martial nature and will establish him as a serious poet. He does not yet deserve "that too-worthy name of *Poet*," but expects that someday he will join the ranks of Samuel Daniel, Ben Jonson, and Michael Drayton. Between 1615 and 1619, a time when he published no new works and his whereabouts are unclear, Wither seems to have been preparing for this new stage in his career. His poetry's more serious strain, however, turned out not to be the traditional martial epic, but rather the versifying of Biblical song. He was probably attracted to this task by its high and serious nature, King James's interest in such activity, and because it, unlike his satires, would be relatively uncontroversial. The new stage in his career was heralded by the publication of *A Preparation to the Psalter* in 1619, a long and learned prose discussion of the psalms and a defence of the translating of them into English verse. This impressive folio volume clearly was meant to introduce a major poetic work. However, *The Psalmes of David* was not published until 1632, and then in Holland after attempts to print it in England had failed because of the monopoly of the Stationers' Company on the printing of all metrical Psalters. In 1620 Wither freely published *Exercises upon the First Psalme*, an in-depth study and translation of a single psalm. He followed this by versifying many other Old Testament songs; these were published as *The Songs of the Old Testament* (1621), and *Cantica Sacra* (1623?), and then *Hymnes and Songs of the Church* (1623), which included both Old Testament songs and original compositions. This work was in effect an English hymnal, published along with music by Orlando Gibbons and intended for congregational worship. It ranks as an early but unsuccessful attempt to add hymnody to the psalmody then in place in the English Church. Toward this end it was granted a special fifty-one year patent by King James that specified it must be appended to all new publications of the traditional Sternhold and Hopkins Psalter. However, the Stationers' Company strongly resisted this injunction, and without their cooperation extensive distribution was impossible. In response to their opposition, Wither clandestinely published the prose work *Schollers Purgatory* (1624) in which he defended his hymns and attacked the monopolies and policies of the Stationers.

In the midst of this religious verse, Wither published *Wither's Motto* (1621), another long satiric poem, in which he asserted his disdain for the follies of the world. Once again the work was perceived as seditious. In this case, it was likely his implicit criticism of England's failure to support the Elector Frederick in his bid for Bohemia that landed him in the Marshalsea. As with *Abuses Stript, and Whipt*, the controversy surrounding the work helped to establish Wither's name and ensured the work a wide readership. *Faire-Virtue, the Mistresse of Phil'Arete* (1622), is a pastoral work celebrating the female figure "Faire-Virtue," who in spite of her name seems to reflect a real woman rather than an abstraction. The poet may have written parts of it much earlier. Wither signaled that the immature stage of

his poetic career was over at this point by publishing his *Juvenilia* (1622) which included all his nonreligious work that had already appeared in print. *The Workes of Master George Wither*, published in 1620, had been a pirated collection of Wither's early poetry, and included his paraphrase on the Apostles' Creed and the Lord's Prayer. His widespread fame at this time is shown not only by the pirating of his works in this way, but also by the fact that Ben Jonson satirized him as the character Chronomastix in the masque *Time Vindicated to Himself and to his Honors* in 1623.

In the early 1620s Wither's hope had rested largely upon the beneficence of King James and their mutual interest in the metrical psalms. However, Wither was among those who loathed and distrusted the king's favorite, George Villiers, who became duke of Buckingham in 1623 and whose continuing influence on King Charles after the death of James in 1625 lay behind much of Wither's warning to the king in *Britain's Remembrancer* (1628). This lengthy work presented the bubonic plague of 1625 as God's judgment upon England. The poet claims to have been called by God to remain in London in order to bear witness to the progress of the plague. An early version of the work was prepared in manuscript in 1625-1626, but the work was not published until a longer version appeared in 1628. The delay may have been due to Wither's difficulties with the Stationers, or the danger in publishing the work before Villiers's death on 23 August of that year. As with his other, later prophetic works, Wither presents contemporary troubles as God's warning to England, yet he has little confidence that either the people or the king will pay the plague itself, or Wither, its "remembrancer," much attention. However, the work shows Wither's faith that he will be read and vindicated long after his death for the accuracy of his prophecies. *Britain's Remembrancer* goes on for nearly three hundred pages that are divided into eight cantos; it begins as an epic with a conference between God and the allegorical figures of Justice and Clemency, but after the first few cantos the organization becomes much looser and the poet's Muse "at random flyes," as Wither describes it. Generally the work reveals a moderate position, cautious between the extremes of papism and iconoclastic puritanism. As Wither's first prophetic work, *Britain's Remembrancer* exhibited traits which were to be found throughout his later prophecies: an emphasis on personal sin lead-

Frontispiece from Wither's Collection of Emblemes *(1635). This work, together with Francis Quarles's* Emblems *(1635), established a new vogue for the genre in England.*

ing to national ruin, a conviction that the author's words would not be heeded, and a disregard for poetic structure. For taking this prophetic stance Wither was occasionally praised, but more frequently mocked.

Wither maintained a relatively low public profile throughout the 1630s. The list of his works in *Fides-Anglicana* suggests that in this period he wrote a significant number of works that were never published. For some time between 1628 and 1632 he served as steward to John Howson, Bishop of Durham. He visited The Hague to present a copy of his *Psalmes of David* to Elizabeth, now the exiled queen of Bohemia, and it is possible that more of his time was spent in the Low Countries. By 1635 he considered him-

self to have lost, through death or betrayal, nearly all his friends at court, and the dedicatory poems to *A Collection of Emblemes* (1635) show Wither at his most obsequious. For this work Wither composed new verses for the plates from Gabriel Rollenhagen's *Nucleus Emblematum Selectissimorum* (1611). Wither had begun composing English verses for these emblems nearly twenty years earlier. Published the same year as Francis Quarles's *Emblems* (1635), the two works established a new vogue for the genre in England. Wither's emblems were designed to be used as exercises in personal edification or guidance: at the end of the volume there was a dial that the reader was to spin in order to be directed to an appropriate emblem for the day. Wither's other major work of the 1630s, a translation of Nemesius's *The Nature of Man* (1636), shows a scholarly and humanist side to Wither which is often overlooked. The later years of the decade were spent largely at Farnham Cottage in Surrey. This seems to have been a time of comparative peace and prosperity for Wither; he was later to claim that his household before the Civil War contained more than sixteen servants.

Wither's life took on a new cast with the events of the early 1640s leading up to the Civil War. He had fought with King Charles against the Scots in 1639, but in 1642 he came down clearly on the side of Parliament. Wither had always venerated the members of the royal family, but generally despised those who surrounded the king. Given this inclination it is not surprising that he was an early and consistent supporter of Parliament, which, at least for the first few years of the Civil War, insisted that it was fighting the courtiers who had misled Charles rather than the king himself. Even in a work written more than ten years later, *Westrow Revived* (1653), Wither would admit a grudging respect for Charles's attempts to bring about justice and public piety. Throughout the 1640s "Captain Wither" and then "Major Wither" was a well-known figure: he was mocked by Royalist writers, quoted by John Lilburne, and featured as one of the poet/jurors in the anonymous *The Great Assizes Holden at Parnassus* (1645, some early bibliographers attributed this work to Wither).

With the Root and Branch Petition of December 1640 (calling for the abolition of episcopacy) and the increasing power of Parliament in the first half of 1641, Wither saw a new chance for introducing his hymns into the English church. His collection of hymns, *Halelujah*, was published in June 1641, and dedicated to "The thrice Honorable, and high Courts of Parliament" rather than to any member of the royal family, as had been the case with his *Hymnes and Songs of the Church*. Clearly, Wither perceived a possible place for his poetry in the new ecclesiastical arrangement that seemed to be pending, but once again his attempts in this area came to nothing, as the matter of appropriate hymns and psalms for the church got bogged down in the Westminster Assembly.

Wither's justification for his pro-Parliament stance is presented in *Campo-Musæ* (1643), a work in which he also explains his forsaking of the pen for the sword. In October 1642 Captain Wither was appointed as the commander of the parlia-

mentary garrison at Farnham Castle in Surrey. When it was threatened by Royalist forces in November of the same year, Wither abandoned the castle. Both it and his own cottage were plundered. This action put Wither at the center of public controversy for a good time to come. In *Se Defendendo* (1643) Wither rebutted critics of his actions at Farnham by claiming that he had received orders to withdraw. In *Aqua-Musae* (1645) John Taylor, a Cavalier poet, mocked both Wither's support of the parliamentary cause and his involvement in the fiasco at Farnham. Both Taylor and the anonymous author of *Withers Remembrancer* (1643) quoted Wither's previous statements of unshakable loyalty to the king in *Britain's Remembrancer*. Also in *Aqua-Musae* Taylor suggested that Wither's consistent motivation had been self-interest and that throughout his life he purposely maligned important figures in order to attract attention to his poetry.

Even after the debacle at Farnham, Wither continued to be active militarily, eventually rising to the rank of major. He took part in relieving Gloucester from the Royalist siege in September 1643, and in August of the following year he was put in charge of all forces in the eastern and middle divisions of Surrey. In the same year he was appointed a justice of the peace for Surrey. In 1645 he was offered the governorship of the Somers Islands, but refused because of financial problems. In the same year an attempt by Wither to gain a seat in Parliament failed. However, throughout the Civil War, Wither's official duties seem to have remained secondary to his writing, both prose and verse.

The events at Farnham continued to haunt Wither; he eventually came to blame the whole escapade on his superior, Sir Richard Onslow, for failing to properly fortify the castle. In the prose work *Justitiarius Justificatus* (1646) Wither went so far as to imply that Onslow was a covert Royalist. For slandering Onslow, a prominent member of Parliament, Wither was brought before the Committee of Examinations. While under investigation in the summer of 1646 he wrote and published *Opobalsamum Anglicanum*, in which he more generally attacked those in Parliament who he felt were attempting to establish a tyranny and repressing any public discussion of their faults. In response there appeared the anonymous *A Letter Sent to George Wither* (1646), which accused him of selfishness and spite in all his actions and writings during the Civil War. In August 1646 the Committee of Examinations declared that the poet was guilty of libeling Onslow. He was imprisoned in Newgate for over a year, fined five hundred pounds, and his book was publicly burned.

Many of Wither's works of the 1640s make reference, some directly, to a persistent grievance of his: that many who were neutral or even Royalists in the conflict came to be treated better than those who, like himself, had wholeheartedly embraced the parliamentary cause from the beginning. Under a parliamentary order of 9 February 1643, Wither was authorized to confiscate land and goods of his Royalist neighbors to make up for his own losses. Among those whose estates he was authorized to seize were lands belonging to Winchester Cathedral and the estates of his fellow-poet John Denham, who had participated in the Royalist attack on Farnham. While rumors circulated that he had received more than double his losses in reparation, Wither himself claimed to be frustrated by the long delays in actually receiving such rewards. The matter was bogged down in such parliamentary bodies as the Committee for Sequestration and the Committee for Compounding. Wither petitioned Parliament and the various committees repeatedly on the matter, describing his woeful condition due to the lack of reward. In 1655 he claimed that he had called on Parliament nearly every day for the past twelve years. Various purchases of land that he made in the period show he was not as poverty-stricken as he claimed, and on at least one occasion he implied he was imprisoned for debt, when in truth he was there for the libel against Onslow.

Vox Pacifica (1645) was Wither's major work of the 1640s, promised as forthcoming in *Campo-Musæ* and *Se Defendendo*, and written in the first half of 1645. In style it resembles *Britain's Remembrancer*; in this case "the VOICE" comes repeatedly to Wither, using him as a vehicle to show England that peace can come only through repentance on all sides. The title reflects the words of the prophet Jeremiah to Hananiah, that after prophecies of war, famine, and pestilence, would come prophecies of peace. Written over a period of six months, the poem reflects the growing success of the parliamentary side. However, Wither criticizes both sides in the Civil War: while Parliament has the "better cause," it too has sinned. Of considerable interest in the work is Wither's critique of the reigns of both James and Charles: much that was obliquely castigated in earlier satiric and prophetic works is here made explicit. He blasts James's overspending and Charles's fail-

ure to investigate the rumors of his father's death and his marriage to a Catholic queen. At the end of the work "the Voice" promises to return again, but Wither's imprisonment for the Onslow libel convinced him that England was still far from peace and justice. From prison he wrote the bitter *What Peace to the Wicked?* (1646) where he concentrates on criticizing the parliamentarians. A notable change in style comes with *Amygdala Britannica* in 1647: Wither still plays the part of remembrancer or prophet to the nation, but here his language is complex and symbolic, nearly apocalyptic in imagery. Similar to *Vox Pacifica* was the 1648 work *Prosopopœia Britannica* in which "Britain's Genius" speaks to Wither; in the first half it explains how the king can still repent, and in the second turns to advise Parliament on how it should proceed. The "Genius" ends by prophesying the course English government will take: after tyranny and chaos, eventually a king will come to bring peace. Both "the Voice" and "Britain's Genius" are thin poetic devices that are unsuccessful in convincing us that we are hearing anything but Wither's own thoughts.

The majority of Wither's writings from the 1640s are of a personal and particular nature, most interesting in their illustration of Wither's careful maneuvering among the various factions within the parliamentary camp. Until at least 1645 or 1646 Wither clearly tended toward the Presbyterians; he praises the Scots and urges the English to observe the Covenant. He had always been relatively happy with the liturgical forms of the established church, apart from its failure to include his own hymns and psalms. He doubted the more Puritan desire to do away with all set form in worship and church polity, but in *Prosopopœia Britannica* he declined from the view that there was only "one outward forme of Discipline." Wither's only significant quarrel with the established church was the abuse of prelatic power. In theology, he disdained the Presbyterian doctrine of foreordination and reprobation. He sided with the Presbyterians because they, at least through the first years of the Civil War, offered the most likely hope for a fair and stable government, one in which some reconciliation with the king would be possible. In 1646 or early 1647 *The Doubtfull Almanack* appeared under Wither's name. This work attacks the Independents, blaming them for the failure to achieve reconciliation. In *Major Wither's Disclaimer* (1647) Wither denied that he had anything to do with the work, pointing out that he always found fault with both

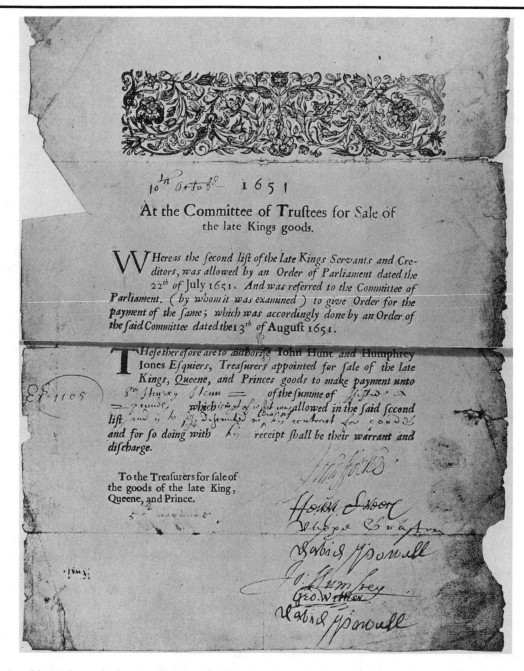

Warrant signed by Wither and other commissioners entrusted with selling the personal effects of the late King Charles I (Harvard College Library)

sides in any dispute and attempting to show that the work was really Royalist propaganda meant to divide the parliamentarians. In support of Wither, it must be noted that *The Doubtfull Almanack* is unlike his usual work in that it includes numerous Latin quotations. On the other hand, *Major Wither's Disclaimer* may reflect Wither's attempt to retract a work so critical of the side that was now becoming dominant. Wither's continual ability to support whatever regime was in place can be seen cynically as mere opportunism, or it can be explained as being due to his faith that whoever governed did so only through the support of God. That he was willing to also critique any regime shows he was not a mere flatterer. In a 9 August 1661 letter to Edward Hyde, Earl of Clarendon and lord chancellor, Wither wrote that he "was never of any faction, but mischeeved by all and litle favoured by any," an assessment which certainly rings true.

With the reduction of Parliament to the Rump in December 1648 and the execution of King Charles the next month, Wither adjusted his political stance to agree with the times. That he was silent at the time of Charles's execution, as he was at the beginning of the Protectorate four years later, reflects the uncertainty of a man who believed that those in power had their authority from God. Generally, he fared well under the Commonwealth and the early stages of the Protectorate in comparison to the Civil War years. While his attempts to gain compensation for his plundered estate continued, he received financial assistance first from John Bradshaw, the president of the commission that convicted King Charles, and then from Thomas Westrow. He honored Westrow with the elegiac *Westrow Revived* in 1653, which was as taken up with Wither's suffering as with the kindness of the benefactor who alleviated it. During the early 1650s Wither was also granted several official positions. Early in 1649 he may have been appointed a commissioner for wine licenses. During the Commonwealth years he lived primarily at Hambledon in Hampshire, and on 6 May 1650 he became a justice of the peace in that county. By 10 October 1651 he became a trustee for the sale of the late king's goods. It may have been at this time that the rumor began that he once irreverently robed himself in the royal garments. In 1654 or 1655 Wither moved to London to take up official duties as a master of the statute office.

Throughout the time of the Commonwealth and Protectorate, Wither seems to have been a strong supporter of Oliver Cromwell and in particular of his military policies. He celebrated Michael Jones's victory in Ireland with *Carmen Eucharisticon* (1649) which he presented to members of Parliament, "in hope they would have sung it the day after, being the thanksgiving day appointed." He wrote *Three Grains of Spirituall Frankincense* (1651), a collection of three hymns, to celebrate the anniversary of the 30 January 1649 execution of Charles I. These were dedicated to Bradshaw, again in the hope that they would be sung in Parliament on the anniversary. For the same occasion Wither produced *The British Appeals* (1651).

Wither accepted the dismissal of the Rump of the Long Parliament in 1653 as the will of God but expected that the military administration would merely be a transitional stage on the road to the rule of the saints and eventually the personal rule of Christ on earth. These expectations show Wither to be among those radical Independents inclined to Fifth Monarchist ideas. Early 1653 saw the publication of the enigmatic work *The dark Lantern* in which Wither declared that England should unite with the other Protestant nations of northern Europe in anticipation of the coming reign of Christ. In April 1653, when the Rump was dissolved and the Nominated (or Barebones) Assembly was called, Wither offered his advice in *A Perpetuall Parliament*; he proposed a fixed constitution, the annual election of two members from each constituency from which one would be chosen by lot, and salaries for members of the House. As always, however, Wither came to accept the actual regime which came to rule, in this case the Protectorate, as doing so by the will of God. In 1655 he published *Vaticinium Causuale* where he denies that Cromwell's recent carriage accident was in any way a sign that he was acting wrongly. He praised Cromwell in *The Protector* (1655), but warned him against taking the crown, a warning repeated two years later in *A Suddain Flash* (1657). In these years Wither seems to have been in fairly close contact with Cromwell, but the lord protector had little time for the poet's political advice. Once again Wither was frustrated by a ruler who failed to recognize his prophetic role. By 1657 his petitions show a certain dissatisfaction with the regime, as he found himself treated no better than he had been under king or Parliament. In the works written between the death of Oliver Cromwell and the Restoration, Wither shows considerable uncertainty; he lends qualified support to the lord protector's son, Richard Cromwell, the Rump, the army, and General George Monk in turn. *Salt upon Salt* (1659), written shortly after the death of Oliver Cromwell, shows Wither pulling back from his association with the lord protector, apparently to be open to whatever new rulers emerged. However, to Wither's credit, in *A Cordial Confection* (1659) his criticism is so broad as to antagonize nearly any possible new regime. In *Speculum Speculativum* (1660) he accepts the return of Charles II as the will of God but does not celebrate the event.

With the Restoration, Wither's fortunes took their final downward turn. Many of the Royalist and ecclesiastical lands he had gained through his endless petitioning and court actions were confiscated. At this point he probably was truly desperate. However, it did not take him long to offend the new authorities. In August 1661 his rooms were entered and papers seized,

Portrait from the second edition (1626) of Wither's Juvenilia

including his manuscript copy of *Vox Vulgi*. This work vigorously attacks certain elements in the Restoration Parliament while moderately praising Charles II. Although Wither claimed that he had no intention of publishing it without Lord Chancellor Clarendon's approval, he was once again imprisoned at Newgate, tried in March of 1662, and after conviction imprisoned in the Tower until July 1663. He humbly appealed for mercy in *A Declaration of Major George Wither* (1662) and *Verses Intended to the King's Majesty* (1662)). However, his mere survival of imprisonment once again confirmed his view that he was called to prophetic work. Thus, he confidently transformed his suffering into further writings: in this case *An Improvement of Imprisonment* (1661), *A Triple Paradox* (1661), *Joco-Serio* (1661?), *Paralellogrammaton* (1662), *A Proclamation in the Name of our King of Kings* (1662), and *The Prisoners Plea* (1661). In *The Prisoners Plea* he restates his conviction that poets are called to be outspoken critics, and outlines the difference between such criticism and libel.

The majority of these works from prison continue Wither's habit of combining prophecy and the bemoaning of personal misfortune. Once

again in *A Proclamation in the Name of our King of Kings* and *Paralellogrammaton* he relies on biblical parallels as the basis for his own crying out against the sins of England. More so than ever, religious concerns are central to his writings in the early 1660s. Wither had never been a proponent of strict religious unity, and in the 1660s he expressed an increased desire for diversity among those sects who upheld the essentials of Christianity. He exhibited sympathy for the Quakers, much persecuted at the time, and in his reference in *The Prisoners Plea* to that "*Light* within me, which beameth from the *Light Eternal*," the influence of Quakerism or other radical Protestants is clear. About the time of the Restoration, Wither had modified his view about the coming reign of Christ: he now expected it to begin in 1700 rather than 1666. In *Fides-Anglicana* he denied that he was a Fifth Monarchist; yet in the same work he showed considerable sympathy for their recent uprising. However, in *Paralellogrammaton* he rejected their use of the sword in attempting to bring about the millennium. In spite of his prophetic stance and sympathy for radical sectaries, Wither at this time seems to have continued to participate in Church of England worship.

Hostilities between the English and Dutch in the mid 1660s elicited the prophetic works *Tuba-Pacifica* (1664), *Three Private Meditations* (1666), and *Sighs for the Pitchers* (1666); for the last work Wither was once again arrested for sedition. The plague of 1665, like that of 1625, provided Wither with an opportunity to castigate England for its sins, which he did in *A Memorandum to London* (1665). With death approaching, Wither selected passages from his various poetic works and published the whole as *Ecchoes from the Sixth Trumpet* (1666). In it he tries to show how his earlier works have been justified by the actual events that followed. The title reflects Wither's apocalyptic preoccupations; although he no longer expected 1666 to mark the return of Christ, he believed it would nevertheless be a significant year of upheavals. Wither died on 2 May 1667 in his London house in the Savoy and was buried at the chapel of the Savoy Palace. He was survived by his wife, Elizabeth, his son, Robert, who went through the Inns of Court and then settled at Bentworth, and his daughter Elizabeth Barry of London. Wither's papers passed into his daughter's hands at his death, and from them she published his *Divine Poems* in 1688.

Even before his death, Wither's name had became a byword for hastily written and sloppy poetry, but his disrepute probably owed more to his political stance in the Interregnum than to the quality of his verses. Samuel Butler's dismissal of him in *Hudibras* (1663-1678) was echoed by both Jonathan Swift and Alexander Pope. Among some readers of the later seventeenth century, however, he was recognized as the prophet he always said he would be. Canto Eight of his *Britain's Remembrancer* was republished in 1683 and 1734 as an example of fulfilled prophecy. The prophetic section of *Prosopopœia Britannica* was reprinted three times immediately following the Glorious Revolution of 1688, which to many it seemed to have heralded. Similarly, a passage from *Speculum Speculativum* was republished in 1689. Daniel Defoe was a frequent reader of Wither's poems, and it has been suggested that he drew heavily upon *Britain's Remembrancer* for his *Journal of the Plague Year* (1722). Through the early eighteenth century, while Wither may have been occasionally disparaged, he was rarely read. Not until his inclusion in Thomas Percy's *Reliques of Ancient English Poetry* (1765) was there a renewed appreciation for his poetry, and then it was for his early pastoral verse. This same verse was much admired by Charles Lamb, Robert Southey, and Samuel Taylor Coleridge for its simple and rustic nature. His religious verse, especially his hymns, was highly praised by Robert A. Willmott in 1834, and his opinion set the tone for many later critics of the nineteenth century. Nineteenth- and early-twentieth-century readers of Wither tended to praise the early work and dismiss the later for being overly topical and concerned with the poet's own misfortunes. Readers then and now are frequently put off by the sheer volume of Wither's writings. While there has been significant scholarly interest of late in the political and prophetic works of the 1640s, Wither's poems and pamphlets have generally not been among those turned to. While Wither has received scant attention from scholars, since the nineteenth century he has attracted even fewer general readers. A single lyric, "Shall I wasting in despair," is the only poem regularly anthologized, and it hardly represents the prophetic word for which Wither expected to be remembered.

Biography:

Robert A. Willmott, *Lives of the Sacred Poets*, (London: John Parker, 1834).

References:

P. B. Anderson, "George Wither and the 'Regalia,'" *Philological Quarterly*, 14 (October 1935): 366-368;

Reginald Bigg-Wither, *Materials for a History of the Wither Family* (Winchester: Warren, 1907);

Thomas O. Calhoun, "George Wither: Origins and Consequences of a Loose Poetics," *Texas Studies in Literature and Language*, 16 (Summer 1974): 263-279;

Norman Carlson, "George Wither: A Troublesome Litigious Man," Ph.D. dissertation, Rutgers State University, 1962;

Carlson, "Wither and the Stationers," *Studies in Bibliography*, 19 (1966): 210-215;

Jocelyn C. Creigh, "George Wither and the Stationers: Facts and Fiction," *Papers of the Bibliographical Society of America*, 74 (First Quarter 1980): 49-57;

Sir Charles Firth, "George Wither," *Review of English Studies*, 2 (October 1926): 457-459;

J. M. French, "Four Scarce Poems of George Wither," *Huntington Library Bulletin*, no. 2 (November 1931): 91-121;

French, "George Wither," Ph.D. dissertation, Harvard University, 1928;

French, "George Wither in Prison," *PMLA*, 45 (December 1930): 959-966;

French, "George Wither's Verses to Dr. John Raven," *PMLA*, 63 (June 1948): 749-751;

French, "Thorn Drury's Notes on George Wither," *Huntington Library Quarterly*, 23 (August 1960): 379-388;

Charles S. Hensley, *The Later Career of George Wither*, (The Hague: Mouton, 1969);

Christopher Hill, "George Wither and John Milton," *English Renaissance Studies* (Oxford: Clarendon Press, 1980), pp. 212-227;

Lyle H. Kendall, Jr., "Wither's Authorship of The Great Assises," *Notes and Queries*, 198 (March 1953): 102;

Kendall, "An Unrecorded Prose Pamphlet by George Wither," *Huntington Library Quarterly*, 20 (February 1957): 190-195;

David Norbrook, "Leveling Poetry: George Wither and the English Revolution, 1642-1649," *English Literary Renaissance*, 21 (Spring 1991): 217-256;

Norbrook, *Poetry and Politics in the English Renaissance*, (London: Routledge & Kegan Paul, 1984);

Allan Pritchard, "Abuses Stript and Whipt and Wither's Imprisonment," *Review of English*

Studies, new series 14 (November 1963): 337-345;

Pritchard, "George Wither," Ph.D. dissertation, University of Toronto, 1957;

Pritchard, "George Wither: The Poet as Prophet," *Studies in Philology*, 59 (April 1962): 211-230;

Pritchard, "George Wither and the Somers Islands," *Notes and Queries*, new series 8 (1961): 428-430;

Pritchard, "George Wither's Quarrel with the Stationers: An Anonymous Reply to *The Schollers Purgatory*," *Studies in Bibliography*, 16 (1963): 27-42;

Pritchard, "A Manuscript of George Wither's

Psalms," *Huntington Library Quarterly*, 27 (November 1963): 73-77;

Pritchard, "An Unpublished Poem of George Wither," *Modern Philology*, 61 (November 1963): 120-121;

Pritchard, "Wither's *Motto* and Browne's *Religio Medici*," *Philological Quarterly*, 40 (April 1961): 302-307;

Percy Simpson, "Walkley's Piracy of Wither's Poems in 1620," *Library*, new series 6 (December 1925): 271-277;

W. D. Templeman, "Some Commendatory Verses by George Wither," *Notes and Queries*, 188 (July 1942): 365-366.

Sir Henry Wotton

(30 March 1568 - 5 December 1639)

Ted-Larry Pebworth
University of Michigan—Dearborn

BOOKS: *Ad illustrissimum virum Marcum Velserum duumvirum Augustæ Vindeliciæ H. Wottonij epistola* (London, 1612);

The Elements of Architecture, Collected from the Best Authors and Examples (London: Printed by J. Bill, 1624);

A Meditation upon the XXIIth [sic] *Chapter of Genesis* (Printed by A. Mathewes for G. Baker, 1631);

Ad regem è Scotia reducem Henrici Wottonij plausus et vota (London: Typis A. Mathusij, 1633); translated as *A Panegyrick of King Charles; being Observations upon the Inclination, Life and Government of Our Soveraign Lord the King* (London: Printed for Richard Marriot, 1649);

A Parallel betweene Robert Late Earle of Essex, and George Late Duke of Buckingham (London, 1641);

A Short View of the Life and Death of George Villers, Duke of Buckingham (London: Printed for W. Sheares, 1642);

Reliquiæ Wottonianæ. Or, a Collection of Lives, Letters, Poems: with Characters of Sundry Person-

ages: And other Incomparable Pieces of Language and Art. By the curious Pensil of the Ever Memorable Sr Henry Wotton, K[t], Late Provost of Eton Colledg (London: Printed by T. Maxey for R. Marriot, G. Bedel & T. Garthwait, 1651; second edition, enlarged, London: Printed by Thomas Maxey for R. Marriot, G. Bedel & T. Garthwait, 1654; third edition, London: Printed by T. Roycroft for R. Marriott, F. Tyton, T. Collins & J. Ford, 1672; fourth edition, enlarged, London: Printed for B. Tooke & T. Sawbridge, 1685);

The State of Christendom: or, A Most Exact and Curious Discovery of Many Secret Passages, and Hidden Mysteries of the Times (London: H. Moseley, 1657).

Editions: *Poems by Sir Henry Wotton*, edited by Alexander Dyce (London: Percy Society, 1843);

Poems by Sir Henry Wotton, Sir Walter Ralegh and Others, edited by John Hannah (London: Pickering, 1845); revised as *The Courtly Poets from Raleigh to Montrose* (London: Bell & Daldy, 1870); republished as *The Poems of Sir Walter*

Henry Wotton (portrait attributed to Gheeraedts; location of original unknown; reproduced from a negative on file at the National Portrait Gallery, London)

Raleigh, Collected and Authenticated with those of Sir Henry Wotton and Other Courtly Poets from 1540 to 1650 (London: Bell, 1885).

OTHER: "O Faithles World . . . ," in *A Political Rapsody*, by Francis Davison and others (London: Printed by V. Simmes for J. Baily, 1602);

"The Character of a Happy Life," in *A Wife, Now a Widowe*, by Sir Thomas Overbury, third edition (London: Printed by E. Griffin for L. Lisle, 1614);

"On a Banck as I sate a Fishing . . . ," in *The Compleat Angler*, by Izaak Walton (London: Printed by T. Maxey for Rich. Marriot, 1653).

Sir Henry Wotton is remembered today primarily as a diplomat and letter writer during the reign of James I, as provost of Eton during the reign of Charles I, and as the author of two of the most frequently anthologized poems of the earlier seventeenth century, a characterization of the happy life and a tribute to Elizabeth Stuart, the ill-fated queen of Bohemia. Well known for his wit as well as for his political acumen, he once defined an ambassador as one "sent to lie abroad for his king," and he wished to be remembered as the author of the all-too-accurate warning, "Disputandi pruritus fit Ecclesiarum scabies" (The itch of disputation will prove the scab of the Church). Throughout his interesting and active life, Wotton wrote hundreds of letters (both official and personal) and several fine lyric poems; in his later years, he turned his considerable creative talents to history, biography, and social and political commentary. More than a thousand of his letters survive, and all are witty, lively, and informative. His historical writings include *Parallel Lives* of Robert Devereux, second Earl of Essex, and George Villiers, first Duke of Buckingham (1641), written on the model of Plutarch, and a separate *Short View of the Life and Death of George Villers, Duke of Buckingham* (1642), as well as sketches of William the Conqueror and Henry VI written for a history of England that was never completed. His theoretical works include insightful treatises on politics, education, and architecture. He was a friend of John Donne, Isaac Casaubon, and Izaak Walton and was much admired by Francis Bacon, Ben Jonson, and George Herbert. Wotton was also the first Englishman to record an appreciation of the young John Milton's genius, remarking of *Comus* (1634) in a 13 April 1638 letter, "I should much commend the Tragical part, if the Lyrical did not ravish me with a certain Dorique delicacy in your Songs and Odes, whereunto I must plainly confess to have seen yet nothing parallel in our Language." And it was because of Wotton's procrastination in writing a life of his friend Donne that Wotton's fishing companion Izaak Walton became a biographer.

A younger son in a prominent Kentish family, Wotton, the only child of Thomas Wotton by his second wife, Eleanor (née Fitch), was educated at Winchester School and at New College and Queen's College, Oxford, receiving a bachelor of arts degree in 1588. While at Oxford he probably established what was to become a lifelong friendship with Donne. Wotton spent several years touring the Continent (1588-1594), where he perfected his skills in modern languages and observed the European political scene. Shortly after his return to England, he entered the service of the earl of Essex, Queen Elizabeth's favorite, acting as secretary and agent. In 1595 he entered the Middle Temple, though he was never to be called to the bar. Under Essex, Wotton took part, along with Donne, in the Cádiz expedition of 1596 and the Azores expedition in 1597. In 1599 he accompanied Essex on the disastrous expedition to Ireland and was one of the principal negotiators of the truce with Hugh O'Neill, second Earl of Tyrone, the rebel leader. After returning to England with Essex, Wotton recognized the growing rashness of his employer and soon left his service, going back to the Continent and thereby avoiding participation in Essex's rebellion and fall (1600-1601). Knighted by King James in 1603, Wotton served three terms as ambassador to Venice (1604-1612, 1616-1619, and 1621-1624), and he negotiated the ultimately ineffectual treaty of Xanten in 1614. While in public service, Wotton became acquainted with the successive favorites of King James, Robert Carr (or Ker), later Earl of Somerset, and George Villiers, later first Duke of Buckingham; for a time he served as Buckingham's agent in Italy, procuring Italian paintings and

Greek manuscripts for his young patron. During one of his several journeys to the Continent, Wotton also became a friend of Casaubon. Under the patronage of Buckingham, Wotton was awarded the provostship of Eton College in 1624, and he served in that office with considerable distinction until his death in 1639. In 1627 he was ordained deacon in the Church of England.

Wotton's poems, though relatively few in number, encompass a wide range of lyric genres—amorous, commendatory, political, religious, and reflective—and all are of very high quality. Jonson, one of the two best English poets of the earlier seventeenth century and the most perceptive literary critic of the age, told William Drummond of Hawthornden in 1619 that he much admired and knew "by Heart" Wotton's poem on the happy life, written about 1612. Wotton's ode to Charles I, written in 1633, was ironically honored by inclusion in the posthumously published 1640-1641 folio edition of Jonson's *Workes*. Several of Wotton's poems were set to music by important seventeenth-century composers; several were pirated by unscrupulous publishers; several were imitated, translated, and adapted to new uses by various hands; and, judging by the frequency of their appearance in manuscript miscellanies of the period, several of Wotton's lyrics were among the most widely circulated and universally appreciated poems of his age. Wotton is not a major poet, but he is a significant and central one. His centrality stems from the enormous influence of several of his poems and from his connections with such important seventeenth-century figures as the first two Stuart kings, Buckingham, Bacon, Donne, Jonson, Herbert, and Milton. His poems reflect his active involvement in the political and literary life of his time. Moreover, the intrinsic merits of his poetry are considerable, exemplified most fully by his frequently anthologized poem to the queen of Bohemia, among the most beautiful commendatory lyrics of the seventeenth century.

More than half of Wotton's lyrics are occasional poems that stem directly from his active involvement in public life. Two of these, the verse letter to Donne beginning " 'Tis not a coate of gray, or Shepheards life" and the characterization of a happy life beginning "How happy is he borne, or taught," are general reflections on the difficulty of remaining both moral and contented in the generally immoral and frantic environment of a late-Renaissance royal court. The poem on the fall of Somerset, beginning "Dazeld thus with hight of

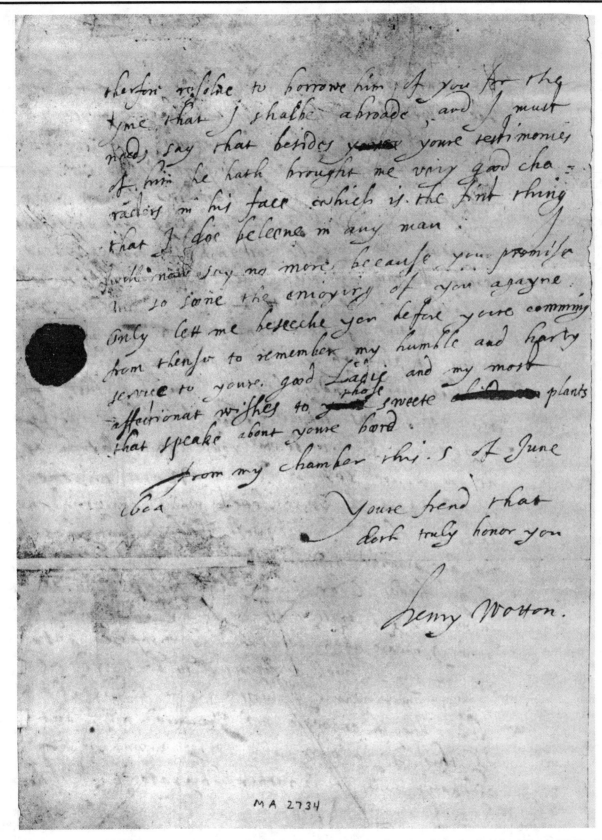

Second page of Wotton's 5 June 1604 letter to a friend (possibly Sir Henry Fanshawe), written shortly before Wotton left England to serve his first term as ambassador to Venice (Pierpont Morgan Library; MA 2734, purchased as the gift of Mrs. J. Carter Brown)

place," is both a reflection on the vagaries of fortune and a warning to would-be favorites of great men. Another poem, addressed to George Villiers, first Duke of Buckingham, successor to Somerset as the king's favorite, is a thinly veiled begging letter from client to patron. "A short Hymn upon the Birth of Prince CHARLES" expresses measured hope for the Stuart monarchy. The ode written to commemorate King Charles's return from his Scottish coronation is an epithalamic hymn to the royal couple that tactfully ignores political disaster by concentrating on domestic triumph. The best known and most highly praised of Wotton's poems today is a verse compliment to Elizabeth Stuart, daughter of James I, written shortly after her husband had accepted the Bohemian throne.

The verse epistle to Donne, written during the summer of 1598, is a sharp response to Donne's own well-intentioned verse letter to Wotton beginning "Here's no more newes then vertue." At the time, Donne, secretary to Lord Keeper Thomas Egerton, seemed more securely placed in public life than Wotton, whose patron and employer Essex was in temporary disgrace. Writing from court to his friend in the country, Donne catalogued the vices of courtiers and concluded that it is better for one's moral health to be "From Court" rather than "At Court." Although Donne had obviously meant to console his rusticating friend, Wotton must have been more annoyed than comforted by the poem, for he immediately answered it with a poem beginning " 'Tis not a coate of gray, of Shepheards life, / 'Tis not in feilds or woods remote to lyve, / That adds or takes from one that peace or strife / Which to our dayes such good or ill doth give." Echoing one of the more popular poems of the period, Edward de Vere, Earl of Oxford's "My Mind to Me a Kingdom Is," Wotton rejects Donne's implicit advice that he abandon courtly ambitions by outlining an alternative means of coping with possible disappointment, one that does not necessarily require him to be away "From Court." Judging it "vayne, if wee to desarts goe / To seek our bliss, or shroud us from annoy," Wotton advocates instead a moderation of the "extreames" of "desires" by a deliberate change of "Will" directed toward freeing the "mynd of passions." He upholds as more efficacious than retirement from the public arena the time-honored Stoic recipe for contentment in the face of inevitable adversity, the cultivation of an indifference toward both fortunate and unfortunate worldly

events. His answer to Donne's complaint about false friends is that it is the chooser's fault, not the supposed friend's, if the latter proves untrue. And he transparently excuses the didactic tone taken toward his friend by concluding, "Yet 'tis no harme mortality to preach, / For men do often learne when they do teach." Donne must have been stung by the rebuke implicit in Wotton's poem, for he immediately replied with one of his most moving verse letters, beginning "Sir, more then kisses, letters mingle soules." In that reply, he gracefully begs pardon for his earlier presumption, and—implicitly acknowledging the validity of his friend's corrective—conflates his earlier stance with Wotton's, concluding that since all locales on earth are filled with temptation and turmoil, the wise man should "Be . . . thine owne home, and in thy selfe dwell." The verse letter to Donne marks Wotton's emergence as a reflective poet, and it is of considerable interest that Wotton and not Donne controls the exchange.

Wotton's better-known and more comprehensive contemplation of living well, most commonly titled "The Character of a Happy Life," was written some fifteen years later, at a time when the diplomat-poet was in temporary disfavor with King James for having written the witty though impolitic epigram defining an ambassador. Composed in the Horatian *beatus ille* tradition, informed by Christian Stoicism, and influenced by the revival of interest in the Theophrastan character, the poem catalogues the personal attributes and the accompaniments necessary for a happy life: an independence of will, the love of truth, control of the passions, an indifference to the things of the world, freedom from rumor and envy, the desire for a middle station in life, the love of good and hatred of vice, a prayerful attitude toward God, and "a well-chosen booke, or freind [*sic*]." The person who has all these, Wotton concludes, "is free from servile bandes / Of hope to rise, or feare to fall; / Lord of himselfe, though not of landes: / And having nothing, yet hath all." The one element missing in Wotton's poem but present in the dozens of other characterizations of the happy life written during the Renaissance is a loving and helpful wife. Despite that omission, Wotton's "Character" became one of the most frequently copied poems of the century, surviving in dozens of manuscript miscellanies and commonplace books; it was expanded and answered by anonymous copyists, translated into German by Georg Rudolph

Weckherlin, and set to music. Simple in its surface, yet elegantly and movingly written, the poem encapsulates the ideals of the Stoic revival of the late Renaissance.

Almost as popular with his contemporaries is another of Wotton's poems written during the same period, a cautionary reflection occasioned by the fall of the earl of Somerset, the favorite of James I who was implicated in the murder of Sir Thomas Overbury, convicted, and imprisoned in the Tower of London (1615-1622). It, too, is deceptively simple on the surface, yet insightful in its picture of the self-centered courtier: "Dazeld thus with hight of place, / Whilst our hopes our witts beguile, / No man markes the narrow space / 'Twixt a prison, and a smile." Warning that "fortunes favours fade" and that "the hearts of kinges are deepe," Wotton offers this advice to those temporarily raised up by the whim of royal favor: "if greatnes bee so blind / As to trust in Towers of ayer, / Lett it bee with goodnesse lin'd / That at least the fall bee faire." Then, "When frends fayle and princes frowne," as they inevitably will, the fallen favorite can rest in the knowledge that though "Virtue is the roughest way," it proves "att night a bedd of downe." Although the poem was written specifically on the fall of Somerset, its applicability to all fallen courtiers was immediately recognized. Seventeenth-century copies of the poem variously apply it to the fall of Secretary William Davison, the scapegoat used by Queen Elizabeth in the unpopular execution of Mary, Queen of Scots, and of Francis Bacon, who was disgraced by accusations of bribery. One manuscript copy even puts the poem in the mouth of the assassinated duke of Buckingham, making it literally his confessional swan song. Such uses speak eloquently to the truth of Wotton's observations and conclusions, as well as to the adaptability of seventeenth-century political verse.

A decade later Wotton wrote a poem to Somerset's successor as royal favorite, George Villiers, first Duke of Buckingham. At the time, Wotton was in debt, wearied with public life, and desperately seeking the provostship of Eton College. Buckingham, who had used Wotton's assistance in the procurement of manuscripts and paintings and who had the major influence in the king's selection of the new provost, was plagued with a serious fever. Although the poem is clearly intended to remind Buckingham of Wotton's suit, it does so with wit and indirection. Initially addressing not the duke but the "Untimely . . . rude insult-

ing" fever itself, Wotton asks, "How durst thou in such inharmonious heate / Dare to distune his well composed rest / Whose hart so just, so noble stroakes did beate?" He glances at Buckingham's role as lord high admiral by asking if the blood let three times by his physicians had not "Beene better treasur'd for some better day, / At farthest west to paint the liquid feild / And with new worlds his Masters love to pay?" He concludes by asking the young favorite to "pardon these poore rimes that would beguile / With mine owne griefe some portion of thy paine." The poem is saved from crass sycophancy by its wit and the genuineness of its concern for Buckingham's health. Although Wotton was not blind to the duke's faults (as witness his two biographical sketches of the ill-fated young man), he nevertheless had a genuine admiration and affection for his "Sweet Lord." The poem, while no doubt self-interested, is not merely selfish.

Wotton wrote three poems on members of the royal family, a hymn celebrating the birth of Prince Charles (later Charles II) in May of 1630, an ode to King Charles I on returning from his coronation in Scotland, and a tribute to the queen of Bohemia, sister of Charles I. All three are remarkable in that they largely avoid direct political comment and focus instead on familial and personal concerns. They contribute to the seventeenth-century discourse on the divine right of monarchs; yet they eschew extreme claims in favor of an approach that humanizes the royal personages.

Placed beside the poems commemorating the same event by more extravagant panegyrists of the Stuart monarchy, Wotton's "A short Hymn upon the Birth of Prince CHARLES" seems subdued and cautious. Where they had made much of the star shining at noon that—miraculously—heralded the new prince's birth, Wotton only glances at the phenomenon, then turns to praise God "From whom our *Joy* descends," and to pray for blessings on the newborn: "Upon this Royal flower, / Sprung from the Chasteste Bed, / Thy glorious swetness shower, / And first let *Myrtles* crowne his head, / Then *Palmes* and *Lawrels* wreath'd betweene; / But let the *Cypresse* late be seen." Having invoked love, piety, victory, and long life to attend the infant, Wotton then leaves it to "succeeding men," when they have seen the "fulness" of this new prince's accomplishments, to "Celebrate his *Praise* above." Experienced in the vagaries of politics, Wotton knew, even in 1630, that the Stuart monarchy was facing troubled times. He was obviously too wise to celebrate with uncritical optimism the birth of a royal heir as yet untried.

Wotton may well have been commissioned to write "An Ode Upon King Charles's returne to the Queene from his Coronation in Scotland" in 1633. A triumphal entry into London was planned, and the existence in manuscript of a musical setting of Wotton's poem suggests that it was intended to be performed during that celebration. Because of fiscal austerity, however, the event was canceled; and it is likely that Wotton's ode was never sung before its proposed audience. As with the birth of Prince Charles, many poets rushed to write uncritical encomia of the king's supposedly triumphal coronation in Scotland, but the journey was in actuality a political disaster. Charles was accompanied by Archbishop William Laud, who infuriated the Scots with his imposed liturgies, and Charles left his northern kingdom less liked than he had been from a distance. Again, Wotton approached his subject tactfully. Instead of praising Charles's accomplishments on the journey, which were dubious at best, he mixed the Horatian ode with the Catullan epithalamion to celebrate the reunion of the royal couple. "Make first a song of joy, of love / Which chastly flames in Royall eyes," Wotton commands his "gentle Muse"; and each stanza is concluded with the epithalamic "Chorus": "Long may they both contend to prove / The best of crowns is such a love." Wotton does not neglect the political altogether, but Charles is praised more for his person than for his political skill: "Long may he live, whose life doth bound / More then his lawes, and better leade / By high example then by dread." The emphasis of the poem is on the familial; and it offers only a prayer, rather than a prediction, for the future: "Long may he round aboute him see / His Roses and his lillies blowne; / Long may his only Deare and Hee / Joy in Idea's of theire owne, / And Kingdomes hopes see timely sowne." The poet is too politically astute to ignore the problems facing the monarchy and too truthful to lie about them. Although his reticences themselves constitute a political statement, he diplomatically focuses on aspects of the royal couple—their love, fidelity, and fruitfulness—that he can praise without reservation.

Wotton's poem addressed to Elizabeth Stuart, after 1619 Queen of Bohemia, has the distinction of being one of the most popular poems of its age. It is preserved in more than ninety seventeenth-century sources, in both print and manuscript; it was subjected to at least ten nonauthorial adaptations during the century, incorporating permutations of thirteen additional stanzas; it was translated twice into Latin verse by anonymous hands, and it was set to music by six seventeenth-century composers as well as one in the early eighteenth century. The popularity of the poem and its adaptability to new uses are easy to explain. With the possible exception of the final stanza (and even that might be accounted for as acceptable hyperbole), Wotton's encomium could very well be taken as a love poem (and very often was), celebrating the physical charms of its subject in a series of comparisons that almost invites imitation: first, she is the paragon of celestial lights, then of flowers, then of birds. It is no wonder, then, that adapters added a stanza on jewels and tried their hands at additional stanzas variously combining lights, flowers, birds, and jewels. Wotton's original is elegantly simple. What are the stars, he asks, "when the Moone shall rise?" What are the violets "when the Rose is blowne?" What are the "wandering chanters of the wood / . . . / When *Philomel* her voyce shal rayse?" It is only in the fourth and final stanza that Wotton makes any specific references to Elizabeth as a public person: "So when my mistris shall be seene / In sweetnes of her looks and mind, / By nature first, then choyce a Queene, / Tell me if she were not design'd / Th'Eclipse and glory of her kind." Wotton's compliment to Elizabeth is witty. Although she had been born a royal princess, Elizabeth had married not a king but Frederick, Prince of the Palatinate, in 1613; and although she had been made a queen by "nature," according to Wotton, she literally became a queen only by "choyce" when her consort Frederick chose to accept the offer of the crown of Bohemia in 1619. Wotton knew Elizabeth personally, and his nephew Albertus Morton was her secretary for a time. The poem was obviously written during the short period that Elizabeth shared the Bohemian throne. Frederick and she were soon deposed, and she spent the rest of her long life in exile, variously called the Queen of Hearts and the Winter Queen by her adherents. Beautiful in its simplicity and charm, Wotton's poem to the Queen of Hearts is a delightful celebration of Elizabeth as the epitome of "her kind."

Like his friend Donne, Wotton resolved on entering holy orders to put his pen to the service of God, and three of his last poems are hymns,

Wotton after he was appointed provost of Eton College (portrait by an unknown artist; National Portrait Gallery, London)

while another is a celebration of the coming of spring that closely approaches the religious in its rejoicing at the annual renewal of nature.

The first of the three hymns is "A Translation of the CIV. Psalm to the Originall Sense." Probably because of its emphasis on the bounty and beneficence of creation, Psalm 104 was a popular subject for English versification throughout the Renaissance. Wotton's decision to turn the psalm into verse was probably occasioned by the 1625 publication of Bacon's version in *The Translation of Certaine Psalmes*. Bacon's rendering is expansive, interpolating much original material into the biblical text. The title of Wotton's version, promising to translate the work "to the Originall Sense," suggests a reaction to Bacon's verbosity. Wotton's rendering is charmingly simple, yet witty and lively. The stanza translating verses 20-23 of the original is typical of the whole:

> Thou mak'st the *Night* to over-vail the *Day*;
>> Then savage Beasts creep from the silent *Wood*,
> Then Lions whelps lie Roaring for their Prey,
>> And at Thy powerfull Hand demand their *food*.

> Who when at *Morn* they *All* recouch again,
> Then toiling *Man* till *Eve* pursues his pain.

The exuberance of the descriptive elements and the wordplay on "Eve," coupled with "toiling" and "pain," are good examples of the style of the whole.

For sheer exuberance in nature and its annual renewal, however, nothing in Wotton's poetic canon can match his "On a Banck as I sate a Fishing, A Description of the Spring," written in his old age. The poem opens joyously: "This day Dame nature seem'd in love: / The lusty sapp began to move, / Fresh juice did stirre th'imbracinge vines, / And Birds had drawne their valentines." Wotton's lifelong passion, angling, and the fishing companion of his later years, Izaak Walton, are present in the scene: "The jealous Trout that low did lye / Rose at a well dissembled fly; / There stood my frend with patient skill / Attendinge on his Tremblinge quill." Barn swallows, nightingales, tulips, crocuses, violets, and the "modest Rose" populate this verdant world; and youthful love has a place as well: "*Joane* takes her neat rub'd pale and now / Shee trips to milke the sand red Cow, / Where, for some sturdy football Swayne, / *Joane* stroaks a Sillibub or twayne." The poem concludes in a summary statement, "Thus all looks gay, and full of cheere / To wellcome the new livery'd yeare." It is appropriate that this paean to spring found an honored place in Walton's *The Compleat Angler* (1653); and because it did, it has become Wotton's most frequently published poem.

Wotton wrote two original hymns. Though the second of them, beginning "Eternall mover, whose diffused glorie," was alleged in *Reliquiæ Wottonianæ* (1651) to have been written when Wotton "was an Ambassadour at Venice, in the time of a great Sickness there," both were in fact written during his final illness, and both are contemplations of imminent death. They are clearly companion poems. The first, beginning "Oh thou great power in whom wee move," concentrates on the meaning of the Passion. The speaker asks God to "cleanse my sordid soule within / By thy Christs blood: the Bathe of sinn" and affirms his belief that "One Rosye dropp from Davids seed / Was worlds of seas to quench thyne Ire, / Oh pretious ransom, which once payd, / That *Consummatum est* was said." The second chastises the vainglory of man, who considers himself "thy proudest Creature . . . The worlds contracted Summe: the little all." Echoing Donne's "First Anniversary," the speaker asks, "For what are wee but Lumpes of Walkinge Clay. / Where are our vauntes: whence should our Spirits rise? / Are not bruite beasts as stronge, and birds as gaye, / Trees longer liv'd, and creepinge thinges as wise?" Then, for comfort, the speaker turns to thoughts of the Second Coming and the Last Judgment: "Therefore my Soule, Joye in the midst of payne. / Thy Christ that conquer'd Hell shall from above / With greater triumphs yet returne againe / And conquer his owne Justice with his love, / Commandinge Earth and Seas to render those / Unto his blisse, for whom hee payed his woes." Secure in the belief that Christ will "conquer his owne Justice with his love," the speaker resigns himself to death: "Thy words are true, thy Promises are Just, / And thou wilt know thy marked flocke in dust." Simple in their wording yet profound in their faith, Wotton's two hymns are moving testimony to his skill as a poet.

Of Wotton's four other poems, two are youthful love lyrics; one is a lament for the death of his nephew Albertus Morton; and one is a brief tribute to James Howell prefixed to Howell's politi-

cal allegory *Dodona's Grove, or, The Vocall Forrest* (1640). The last of these is certainly Wotton's final poetic effort. Obviously written while Howell's book was still in manuscript, it is remarkable for avoiding comment on the political content of Howell's work altogether, focusing instead on the "rich *English* Prose" that the author has taught "The *Olive, Ivie, Mulbery,* and *Pine,*" and concluding, "Who makes *Trees* speak so well, deserves the *Bay.*"

Perhaps Wotton's earliest surviving poem, first published in 1602 in Francis Davison's *A Poetical Rapsody*, is the lyric beginning "O Faithles World, and thy most faithles part, / A Woman's Harte" and concluding "thinke thy gaine, / To know that Love, lodg'd in a Womans Brest, / Is but a Ghest." Although the sentiments expressed are common to the misogynistic love elegy of the period, Wotton's poem is of considerable technical interest because it is written in epodic couplets and is thus a novel blend of the love elegy and the satiric epode. The second of his love lyrics is addressed to a "Noble, lovely, vertuous Creature, / Purposely so fram'd by nature / To enthrall your servants wits" and is written in alternating stanzas by Wotton and an early friend of his, the prolific John Hoskins. In each of the four pairs of brief stanzas, Hoskins speaks first, in a thoroughly conventional fashion, and Wotton second, inevitably inserting a twist that darkens an otherwise straightforward courtship. What is most interesting about the poem is the way that Wotton, though always speaking second, controls the discourse.

Aside from the two hymns written during his last illness, perhaps the most personal of Wotton's poems is the lament occasioned by the death in 1625 of his nephew Sir Albertus Morton, for whom he had a strong attachment. After pleading that "Silence, in truth, would speake my sorrow best," Wotton nevertheless seeks to "ingrave / These bleeding Numbers to adorne" Morton's "sable stone," vowing "Heere will I print the Characters of woe." Wotton's mourning does eventually end in Christian consolation: "Dwell then in endless light thou freéd soule, / Discharg'd from Natures and from Fortune's trust"; but it is a consolation that has little power to take away the very human feelings of emptiness and paralysis in the survivors: "While on this fluent globe our glasses rowle, / And run the rest of our remaining Dust."

It is obvious that Wotton did not consider himself as primarily a poet. Like so many of his generation, he was a man of affairs who liked poetry and who occasionally expressed himself in verse. Yet, also like many of his contemporaries, he was extremely skillful in the writing of those few poems. He was by turns, as the occasion demanded, satiric, witty, sober, pious, mournful, didactic, admiring, joyous, cautious, or tactful. In all those moods he managed to strike chords that ring true to the human condition while expressing himself in a deceptively simple yet elegant language. Although he experimented with form and often played with multiple meanings of words, his poetry is not eccentric in the way that his friend Donne's often is. Wotton wrote the occasional verse of a Renaissance public figure who was also a Christian humanist. While his canon is too small and his talent too limited to make Henry Wotton a major poet, he is an accomplished minor poet in an age of excellent minor poetry.

Letters:

Letters of Sir Henry Wotton to Sir Edmund Bacon (London: Printed by R. W. for F. T., 1661);

Letters and Dispatches from Sir Henry Wotton to James the First and His Ministers, in the Years MDCXVII-XX (London: Printed by W. Nicol, Shakespeare Press, 1850);

Logan Pearsall Smith, *The Life and Letters of Sir Henry Wotton*, 2 volumes (Oxford: Clarendon Press, 1907);

A. M. Crinò, *Fatti e figure del Seicento anglo-toscano* (Florence: L. S. Olschki, 1957).

Biographies:

Izaak Walton, "The Life of Sir Henry Wotton," in *Reliquiæ Wottonianæ* (London: Printed by T. Maxey for R. Marriot, G. Bedel & T. Garthwait, 1651; revised and enlarged in the second edition, 1654); revised again, in Walton's *The Lives of Dᵣ John Donne, Sir Henry Wotton, Mᵣ Richard Hooker, Mᵣ George Herbert* (London: Printed by Tho. Newcombe for R. Marriot, 1670); revised and enlarged again, in *Reliquiæ Wottonianæ*, third edition (London: Printed by T. Roycroft for R. Marriot, F. Tyton, T. Collins & J. Ford, 1672); revised again, in *The Lives of Dᵣ John Donne, Sir Henry Wotton, etc.*, second edition (London: Printed by Thomas Roycroft for Richard Marriot, 1675);

Logan Pearsall Smith, *The Life and Letters of Sir Henry Wotton*, 2 volumes (Oxford: Clarendon Press, 1907).

References:

J. B. Leishman, " 'You Meaner Beauties of the Night': A Study in Transmission and Transmogrification," *Library*, fourth series 26 (September-December 1945): 99-121;

Wolfgang Lottes, " 'On this Couch of tears': Meditationen in schwerer Krankheit von Donne, Wotton, Latewar, Isham und Philipot," *Literatur in Wissenschaft und Unterricht*, 8 (August 1975): 56-70;

C. F. Main, "Wotton's 'The Character of a Happy Life,' " *Library*, fifth series 10 (December 1955): 270-274;

Ted-Larry Pebworth, "New Light on Sir Henry Wotton's 'The Character of a Happy Life,' " *Library*, fifth series 33 (September 1978): 223-226;

Pebworth, "Sir Henry Wotton's 'Dazel'd Thus, with Height of Place' and the Appropriation of Political Poetry in the Earlier Seventeenth Century," *Papers of the Bibliographical Society of America*, 71 (April-June 1977): 151-169;

Pebworth, "Sir Henry Wotton's 'O Faithless World': The Transmission of a Coterie Poem and a Critical Old-Spelling Edition," *Analytical & Enumerative Bibliography*, 5, no. 4 (1981): 205-231;

Pebworth and Claude J. Summers, " 'Thus Friends Absent Speake': The Exchange of Verse Letters between John Donne and Henry Wotton," *Modern Philology*, 81 (May 1984): 361-377.

Papers:

No autograph copies of Wotton's poems are known to exist. Copies of his poem on the happy life and his verse tribute to the queen of Bohemia in the handwriting of William Parkhurst, Wotton's secretary during the first embassy to Venice, are preserved in the Burley manuscript (Leicestershire Record Office, DG. 7/Lit.2). For the other early manuscript copies of Wotton's poems, see volume 1, part 1 of Peter Beal's *Index of English Literary Manuscripts* (1980), pp. 561-587, 635-636.

Lady Mary Wroth

(18 October 1587 - circa 1653)

Josephine A. Roberts
Louisiana State University

BOOKS: *The Countesse of Mountgomeries Urania* (London: Printed by Augustine Mathewes for John Marriott & John Grismand, 1621).

Editions: *Pamphilia to Amphilanthus by Lady Mary Wroth*, edited by G. F. Waller (Salzburg: Institut für Englische Sprache und Literatur, Universität Salzburg, 1977);

The Poems of Lady Mary Wroth, edited by Josephine A. Roberts (Baton Rouge & London: Louisiana State University Press, 1983);

Lady Mary Wroth's 'Love's Victory': The Penshurst Manuscript, edited by Michael G. Brennan (London: Roxburghe Club, 1988).

Lady Mary Wroth was the first Englishwoman to write a complete sonnet sequence as well as an original work of prose fiction. Although earlier women writers of the sixteenth century had mainly explored the genres of translation, dedication, and epitaph, Wroth openly transgressed the traditional boundaries by writing secular love poetry and romances. Her verse was celebrated by the leading poets of the age, including Ben Jonson, George Chapman, Josuah Sylvester, and others. Despite the controversy over the publication in 1621 of her major work of fiction, *The Countesse of Mountgomeries Urania*, Wroth continued writing a second part of her romance and composed a five-act pastoral drama, *Love's Victory.*

The eldest daughter of Sir Robert Sidney and Lady Barbara Gamage, she was probably born on 18 October 1587, a date derived from the Sidney correspondence. She belonged to a prominent literary family, known for its patronage of the arts. Her uncle, Sir Philip Sidney, was a leading Elizabethan poet, statesman, and soldier, whose tragic death in the Netherlands elevated him to the status of national hero. Wroth was influenced by some of her uncle's literary works, including his sonnet sequence *Astrophil and Stella* (1591); a prose romance, intermingled with poetry, *The Countess of Pembroke's Arcadia* (existing in two distinct versions, the second of which was published in 1590); and a pastoral entertainment, *The Lady of May* (written in 1578 or 1579).

Wroth's father, Sir Robert Sidney, was also a poet (his verse survived in a single manuscript and did not appear in print until 1984). Following the death of Philip, Robert was appointed to fill his brother's post as governor of Flushing in the Netherlands, where he served throughout much of Wroth's childhood. He kept in close touch with his family through visits and letters; his friend and adviser Rowland Whyte wrote Sidney frequent reports concerning his eldest child, whom he affectionately nicknamed "little Mall."

One of the most powerful forces in shaping Wroth's literary career was her aunt and godmother, Mary Sidney, who was married to Henry Herbert, second Earl of Pembroke. Her country estate at Wilton served as a gathering place for a diverse number of poets, theologians, and scientists. The countess of Pembroke wrote poetry and translations from French and Italian, but even more important, she boldly published her works at a time when few women dared: her *Antonius*, a translation of Robert Garnier's French drama, appeared in print in 1592, along with her translation of Philippe Duplessis-Mornay's treatise *A Discourse of Life and Death*. She also assumed an active role as editor of the surviving works of her brother Philip and as a literary patron. One of her crowning achievements was the completion of the metrical version of the Psalms she had begun as a joint project with Philip; she heavily revised his first 43 psalms and then added 107 of her own. Her experiments in a variety of metrical and verse forms probably helped inspire Wroth's own interest in lyrical technique. Wroth offered highly sympathetic portraits of her aunt as the Queen of Naples in the *Urania*, where she is described as "perfect in Poetry, and all other Princely vertues as any woman that ever liv'd," and as Simena (an anagram for Mary Sidney) in *Love's Victory.*

Wroth's education was largely informal, obtained from household tutors under the guid-

Lady Mary Wroth (portrait by an unknown artist; Collection of Viscount de L'Isle, Penshurst Place)

ance of her mother. Rowland Whyte reported in 1595 that "she is very forward in her learning, writing, and other exercises she is put to, as dawncing and the virginals." Whyte's letters make frequent reference to her musical education; he reassured her absent father that the children "are kept at ther bookes, they dance, they sing, they play on the lute, and are carefully kept unto yt." It is also likely that Wroth learned French during her childhood trips to the Lowlands with her family.

Negotiations for her marriage began as early as 1599, and she eventually married Sir Robert Wroth, the son of a wealthy Essex landowner, at Penshurst on 27 September 1604. Disagreements between the couple began almost immedi-

ately. In a letter Sir Robert Sidney described his unexpected meeting in London with the bridegroom, who was greatly discontented with his new wife. Fundamental differences of temperament and interests quickly became apparent.

Sir Robert Wroth, knighted by James I in 1603, rapidly advanced in the king's favor because of his skill in hunting. He maintained country homes at Durrance and Loughton Hall, which the king visited on hunting expeditions with his friends. Ben Jonson commemorated the visits in his poem "To Sir Robert Wroth," in which he described how James I "makes thy house his court." Unlike his wife, who served as an important patron of the arts, Wroth appears to have had few literary interests. During his entire career, only one book was dedicated to him—a treatise on mad dogs.

Ben Jonson in his Conversations with William Drummond succinctly observed that Mary Wroth was "unworthily maried on a Jealous husband." More unflattering testimony is offered by Sir John Leeke, a servant of Mary Wroth's, who described a relative's husband as "the foulest Churle in the world; he hath only one vertu that he seldom cometh sober to bedd, a true imitation of Sir Robert Wroth." Indeed, the experience of an unhappy marriage seems to have inspired many episodes in Mary Wroth's prose fiction, especially those involving arranged marriages established primarily for financial reasons. On the other hand, her husband's favor with James I helped place Mary Wroth in the center of court activities. She gained one of the most coveted honors, a role in the first masque designed by Ben Jonson in collaboration with Inigo Jones, *The Masque of Blackness*, performed at Whitehall on 6 January 1605. She joined Queen Anne and eleven of her closest friends in disguising themselves as black Ethiopian nymphs. She also appeared with the queen in *The Masque of Beauty*, performed at Whitehall on 10 January 1608. She may have acted in other court masques for which the performance lists are incomplete, and it is likely that she attended masques such as *Hymenaei* (performed in 1606), *The Masque of Queens* (performed in 1609), and *Oberon* (performed in 1611). In the *Urania* she alluded to *Lord Hay's Masque* (performed in 1607) by Thomas Campion and probably to *Tethys' Festival* (performed in 1610) by Samuel Daniel. She also included descriptions of imaginary masques, complete with spectacular stage effects, in the second part of her romance.

By 1613 Wroth had begun her writing career—as revealed in Josuah Sylvester's elegy for Prince Henry, *Lachrymæ Lachrymarum* (1613), in which he refers to her verse and praises her as "AL-WORTH Sidnëides / In whom, her *Uncle's* noble Veine renewes." Her poems apparently circulated in manuscript long before their publication in 1621. Ben Jonson refers to "exscribing," or copying out, her verses in one of his poems addressed to her (*Underwood* 28). An early version of her sonnet sequence *Pamphilia to Amphilanthus* survives in a single manuscript, neatly copied in Wroth's own formal italic hand, now at the Folger Shakespeare Library.

This autograph version of Wroth's sequence consists of 110 songs and sonnets, plus 7 miscella-

neous pieces. The sequence opens with the dream vision of Pamphilia, whose name means "all-loving," in which she describes the triumph of Venus and Cupid over her heart. The first section of 55 poems reveals Pamphilia's conflicting emotions as she attempts to resolve the struggle between passionate surrender and self-affirmation. The Petrarchan model of the male lover wooing a cold, unpitying lady posed a genuine challenge to Wroth, who could not simply reverse the gender roles. Instead of presenting her female persona in active pursuit of Amphilanthus, whose name means "lover of two," Wroth completely omits the Petrarchan rhetoric of wooing and courtship. She addresses most of the sonnets to Cupid, night, grief, fortune, or time, rather than directly to Amphilanthus, whose name appears only in the title of the sequence.

A revised version of the sonnet cycle, printed at the end of the prose romance *Urania* (1621), consists of eighty-three sonnets and twenty songs. Wroth tightened the structure of the sequence by rearranging the poems in four distinct yet interrelated sections. While the order of the first group of fifty-five poems was left relatively unchanged, the second was heavily revised to explore the darker side of passion, especially through the use of the blind boy Cupid as a symbol of infantile, self-centered, sensual emotion. Pamphilia's harsh mockery of Cupid produces a guilty reaction when she suddenly repents of treason against the god of love and vows to reward him with a "Crowne" of praise, a group of fourteen sonnets imitating the Italian verse form the *corona*, in which the last line of the first sonnet serves as the first line of the next.

Wroth's "Crowne of Sonnets" represents a technical tour de force, as well as a central turning point in Pamphilia's inner debate. In this third section the persona attempts to redirect her thoughts to glorify Cupid as a fully mature monarch, a figure of divine love. Critics differ in their interpretations of this section, with some regarding Pamphilia as achieving an ascent to heavenly love. Others maintain that Pamphilia ends as she began, trapped in fearful perplexity: "In this strang labourinth how shall I turne?" (the line that opens and closes the "Crowne").

Some of the sonnets in the final group of the sequence are extremely melancholy in tone, with predominant imagery drawn from the winter world of clouds, shadows, and darkness. Yet a fragile hope emerges in the last two sonnets, where Pamphilia claims that her suffering has

A crowne of Sonetts
dedicated to Loue s

In this strang labourinth how shall I turne
wayes are on all sides while the waye I miss:
if to the right hand, ther in loue I burne;
lett mee goe forward, therin danger is;

If to the left suspition hinders bliss,
lett mee turne back, shame cries I ought returne
nor faynte though crosses w{th} my fortunes kiss;
stand still is harder, allthough sure to mourne;

Thus lett mee take the right, or left hand way;
goe forward, or stand still, or back retire;
I must thes doubts indure w{t}out allay
or help, butt traueile find for my best hire;

yett that w{ch} most my troubled sence doth moue
is to leaue all, and take the thread of loue,

Is to leaue all and take the thread of loue
w{ch} line straite leads vnto the soules content
wher choyce delights w{th} pleasures wings doe moue
and idle phantsie neuer roome had lent,

When chaste thoughts guide vs then our minds ar bent
to take that good w{ch} ills from vs remoue,
light of true loue brings fruite w{ch} none repent
butt constant louers seeke and wish to proue;

Loue is the shining starr of blessings light;
the feruent fire of zeale, the roote of peace,
the lasting lampe fed w{t} the oyle of right;
Image of faith and wombe for ioyes increase

                                           Loue

Opening page of an early draft for Pamphilia and Amphilanthus *(Folger Shakespeare Library, MS V.a. 104, f. 43)* taught her how to value spiritual love, and in her farewell poem she vows to leave behind the discourse of Venus and Cupid.

In many of the songs found throughout the sequence, Wroth adopts the pastoral mode, wherein Pamphilia speaks as a lovelorn shepherdess. The pastoral disguise allowed Wroth to set a vision of idyllic, innocent love alongside the actuality of the corrupt and inconstant passion of the court. As Ann Rosalind Jones has argued, the pastoral mode provided Wroth and other women poets with a vehicle to criticize sexual politics and masculine power. For example, one of Wroth's late songs, "Come merry spring delight us," begins with a cheerful invocation of spring and the renewal of nature, but the final stanza turns to the image of Philomela, who had been transformed into a nightingale following her rape by Tereus. Unlike her male predecessors, Wroth insists upon Philomela's continued pain and suffering, which memory cannot erase. Significantly, Wroth incorporated the pastoral mode in all three of her major works—her sonnet sequence, prose fiction, and drama.

Because Wroth composed her sequence long after the Elizabethan rage for sonneteering in the 1590s had passed, she had many earlier models at her disposal. Her father's unpublished collection of sonnets served as a particularly important influence. These love poems addressed to a lady named Charys, probably written during Robert Sidney's wartime exile from England, express a dark atmosphere of brooding hopelessness and death. Sidney attempted to write a *corona* as part of his sequence, but completed only four poems and a quatrain of a fifth. Perhaps Wroth regarded this unfinished "Crowne" as a challenge for her poetic talents in writing her own version. Also various verbal echoes of her father's imagery can be found in other poems. Similarly, Wroth appears to have drawn on her uncle's *Astrophil and Stella*, especially for the treatment of wayward Cupid and for verse forms. Yet Wroth avoids Philip Sidney's ironic raillery by creating instead a tone of more repressed anger and restrained sorrow.

Another influence on Wroth may have been the verse of her first cousin and lover, William Herbert, third Earl of Pembroke. Some of his surviving lyrics, which were not printed until 1660—such as his poem beginning, "Can you suspect a change in me, / And value your own constancy?"—can be read as answers or comments on Pamphilia's constancy. Wroth knew Pembroke from childhood, when she met him at family gatherings at Wilton and at Baynard's Castle, the London home of the Pembrokes. His younger brother, Philip, actually lived for a while in the Sidney household, and William visited three or four times a week.

Although Wroth and Pembroke shared close ties of kinship, they were separated by a great disparity in wealth. Because Pembroke was one of the richest peers in England, his family anticipated a marriage that would enhance his vast holdings of property, but he appears to have resisted their efforts to select a bride; instead he conducted an affair with the courtier Mary Fitton, who bore his child. When he steadfastly refused to marry her, he was sent to Fleet Prison for a brief period in 1601. After his father's death, Pembroke negotiated his own marital settlement with Mary Talbot, who was coheir to the immense wealth of Gilbert Talbot, seventh Earl of Shrewsbury. In *The History of the Rebellion and Civil Wars in England* (1702-1704), Edward Hyde, first Earl of Clarendon, commented on Pembroke's financial motivation, "for he paid much too dear for his wife's fortune, by taking her person into the bargain." They were wed on 4 November 1604, less than three months after Mary Wroth's marriage.

It is clear from the Sidney correspondence that Mary Wroth's relationship with Pembroke continued after her marriage, for he was a visitor at her home, Loughton Hall, and participated in many of the same family and court gatherings. During this period Pembroke steadily progressed in royal favor, becoming a leading statesman under James I, and serving successively as lord chamberlain and lord steward. He also became a distinguished patron of Jonson and William Shakespeare; the first folio of Shakespeare's plays was jointly dedicated to Pembroke and to his brother Philip Herbert, Earl of Montgomery.

One of the few concrete means of identifying Pembroke as the "Amphilanthus" of Wroth's sequence occurs in the text of the second part of the prose romance *Urania*. Here Wroth assigns to the character Amphilanthus a poem that was identified as Pembroke's in three early seventeenth-century manuscript collections: "Had I loved butt att that rate." Wroth did not risk explicitly identifying Pembroke within the sonnet cycle itself, however, and only in the final sonnet is there even a possibility of a pun on his first name: "The endless gaine which never *will* remove" (italics added).

Pembroke's presence may certainly have contributed to the unhappiness of Mary Wroth's marriage, but Robert Wroth's last testament suggests that her husband finally rested on good terms with both parties. He specifically chose Pembroke as one of the overseers of his will and left him a bequest of silver plate. Wroth described Mary as a "deere and loving wife," who deserved far better recompense than his debts would allow. He made special provision in his will to assign Mary "all her books and furniture of her studdye and closett." Wroth's husband died on 14 March 1614, only a month after the birth of her first child, James, who was named in honor of the king and christened with Pembroke and her mother in attendance.

Wroth's financial situation was radically altered after her husband's death, for she found herself with a young child and an estate charged with a twenty-three-thousand-pound debt. When her son died on 5 July 1616, her predicament was made even more difficult because much of the estate fell to Robert Wroth's uncle, John Wroth.

As a widow, Wroth appears to have lived for a period at Pembroke's London home, Baynard's Castle, for its name appears on several of her letters, and one of her correspondents refers to her "study" there. During this period she bore Pembroke two illegitimate children, whose births are recorded in a manuscript history of the family compiled by Sir Thomas Herbert of Tintern, which is now at the Cardiff Central Library. One was a son, William, who later became a captain under Sir Henry Herbert and a colonel under Prince Maurice; the other was a daughter, Catherine, who married a Mr. Lovel living near Oxford. The dates of their births are not listed, but Edward, Lord Herbert of Cherbury, sent a congratulatory poem to Mary Wroth which includes a likely reference to one of the children: "A Merry Rime Sent to Lady Mary Wroth upon the birth of my Lord of Pembroke's Child. Born in the spring." He may have sent a copy to Pembroke, who wrote a letter, dated 28 March 1620, thanking him for "congratulating with me yo'r little cousin." However, the evidence for dating the births of the children is very inconclusive.

Following her husband's death, Wroth suffered a decline in royal favor. She lost her place among Queen Anne's intimate circle of friends, although the exact cause of her downfall is uncertain. In some of the autobiographical episodes in the *Urania*, Wroth attributed her loss of the queen's favor to slander spread by envious rivals. Her relationship with Pembroke may have fueled the gossip, but certainly after her husband's death she lacked the financial ability to participate in the lavish court entertainments. She was, however, named as a member of the official procession of the state funeral for Queen Anne in 1619, and James I showed her a small measure of favor by issuing a warrant in 1621 to William Cecil, second Earl of Salisbury, to provide her with deer from the king's forest.

Wroth maintained her close ties to the Sidney family, as Anne Clifford recorded in her diary, where she mentions seeing Wroth at Penshurst, the Sidney home, and hearing her "news from beyond sea." One of Wroth's sources of foreign information was probably Dudley Carleton, ambassador to the Hague, with whom she corresponded in 1619. In these letters she mentions his recent presence at Loughton Hall, refers to some "rude lines" she had given him, and thanks him profusely for a gift. During this time there was also some speculation that Wroth might marry Henry de Vere, eighteenth Earl of Oxford (1593-1625), but he eventually married Diana Cecil.

The earl of Oxford's sister was Wroth's closest friend: Susan Vere, the first wife of Sir Philip Herbert, Earl of Montgomery (Pembroke's brother). The two women had known one another as early as 1605, when they participated together in *The Masque of Blackness*, and they exchanged frequent visits. As Pembroke's sister-in-law, Susan was a part of a tightly knit circle. She was also known for her literary patronage, extending from religious works (John Donne sent her a copy of one of his sermons) to secular prose romances of all types. In the dedication to a translation (1619) of the fourteenth-century Spanish romance *Amadis de Gaule*, Anthony Munday thanked the countess for her help in obtaining the best Spanish editions of the romance. Among other fiction, the first English translation (1620) of Honoré d'Urfé's *Astrée* (1607-1627) was dedicated to the countess and her husband.

When Wroth began to compose her own prose romance in the period 1618-1620, the countess of Montgomery was the logical dedicatee of her work. Wroth also paid her the highest compliment in creating the fictional character Urania in her honor. Named after the heavenly muse, Urania appears in the opening scene of the romance as a grief-stricken shepherdess who has just learned that the country couple who reared her

Title page for Wroth's prose romance about the personae of her sonnet sequence, Pamphilia and Amphilanthus

from childhood are not her actual parents. To discover her true identity, she must undertake an arduous quest, which eventually leads to a climactic scene late in the romance when she receives a book describing her royal heritage. Wroth's characterization of Urania is the first extended portrait of a woman by a woman in English. In addition, Wroth's treatment of the friendship between Urania and Pamphilia provides one of the most important links in a vast panorama of tales and tellers.

Wroth's sonnet cycle describing the intense, ambivalent passion of Pamphilia for Amphilanthus appears to have furnished the nucleus for her fiction, in which she developed the background and motivation of each of the central characters in far greater detail. In the prose romance, Pamphilia, the eldest daughter of the King of Morea, is designated by her unmarried

uncle as the heir to his kingdom of Pamphilia (located on the south coast of Asia Minor). Despite her feelings for Amphilanthus, she vows to remain a virgin monarch and to dedicate her life to the service of her country, undoubtedly in imitation of Elizabeth I. Her beloved Amphilanthus, the eldest son of the King of Naples, is crowned King of the Romans and eventually emperor, but despite his many virtues, he has one major flaw, his inconstancy. In the course of the *Urania* he betrays Pamphilia with a variety of female characters but returns each time begging her forgiveness.

The title page of the *Urania* features an engraving of one of the central episodes of the fiction, the Throne of Love. The Dutch artist Simon van de Passe based his engraving on Wroth's detailed description of an adventure in Cyprus, the traditional habitation of Venus (according to poets from Ovid to Petrarch). Wroth describes how a violent tempest shipwrecks the major characters on the island, where they soon discover a splendid palace high on a hill, which may be reached only by means of a bridge topped by three towers. The first tower to the left is Cupid's Tower, or the Tower of Desire, reserved as a place of punishment for false lovers. The second, belonging to Venus, is the Tower of Love, which may be entered by any suitors able to face such threats as Jealousy, Despair, and Fear. The third tower, guarded by the figure of Constancy, cannot be entered until the other obstacles have been overcome. Constancy holds the keys to the Throne of Love, a palace that is open to a very few. This episode not only provides a central point of reference for the entire romance, but it also functions as a landmark to measure the central couple's troubled relationship.

The end of the first book seems to affirm the special status of Pamphilia and Amphilanthus as heroic lovers. Despite all their misunderstandings, the pair returns to Cyprus, where they are able to free their female friends who are trapped inside the first two towers. When Pamphilia holds the keys to Constancy, the statue on the third tower actually metamorphoses itself into her breast. Although the Throne of Love may at first appear to be an idealized vision of the relation between the sexes, Wroth soon shows that it is a delusion that frustrates and thwarts the major characters. The anticipated marriage between the King of Cyprus and the Princess of Rhodes fails to materialize, as do most of the other promised unions, including that of the central pair of lovers. At the end of the second book Pamphilia herself falls prisoner at the enchanted Theater of the Rocks, so that her role is transformed from that of rescuer to victim. When Amphilanthus comes to her aid, he appears arm-in-arm with two other women, emblems of his infidelity. In the fourth book Wroth presents the "Hell of Deceit," in which each lover sees the other undergoing torture but is powerless to intervene; the insurmountable wall of doubt and suspicion is never overcome, even in the second, unpublished part of Wroth's romance.

The complete *Urania* includes more than three hundred characters, and thus a brief summary does not do justice to its intricate plot with many first-person narratives and inset tales. Wroth emphasizes the social conditions that oppressed early-seventeenth-century women, especially their lack of freedom to choose a marital

partner. She offers tales describing the horrors of enforced marriage, where a woman's consent might be obtained by means of physical or psychological abuse. Wroth also presents female figures who demonstrate active resistance to parental authority, although their acts of self-determination are often fraught with tragedy. As Maureen Quilligan has argued, one of the most important underlying concerns in the *Urania* is the "traffic in women," whereby males freely exchange females as property.

Some of the tales appear to be autobiographical, but Wroth mingled fact and fantasy in the portraits of herself, carefully modifying and refashioning the major events of her life. Pamphilia herself tells the tale of Lindamira (an anagram for Lady Mary), "faigning it to be written in a French Story," but at the conclusion her audience suspects that it is "some thing more exactly related then a fixion." In this tale Wroth traces her own career as a courtier and poet, including her loss of royal favor, which she protests as unjust. Lindamira concludes with a group of seven sonnets, an exact mirror of the larger *Urania*, with its appended sonnet sequence. The tale of Bellamira also seems to be largely autobiographical, although it includes a fictional subplot involving her father. Wroth's multiple self-portraits within the *Urania*—Pamphilia, Lindamira, Bellamira, and others—suggest a continuous struggle of self-representation, in which the author seeks to assert and justify her behavior in the face of a hostile, disapproving court.

Throughout the text of the *Urania*, Wroth intersperses a total of fifty-six poems, which underline key moments of crisis or discovery. Ranging in genre from sonnets to madrigals, dialogues, ballads, and pastoral narratives, the poems reveal experimentation in a variety of meters, most notably sapphics. Wroth adapts the poems to fit the different personalities of her characters, from the nervous, high-strung Antissia to the comically loquacious Florentine. She also includes poems specifically based on her uncle's *Arcadia*, such as a sonnet Pamphilia carves on the bark of an ash tree. Despite the outward similarity of this poem to Sidney's, Wroth recasts the view of woman from a passive subject of love's mastery to an active, controlling artist.

Indeed, many of Wroth's borrowings from earlier sources reveal an effort to transform the original material by reversing major conventions. In the first scene of her romance Wroth alludes to the opening of Sidney's revised *Arcadia*, in which two shepherds lament the disappearance of the mysterious shepherdess Urania, who never actually appears in Sidney's fiction. Wroth, however, creates her Urania as a fully human female, who refuses to accept society's narrow roles. When Perissus mistakes her for a spirit, he apologizes, saying, "but now I see you are a woman; and therefore not much to be marked." Urania disputes his sexist judgment by demonstrating her ability to save him, a pattern that is continually repeated in the romance.

Other sources include *Amadis de Gaule*, which provided Wroth with details for some of the major enchantments. Edmund Spenser's *Faerie Queene* (1590, 1596) furnished the inspiration for some episodes, including the account of the Hell of Deceit at the end of the published *Urania*. D'Urfé's *Astrée*, with its portrayal of the inconstant male figure Hylas, may have influenced Wroth's treatment of Amphilanthus. Another Continental romance, Jorge de Montemayor's *Diana*, translated by Bartholomew Yong (1598), includes a female seer, Felicia, who probably served as a model for Wroth's Mellissea. Finally, the appearance of Miguel de Cervantes' *Don Quixote* (1605), translated into English in 1612, popularized the satirical, self-critical romance, a mode which clearly appealed to Wroth in shaping the *Urania*.

Another significant development in the genre was the roman à clef, which includes allusions to actual persons and places. Marguerite de Navarre's *Heptaméron* (1558) as well as Sidney's two *Arcadia*s include thinly veiled characters, but John Barclay's *Argenis* (1621) was a systematic roman à clef, which commanded a wide audience at the Jacobean court. Wroth seems to have based the major characters of the *Urania* on members of the Sidney-Herbert family, although she exercised considerable artistic freedom. In addition, Wroth derived subplots from court figures and scandals. Her contemporaries recognized the allusions, as revealed in John Chamberlain's letters and in Sir Aston Cokayne's verse: "The Lady Wrothe's Urania is repleat / With elegancies, but too full of heat."

One of the courtiers who identified himself in the fiction was Sir Edward Denny, Baron of Waltham, who was outraged to find his personal affairs recounted in the episode of Seralius and his father-in-law. He responded by launching a vicious attack against the *Urania* and its author, with his complaints eventually reaching the ears of the king. He even wrote an insulting poem, addressed "To Pamphilia from the father-in-law of Seralius," in which he vilified Wroth as "Hermophradite in show, in deed a monster / As by thy words and works all men may conster." Undaunted, Wroth returned his insults in rhymes which match his, word for word: "Hirmophradite in sense in Art a monster / As by your railing rimes the world may conster."

Writing to her friends in an effort to rally support, she assured King James's favorite, George Villiers, first Duke of Buckingham, that she never meant her work to offend and volunteered to stop the sale of it. Her letter is especially revealing because she states that the books "were solde against my minde I never purposing to have had them published" (15 December 1621). It is clearly possible that her manuscript may have been pirated and entered for publication in the Stationers' Register without her permission; the absence of any dedicatory epistles or prefatory matter in the book is very unusual. On the other hand, Wroth admitted sending the duke of Buckingham her own personal copy, and the illustration for the title page was chosen by someone very familiar with the nature of her romance.

Following the storm of criticism, the book was never reprinted, but it continued to be read throughout the seventeenth century. The *Urania* may have furnished the dramatist James Shirley with plot material for his play *The Politician* (1655). Edward Phillips, John Milton's nephew, listed Wroth in his catalogue of "Women Among the Moderns Eminent for Poetry" (*Theatrum Poetarum*, 1675). Nor was she forgotten by other women writers, for Margaret Cavendish, Duchess of Newcastle, quoted the final couplet from Denny's diatribe against Wroth in the preface to her *Sociable Letters* (1664); Cavendish was the first woman to publish her fiction in more than forty years after the controversy over *Urania*.

Wroth herself was not completely silenced by the quarrel, for she continued writing a second, unpublished part of the *Urania*, which survives in a holograph manuscript of nearly 240,000 words at the Newberry Library in Chicago. The manuscript is divided into two volumes and picks up immediately with the final word of the printed book. This unfinished, second part of the *Urania* describes the continuing struggles of Pamphilia and Amphilanthus, along with a second generation of princes and princesses. Of special interest is Wroth's account of several children, born out of wedlock, who occupy important positions by virtue of individual merit

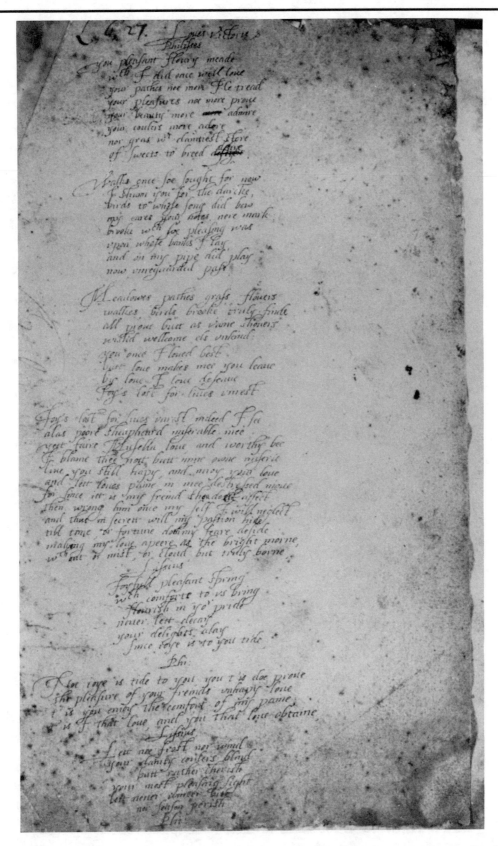

Page from the manuscript for Love's Victorie *in Wroth's formal script. The play depicts four contrasting couples who demonstrate a variety of human responses to love (The Huntington Library, Huntington MS HM 600, f. 1).*

lett them alone, and lett themselues beguile
they shall haue tormentts when they striue to smile
they are nott yett in pride of all theyr scorne
~~but~~ ere they haue theyr pleasures haulfway worne
they shall both cry, and waile, and creepe
and for our mercy shall most humbly creepe
loue hath most glory when as greatest sprites
hee downeward throwse unto his owne delights
then take noe care loues victory shall shine
when as your honor shall bee raisd by mine

               Venus

Thankes Cupid if thou doe performe thy oathe
and nede you must for gods must vaine noe trothe
lest mortalls neuer thinke ist, od or vaine
                  heere
is ~~knowne~~ thee soue can in all spiritts raine
prinses as nott exempted from our mights
              much
~~which~~ ler should sheapheards scorne us, and our rights
though they as well can loue and like affects
they must nott therfor our commands reiect

               Cu:

Nor shall and mark butt what my vengeance is
Ile miss my force or they shall vant theyr bliss
and arrows heere I haue of purpose fronid
wch as they qualities for are they named
                     leaue
Ioue, iealousie, malice, ~~loue~~ and mistrust
                     ^att last
yet all this shall att last incounter lust
harme shall bee non, yett shall they harme indure
for som small season then of ioy bee sure
like you this mother, ve: sure I like this well
and faile nott now in least part of this spell; &

                     &

Page from the manuscript for Love's Victorie *in the informal script Wroth used for the speeches of Cupid and Venus, which appear to have been written last and inserted into the rest of the text (The Huntington Library, Huntington MS HM 600, f. 5)* rather than birth. Wroth also tells how the major couple falls victim to the manipulations of a lying servant, who tricks each partner into believing in the other's betrayal. Pamphilia's marriage to the Tartarian king, Rodomandro, is described in great detail as is Amphilanthus's wedding to the Princess of Slavonia. Only near the very end of the manuscript do the characters rejoin on the island of Cyprus, where amid reminders of the earlier enchantment of the Throne of Love, they achieve a reconciliation as Platonic lovers. The manuscript breaks off shortly after in midsentence, with Amphilanthus left in search of one of the illegitimate children, the mysterious Faire Designe.

While writing the second part of *Urania* in the 1620s, Wroth was probably also at work on her play *Love's Victory*, since the two works share a common plot and characters. In the second volume of the *Urania* manuscript, Wroth describes a group of eight lovers, led by a distinguished brother and sister who excel in writing poetry. Appearing in both works are the disguised shepherds Arcas and Rustick, along with the fickle Magdaline (her name is shortened to Dalina in the play), and in both works the young lovers suffer as a result of Cupid's revenge. Wroth's drama is a pastoral tragicomedy, probably written for private presentation, although no record of its performance has been discovered so far.

It is not surprising that Wroth would undertake a play, given her interest in dramatic entertainments. In addition to performing in masques, she was a participant in Ben Jonson's nonextant pastoral drama *The May Lord*, according to William Drummond's Conversations, recorded in 1619. Jonson himself dedicated to her one of his finest plays, *The Alchemist* (1612). Her writings include many allusions to playacting, with several specific references to the cross-dressed boy actors. Pembroke's London home, Baynard's Castle, where Wroth frequently stayed, was located next to the private theater Blackfriars; immediately across the Thames was the Globe. Pembroke himself was directly involved with the players both as patron of an acting company, Pembroke's Men, and in his official capacity as lord chamberlain.

Wroth's drama depicts four contrasting couples who illustrate a variety of human responses to love. The virtuous lovers Philisses and Musella triumph over a period of serious misunderstanding as well as parental interference. The second couple, Lissius and Simena, must learn to overcome baser emotions—scornful pride and jeal-ousy. At the other end of the spectrum are the Neoplatonic lovers, the Forester and Silvesta, who have dedicated themselves to chastity. Their comic counterparts are Rustic and Dalina, who frantically pursue earthly pleasures. Three rival lovers complicate the plot (Lacon, Climena, and Fillis), together with the villainous shepherd Arcas.

Presiding over the action are the mythological figures Venus and Cupid, who serve as internal commentators and appear before each act of the play. Because Venus believes that humans disdain their immortal power, she urges Cupid to make the young lovers suffer by shooting them with arrows of jealousy, malice, fear, and mistrust. The opening of Wroth's play echoes one of the best-known dramatic pastorals, Torquato Tasso's *Aminta* (1573), where a belligerent Cupid appears as prologue to the play. Many subsequent dramatists copied Tasso's device, including Ben Jonson, who placed Cupid as a commentator in several of his masques and plays, especially *Cynthia's Revels* (1601). Wroth's patterned design of multiple pairs of lovers also shows the influence of earlier pastoral dramas such as Giovanni Battista Guarini's *Il Pastor Fido* (1590), John Fletcher's *The Faithful Shepherdess* (1609?), and Samuel Daniel's *Hymen's Triumph* (1615). Wroth's use of the sleeping potion in the fifth act may derive from Shakespeare's *Romeo and Juliet* (1597), although it was a common stage device.

Wroth's play survives in two versions: a complete fair copy at Penshurst, and an incomplete, earlier version at the Huntington Library (which omits the opening dialogue between Venus and Cupid, their dialogue at the end of act 3, and most of the fifth act). The incomplete version, however, provides a clear indication of Wroth's methods of composition, in which the mythological parts appear to have been written last and inserted into the rest of the text. Wroth also developed the play's setting to provide for Venus's temple and a chorus of priests, as well as some further stage directions, such as the appearance of Venus and Cupid in the clouds (a masquelike feature).

Wroth's pastoral drama resembles her other works by including thinly disguised personal allusions. The name of the protagonist Philisses probably refers to her uncle Sir Philip Sidney, while Musella combines the muse of poetry with the Stella of Sidney's sonnet sequence. Philisses' sister, Simena, resembles Mary Sidney, Countess of Pembroke, who after her husband's death was linked with the London physician Dr. Matthew Lister (possibly Lissius). The drama thus includes family associations appropriate to the intimacy of private theatricals performed in country houses.

The later period of Wroth's life seems to have been devoted largely to settling her financial difficulties. To forestall her creditors, she repeatedly applied to the crown for warrants of protection, which were granted at regular intervals. In one case Sir Edward Conway (principal secretary of state under James I and Charles I) wrote to her father requesting that he pressure Wroth for immediate payment of outstanding bills. To his credit Sir Robert Sidney defended his daughter by stating that she was handling her own affairs and planned to discharge all of her debts. She appears to have continued living at Loughton Hall, and her father visited her there. Little evidence survives of her two children by Pembroke, but in 1640 one of Wroth's former servants, Sir John Leeke, wrote that "by my Lord of Pembroke's good mediation," the king had provided her son with a "brave livinge in Ireland." Because Pembroke died in 1630, Leeke is here referring to Philip Herbert, Earl of Montgomery, who succeeded to his brother's title. Wroth apparently spent the last years of her life in Woodford, where her name appears in connection with the sale of lands and in tax rolls. The only record of Wroth's death occurs in a Chancery deposition of 1668, in which the event is said to have occurred in 1651, or more likely in 1653. No literary works survive from the last thirty years of her life.

Wroth's creative accomplishments are still impressive. She created a pair of female heroes whose friendship lies at the center of the *Urania*, an encyclopedic romance of nearly six hundred thousand words in length. Her sonnet sequence, justly praised by Ben Jonson for its psychological insight, surmounted the gender constraints of the Petrarchan form and opened the possibilities for women writers of succeeding generations.

Letters:
"The Correspondence of Lady Mary Wroth" in *The Poems of Lady Mary Wroth*, edited by Josephine A. Roberts (Baton Rouge & London: Louisiana State University Press, 1983), pp. 233-245.

Bibliography:
Elizabeth H. Hageman, "Recent Studies in Women Writers of the English Seventeenth Century," in *Women in the Renaissance*, edited by Kirby Farrell, Elizabeth H. Hageman, and Arthur F. Kinney (Amherst: University of Massachusetts Press, 1990), pp. 279-280, 301-304.

References:
Elaine V. Beilin, "Heroic Virtue: Mary Wroth's *Urania* and *Pamphilia to Amphilanthus*," in her *Redeeming Eve: Women Writers of the English Renaissance* (Princeton: Princeton University Press, 1987), pp. 208-243;

Ann Rosalind Jones, "Feminine Pastoral as Heroic Martyrdom: Gaspara Stampa and Mary Wroth," in her *The Currency of Eros: Women's Love Lyric in Europe, 1540-1620* (Bloomington: Indiana University Press, 1990), pp. 118-154;

Mary Ellen Lamb, *Gender and Authorship in the Sidney Circle* (Madison: University of Wisconsin Press, 1990);

Janet MacArthur, "'A Sydney, Though Unnamed': Lady Mary Wroth and her Poetical Progenitors," *English Studies in Canada*, 15 (March 1989): 12-20;

Margaret Anne McLaren, "An Unknown Continent: Lady Mary Wroth's Forgotten Pastoral Drama, *Love's Victorie*," in *The Renaissance Englishwoman in Print: Counterbalancing the Canon*, edited by Anne M. Haselkorn and Betty S. Travitsky (Amherst: University of Massachusetts Press, 1990), pp. 295-310;

Naomi Miller, " 'Not much to be marked': Narrative of the Woman's Part in Lady Mary Wroth's *Urania*," *Studies in English Literature* 29 (Winter 1989): 121-137;

Miller, "Rewriting Lyric Fictions: The Role of the Lady in Mary Wroth's *Pamphilia to Amphilanthus*," *The Renaissance Englishwoman in Print: Counterbalancing the Canon*, pp. 295-310;

Miller and Gary F. Waller, eds. *Reading Mary Wroth: Representing Alternatives in Early Modern England* (Knoxville: University of Tennessee Press, 1991);

John J. O'Connor, "James Hay and the Countess of Montgomery's *Urania*," *Notes and Queries*, 200 (April 1955): 150-152;

Graham Parry, "Lady Mary Wroth's *Urania*," *Proceedings of the Leeds Philosophical and Literary Society*, 16 (July 1975): 51-60;

May Nelson Paulissen, *The Love Sonnets of Lady Mary Wroth: A Critical Introduction* (Salzburg:

Institut für Englische Sprache und Literature, Universität Salzburg, 1982);

Maureen Quilligan, "The Constant Subject: Instability and Female Authority in Wroth's *Urania* Poems," in *Soliciting Interpretation: Literary Theory and Seventeenth-Century English Poetry*, edited by Elizabeth D. Harvey and Katharine Eisaman Maus (Chicago: University of Chicago Press, 1990), pp. 307-335;

Quilligan, "Lady Mary Wroth: Female Authority and the Family Romance," *Unfolded Tales: Essays on Renaissance Romance*, edited by George M. Logan and Gordon Teskey (Ithaca: Cornell University Press, 1989), pp. 257-280;

Josephine A. Roberts, "The Biographical Problem of *Pamphilia to Amphilanthus*," *Tulsa Studies in Women's Literature*, 1 (Spring 1982): 43-53;

Roberts, "The Huntington Manuscript of Lady Mary Wroth's Play, *Loves Victorie*," *Huntington Library Quarterly* 46 (Spring 1983): 156-174;

Roberts, "Radigund Revisited: Perspectives on Women Rulers in Lady Mary Wroth's *Urania*" in *The Renaissance Englishwoman in Print: Counterbalancing the Canon*, pp. 187-207;

Paul Salzman, "Contemporary References in Mary Wroth's *Urania*," *Review of English Studies*, new series 29 (May 1978): 178-181;

Salzman, "*Urania* and the Tyranny of Love," in his *English Prose Fiction, 1558-1700: A Critical History* (Oxford: Clarendon Press, 1985), pp. 138-144;

Michael Shapiro, "Lady Mary Wroth Describes a 'Boy Actress,'" *Medieval and Renaissance Drama in England*, 4 (1987), 187-194;

Carolyn Ruth Swift, "Feminine Identity in Lady Mary Wroth's Romance *Urania*," *English Literary Renaissance*, 14 (Autumn 1984): 328-346;

Swift, "Feminine Self-Definition in Lady Mary Wroth's *Love's Victorie* (c.1621)," *English Literary Renaissance*, 19 (Spring 1989): 171-188;

Gary Waller, "Mother/Son, Father/Daughter, Brother/Sister, Cousins: The Sidney Family Romance," *Modern Philology*, 88 (May 1991): 401-414.

Papers:

The second part of Lady Mary Wroth's prose romance the *Urania* survives in a two-volume manuscript in Wroth's hand, at the Newberry Library, Chicago. An early version of the sonnet sequence *Pamphilia to Amphilanthus*, also in Wroth's hand, is at the Folger Shakespeare Library in Washington, D.C. A complete manuscript of Wroth's play *Love's Victory* is at Penshurst Place, and an incomplete version is at the Henry E. Huntington Library in San Marino, California. Copies of individual poems by Wroth also survive at the British Library and the University of Nottingham Library.

APPENDIX
Minor Poets of the Earlier Seventeenth Century

Minor Poets of the Earlier Seventeenth Century

Ernest W. Sullivan, II

Texas Tech University

The eight poets discussed below represent only a few of the hundreds of lesser-known poets in the seventeenth century. All are "minor" in the sense that they have attracted very little critical attention and are very little read at present. Even so, a fuller understanding of seventeenth-century poetics will come about with further attention to such poets because present understanding reflects a privileging of lyric verse more than the reality of the diversity of seventeenth-century verse and its cultural role. The particular authors selected for discussion have suffered the vagaries of twentieth-century critical prejudices: some are little thought of as poets because their other accomplishments overshadowed their verse, others because their work has only been published in nineteenth- and twentieth-century works of chiefly antiquarian interest, others because their religion prevented significant circulation of their work, most because they wrote in genres (historical narratives, romances, religious meditations, epigrams, verse translations) little valued today.

Gervase Markham

(1568? - 1637)

SELECTED BOOKS: *A Discovrse of Horsmanshippe* (London: Printed by J. Charlewood for R. Smith, 1593); enlarged as *How to chuse, ride, traine and diet both Hunting-horses and running Horses* (London: Printed by J. Roberts for R. Smith, 1595);

The Most Honorable Tragedie of Sir Richard Grinuile, Knight (London: Printed by J. Roberts for Richard Smith, 1595);

The Poem of Poems, Or, Sions Muse, contayning the diuine Song of King Salomon (London: Printed by Iames Roberts for Matthew Lownes, 1595);

The Teares of the Beloved: Or, the Lamentation of Saint John (London: Printed by Simon Stafford, sold by J. Browne, 1600);

Marie Magdalens Lamentations for the Losse of her Master Iesus (London: Printed by Adam Islip for Edward White, 1601);

A most exact, ready and plaine discourse, how to trayne and teach horses to amble (London: Printed by G. Eld for E. Blount, 1605);

Cauelarice, or the English Horseman (London: Printed by E. Allde & W. Jaggard for Edward White, 1607; second edition, revised, London: Printed by E. Allde for Edward White, 1617);

The English Arcadia, Alluding his beginning from Sir Philip Sydneys ending (London: Printed by Edward Allde, sold by H. Rocket, 1607);

The shape and porportion of a perfit horse (London: Printed for E. White, 1607);

The Dumbe Knight, by Markham and Lewis Machin (London: Printed by N. Okes for J. Bache, 1608);

Markhams maister-peece. Or, what doth a horse-man lacke (London: Printed by N. Okes, sold by W. Welby, 1610);

The English Husbandman (2 volumes, London: Printed by T. Snodham for J. Browne, 1613, 1614; 1 volume, London: Printed by A. Mathewes and J. Norton for W. Sheares, 1635);

Hobsons Horse-load of Letters: or a president for epistles (London: Printed by T. Snodham for R. Hawkins, 1613; enlarged edition, London: Printed by G. Purslow for R. Hawkins, 1617);

The Second and Last Part of the First Booke of the English Arcadia, making a Compleate End of the First History (London: Printed by N. Okes for T. Saunders, 1613);

Cheap and Good Husbandry (London: Printed by T. Snodham for R. Jackson, 1614);

Countrey Contentments, in two bookes: the first, of riding great Horses. Likewise of hunting, hawking . . . The second, The English huswife (London: Printed by J. Beale for R. Jackson, 1615); second book enlarged as *Country Contentments, or the English Huswife.* (London: Printed by J. Beale for R. Jackson, 1623); first book

The beginning of one of seven lamentations on the death of Christ as it appeared in the first edition of Marie Magdalens Lamentations for the Losse of her Master Jesus *(1601)*

revised as *Country Contentments: or, the husbandmans recreations* (London: Printed by N. Okes for J. Harison, 1631);

A Schoole for young souldiers (London: Printed for J. Trundle, 1615);

Markhams Farwell to Husbandry, or the Inriching of all sorts of Barren and sterill Grounds (London: Printed by J. Beale & A. Mathewes for R. Jackson, sold by P. Nevill, 1620);

Hungers Prevention: or, the whole Arte of Fowling (London: A. Mathewes for A. Helme & T. Langley, 1621);

The True Tragedy of Herod and Antipater, by Markham and William Sampson (London: Printed by G. Eld for M. Rhodes, 1622);

Honovr in his Perfection: or, a Treatise in Commendations of the vertues and reknowned virtuous undertakings of the illustrious and heroyicall princes Henry Earle of Oxenford. Henry Earle of Southampton. Robert Earle of Essex, and the euer praiseworthy and much honored lord, Robert Bartve, Lord Willoughby of Eresby (London: Printed

by B. Alsop for Benjamin Fisher, 1624);

The Inrichment of the Weald of Kent (London: G. Purslowe for R. Jackson, 1625);

The Souldiers Accidence: Or an Introduction into Military Discipline (London: Printed by J. Dawson for J. Bellamie, 1625);

The Souldiers Grammar (2 volumes, volume 1, London: Printed by A. Mathewes for W. Shefford, 1626; volume 2, London: Printed by A. Mathewes for H. Perry, 1627; 1 volume, London: Printed by J. Norton for H. Overton, 1639);

The Art of Archerie (London: Printed by B. Alsop & T. Fawcett for B. Fisher, 1634);

The Souldiers Exercise: in three bookes (London: Printed by J. Norton for J. Bellamy, H. Perry, & H. Overton, 1639; facsimile, Amsterdam: Theatrum Orbis Terrarum / Norwood, N.J.: W. J. Johnson, 1974).

Editions: *The last fight of the Revenge at sea; under the command of Vice-Admiral Sir Richard Gren-*

William Herbert, third Earl of Pembroke (Engraving by Simon van de Passe)

ville, edited by Edward Arber (London, 1871);

The English Housewife, edited by Michael R. Best (Kingston, Ontario: McGill-Queen's University Press, 1986);

The Teares of the Beloued and Marie Magdalen's Lamentations for The Losse of Her Master. 1601, edited by Alexander B. Grosart, volume 2 of the Miscellanies of the Fuller Worthies' Library (London, 1871);

A Critical Edition of The True Tragedy of Herod and Antipaster, edited by Gordon Nicholas Ross (New York: Garland, 1979);

The Muster-Master, edited by Charles L. Hamilton (London: Royal Historical Society, 1975).

OTHER: *The Gentlemans Academie. Or, the Booke of S. Albans*, edited by Markham (London:

Printed by V. Sims for Humfrey Lownes, 1595);

Madame Geneviève Pétau Maulette, *Deuoreux. Vertues Teares for the lossse of the most christian King Henry, third*, translated by Markham (London: Printed by J. Roberts for T. Millington, 1597);

Ludovico Ariosto, *Rodomonths Infernall, or The Divell Conquered. Ariastos conclusions. Of the Marriage of Rogero with Bradamanth his Loue, & the fell fought Battell betweene Rogero and Rodomonth the neuer-conquered Pagan. Written in French by Phillip de Portes and paraphrastically translated by G. M.* (London: Printed by V. Simmes for N. Ling, 1607);

The Famous Whore, or Noble Curtizan: conteining the Lamentable Complaint of Paulina, the famous Roman Curtizan, sometime Mrs. unto the great

Cardinall Hypolito of Est, translated by Markham (London: Printed by N. Okes. for John Budge, 1609);

Ariostos Seven Planets Governing Italie, translated by Markham (London: Printed by W. Stansby for R. Jackson, 1611);

The most famous and renowned historie of that woorthie knight Mervine, translated by Markham (London: Printed by R. Blower & V. Sims, 1612);

Conrad Heresbach, *The Whole Art of Hvsbandry*, translated by Barnabe Googe, edited by Markham (London: Printed by T. Cotes for R. More, 1631);

Charles Estienne and Jean Liebault, *Maison Rustique, or, The Country Farm*, translated and edited by Markham (London: Printed by A. Islip for J. Bill, 1616);

Conrad Heresbach, *The whole Art of Husbandry in four bookes*, edited by Markham (London: Printed by T. Cotes for R. More, 1631).

Markham's works endlessly repeat themselves, and (like many other writers) he republished unsold copies of old books under new titles; sorting out all the bibliographical details of his works will provide steady employment for someone. The Company of Stationers' Register (23 April 1953) lists him as having revised for the press a poem, *Thyrsis and Daphne*, but the poem is not extant. *Conceyted Letters, newly layde open* (1618) has a preface signed "I. M.," but is now generally assigned to Nicholas Breton. *Ariosto's Satyres* (1608) is sometimes considered Markham's, though Robert Tofte claimed authorship in his *Blazon of Jealousy* (1615). Barnaby Rich's *Allarme to England* (1578), republished as *Vox Militis* (1625), is now assigned to G. Marcelline instead of Markham.

Markham's *The Most Honorable Tragedie of Sir Richard Grinuile, Knight* (1595) is dedicated to Charles Blount, the eighth Lord Mountjoy, and includes a sonnet addressed to Henry Wriothesley, third Earl of Southampton, that Frederick Gard Fleay uses to argue a competition between Markham and William Shakespeare for Southampton's favor. Fleay also contends that Shakespeare alludes to Markham in his sonnets. Readings in Alfred, Lord Tennyson's poetic account of Sir Richard Grenville's fight, "The Revenge" (1880), show that Tennyson's poem probably owes some debt to Markham's: where Markham has "Sweet maister gunner, split our

keele in twaine," Tennyson has "Sink me the ship, master gunner; sink her—split her in twain."

Markham's *The Poem of Poems* (1595) is dedicated to Elizabeth, daughter of Sir Philip Sidney. Markham describes his verse adaptation in a preface: "I made loue to Salomons holy Song, & dissoluing my spirits in applause of that excellence, sought to attract it within the compasse of our most usuall stanzas." His translation of *Devoreux* (1597) laments the loss of Henry III of France and of the second earl of Essex's brother, Walter Devereux, who was slain before Rouen. *Devoreux* is dedicated to Dorothy Percy, Countess of Northumberland, and Penelope, Lady Rich, Robert Devereux's sisters. R. Allot and E. Guilpin provide prefatory sonnets. *The Teares of the Beloved* (1600) is a long lament in six-line stanzas for the death of Christ. *Marie Magdalens Lamentations for the Losse of her Master Jesus* (1601) is a series of seven lamentations in the voice of Mary Magdalene on the death of Christ followed by a conclusion. The two volumes of Markham's *English Arcadia* (1607, 1613) are primarily prose mixed with some verse.

Gervase Markham was the brother of Francis Markham and third son of Robert Markham of Cottam, Nottinghamshire. He began a career as a soldier in the Low Countries and was a captain under the earl of Essex in Ireland. Markham's scholarly interests prevailed, however, and he turned to literature to support himself. He owned valuable horses and is thought to have imported the first Arabian horse. He sold an Arabian horse to James I for five hundred pounds. He was a prodigiously prolific writer: on 24 July 1617 the booksellers, no doubt fearing for the wear on their type, got him to sign a paper promising to write no more books on the treatment of the diseases of horses and cattle. In his Conversations with William Drummond of Hawthornden, Ben Jonson declared Markham "not of the number of the Faithfill .j. Poets and but a base fellow." Markham married a daughter of J. Gelsthorp, but no record of children exists. He was buried at St. Gile's, Cripplegate, on 3 February 1637.

Papers:
The only holograph of Markham's known to exist is an undated letter to his uncle Sir John Markham of Ollerton. The letter is located at Lambeth Palace, London (MS. 709, p. 65).

Bibliography:

F. N. L. Poynter, *A Bibliography of Gervase Markham, 1568?-1637* (Oxford: Oxford Bibliographical Society, 1962).

References:

Frederick Gard Fleay, *A Biographical Chronicle of the English Drama 1559-1642*, 2 volumes (London: Reeves & Turner, 1891);

Robert Gittings, *Shakespeare's Rival: A Study in Three Parts* (London: Heineman, 1960);

John Thomas Godfrey, *Four Nottinghamshire Dramatists* (Nottingham, 1895);

Gerard Langbaine, *An Account of the English Dramatick Poets*, edited by John Loftis, 2 volumes (Los Angeles: William Andrews Clark Memorial Library, 1971), II: 340-341;

John Henry Hobart Lyon, *A Study of The Newe Metamorphosis written by J. M.* (New York: Columbia University Press, 1919).

Sir Benjamin Rudyerd

(26 September 1572 - 31 May 1658)

BOOKS: *Benjamin Rudyerd, Five speeches* (London: Printed by H. Dudley for Henry Seile, 1641);

Sir Beniamin Rvdyerds speech; concerning bishops (London, 1641);

A Speech concerning a West Indie association (London, 1641);

A speech delivered in Parliament (London: Printed for Tho. Banks, 1641);

Sir Beniamin Rudyerd his speech made concerning the French and Spanish embassadors . . . August 28. (London, 1641);

Sir Beniamin Rudyerd his speech made in answer to the French and Spanish embassadors request for our souldiers at their disbanding, August 28. 1641 (London, 1641);

The speech of that worthy knight (London: Printed for W. Ley, 1641);

The speeches of Sr. Benjamin Rudyer in the high court of Parliament (London: Printed for Thomas Walkly, 1641);

Two speeches by Sir Beniamin Rudyard concerning the Palatinate (London: Printed for Francis Constable, 1641);

Sir Benjamin Rudyard. His learned speech in Parliament on Wednesday, being the twenty ninth day of December 1641 (London: Printed for Iohn Thomas, 1642);

Sir Benjamin Rudyerd his speech for propositions of peace (London: Printed by L. N. and R. C. for William Sheares, 1642);

A most worthy speech spoken . . . Iuly 9th. 1642 (London: Printed for N. Allen, 1642);

A worthy speech spoken in the honourable House of Commons, by Sir Benjamin Rudyard this present July, 1642 (London: Printed for R. Thrale, 1642);

Two speeches in Parliament (London: Printed by B. A. for Henry Seile, 1642);

Two speeches in the House of Commons (London, 1642);

Sir Benjamin Rudyerd his speech in the high court of Parliament the 17. of February (London: Printed for Michael Young, 1643);

Two worthy speeches (London: Printed for Anthony Vincent, 1643);

Le Prince d'Amour (London: Printed for William Leake, 1660);

Poems, Written by the Right Honorable William Earl of Pembroke, Lord Steward of his Majesties Houshold. Whereof Many of which are answered by way of Repartee, By Sr Benjamin Ruddier, Knight. With several Distinct Poems, Written by them Occasionally, and Apart, edited by John Donne, Jr. (London: Printed by Matthew Inman, sold by James Magnes, 1660).

Editions: *Poems of William Herbert, third Earl of Pembroke, K. G., and Sir Benjamin Rudyard*, edited by Samuel Egerton Brydges (London: Printed by Bensley & Son for R. Triphook, 1817);

Memoirs of Sir Benjamin Rudyerd, Knt., containing his Speeches and Poems, edited by James Alexander Manning (London: T. & W. Boone, 1841).

Although his poems were not printed until after his death, Rudyerd's contemporary reputation as poet and critic brought him association with Ben Jonson, John Hoskyns, John Owen, and William Herbert, third Earl of Pembroke. Epigrams 121, 122, and 123 in Jonson's 1616 *Workes* are addressed to Rudyerd and praise his virtues, friendship, and "learned muse." A poem written on seeing Rudyerd's portrait has been attributed to John Owen and Sir Henry Wotton. The canon of Rudyerd's poems is uncertain, mixed as his poems are with those of William Herbert, third Earl of Pembroke, and others in *Le Prince d'Amour* (1660) and *Poems* (1660); however, the poems in these collections are witty lyrics.

Rudyerd was the son of James Rudyerd of Hartley, Hampshire, by Margaret, daughter and heiress of Lawrence Kidwelly of Winchfield. He was educated at Winchester school and matriculated as a member of St. John's College, Oxford, on 15 January 1588 but may not have graduated. Anthony Wood dates his matriculation as 4 August 1587. On 18 April 1600 he was admitted to the Inner Temple; on 24 October 1600 he was called to the bar. He married Elizabeth, daughter of Sir Henry Harington and a kinswoman of William Herbert. They had one son, William. Rudyerd was knighted on 30 March 1618 and granted on 17 April 1618 the post of surveyor of the court of wards for life. In 1647 he was granted six thousand pounds to compensate for the abolition of the post by the Long Parliament. In Parliament Rudyerd represented the boroughs of Portsmouth in 1620, 1624, and 1625, Old Sarum in 1626, Downton in 1628, and Wilton in 1640. Generally Rudyerd supported Charles I, but he occasionally supported the rights of the individual against the monarchy. On 4 December 1630 he was one of the original incorporators of the Providence Company, one of many companies which financed colonization in America. His support for the Presbyterians led to his arrest and brief imprisonment on 6 December 1648. He was buried in the church of West Woodhey in Berkshire. He wrote his own epitaph, which begins "Fond world leave off this foolish trick / Of making epitaphs upon the dead; / Rather go write them on the quick."

Charles Fitzgeffrey

(1575? - 24 February 1638)

BOOKS: *Sir Francis Drake, His Honorable lifes commendation, and his Tragicall Deathes lamentation* (Oxford: Joseph Barnes, 1596; revised and enlarged edition, Oxford: Printed by Joseph Barnes, sold by J. Broome, London, 1596);

Caroli Fitzgeofridi Affaniae: sive Epigrammatum libri tres. Ejusdem Cenotaphia (Oxford: Printed by Joseph Barnes, 1601);

Deaths Sermon vnto the Living. Delivered at the funerals of the ladie Phillipe, late wife vnto S. *Anthonie Rovs* (London: Printed by W. Stansby for J. Parker, 1620);

Elisha his Lamentation, for his losse (London: Printed by W. Stansby for J. Parker, 1622);

The Curse of Corne-horders: with the Blessing of seasonable Selling. In three sermons (London: Printed by J. Beale for M. Sparke, 1631); republished as *God's Blessing upon the Providers of Corne* (London: Printed for M. S., 1648);

The Blessed Birth-Day celebrated in some Pious Meditations on the Angels Anthem (Oxford: Printed by J. Lichfield, sold by E. Forrest, 1634);

Compassion towards Captives, chiefly towards our Bretheren in bondage in Barbarie. In three sermons (Oxford: Printed by L. Lichfield for E. Forrest, 1637).

Edition: *The Poems of the Rev. Charles Fitzgeoffrey*, edited by Alexander B. Grosart, Occasional Issues of unique or very rare books, no. 34 (Manchester: C. E. Simms, 1881).

OTHER: Thomas Storer, *The Life and Death of Thomas Wolsey, cardinall*, includes commendatory verses by Fitzgeffrey (London: Printed by V. Simmes for T. Dawson, 1599);

John Davies of Hereford, *Microcosmos*, includes commendatory verses by Fitzgeffrey (Oxford: Printed by Joseph Barnes, sold by John Barnes, 1603);

Bartas his Devine Weekes and Workes, translated by Josuah Sylvester, includes commendatory verses by Fitzgeffrey (London: Printed by H. Lownes, 1605);

William Vaughan, *The Golden-Grove*, includes commendatory verses by Fitzgeffrey (London: Printed by S. Stafford, 1608);

Academiæ Oxoniensis Pietas erga serenissimvm et potentissimvm Iacobvm, includes ten Latin poems by Fitzgeffrey (Oxford: Printed by Joseph Barnes, 1603);

Oxoniensis Academiæ Funebre Officium in Memoriam . . . Elisabethæ, Reginæ, includes one Latin poem by Fitzgeffrey (Oxford: Printed by Joseph Barnes, 1603).

John Dunbar's *Epigrammaton Joannis Dunbari Megalo-Britanni Centuriæ Sex* (1616) includes an epigram to Charles Fitzgeffrey, and Thomas Campion addressed two epigrams to him in *Epigrammatum libri II* (1619). Fitzgeffrey's *Sir Francis Drake* (1596) was dedicated to Queen Elizabeth, with commendatory verses by Richard Rous, Francis Rous, "D. W.," and Thomas Mychelbourne. Francis Meres, in *Palladis Tamia* (1598), mentions "yong Charles Fitz-Ieffrey, that high touring falcon"; several quotations from the poem appear in *England's Parnassus* (1600). Fitzgeffrey's *Caroli Fitzgeofridi Affaniae* (1601) includes epigrams to Campion, Michael Drayton, Samuel Daniel, Sir John Harington, Ben Jonson, Thomas Nashe, Thomas Overbury, William Herbert, William Percy, and Josuah Sylvester as well as an epitaph on Edmund Spenser. Fitzgeffrey's closest friends were the brothers Edward, Laurence, and Thomas Mychelbourne—frequently mentioned in Campion's Latin epigrams. An epigram, "To my deare freind Mr. Charles Fitz-Ieffrey," appears among the poems "To Worthy Persons" appended to John Davies of Hereford's *Scourge of Folly* (1611). Robert Chamberlain has some verses to his memory in *Nocturnall Lucubrations* (1638). Robert Hayman's *Quodlibets, lately come over from New Britaniola. Epigrams and other small parcels* (1628) includes an epigram suggesting that Fitzgeffrey was blind in one eye:

> To the reverend, learned, acute and witty master Charles Fitz-Geoffrey, bachelor in divinity, my especiall kind friend, most excellent poet:

> Blind Poet Homer you doe equalize
> Though he saw more with none, then with most eyes:
> Our Geoffrey Chaucer, who wrote quaintly neat,
> In verse you match, equall him in conceit:
> Featur'd you are like Homer in one eye,
> Rightly surnam'd the sonne of Geoffrey.

Fitzgeffrey experimented with a variety of genres. His *Sir Francis Drake* attempts to create an English historical epic:

> Let famous Red Crosse yeld to famous Drake,
> And good Sir Gvion give to him his launce;
> Let all the Mortimers surrender make
> To one that higher did his fame advance;
> Cease Lancasters, & Yorkes iars to enhaunce;
>   Sing all, and all to few to sing Drakes fame;
>   Your Poems neede no laurell save his name.

His epigrams are witty and personal, rather than satirical like those of John Donne and Ben Jonson. *The Blessed Birth-Day* (1634) is a long meditational poem with refrains.

Fitzgeffrey was the son of Alexander Fitzgeffrey, a clergyman, and was born at Fowey in Cornwall about 1575. He entered Broadgates Hall (now Pembroke College), Oxford, in 1590 and proceeded to get a B.A. on 31 January 1597 and an M.A. degree on 4 July 1600. By 1610 he was evidently in orders. His friend Sir Anthony Rous presented him with the living of St. Dominic, Eastwellshire. He is buried under the communion table of his church.

Papers:
A letter from Fitzgeffrey, dated from Fowey, March 1633, is preserved at Kimbolton Castle, Huntingdonshire.

William Herbert, Third Earl of Pembroke
(8 April 1580 - 10 April 1630)

BOOK: *Poems, Written by the Right Honorable William Earl of Pembroke, Lord Steward of his Majesties Houshold. Whereof Many of which are answered by way of Repartee, By Sr Benjamin Ruddier, Knight. With several Distinct Poems, Written by them Occasionally, and Apart*, edited by John Donne, Jr. (London: Printed by Matthew Inman, sold by James Magnes, 1660).

Editions: *Poems of William Herbert, third Earl of Pembroke, K.G., and Sir Benjamin Rudyard*, edited by Samuel Egerton Brydges (London: Printed by Bensley & Son for R. Triphook, 1817);

Poems Written by the Right Honourable William Earl of Pembroke, edited by Gaby E. Onderwyzer (Los Angeles: William Andrews Clark Memorial Library, 1959);

Ernest W. Sullivan, II, *The First and Second Dalhousie Manuscripts: Poems and Prose by John Donne and Others* (Columbia: University of Missouri Press, 1988).

OTHER: Robert Chamberlain, ed., *The Harmony of the Muses*, includes two poems by Pembroke (London: Printed by T. W. for William Gilbertson, 1654; facsimile, Hants, England: Scolar Press / Brookfield, Vt.: Gower, 1990).

The poetic canon of William Herbert, third Earl of Pembroke, is extremely uncertain. The younger John Donne, who edited Pembroke's *Poems* (1660), is ambiguous about the sources of the manuscripts he used: in his dedication to Christiana Cavendish, Countess of Devonshire, the editor claims that he used manuscripts from her hand; in the preface to the reader, he states that the poems were from Henry Lawes and Nicholas Lanier. Gaby E. Onderwyzer speculates that the poems on the first twenty-eight pages may be from Christiana, with the poems in the remainder of the volume (which has poems by Pem-

The beginning of Beaumont's "To the Countesse of Rutland" as it appears in the second Dalhousie manuscript (Texas Tech University Library, Dalhousie II, F. 26)

broke mixed with unattributed poems by Sir Edward Dyer, Henry Wotton, Sir Walter Ralegh, Henry King, Thomas Carew, John Corbet, John Grange, Sir Thomas Nevill, and William Strode) possibly supplied by Lawes and Lanier. *The British Library Catalogue* ascribed *Of the Internal and Eternal Nature of Man in Christ* (1654) to Pembroke on the basis of a manuscript note by George Thomason, but the attribution is doubtful.

William Herbert was born at Wilton in Wilts and was the eldest son of Henry Herbert, second Earl of Pembroke, by his third wife, Mary Herbert. Tutored in childhood by Samuel Daniel, he matriculated on 8 March 1593 from New College, Oxford, where he studied for two years. He seems to have moved to London in 1598 to attend Queen Elizabeth. Prior to his father's death on 19 January 1601, William impregnated Mary Fitton, a lady of the court and a favorite of the queen, but refused to marry her, and his son died soon after birth. Pembroke was committed to the Fleet prison and later banished from court. On 4 November 1604 he married Lady Mary, the wealthy daughter of Gilbert Talbot, seventh Earl of Shrewsbury.

Pembroke traveled in elevated literary circles: Sir Philip Sidney was his uncle and George Herbert his kinsman; Samuel Daniel, John Donne, Sir John Harington, Philip Massinger, Inigo Jones, and, particularly, Ben Jonson were his friends. Jonson told William Drummond that "every first day of the new year he had 20lb sent him from the Earl of Pembrok to buy books." Jonson dedicated *Catiline His Conspiracy* (1611) and his *Epigrams* (1616) to Pembroke and addressed Epigram 102 to him. Pembroke also deserves credit for inspiring Jonson's song, "That Women Are But Mens Shaddowes": "Pembrok and his Lady discoursing the Earl said the Woemen were mens shadowes, and she maintained y^m, both appealing to Johnson, he affirmed it true, for which my Lady gave a pennance to prove it jn Verse, hence his Epigrame." Chapman inscribed a sonnet to him in his translation of the first 12 books of *The Iliad* (1609) and Francis and Walter Davison's *Poetical Rhapsody* (1602) is dedicated to him. He and his brother Philip are "the incomparable pair of brethren" to whom Shakespeare's First Folio (1623) is dedicated; they had known Shakespeare as a member of James I's company of actors. Pembroke's role as the "W. H." of

Shakespeare's sonnets has been the subject of debate, though not now credited. In *Athenæ Oxonienis*, Anthony Wood describes Pembroke's status among his contemporaries: "He was not only a great favourer of learned and ingenious men, but was himself learned, and endowed to admiration with a poetical geny, as by those amorous and not inelegant aires and poems of his composition doeth evidently appear; some of which had musical notes set to them by Hen. Lawes, and Nich. Laneare."

On 25 June 1603, Pembroke was made a Knight of the Garter. He accompanied King James to Oxford in August of 1605 and was granted an M.A. degree. Pembroke had a great interest in explorations of America as shown by his membership in various companies that financed colonization. From 1614 he was a member of the East India Company; he became a member of the king's council for the Virginia Company on 23 May 1609; an incorporator of the North-West Passage Company on 26 July 1612; of the Bermudas Company on 29 June 1615; and of the Guiana Company on 19 May 1627. A part of the Bermudas was named for him, and the Rappahannock River in Virginia was once the Pembroke river. He became chancellor of Oxford University on 29 January 1617, and in 1624 Broadgates Hall was replaced by Pembroke College. In April 1621 he defended Francis Bacon against charges of corruption. In March 1625 Pembroke attended the deathbed of James I at Theobalds. He carried the crown at Charles I's coronation on 2 February 1626. In 1629 Pembroke donated part of the Barocci library (some 250 Greek manuscripts) to the Bodleian Library, specifically requesting that the manuscripts should be borrowed by students. According to Wood, Pembroke died suddenly at his London house, Baynard's Castle, "of an apoplexy after a full and chearful supper." He was buried in the family vault in Salisbury Cathedral. His funeral sermon by T. C., *The Just Man's Memorial, as it was delivered at Baynard's Castle before the interment of the Body*, was published in 1630.

References:

William Archer, "Shakespeare's Sonnets. The Case against Southampton," *Fortnightly Review*, 62 (December 1897): 817-834;

Donald W. Foster, "Master W. H., R.I.P.," *PMLA*, 102 (January 1987): 42-54;

"Ben Jonson's Conversations with William Drummond of Hawthornden," in volume 1 of *Ben Jonson*, edited by C. H. Herford and Percy Simpson (Oxford: Clarendon Press, 1925);

Andreas Gebauer, *Leben und Werk William Herberts, des dritten Earls von Pembroke*, Heidelberger Forschungen, 28 (Heidelberg: C. Winter, 1987);

Sir Sidney Lee, "Shakespeare and the Earl of Pembroke," *Fortnightly Review*, 63 (February 1898): 210-223;

John Padel, "Shakespeare's Sonnets, the Sidney and Herbert Families," *Sidney Newsletter*, 3 (1982): 3-12;

Thomas Tyler, *The Herbert-Fitton Theory of Shakespeare's Sonnets: a reply* (London: D. Nutt, 1898);

Barrie Williams, "A Welsh Connection in Stuart Salisbury: John Williams and the Herberts," *Hatcher Review*, 2 (Autumn 1985): 480-488.

Papers:

Manuscripts of Pembroke's poem, "When my Carliles Chamber was on fire," are located at the British Library (Add. MS. 18647, f. 109v), Cambridge University Library (Add. MS. 4138, f. 49v), Trinity College Library, Dublin (MS. 877, 2nd collection, f. 189v), and the Bodleian Library (Rawlinson poet. MS. 116, f. 49v).

Sir John Roe

(5 May 1581 - 1608)

WORKS: John Donne, *Poems*, second edition, enlarged; includes six poems by Roe attributed to Donne (London: Printed by M. Flesher for John Marriot, 1635; revised edition, includes a seventh poem by Roe attributed to Donne, London: Printed by T. N. for Henry Herringman, 1669);

Sir Benjamin Rudyerd, *Le Prince d'Amour*, includes a poem by Roe (London: Printed for William Leake, 1660);

H. J. C. Grierson, ed., *The Poems of John Donne*, includes poems by Roe, 2 volumes (Oxford: Oxford University Press, 1912);

Alexander B. Grosart, ed., *The Complete Poems of John Donne*, includes poems by Roe, 2 volumes (London: Robson, 1872, 1873);

Ernest W. Sullivan, II, *The First and Second Dalhousie Manuscripts: Poems and Prose by John Donne and Others* (Columbia: University of Missouri Press, 1988).

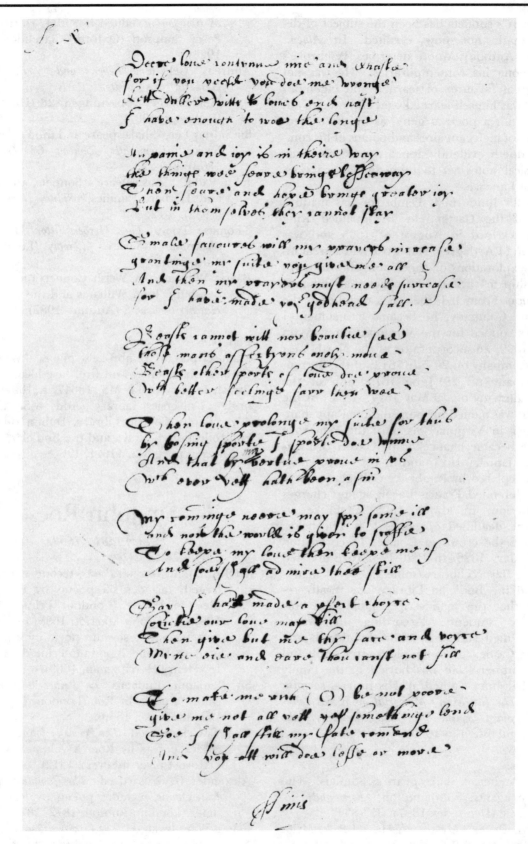

Roe's "Deare loue contynue nice and chaste" as it appears in the second Dalhousie manuscript (Texas Tech University Library, Dalhousie II, F. 20v)

Seven of Sir John Roe's nine poems appear in various of the seventeenth-century collected editions of John Donne's poems: "Song" ("Deare Love, continue nice and chaste"); "An Elegie. Reflecting on his passion for his mistrisse" ("Come, Fates; I feare you not"); "Satyre" ("Men write that love and reason disagree"); "To Ben. Iohnson, 6 Ian. 1603" ("The state and mens affaires are the best plaies"); "To Ben. Iohnson, 9. Novembris, 1603" ("If great men wrong mee I will spare my selfe"); and "To Sir Tho. Roe 1603" ("Tell her if shee to hired seruantes shewe") all appeared in the editions of Donne's *Poems* between 1635-1669; "Satyre" ("Sleep, next society and true friendship") appeared in the 1669 edition. Roe's "Shall I goe force an Eligie" appears anonymously in *Le Prince d'Amour*, by Benjamin Rudyard (1660), and his "Elegie. 'True Love findes witt'" was attributed to Donne and first printed by Alexander B. Grosart. For a discussion of the authorship of the poems, see H. J. C. Grierson's "Canon of Donne's Poems" in his edition of *The Poems of John Donne* (1912).

Sir John Roe was the cousin of Sir Thomas Roe and eldest son of William Roe (or Rowe) of Higham Hill, near Walthamstow, in the county of Essex. He matriculated at Queen's College, Oxford, on 14 October 1597. According to Grierson, Roe may have served under and been knighted by Robert Devereux, second Earl of Essex, in Ireland in 1599. On 13 May 1605, Charles Blount, Earl of Devonshire and eighth Lord Mountjoy, wrote to Sir Ralph Winwood, ambassador to the United Provinces, to recommend Roe as a soldier; Mountjoy wrote again to Winwood on 7 November 1605 to thank him for helping Roe. Roe was severely wounded in the Netherlands in 1605. A list of captains discharged in Ireland since 1603 confirms Roe's death in 1608.

The poems of Roe and Ben Jonson make it clear that they were together in London in 1603, and Jonson's Epigram 32 shows that Roe served in Russia, Ireland, and Belgium:

> What two brave perills of the private sword
>   Could not effect, not all the furies doe,
> That selfe-devided *Belgia* did afford;
>   What not the envie of the seas reach'd too,
> The cold of *Mosco*, and fat *Irish* ayre,
>   His often change of clime (though not of mind)
> What could not worke; at home in his repaire
>   Was his blest fate, but our hard lot to find.
> Which shewes, where ever death doth please
>   t'appere,

> Seas, serenes, swords shot, sicknesse, all
>   are there.

Jonson presented a copy of Isaac Casaubon's *Persius* to Roe with the following inscription: "D. Joanni Roe, Amico Probatissimo, Hunc amorem et delicias Suas, Satiricorum doctissimum, Persium, com doctissimo Commentario Sacravit Ben Jonsonius." In his Conversations with William Drummond, Jonson describes Roe's death: "Sr John Roe was ane jnfinit Spender & and used to Say when he had no more to spend he could die. he died jn his [Jonson's] armes of the pest & he furnished his charges 20 lb, which was given him back."

The wit, obscurity, and licentiousness of Roe's lyrics, satires, and verse letters (generally to Jonson) likely account for their regular attribution to Donne; however, the poems bear more resemblance to Jonson's in their sense of the seedy side of London life.

References:

"Ben Jonson's Conversations with William Drummond of Hawthornden," in volume 1 of *Ben Jonson*, edited by C. H. Herford and Percy Simpson (Oxford: Clarendon Press, 1925);

Jennifer Brady, "Jonson's Elegies of the Plague Years," *Dalhousie Review*, 65 (Summer 1985): 208-230.

Papers:

For texts and manuscript locations of Roe's poems, see *The Poems of John Donne*, edited by H. J. C. Grierson (1912), I: xxiv, 401-417, and *The First and Second Dalhousie Manuscripts*, edited by Ernest W. Sullivan, II (1988), pp. 76, 78-83, 162.

Francis Beaumont
(1584 - 6 March 1616)

See also the Beaumont and John Fletcher entry in *DLB 58: Jacobean and Caroline Dramatists.*

SELECTED BOOKS: *The Masque of the Inner Temple and Grayes Inne* (London: Printed by F. Kingston for G. Norton, 1613);

Poems: By Francis Beavmont, Gent. Viz. The Hermaphrodite. The Remedie of Love. Elegies. Sonnets, with other Poems (London: Printed by Richard Hodgkinson for W. Wethered & L.

Blaikelocke, 1640; enlarged edition, London: Printed for Laurence Blaikelock, 1653); republished as *Poems. The Golden Remains Of those so much admired Dramatick Poets, Francis Beaumont & John Fletcher* (London: Printed for William Hope, 1660);

Comedies and Tragedies written by Francis Beavmont and Iohn Fletcher, Gentlemen. Never printed before, and now published by the Authours Originall Copies (London: Printed for Henry Robinson & Humphrey Moseley, 1647).

Editions: *The Works of Beaumont and Fletcher*, edited by Alexander Dyce, 11 volumes (London: Moxon, 1843-1846);

Ernest W. Sullivan, II, *The First and Second Dalhousie Manuscripts: Poems and Prose by John Donne and Others* (Columbia: University of Missouri Press, 1988).

OTHER: John Beaumont, *The Metamorphosis of Tabacco*, includes prefatory verse by Francis Beaumont (London: Printed by F. Kingston for J. Flasket, 1602);

Ovid, *Salmacis and Hermaphroditus*, translated by Beaumont (London: Printed by S. Stafford for J. Hodgets, 1602);

Benjamin Jonson, *Ben: Jonson his Volpone or the foxe*, includes a commendatory poem by Beaumont (London: Printed by G. Eld for T. Thorppe, 1607);

Jonson, *Catiline His Conspiracy*, includes a commendatory poem by Beaumont (London: Printed by W. Stansby for W. Burre, 1611);

Henry Fitzgeffrey, *Certain Elegies, Done by Svndrie Excellent Wits*, includes poems by Beaumont (London: Printed by B. Alsop for Miles Partriche, 1618);

Jonson, *Epicoene*, includes a commendatory poem by Beaumont (London: Printed by W. Stansby, sold by J. Browne, 1620);

Robert Chamberlain, *The Harmony of the Muses*, includes a poem by Beaumont (London: Printed by T. W. for William Gilbertson, 1654; facsimile, Hants, England: Scolar Press / Brookfield, Vt.: Gower, 1990).

The seventeenth-century editions of Francis Beaumont's poems include unattributed verse by other authors; thus, the canon is uncertain. For example, the 1653 edition and later collections include "A Song," which is the first two stanzas of John Donne's "Song. Goe, and catch a falling star," and Thomas Carew's "Secresie Protested." Peter Beal in *Index of English Literary Manuscripts*

(1980) accepts the verse canon established by Beaumont's editor Alexander Dyce with the following modifications: "Like a ring without a finger" reassigned to Sir Walter Ralegh; "On the Life of Man" reassigned to Henry King; "On the Tombs in Westminster" reassigned to William Basse. "On Madame Fowler desiring a sonnet to be writ on her," "To Mr B[en]. J[onson]," and "Why should not pilgrims to thy body come" are added to the canon by Beal.

Francis Beaumont, the third son of Francis Beaumont, judge of the common pleas, and younger brother of Sir John Beaumont, was born at Grace-Dieu, Leicestershire, the family seat. He entered as a gentleman commoner at Broadgates Hall (now Pembroke College), Oxford, at age twelve on 4 February 1597. When his father died on 22 April 1598 he and his brothers, Henry and John, left the university without taking degrees. Francis became a member of the Inner Temple on 3 November 1600 but did not pursue legal studies. Sir John and Francis were close friends of Michael Drayton and Ben Jonson.

No record survives of the initial meeting of Beaumont and John Fletcher, but John Aubrey has described their early friendship: "There was a wonderfull consimility of phansey between him and Mr. John Fletcher, which caused that dearnesse of friendship between them.... They lived together on the Banke side, not far from the Play-house, both batchelors; lay together; had one Wench in the house between them, which they did so admire; the same cloathes and cloake, &c.; betweene them." About 1613 Beaumont married Ursala, daughter and coheiress to Henry Isley of Sundridge in Kent; the Beaumonts had two daughters, Elizabeth and Frances. On 6 March 1616 Beaumont was interred in Westminster Abbey. Bishop Richard Corbett wrote of him: "So dearly hast thou bought thy precious lines; / Their praise grew swiftly, as thy life declines. / Beaumont is dead, by whose sole death appears, / Wit's a disease consumes men in a few years." Although Beaumont and Jonson are usually thought to have been good friends, Jonson in his Conversations with William Drummond of Hawthornden, noted Beaumont's ego: "Francis Beaumont loved too much himself & his own verses."

Bibliographies:
Samuel A. Tannenbaum, *Beaumont and Fletcher: A Concise Bibliography* (New York: Privately printed, 1938); supplement, Samuel A. and

Engraved title page bearing a 1623 date for the 1624 first edition of Bolton's life of Nero

Dorothy R. Tannenbaum (New York: Privately printed, 1946);

C. A. Pennel and William P. Williams, *Elizabethan Bibliographies, Supplement VIII: Francis Beaumont and John Fletcher, 1937-1965* (London: Nether Press, 1968).

Reference:

John Aubrey, *Brief Lives*, edited by Oliver Lawson Dick (Ann Arbor: University of Michigan Press, 1957).

Papers:

For manuscript locations of Beaumont's poems, see *Index of English Literary Manuscripts*, edited by Peter Beal (1980), I: i, 69-79, and *The First and Second Dalhousie Manuscripts*, edited by Ernest W. Sullivan, II (1988), p. 206.

Sir Francis Kynaston

(1587 - 1642)

BOOKS: *Corona Minervæ, Or a masque* (London: Printed for W. Sheares, 1635);

The Constitutions of the Musæum Minervæ (London: Printed by T. Purfoot for T. Spencer, 1636);

Leoline and Sydanis, a poetical Romance (London: Printed by Richard Hearne, 1642).

Edition: George Saintsbury, *Minor Poets of the Caroline Period, Leoline and Sydanis* (Oxford: Clarendon Press, 1906), II: 70-173.

OTHER: *Amorum Troili et Creseidæ Libri Duo priores Anglico-Latini*, Geoffrey Chaucer's *Troilus and Criseyde* translated into Latin by

Kynaston (Oxford: Printed by J. Lichfield, 1635); also published as *Amorum Troili et Creseidæ liber primus (secundus) Latinè versus* (Oxford: Printed by J. Lichfield, 1635);

Arthur Johnston, *Musæ Querlæ*, translated by Kynaston (London: Printed by T. Harper for N. Butter, 1633);

Arthur Johnston, *Musae Aulicae*, translated by Kynaston (London: Printed by T. Harper for N. Butter, 1635).

In his *Specimens of Early English Poets* (1790), George Ellis quotes from a 1641 edition of the sonnets by Sir Francis Kynaston that were later included in *Leoline and Sydanis* (1642); thus, the sonnets may have been published separately.

Leoline and Sydanis is a heroic romance in verse containing some of the legendary history of Wales and Anglesey. The sonnets, addressed to a "Cynthia," are not technically sonnets, but are described in the *Dictionary of National Biography* as "often of genuine merit." William Strode, William Cartwright, Dudley Digges, and other Oxford writers prefaced fifteen poems to Kynaston's translation (1635) of *Troilus and Criseyde*.

Sir Francis Kynaston was born in 1587 to Sir Edward Kinaston and Isabel, daughter of Sir Nicholas Bagenall, at Oteley, Shropshire. Sir Edward was sheriff of Shropshire in 1599. On 11 December 1601 Francis matriculated at Oriel College, Oxford, and graduated with a B.A. from St. Mary Hall on 14 June 1604. According to Anthony Wood, he was more addicted "to the superficial parts of learning, poetry and oratory, (wherein he excell'd), than logic and philosophy." Kynaston graduated with an M.A. from Trinity College, Cambridge, in 1609, was incorporated M.A. at Oxford on 11 November 1611, and was called to the bar at Lincoln's Inn in 1611. In 1613 he married Margaret, daughter of Sir Humphrey Lee, baronet, and had one son. He was knighted by James I on 21 December 1621, served as a member of Parliament for Shropshire in 1621-1622, as taxor of Cambridge University in 1623 and as proctor in 1634. He became esquire of the body to Charles I on his accession. In 1635 Kynaston founded an academy of learning, the Musæum Minervæ, for which he obtained a license under the great seal, a grant of arms, and a common seal. Kynaston gave his own house in Bedford Street, Covent Garden (now Kynaston's Alley, Bedfordbury) for the museum. Kynaston was regent and his friends Edward

May, Nicholas Mason, Thomas Hunt, Nicholas Phiske, John Spiedel, and Walter Salter comprised the faculty. Wood records an example of Kynaston's scientific interests: "This is the person also who by experience falsified the alchymist's report that a hen being fed for certain days with gold, beginning when Sol was in Leo, should be converted into gold, and should lay golden eggs; but indeed became very fat." On 27 February 1636 Prince Charles and the duke of York visited the museum, and Kynaston's masque *Corona Minervæ* (1635) was performed in their presence. The museum perished with its founder.

References:

Richard Beadle, *The Virtuoso's Troilus*, in *Chaucer Traditions: Studies in Honor of Derek Brewer*, edited by Barry Windeatt and Toshiyuki Takamiya (Cambridge: Cambridge University Press, 1990);

George Ellis, *Specimens of the Early English Poets*, fifth edition, revised (London: H. Washbourne, 1845);

Judith May Newton, "Another Text of Troilus: Kynaston's Version of Book II," *Tohoku Gakuin University Review: Essays and Studies in English Language and Literature*, 72 (November 1981): 41-55;

Newton, "A Glimpse of Chaucer in a Toga: Kynaston's Version of Troilus and Criseyde, Book I (Part Two)," *Journal of the English Institute*, 16 (1987): 1-56;

Lawrence V. Ryan, "Chaucer's Criseyde in Neo-Latin Dress," *English Literary Renaissance*, 17 (Autumn 1987): 288-302;

Ryan, "A Neo-Latin Version of Robert Henryson's Testament of Cresseid," in *Acta Conventus Neo-Latini Sanctandreani: Proceedings of the Fifth International Congress of Neo-Latin Studies*, edited by I.D. McFarlane (Binghamton, N.Y.: Medieval & Renaissance Texts & Studies, 1986), pp. 481-491.

Edmund Bolton
(1575? - 1633?)

BOOKS: *Tricorones, sive soles gemini in Britannia* (London: Printed by Eliot's Court Press, 1607);

The Elements of Armories (London: Printed by G. Eld, 1610);

Hypercritica, or a Rule of Judgment for writing or reading our History's: Delivered in four

Supercensorian addresses by occasion of a Censorian Epistle, prefix'd by Sir Henry Savile, knight, to his Edition of some of our oldest Historians in Latin, dedicated to the late Queen Elizaabeth (London, 1618?);

Nero Cæsar, or Monarchie depraved. An historicall worke. Dedicated, with leaue, to the Dvke of Bvckingham, Lord Admirall. By the Translator of L. Florvs (London: Printed by T. Snodham & B. Alsop for T. Walkley, 1624; second, enlarged edition, London: Printed by A. Mathewes, 1627);

The Cities Advocate, in this Case of Honor and Armes; Whether Apprentiship extinguisheth Gentry? (London: Printed by M. Flesher for W. Lee, 1629); republished as *The Cities great concern, in this Case of Question of Honour and Arms, Whether Apprentiship extinguisheth Gentry? Discoursed; with a clear refutation of the pernicious error that it doth* (London: Printed by William Godbid, 1674).

Editions: Anthony Hall, *Nicolai Triveti Annalium Continuatio; ut et Adami Murimuthensis Chronicon*, includes *Hypercritica* (Oxford, 1722);

Joseph Haslewood, *Ancient Critical Essays upon English Poets and Poesy*, second volume includes *Hypercritica* (London: Harding & Wright for Robert Triphook, 1815);

Hugh MacDonald, ed., *England's Helicon* (Cambridge: Harvard University Press, 1950);

J. E. Spingarn, ed. *Critical Essays of the Seventeenth Century*, 3 volumes, contains *Hypercritica* (Oxford: Clarendon Press, 1908): I, 82-115.

OTHER: John Bodenham, ed., *Englands Helicon*, includes five poems by Bolton (London: Printed by J. Roberts for J. Flasket, 1600; enlarged edition, London: Printed by T. Snodham for R. More, 1614);

Benjamin Jonson, *Ben: Jonson his Volpone or the foxe*, includes Latin prefatory verse by Bolton (London: Printed by G. Eld for T. Thorppe, 1607);

The Roman Histories of Lucius Iulius Florus, from the foundation of Rome, till Caesar Augustus, for aboue DCC yeares, divided by Florus into IV ages, translated by Bolton (London: Printed by W. Stansby, 1618).

Edmund Bolton's *The Cities Advocate* (1629) is often incorrectly attributed to John Philipot. Bolton may have written the sonnet "To the Excellent and most accomplish'd Ladie, Lucie

Countesse of Bedford" prefixed to Michael Drayton's *Mortimeriados* (1596). According to the *Dictionary of National Biography*, Bolton prepared *Vindiciæ Britannicæ, or London righted by rescues and Recoveries of antiquities of Britain in general, & of London in particular, against unwarrantable prejudices, and historical antiquations amongst the learned; for the more honour, & perpetual just uses of the noble island & the city* for press, but it was never printed. According to Anthony Wood, Bolton's *Life of King Henry II* was intended for insertion in John Speed's *Historie of Great Britaine* (1611) but was rejected for its too favorable account of Saint Thomas à Becket.

Bolton's poems appear in *Englands Helicon* (1600) with those of Philip Sidney, Edmund Spenser, Michael Drayton, Thomas Lodge, Nicholas Breton, George Peele, Henry Howard, Earl of Surrey, William Shakespeare, Edward Dyer, and Christopher Marlowe, among others. Bolton's five contributions are all pastorals: "Theorello: A Sheepheards Edillion," "A Palinode," "A Canzon Pastorall in honour of her Maiestie," "A Pastorall Ode to an honourable friend," and "The Sheepheard's Song: a Caroll or Himne for Christmas."

Bolton's birth is dated from his signature in a British Library manuscript (Harley MS. 6521), "Edmundus Maria Boltonus, aetatis 47, 1622." He may have been descended from the family of Basset and have been a distant relation of George Villiers, first Duke of Buckingham. He was raised and remained a Catholic. Bolton was for some years a free commoner at Trinity Hall, Cambridge, and then lived at the Inner Temple. He was married about 1606 and eventually had three sons. Bolton earned respect in his own time as a historian and antiquarian and became friends with William Camden; however, his religion thwarted any hopes of advancement throughout his life until, assessed as a recusant in 1628, he could not pay the six-pound fine because he was a prisoner in the Fleet. Nor could he pay in 1629 when his place of detention was the Marshalsea. He is last heard from in a letter to Henry, Lord Falkland, on 20 August 1633.

Papers:
Bolton manuscripts are held by Christ Church, Oxford, the Bodleian Library (MS. Rawlinson Misc. 1), the British Library (Cotton MS. Titus A, xiii, 178-184; Harley MS. 6521; Royal MS. 18 A, lxxi), and the State Papers Office.

Checklist of Further Readings

Aers, David, Bob Hodge, and Gunther Kress. *Literature, Language and Society in England 1580-1680.* Dublin: Gill & Macmillan / Totowa, N.J.: Barnes & Noble, 1981.

Alden, Raymond M. *The Rise of Formal Satire in England Under Classical Influence*, Publications of the University of Pennsylvania Series in Philology, Literature, and Archaeology, 7, no. 2. Philadelphia: University of Pennsylvania, 1899.

Allen, Don Cameron. *Doubt's Boundless Sea: Skepticism and Faith in the Renaissance.* Baltimore: Johns Hopkins Press, 1964.

Ashley, Maurice. *England in the Seventeenth Century*, revised. New York: Barnes & Noble, 1980.

Aubrey, John. *Aubrey's Brief Lives*, edited by Oliver Lawson Dick, third edition, revised. London: Secker & Warburg, 1958.

Baker, Herschel C. *The Wars of Truth: Studies in the Decay of Christian Humanism in the Earlier Seventeenth Century.* Cambridge: Harvard University Press, 1952.

Bennett, Joan. *Five Metaphysical Poets: Donne, Herbert, Vaughan, Crashaw, Marvell*, third edition. Cambridge: Cambridge University Press, 1964.

Bethell, Samuel Leslie. *The Cultural Revolution of the 17th Century.* London: Dobson, 1951.

Bradbury, Malcolm, and David Palmer, eds. *Metaphysical Poetry.* London: Arnold, 1970.

Bush, Douglas. *English Literature in the Earlier Seventeenth Century 1600-1660*, second edition, revised. Oxford: Clarendon Press, 1962.

Cain, T. G. S., and Ken Robinson, eds., *"Into Another Mould": Change and Continuity in English Culture, 1625-1700.* London & New York: Routledge, 1992.

Carlton, Charles. *Charles I, the Personal Monarch.* London & Boston: Routledge & Kegan Paul, 1983.

Chambers, A. B. *Transfigured Rites in Seventeenth-Century English Poetry.* Columbia: University of Missouri Press, 1992.

Colie, Rosalie L. *Paradoxia Epidemica; The Renaissance Tradition of Paradox.* Princeton: Princeton University Press, 1966.

Colie. *The Resources of Kind; Genre-Theory in the Renaissance*, edited by Barbara K. Lewalski. Berkeley: University of California Press, 1973.

Cook, Elizabeth. *Seeing Through Words: The Scope of Late Renaissance Poetry.* New Haven: Yale University Press, 1986.

Cruttwell, Patrick. "The Metaphysical Poets and their Readers," *Humanities Association Review*, 28 (Winter

1977): 20-42.

Cruttwell. *The Shakespearean Moment and its Place in the Poetry of the 17th Century*. London: Chatto & Windus, 1954.

Davies, Horton. *Worship and Theology in England*, 5 volumes. Princeton: Princeton University Press, 1961-1975.

Eliot, T. S. "The Metaphysical Poets," in *Selected Essays*, third edition, enlarged. London: Faber & Faber, 1951, pp. 281-291.

Ellrodt, Robert. *L'Inspiration personelle et l'esprit du temps chez les poétes mètaphysiques anglais*, 3 volumes. Paris: J. Corti, 1960-1973.

Ezell, Margaret J. M. *The Patriarch's Wife: Literary Evidence and the History of the Family*. Chapel Hill: University of North Carolina Press, 1987.

Ferry, Anne. *All in War with Time: Love Poetry of Shakespeare, Donne, Jonson, Marvell*. Cambridge: Harvard University Press, 1975.

Fish, Stanley E. *Self-Consuming Artifacts: The Experience of Seventeenth-Century Literature*. Berkeley: University of California Press, 1972.

Fowler, Alastair. *A History of English Literature*. Cambridge: Harvard University Press, 1987.

Fowler, ed. *The New Oxford Book of Seventeenth Century Verse*. Oxford & New York: Oxford University Press, 1991.

Fraistat, Neil, ed. *Poems in their Place: The Intertextuality and Order of Poetic Collections*. Chapel Hill: University of North Carolina Press, 1986.

Fraser, Russell A. *The War Against Poetry*. Princeton: Princeton University Press, 1970.

Freeman, Rosemary. *English Emblem Books*. London: Chatto & Windus. 1948.

Goldberg, Jonathan. *James I and the Politics of Literature: Jonson, Shakespeare, Donne, and their Contemporaries*. Baltimore: Johns Hopkins University Press, 1983.

Gordon, D. J. *The Renaissance Imagination: Essays and Lectures*, edited by Stephen Orgel. Berkeley: University of California Press, 1975.

Gottlieb, Sidney, ed. *Approaches to Teaching the Metaphysical Poets*. New York: Modern Language Association of America, 1990.

Grant, Patrick. *The Transformation of Sin: Studies in Donne, Herbert, Vaughan and Traherne*. Montreal: McGill-Queen's University Press / Amherst: University of Massachusetts Press, 1974.

Grierson, H. J. C. *Cross Currents in English Literature of the XVIIth Century: or, the World, the Flesh, & the Spirit, their Actions and Reactions*. London: Chatto & Windus, 1929.

Halewood, William H. *The Poetry of Grace; Reformation Themes and Structures in English Seventeenth-Century Poetry*. New Haven: Yale University Press, 1970.

Hammond, Gerald. *Fleeting Things: English Poets and Poems, 1616-1660*. Cambridge: Harvard University Press, 1990.

Harris, Victor. *All Coherence Gone*. Chicago: University of Chicago Press, 1949.

Haselkorn, Anne M., and Betty S. Travitsky, eds. *The Renaissance Englishwoman in Print: Counterbalancing the Canon*. Amherst: University of Massachusetts Press, 1990.

Haydn, Hiram C. *The Counter-Renaissance*. New York: Scribners, 1950.

Helgerson, Richard. *Forms of Nationhood: The Elizabethan Writing of England*. Chicago: University of Chicago Press, 1992.

Hill, Christopher. *Puritans and Revolution: Studies in Interpretation of the English Revolution of the 17th Century*, edited by Donald Pennington and Keith Thomas. Oxford: Clarendon Press, 1978.

Hill. *Society and Puritanism in Pre-Revolutionary England*. London: Secker & Warburg, 1964.

Holden, William P. *Anti-Puritan Satire, 1572-1642*. New Haven: Yale University Press, 1954.

Hollander, John. *The Untuning of the Sky: Ideas of Music in English Poetry 1500-1700*. Princeton: Princeton University Press, 1961.

Joseph, B. L. *Shakespeare's Eden: The Commonwealth of England, 1558-1629*. London: Blanford Press, 1971.

Kahn, Victoria. *Rhetoric, Prudence, and Skepticism in the Renaissance*. Ithaca: Cornell University Press, 1985.

Kay, Dennis. *Melodious Tears: The English Funeral Elegy from Spenser to Milton*. Oxford: Clarendon Press / New York: Oxford University Press, 1990.

Keast, William R., ed. *Seventeenth-Century English Poetry; Modern Essays in Criticism*. New York: Oxford University Press, 1962.

Kernan, Alvin B. *The Cankered Muse; Satire of the English Renaissance*. New Haven: Yale University Press, 1959.

Knights, L. C. *Drama and Society in the Age of Jonson*. London: Chatto & Windus, 1937.

Lamont, William M. *Godly Rule: Politics and Religion, 1603-60*. London: Macmillan / New York: St. Martin's, 1969.

Lecocq, Louis. *La Satire en Angleterre 1588 à 1603*. Montreal, Paris, Bruxelles: Didier, 1969.

Lee, Maurice, Jr. *Great Britain's Solomon: James VI and I in His Three Kingdoms*. Urbana: University of Illinois Press, 1990.

Lee, ed. *Dudley Carleton to John Chamberlain, 1603-1624; Jacobean Letters*. New Brunswick: Rutgers University Press, 1972.

Leishman, J. B. *The Metaphysical Poets: Donne, Herbert, Vaughan, Traherne*. Oxford: Clarendon Press, 1934.

Lewalski, Barbara K. *Protestant Poetics and the Seventeenth-Century Religious Lyric*. Princeton: Princeton University Press, 1979.

Lovejoy, Arthur O. *The Great Chain of Being; A Study of the History of an Idea*. Cambridge: Harvard University Press, 1936.

Low, Anthony. *Love's Architecture: Devotional Modes in Seventeenth-Century English Poetry*. New York: New York University Press, 1978.

Lyons, Bridget Gellert. *Voices of Melancholy: Studies in Literary Treatments of Melancholy in Renaissance England*. London: Routledge & Kegan Paul, 1971.

Lyons, John D., and Stepen G. Nichols, Jr., eds. *Mimesis, from Mirror to Method, Augustine to Descartes*. Hanover: University Press of New England, 1982.

Mahood, Molly M. *Poetry and Humanism*. London: Cape, 1950.

Manley, Lawrence. *Convention, 1500-1750*. Cambridge: Harvard University Press, 1980.

Martines, Lauro. *Society and History in English Renaissance Verse*. Oxford: Blackwell, 1985.

Martz, Louis L. *The Poetry of Meditation: A Study in English Religious Literature of the Seventeenth Century*. New Haven: Yale University Press, 1954.

Mazzaro, Jerome. *Transformations in the Renaissance English Lyric*. Ithaca: Cornell University Press, 1970.

Mazzeo, Joseph A. *Renaissance and Revolution: Backgrounds to Seventeenth-Century English Literature*. New York: Pantheon, 1967.

Mazzeo. *Renaissance and Seventeenth-Century Studies*. New York: Columbia University Press, 1964.

McCanles, Michael. *Dialectical Criticism and Renaissance Literature*. Berkeley: University of California Press, 1975.

McClung, William Alexander. *The Country House in English Renaissance Poetry*. Berkeley: University of California Press, 1977.

Miner, Earl. *The Cavalier Mode From Jonson to Cotton*. Princeton: Princeton University Press, 1971.

Miner. *The Metaphysical Mode from Donne to Cowley*. Princeton: Princeton University Press, 1969.

Miner, ed. *Seventeenth-Century Imagery: Essays on Uses of Figurative Language from Donne to Farquhar*. Berkeley: University of California Press, 1971.

Mulder, John R. *The Temple of the Mind: Education and Literary Taste in Seventeenth-Century England*. New York: Pegasus, 1969.

Neale, J. E. *The Age of Catherine de Medici and Essays in Elizabethan History*. London: Jonathan Cape, 1943.

Nicolson, Marjorie Hope. *The Breaking of the Circle: Studies in the Effect of the "New Science" upon Seventeenth-Century Poetry*, revised edition. New York: Columbia University Press, 1962.

Owens, W. R. ed. *Seventeenth-Century England: A Changing Culture*, volume 2. London: Ward Lock Educational, in association with the Open University Press, 1980.

Parfitt, George. *English Poetry of the Seventeenth Century*. London & New York: Longman, 1985.

Parry, Graham. *The Seventeenth Century: The Intellectual and Cultural Context of English Literature, 1603-1700*. London & New York: Longman, 1989.

Patrides, C. A., and Raymond B. Waddington, eds. *The Age of Milton: Backgrounds to Seventeenth-Century Literature*. Manchester: Manchester University Press / Totowa, N.J.: Barnes & Noble, 1980.

Patterson, Annabel. *Censorship and Interpretation: The Conditions of Writing and Reading in Early Modern England*. Madison: University of Wisconsin Press, 1984.

Praz, Mario. *Studies in Seventeenth-Century Imagery*, 2 volumes, second edition, enlarged. Rome: Edizioni di storia e letteratura, 1964, 1974.

Ricks, Christopher, ed. *English Poetry and Prose, 1540-1674*. London: Barrie & Jenkins, 1970.

Rivers, Isabel. *Classical and Christian Ideas in English Renaissance Poetry: A Students' Guide*. London & Boston: Allen & Unwin, 1979.

Ross, Malcolm M. *Poetry and Dogma: The Transfiguration of Eucharist Symbols in Seventeenth Century English Poetry*. New Brunswick: Rutgers University Press, 1954.

Rostvig, Maren-Sofie. *The Happy Man: Studies in the Metamorphoses of a Classical Ideal*, 2 volumes, revised. Oslo: Norwegian Universities Press, 1962, 1971.

Scodel, Joshua. *The English Poetic Epitaph: Commemoration and Conflict from Jonson to Wordsworth*. Ithaca: Cornell University Press, 1991.

Selden, Raman. *English Verse Satire, 1590-1765*. London & Boston: Allen & Unwin, 1978.

Sharp, Robert L. *From Donne to Dryden: The Revolt Against Metaphysical Poetry*. Chapel Hill: University of North Carolina Press, 1940.

Sharpe, Kevin, and Steven N. Zwicker, eds. *Politics of Discourse; The Literature and History of Seventeenth-Century England*. Berkeley: University of California Press, 1987.

Shawcross, John T. *Intentionality and the New Traditionalism: some liminal means to Literary Revisionism*. University Park: Pennsylvania State University Press, 1991.

Sinfield, Alan. *Literature in Protestant England, 1560-1660*. London: Croom Helm / Totowa: Barnes & Noble, 1983.

Smith, A. J. *Metaphysical Wit*. Cambridge & New York: Cambridge University Press, 1991.

Smith. *The Metaphysics of Love: Studies in Renaissance Love Poetry from Dante to Milton*. Cambridge & New York: Cambridge University Press, 1985.

Smith, James. "On Metaphysical Poetry," *Scrutiny*, 2 (December 1933): 222-239.

Sorlien, Robert Parker. *The Diary of John Manningham of the Middle Temple, 1602-1603*. Hanover: Published for the University of Rhode Island by the University Press of New England, 1976.

Spingarn, J. E., ed. *Critical Essays of the Seventeenth Century*, 3 volumes. Bloomington: Indiana University Press, 1957.

Stewart, Stanley. *The Enclosed Garden; The Tradition and the Image in Seventeenth-Century Poetry*. Madison: University of Wisconsin Press, 1966.

Stone, Lawrence. *The Causes of the English Revolution, 1529-1642*. New York: Harper & Row, 1972.

Stone. *The Family, Sex and Marriage in England, 1500-1800*. New York: Harper & Row, 1977.

Summers, Claude, and Ted-Larry Pebworth. *The Eagle and the Dove: Reassessing John Donne*. Columbia: University of Missouri Press, 1986.

Summers and Pebworth, eds., *"Bright Shootes of Everlastingnesse": the Seventeenth-Century Religious Lyric*. Columbia: University of Missouri Press, 1987.

Summers and Pebworth, eds., *"The Muses Common-Weale": Poetry and Politics in the Seventeenth Century*. Columbia: University of Missouri Press, 1988.

Summers, Joseph H. *The Heirs of Donne and Jonson*. New York: Oxford University Press, 1970.

Swardson, H. R. *Poetry and the Fountain of Light: Observations on the Conflict Between Christian and Classical Traditions in Seventeenth-Century Poetry*. London: Allen & Unwin, 1962.

Tayler, Edward William. *Nature and Art in Renaissance Literature*. New York: Columbia University Press, 1964.

Thomson, Elizabeth M., ed. *The Chamberlain Letters; A Selection of the Letters of John Chamberlain Concerning Life in England from 1597 to 1626*. New York: Putnam, 1965.

Tuve, Rosemond. *Elizabethan and Metaphysical Imagery; Renaissance Poetic and Twentieth-Century Critics*. Chicago: University of Chicago Press, 1947.

Vickers, Brian. *Classical Rhetoric in English Poetry*. London: Macmillan / New York: St. Martin's Press, 1970.

Wallerstein, Ruth C. *Studies in Seventeenth-Century Poetic*. Madison: University of Wisconsin Press, 1950.

Willey, Basil. *The Seventeenth Century Background; Studies in the Thought of the Age in Relation to Poetry and Religion*. London: Chatto & Windus, 1934.

Williamson, George. *The Donne Tradition; A Study in English Poetry from Donne to the Death of Cowley*. Cambridge: Harvard University Press, 1930.

Wilson, F. P. *Elizabethan and Jacobean*. Oxford: Clarendon Press, 1945.

Wilson, Katharina M. and Frank J. Warnke, eds. *Women Writers of the Seventeenth Century*. Athens: University of Georgia Press, 1989.

Wood, Anthony. *Athenæ Oxonienses*, 5 volumes, edited by Philip Bliss. London: Printed for F. C. & J. Rivington, 1813-1820.

Contributors

Robert D. Beckett..*Southwest Missouri State University*

Sandra Bell..*Queen's University at Kingston*

Brian M. Blackley ....*University of Kentucky*

Jean R. Brink..*Arizona State University*

Helen B. Brooks ....*Stanford University*

Ronald Corthell ....*Kent State University*

Theresa M. DiPasquale ....*Florida International University*

James Doelman..*Centre for Reformation and Renaissance Studies, University of Toronto*

Robert C. Evans ....*Auburn University at Montgomery*

Gary R. Grund...*Rhode Island College*

Charles A. Huttar..*Hope College*

Frank S. Kastor ....*Wichita State University*

Frances M. Malpezzi ....*Arkansas State University*

Edmund Miller ....*C. W. Post Campus, Long Island University*

Mary Norton..*Western Carolina University*

Patricia Panek..*Wilmette, Illinois*

Mary Arshagouni Papazian...*Oakland University*

Ted-Larry Pebworth...*University of Michigan—Dearborn*

James A. Riddell..*California State University, Dominquez Hills*

Josephine A. Roberts..*Louisiana State University*

Deborah Rubin..*Nassau Community College, State University of New York*

A. J. Smith ....*University of Southampton*

Gerald Snare...*Tulane University*

Ernest W. Sullivan, II ....*Texas Tech University*

Frederick Waage ....*East Tennessee State University*

Susanne Woods ....*Franklin and Marshall College*

Julie W. Yen...*California State University, Sacramento*

Cumulative Index

Dictionary of Literary Biography, Volumes 1-121
Dictionary of Literary Biography Yearbook, 1980-1991
Dictionary of Literary Biography Documentary Series, Volumes 1-9

Cumulative Index

DLB before number: *Dictionary of Literary Biography*, Volumes 1-121
Y before number: *Dictionary of Literary Biography Yearbook*, 1980-1991
DS before number: *Dictionary of Literary Biography Documentary Series*, Volumes 1-9

A

C

E

G

H

I

J

K

L

N

O

P

Q

R

S

U

V

Y

Z

ISBN 0-8103-7598-2

90000

9 780810 375987